THE LAW-MAKING PROCESS

This book presents a critical, in-depth analysis of the law-making process.

Now in its ninth edition, this leading textbook presents a complete overview of the law-making process in the UK. Written by Michael Zander KC, one of the foremost authorities on the workings of the legal system, it combines critical and clear commentary with a well-chosen and wide-ranging selection of materials so that students have at their fingertips everything they need to know about the law-making process.

Dealing with every stage and all forms of law-making, it looks at:

- the preparation of legislation;
- its passage through Parliament;
- statutory interpretation;
- the operation of the rules of precedent in judicial decision-making;
- the many facets of judicial law-making; and
- the machinery of law reform.

The ninth edition has been updated to include the latest information and commentary about government action, case-law, legislation, official reports and a great range of legal and political journals. It provides extensive coverage of the law-making process post-Brexit and analysis of the changing character of the Supreme Court.

The Law-Making Process

Ninth Edition

Michael Zander KC

• HART •
OXFORD • LONDON • NEW YORK • NEW DELHI • SYDNEY

HART PUBLISHING

Bloomsbury Publishing Plc

Kemp House, Chawley Park, Cumnor Hill, Oxford, OX2 9PH, UK

1385 Broadway, New York, NY 10018, USA

Bloomsbury Publishing Ireland Limited, 29 Earlsfort Terrace, Dublin 2, D02 AY28, Ireland

HART PUBLISHING, the Hart/Stag logo, BLOOMSBURY and the Diana logo are trademarks of Bloomsbury Publishing Plc

First published in Great Britain 2025

1

A catalogue record for this book is available from the British Library.

A catalogue record for this book is available from the Library of Congress.

Library of Congress Control Number: 2025939033

ISBN: PB: 978-1-50998-650-7
ePDF: 978-1-50998-653-8
ePub: 978-1-50998-652-1

Typeset by Compuscript Ltd, Shannon
Printed and bound in Great Britain by CPI Group (UK) Ltd, Croydon CR0 4YY

MIX
Paper | Supporting responsible forestry
FSC® C013604

For product safety related questions contact productsafety@bloomsbury.com

To find out more about our authors and books visit www.hartpublishing.co.uk. Here you will find extracts, author information, details of forthcoming events and the option to sign up for our newsletters.

Preface to the Ninth Edition

This book was first published in 1980, exactly 45 years ago, in the Law in Context Series, founded and edited by Robert Stevens and William Twining. The publisher of the series originally was Weidenfeld & Nicolson, before transferring first to Butterworths, and then to Cambridge University Press. The sixth edition was published with Cambridge University Press in 2004 and there it remained until 2015 when Hart Publishing decided to give the book new life. It now proceeds on its own, no longer part of the great Law in Context series. Roughly a tenth of the book is new text since the last edition, but through some judicious pruning its length is slightly reduced. Some new material is the result of the addition of new sections, some is addition to existing sections, some is re-writing of sections. Brexit required considerable new material. There have been significant judicial decisions, reports of parliamentary Select Committee, empirical research, articles in learned journals – and events.

The Preface to the first edition said that the aim was to produce a book that was of value to anyone interested in understanding how the law-making process actually works. That remains the purpose. The book presents a large number of original texts from a great variety of sources – official reports, statutes, cases, articles, books, speeches and empirical studies, together with the author's commentary and reflections.

The text is up to date as of 1 July 2025.

Acknowledgements

The materials excerpted here are included with the kind permission of those who hold the copyright. A book of this kind would be impossible without their help and I am most indebted to all those who consented to this use of their material. They may be divided into four main groups. There are, first, those who hold copyright over official publications and law reports – the Controller of Her Majesty's Stationery Office, and the Incorporated Council of Law Reporting for England and Wales in relation to the *Law Reports* and the *Weekly Law Reports*, and Butterworths in relation to the *All England Law Reports*. The second group are the publishers and editors of journals from which extracts have been taken – *Australian Law Journal, British Tax Review, Canadian Bar Review Counsel, Current Legal Problems, International and Comparative Law Quarterly, Israel Law Review, Journal of the Society of Public Teachers of Law, Law Quarterly Review, Law Society's Gazette, Michigan Law Review, Modern Law Review, New Law Journal, New Society, New Zealand Law Review, Parliamentary Affairs, Public Law, Statute Law Review, The Lawyer* and *William and Mary Law Review*. The third group are publishers of extracts in books: Oceana Press, for the extracts from Karl Llewellyn's *Bramble Bush*; the Yale University Press, for extracts from Benjamin Cardozo's *The Nature of the Judicial Process*; the BBC, for extracts from a broadcast on the background to the Criminal Justice Bill which was later published in *Beyond Westminster*, edited by Anthony King and Anne Sloman; the Institute of Criminology, Cambridge, for extracts from a paper by Mr Michael Moriarty published in a Cropwood booklet; Hamish Hamilton Ltd, for extracts from the late Lord Radcliffe's book *Not in Feather Beds*, Hamish Hamilton and Jonathan Cape Ltd, for an extract from *Diaries of a Cabinet Minister* by the late Richard Crossman; LexisNexis for permission to publish extracts from Lord Neuberger's chapter on Law Reporting from the *Centenary Essays 2007 for Halsbury's Laws of England*; and Hart Publishing for many extracts from Professor Alan Paterson's *Final Judgment The Last Law Lords and the Supreme Court*. Fourthly there are the individual authors themselves (some since deceased): Mr E Angell, Mr GW Bartholomew, Mr Francis Bennion, Lord Carlisle QC, Dr Ernst Cohn, Sir Rupert Cross, Sir William Dale, Mr Edmund Dell MP, Lord Devlin, Lord Elwyn-Jones, Sir George Engel, Sir Terence Etherton, Professor MDA Freeman, Ms G Ganz, Lord Goff of Chieveley, Dr Lewis Graham, Professor JAG Griffith, Dr HR Hahlo, Sir Michael Kerr, Professor Anthony King, Professor HK Lücke, Professor Kate Malleson, Professor Sir Basil Markesinis, Professor Norman Marsh, Mr Michael Moriarty, Professor RJC Munday, Lord Neuberger of Abbotsbury, Mr Justice Nicol, Professor Martin Partington, Professor Alan Paterson, Dr Stephanie Pywell, Lord Russell of Killowen, Lord Scarman, Mr IML Turnbull, Mr DAS Ward, Professor J Willis, and Mr William Wilson. I am extremely grateful to all those listed and finally to Mrs Sonia Llewellyn for permission to use extracts from her late husband's work, *The Bramble Bush*.

Contents

Books, Pamphlets, Memoranda and Articles Excerpted

Note: Listed here are those works from which substantial excerpts are reproduced in the text.

Table of Cases

Practice Directions, Notes, Statements

Australia

Canada

Court of Justice of the European Union

European Court of Human Rights

Germany

India

United States of America

1

Legislation: The Whitehall Stage

One of Parliament's chief functions is the passing of legislation. Most legislation is initiated by the government of the day. This first chapter deals with what is involved in the stages leading to the introduction of government legislation into the parliamentary process. The work at this stage takes place not in Parliament but in government departments. Thus the title of the chapter.[1]

1.1. The Preparation of Legislation

1.1.1. The Sources of Legislation

The belief that most government bills derive from its manifesto commitments is mistaken. There is no recent research, but only 8 per cent of the Conservative government's bills in the period from 1970 to 1974 came from election commitments and in the 1974–79 period of a Labour government the proportion was only a little higher at 13 per cent.[2] The great majority of bills originate within government departments.

A considerable number of bills derive from the recommendations of independent advisory commissions or committees. Some of these are ad hoc – such as Royal Commissions, Departmental and Inter-Departmental Committees. Others are standing bodies, notably the Law Commission.[3] A study of twenty-five years of legislation showed that as many as a quarter to a third of all statutes that could have been preceded by the report of an independent advisory committee or commission were the result of such a report. Dr Helen Beynon studied all the Public Bills that received Royal Assent between 1951 and 1975 (a total of 1,712 statutes). She excluded from the study: (1) legislation that did not change the law, such as consolidation or statute law revision legislation, or re-enactment legislation; (2) emergency legislation rushed through to deal with some unexpected crisis; (3) certain financial legislation such as the Appropriation Acts which authorise the bulk of annual

[1] In common usage, the word 'Whitehall' is known to refer to government, while the word 'Westminster' refers to Parliament.

[2] Richard Rose, *Do Parties Make a Difference?* 2nd edn (Macmillan, 1984) 72–73. Moreover, as will be seen below (p 4), manifesto commitments are often themselves based on ongoing Whitehall processes. See also RI Hofferbert and I Budge, 'The party mandate and the Westminster model: election programmes and government spending in Britain 1948–85' 22 *British Journal of Political Science*, 1992, 151.

[3] Chapter 9 below is mainly about the Law Commission.

expenditure and Consolidated Fund Acts authorising interim and supplementary expenditure; (4) legislation concerning the Civil List which pays for the monarchy; and (5) statutes to give effect to treaties and other international commitments. When these were eliminated, there remained 1,335 statutes. In no less than 380 cases (28 per cent) the statute was preceded by a report of an independent advisory committee or commission.[4]

Very little has been written about the process of preparing legislation as seen from Whitehall's perspective. A rare instance was a paper by a senior Home Office official speaking at a Cambridge conference on penal policy-making in December 1976. (In those days, unlike the present era, penal policy was not a hot party political issue.) The paper is based on work done several decades ago but it gives an idea of the wide range of influences that often lies behind a major piece of legislation. That will be likely as true today as then.

Michael Moriarty, 'The policy-making process: how it is seen from the Home Office' in Nigel Walker (ed), *Penal Policy-Making in England*, Cropwood Conference (University of Cambridge, Institute of Criminology, 1977, 132–39.

> In general it is unusual for an incoming government to bring with it anything approaching a detailed blueprint of penal policy …
>
> The absence, usually, of a strong and detailed Party programme on penal matters does not mean that an incoming Home Secretary (or other Home Office Minister) may not have its own well-formed objectives and priorities. A recent example is the Ministerial commitment, since March 1974, to improving bail procedures and developing the parole system. But time and again the Ministerial contribution to penal policy-making, at least as it appears to the observer and participant within the Home Office, lies not in the Minister's bringing in his own fresh policy ideas, but in his operating creatively and with political drive upon ideas, proposals, reports etc, that are, so to speak, already to hand, often within the department but sometimes in the surrounding world of penal thought.
>
> *Sources of the Criminal Justice Act 1972*
>
> The year 1970 was notable for a sharp rise in the prison population to what was then a peak of 40,000,[5] which gave rise to intensified policy discussions within the Department of ways of developing alternative measures. The Report of the Advisory Council on the Penal System (ACPS) on Non-Custodial Measures (the 'Wootton Report')[6] contained a number of relevant proposals, notably a proposal that offenders should carry out community service. The Department instituted an urgent study of the practicalities by a working group with substantial probation service representation. Two other working groups were set up at the same time: one on use of probation resources, the other on residential accommodation for offenders. The main production of the first of these was a proposal to establish experimentally some day training centres, on a model originating in the United States, interest in which had been stimulated by the Howard League for Penal Reform among others. The other group developed ideas for running probation hostels: a substantial adult hostel building programme was established in 1971, following a small-scale experiment promoted by the Department in extending this method of treatment to those over 21. Detailed work on the proposals in the ACPS report on Reparation – the 'Widgery Report'[7] – was also going on.
>
> Thus the Criminal Justice Bill of 1971/2 could be said to be born from a fusion of a Ministerial desire to be active in the criminal justice field, along lines which were identified but not too

[4] H Beynon, 'Independent advice on legislation', unpublished PhD thesis, Oxford University (1982), Table 11, p 21.

[5] In December 2024 the prison population was 86,059. (ed).

[6] *Non-custodial and Semi-custodial Penalties* (HMSO, 1970).

[7] *Reparation by the Offender* (HMSO, 1971).

rigidly pre-determined by them, with a supply of departmental and other raw material that was lying ready or in process of being worked up. Much of the Widgery Report was in tune with a political objective that offenders should recompense their victims. From the Wootton Report, the community service proposal appealed partly for its reparatory element, partly because it was a non-custodial penal measure (Ministers were already well aware of the need to try to bring down the prison population) that would appeal to those who were suspicious of 'softness'. The form in which the community service proposals appeared in the Bill owed something to the specific intention of Ministers that the new measure should be seen as a credible alternative to custodial sentences.

In fact recommendations from the two ACPS reports made up much of the 'core' of the Bill – Part I entitled 'Powers for Dealing with Offenders'. In the form in which it received Royal Assent, Part I comprised 24 sections (and one linked Schedule) which related to the main sources of the Bill roughly as … [indicated in Table 1.1]:

Table 1.1 Sources for the Criminal Justice Bill 1972

Section	Subject	Origin
1–6	Compensation	Widgery Report
7–10	Criminal Bankruptcy	– do –
11–14	Suspended prison sentences etc	Ministerial/Departmental (s 12 from Wootton Report)
15–19	Community Service	Wootton Report
20	Day Training Centres	Departmental
21	Breach of Probation	Departmental
22	Deferment of Sentence	Wootton Report
23	Forfeiture of Property	– do –
24	'Criminal' driving disqualification	– do –

Not all the sections listed … [in Table 1.1] were in the original 'core': the origin of some of the later starters is illustrative of how penal policy is formed. What became section 14, extending the principle of the First Offenders Act to a wider range of adult offenders, was devised during the preparatory stage as a counter-weight to the ending of mandatory suspension of sentence. Other provisions owed their origin, or final form, to the Parliamentary proceedings on the Bill.

However, the bulk of the Bill was devoted to provisions aptly described as Miscellaneous and Administrative Provisions (sections 28 to 62). Some of these supported Part 1 provisions (eg administrative aspects of community service) or were otherwise related to its main themes (eg probation hostel provision; legal aid before first prison sentence). Others covered a wide range of topics of varying importance. In source they were hardly less diverse. At least one – increase in penalties for firearms offences – was a 'core provision'; some came from organisations close to the Home Office such as the Justices' Clerks. The provision giving 'cover' for the police to take drunks to a detoxification centre (section 34) had its origin in the report of the Working Party on Habitual Drunken Offenders.[8] Others came from the famous pigeon holes of Whitehall – and these in turn can be sub-divided into, on the one hand, tidying up and, on the other, more substantial though minor changes – for example simplification of parole procedure (section 35).

… In 1970–1 much detailed work was done on community service and criminal bankruptcy in particular, but to a lesser degree on the other major Bill proposals in working parties by the Home

[8] (HMSO, 1971).

> Office which brought into consultation others whose advice and co-operation were needed. The community service working group included representatives of the probation service, magistracy and voluntary service movement; the criminal bankruptcy group included lawyers of both the Home Office and Lord Chancellor's Office and officials from the Bankruptcy Inspectorate of the (then) Board of Trade.
>
> Beyond this area of activity there was (to move on to a second point) a wider and continuing process of consultation, on particular proposals and on ways of giving effect to them, with many official and non-official interests. A number of Bill proposals affected other Government departments – for instance, Transport and Health and Social Security – in addition to those already mentioned. On any penal policy it is necessary to keep the Scottish and Northern Ireland Offices in close touch. The Director of Public Prosecutions was closely involved in the criminal bankruptcy scheme and other Bill matters, at least one of which owed much to his suggestion. Consultation also went on with the police and probation services (the prison service was not greatly affected by the Bill, except as a hopeful beneficiary), the judiciary, magistrates and justices' clerks. The various representative organisations of course play an active part in the consultation process; and the burden on them can be a heavy one, especially as the pace quickens. The task of keeping the consultation process on the move while doing all the other preparatory work also makes considerable demands on the small team of officials working on a Bill.

Professor Edward Page of the London School of Economics examined the role of civil servants in the legislative process, a subject on which there has been a signal dearth of knowledge and writing.[9] The study was an investigation, through interviews with civil servants, of four bills that became Acts in 2002: The Employment Bill ('Employment'); the Adoption and Children Bill ('Adoption'); the Proceeds of Crime Bill ('Crime'); and the Land Registration Bill ('Land').

In each case there was a manifesto pledge covering significant portions of the bill but Page says that in each case the manifesto commitment 'resulted to a great or lesser degree from the ongoing Whitehall process'.[10] In two of the four cases – the Crime and Land bills – civil servants who served on the eventual bill team played a pivotal role in placing items on the political agenda and seeking to make sure that the government committed itself to legislation. With land registration, the subject had been under discussion since the 1960s but it was a particular individual (Charles Harpum, who became a Law Commissioner in 1994) who caused a viable proposal for major reform to emerge through collaboration between the Law Commission and the Land Registry. Two members of the eventual departmental bill team were involved in the Law Commission/Land Registry working party. In the case of the Crime Bill, 'the activism of officials created proposals for change which the government later accepted'.[11] Three of the Home Office officials who were on the 1998 Working Group on Confiscation, on whose Third Report the legislation was based, were members of the later bill team, including the head of the team. In 2000 the Performance and Innovation Unit (PIU) in 'Number 10' produced a report, *Recovering the Proceeds of Crime*, that helped to get political attention for the issue. Two Home Office officials who had worked on the Home Office Working Group and later on the bill team were also members of the PIU team.

The Employment Bill, dealing with a variety of topics, Page says, originated above all in units within the relevant departments. The Adoption Bill arose more closely from a

[9] EC Page, 'The civil servant as legislator: law making in British administration' 81 *Public Administration*, 2003, 651.

[10] Ibid, 656.

[11] Ibid, 657.

Prime-Ministerial initiative. The Prime Minister, Tony Blair, personally committed himself to reform the adoption system, partly at least, as he later said, as a result of his own experience – his father was fostered. A report in 2000, again, from Number 10's PIU, Page says, 'served the major function of reviving further political interest in adoption reform'.[12]

Summarising, Page stated:

> On the basis of the experience of these four bills, civil servants routinely play a major role in the development of the policy behind legislation, *even helping to ensure the legislation reaches the party election manifesto*.[13]

In a later paper[14] Page drew attention, however, to the increasing role in the development of policy, of external consultants,[15] political advisers[16] and think-tanks linked to political parties.[17]

See also EC Page and Bill Jenkins, *Policy Bureaucracy, Government with a Cast of Thousands* (Oxford University Press, 2005) in which the authors investigated the important role in policy making of the 100,000 or more middle-ranking civil servants. See also Professor Page's book, *Governing by Numbers: Delegated Legislation and Everyday Policy-Making* (Hart Publishing, 2001), an exploration of the processes that lead to statutory instruments; and a detailed study of the stages of 12 Bills enacted between 2005 and 2012: and M Russell and D Gover, *Legislation at Westminster* (Oxford University Press, 2017) 52–57.[18]

The Home Office 1782–2007 (Strathmore Publishing, 2024) includes 'witness seminars' bringing together people who played a variety of significant roles in the development of the Criminal Justice Act 1991 (pp 83–134) and the Police and Criminal Evidence Act 1984 (pp 189–235).

1.1.2. The Role of the Civil Servants – The Bill Team

Professor Page distinguishes three separate tasks involved in putting a bill onto the statute book – deciding the policy; producing the clauses of the bill; and handling the parliamentary process. Civil servants are actively involved in all three stages.

The government department responsible for the legislation first sets up a 'bill team'. The size of the bill team depends on the nature of the case. In Page's study it varied from four to eleven. The variation in size depended not only on the size and scope of the bill but also on whether it was a *policy* bill team or a *handling* bill team. A policy team is one in which all three tasks involved in producing legislation are carried out by members of the team.

[12] Later the Prime Minister, responding to a highly publicised case of inter-country adoption, committed the government to 'introduce legislation on it this session' (HC, *Hansard*, 17 January 2001) – which led to a 'flurry in Whitehall among officials who did not expect adoption legislation until after the election and who were still consulting on proposals in a white paper published in December' (Page, 'The civil servant as legislator' (n 9 above) 659).

[13] 'Civil servant as legislator' (n 9 above) 660; emphasis added.

[14] EC Page, 'Has the Whitehall Model survived?' 76 *International Review of Administrative Sciences,* 2010, 407.

[15] Expenditure of hundreds of millions of pounds annually to firms such as Accenture, KPMG, PWC, Deloitte, Ernst & Young etc.

[16] In 1997 there were 38 advisers; the number grew to 70 in 1998, increased to 82 in 2004 before slipping back to its 2008 level of 73. (Page, 'Has the Whitehall Model survived' (n 14 above) 415.)

[17] The Centre for Policy Studies for the Conservatives and DEMOS and the Institute for Public Policy Research for the Labour Party.

[18] The chapters of the book include: 'The origins of regulations', 'Ministers on top', 'Drafting SIs: the joint effort of administrators and lawyers', 'Consulting outside interests' and 'The discreet impact of parliamentary scrutiny'.

A handling team is one that concentrates on stewarding the legislation through its parliamentary stages, with policy being handled by 'policy lead' civil servants who are not formally in the team. Working closely with each bill team, full-time or part-time, is one or more departmental lawyer, acting as legal adviser.

The lead time from the setting up of the bill team to introduction of the bill into Parliament varies greatly. In Page's study of four bills, in the case of two it was only three months, in one it was ten months and in the fourth it was eleven months.

The government's legislative programme for the coming parliamentary session is controlled by a Cabinet sub-committee. This is called the Parliamentary Business and Legislation (PBL) Committee.[19] PBL is chaired by the Leader of the House of Commons. Its members include the other business managers – the Leader of the House of Lords and the Government Chief Whips from both Houses. Sometimes clearance for going ahead with a bill is required not only from the PBL Committee but from the Cabinet's policy sub-committee on that general topic, if there is one.[20]

The bill will eventually be drafted by Parliamentary Counsel, specialist lawyers who draft all government bills (see 1.2.1 below). They work from Instructions prepared by the department, which are normally drafted by departmental lawyers. The job of the bill team, together with the lawyers, is to work out the detail for the Instructions to Parliamentary Counsel.

The bill team is also responsible for preparing the Explanatory Notes that accompany both the bill and the Act. The Cabinet Office's *Guide to Making Legislation* states that the purpose of the Explanatory Notes was to make the bill accessible to readers who may not be legally qualified or have specialised knowledge of the subject area.[21] The notes were not intended to be an exhaustive description of the bill or to be a substitute for it. The point of the Explanatory Notes was to provide additional information not to duplicate the legislation or repeat or paraphrase the words in a clause. The Commentary section in the Explanatory Notes should provide factual background, cross-references to other relevant legislation and examples of how the bill would work in practice.

Explanatory Notes are published not by the Government but by the House authorities and it is open to them to refuse to publish them. The *Guide to Making Legislation* says that the House authorities have made it clear that they will do so if the Notes attempt to 'sell' the bill, that is, go beyond a neutral account of the bill and into promoting it.[22]

The bill team also has further responsibilities:

Impact assessment Impact assessments are generally required for all UK Government interventions of a regulatory nature that affect the private sector, civil society organisation or public services. The impact assessment includes an assessment of economic, social and environmental impacts. In particular, there is a legal requirement for public bodies to demonstrate they are considering their responsibilities under the Equality Act 2010 (ie in relation to age, disability, gender reassignment, pregnancy and maternity, race, religion or belief, sex, sexual orientation).

[19] It was known before as the Legislative Programme Committee and before that as the Future Legislation Committee.

[20] See 'Securing a slot in the legislative programme' in the Cabinet Office's *Guide to Making Legislation* 2025 s 5, pp 29–33.

[21] Cabinet Office, *Guide to Making Legislation*, 2025, para 10.1. For the use that can be made of Explanatory Notes in the interpretation of statutes see 3.5.9 below.

[22] Cabinet Office, *Guide to Making Legislation*, 2025, para 10.34.

Compatibility with the ECHR Section 19 of the Human Rights Act 1998 requires that, for every government bill, the minister in charge in each House make a statement that, in his or her view, the bill's provisions are compatible with the European Convention on Human Rights.[23] Alternatively, if he or she is not able to provide that personal assurance, the Minister must state that, nevertheless, the Government wishes the House to proceed with the bill. That was the statement made in May 2024 by Home Secretary James Cleverly when introducing the Conservative Government's controversial Safety of Rwanda (Asylum and Immigration) Bill.[24] Consideration of the impact of legislation on Convention rights therefore has to be an integral part of the policy-making process. The *Guide to Making Legislation* warns that the Joint Committee on Human Rights may report on the ECHR issues raised by a bill and 'that it is likely to examine closely the arguments put forward by the department justifying interference with a Convention right'.[25]

Other legal issues Pre-Brexit, the bill team had to check whether the bill had any European Union implications and especially whether there was a possibility of conflict with EU law. The 2022 edition of the Cabinet Office Guide, post-Brexit, says 'Departments should consider any implications for the UK's international legal obligations, including in relation to WTO rules and any legal obligations arising as a result of UK withdrawal from the EU'.[26]

The concern is to reduce the risk of legal challenge to the provisions of the bill by judicial review or otherwise. It will have regard to the separate devolution arrangements made with Scotland, Wales and Northern Ireland and will consider whether any of the provisions of the bill touch on topics that have been devolved, reserved or transferred under the separate settlements – as to which see 2.16 below.

1.1.3. Consultation

The government department with responsibility for the legislative project will need to decide how much to consult during the gestation process leading to the introduction of the bill in Parliament. If the proposed legislation impinges on the responsibilities of other government departments or governmental agencies they will have to be consulted. But the question here is whether and, if so, to what extent persons or bodies outside the governmental machine should be consulted prior to publication of the bill.

The traditional Whitehall view was that non-governmental persons and bodies should not normally be consulted at that stage – the time for consultation was later, when the bill had been introduced in Parliament. The effect of this was that consultation only started when it was generally too late to influence the basic shape of the legislation.

[23] Statement under s 19(1)(a) of the Human Rights Act 1998: 'In my view the provisions of the …. Bill are compatible with the Convention rights. [signed] … … …. Secretary of State / Minister for … … ….'

[24] 'Secretary James Cleverly has made the following statement under section 19(1)(b) of the Human Rights Act 1998: I am unable to make a statement that, in my view, the provisions of the Safety of Rwanda (Asylum and Immigration) Bill are compatible with the Convention rights, but the Government nevertheless wishes the House to proceed with the Bill.' The legislation provided for the removal of asylum seekers to Rwanda. It became law just before the 2024 General Election. The incoming Labour Government stated that the Act would not be implemented. For a series of articles by the writer about the progress of the Bill through Parliament see 'Tracking the Rwanda Bill', *New Law Journal*, 9 February 2024, 8 March 2024, 3 May 2024.

[25] Cabinet Office, *Guide to Making Legislation*, 2025, para 11.30.

[26] Cabinet Office, *Guide to Making Legislation*, 2025, p 115.

Until 1967, Consultation was normally limited to individuals and organisations most immediately concerned. In 1967, for the first time, Government issued a Green Paper:

> [F]or the first time in the history of British public administration, an official government document was published which went out of its way to point out that it did not, at any rate at the time of publication, represent declared government policy. The method used was to invite public discussion on the memorandum which the Green Paper contained and which the Government had previously sent to the National Economic Development Council and the regional planning councils for their comments.[27]

Since then, there has been a huge growth in the amount of consultation. The Hansard Society, in *Making the Law*, its wide-ranging and influential 1992 Report on the Legislative Process,[28] said that there were many complaints about the way that government carried out consultation in regard to legislation. ('The overwhelming impression from the evidence is that many of those most directly affected are deeply dissatisfied with the extent, nature, timing and conduct of consultation on bills as at present practised'.[29]) Ten years later, the Hansard Society returned to the subject in *Making Better Law*.[30] The situation had been transformed. At that time, there was plenty of consultation. But the consultation, it said, more often sought opinion, rather than evidence. 'Good consultation requires asking the right people the right question at the right time'.[31] Unsurprisingly, external stakeholders strongly preferred consultation to take place as early in the policy-making process as possible.[32]

> With policy still in flux it gives outsiders a greater chance of making their voice heard and influencing the final decision. Once a proposal is on the table the politics and the dynamics of the consultation process inevitably change; ministers and civil servants become more proprietorial towards it.[33]

Public consultation will normally take the form of a Green Paper, which is to be distinguished from a White Paper. The difference between those two forms of government statement, and a discussion of their function in the context of tax legislation, appeared in the *British Tax Review* in 1980.

Cedric Sandford, 'Open government: the use of green papers' *British Tax Review*, 1980, 351:

> Green Papers were invented by the Labour Government in 1967. White Papers are of much earlier vintage. It is generally held that 'White Papers announce firm government policy for implementation. Green Papers announce tentative proposals for discussion.'[34]

[27] A Silkin, 'Green papers and changing methods of consultation in British government' 51 *Public Administration*, 1973, 427.

[28] *Making the Law* (Hansard Society, 1992). The report was the work of a Commission appointed by the Society whose prestigious membership included a former Permanent Secretary to the Home Office, a former First Parliamentary Counsel, a former Director-General of the Royal Institute of Public Administration, a former Clerk of Committees of the House of Commons, the Director of Legal Affairs of the Consumers' Association, the General Secretary of the Association of First Division Civil Servants and a sitting Law Lord. The chairman was Lord Rippon. (It is sometimes referred to as the Rippon Report.)

[29] *Making the Law* (n 28 above) 30.

[30] Ruth Fox and Matt Korris, *Making Better Law* (Hansard Society, 2010).

[31] Ibid 57.

[32] Ibid.

[33] Ibid.

[34] John E Pemberton, 'Government green papers' LXXI, *Literary World*, 1969, 830.

Sir Harold Wilson wrote:

> 'A White Paper is essentially a statement of government policy in such terms that withdrawal or major amendment, following consultation or public debate, tends to be regarded as a humiliating withdrawal. A Green Paper represents the best that the government can propose on the given issue, but, remaining uncommitted, it is able without loss of face to leave its final decision open until it has been able to consider the public reaction to it.'[35]

As applied to taxation these distinctions are at best over-simplifications. Where Green Papers were not issued, the proposals of the White Paper were often subject to change on major issues. Thus, with selective employment tax the treatment of charities, agriculture and mining was all changed within a fortnight of the publication of the White Paper, whilst with capital transfer tax a lower rate of tax for life-time gifts was adopted during the passage of the Finance Act in direct contradiction to the White Paper. On the other hand, important elements in some of the Green Papers have been presented as 'hard'. As Grant Gordon puts it: 'One believes that one knows the difference between White Papers, Green Papers and their kin, but under close examination they often tend to merge to a uniform grey.'[36]

The Lords Constitution Committee in 2017 urged that there should normally be a Green and a White Paper for government legislation. It welcomed the statement by Mrs Theresa May, as Prime Minister, that she would normally expect a Minister, before having legislation, 'to have gone through a Green Paper stage for discussion and then a White Paper stage to set out policy'.[37]

In 1998, the Cabinet Office had published *How to Conduct a Written Consultation Exercise*.[38] Two years later, in November 2000, it published a *Code of Practice on Written Consultation*.[39] This later morphed into Consultation Principles, the latest version of which was published in July 2018:

A. Consultations should be clear and concise. Use plain English and avoid acronyms. Be clear what questions you are asking and limit the number of questions to those that are necessary. Make them easy to understand and easy to answer. Avoid lengthy documents when possible and consider merging those on related topics.
B. Consultations should have a purpose. Do not consult for the sake of it. Ask departmental lawyers whether you have a legal duty to consult. Take consultation responses into account when taking policy forward. Consult about policies or implementation plans when the development of the policies or plans is at a formative stage. Do not ask questions about issues on which you already have a final view.
C. Consultations should be informative. Give enough information to ensure that those consulted understand the issues and can give informed responses. Include validated impact assessments of the costs and benefits of the options being considered when possible; this might be required where proposals have an impact on business or the voluntary sector.
D. Consultations are only part of a process of engagement. Consider whether informal iterative consultation is appropriate, using new digital tools and open, collaborative

[35] Harold Wilson, *The Labour Government 1964–70* (Weidenfeld and Nicolson, 1971) 380.
[36] Grant Gordon, 'Grey papers' 48 *Political Quarterly*, 1977, 1.
[37] Lords Constitution Committee, *Preparing Legislation for Parliament*, 4th Report, 2017–19, October 2017 HL 27, paras 38,41.
[38] Drawing on the work of the National Consumer Council's *Government Consultation: Not Just a Paper Exercise* (National Consumer Council, 1997).
[39] This had been proposed by the Hansard Society in 1993.

approaches. Consultation is not just about formal documents and responses. It is an on-going process.

E. Consultations should last for a proportionate amount of time. Judge the length of the consultation on the basis of legal advice and taking into account the nature and impact of the proposal. Consulting for too long will unnecessarily delay policy development. Consulting too quickly will not give enough time for consideration and will reduce the quality of responses.

F. Consultations should be targeted. Consider the full range of people, business and voluntary bodies affected by the policy, and whether representative groups exist. Consider targeting specific groups if appropriate. Ensure they are aware of the consultation and can access it. Consider how to tailor consultation to the needs and preferences of particular groups, such as older people, younger people or people with disabilities that may not respond to traditional consultation methods.

G. Consultations should take account of the groups being consulted. Consult stakeholders in a way that suits them. Charities may need more time to respond than businesses, for example. When the consultation spans all or part of a holiday period, consider how this may affect consultation and take appropriate mitigating action, such as prior discussion with key interested parties or extension of the consultation deadline beyond the holiday period.

H. Consultations should be agreed before publication. Seek collective agreement before publishing a written consultation, particularly when consulting on new policy proposals. Consultations should be published on gov.uk.

I. Consultation should facilitate scrutiny. Publish any response on the same page on gov.uk as the original consultation, and ensure it is clear when the government has responded to the consultation. Explain the responses that have been received from consultees and how these have informed the policy. State how many responses have been received.

J. Government responses to consultations should be published in a timely fashion. Publish responses within 12 weeks of the consultation or provide an explanation why this is not possible. Where consultation concerns a statutory instrument publish responses before or at the same time as the instrument is laid, except in very exceptional circumstances (and even then publish responses as soon as possible). Allow appropriate time between closing the consultation and implementing policy or legislation.

K. Consultation exercises should not generally be launched during local or national election periods. If exceptional circumstances make a consultation absolutely essential (for example, for safeguarding public health), departments should seek advice from the Propriety and Ethics team in the Cabinet Office.

This document does not have legal force and is subject to statutory and other legal requirements.

Until 2012, the code of practice governing government consultations recommended a 12-week period for consultations. In 2012, the government 'Consultation Principles', replacing the 2008 code of practice also replaced the default 12-week period with a principle that 'consultations should last for a proportionate amount of time'. Giving evidence to the Lords Constitution Committee, the Bingham Centre for the Rule of Law called for the 12-week period to be reinstated as the default. The Committee said that, save for exceptional circumstances, six weeks should be regarded as the 'minimum feasible consultation period'.[40] This recommendation has not been adopted.

[40] Ibid, para 58.

A study of set-piece consultations in which the Government seeks views about its intentions from interested bodies and individuals was carried out by Professor Edward Page. His conclusion was that respondents regard it to be worthwhile even though they do not have high hopes of influencing government:

> Set-piece consultations are a distinctive and limited form of pluralism which strongly privilege the perspective already reached by the government but which offer sufficient prospects that the government will change details to make the whole process worthwhile for the large number of interest groups that respond to them. There are distinct issues that are handled at the set-piece consultation stage, and while it helps to have had other direct contacts to make sure your views are given sufficient weight, even those without such contacts feel good enough about the process, and feel they have been taken seriously enough in the past, to believe that they are in with a chance to shape the details next time around.[41]

Considering that such consultation takes time and resources and only rarely results in significant changes of policy, the value for the Government, Page suggests, is gaining the legitimising effect of consultation, having a means of giving notice of its intentions, making sure that it has not overlooked any important aspect of the issue, some fine-tuning of the proposals and reducing the risk of unintended consequences.[42]

Regardless of whether there has been or has not been a formal consultation stage, interest groups and experts may of course try to influence policy by lobbying Ministers, other MPs and civil servants after the bill has been published.

1.1.4. Cabinet Control

To what extent is the process of the preparation of legislation controlled or supervised by the Cabinet and its sub-committees?[43] Little is known of this. A glimpse of what goes on behind the scenes was given in a lecture in 1951 by Sir Granville Ram, the then First Parliamentary Counsel in charge of the Office of Parliamentary Counsel. Comparison between Sir Granville's description of the system then with that in the Cabinet Office's *Guide to Making Legislation* shows that little of substance has changed other than arrangements for annual sessions of Parliament.[44]

Within a five-year Parliament there will generally be five sessions lasting a year each, though some recent sessions have lasted two years. The 'Brexit parliamentary session' that began in June 2017 lasted over two years. It was finally prorogued on 8 October 2019[45] and the new session which began with the Queen's Speech on 14 October 2019 only lasted a few days before it ended with Parliament's decision to call a general election by means of

[41] EC Page, 'Groups and the limited plurism of the set-piece consultation' *British Journal of Politics and International Relations*, 2011, 175, 185.

[42] Ibid.

[43] The list of Cabinet sub-committees and their members is accessible online – www.gov.uk (ed).

[44] The Fixed-term Parliaments Act 2011 provided that general elections should take place every five years on the first Thursday in May. However, the Fixed-term Parliaments Act was repealed by the Dissolution and Calling of Parliament Act 2022 which provides only that a Parliament cannot last longer than five years from the day it began.

[45] Prime Minister Boris Johnson's earlier attempt to prorogue Parliament for seven weeks had been declared unlawful by the unanimous decision of the eleven Justices of the Supreme Court – *R (Miller and others) v Prime Minister* [2019] UKSC 41.

legislation rather than under the Fixed-term Parliaments Act 2011.[46] Subject to minor indicated changes, the passage that follows is still an authoritative description of the process.

Sir Granville Ram, 'The improvement of the statute book' 1 *Journal of the Society of Public Teachers of Law*, NS, 1951, 442, 447–49:

> [A]bout six weeks after the beginning of each session the Cabinet Office asks Departments to send in lists of the Bills likely to be required for introduction in the *next* session, together with their observations as to the urgency of any Bill included in the lists, an estimate of its magnitude, and a forecast of the date on which instructions to Parliamentary Counsel can be ready.
>
> I must make it plain that all these proposals, observations and forecasts relate not to the session that has just begun but to the next one which will begin nearly eleven months later. When they have been received from Departments they are collated and submitted to a Cabinet committee, known as the Future Legislation Committee [now, as has been seen, called the Parliamentary Business and Legislation (PBL) Committee (ed)], which always includes in its membership the Leaders of both Houses and the Chief Whip,[47] because the drawing up and control of the legislative programme must be closely related to the arrangement of Parliamentary business. Soon after Christmas the Committee examines the Department's proposals in detail, and draws up a tentative list of Bills for discussion with the Ministers who have put forward the proposals. The Committee then holds a meeting at which those Ministers are present, and after consultation with them and with the First Parliamentary Counsel, draws up a provisional list of Bills for the session due to begin in the following autumn. This list is prepared with careful regard to the amount of time likely to be available for legislation during the session and, in drawing it up, the Committee makes allowances for the subsequent inclusion of Bills the need for which has not yet been foreseen, and for annual Bills (such as Finance Bills, Army and Air Force (Annual) Bills and Expiring Law Continuance Bills).[48]
>
> The Bills recommended for inclusion in the programme are placed in order of priority, having regard to the dates when instructions to Parliamentary Counsel can be ready, to the time that drafting may be expected to take, and to the Chief Whip's estimate of the approximate dates on which the Bills must, respectively, be introduced in order to pass through their successive stages under the arrangements he will have to make for the Parliamentary business of the session. The list is then submitted to the Cabinet, and when the Cabinet has approved the recommendations of the Committee, with or without alterations, the Bills remaining in the list become the Government's provisional programme of legislation for the following session. [When a new government is elected after a general election the normal five months or so that it takes to prepare the legislative programme has to be telescoped into days (ed).]
>
> The need for determining the lines of a session's programme so long before the session starts is obvious because Bills take time to draft, but there remains much for the [PBL Committee] to do before the programme is finally completed and its main features are announced in the Queen's Speech at the opening of the new session. Between Easter and the summer recess the Committee

[46] The Fixed-term Parliaments Act provided that an early election could be called if either it was approved by more than a two-thirds majority of MPs or after a No-confidence motion in the government. On Monday 29 October 2019, the Early Parliamentary General Election Bill providing for an election on 12 December went through all its stages in the House of Commons and was approved on the Third Reading by 438 votes to 20. It went through all its stage in the Lords on Tuesday 30th and received Royal Assent on Wednesday 31st. The session ended on November 5, when Parliament was prorogued for the 25 days prescribed for a general election campaign. (The Conservative Party's Election Manifesto (p 48) promised that the Fixed-term Parliaments Act would be repealed – and, as noted above, it was.)

[47] The whips enforce party discipline. The Leader of the House and Chief Whip and their Shadows are known as 'the usual channels'. They play a crucial role in managing the timetabling and organisation of parliamentary business (ed).

[48] Today there are no annual bills apart from the Finance Bill. The Army, Navy and Air Force Acts are now continued from year to year by Order in Council. An Armed Forces Bill is required every five years (ed).

reviews the progress of the Bills decided upon, and considers any proposals made by Ministers for the addition to the programme of Bills that have not been previously foreseen. Early in June Departments will be asked by the Cabinet Office for particulars of any such Bills, but the Departments anticipate this request whenever possible by giving information to the Cabinet Office as soon as it becomes reasonably clear that any Bill not already included in the provisional programme is likely to be wanted. During this period between Easter and the end of July the [PBL Committee] also controls the flow of instructions to Parliamentary Counsel so as to secure, so far as possible, that it shall conform to the order of priority approved by the Cabinet. Finally after the summer recess the [PBL Committee] presents to the Cabinet, when they are considering the Queen's Speech for the opening of Parliament, a complete classified programme.

Upon the opening of a new session, control of the programme for that session passes to another Cabinet committee called the Legislation Committee. [This too has changed. It is done today by the same PBL Committee that considered bids from departments at the outset (ed).] That Committee performs functions in relation to the examination of draft Bills …, but it also exercises control over the programme for the current session … In this capacity it reviews every month the progress of all Bills in the programme for the current session, and regulates both the flow of instructions to Parliamentary Counsel and the flow of Bills to the two Houses according to the progress made. Applications for the admission of new Bills to the programme are made to this Committee through the Cabinet Office, and any necessary adjustments, whether by way of changes in priority or of addition to, or deletions from, the programme are authorised by the Committee.

This machinery for obtaining a place in the programme is the product of many years of experience and has proved far more effective than anything previously devised. The simple requirements it imposes on Ministers and their Departments are necessary to prevent a return to the chaotic conditions which existed before it was invented, but it is designed to deal with ordinary cases, and like most human institutions, it would be capable of abuse if it were too rigidly applied to cases that are not ordinary. A sudden emergency or an unexpected change of circumstances may necessitate the production of a Bill at such short notice that some deviation from the usual procedure is essential. Circumstances do, therefore, sometimes arise in which the normal procedure may have to be either anticipated or short-circuited, and in such cases strict compliance with it may be dispensed with by the Chairman of the [PBL] Committee …

When the Bill is ready for presentation it becomes necessary to submit the latest draft of it with a covering memorandum initialled by the Minister to the [PBL Committee] … The meetings of the Committee are attended by any Ministers who may be concerned with items on the agenda, and papers for the Committee are circulated to all Departments, so that any Ministers who may not have been expressly invited may have an opportunity to attend. The Parliamentary Counsel are in attendance, and any departmental officials whose presence is necessary accompany their Ministers. As has been said, the Committee has control of the legislative programme for the current session, and holds a special meeting once a month to review its progress, but at the ordinary weekly meetings the main business is to go through the draft Bills submitted to it. This it does in some detail, and any points that have occurred to the Ministers present, the Law Officers, or the Chief Whip are raised and discussed with the Minister in charge of the Bill.

When the Committee has considered the Bill it decides whether it may be presented to Parliament, and if so, in which House.[49] The choice of House is often a matter of convenience depending on the state of parliamentary business and the time of year, but Bills which contain many clauses providing for fresh expenditure and Bills which consist largely of provisions imposing 'charges on the people', whether by way of rates or taxes, may not be introduced in the House of

[49] ['For a number of reasons Lords introduction is generally reserved for lower-profile, less controversial Bills with high-profile ones introduced in the Commons. Senior ministers are concentrated in the Commons, the chamber receives more media attention, and the government's primary accountability is to elected MPs.' (M Russell and D Gover, *Legislation at Westminster* (Oxford University Press, 2017) 62. (ed)]

> Lords because, although there are various expedients for enabling that House to avoid questions of privilege where such provisions appear only as minor and subsidiary features of a Bill, legislation which is substantially of that character cannot be dealt with by the Lords without infringing the privileges of the Commons. The Committee also decides the date of presentation, which will depend partly on the Chief Whip's plans, and, of course, upon the amount of redrafting that may be necessary as a result of the Committee's deliberations. The Committee sometimes gives provisional approval to a draft Bill subject to questions of law or of drafting being settled by the Lord Chancellor and the Law Officers in consultation with the Parliamentary Counsel, or subject to minor points raised by Ministers being adjusted by subsequent discussion; but if differences arise on major points of policy, the issues are referred to the Cabinet and the [PBL] Committee postpones a decision as to the presentation of the Bill.

The formal recital of the stages of the process gives little clue as to whether the process functions effectively. How much control does the Cabinet, either itself or through its committees, actually exert over the details of legislation? A vivid impression of how it works in practice (at least then) was given in the late Richard Crossman's *Diaries of a Cabinet Minister*. (Crossman was successively Minister of Housing, Lord President of the Council and Leader of the House of Commons, and Secretary of State for Social Services. Previously he had been both a journalist and an Oxford don.) The impression that Crossman conveys is that neither the Cabinet nor the Future Legislation Committee (as it was then called) actually exercised much real scrutiny.

Lord Simon of Glaisdale, speaking with experience as a former minister, law officer and judge, told the Hansard Society's inquiry into the legislative process that he would like to see the Legislation Committee 'giving closer attention to the way bills were drafted'. According to him, the Committee used to be chaired by the Lord Chancellor and acted as a scrutiny committee, 'looking carefully at constitutional points as well as drafting', but now it was chaired by the Leader of the House of Commons 'and operated more as a business management committee'.[50]

For further reading on the stages leading to the formulation of legislative proposals, see, for instance, MJ Barnett, *The Politics of Legislation: The 1957 Rent Act* (London School of Economics and Political Science, 1969); K Hindell, 'The genesis of the Race Relations Bill' 40 *Political Quarterly*, 1965, 390; JJ Richardson, 'The making of the Restrictive Trade Practices Act, 1956' *Parliamentary Affairs*, 1967, 101; Victor Bailey and Sheila Blackburn, 'The punishment of Incest Act 1908: a case study of law creation' *Criminal Law Review*, 1979, 708. See also Sir Noel Hutton, 'Mechanics of law reform' 24 *Modern Law Review*, 1961, 18.

1.2. Drafting Legislation

1.2.1. The Office of Parliamentary Counsel

Government bills are drafted by Parliamentary Counsel acting on the instructions of whichever government department is responsible for the legislation. (The website is www.gov.uk/

[50] Hansard Society, *Making the Law* (n 28 above) 47.

government/organisations/office-of-the-parliamentary-counsel).[51] Bills relating solely to Scotland and the Scottish provisions of United Kingdom bills are drafted by the Lord Advocate's Department.

The Office of Parliamentary Counsel (OPC) was established in 1869. Prior to that legislative drafting was done by barristers in private practice. (For a celebration of the significance of the establishment of the Office of Parliamentary Counsel see Lord Justice Sales [now Lord Sales], 'The contribution of legislative drafting to the rule of law'.[52]

The head of the office is First Parliamentary Counsel. Traditionally, First Parliamentary Counsel was someone with long experience as a drafter.[53] That may or may not still be the case. Richard Heaton who was appointed to the office in 2012 had never worked as Parliamentary Counsel. A former Home Office lawyer, he came to OPC from senior administrative posts in different government departments. By contrast, Elizabeth Gardiner had been with OPC for some 20 years when she succeeded him in 2015. Since 2012, First Parliamentary Counsel is also Permanent Secretary of the Government in Parliament Group in the Cabinet Office.

The fact that the head of the office may now be an administrator reflects the recent growth in its size which in turn reflects the workload. Remarkably, for the first fifty or so years of OPC's existence there were only two draftsmen employed. A hundred years later, by the end of the twentieth century it had grown to almost thirty and it is now around fifty, several of whom are seconded to the Law Commission and to the devolved legislatures of Wales and Northern Ireland. Scotland has always had its own cadre of drafters.

To join OPC as a drafter one must be a qualified lawyer.[54] Most come from private practice. Originally only barristers could become Parliamentary Counsel. Today the position is of course open also to solicitors. The posts are highly prized. The recruitment exercise in Spring/Summer 2014 – the first in six years – attracted some 300 applicants for four posts.[55]

In his 1951 lecture, Sir Granville Ram, First Parliamentary Counsel, spoke proudly of the quality of members of the office:

> As to the standard required I should be misleading you if I allowed any false modesty to prevent me from saying that only men and women of first-class ability can do the work. Among past and present members of the Office there have been a few who have not taken their university degrees with first-class honours, but the great majority have done so, and I may say that my three immediate predecessors in the Office of First Parliamentary Counsel all had the distinction of being Fellows of All Souls. As a result of the standard that has been maintained I can say without fear of contradiction that the members of the Office are unquestionably recognised by the Civil Service Legal Departments as a *corps d'élite*; if it were not so, satisfactory relations between them and the Office would be impossible.[56]

[51] A great deal of information as to the way OPC operates is now available on its website. See especially *Working with Parliamentary Counsel* written for the guidance of civil servants.

[52] 77(3) *Cambridge Law Journal*, 2018, 630–35. Lord Sales became a Justice of the Supreme Court in 2019.

[53] The term 'draftsman' has recently given way to the gender-neutral term 'drafter'.

[54] The Job Specification dated March 2014 said applicants should have a good honours degree '(2:1 or above or an overseas equivalent)' and be qualified to practise as a solicitor or barrister in England and Wales. They must have completed a training contract/pupillage or have been exempted.

[55] The selection process begins with an online Critical Reasoning Test to be completed at home within one week. Those selected for interview are asked to undergo a psychological assessment 'to identify key behavioural strengths as well as any associated areas for development'. On the day of the interview they are also asked to undertake a written exercise based on a spoof bill full of issues designed to test analytic skills.

[56] Granville Ram, 'The improvement of the statute book' 1 *Journal of the Society of Public Teachers of Law*, NS, 1951, 442, 444.

The training of a legislative drafter takes a long time – normally some six years before a person appointed as Assistant Parliamentary Counsel will be considered for promotion to the next level of Parliamentary Counsel. There is a formal induction programme. Traditionally, after that the training was mainly by the one-to-one exposure of working as the junior in a two- or three-person drafting team. The old system was that the trainee was attached to a particular senior for a lengthy period which could be anything from one to several years. Nowadays, the junior will work with any of the seniors in the team to which they are attached. Traditionally there was no specialisation in subject areas. A drafter was expected to be able to work on any subject matter. Today Parliamentary Counsel are organised into teams, known by the name of the team leader. Each team is allocated to the legislative projects of several government departments. So some specialisation does develop. Drafters typically spend two or three years in a team before being assigned to another team as part of career development to gain a different range of experience.

In October 2010 OPC produced a lengthy drafting manual – *Drafting Guidance* – which now plays a significant part in the training of drafters, as well as promoting best practice and uniformity of style in the office generally.[57] When a bill has been drafted, before it gets published, it will normally be subjected to internal peer review by OPC colleagues who were not involved in the drafting. This provides a further form of training.

The role of Parliamentary Counsel goes well beyond drafting. They review Explanatory Notes to Bills and Acts and sometimes subordinate legislation prepared by departmental lawyers. They also advise government on legal, parliamentary and constitutional questions.

> Parliamentary Counsel are more than just instruments of the executive's will, a specialist cadre whose professional skill lies in translating the Government's intentions into legislative form. They also act as internal guardians of values customarily regarded as integral to the legal order, such as non-retrospection, proper use of delegation, and respect for the liberties of the subject.[58] Faced with a conflict between their instructions and what they interpret as their duty to the law and the statute book, they have the power to refer their instructions to the Law Officers, who have a special responsibility for 'legislative policy' within government and who can if they agree with Counsel take up the matter with the minister whose Bill it is … [I]n the absence of a higher law by which a sovereign Parliament is bound, the concept of 'legal policy' as interpreted by Parliamentary Counsel is as close as our system has traditionally come to a check on the 'constitutionality' of legislation.[59]

However, Daniel Greenberg, a former member of OPC, regrets that that may no longer be the case:

> There was a close relationship between the Parliamentary Counsel and the Attorney General. Faced with a proposal which Counsel considered contrary to principle, he or she could and frequently did refer the matter to the Attorney, who routinely endorsed Counsel's view and gave it the support required to ensure that it prevailed within Government. The language of correspondence between Counsel and the Attorney would include language reflecting the broad range of principles that could be engaged: 'proper', 'improper', 'fair' and 'unfair' were all descriptions that

[57] At the time of writing the latest version, 112 pages, was dated March 2024 – accessible on www.gov.uk/government/publications/drafting-bills-for-parliament. For an instructive (as well as entertaining) contribution to understanding the work of drafting legislation, including the training of drafters, see Sir Geoffrey Bowman's lecture to the Statute Law Society published as 'Why is there a Parliamentary Counsel Office?' 26 *Statute Law Review*, 2005, 69.

[58] Other such principles mentioned by the authors of this passage included compliance with international law, clarity, proportionality and the restriction of expected powers of scrutiny of subordinate legislation.

[59] T Daintith and EC Page, *The Executive in the Constitution* (Oxford University Press, 1999) 255.

> might be applied to legislation. It was not considered necessary to appeal to particular technicalities, such as the European Convention on Human Rights or to formal Government documents; Counsel's feeling as to what was good and bad legislation would carry considerable weight.
>
> This particular aspect of self-regulation has been largely replaced by the concentration since the enactment of the Human Rights Act 1998 on compliance with the European Convention on Human Rights. Compatibility with the Convention rights, as construed by the jurisprudence of the European Court of Human Rights in a variety of political, constitutional and social contexts (not all of which reflect those of the UK), has to a significant extent replaced open principles of propriety and fairness as the principal language of fundamental legislative acceptability.
>
> The concept of a close group of legislative drafters imposing discipline on themselves has broken down significantly within the last two decades for a variety of reasons.[60]

One reason, he suggested, was the shift from training by one-to-one person tutorship to reliance on office manuals and 'similar techniques for imposing uniformity'. ('This change of approach may have arisen as a function of the changing size of the Office or for other reasons; but whatever the reason for it, it contributes to the changing perception and self-perception of Parliamentary Counsel as a group of independent, self-regulating and self-disciplining guardians of legislative propriety'.[61])

A new project for a bill or draft bill used to be sent by the Department to First Parliamentary Counsel who allocated it to a team. Today, the department sends the Instructions direct to the leader of the team covering that department. Individual Counsel may be involved in more than one legislative project at the same time, sometimes in differently constituted teams.

Parliamentary Counsel's work includes the drafting of government amendments as the bill is going through parliament.[62] Where the government accepts an amendment moved originally by a backbencher, the amendment will normally be re-drafted by Parliamentary Counsel. By the same token, Parliamentary Counsel will often re-draft Private Members' Bills to which the Government has offered support, and will consider whether re-drafting is required of other Private Members' Bills that are likely to become law. Help with drafting may also be provided by the Public Bill Office.

1.2.2. The Process of Drafting

Departments are advised by OPC to send detailed instructions in narrative form – *not* in the form of first drafts: 'OPC does not welcome "instructions in the form of a draft"; but it is important to explain why that is. It is not a demarcation matter. It is because the drafter needs instructions that do not inhibit the proper performance of the drafter's functions.'[63] The function at the initial stage is to master the brief – to identify the concept behind the

[60] D Greenberg, 'Dangerous Trends in Modern Legislation', *Public Law*, 2015 (1), 96–110, 97.

[61] Ibid 97.

[62] Government amendments can add very considerably to the length of Acts. For example the total length of five key bills introduced in the 1987–88 session was 714 pages but by the time they reached Royal Assent the five Acts were 1,084 pages long – an increase of 53 per cent. In session 1988–89, eight key bills totalling 1,160 pages on introduction increased in length by 43 per cent to 1,663 pages on enactment. (Statistics produced by Lord Howe in a speech to the Statute Law Society, May 1991, quoted in the Report of the Hansard Society, *Making the Law* (n 28 above) 45–46.)

[63] OPC, *Working with Parliamentary Counsel*, 2011 para 158.

proposed legislation. The drafter has to work out how best to approach it. Sir Granville Ram's description in his 1951 lecture of the process that ensues after the drafters have been assigned is still largely true today. (Text in square brackets indicates where the position has changed since 1951.)

> When the draftsman has had time to digest his instructions and inform himself as to the existing law relating to the subject in hand he usually begins by asking for a conference with the department officials in charge of the Bill, and this will be the beginning of many close interchanges between them. At this point it is desirable to define their respective responsibilities. The departmental staff [the bill team (ed)] are responsible to their Minister for the substance of the Bill and for any questions of policy that may arise. The draftsman is responsible to the Minister, to the Treasury, to the Cabinet, and to Parliament, for producing the desired result in the correct form and in language that is aptly chosen to produce the legal effect intended. He also carries responsibility for the integration and coherence of the Statute Book itself. But substance, form, policy and law, are almost inextricably mixed up. Fortunately on the one hand the draftsman will be not altogether unversed in administrative and political ways, and on the other hand the departmental staff will generally have had previous experience in the preparation of Bills. Moreover they, and especially their departmental legal adviser, will also have an intimate knowledge of such particular aspects of the law as concern their daily work. It is important that the departmental officials who confer with the draftsman should be of sufficient standing to give, or obtain speedily, authoritative answers to the many questions which he will have to put, for the process of drafting invariably throws up difficulties that have until then lain hidden below the surface. It will not be a surprise to you as lawyers, but it seems constantly to surprise laymen, to discover that, even with the most carefully thought out schemes, there are almost always innumerable points which are found to require further consideration when drafting begins. It is largely for this reason that a Parliamentary draftsman requires years of training and experience …
>
> As soon as the draftsman, with the help of the departmental officials, has sufficiently clarified the situation to enable him to prepare the first draft of the Bill he does so and sends them as many copies of it as they have asked for. There then ensues a series of conferences, telephone calls, and letters [or nowadays, emails (ed)[64]], which often call for much hard thought, many late hours, and a great deal of work on the part of all concerned. Eventually, probably after many further drafts have been prepared, criticised, and revised, the time comes when the draft Bill is in a fit state to be shown to the Minister. If the Minister interests himself closely in the preparation of his Bill, he will at this stage hold conferences upon it, which his own officials and the draftsman will be required to attend, either in his office or at the House. Time and effort devoted by a Minister to all points of importance that are thrown up in the course of the drafting is usually more than repaid to him during the passage of the Bill through Parliament.
>
> Not infrequently, while a Bill is being drafted, some point of policy or political tactics arises of such importance that reference to the Cabinet or to a Cabinet committee is necessary. Whether this step should be taken or not is, of course, a question for the Minister and one on which he may very likely seek advice from the Cabinet Office. It often saves delay to make such a reference as soon as the point emerges rather than have questions raised at the last moment when the drafting of the Bill is by way of being completed.
>
> If this picture of the labours of those engaged upon the drafting of a Bill has given the impression that the process is as leisurely as it ought to be it is indeed a false one. The drafting of a Bill

[64] 'Nowadays, instead of lengthy letters that have taken a considerable time to prepare, have been proof-read before being sent out, and which deal with a number of issues, the norm is to receive short and sharp emails, sent with such rapidity that it is impossible that the questions to which they reply can possibly have been fully appreciated, let alone a careful answer prepared' (D Greenberg, *Laying Down the Law* (Sweet & Maxwell, 2011) 138–39). As noted above, the author was formerly a member of OPC (ed).

is essentially a task that *ought* to be carried out under conditions which allow sufficient time for deliberate thought and research upon the innumerable points that invariably arise, but unfortunately such work has almost always to be done under exactly the opposite conditions.[65] To those who devote their lives to the business it is a constant source of wonder how it is that even the most experienced Ministers and civil servants never seem to appreciate that drafting always takes longer than was expected. I can say little to suggest a remedy. I can only regret that, despite many efforts, I have so often failed to impress Ministers and others with the simple fact that the drafting of a Bill does take a considerable time. How much time depends, of course, upon the length and difficulty of the Bill as well as upon the preparedness of the Department in whose charge it is. A Bill of moderate length will take several months to draft and even the shortest Bills often give rise to many difficulties and the need for much research and consultation. It is true that, in emergencies, Bills are sometimes produced with astonishing speed, but a *tour de force* of this kind disturbs the progress of other Bills in the programme, and involves an almost intolerable strain upon all who are called upon to co-operate in achieving it. Unfortunately the more experienced a Minister is the more likely it is that he will have seen Bills spring into being in this way and – well – watching a conjurer produce rabbits out of a hat is not the best training in midwifery.

There has been some writing on the actual problems faced by the parliamentary draftsman. One example is a paper written by FAR Bennion, a notable figure in this field who for many years was himself a parliamentary draftsman.[66] In his paper Bennion identified the parameters within which the draftsman had to work:

Legal effectiveness The draftsman must express the government's intentions in such a way that the statute will have its desired effect.

Procedural legitimacy The bill must comply with the procedural requirements of each House of Parliament. Parliamentary procedure governs the form of the bill. It decrees, for instance, that a bill have a long title and be divided into clauses. It allows a preamble and Schedules but no other type of formulation. It requires amendments to be in a certain form.

Timeliness The Future Legislation Committee [now the Parliamentary Business and Legislation (PBL) Committee (ed)] of the Cabinet is responsible for the government's timetable of legislation. Usually this is such as to create serious pressure on the draftsman. The pressure of time exists not merely in the period before first publication of a bill but equally after publication for the preparation of amendments.

Certainty It is usually desired that the text have one construction only. But sometimes it is intended to leave things deliberately somewhat vague – often because those responsible for the bill were themselves unable to agree as to how it should be handled.

Comprehensibility Most statute-users are lawyers or experts, but most politicians are non-lawyers and non-experts. The bill must be comprehensible to both categories.

Acceptability The language must not excite opposition; the prose style is flat; traditional and often verbose forms are normally preferred. (Bennion described how he incurred considerable criticism when he once used the phrase 'tried his best' instead of the more familiar 'used his best endeavours'.)

[65] [Normally there is a deadline in the form of a date by which the bill is required to be ready for consideration by the PBL (ed).]

[66] 'Statute law obscurity and the drafting parameters' 5 *British Journal of Law and Society*, 1978, 235.

Brevity Draftsmen are encouraged to be as brief as possible. In particular they are desired to keep down the number of clauses because MPs have the right to debate each clause if they wish.

Debatability The bill must be so framed as to allow the main points of policy to be debated. ('If they are buried in confused verbiage, it becomes difficult for Members to perceive what they are and deploy argument.')

Legal compatibility The bill when it becomes law should fit as well as possible with existing law. The language used in one statute should be the same as that used in other statutes to describe the same subject-matter. The draftsman should also indicate in their bill what its effect is on other statutory provisions – by way of repeal or amendment. Another consideration is who is the audience for the statute? The draftsman needs to have in mind whether the statute is likely to be read by other than specialists. That the statute is aimed mainly at persons familiar with the subject matter does not mean that it is drafted badly. But there is a difference if the reader may be completely innocent of any knowledge of the subject.[67]

In an address in autumn 1981, Sir George Engle, First Parliamentary Counsel, said that there were three main restraints on the preparation of bills: 'the fact that they were legal documents, shortage of time and the impracticability of continuous design'.

Sir George Engle, 'Bills are made to pass as razors are made to sell: practical constraints in the preparation of legislation' 4 *Statute Law Review*, 1983, 7, 10–15:

> ACTS OF PARLIAMENT ARE LEGAL DOCUMENTS
>
> The fact that Acts of Parliament are legal documents marks them off from other kinds of writing with which they are sometimes unfavourably compared, such as works of literature, text-books, political manifestos and journalism. Their special character is well described by Sir Bruce Fraser in his revision of Gowers' *The Complete Plain Words*:
>
>> 'The legal draftsman', he says, '… has to ensure to the best of his ability that what he says will be found to mean precisely what he intended, even after it has been subject to detailed and possibly hostile scrutiny by acute legal minds …'
>>
>> 'Legal drafting must therefore be unambiguous, precise [and] comprehensive … If it is readily intelligible, so much the better; but it is far more important that it should yield its meaning accurately than that it should yield it on first reading, and the legal draftsman cannot afford to give much attention, if any, to euphony or literary elegance. What matters most to him is that no one will succeed in persuading a court of law that his words bear a meaning he did not intend, and, if possible, that no one will think it worthwhile to try.'
>
> Our statute book goes back to the year 1235. A great deal of the dead wood has been cleared away; but over the centuries there is hardly a topic that has not attracted its share of legislation. Once there has been legislation on a given topic, it is only a matter of time before a further round of legislation on the same topic is found to be necessary; and the nearer one gets to the present, the shorter is the interval between one round and the next.
>
> This proliferation of statute law on every topic means that each new change in the law has to be meticulously knitted into the existing fabric; and this in turn means that the draftsman's room for manoeuvre is more often than not severely limited by the need to make what he has to say fit in with, and match, the structure and language of existing statute law. In my experience it is

[67] See Francis Bennion, 'If it's not broke don't fix it: a review of the New Zealand Law Commission's proposals on the format of legislation' 15 *Statute Law Review*, 1994, 165.

> comparatively rare for the draftsman to be entirely free of this particular form of constraint for more than a few lines at a time.

As will be seen below, the process of re-drafting and amendment may be influenced not only by all the other forms of lobbying, but by reports of parliamentary committees such as the Joint Committee on Human Rights, the House of Commons Home Affairs Committee, the House of Lords Constitution Committee etc.

1.3. Criticism of the Quality of Drafting

The 1975 Report of the Renton Committee (*The Preparation of Legislation*, Cmnd 6053) said that criticism of the quality of drafting of statutes was common centuries ago:

> 2.8 As long ago as the 16th and 17th centuries there were in England many expressions of dissatisfaction with, and projects for reforming, the drafting of statutes and the shape of the statute book. These early critics included Edward VI ('I would wish that … the superfluous and tedious statutes were brought into one sum together, and made more plain and short, to the intent that men might better understand them'), Lord Keeper Sir Nicholas Bacon ('a short plan for reducing, ordering, and printing the Statutes of the Realm'), James I ('divers cross and cuffing statutes … [should] be once maturely reviewed and reconciled; and … all contrarieties should be scraped out of our books'), and Sir Francis Bacon, when Attorney General ('the reducing of concurrent statutes, heaped one upon another, to one clear and uniform law').

Lord Justice Harman gave colourful expression to such exasperation in a case in 1964:

> To reach a conclusion on this matter involved the court in wading through a monstrous legislative morass, staggering from stone to stone and ignoring the marsh gas exhaling from the forest of schedules lining the way on each side. I regarded it at one time, I must confess, as a Slough of Despond through which the court would never drag its feet but I have, by leaping from tussock to tussock as best I might, eventually, pale and exhausted, reached the other side.[68]

Increasingly such criticism mounted.[69] In 1973 the government set up the Committee under the chairmanship of Sir David Renton (later Lord Renton). Its terms of reference were: 'With a view to achieving greater simplicity, and clarity in statute law to review the form in which Public Bills are drafted, excluding consideration of matters relating to policy formulation and the legislative programme; and to consider any consequential implications for Parliamentary procedure.'

The Report of the Renton Committee on the *Preparation of Legislation* (1975) said that it had received evidence from judges, bodies representing the legal and other professions, from non-professional bodies and from prominent laymen, that much statute law lacked simplicity and clarity. The complaints, it said (p 27), fell into four main categories:

(*a*) *Language* It was said that the language used was obscure and complex, its meaning elusive and its effect uncertain. The Statute Law Society criticised the language of statutes as: 'legalistic, often obscure and circumlocutious, requiring a certain type of

[68] *Davy v Leeds Corporation* [1964] 1 WLR 1218, 1224.

[69] See, for instance, Statute Law Society, *Statute Law Deficiencies* (Sweet & Maxwell, 1970), and *Statute Law: The Key to Clarity* (Sweet & Maxwell, 1972).

expertise in order to gauge its meaning. Sentences are long and involved, the grammar is obscure, and archaisms, legally meaningless words and phrases, tortuous language, the preference for the double negative over the single positive, abound.'

(b) *Over-elaboration* It was said that the desire for 'certainty' in the application of legislation leads to over-elaboration. The parliamentary drafter tried to provide for every contingency. The committee said that this was because of concern on the part of the legislature to ensure against the possibility that the legislation will be construed by someone, in some remote circumstances, so as to have a different effect from that envisaged by those preparing the bill in question. (p 29).

(c) *Structure*

> Many of the witnesses have said that more attention should be paid to the logical sequence of the provisions of statutes, and that there should be a consistent approach to such questions as what kind of provision should go in the main body of the Act and what in the Schedules, so that people could more easily find their way about them. There is also the criticism that sentences are sometimes too long, and complicated by too many subordinate phrases, and that there should be greater readiness to break up clauses into separate subsections. (pp 30–31)

(d) *Arrangement and amendment* The chronological arrangement of the statutes and the lack of clear connection between various Acts bearing on related subjects were said to cause confusion and made it difficult to ascertain the current state of the law on any given matter. This confusion was increased by the practice of amending an existing Act, not by altering its text (and reprinting it as a new Act) but by passing a new Act which the reader had to apply to the existing Act and work out the meaning for themself:

> … there is another problem. New laws frequently amend existing statutes. Such amendment, however, by no means always takes the form of substituting a fresh and amended text in the statute which is being amended. The 'non-textual' amendment of legislation has been criticised by many of our witnesses, though some of them conceded that its use may be unavoidable. Amendments drafted non-textually have been described as being:
>
> > Drafted in a narrative or discursive style producing an inter-woven web of allusion, cross-reference and
>
> The other method of amending previous legislation which several witnesses have commended to us is the system of 'textual amendment'. By using this method new statutes which alter the provisions of earlier Acts give effect to such alterations by enacting fresh portions of text which are then added to or substituted for the earlier version.

The non-textual form of amendment was more difficult for the ordinary user since it not only required reference to earlier legislation but often left considerable doubt as to how the two provisions should be read together (conflated). By contrast, the textual form of amendment enabled the reader to see exactly how the old law had been amended, providing only they had both the old and the new before them. The Committee said textual amendments were generally preferable.[70]

A possible solution to this problem is what is called 'a Keeling Schedule' – a schedule to the Act setting out the text as amended.[71] However, for whatever reason, Keeling Schedules are used very rarely. In fact, as will be seen, non-textual amendment has fallen

[70] See JM Keyes, 'Incorporation by reference in legislation' 25 *Statute Law Review*, 2004, 180.

[71] So-called because it was the suggestion of Mr EH Keeling, MP for Twickenham, in 1938. For an example of a Keeling Schedule see the London Local Authorities Act 2012 Sch 2.

into disrepute. Textual amendment is now the norm. Today, for those with access to Westlaw or LexisNexis, these problems have disappeared as they provide online access to statutes as amended.

In 1997, Sir William Dale published a study in which he compared the approach to legislative drafting in France, Germany, Sweden and the United Kingdom. Sir William, a former legal adviser to the Commonwealth Office, concluded that our system was the least satisfactory:

Sir William Dale, *Legislative Drafting: A New Approach* (Butterworths, 1977) 331–33.

> [Sir William summarised the features that appeared to make for obscurity or length or both in United Kingdom statutes:]
>
> *(a)* long, involved sentences and sections;
> *(b)* much detail, little principle;
> *(c)* an indirect approach to the subject-matter;
> *(d)* subtraction – as in 'Subject to …', 'Provided that …';
> *(e)* centrifugence – a flight from the centre to definition and interpretation clauses;
> *(f)* poor arrangement;
> *(g)* schedules – too many and too long;
> *(h)* cross-references to other Acts – saving space, but increasing the vexation.
>
> In contrast, lucid and often succinct drafting is to be found in the countries on the European continent, represented in this study by France, Germany and Sweden. The continental lawmakers, influenced by their heritage of codes, think out their laws in terms of principle, or at least of broad intention, and express the principle of intention in the legislation. This is the primary duty of the legislator – to make his general will clear. An orderly unfolding of the concepts and rules follows; and whenever it is necessary to give the meaning of a term, it is done when that term first makes its appearance.
>
> The characteristics of French drafting are clarity of principle, of form and of word, a logical development, economy of expression, and a resultant brevity. The French, as their President has observed, 'like things to be said and done clearly, on the basis of an overall concept'.
>
> In Sweden the laws are drafted in layman's language, often with some generality of expression and even greater brevity. Technical terms are likely to be in the legislative material, the *Proposition*, to which recourse is constantly had. In some laws in the social field the policy is to use general language, set up special courts, and leave them to develop the law in the light of varying circumstances and changing conditions.
>
> In Germany the practice is to state a principle, and then to fill in the detail with, very often, great thoroughness. There is necessarily some length, but a systematic arrangement. At times one finds thick clusters of sentences. Some contain matter which in the United Kingdom would be put into regulations: German statutes rarely contain a regulation-making power.

Sir William Dale identified one problem as being the lack of any adequate process of revision or review of draft legislation (pp 334–35):

> In France all draft laws are examined and revised as necessary by the Conseil d'Etat; in Sweden many are referred to the Law Council; in Germany there is no similar body, the Ministry of Justice performing an examining and co-ordinating role for all Federal draft laws.
>
> Parliamentary committees then closely scrutinise all draft Bills, in round-the-table discussions attended by ministers and civil servants, and report on the Bills, with draft amendments proposed, to the House. In Germany the scrutiny by the committees of the Bundesrat, the second Chamber, to which the Government *must* under the Constitution first send all its Bills, is particularly efficacious.

As will be seen, government draft bills are now sometimes published as part of the consultation process (see 2.8 below).

See to same effect Sir William Dale, 'A London particular' 6 *Statute Law Review*, 1985, 11. Similar thoughts on the contrast between English and continental methods were expressed by Professor Clarence Smith of the University of Ottawa: JA Clarence Smith, 'Legislative drafting: English and continental' 1 *Statute Law Review*, 1980, 14.

Mr T Millett, Legal Secretary at the Court of Justice of the European Communities, analysed the differences between the English and French Nationality Acts as an illustration of the national styles of legislative drafting: Timothy Millett, 'A comparison of British and French legislative drafting (with particular reference to their respective Nationality Laws)' 7 *Statute Law Review*, 1986, 130, 158–60.

See further, Institute of Advanced Legal Studies, *British and French Statutory Drafting: Proceedings of the Franco-British Conference, April 1986* (The Institute, 1986); Sir William Dale, 'The European legislative scene' 13 *Statute Law Review*, 1992, 79; FAR Bennion, 'How they do things in France' 16 *Statute Law Review*, 1995, 90; and J Massot, 'Legislative drafting in France: the role of the Conseil'd'Etat' 22 *Statute Law Review*, 2001, 96.

For reflections on the differences between the United States and the United Kingdom in regard to drafting of statutes – rather to the advantage of the latter – see Reed Dickerson, 'Legislative drafting in London and Washington' 17 *Cambridge Law Journal*, 1959, 49.

1.4. What to do about the Quality of the Statute Book?

Sir William Dale offered a number of possible remedies for the condition of the statute book:

(1) *Changes in drafting technique* 'We need at least to reduce the verbal impedimenta; to be less fussy over detail, to be more general and concise; and to situate each rule where it belongs, in an orderly and logical development. On this level, the question is largely a matter of style and arrangement. A more profound change is also desirable: a determination to seek the principle, to express it, and to follow up with such detail, illuminating and not obscuring the principle, as the circumstances require' (Dale, *Legislative drafting*, 335).

(2) *The establishment of a Law Council* To advise the government on draft bills. It would include judges, practising lawyers, academics, lay authors, members of consumer councils, etc. 'Its duty would be to examine [draft bills] from the point of view of coherent and orderly presentation, clarity, conciseness, soundness of legal principle, and suitability for attaining the Government's objective' (Dale, *Legislative drafting*, 336). It would report to the minister responsible. The role of the Law Council would be similar to that played in France by the Conseil d'Etat, which reviews all draft legislation in discussion with an official of the initiating department. If the ministry is not prepared to accept an amendment proposed by the Conseil d'Etat, it states its reasons and the matter is determined by the Council of Ministers.

Technically, the French government was not bound to submit to views put by the Conseil d'Etat, but in practice it normally did so, especially on matters of form. In regard to substance the government also normally followed the advice given when it concerned legal points. If the matters raised concern policy, the government might or might not follow the advice given.

Also the fact that everyone knew that the Conseil d'Etat had to be brought in at the end of the process before it went to Parliament meant that there were indirect effects. Civil servants obviously tried to anticipate objections that might be made and so avoid them in advance. According to M Ducamin, the fact that the Conseil d'Etat was there as a check was a matter of security for both civil servants and ministers. The power was exercised in a restrained and responsible manner and was generally highly respected.

(3) *A greater hand in the drafting process to be given to experts in the subject-matter rather than experts in drafting* Instead of all drafting being done by Parliamentary Counsel, at least some should be done within departments, as was the case in continental countries and was the case in the United Kingdom for delegated legislation.

(4) *Improved system for parliamentary examination of legislation* 'A legislative body is wise to arm itself with the means of criticising and revising the draft Bills laid before it; and this the continental system of parliamentary working parties provides' (Dale, *Legislative drafting*, 340). The report of such a committee, reflecting discussions with ministers and civil servants and setting out amendments, would be a helpful guide to the House when the bill came to be debated.

The Renton Committee also made many proposals for possible reforms. Most of its proposals related to matters too detailed to consider here (regarding the layout of statutes, punctuation, internal cross-referencing, the use of definitions, etc). The Committee thought, however, that consideration should be given to providing a training course for legislative drafting (para 8.16), and that more draftsmen should be recruited 'as a matter of high priority' (para 8.22). The use of statements of principle should be encouraged – where detailed guidance was called for in addition, it should be given in Schedules (para 10.13). More use might be made of examples in Schedules to show how a bill was intended to work in particular situations (para 10.07). Long un-paragraphed sentences should be avoided (para 11.12). Statements of purpose should be used when they were the most convenient method of clarifying the scope and effect of legislation (para 11.8).

The Renton Committee considered but rejected the idea that there should be some form of prior scrutiny of draft bills. It concluded that 'it must be left to government departments themselves to decide what advice they should seek before presentation [of legislation] from advisory bodies on the drafting'.[72]

Nor was the Committee persuaded that there should be such scrutiny machinery after a bill had been published. ('Having weighed the arguments on both sides, we do not think that there is any practical scope for introducing a new scrutiny stage during the Parliamentary process. This would in our opinion impose strain on a Parliamentary machine which is already under great pressure, and would also add to the labours of the draftsmen who have more than enough to do as it is to keep pace with the legislative programme' (para 18.33, p 131).)

[72] Renton Report, *Preparation of Legislation* (HMSO, 1975), p 130, para 18.29.

Francis Bennion, himself a sharp critic of the condition of the statute book, was not convinced that Sir William Dale was right to think that the style of continental drafting was preferable to our own. In a review of Sir William's book (1 *Statute Law Review*, 1980, 61), he said:

> Sir William holds that a statute should be drafted so that it can be understood by all affected by it. An author should be able to understand a statute on copyright, a family man a statute on family law, a land owner a statute on land law, and so on. This sounds fine until we look more closely. Copyright law applies to every sort of creator or performer, from the writer of an article in a parish magazine to the man who does lightning sketches on the pier. We are all family men or women, and most of us are at some time landowners or tenants. Thus Sir William might as well have said statute law should be drafted so that it can be understood by all. That only has to be stated for its impracticability to be apparent. Yet the Swedes don't find it impracticable. They draft in layman's language, Sir William tells us. His first extract from a Swedish statute deals with copyright. 'The performance of a work at a place of business for a comparatively large closed group of people shall be considered a public performance.'
>
> It would be interesting to hear laymen discussing whether a public hall hired by a firm for a staff party is a 'place of business', or 43 persons consisting of the firm's staff with a few relatives and friends is a 'comparatively large closed group'. To find the answer the Swedes might go, like most continental users, to the *travaux préparatoires*. For Sir William tells us that 'the legislature has often deliberately left it to the inquirer, whether citizen, lawyer or judge, to go to the legislative material to find out more precisely what was intended.'
>
> What are the essential features of continental drafting? The book does not give a clear answer, perhaps because the concept is not as definite as is sometimes thought. One element is the background presence of a general code: 'Codification, willy-nilly, involves – nay, is – the continental style.' Another element, leading from the first, is the tendency to state a principle.
>
> > 'The continental lawmakers, influenced by their heritage of codes, think out their laws in terms of principle, or at least of broad intention, and express the principle or intention in the legislation. This is the primary duty of the legislator – to make his general will clear. An orderly unfolding of the concepts and rules follows …'
>
> Sir William castigates the British Copyright Act of 1956, for example, because it nowhere states the principle of what copyright is, but merely lists the acts restricted by the existence of copyright in a work. He overlooks the fact that the pragmatic British are chary of statements of principle. They mistrust them because they invariably have to be qualified by exceptions and conditions before being fitted for real life. Sir William, quoting the rule in *Leviticus* that when one man strikes another and kills him, he shall be put to death, adds: 'We observe the complete generality, and the utter certainty.' In fact of course, as to some degree he admits later, there is no such certainty. Suppose the striking is accidental, or the striker is insane? Suppose death occurs after a long interval, or the sufferer was already mortally ill? What does 'strikes' mean? Does it include riding a horse at a man, or pulling down his house about his ears? What is the value of a statement of principle that later has to be qualified almost out of existence? In the rare case where statements of principle are possible without suffering this defect they are often made by British draftsmen. Sir William recognises this when he praises the long title to the Consumer Credit Act 1974.
>
> Another feature of continental drafting is willingness to leave more to the courts. Sir William extols this, but it has two undesirable aspects. One is that until a court has had an opportunity of pronouncing on the point the law is uncertain. The other is that too much of the legislative power may thereby pass from Parliament to the judges. Those who hanker for a revival of judge-made law need to remember that the greatness of the common law lay in its defence of the citizen against

> despotic monarchs. A democratic Parliament cannot sensibly be likened to a despotic monarch. We do not need, nor do most of us desire, to be saved by our judges from the intentions of our Parliament. Sir William records that the French, on the other hand, 'have, under the influence of Gény, allowed the judge to soar from the text into the headier regions of ethics, political science, sociology and the like.' There are those, led by Lord Scarman … who aim at a similar ascent by the British judiciary …
>
> The book gives no proof that we would benefit from going over to the continental system; it could scarcely be expected to. It requires the background presence of a code, which we do not have and are not likely to get. It requires legislation to be prefaced by the statement of principles, which is foreign to British temperament. It produces a considerable degree of uncertainty. It does not enable Parliament to assert its will with the particularity British political conditions require. It gives too much legislative power to non-elected judges. Also to be considered is the fact that if a change-over were made we would have a dual system for many years while the existing body of statute law was replaced.

Speaking to the Statute Law Society in April 1978, Lord Renton said that little had been done to implement the recommendations of his Committee. The Committee had recommended that statements of purpose should be included in statutes but there had been 'scarcely any statements of purpose occurring in legislation since we published in May 1975'.

More important, the Cabinet had decided not to accept the recommendation that the Statute Law Committee keep 'the structure and language of statutes under continuous review'. (See 'Failure to implement the Renton Report', speech of Sir David Renton, in *Renton and the Need for Reform* (Sweet & Maxwell on behalf of the Statute Law Society, 1979) 2–8.)

It is likely that the failure of the Renton Committee's proposals was due as much as anything to the powerful lobbying of Parliamentary Counsel's Office. If they are against an idea affecting their work it is difficult for it to come to fruition. Technically it is part of the Cabinet Office under the authority of the Prime Minister but in practice it is effectively not accountable to anyone. Obviously the draftsmen on a particular bill work for the minister in charge of that bill. But there is no minister who has the power or the position to instruct the Office of Parliamentary Counsel as to how they should perform their duties. (In 1964–65 Lord Gardiner, Lord Chancellor in Harold Wilson's government, proposed that responsibility for Parliamentary Counsel be taken over by the Lord Chancellor. But this proposal 'aroused a storm of protest in Whitehall' and Gardiner dropped the idea.[73])

The Hansard Society's 1992 *Report on the Legislative Process Making the Law* said that it had rejected Sir William Dale's proposal for pre-natal scrutiny of bills to consider drafting, constitutional, legal and other non-policy matters. First, it thought it best if the drafting style of statutes should be consistent, which might suffer if such a system were in place. Secondly, the scrutiny body would not have sufficient expertise to undertake the task since all the experts were in Parliamentary Counsel's Office. Thirdly, the interposition of the scrutiny process would introduce unacceptable additional delay into the process (pp 49–50).

However, the Hansard Society's Report said (p 50) that there was a danger of complacency and that it might be a good thing 'for someone to keep an eye on Parliamentary Counsel'. It was not enough to leave responsibility with ministers in charge of individual bills – 'neither the Minister or the officials … will have time to read each bill with the care

[73] S Cretney, 'The Law Commission: true dawns and false dawns' 59 *Modern Law Review*, 1996, 631, 636–37.

required to test the drafting' (ibid). Also 'maintenance of good drafting standards across the board will not be achieved by having each bill scrutinised in the department that is preparing that bill'. Some central responsibility was required. This function, it thought, should be performed by the Cabinet's Legislation Committee (now the Parliamentary Business and Legislation Committee) – but given the way that Committee operates this seems an unrealistic recommendation.

The Hansard Society Report also recommended (p 51) that the Attorney-General rather than the Cabinet Office should be responsible for the establishment and expenses of Parliamentary Counsel, though the most senior appointments should continue to be made by the Prime Minister. The Attorney-General should have ministerial responsibility for the work of Parliamentary Counsel 'and particularly for oversight of the drafting methods employed and scrutiny of the drafting of all Government Bills' (p 51). First Parliamentary Counsel would be accountable to the Attorney-General for the day-to-day work of the Office but they would remain responsible to the Chairman of the Legislation Committee for the delivery of drafted bills.

In regard to the style of drafting, the Hansard Society's Report did not agree with Sir William Dale and the Renton Committee that statements of general principle in statutes would help. It shared the view expressed by Conservative Attorney- General, Sir Patrick Mayhew (later Lord Mayhew), who said, 'I confess to great difficulty in seeing how a general statement of principle or purpose could enable the law to be developed by the judges, and thereby affect the public's rights, in a way foreseeable with sufficient accuracy by that public'.[74]

1.4.1. Plain Language Drafting

Mr Martin Cutts in 1979 co-founded the Plain English Campaign. In the early 1980s he had meetings with two successive First Parliamentary Counsel to discuss the prospects for plain language in English statutes. They did not encourage him to think that they were persuaded by his suggestion that the statute book could benefit from radical changes in drafting style. But they challenged him to try to produce his own draft of an actual statute. Mr Cutts responded to this challenge. In 1993 he circulated *Unspeakable Acts?* as a discussion paper based on his attempted redraft of the Timeshare Act 1992. (His version, cheekily, was entitled 'The Clearer Timeshare Act 1993'.) In the light of comments (including eleven and a half pages of comments from the drafter of the original act – see p 29 below), Mr Cutts produced a revised text. The Cutts version had a great variety of changes in regard to structure, typography, lay-out and, above all, drafting. For example:

Defined terms were listed on each page so that the reader could see at a glance whether anything on the page was defined in the definition section.

Definitions were all collected in one section at the end instead of being scattered in more than one section as before.[75]

[74] Sir Patrick Mayhew, 'Can legislation ever be simple, clear, and certain?' 11 *Statute Law Review*, 1990, 1, 7.

[75] In the 1997–98 parliamentary session such an index to definitions was used in the Government of Wales Act, the Government of Scotland Act, the Schools and Standards Framework Act and the Data Protection Act which respectively had 42, 57, 67 and 44 defined expressions. But in the same session the government resisted attempts to

Sections were grouped with a group heading.

Headings were used more than in ordinary statutes. They were also more informative.

Section numbers were in the form 1.1, 1.2, etc. Further subdivisions however used the present form – thus 1.1(a)(ii).

Section headings were in bold type.

Footnotes were used to indicate cross-references to other Acts and regulations.

Spacing between sections and subsections was more generous than in ordinary statutes.

Typeface was changed to improve appearance.

Type size was somewhat larger. The Schedule was in the same size type as the main part of the Act, instead of smaller as is the normal style.

Running heads at the top of each page indicated the sections dealt with on that page.

Simpler language was used throughout. Thus, for illustration, section 2 of the Act stated:

> 2. (1) A person must not in the course of a business enter into a timeshare agreement to which this Act applies as offeror unless the offeree has received, together with a document setting out the terms of the agreement or the substance of those terms, notice of his right to cancel the agreement.
>
> (2) A notice under this section must state—
>
> (a) that the offeree is entitled to give notice of cancellation of the agreement to the offeror at any time on or before the date specified in the notice, being a day falling not less than fourteen days after the day on which the agreement is entered into, and
>
> (b) that if the offeree gives such a notice to the offeror on or before that date he will have no further rights or obligations under the agreement, but will have the right to recover any sums paid under or in contemplation of the agreement.

The equivalent section in the Cutts' version stated:

> 2 Seller's duty to give information about a timeshare agreement
>
> 2.1 Before a seller enters into a timeshare agreement, the seller must give the customer a right-to-cancel notice and a document setting out the terms of the agreement or the substance of its terms.
>
> 2.2 The right-to-cancel notice must show that:
>
> (a) the customer may cancel the agreement by giving the seller a notice of cancellation on or before the date specified in the right-to-cancel notice, which must be at least fourteen days after the agreement is entered into; and
>
> (b) the customer who cancels has no further rights or duties under the agreement, except to get back any money paid to the seller under the agreement or while considering entering into it.

For a commentary on Martin Cutts' draft by the Parliamentary Counsel who drafted the Timeshare Act, see Euan Sutherland, 'Clear drafting and the Timeshare Act 1992: a response from Parliamentary Counsel to Mr Cutts' 14 *Statute Law Review*, 1993, 163. Martin Cutts,

introduce such an index into the Competition Act which had 59 defined expressions – on the grounds that 'it would be unhelpful to users'! (See Lord Brightman, 'Drafting quagmires' 23 *Statute Law Review*, 2002, 1, 9–10.)

after amending his draft in response to criticisms, replied in 'Plain English in the law' 17 *Statute Law Review*, 1996, 50. He reported that when his version was tested against the real Act by 91 students on placement with leading law firms, the great majority thought that his was the clearer. When answering questions on the Act, the students using his revision performed better on nine out of twelve questions. (The Law Reform Commission of Victoria reported similar results in a study they undertook.[76]) Cutts concluded that statute law could be clarified markedly without significant loss of accuracy. He returned the challenge originally put to him by First Parliamentary Counsel by asking his successor to say whether, if he were an MP, a judge or an ordinary citizen he would prefer to use the real Act or Martin Cutts' version.

See also J Stark, 'Should the main goal of statutory drafting be accuracy or clarity?' 15 *Statute Law Review*, 1994, 207; I Turnbull, 'Legislative drafting in plain language and statements of general principle' 18 *Statute Law Review*, 1997, 21; Ruth Sullivan, 'Some implications of plain language drafting' 22 *Statute Law Review*, 2001, 175; P Butt, 'Modern legal drafting' 23 *Statute Law Review*, 2002, 12; B Hunt, 'Plain language in legislative drafting: is it really the answer?' 23 *Statute Law Review*, 2002, 24; 'Plain language in legislative drafting: an achievable objective or a laudable ideal' 24 *Statute Law Review*, 2003, 112.

For an account of typographical and other stylistic changes made to New Zealand statutes see R Castler, 'Legislation in New Zealand', *Solicitors' Journal*, 11 August 2000, 755.

1.4.2. The Tax Law Rewrite

Signs that the Plain English campaign had made progress came with the announcement of a major government initiative to simplify tax law. The project, known as the Tax Law Rewrite, had its origins in the mid-1990s. The Finance Act 1995, s 160 required the Inland Revenue to prepare and present to Treasury ministers a report on tax simplification. In November 1995, the then Chancellor of the Exchequer, Mr Kenneth Clarke MP, in the course of his Budget statement, announced that the plan was that 'the Revenue tax code is rewritten in plain English – a major task'.[77] 'The project', he said, 'is as ambitious as translating the whole of "War and Peace" into lucid Swahili. In fact it is more ambitious. I am told that "War and Peace" is only 1,500 pages long. Inland Revenue law is 6,000 pages long and was not written by a Tolstoy'.

The Inland Revenue's report *The Path to Tax Simplification* together with a background report 'The path to tax simplication: a background paper' was published in December 1995. It set out the perceived criticisms of tax legislation – complicated syntax, long sentences, archaic or ambiguous language, obscurity of meaning, the spread of relevant provisions among different statutes, the principles underlying the rules not being apparent, excessive detail, especially in primary legislation. The techniques envisaged included the use of plain language, rationalisation of definitions, reordering and renumbering, omitting outdated or unnecessary material and better design and layout. The Inland Revenue would lead but there would be full consultation with experts and with users.

[76] See P Butt, 'Modern legal drafting' 23 *Statute Law Review*, 2002, 12, 22.
[77] HC *Hansard*, November 28 1995, vol 1995–96, col 1066.

In July 1996 the Revenue published *The Tax Law Rewrite: The Way Forward.* This stated that arrangements had been made for a novel, formalised pre-parliamentary consultative process. This involved the creation of three distinct bodies: the Project Team, the Consultative Committee and the Steering Committee. The task of devising and carrying out the programme of work, including setting of priorities, was for the Project Team.[78] The Consultative Committee's job was to secure maximum consultation.[79] The Steering Committee, under the chairmanship of former Chancellor of the Exchequer, Lord Howe of Aberavon, supervised the whole operation.[80] The Project Team actually doing the work consisted of some forty persons.[81]

There was public consultation in the form of a series of Exposure Drafts which published clauses in draft, and draft bills were published for further consultation.

The Inland Revenue estimated that the Rewrite would be even longer than the 6,000 pages of statutory material it was replacing. When the Project began in 1996 it was suggested that the first Rewrite Bill would be enacted by 1998 and that the whole operation would take some four to five years. This timetable proved considerably over-optimistic. Professor Roger Kerridge of Bristol University, commenting in 2003 on the Income Tax (Earnings and Pensions) Act 2003 (ITEPA) wrote, 'The whole process has proved much slower, more time consuming, and more expensive, than originally envisaged'.[82] The project was still going 13 years later, in 2009, at which point the Labour Government announced that it would be brought to an end in 2010. By then there had been seven Rewrite Acts.[83]

Was all the time, effort and expense worthwhile? The object, Professor Kerridge said, had been to set out the relevant legislation in such a way as to give it a new, more logical structure, to use modern language, shorter sentences, better use of definitions, better sign-posting and a new format and layout to make it easier to read, but without changing the substance.

> In these terms, the 2003 Act is a success ... *but*, and this is the caveat, there is only a limited amount that can be achieved with no change of substance ... The Act is not short. It consists of 725 sections plus a further 8 schedules ... The layout is relatively easy to follow and a huge improvement on what it replaces. Having said this, the suggestion made in the Joint Parliamentary Committee, that someone new to the subject ... would only have to buy a copy of the Act and read it, to obtain straightforward enlightenment, seems a bit optimistic. The layout is clear, the sentences are short, the English is modern, but the obvious disincentive, for the would-be reader new to the subject, is the enormity of it all ... Those who really will welcome this rewritten legislation will *not* be novice readers; they will be those who had a reasonable acquaintance with what went before. For them, this is a clear improvement.[84]

[78] Mainly persons drawn from HM Revenue and Customs (HMRC) and from the Office of Parliamentary Counsel.

[79] Most of the 20 or so members were tax practitioners.

[80] The membership consisted of some eight to ten persons at any one time drawn from the Houses of Parliament, the judiciary, the tax, legal profession and business.

[81] A Drafting team and four Rewrite teams. The Rewrite teams researched the existing legislation, extra statutory concessions, practice and other relevant material on the basis of which they prepared instructions for the Drafting Team. (Q1 of the Evidence of the Rewrite team to the Joint Committee on Tax Law Rewrite Bills, 14 January 2003 appended to the Committee's Report, 24 January 2003).

[82] R Kerridge, 'The Income Tax (Earnings and Pensions) Act 2003' *British Tax Review*, 2003, 257.

[83] Capital Allowances Act 2001; Income Tax (Earnings and Pensions) Act 2003; Income Tax (Trading and Other Income) Act 2005; Income Tax Act 2007; Corporation Tax Act 2009; Corporation Tax Act 2010; Tax (International and Other Provisions) Act 2010.

[84] Kerridge, 'The Income Tax (Earnings and Pensions) Act 2003' (n 82 above) 258.

Professor Kerridge said, if this rewritten legislation were looked at by someone from another country what would probably strike them was '(i) the enormous amount of petti-fogging detail and (ii) the apparent lack of any underlying logic'.[85] United Kingdom tax law had been described as 'a shambles'. To explain it, it was usually best to begin with its history. But the Rewrite actually made it more, rather than less, difficult to follow the history of the provisions. The rules had been taken further out of their historical context and had been reassembled neatly. 'But if an outsider were now to attempt to guess *why* particular rules had been enacted in the first place, he or she would generally have no clue … In some ways the tidying up operation has disguised the underlying incoherence, in other ways it has highlighted it.'[86] Or, as M Parry-Wingfield put it in an earlier comment, 'we now find that the Rewrite cruelly exposes tax laws that are inconsistent, irrational or fundamentally complex'.[87]

The big question, Professor Kerridge said, was whether the Rewrite represented the start of something much grander – actual simplification of tax law? This could involve purposive redrafting – assuming that its purposes could be discerned. He considered that although this was theoretically possible, it was too big a step to take at the present time. 'It would involve too much change and would take too long.' But it would be possible to have something between a purposive redraft and the present Rewrite. What was needed was to set in train a process whereby the legislation was first rewritten and then simplified.[88]

There seems to be general agreement that the Tax Law Rewrite did produce legislation that was clearer and easier to use with a more logical and easily navigable structure and more accessible language. But it was far from clear that on balance it had been worthwhile. It had tied up a large number of experts for years, at enormous cost estimated to be some £40 million pounds. The fact that the project stopped before it was completed meant that tax law was partly rewritten and partly old-style. The re-written law was easier to use for new users, but those who knew their way around the old-style did not necessarily welcome having to master the new product. For one thing, as had been foreseen by the Revenue, the Rewrite was significantly longer than the legislation it replaced. Anyone familiar with the old system had to master the significantly different new system. Once the project came to an end there was anyway the possibility that the tax legislation system would gradually revert to the previous way of proceeding. But above all, the Tax Law Rewrite had only aimed at making the law clearer it had not purported to make it simpler.

In March 2010, the month that the Rewrite was brought to an end, the Law Society in its paper *Tax: Good Governance and Better Law Making: A Manifesto for Improving Tax Law*, wrote that tax law in the UK was 'unclear and complex', that much of it 'still lacks simplicity and clarity' and that, arguably, the Rewrite had made more obvious the underlying problems of tax legislation, namely 'its volume, frequency of change and sheer complexity'. In 2017, the Lords Constitution Committee quoted a discouraging assessment of the long-term effect of the Tax Law Rewrite project by the Institute of Chartered Accountants in England and Wales: 'It is also unfortunate that the lessons of the Tax Law Rewrite project have not been remembered. For a short period, legislation was drafted in better English, making it more manageable. Lack of resource is presumably why this is no longer happening, but the consequences for those who seek to apply it, accountants, lawyers

[85] Ibid.
[86] Ibid, 258–59.
[87] M Parry-Wingfield, 'The chicken or the egg?' *British Tax Review*, 2000, 597, 598.
[88] Kerridge, 'The Income Tax (Earnings and Pensions) Act 2003' (n 82 above) 262.

and the general public who are governed by it, are that it takes longer to work with and interpret, and mistakes are made.'[89] *Craies on Legislation*, concluding the section on the Tax Law Rewrite says 'there is no sign that it has ushered in a new dawn of legislative drafting and composition, either generally or even in relation to tax legislation'.[90]

In July 2010 the Coalition Government established a new Office of Tax Simplification to advise government, with members drawn partly from the Treasury and HMRC and partly from the private sector. The OTS was made a permanent independent Office of HM Treasury in 2015 and was placed on a statutory basis in ss 184 to 189 of, and Schedule 25 to, Finance Act 2016.

1.5. The 'Good Law' Initiative

In April 2013 the Institute for Government hosted a seminar in collaboration with the Cabinet Office and the Office of Parliamentary Counsel (OPC) to launch the Good Law initiative, the purpose of which was to improve legislation generally and make it more understandable. Richard Heaton, then First Parliamentary Counsel, explained:

> [P]eople are using legislation – reading, searching, accessing, downloading – in a way that has never happened before. Between 2 and 3 million people log on to the legislation.gov.uk website every month and there are getting on for half a billion page downloads a year … How does a reader make sense of a complicated network of statute law? Is it possible to reduce complexity, or improve accessibility, or both.
>
> 'Good law', he said, was a call to potential partners in the fields of policy, law-making, and law-publishing How can we, in our own fields or working together, promote law that is clear, necessary, coherent, effective and accessible?

At a follow-up meeting that autumn, Richard Heaton described areas in which he said there would be progress:

- Better design of statutes
- A new tool for drafting, amending and publishing legislation, functioning in a standard web browser.
- Improved Explanatory Notes
- Bringing statutes on www.legislation.gov.uk up-to-date by including amendments.
- Mapping the entire statute book

[89] Lords Constitution Committee, *Preparing Legislation for Parliament*, 4th Report, 2017–19, October 2017, HL 27, para.114. See also D Salter, 'The Tax Law Rewrite in the United Kingdom – plus ça change, plus c'est la même chose', *British Tax Review*, 2010 (6), 671–87 and D Salter, 'The Ipsos MORI review of rewritten income tax legislation – contrasting and converging viewpoints', *British Tax Review*, 2011 (6), 622–25, on the results of a study of the results of the project drawn from the view of tax lawyers and accountants. For the first case to reach the Supreme Court involving the Tax Rewrite see *R (Derry) v Commissioners for HM Revenue and Customs* [2019] UKSC 19 and commentary on the case in *British Tax Review*, 2019(5) 593–605. ('The Court was unanimous in concluding that the effect of the Rewrite Project is such that a taxpayer should be able to expect that the rewritten law would constitute a "self-contained code" unless it contains a "direct reference or signpost" to the contrary.').

[90] *Craies on Legislation*, 11th edn, 2017, 1.11.8. (The editor is Daniel Greenberg, former member of the Office of Parliamentary Counsel.)

Richard Heaton developed his thinking when he gave the annual lecture in Sir William Dale's memory.[91] Dale, he said, had advocated legislation that was accessible and easy to understand, written in terms comprehensible to non-lawyers. Word for word the Government's Good Law Project had adopted Dale's manifesto. Laws should be 'effective, clear, necessary, coherent and accessible'. Drafting techniques were being refined and improved: textual amendments, navigational aids to help users, increasing use of short sentences and tables.

With regard to better access, Mr Heaton said, changes made on www.legislation.gov.uk meant that users could now compare the original text of legislation with the latest version and view a timeline of changes using a slider for navigation. Once new legislation was on the database it was convertible from one format to another which created opportunities for large commercial legal publishers but also for new publishing entrants and legal start-ups. ('We are seeing a quiet revolution in the legal sector: a new breed of providers and applications of legal data we could not have imagined a few years ago.')

The Good Law project had a website – www.gov.uk/good-law – but this was closed in January 2020. On enquiring, the writer was informed:

> The project no longer exists as a separate entity, but the principles of the project continue to be promoted by OPC. They are flagged on our gov.uk page – and are now reflected in our priorities (also shown on our gov.uk page). Our drafting guidance reflects the importance we continue to place on the principles of good law and on making sure that our approach to drafting is consistent with them.[92]

(Note: The Government's Good Law Project is not to be confused with the non-governmental campaigning Good Law Project which states 'Our mission is to use the law to hold power to account, protect the environment, and ensure no one is left behind'.)

Is Plain Language necessarily Good Law?

For some scepticism about the Plain Language/Good Law project see Thomas E Webb and Robert Geyer, 'The drafters' dance: The complexity of drafting legislation and the limitations of plain language and good law initiatives', 41 *Statute Law Review*, 2020 (2), 129–58. It is not that they are against improved drafting. Their point is that if the issues covered by the law are complex, then complexity in the drafting may be essential and attempts to render the text simple may be counter-productive.

> Laws should be as clear, simple and accessible as possible. However, clarity, simplicity, and accessibility all come with various trade-offs and are not inherently better than more complicated and complex laws or policies. If law is required to be complicated, such that one would quite reasonably be concerned that the ordinary lay person, or indeed specialist non-lawyer, would struggle to grasp the meaning of the law to them at first glance, then we need to think about the accessibility of legal advice. The requirements society imposes on the law – in particular that the law is sufficiently rigorous as to allow it to be observed and enforced as intended – should not yield to the goal of simplifying and clarifying the law for lay people if this ultimately harms the interests of those very same people; for example, by weakening environmental protections or food safety standards … PL/GL [Plain Language/Good Law] initiatives are often focused on the needs of business and can be used as a cloak for deregulatory political agendas that other stakeholders (consumers, workers,

[91] R Heaton, 'Innovation and continuity in law-making', www.gov.uk/government/speeches/innovation-and-continuity-in-law-making, 14 May 2014.

[92] Email 25 September 2024 from PPS to First Parliamentary Counsel.

> etc.) would be strongly opposed to, or certainly would wish to actively consent to before they were advanced. Hence, claims that simple laws are inherently beneficial and somehow less political than 'normal' complex laws are clearly overstated, perhaps even disingenuous …
>
> [W]e fear that, in addition to acting as a cloak for certain political groups, it unnecessarily constrains drafters, legislators, and the law in responding to the normal complexity of everyday life. This limits the adaptability, flexibility, and viability of the legal system and legislative process, and could lead to a distancing of the law and legislative process from the very people that PL/GL initiatives claim to be interested in connecting with.

Is it the draftsmen's fault?

Professor John Spencer of Cambridge University, in a lecture to the Judicial Studies Board, asked whether the draftsmen were responsible for the fact that so much criminal legislation was so difficult to understand.[93] He suggested that if Parliamentary counsel were to blame they were only partly so and that the real roots of the problem lay elsewhere. In his view the first and main reason was 'binge law-making' – that politicians could not resist making too much criminal law, too quickly. In the eleven years from 1997 to 2008 there had been 57 Acts of Parliament altering the rules of criminal justice for England and Wales. The Criminal Justice Act 2003 had 339 sections and 38 Schedules; the Serious Organised Crime and Police Act 2005, 179 sections and 17 Schedules; the Sexual Offences Act 2003, 143 sections and 7 Schedules; the Serious Crime Act 2007, 95 sections and 14 Schedules; the Criminal Justice and Immigration Act 2008, 154 sections and 28 Schedules. It had been estimated that Tony Blair's government created over 3,000 new criminal offences. 'When so much legislation is passed so rapidly, Parliament does not have the time it needs to scrutinise the text'.[94]

Further reading on drafting

FAR Bennion, *Understanding Common Law Legislation: Drafting and Interpretation* (Oxford University Press, 2001); *Thornton's Legislative Drafting* 6th edn (Bloomsbury Professional, 2023); C Stefanou and H Xanthiki (eds) *Drafting Legislation: A Modern Approach* (Ashgate, 2008), a collection of 20 essays in memoriam Sir William Dale; U Karpen, *Legislation in Europe: A Comprehensive Guide for Scholars and Practitioners* (Hart, 2017); R Cormacain, *The Form of Legislation and the Rule of Law* (Hart, 2022).

1.6. Final Approval before Introduction in Parliament

The last hurdle before a Public Bill is introduced in one or other House of Parliament is approval by the Parliamentary Business and Legislation (PBL) Committee. The Cabinet Office's *Guide to Making Legislation* (para. 3.26) says that when a bill is ready for introduction it must be circulated to the PBL Committee accompanied by: a covering memorandum explaining the contents of the bill; the Explanatory Notes; the Regulatory Impact Assessment

[93] JR Spencer, 'The drafting of criminal legislation: need it be so impenetrable?' 67 *Cambridge Law Journal*, 2008, 585.

[94] Ibid, 587.

showing in particular the effect of the bill on different groups (eg race, gender, disability[95]); the required memorandum on compatibility with the European Convention on Human Rights cleared with the Law Officers; a note regarding the strategy for parliamentary handling in both Houses that has been agreed with the Government Whips Office; and, if relevant, the required delegated powers memorandum explaining the purpose and justification for any such powers included in the bill.

At the meeting, the bill minister is asked to summarise the main provisions of the bill, confirm that it is ready for introduction and set out any particular handling issues. If there are no outstanding issues, it is likely that the Committee will then approve the bill for introduction on the agreed date 'subject to any minor or drafting amendments'. The Committee will also decide whether the bill should be introduced in the House of Commons or House of Lords. Policy issues are not normally addressed at that stage unless they give rise to a significant handling issue. Policy has to be cleared by Cabinet or the relevant Cabinet policy committee before the bill is presented to the PBL Committee.

[95] There is a legal requirement for public bodies to demonstrate they are considering their responsibilities under the Equality Act 2010 (ie in relation to age, disability, gender reassignment, pregnancy and maternity, race, religion or belief, sex, sexual orientation). An impact assessment includes a full assessment of economic, social and environmental impacts.

2

Legislation: The Westminster Stage

Legislation takes the form either of Public or Private Acts. Most Acts are Public General Acts that affect the whole public. Private Acts are for the particular benefit of some person or body of persons such as an individual or company. Private Acts must not be confused with Private Members' Acts which are initiated by Members of Parliament – for which see 2.1.7 below. Private Acts sometimes deal with the affairs of local authorities and are then called Local Acts. To confuse matters, Local Acts are sometimes the result of Public Bills, but any Public Bill which affects a particular private interest in a manner different from that of other similar private interests is technically called a Hybrid Bill (see 2.1.6 below). The significance of the difference between Public Bills, Private Bills and Hybrid Bills lies in the parliamentary procedure adopted in each case. This book concerns itself primarily with Public Bills.

In the 22 years from 1999 to 2021, there was a total of 534 Public Bills introduced by government, of which 338 started in the House of Commons and 196 started in the House of Lords. The average per year was 22. Of those that started in the Commons, 322 (95 per cent) received Royal Assent; of those that started in the Lords, 173 (88 per cent) received Royal Assent.[1]

In addition to Acts of Parliament, there are also very large numbers of statutory instruments (SIs; see 2.17–2.19 below). In the early years of last century the number of statutory instruments was in the hundreds; since the Second World War it has been in the thousands.[2]

The authoritative guide to parliamentary practice and procedure is Erskine *May, Parliamentary Practice*, 25th edn (Butterworths LexisNexis, 2019) 1,281pp. *Erskine May*, as it is known, was first published in 1844.[3] In July 2019 it became available online free to all.

The House of Commons Library is an invaluable source of information through briefing papers, reports and statistics accessible online.

[1] Figures calculated from House of Lords, *Public Bill Sessional Statistics for Session 2019–21*. The report gives the figures for each session, all but two of which were one year sessions. The exceptions were 2017–19 and 2019–21.

[2] See *Acts and Statutory Instruments: the volume of UK legislation* 1850 to 2019, House of Commons Library Briefing Paper No.7438, June 2019, para. 5.1.

[3] Updates are added twice a year. (In 1844, Thomas Erskine May was a junior in the House of Commons Library when he produced the first edition of 'Erskine May'. He rose to become the Senior Clerk and produced the first nine editions.).

2.1. The Legislative Process

2.1.1. Procedure for Public Bills

The sequence of events in the legislative process from the introduction of a bill to Royal Assent was described in 1985 for the second edition of this book by a senior member of the office of Clerk to the House of Commons.[4] Though some things have changed, it is still apt 40 years later. (Headings, editorial notes and footnotes have been added. Comparison of this description against the Cabinet Office's *Guide to Making Legislation*[5] shows that little of substance has changed.[6])

> *Three Readings* A bill must be given 'three readings' in each House before it can be submitted for Royal Assent. The First Reading is purely formal when the Clerk of the House reads the title from a dummy bill and a day is named for Second Reading. For government bills, the day named is 'tomorrow'. Although the bill will appear amongst the remaining orders of the day for the next sitting, the government will not move the Second Reading until a later date, which is announced in advance in the weekly business statement and which will be a sufficient time after presentation to give members an opportunity to consider the text.[7] [The Bill and the Explanatory Notes will both be published either on the day of the First Reading or on the next day, and are then available on the parliament website: www.parliament.uk/business/bills-and-legislation (ed).]
>
> *Second Reading* The debate on Second Reading is the main consideration of the general principles of a bill, at the end of which a vote (though it need not) may be taken on the bill as a whole. Although a bill can be lost at many stages in its career, the Second Reading is undoubtedly the most important, and the vast majority of bills which get a Second Reading and proceed into committee also get on to the statute book. For government bills, the Minister in charge of the department concerned usually opens the debate, and one of his junior Ministers replies at the end. Front-bench opposition speakers follow the ministerial opening, and precede the winding-up.
>
> *Committee stage* Unless a member moves that the bill be sent to a committee of the whole House[8] (or to a Select Committee [see 2.2.5 below] if a detailed examination with witnesses is required or to a Special Standing Committee [see 2.2.1 below] which combines both Select Committee and [Public Bill] Committee procedure) all bills after Second Reading (with the exception of certain financial measures) are automatically sent upstairs to a [Public Bill] Committee.[9]

[4] To my regret he insisted on remaining anonymous (ed).

[5] www.gov.uk/government/publications/guide-to-making-legislation (2022).

[6] See also the very informative chapter 8 entitled 'Legislation' in T Daintith and E Page, *The Executive in the Constitution* (Oxford University Press, 1999) 240–86.

[7] The convention is that, save in emergency situations, the Second Reading debate should not take place until two weekends have passed following the publication of the Bill. (ed).

[8] There are four main categories of bills where the committee stage is or includes the whole House: (1) bills of constitutional importance; (2) bills of major political importance; (3) bills which require no consideration where it would be a waste of time to establish a committee – such as consolidation bills; (4) bills which the government wishes to rush through Parliament. The committee stage of the annual Finance Bill always begins in the whole House. And sometimes a bill is sent to a committee of the whole House in order to prevent the taking of evidence. (ed).

[9] Standing Committees were renamed Public Bill Committees in 2007 following the Select Committee on Modernisation's report *The Legislative Process* (2006, HC 1097). The main difference is that a Public Bill Committee can take both oral and written evidence before starting its examination of the bill. The Lords Constitution Committee said in 2019: 'Evidence-taking on bills has strengthened Parliament's scrutiny of bills. It has increased the knowledge of MPs serving on public bill committees and provided an opportunity for the public

These committees consist of from sixteen to fifty members. In a session over 500 members are called upon to serve on them. Appointments to [Public Bill] Committees are made by a Select Committee, called the Committee of Selection,[10] which is charged with having regard to the 'qualifications of those members nominated and to the composition of the House'. The government thus keeps its majority, but the opposition and minority parties so far as possible are fully represented. The chair is taken by a member selected by the Speaker from a panel of chairmen, who maintains the same standard of impartiality in Committee as the Speaker does in the House. The task of the Committee is to go through the bill and amend it where desirable, bearing in mind that the general principles of the bill have been approved by the House.[11]

A bill in Committee is considered clause by clause and the question that the clause 'stand part of the bill' is put on each one. Before the question is put on a clause, however, amendments may be moved – provided that they are relevant, not 'wrecking', and conform to various technical requirements, such as the limitation imposed by any accompanying financial resolution passed by the House.[12]

Amendments Members of most [Public Bill] Committees are showered with suggestions for amendments from interested bodies – to add to any ideas of their own for amendment of the bill. The government's amendments are drafted by Parliamentary Counsel; a private member [steering a Private Member's Bill] usually seeks the advice of the Public Bill Office. The office, which is staffed by clerks in the service of the House (the counterpart in parliamentary terms of the administration group in the civil service), has charge of a bill throughout its passage; checks that the text is in accordance with the title and otherwise in order; provides the clerk for the [Public Bill] Committee; and supervises the bill through its remaining stages. The Committee clerk not only helps members with their amendments, but advises the chairman on their orderliness and assists him in the exercise of his power to select which amendments shall be debated. He then attends the meetings of the Committee to keep the minutes[13] and advise the chair and members of the Committee, without distinction of party, on any matter of order that may arise. He keeps the authoritative copy of the bill and enters any amendments as they are made.

Report and Third Reading A bill which has been considered by a committee of the whole House and emerges unamended goes straight on to Third Reading. Any other bill must have a consideration or 'Report' stage, when further amendments may be moved, and attempts made either

and external organisations to contribute directly to the legislative process.' (Lords Constitution Committee, *The Legislative Process: The Passage of Bills through Parliament*, 24th Report 2017–19, July 2019, HL 393, para 120.) Evidence taking on bills does not take place in the Lords. The Constitution Committee recommended in its 2019 report (para 121) that it be extended to bills that start in the Lords. The Government Response (4 November 2019) said, without giving reasons, that it did not support public evidence taking during Committee stage in the House of Lords. However, in its response (16 April 2018) to the Committee's report, *Preparing Legislation for Parliament*, (4th Report, 2017–19, October 2017, HL 27), the government referred to the What Works Network set up by the Cabinet Office in 2013 to provide government departments, ministers and others with independent assessments of the available evidence in different policy areas (health, social care, policing etc).The Network had 10 What Works Centres and a central team in the Cabinet Office to help bring their findings to the attention of policymakers. (ed).

[10] The Select Committee on Selection is dominated by the whips. In practice, for government bills, the Committee of Selection accepts the teams nominated by the whips on either side. Membership of PBCs reflects the strength of the parties. It does not necessarily reflect the balance of opinion in the respective parties. Rebels against a party are usually excluded. Government whips will also often exclude 'experts' for fear that they will not follow the party line. (ed).

[11] The proceedings of the committee stage of bills have been accessible on the web since the 1997/1998 session at www.publications.parliament.uk/pa/cm/stand.htm or http://www.parliament.uk/business/publitions/ hansard/ commons/bill-committee-debates. One chooses the required session and then selects the relevant committee, by the topic concerned or by the title of the legislation. (ed).

[12] For a detailed description of the committee stage see the Cabinet Office, *Guide to Making Legislation*, 2025, s 29, p 221. See also R Blackburn, *Griffith and Ryle on Parliament*, 2nd edn (Thompson, 2003) (hereinafter *Griffith and Ryle on Parliament*) paras 6-131–6-13.9. (ed).

[13] As just noted, the proceedings are all accessible online. (ed).

to restore parts lost in Committee or to remove parts added. The government frequently use the Report stage to introduce, in a form acceptable to them, amendments the principle of which they have accepted in Committee. The members who have been through the Committee stage together very often dominate the debates on Report stage. This is partly because many of the points at issue were postponed in the Committee at the request of the government, and partly because these members are by now (if they were not before) specialists in the subject, which may make it difficult for an 'outsider' to break in. The Report stage is a useful safeguard, however, against a small Committee amending a bill against the wishes of the House, and a necessary opportunity for second thoughts. The Speaker takes account of the time spent on amendments in Committee when selecting what is to be discussed. A large bill may take two or even three days on Report, amounting to ten hours' consideration or more.[14]

There remains Third Reading; and here, unlike Second Reading, when a bill may be reviewed in the context of the subject to which it relates, debate must be confined to the contents of the bill. [Substantive amendments are not permitted at Third Reading (ed)] Generally by this stage the battle is recognised to be over, and apart from a few set-piece occasions when a formalised debate precedes a vote, a few minutes only are spent reviewing the victories and defeats of the campaign, and in paying compliments to the opponents.[15] Since 1967, the Third Reading may be taken without debate unless at least six members table a motion, 'that the Question be not put forthwith'. Although a vote may be called on a bill at this stage it would amount almost to a parliamentary accident for a bill which had been given a Second Reading to fall at this final stage.

Safely read the third time, a bill is endorsed *soit baille aux Seigneurs* and tied up in a green ribbon together with a message asking the Lords' concurrence. The Clerk of the House proceeds to the 'other place' and hands in the bill at the bar of the House.

House of Lords procedure Since the House of Lords is not weighed down with as great a burden of business as the Commons, and is not to the same extent a political battleground, it does not have the same highly developed procedural rules which control the way in which proceedings are conducted. Their lordships use their own discretion as to what they will say, and are prepared, for example, to make amendments on the Third Reading of a bill, if it will improve it, in a way quite breathtaking to newly ennobled former members of the Commons. Basically, however, the legislative process of the two Houses is the same, and the greatest practical difference in the field of legislation is that in the Lords there is no equivalent of the [Public Bill] Committee with defined and limited membership. This means that any member can put down amendments, and on a highly controversial measure this can result in a very protracted Committee stage. Bills get a formal First Reading, a Second Reading, consideration in Committee and on Report and then a Third Reading. [It is very common in the Lords for Opposition amendment to be moved in the Committee stage but not to be put to a vote until the Report stage. (ed)] They must also finally survive a formal motion, 'That this bill do now pass'. Although bills may generally get a smoother passage in the Lords than through the Commons,[16] the Lords have increased their work-load in recent years. Perhaps because many peers are former members of the House of Commons, proceedings have taken on a more similar character to those in the Commons.[17]

[14] On the Report stage see Cabinet Office, *Guide to Making Legislation*, 2025 s 30, p239. See also *Griffith and Ryle on Parliament* (n 12 above) paras 6-140–6-144. (ed).

[15] In the 2002–03 session the longest Third Reading lasted 1 hour and 21 minutes. Twelve bills had a Third Reading lasting under half an hour – Committee on the Modernisation of the House of Commons, *The Legislative Process*, HC 1097, July 2006, para.94. The Third Reading normally takes place on the same day as the Report stage and is usually very brief. The Committee recommended that where a bill has been significantly amended, the Third Reading should be programmed for a different day. (ed).

[16] That proposition would be a surprise to many Ministers. (ed).

[17] On the various stages of proceedings in the House of Lords see the Cabinet Office, *Guide to Making Legislation* ss 32–36. (ed).

'Ping-pong' After a Commons bill has been through the Lords, it is returned with the Lords Amendments to it, which then must be considered in the House.[18] On any bill, the two Houses must finally reach agreement on the amendments made by each other if the bill is not to fall during that Session.[19] Under the Parliament Acts 1911 and 1949, disagreement between the two Houses can delay a bill for a year if the Commons persist with it;[20] and in the case of a money bill,[21] a bill passed by the Commons can go for Royal Assent after only one month's delay.[22] [This therefore does not apply to bills that start in the Lords. (ed)] Where one House cannot agree to the other's amendments, it sends a message to that effect giving reasons. The 'ping pong' between the two Houses can go back and forth several times,[23] but it is only rarely that a bill has had to be reintroduced in a second Session because of the failure of the two Houses to agree. The last occasions were the [War Crimes Act 1991, the European Parliamentary Elections Act 1999 and the Sexual Offences (Amendment) Act 2000. (ed)][24]

[The' ping-pong' stage of Bills between the two Houses takes on a particular aspect at the end of a parliament when several bills typically are taken through their final stages in a rush between the calling of the general election and the proroguing of parliament. This stage, known as 'wash-up', by definition means that the bills that are scrambled through do not have proper scrutiny.[25] (ed)]

Royal Assent The final stage in the enacting process is Royal Assent [as to which see 2.1.3 below].

From this account of the customary procedures for the passage of a bill, it will be seen that, if proper consideration is given at each stage to a substantial measure, whether or not it is opposed in principle, its passage takes a considerable time. In fact major bills will take six months or more to pass. On the other hand, a small bill can, if urgency requires it, pass through both Houses in a day.[26]

The key to the productivity of parliament lies in control of the timetable of the House of Commons by the government[27] and the willingness of the House to entrust the Chair with discretion to select amendments for debate, and to accept or reject motions for the closure of debate.

[18] See Cabinet Office, *Guide to Making Legislation*, 2025, s 37 and *Griffth and Ryle on Parliament* (n 12 above) paras 6-146–49 (ed).

[19] Under what is called 'the Salisbury Convention' the Lords traditionally do not destroy or alter beyond recognition bills that derive from manifesto commitments – see R Brazier, 'Defending the hereditaries: the Salisbury convention' *Public Law*, 1998, 371. (ed).

[20] See 2.12 below (ed).

[21] A Money Bill is not defined in the 1911 Act but s 3 provided that the certificate of the Speaker of the House of Commons is 'conclusive for all purposes'. (ed).

[22] The bill as introduced in the second session must be the same as when it was first introduced except that it may contain alterations necessary owing to the elapse of time and it may also include amendments made in the Lords in the first session. If the bill is rejected again by the Lords, it is automatically presented for Royal Assent notwithstanding the Lords disagreement, unless the Commons directs to the contrary. (ed).

[23] The Lords finally backed down having six times rejected the government's European Parliamentary and Local Elections (Pilots) Bill to permit postal voting trials. The record however seems to be the Corporate Manslaughter and Corporate Homicide Act 2007 which went back and forth seven times before becoming law. (ed).

[24] The Parliament Acts (Amendment) Bill 2001, introduced by Lord Donaldson, sought to validate the Parliament Acts. It also stated that the Parliament Acts could not be used for amending or repealing the 2001 (Act) or amending the Parliament Acts 1911 and 1949. (See HL, *Hansard*, vol. 620, col. 1308, 19 January 2001.) The Royal Commission on the Reform of the House of Lords had recommended that the Parliament Acts should be amended to exclude the possibility of their being further amended by use of the Parliamentary Acts procedure (Cm 4534, 2000, p 52, paras 5.13–16). But the 2001 Bill was lost on the dissolution of Parliament for the general election. On the Parliament Acts 1911 and 1949 see further 2.12 below (ed).

[25] For an analysis of the political, legislative and constitutional issues and consideration of possible reforms see R Fox and M Korris, 'Reform of the wash-up: managing the legislative tidal-wave at the end of a parliament' 63 *Parliamentary Affairs* 2010, 558. The article focuses especially on the 2010 wash-up when 14 Government Bills and 4 Private Members Bills were approved. (ed).

[26] Not only 'small bills'! – see 2.13 below (ed).

[27] On timetabling ('guillotining') and programming of bills see 2.11 below (ed).

2.1.2. Making the Legislative Committee System Work Better

The procedure of the two Houses differs in many ways. One such is in the way they organise themselves for the scrutiny of legislation, described by the Lords Constitution Committee:

> The approaches of the Commons and the Lords to scrutinising legislation differ. While the main stages for considering bills are formally the same in both Houses … each House has its own style, mechanisms and conventions for scrutinising legislation. For example, committee stage in the House of Commons predominantly takes place in a committee room, away from the Chamber, on a set timetable, with the membership of the committee chosen by the party whips and evidence sessions prior to formal scrutiny of the bill itself. In the House of Lords, committee stage, whether in the Chamber or Grand Committee, allows all members to participate and has no time limit, meaning that all amendments can be debated; but no evidence is taken.[28]

In 2017, the Lords Constitution Committee said: 'The PBL Committee, and the Leader of the House of Commons in particular, will continue to play an important role in upholding the standard of legislation', but that it was also 'in the interest of all parties to ensure that standards of legislation do not depend so heavily on the regularly changing holders of the office of the Leader of the House of Commons'.[29] There should be a select or joint committee whose remit was legislative standards. In 2019, the Committee revisited that recommendation:

> We reiterate this recommendation as the Parliamentary Business and Legislation (PBL) Cabinet Committee, which is responsible for carrying out this task in Government, has not always rigorously ensured that bills are fit for purpose before introduction … The existence of a Legislative Standards Committee would encourage the Government to ensure that bills are thoroughly prepared before introduction to Parliament to avoid the risk of critical reports and potential delays.[30]

The Government Response[31] was that it believed such a committee was 'unnecessary'. ('The Government already follows a stringent process ahead of a bill's introduction, whereby bills need to be cleared by the Parliamentary Business and Legislation Cabinet Committee.')

A much more critical analysis of the shortcomings of Public Bill Committees was made in 2013 by the prestigious Constitution Unit of University College, London. The Executive Summary of its 60-page Report[32] began: 'Parliamentary scrutiny of bills is arguably where the House of Commons is at its weakest – and the committee stage is central to that weakness.' The Summary continued:

> Crucially, public bill committees (PBCs) are nonspecialist and temporary, being created for the duration of every bill, and then disbanded. Their members have little opportunity to develop

[28] Lords Constitution Committee, *The Legislative Process: The Passage of Bills through Parliament*, 24th Report 2017–19, July 2019, HL 393, para 18.

[29] Lords Constitution Committee, *Preparing Legislation for Parliament*, 4th Report, 2017–19, October 2017, HL 27, para 177.

[30] Lords Constitution Committee, *The Legislative Process: The Passage of Bills through Parliament*, 24th Report 2017–19, July 2019, HL 393, para 46.

[31] Published on the Parliament website, 4 November 2019.

[32] M Russell, B Morris and P Larkin, *Fitting the Bill – Bringing Commons Legislative Committees into Line with Best Practice*, UCL Constitution Unit, June 2013.

> expertise in the subject area, or effective working relationships with each other, particularly across party lines. Another key concern is that their members are effectively chosen by the whips, with no accountability to the House as a whole.
>
> This is all in stark contrast to the House of Commons select committees, which are permanent, specialist, and valued for their consensual cross-party working.[33] Over recent years these committees have gained in resources, strength and reputation. Since 2010, their members have also been elected. These and other changes make the public bill committees appear increasingly out of step …
>
> We therefore set out three potential models of legislation committees for piloting, suited to departments with different loads. These include new permanent committees in heavy legislating departments, and select committee consideration of bills from departments where legislation is rare. In most departments the existing PBC system could be reformed, through formalising overlap with the select committee, democratising membership.[34]

The proposed three models were not piloted or adopted and the membership of PBCs and select committees has not been formalised, though select committee members with relevant expertise do sometimes serve on a PBC.

A report in 2022 considered whether there would be merit in abolishing the Public Bill Committee system and leaving scrutiny of bills to departmental select committees. That was the system in all the devolved legislatures, but, having considered the possible advantages, it concluded that this would not be wise:

> [G]iving select committees a formal role in the legislative process would fundamentally change their nature, in ways that could undermine their effectiveness. Since the introduction of elections for select committee chairs, they have become increasingly independent of government. Chairs from the governing party have been increasingly willing to publicly criticise government policy, members have continued to develop good cross-party relationships, and an increased focus on impact has meant that they are arguably one of parliament's most effective tools for influencing government policy. Changes to their role should be carefully balanced against their potential consequences. Lessons from Scotland and Wales suggest that departmental committees with a role in legislative scrutiny are less independent than Westminster select committees. The whips take a greater interest in the membership of such committees, meaning members of key committees may be chosen for their party loyalty. Interviewees told us that while there was often good cross-party working during non-legislative inquiries and during the evidence-taking stage of bill scrutiny when it came to line-by-line scrutiny and votes, members fall back into political party divides.[35]

The report recommended instead:

- That House of Commons Standing Orders should require that bill committees include a minimum of two or three select committee members.
- That select committees should be entitled to request a 'select committee stage' on all programmed bills between second reading and committee stage.

[33] 'Rather than bills being considered by groups of members who know each other well, and must work together again, PBC members have few incentives to behave constructively rather than making party points. This is worsened by the fact that some members may have no particular commitment to the subject area, that they discuss the bill after a high-profile partisan debate has already taken place, and that members whose views diverge from the party line may be intentionally excluded from the committee.' (Ibid, 44).

[34] The proposed formalisation would include a rule that all PBCs include at least two members from the departmental select committee.

[35] Bennett Institute for Public Policy and Institute for Government, *The Legislative Process: How to Empower Parliament*, Jess Sergeant and Jack Pannell, December 2022, p 48.

> This would allow select committees to hold an inquiry or one-off evidence sessions on a bill, and produce a statement or report on what they consider to be the key issues or problems with the bill. They may wish to include draft amendments in these outputs, as is current practice in the Northern Ireland assembly, which can be tabled at a later stage of the bill ...
>
> Formalising a role for select committees would bring them into the legislative process itself, and ensure their scrutiny takes place on a timescale and in a format that would allow it to inform scrutiny at committee stage. As select committees already have relationships with key stakeholders in their area it would also allow members to hear from a broader range of witnesses than those determined at short notice through the usual channels.[36]

2.1.3. Royal Assent

The final stage is that the monarch is informed by the Lord Chancellor of the Bills that have completed the parliamentary stages and that are therefore ready for Royal Assent. Strangely, the monarch only receives the short title. What they sign is not the Act but Letters Patent signifying assent to the Act.[37]

Under the procedure introduced by the Royal Assent Act 1967, assent is now normally notified by the Speaker of each House reading the title of bills that have received Royal Assent. The Clerk of the Parliaments subsequently endorses the Acts with the customary Norman French formulae.[38] These are written on the text of the Act. They are not spoken.

In 2019, during the Brexit crisis, the question was raised whether the government could refuse to put forward for Royal Assent a bill that had completed all its parliamentary stages. The question became of moment when backbenchers twice took control of the Order Paper and succeeded in getting Bills through Parliament despite the fierce opposition of first, the Theresa May government and then of the Boris Johnson government. (See p 423 below.) Could the government thwart the Brexit rebels who were trying to force the Prime Minister to seek an extension of notice of withdrawal from the EU either by not putting the Bills forward for Royal Assent or delaying such that the purpose of the legislation would be defeated? In the event, the executive put forward both Bills without any delay. The correct view in the writer's view, is that constitutionally the executive had no choice. It did what it had to do. That will remain the correct view unless one day it is displaced by the executive doing otherwise without such action being successfully challenged in the courts.

There is no case of refusal of Royal Assent since 1707 when Queen Anne refused to approve the Scotch Militia Bill. Refusal of Royal Assent did occur in earlier times.[39]

[36] Ibid, p 49.

[37] For a description of the actual process see F Bennion, 'Modern Royal Assent Procedure at Westminster' 2 *Statute Law Review*, 1981, 133 and BS Jackson, 'Who enacts statutes?' 18 *Statute Law Review*, 1997, 177.

[38] For most public and private Acts, 'La Reine le veult'. For Acts providing aids and supplies to the Crown, 'La Reine remercie ses bons sujets, accepte leur benevolence, et ainsi le veult'. For personal Acts, 'Soit fait comme il est désiré. (Erskine May, *Parliamentary Practice*, 25th edn, 2019, para 30.38.).

[39] 'Elizabeth I declined Royal Assent in each of her ten Parliaments, and in the 1597–98 session she vetoed 48 out of 91 Bills presented to her.' (G Wheeler, 'Royal Assent in the British Constitution' 132 *Law Quarterly Review*, 2016, 495–505, 495.).

The question of whether and, if so, in what circumstances Royal Assent could be refused, has been debated.[40]

For a learned consideration of the implications of a statute which includes what is manifestly a mistake see Diggory Bailey, 'What is an Act of Parliament?' *Public Law*, 2024, 316–34. The author considers how the courts approach the question of the validity of a statute and who decides on the content of a statute.

2.1.4. King's/Queen's or Prince's Consent

Royal Assent is to be distinguished from King's/Queen's or Prince's Consent. King's Consent is required if the bill affects the prerogative of the Crown or the interests (hereditary revenues, personal property or other personal interests) of the Crown, the Duchy of Lancaster and the Duchy of Cornwall.[41] It authorises the discussion of the provisions of a Bill that requires Consent, as distinct from approves the legislation itself. In the 2010–12 session, for example, Queen's Consent was signified on the Second Reading of the Fixed-term Parliaments Bill 2011[42] and of the European Union Bill.[43] Prince of Wales's Consent is required if the bill affects the Duchy of Cornwall and sometimes for other bills. The Prince of Wales's Consent was, for instance, required for the House of Lords Act 1999 which removed most of the hereditary peers (including him) from the House of Lords.[44]

The topic was considered in 2014 by the House of Commons Political and Constitutional Committee in *The Impact of Queen's and Prince's Consent on the Legislative Process*:[45]

> The Leader of the House of Commons, Rt Hon Andrew Lansley MP, told us in written evidence: 'the process of Queen's and Prince's Consent is subject to the convention that the Sovereign must ultimately accept Ministerial advice.' He also commented: 'A request for Consent carries with it by implication Ministerial advice that Consent should be granted.' In other words, Ministers would tend not to advise the Queen or Prince of Wales to withhold Consent; they would simply not seek Consent in the first place. It seems also that the advice is thus not actual written advice; there is simply a presumption that when Consent is sought by Ministers, it will be granted by the Queen or the Prince of Wales.[46]

[40] See A Twomey, 'The refusal or deferral of Royal Assent' *Public Law*, 2006, 580; R Brazier, 'Royal Assent to legislation' 129 *Law Quarterly Review*, 2013, 184–204; GJ Wheeler, 'Royal Assent in the British Constitution' 132 *Law Quarterly Review*, 2016, 495–505. The last named article ended (505): 'In the absence of a written constitution, it is submitted that the requirement for Royal Assent can safely be allowed to lie on the books – in the hope that no situation will arise in which it needs to be refused, but in the knowledge that the possibility is there if necessary.'

[41] *The Guardian*, 8 February 2021, reported that it had compiled a database of 'at least' 1,062 bills that during her reign had been vetted by the Queen or Prince Charles and that they covered matters ranging from justice, social security, pensions, race relations and food policy through to obscure rules on car parking charges and hovercraft.

[42] HC, Hansard, vol 511, col 621.

[43] HC, Hansard, vol 520, col 191.

[44] The topic was dealt with in *Queen's or Prince's Consent*, a Cabinet Office paper for the guidance of the Office of Parliamentary Counsel, 8 November 2013: www.gov.uk/government/publications/queens-or-princes-consent. See also R Brazier, 'Legislating about the monarchy' 66 *Cambridge Law Journal*, 2007, 86, 95–97; and the Cabinet Office's *Guide to Making Legislation*, 2025, s 17, pp 157–159.

[45] 11th Report of Session 2013–14 HC 784, 26 March 2014.

[46] Ibid, para 11.

The difference between the constitutional requirement that the Monarch and the Prince of Wales act on the advice of Ministers was illustrated in 1970 when the Prince of Wales, as Duke of Cornwall, both consented to the Plymouth and South West Devon Water Bill (a Private Bill) and petitioned against it.

Once Consent has been granted by the King or Prince of Wales, it must be signified in both Houses of Parliament. Consent is normally signified in the Commons at the Third Reading stage of a Bill, but if the Bill fundamentally affects the prerogative or interests, it will usually be signified at Second Reading.[47] Although a bill which needs Consent cannot progress if Consent is not granted, if a bill receives Royal Assent without the need for Consent being noticed, it remains valid.

Since making treaties is a prerogative power one might think that authorising withdrawal from a treaty would require King's/Queen's Consent but Commons Speaker Bercow decided that Queen's Consent was not required for the European Union (Notification of Withdrawal) Bill 2017.[48] It is not known for sure, but it is thought that his reason was that the Supreme Court had ruled that notification of the intention to withdraw under Article 50 of the Treaty on European Union required the authority of Parliament.[49] The same ruling was applied by Speaker Bercow in 2019 to the two Bills introduced when backbenchers took control of the Order Paper to pass legislation requiring the Prime Minister to seek a further extension under Article 50 (as to which see p 423 below).[50]

As to whether King's/Queen's and Prince's Consent should be abolished, the House of Commons Committee in its 2014 Report (above) said (para 41):

> The United Kingdom is a constitutional monarchy. The Queen has the right to be consulted, to advise and to warn. But beyond that she should have no role in the legislative process. Consent serves to remind us that Parliament has three elements – the House of Commons, the House of Lords, and the Queen-in-Parliament – and its existence could be regarded as a matter of courtesy between the three parts of Parliament. Whether this is a compelling justification for its continuance is a matter of opinion.

2.1.5. Private Bill Procedure

The discussion so far has been of public bills, but Parliament passes substantial numbers of so-called private bills as well. The difference between public and private bills is not easy to describe. The original conception of a private bill is one that altered the general law in relation to a particular locality, institution or individual. An example drawn from earlier times (pre-1869) is an Act which granted a divorce before there was any general law of divorce. But today private bills tend to deal with nationalised industries, local authorities, universities, commercial undertakings and other institutions. Personal bills are now rare.

[47] The House of Commons Committee recommended (para 45) that it always be given on Third Reading. The Government's Response said it was a matter for Parliament but that 'given that Consent is sought for certain Bills to be debated, it seems to follow that Consent should be signified in the early legislative stages of those Bills' and that 'The Government agrees that a consistent approach to signifying Consent in both Houses would be desirable.' (Government Response to the Committee's Eleventh Report of Session 2013–14, HC 224, June 16, 2014, para 19.).

[48] One knows that he did so not from *Hansard* at the time because there is no reference there to the decision. One knows because he said so later.

[49] *R (Miller) v Secretary of State for Exiting the European Union* [2017] UKSC 5, [2018] AC 61.

[50] The Speaker's rulings were given respectively on 3 April 2019, HC *Hansard*, cols 1130–31 and 4 September 2019, HC *Hansard*, cols 211–12.

The procedure for private bills is quite different from that for public bills. The main purpose of the rules is to provide proper opportunity for those affected by the legislation to prepare and voice their objections. The procedure was described in a special study by the Study of Parliament Group:

'Private bill procedure: a case for reform' *Public Law*, 1981, 206

A second reading of a public bill indicates approval of the principles of the bill: the second reading of a private bill approves the principles, subject to the need for the bill being proved at the committee stage. Also at the second reading stage a motion may be passed giving certain instructions to the committee nominated to look into the details of the bill.

The committee stage is the most complex and most critical part of the procedure. Composition of the committees varies but there is a common feature: no Ministers are present. The procedure depends upon whether a bill is opposed or unopposed. To take the simplest case first: if a bill arouses no objection the promoters have still to demonstrate at least formal proof of the expediency of the proposed measure. They will be represented by their Parliamentary Agents before the Committee on Unopposed Bills. In the Commons this body in practice normally consists of a Deputy Chairman of Ways and Means together with four backbenchers; in the Lords it comprises the Lord Chairman of Committees and, should he see fit, 'such Lords as he may select from the panel of Deputy Chairmen appointed each Session'.

An opposed bill goes to an ad hoc committee consisting in the Commons of four backbenchers and in the Lords of five peers. There is not the same continuity of knowledge and experience on these ad hoc bodies as on the committees on unopposed bills.

Arguably, where such experience is most needed, it is not available. At an opposed bill committee, promoters and opponents will normally be represented by counsel. A long contentious hearing can be very expensive. The cost, combined with the lack of certainty of success, has in the past deterred smaller local authorities or other bodies from bringing forward their own bills.

Opponents of a bill may present a petition of objection. However, promoters may claim that an objector has insufficient *locus standi* and force a preliminary inquiry into whether the petitioners should be heard. In the Lords the decision is made by the committee due to review the bill: in the Commons the issue is referred to the Court of Referees on Private Bills which consists of the Chairman and Deputy Chairmen of Ways and Means, the counsel to the Speaker and eight backbench MPs.[51]

The committee stage of an opposed private bill has something of a judicial flavour. The conflicting cases are normally presented by counsel; witnesses are examined and cross-examined. The promoters of the bill must first prove their preamble – that is, demonstrate the need for the powers requested – and then follows a clause-by-clause examination. Arguments are not conducted simply on the basis of whether an idea has merit or how far the interests of X will be damaged. The judicial element in the proceedings has become so strong that counsel will quote previous decisions of private bill committees, a type of 'case-law', in order to strengthen their client's case.

A third method of dealing with private bills is used when a bill, although unopposed, is thought to be so important or controversial that it should be treated on the lines of an opposed bill. On such occasions the bill is sent to an Opposed Bill Committee in either or both Houses. The promoters will have to engage counsel and will be expected to provide strong evidence of need for their proposals. The decision to invoke this form of procedure is within the discretion of the Chairman of Ways and Means and the Lord Chairman of Committees.

[51] In 1968, Standing Orders were altered to admit petitions by bodies such as amenity societies 'alleging that the interests which they represent will be adversely affected to a material extent by the provisions contained in the bill'. Before then the plaints of petitioners had to be linked to property rights.

> After the committee stage in the Lords, the bill is sent forward for a third reading. In the Commons there is a report stage unless the bill has not been amended in committee. Third readings are normally a formality. The crux is the committee stage. The fact that a bill has to pass through both Houses *seriatim* involves the possibility of a second lengthy and expensive committee hearing. For any proposal with a semblance of novelty, the outcome is unpredictable. A final opportunity for conflict could arise if the two Houses fail to agree. However, if one House disallows a clause in a private bill, the other House does not reinstate it.

In the past, a very high percentage of private bills involved railways, canals, tramways and the like. Critics argued that it took up too much of the time of Members of Parliament and congested the parliamentary timetable. There was also concern that the procedure did not allow for co-option of expert assessors who could help with the evaluation of technical evidence, such as whether to build a barrage across Cardiff Bay or whether to have a new underground railway in London.

In 1988, a Joint Committee of both Houses recommended that private bill procedure should no longer be used for such legislation.[52] Following a process of consultation, the government put forward the Transport and Works Bill which became an Act in 1992. This established a new procedure under which proposals for light railway, tramway, underground railway schemes, those affecting inland waterways, diversions of rivers, canals and the like can no longer be the subject of a Private Act of Parliament. Instead they have to be authorised by Ministerial Order after procedures involving an opportunity for objectors to make representations and in some cases the holding of a public inquiry.

See further Erskine May, *Parliamentary Practice*, 25th edn (LexisNexis, 2019 and online), 42.1–42.20 and 45.1–45.37; R Blackburn, *Griffith and Ryle on Parliament*, 2nd edn (Sweet & Maxwell, 2003), paras 10-083–084, 12-163–64. See also a House of Commons Library Note on Private Bills: www.parliament.uk/briefing-papers/SN06508/private-bills-in-parliament-house-of-commons-background-paper and a historic Fact Sheet: www.parliament.uk/documents/commons-information-office/l04.pdf.

For the petitioner's perspective see David Watkinson, 'Private Bill Procedure: The Petitioner's Experience' 41 *Statute Law Review*, 2020 (1), 50–63.

2.1.6. Hybrid Bills

Some bills have features of both public and private bills. These are known as hybrid bills. A House of Commons Speaker defined hybrid bills as 'a public bill which affects a particular private interest in a manner different from the private interests of other persons or bodies of the same category or class'. The interests of a local authority in the administration of its area is regarded as a private interest, and a bill is generally regarded as hybrid if it relates to only one named area outside London. Thus bills which propose works of national importance but in a local area are generally hybrid. The British Museum Bill 1962–63 and the Channel Tunnel Bill 1986–87 were examples.[53] At the time of writing, the very controversial Holocaust Memorial Bill is a hybrid bill.[54]

[52] See *Report on Private Bill Procedure*, HC 625; HL Paper 97, 1988. The Government followed this by a consultation paper – *Private Bills and New Procedures: A Consultation Document* (HMSO, 1990).

[53] The Cabinet Office, *Guide to Making Legislation* 2025 deals with Hybrid Bill Procedure in s 41.

[54] The principal controversy is as to the siting of the memorial. The Bill would remove restriction on building a Holocaust Memorial and Learning Centre in Victoria Tower Gardens immediately opposite the Houses

Hybrid bills can be introduced by Private Members as well as by Government. Governments try to avoid hybridity because of the extra requirements of the procedure. One way to do that is to generalise the legislation even though in reality it has a much narrower target. An example was the legislation aimed at closing down Mr Brian Haw's long-standing anti-war demonstration in Parliament Square. The parliamentary debates show clearly that he was the sole target of s 132 of the Serious Organised Crime and Police Act 2005 but the section was drafted so as to ban demonstration near Parliament generally, thus avoiding hybridity.

The steps to be taken vary from bill to bill but usually there will be a need for advertisements in the press, serving of notices on affected persons and depositing of plans and copies of the bill. The Second Reading for a hybrid bill is taken as usual for a public bill. After Second Reading, however, it is committed to a Select Committee made up partly of members chosen by the House and of others chosen by the Committee of Selection.

If no petitions opposing the bill are received, the bill goes to a Public Bill Committee which considers it like any other public bill.

If petitions opposing the bill are received, the Select Committee meets to consider the bill in much the same way as for private bills by hearing submissions and witnesses. There are, however, some differences. One is that the promoters do not need to establish the need for the preamble since this has already been established by the Second Reading.

Once reported by the Select Committee it goes to a Public Bill Committee, Report and Third Reading as for normal public bills.

A hybrid bill, like a private bill, can be carried forward from one session to the next if both Houses agree.

See further www.parliament.uk/publications – Fact Sheet L5 ('Hybrid bills'); Erskine May, *Parliamentary Practice*, 25th edn 2019, 18.16, 26.2, 30.57–74.

2.1.7. Private Members' Bills

Most bills are introduced by government ministers. But each year some time is reserved in the House of Commons for the introduction of bills by Members of Parliament who are not ministers. (As noted above, Private Members' Bills must be distinguished from Private Bills.) There are a variety of different ways in which private Members in the Commons can introduce bills: through the ballot, under Standing Order No 57; under the Ten-Minute Rule; simple presentation; and Lords' bills. Members of the House of Lords, by comparison, have an unrestricted right to introduce Private Members' Bills and provided they begin early enough in the session, time is generally found for their consideration. However, 'consideration' does not mean prospects of becoming law. That is usually not the intention. They are introduced for the record but not proceeded with beyond the First Reading. (In the 22 years from 1999 to 2021, 587 Private Members Bills were introduced in the House of Lords. Only 11 went on to receive Royal Assent.[55] The Cabinet Office, *Guide to Making*

of Parliament. At the time of writing the Bill had completed its passage through the Commons and had had its Second Reading in the Lords on 1 October 2024. The House of Commons Library published a 44-page report on the Bill and its history: *Holocaust Memorial Bill: Progress of the Bill*, 4 September 2024. The report includes description of hybrid bill procedure.

[55] Calculated from House of Lords annual statistics of Public Bills 2019–21 which gives the figures for each session from 1999.

Legislation deals with Private Members' Bill procedure in s 48 – www.gov.uk/government/publications/guide-to-making-legislation.)

Balloted bills Most Private Members' Bills that reach the statute book are balloted bills.[56] A ballot is held each session among backbench MPs – those who hold no form of job as members of the government. Most such MPs take part. Typically more than 400 Members enter. Twenty names are drawn. Those who draw high positions in the ballot have a particularly good chance of getting a bill on to the statute book providing they choose their subject with care. But even those who do not draw high positions may succeed, providing they have government support for their bills or they are unopposed.[57]

Under Standing Order No 57 After the 20 balloted bills have been presented, any MP can present a bill to the House. All that is required is at least one day's notice, and its presentation to the Clerk of the table. The major difference between these bills and balloted bills is that the latter will normally absorb virtually all the time available for debates on Private Members' Bills. The bill cannot make progress if it is opposed. The objection of only one Member is sufficient to put an end to the bill.

Ten-Minute Rule Bills Standing Order No 23 allows any MP to make a speech of up to ten minutes in support of the introduction of a piece of legislation. Two such speeches can be made in any week. A single speech may be given in opposition. If there is opposition, a vote is taken as to whether the bill should be read a first time. If there is none, a date is given for the second reading but this is an empty formality since there is never any time for a second reading debate on a Ten-Minute Rule Bill. The only possibility for such a bill to proceed is if it gets an unopposed second reading without a debate.[58]

Simple presentation MPs may present a bill to the House without debate. The title of the bill is listed on the Order Paper for the day's proceedings and the Speaker calls the MP to present it at the start of public business. It means that the bill can be published and circulated but there is no opportunity for it to be presented by the proposing Member nor for any debate. Anthony Wedgwood (Tony) Benn used this procedure to present the Parliamentary Declaration and Parliamentary Reform Bill in 1997–98 and the Crown Prerogatives (Parliamentary Control) Bill in 1998–99. Those bills made no progress. By contrast, the European Union (Withdrawal (No. 2) Bill presented by his son, Hilary Benn, during the fierce battle over Brexit, did reach the statute book (see p 423 below). Usually, Presentation bills are expressions of individual opinion and they make no further progress. But if they are so uncontroversial that they require no debate they occasionally do go through[59] and, as Hilary Benn showed, they may succeed even when they are controversial.[60]

[56] The House of Commons Library publishes *Private Members Bills introduced since 1983–1984 that have received Royal Assent* which shows the title of the Bill, who initiated the Bill and the category of Private Members Bill.

[57] If there is no opposition to a bill it can go through all its stages 'on the nod'. At the end of the time allotted to private members' bills, the Clerk 'calls over' all the remaining business, consisting of any Motion down on the Order Paper for that sitting. The Speaker will put the question on any motion moved and if it is agreed without any objection, it is passed. If each stage of the bill is called in that way, the bill could be passed without any debate or any vote.

[58] The Bail (Amendment) Act 1993, giving the prosecution a right of appeal against a grant of bail was a Ten-Minute Rule bill. In the 2019–2024 Session of Parliament, there were 48 Private Members Bills that reached the statute book. Only one was a Ten-Minute Rule Bill.

[59] In the 2019–2024 Session as many as nine of the 48 Bills that reached the statute book were Presentation Bills.

[60] The No 5 Bill introduced by Yvette Cooper during the Brexit battle was also a Presentation bill that reached the statute book.

Lords' bills A private MP can take up a bill which has passed the House of Lords. The MP names a day for Second Reading and the bill is printed. But the chances of such a bill actually receiving a Second Reading are slim unless the Government gives the bill time.[61] No Lords' Private Members' bill can achieve Royal Assent unless it is given a Second Reading on the nod, ie, without opposition.

For the list of Private Members' Bills that have reached Royal Assent see *Private Members' Bills introduced since session 1983–84 that have received Royal Assent.*[62]

Figures for the years 1997–98 to 2015–16 show the proportion of the different categories of private members' bills that reached Royal Assent:[63]

	Ballot	Ten-minute rule	Presentation (Commons)	Lords	Government
Introduced:	357	1001	553	241	631
Royal Assent	87	6	5	12	566
	24%	0.6%	0.9%	5%	89.7%

The time available for Private Members' Bills in the Commons is severely limited. Normally there are thirteen Fridays in each session made available for Private Members' Bills. The first seven of these are given over to Second Reading debates. They should therefore at least get a Second Reading for their bills. But if any of these bills is opposed, the opponents commonly prolong the debate on the previous bills so as to prevent any consideration of the contentious measure. Even when it is debated, the sponsoring MP has to make sure that they have enough supporters to defeat the closure motion. Private Members' business ends at 2.30 pm. If the bill's opponents are still speaking just before 2.30 pm, the sponsor moves 'that the Question now be put'. The bill will then be talked out unless there are at least one hundred MPs (plus two tellers) present to vote in favour of the motion.

If the government is actively against a bill, its chances of success are virtually nil. But, as noted above, backbenchers twice took control of the Order Paper in 2019 and succeeded in getting bills through to Royal Assent despite the strong opposition of the government. Both Bills were for the purpose of requiring the Prime Minister to ask for an Article 50 extension of the UK's withdrawal from the EU. (See further p 423 below.)

A Bill that is favoured by the government will normally succeed in reaching the statute book. If there is any prospect of the bill becoming law the government ensures that the drafting is reviewed by Parliamentary Counsel. But this is often only at a late stage. Until then the promoters of Private Members' Bills have to rely on their own resources in the form of legal advice from fellow Members, the help of sponsoring lobbying organisations or the guidance of the clerks in the Public Bill Office. (The House of Commons resolved in 1971 that MPs who drew positions in the first twenty in the annual ballot for Private Members' Bills should receive up to £200 towards the cost of drafting assistance for such bills. In 1986 it was said that the then current value of the £200 allowance was £43.35! In the previous four parliamentary sessions there had been only five applications.[64] The House of Commons

[61] The Census (Amendment) Act 2000 got onto the statute book by this route.

[62] Successful Private Members' Bills since 1983 – House of Commons Library (parliament.uk).

[63] Shota Moriue, '*Support for Private Members' Bills in the United Kingdom and Japan*', 41 *Statute Law Review* 2020 (3), 304–15, Table 1.

[64] Colin T Reid, 'The punctilious punctuator' *Statute Law Review* 7, 1986, 45.

Procedure Committee recommended in November 2003 that the figure should be updated and that it should be index-linked.[65] But that has not yet happened.

MPs who draw high positions in the ballot usually find themselves inundated by suggestions from interest groups hoping to persuade them to adopt their pet projects for law reform. In regard to balloted bills, as has been seen, a high position in the ballot guarantees a Second Reading debate. But it does not by any means guarantee ultimate success. Between 1948 and 1985 there were 259 successful balloted bills. In 37 per cent the MP introducing the measure drew a position in the first six, in 28 per cent the MP's position in the ballot was between seventh and twelfth, and in 35 per cent it was thirteenth to twentieth.[66]

Contrary to conventional wisdom, only a minority of successful Private Members' Bills are due to private initiative. The great majority these days are in reality either government bills (known as 'government handout bills') or bills to enact the recommendations of some official law reform committee or body such as the Law Commission. The major role played by government in Private Members' legislation emerged from analysis of the origins of successful balloted bills in the 15-year period from 1970. There were a total of 140 such bills. Of these, 25 per cent were 'handout' bills suggested to the MP by the Government and drafted by Parliamentary Counsel; 29 per cent were based on the recommendations of an official law reform committee; a further 9 per cent were based on Law Commission reports; a mere 11 per cent were the result of suggestions from interest groups. In 33 cases (23 per cent) the researchers did not discover the origins of the bill.[67]

The role of the government is even greater than appears from the above figures since it is directly or indirectly involved not only in the bills which actually emanate from government departments but also in those which derive from official reports and the Law Commission. So, from 1979 to 1985, a third of successful Private Members' Bills came directly from government departments and a further 31 per cent had their origins in official reports. The role of the Government is also crucial in making time available for any controversial measure. (At the time of writing this applies to the Private Member's Terminally Ill Adults (End of Life) Bill (see n 73 below.)

During the period 1964 to 1970, Private Members' legislation was used to achieve major legislative changes because the Labour government of Harold Wilson with Mr Roy Jenkins as Home Secretary chose to give such measures its support. They included the Abortion Act 1967 liberalising the abortion laws, the Sexual Offences Act 1967 abolishing criminal penalties for homosexual acts between consenting adults, the Theatres Act 1968 reforming the censorship laws and the Divorce Reform Act 1969 introducing the modern concept of 'no fault' divorce. Since those years very few statutes of such major significance have been Private Members' Bills. Most of those that have such potential are defeated. Those that pass tend to be relatively technical and narrow. (But see n 69 below.)

Private Members' Bills (PMBs) can be of value even if they do not become law. In their assessment of the issues, Alex Brazier and Ruth Fox gave various examples:[68]

A means of prodding the Government to change its policy[69]

[65] Fourth Report for 2002–03, HC 333, para 50.

[66] D Marsh and M Read, *Private Members' Bills* (Cambridge University Press, 1988) Table 2.4, p 39.

[67] Ibid, Table 3.4, p 48.

[68] A Brazier and R Fox, 'Enhancing the backbench MP's role as a legislator: the case for urgent reform of Private Members Bills' 63 *Parliamentary Affairs*, 2010, 201.

[69] A succession of PMBs on the rights of the disabled from 1992 onwards eventually resulted in government legislation which became the Disability Discrimination Act 1995. In 1997 Michael J Foster MP introduced the Wild Mammals (Hunting with Dogs) Bill. After a succession of defeats as a PMB, the Government introduced an identical Bill which became law as the Hunting Act 2004.

> Persuading the Government to plug a gap in the law[70]
>
> Introducing new ideas which are taken up later[71]
>
> Capturing public attention at a critical moment[72]
>
> Attracting publicity and building a campaign[73]

Brazier and Fox suggested that the key problems requiring reform were excessive control of time by the executive, the lack of resources available to MPs individually to support legislative initiation and the existence of complex procedural thresholds which enabled even slight opposition to thwart popular bills.[74]

In September 2013 the House of Commons Procedure Committee published a report on Private Members' Bills making a whole raft of recommendations. It said that in terms of the legislation emerging from the process onto the statute book the term Private Members' Bills was a misnomer, as the process was 'Government dominated'.[75] In terms of the debates on Private Members' Fridays, the position was a little better in that Private Members were largely in charge of them but the process was dominated by a small number of Members who understood 'how to use the system and are prepared to play the Friday games necessary to do so'.[76] The Committee said that its aim was to restore the Private Members' Bill procedure as a means of securing debate, scrutiny and decision on genuinely backbench propositions. It recognised that Government had the right, and indeed the duty to oppose Private Members' legislative proposals where it considered that to be necessary. But it should do so openly by a division rather than talking the bill out, thereby preventing the House the opportunity to come to a decision.

The fundamental problem with the Private Member's Bill procedures as they currently operate, the Committee said, was that it was too easy for a small number of Members to prevent a bill from progressing without giving the House as a whole the chance to come to a decision on it.

> Private Member's bill procedures disenfranchise Members who may wish to support a bill being promoted by a colleague and are misleading to the public and to the interest groups who seek to use it to advance legislative change. The lack of transparency in the private Member's bill process

[70] Lord Lester's Forced Marriage (Civil Protection) Bill addressed the issue of forced marriage. After the Bill had received a Second Reading in the Lords the Government moved an amendment which completely re-wrote the Bill and it was the amended version that became law in the Act of 2007.

[71] MP Frank Field's 2002 Housing (Withholding of Benefits) Bill made no progress as a PMB but later emerged in a watered down form in the Government's Welfare Reform Act 2007.

[72] A few days before MP Jim Sheridan's Gangmasters (Licensing) Bill was due to have its Second Reading, 20 Chinese cockle-pickers died in Morecambe Bay which gave the issue immense media attention, as a result of which it was taken over by the government. The Bill became law in a considerably strengthened form.

[73] In 2003 and three subsequent sessions, Lord Joffe introduced PMBs to legalise assisted dying. In 2014, Lord Falconer, former Lord Chancellor, introduced a Bill in the Lords to legalise assisted dying. In 2015 Rob Marris, a Labour MP, introduced a Bill on assisted dying in the Commons. The Commons rejected the Bill by 330 to 118. However, on Friday 29 November 2024, in a free vote, the House of Commons by 330 to 275 gave a Second Reading to the Terminally Ill Adults (End of Life) Bill introduced by backbench Labour MP Kim Leadbeater. It was a ballotted bill. At the time of writing there was no certainty that it would become law, but the indications were that with the Labour Government's assistance, it well might. Public opinion, reflected in the voting of MPs, had changed dramatically since 2015. It was a strange coincidence that the decisive majority in both cases, first against and then for assisted dying, was 330.

[74] For reform proposals by the Speaker of the House of Commons see the speech by Mr John Bercow – 'Parliamentary reform: from here to there', a speech by the Speaker of the House of Commons to the Hansard Society, 24 September 2009. www.hansardsociety.org.uk/files/folders/2188/download.aspx.

[75] House of Commons Procedure Committee, *Private Members' Bills*, Second Report of Session 2013–14, HC 188, 2 September 2013, para 86.

[76] Ibid.

> engenders confusion and unrealistic expectations, and facilitates a situation whereby the Government is able to delay or frustrate progress on a private Members' bill without ever defeating it in a vote. The result is not only a waste of the imagination and good ideas of Members of Parliament, but a missed opportunity for engagement with the public and civil society.[77]

In March 2014 the Procedure Committee published revised proposals in light of the government's unsatisfactory response to its 2013 report.[78] Further reports followed in April[79] and in October[80] 2016. The Procedure Committee remained committed to its proposed reforms to make backbench legislation a sensible working procedure. Its main recommendation was that up to four Bills in each session should be given priority for consideration by the House on the recommendation of the Backbench Business Committee, based on an assessment of their preparation, the prior consultation undertaken on them and the support for the proposition across the House. It said, despairingly, 'If the response to our recommendations is a further period of Government inaction, we believe the House should simply abandon the pretence that there are meaningful opportunities for non-government legislation to be made when that legislation does not have the active support of the Government of the day, no matter what the merits are of the legislation proposed or the level of cross-party support it has.'[81] The government remained unmoved – and there the matter has rested.

On the significance of Private Members' Bills up to 1970 see Peter G Richards, *Parliament and Conscience* (Allen & Unwin, 1971). See generally R Blackburn, *Griffith and Ryle on Parliament*, 2nd edn (Sweet & Maxwell, 2003), especially paras 10-042–075, 12-156–160; and www.parliament.uk – Fact sheet L2 ('Private Members' Bills procedure').

For a vivid account of one such bill by its proposer see Austin Mitchell, 'A house buyer's bill: how not to pass a Private Member's Bill' 39 *Parliamentary Affairs*, 1986, 1.

2.1.8. Consolidation and Statute Law Revision or Repeal

A form of legislation that takes very little parliamentary time is consolidation (putting into one statute what was previously to be found in more than one) and statute law revision or repeal (the repeal of obsolete statutes). Both are dealt with by a special expedited procedure described in the extract that follows. (The Cabinet Office, *Guide to Making Legislation*, 2025, deals with Consolidation Bill procedure in s 42.[82]) The extract that follows tells something of the history:

William Wilson, 'The consolidation of statutes', *Law Society's Gazette*, 30 January 1980, 84

> Consolidation and revision of statutes has been part of the English legal scene for centuries but only comparatively recently has a regular basis of consolidation, revision and repeal of statutes existed.

[77] House of Commons Procedure Committee, *Private Members' Bills*, Second Report of Session 2013–14, HC 188, 2 September 2013, 2–3.

[78] Fifth Report of Session 2013–14, HC 1171, 31 March 2014.

[79] Third Report of Session 2015–16, HC 684, 18 April 2016.

[80] Second Report of Session 2016–17, HC 701, 18 October 2016.

[81] Ibid, Summary, p.3.

[82] www.gov.uk/government/publications/guide-to-making-legislation.

Sir Francis Bacon when Attorney-General became the first law officer to embark upon a scheme of statutory revision and consolidation, but all to no avail. Thomas Carlisle, writing in 1850 regarding the efforts of the Rump Parliament to tidy up the statute book, complained that the committee of that Parliament saw the spring violets become June roses whilst they were still discussing, without resolving, the meaning of 'incumbrances'. Indeed, he went on to add that the committee are 'Perhaps debating it, if so doomed, in some twilight foggy section of Dante's Nether World, to all eternity, at this hour.'

Even at the end of last century, when in a desultory fashion consolidating statutes had been passed for many years, the issue was successfully raised that consolidation could only be effected if the actual words of the consolidated statutes were not changed. It was this theory and the First World War that stopped consolidation of statutes for nearly 25 years. Today, the Joint Select Committee on Bills has 24 members. Twelve each come from the Lords and the Commons. The chairman is usually a member of the House of Lords. Most members are lawyers.

Consolidation with Corrections

In 1949 the Consolidation of Enactments (Procedure) Act was passed. This Act allowed 'corrections and minor improvements' to be made and this ended the argument that consolidation could only be effected if it was pure and unadulterated consolidation. Section 2 of the 1949 Act defines corrections and minor improvements as 'resolving ambiguities, removing doubts, bringing obsolete provisions into conformity with modern practice, or removing unnecessary provisions or anomalies …'.

The 1949 Act enabled consolidation and amendment of Acts to take place on a much greater scale but the preparation of the consolidating Bill was left to a rather 'hit or miss' process of whether there was a parliamentary draftsman available with the knowledge and time to prepare the consolidating Bill. The establishment of the Law Commission in 1965 gave an entirely new impetus and opportunity for consolidation and repeal. Before 1965, where corrections and minor improvements were involved, the originating process was a recommendation by the Lord Chancellor. The Law Commission has power enabling it to make recommendations involving consolidation where more than pure consolidation is involved. More important, the Law Commission is concerned with statute law repeal. To this revision of statute law the Law Commission brings a new criterion when deciding its recommendations to repeal. This new criterion is that of 'practical utility'. This criterion widens considerably the previous criterion which was that of 'obsolete, spent, unnecessary or superseded'.

Procedure

For a Bill to come before this Joint Consolidation Committee it will have originated in the House of Lords who remit the Bill to the committee for consideration. When the draft Bill comes to the committee members it has with it the comments of the draftsman explaining where the Bill is not pure consolidation and also giving a general outline of the Bill's provisions. Where applicable, recommendations of the Law Commission are also provided for the committee members. The draftsman of the Bill (and he may be accompanied by government departmental officers where their particular department is involved) appears before the committee to give oral explanations on the proposed enactment and to answer questions from the committee members. The Bill is taken clause by clause and the draftsman is obliged to satisfy the committee that it is a Bill that has been consolidated in accordance with the law. If the Bill deals with statute repeal then the draftsman has to satisfy the committee that the repealed legislation is truly spent and obsolete and those departments or organisations which may be affected by the repeal do not raise any objections.

The Joint Select Committee on Consolidation Bills, after having considered the Bill and heard and questioned the draftsman and any other witnesses, reports to the Lords and the Commons that either the Bill is pure consolidation or, that corrections or amendments have been made to the previous legislation in accordance with the procedures laid down.

> On a Bill dealing with statute law repeal the committee reports to the Lords and the Commons that only Acts which were obsolete, spent or unnecessary are involved.
>
> The Bills when reported to the Houses are passed through the Houses in a few minutes. There is no debate upon the merits of the particular legislation and only points concerned with the actual alterations that have been made can be raised. In practice this very rarely happens. Any member of the committee soon acquires a profound admiration for the skill and knowledge of Parliamentary draftsmen, but in the consolidation work the members do come to know that even Parliamentary draftsmen make mistakes. Recently the Army Reserve Act 1950 was being consolidated. In a section of that Act it was discovered there was reference to 'Non-commissioned officers and warrant officers'. This is the only time in our statutes that non-commissioned officers have been placed before warrant officers. The Joint Consolidation Committee was solemnly asked to pass an amendment to make 'non-commissioned officers and warrant officers' read 'warrant officers and non-commissioned officers'. The drafting error was corrected and due precedence afforded to warrant officers!

A Report of a Working Party on Consolidation of Statutes set up by the Statute Law Society urged in 1984 that the Law Commission should be somewhat bolder in proposing amendments to consolidation acts. ('Certainly nobody would question that a Bill making use of the streamlined consolidation procedure is not the right vehicle for major or controversial changes. But … we believe that it should be possible to develop a broader and more liberal approach to the problem without destroying Parliament's confidence in the Joint Committee and its assurance that the consolidation procedure will not be abused', 5 *Statute Law Review*, 1984, 169, 174.)

In the view of Lord Etherton, former chairman of the Law Commission, consolidation is of decreasing importance. One reason was that consolidation required that the law being consolidated remained relatively settled while the consolidation was being undertaken – 'an increasingly rare state of affairs'.

> It is also partly because of changes made in the 1970s to the way Parliament amends legislation. This is now routinely done by textual amendment.[83] With modern electronic sources of legislation and existing reference material, anyone wishing to see the latest version of an Act can readily do so. The need to consolidate simply to take account of textual change has largely gone.[84]

Another reason, not mentioned by Lord Etherton (who at that time was Master of the Rolls), is that professionals, which here includes academics and their students, will normally have online access to Westlaw and/or LexisNexis which show the current state of legislation including amendments, so that one can see how an Act looks when amended.

In the 41 years between 1965 and 2006 there were 220 Consolidation Bills. In the 17 years between 2006 and 2023 there were only three. The Law Commission's 2022–23 annual report said (p 69): 'This change reflects the fact that, in a time of reduced funding in most areas of public services, consolidation is perhaps seen by the Government to be a lower priority.'

[83] [As to which see 1.3 (Report of the Renton Committee), item (d) p 22 above. (ed)]

[84] 'Law reform in England and Wales: a shattered dream or triumph of political vision' *Amicus Curiae*, Institute of Advanced Legal Studies, Spring 2008, 3, 10.

The Lords Constitution Committee in 2017 regretted that consolidation did not have a higher priority for government:

> We recommend that the Government should, as a priority, provide the Law Commission with the necessary resources to start consolidating those areas of the law where consistent application of the law is now under threat from the sheer complexity of the existing statute book. The Government should subsequently ensure that the small amount of parliamentary time required is made available to pass the necessary consolidation bills to implement the Law Commission's work. The evidence we received suggested that consolidating immigration and sentencing law in particular would offer real benefits not only in relation to the clarity and ease of application of the law, but in terms of cost and efficiency savings within the justice system.[85]

The Law Commission did recently complete one hugely important piece of consolidation in its Sentencing Code Report together with a draft Sentencing Code Bill (558 pages) published in November 2018. It became the Sentencing Act 2020.The Commission estimated that the Code 'could save up to £250 million over the next decade by avoiding unnecessary appeals and reducing delays in sentencing clogging up the court system'.[86]

> No longer will courts have to make reference to historic versions of legislation, and decipher opaque transitional provisions. For all offenders convicted after the commencement of the Sentencing Code the courts will, by virtue of the clean sweep,[[87]] need to have reference only to the Sentencing Code itself. Even where exceptions to the clean sweep apply, the Sentencing Code will replicate those historic provisions in the Code itself, making clear to which cases they apply. This will avoid the need for users to make reference to, and identify, complex transitional provisions. This represents a considerable departure from current practice and is a change we think will have a significant impact.[88]

Statute law revision, by contrast, goes on year by year. Since 1965 some 3,000 out-of-date statutes have been wholly repealed and many more thousands have been partially repealed.[89]

Alternatives to Consolidation

Sometimes there is a need for consolidation before an actual consolidation is prepared. If one statute amends another it may be exceedingly awkward for citizens and their professional advisers to use the two together. There are three techniques that are sometimes used in this situation. One is to postpone the operation of the amending statute until the consolidation is ready. This is unlikely unless the consolidation is well on the way when the amending statute receives Royal Assent. A second is to include in the amending statute a Keeling Schedule which, as seen above (1.3, text to n 71, p 22 above), gives the text of the law as amended showing typographically the amending passages. (In 2004, the House of Lords Constitution Committee commended Keeling Schedules. In 2019 the Committee

[85] Lords Constitution Committee, *Preparing Legislation for Parliament*, 4th Report, 2017–19, October 2017, HL 27, para.147.

[86] Law Commission, *Annual Report*, 2018–19, 53. For an appraisal of the Code see JV Roberts and U Azmeh, 'Cleansing the Augean Stables: A Commentary on the Law Commission's Sentencing Code for England and Wales' [2019] *Criminal Law Review* (8) 694–705. The authors see the Code 'as constituting a platform for future reform; the consolidation was a necessary first step towards more principled and consistent sentencing.' (694).

[87] ['The clean sweep' was the phrase used by the Law Commission to describe the effect of the Code in sweeping away pre-existing sentencing law. That was achieved by the Sentencing (Pre-Consolidation Amendments) Act 2020. That was followed by the Sentencing Act 2020 which became law on 1 December 2020. (ed)]

[88] Law Commission, *The Sentencing Code*, Vol.1 Report, 2018, 1.27.

[89] Law Commission, *Annual Report* 2018–19, p 33.

said it was disappointed that so little use had been made of them. It recommended 'that the Government produces such schedules or explanatory materials for all bills that substantially amend previous legislation'.[90] The Government Response[91] was brief and to the point: 'We do not support the introduction of Keeling Schedules as a matter of course.')

The third technique is to arrange with the editor of the *Statutes in Force* for publication immediately after Royal Assent of the principal Act as amended. This lacks the full authority of statute but at least it would give members of the public and their advisers the text of an intelligible document. (See Lord Simon of Glaisdale, 'Statute consolidation: interim techniques' *Public Law*, 1985, 352.) Those with access to the online services provided notably by Westlaw and LexisNexis already have the benefit of this third technique.

2.1.9. Special Procedure for Uncontroversial Law Commission Bills

In October 2010 the House of Lords approved a new expedited parliamentary procedure for uncontroversial Law Commission bills that had been recommended by the Procedure Committee.[92] Following First Reading the bill is referred to a 'Second Reading Committee', an innovation for the Lords. Membership of the committee is unlimited. Any member can speak. There is no time limit on debate. No votes can be taken. When the committee reports to the House that it has considered the bill, and assuming there is no opposition, the House votes formally to give it a Second Reading. The bill is then committed to a Special Public Bill Committee. Such committees consist usually of nine or ten members, including the relevant minister and opposition spokesmen. They can take written and oral evidence within a 28-day period. Having taken evidence, they then consider the bill clause by clause and consider amendments in the usual way. The bill is then reprinted as amended and proceeds to Report and Third Reading in the normal way on the floor of the House. It then goes to the full normal procedure in the House of Commons.

2.1.10. Special Procedure for the Tax Law Rewrite

A special procedure was agreed for the Tax Law Rewrite (1.4.2 above) involving the preparation of thousands of pages of primary legislation to replace existing tax laws. It was not possible to use the normal procedure for consolidation because of the substantial changes of language and format involved. On the other hand, it would not have been sensible to apply the ordinary public bill procedure as this would have involved a prohibitively large commitment of parliamentary time. Also, that would have permitted reopening of policy issues that had previously been enacted and established. Moreover, there was an elaborate pre-parliamentary process to prepare the way.

The procedure devised by the Select Committee on Procedure[93] was that the House of Commons should be given an opportunity to give its substantive approval to the principles

[90] Lords Constitution Committee, *The Legislative Process: The Passage of Bills through Parliament*, 24th Report 2017–19, July 2019, HL 393, para.87.

[91] Published on the Parliament website 4 November 2019.

[92] House of Lords Select Committee on Procedure, First Report 2007–08 (HL Paper 63) and Second Report 2010–11 (HL Paper 30).

[93] Second Report of 1996–97, HC 126, 30 January 1997.

underlying the Rewrite before any Rewrite Bills were introduced. Rewrite Bills would be introduced in the House of Commons. The Second Reading would not be on the floor of the House but would instead be in a Second Reading Committee (see 2.2.3 below). The Committee stage would be by a Joint Committee of both Houses. This would permit evidence to be given by Parliamentary Counsel, by Inland Revenue officials, the chairmen of the Steering Committee or the Consultative Committee of the Tax Law Rewrite project and by others. The Joint Committee would have a House of Commons majority from whom the chairman would be drawn. It would determine its own procedure. This was envisaged as having three stages: (1) determination of what evidence was needed and taking such evidence; (2) deliberation by the Committee in private with ministers present; and (3) clause-by-clause examination of the bill, possibly involving hearing further evidence.

After the Committee Stage, Rewrite Bills would go through the Commons with little, if any, further debate and the procedure in the House of Lords would be suitably modified to permit maximum expedition. Just as for normal consolidation bills, the House of Lords plays the dominant role, so here it would be accepted that the dominant role would be played by the House of Commons.

On 20 March 1997, the House of Commons adopted the proposed procedure by Standing Order No 60 for Tax Simplification Bills. The first bill under the Tax Rewrite project, the Capital Allowances Bill, was given a Second Reading on 15 January 2001 and was committed to the Joint Committee. The Committee, comprised of seven MPs and six peers, took evidence on the bill at two meetings and made no amendments to it.[94]

For further description see D Salter, 'Towards a parliamentary procedure for the Tax Law Rewrite' 19 *Statute Law Review*, 1998, 65.

2.2. Legislative Committees

2.2.1. Public Bill Committees (formerly Called Standing Committees)

Standing Committee was the name of the committee that, after the Second Reading, dealt with the clause-by-clause examination of government bills. They were known not by the name of the bill they were considering but as A, B, C, etc. The word 'Standing' was misleading in that the membership changed for each bill. In 2006, the Committee on the Modernisation of the House of Commons recommended that 'Standing Committees' should be called 'Public Bill Committees' and that each Committee be named for the bill it was considering.[95]

Special Standing Committees were introduced in 1980. The 2006 report of the Modernisation Committee recommended that in future Special Standing Committees also be called Public Bill Committees.[96] It recommended further that *all* Public Bill Committees be able to take evidence and that the restrictions on the taking of evidence be removed.[97] Decisions as to what time would be allowed for evidence taking should be made on a

[94] Joint Committee on Tax Simplification Bills, First Report, HC 175 of 2000–01 and HL Paper 24.

[95] Committee on the Modernisation of the House of Commons, *The Legislative Process*, HC 1097, July 2006, para 65.

[96] Ibid.

[97] Ibid.

case-by-case basis. As was previously noted, evidence taking prior to the start of the clause-by-clause examination of the bill is now a normal and valuable part of the process.[98] It only applies to the committees that examine Private Members' Bills if expressly ordered. The Terminally Ill Adults (End of Life) Bill was the first Private Members' Bill to be the subject of such an order, made immediately after the Bill received a Second Reading on 29 November 2024. The taking of evidence does not operate when a bill is committed to the whole House. There are sometimes complaints that a bill has been committed to the whole house expressly so as to avoid the taking of evidence.

The Modernisation Committee 2006 report said that taking evidence had several benefits:

> 53 ... It is first and foremost a mechanism for ensuring that Members are informed about the subject of the bill and that there is some evidential basis for the debate on the bill. Evidence-gathering is also, by its nature, a more consensual and collective activity than debate, and there is evidence that those outside Parliament have a more positive view of select committee proceedings than of debate. So there is a reputational benefit to Parliament in being seen to engage in a more open, questioning and consensual style of law-making, before moving on to the necessary partisan debate.
>
> 54 An evidence-taking stage is also an effective way of engaging the wider public directly in the legislative process. The Law Society argued that it is important that the process for influencing a committee's thinking was as straightforward as possible and suggested that many organisations would value the opportunity to give evidence to a committee considering a bill, even if they had contributed to the Government's consultation exercise.

These important changes were made in 2007. The Modernisation Committee stated that evidence taking by a Public Bill Committee should not be seen as a substitute for pre-legislative scrutiny (as to which see 2.8 below).

> The need to complete both the evidence-taking and the consideration of the bill in reasonable time means that these committees are not a suitable vehicle for exhaustive inquiries, nor are they a substitute for the consultation exercises undertaken by Government before a bill is presented. Where there has been a pre-legislative inquiry, we would expect the Public Bill Committee to take the pre-legislative report as its starting point and not to re-examine the same witnesses on the same issues.[99]

For consideration of the value of the introduction of oral evidence see Hugh H Bochel, 'House of Commons Public Bill Committees and Oral Evidence: A half-step forward?' 77 *Parliamentary Affairs*, 2024(1), 129–48. Drawing on interviews with officials and witnesses, and on data gathered from *Hansard* for the 2017–19 session, the article examined the selection and some of the characteristics of witnesses, witnesses' views of the process and how oral evidence is used in subsequent scrutiny of the legislation. The author concluded;

> [W]hile it might be possible to 'improve' the process, for example with more bills being subject to evidence sessions, including those introduced in the House of Lords, and this might lead to more use of evidence, the combination of process (including the relatively late stage at which public bill committee scrutiny takes place), subject and political factors means that the extent of the use of

[98] See especially n 9 p 38 above. In 2013 the House of Commons Political and Constitutional Reform Committee recommended that there should be a gap of a week between the evidence sessions and the start of the line-by-line examination of the bill so as to give time for the evidence to be considered and amendments to be prepared. *Ensuring Standards in the Quality of Legislation*, 1st Report 2013–14, HC 85, 20 May 2013, para 25.

[99] Committee on the Modernisation of the House of Commons, *The Legislative Process*, HC 1097, July 2006, para 73.

> oral evidence would be likely to vary considerably, while in general its impact on legislation would be likely to remain fairly limited.
>
> As noted above, evidence taking does not apply when the bill is committed to the whole House. Government may take this course as a way of expediting progress on a bill and reducing the opportunities for scrutiny. Of the 47 bills that went to committee stage during the 2019–21 parliamentary session, almost half (23) went to the Committee of the whole House, meaning there was no opportunity to take evidence at all; this was a higher proportion than in other recent sessions. Of the 24 bills that went to public bill committee, 14 did not take oral evidence (seven were private members' bills, and three started in the House of Lords). In total just 10 out of the 47 bills benefited from the 2008 reforms …
>
> Bills should not be put to the Committee of the whole House for the purposes of shortening the bill timetable unless absolutely essential. Doing so curtails opportunities for parliamentarians, the public, civil society and business groups to scrutinise policy. This increases the risk of poor legislation or legislation without broad-based support ending up on the statute book, meaning policies are less likely to succeed and more likely to be reversed.[100]

2.2.2. First Reading Committees

The House of Commons Modernisation Committee established by the Blair government in 1997 proposed in its first report[101] that some bills should be referred for examination by a First Reading Committee prior to Second Reading – as recommended by the Hansard Society's 1992 Report *Making the Law*. The thinking was that ministers might be more receptive to suggested improvements at that stage than once the bill had received its Second Reading. However, this proposal has not been implemented.

2.2.3. Second Reading Committees (House of Commons)

Second Reading Committees are occasionally used for technical or uncontroversial bills. Under this procedure the bill is referred for its Second Reading to a special committee of something between 16 and 50 MPs appointed in the usual way by the Select Committee of Selection. They observe the normal rules that apply to Second Readings – one of which is that no Member may speak more than once without leave of the Committee. After they recommend that the bill be read a second time, the vote on that question is taken by the full House without any debate. The procedure was initiated in 1965 at the time of the setting up of the Law Commission. Law Commission Bills are automatically referred to Second Reading Committee.[102]

2.2.4. Grand Committees (Both Houses)

In the House of Lords the term Grand Committee is used for consideration of bills off the floor of the House in a committee room. But all peers are still free to take part. No

[100] Bennett Institute for Public Policy and Institute for Government, *The Legislative Process: How to Empower Parliament*, Jess Sergeant and Jack Pannell, December 2022, pp 46, 50.

[101] After Labour's defeat in 2010 the \Modernisation Committee ceased to exist until the return of Labour in 2024.

[102] Erskine May, *Parliamentary Practice* (25th edn 2019) 28.54.

votes are allowed in Grand Committees so amendments can only be made if approved unanimously.

The procedure was proposed in a 1994 report on Sittings of the House chaired by Lord Rippon. The Rippon report envisaged that the procedure would be used for 'all but the most important Government bills' and that it would lead to considerable saving of time on the floor of the House. However this has not happened. The procedure has not been used to any great extent.[103]

2.2.5. Select Committee on Bills

Very exceptionally a public bill is sent to a Select Committee. This occurred in 2004 with the Constitutional Reform Bill which provided for the abolition of the office of Lord Chancellor and of the judicial functions of the House of Lords and the creation of a Supreme Court and a Judicial Appointments Commission. The Government opposed the reference but it was defeated.

The Report of that Select Committee stated that the practice of committing a government bill to a Select Committee had been very rarely used in recent times (though it was not unusual in respect of contentious Private Members' Bills). The Hare Coursing Bill had been referred to a Lords Select Committee against the Government's wishes in 1975. The most recent precedents where it had been done by agreement lay in the period during and just after the First World War.[104]

Such a Select Committee has power to receive evidence on the policy of the bill and to determine whether or not the bill should proceed. The Committee also has the power to amend the bill – which it does in private session. The bill is then reprinted as amended and re-committed to a Committee of the whole House.

2.2.6. The Role of Departmental Select Committees in Legislation

Public Bill Committees on bills must be distinguished from Departmental Select Committees which are entirely different. These owe their existence to the report of a Select Committee on Procedure in 1978 which criticised the House of Commons for its inadequate system of scrutinising the activities of the executive. Against the instincts of frontbenchers on both sides, backbench Members of Parliament forced the acceptance of the new concept of select committees with responsibility for scrutinising the executive within their respective field. MPs voted for the new system in June 1979. The Liaison Select Committee was later added, consisting of the chair person of the individual select committees.

Most House of Commons select committees shadow the work of particular departments; some pursue cross-cutting themes such as Women and Equality, Science and Technology, Public Accounts, Environmental Audit. In the House of Lords all the select committees are related to subjects rather than to government departments. Departmental Select Committees frequently issue reports commenting on pending legislation. The House of Commons Home Affairs Committee, the Lords Delegated Powers and Regulatory Reform

[103] The number of bills referred to a Lords Grand Committee in the eight sessions from 1994 to 2002 was 1, 5, 3, 6, 5, 9, 2, 3 – *Griffith and Ryle on Parliament* (n 12 p 39 above) 724.

[104] *Report of the Select Committee on the Constitutional Reform Bill*, July 2004, HL 125-I, para 4.

Committee,[105] Constitution Committee and the Joint Committee on Human Rights[106] in particular do so.

The significant contribution that can be made by select committees came to the fore during the several years of travail over Brexit. As this extract from an important article explains, it began even before Theresa May's government had triggered Article 50 to begin the process of withdrawal from the EU:

> The House of Lords Constitution Committee issued three reports [on the European Union (Withdrawal) Bill], the first of which was anticipatory, published in March 2017, before even notification of intention to withdraw under Article 50 of the Treaty on European Union had been issued. In this report the Committee sought to flag up the main constitutional issues which were likely to be raised by the then-forthcoming Bill and to which Parliament ought to be attentive.[107] Having seen the published Bill, the Committee produced a second (interim) report to coincide with the Bill's second reading in the House of Commons,[108] assessing the Bill in light of its earlier recommendations and drawing attention to the fact that many of the problems anticipated by the Committee had materialised in the Bill itself. The timing of this report is indicative of how the two houses can work together when important constitutional issues are at stake. The Lords is conscious that it lacks the democratic legitimacy of the Commons, but its committees were able to supply the ammunition of constitutional critique which was then fired with more political authority by the Commons. The Constitution Committee, following its own inquiry into the Bill, and taking account of the preceding Commons stages, published a final and detailed report on the Bill ahead of second reading in the Lords.[109]
>
> Other committees were also active in assessing many aspects of the Bill – in particular, the Commons' European Scrutiny Committee and Public Administration and Constitutional Affairs Committee, and the Lords' EU Committee and Delegated Powers and Regulation Reform Committee. At the same time scrutiny was enabled by a number of important analyses of the Bill's key provisions produced by the House of Commons library and the devolved legislatures. As we assess the evolution of the Bill in this article, it will be apparent just how much its development was the consequence of interplay between Parliament in plenary session and the information it derived from its committees, the latter also in dialogue directly with the Government through evidence sessions and discussion seminars taking place both in public and private as part of ongoing inquiries into the Bill as a whole or particular aspects of it.[110]

Departmental Select Committees determine their own agenda, call and examine witnesses (including ministers[111] and judges![112]) and appoint specialist advisers. They have their

[105] The Committee was originally called the Delegated Powers and Deregulation Committee. Its work was described by its Clerk, in P Tudor, 'Secondary legislation: second class or crucial?' 21 *Statute Law Review*, 2000, 149. See further below.

[106] For a helpful review of the Joint Committee's work by its Legal Adviser see D Feldman, 'Parliamentary scrutiny of legislation and human rights' *Public Law*, 2002, 323. See also D Feldman, 'The impact of Human Rights on the UK legislative process' 25 *Statute Law Review*, 2004, 91.

[107] Lords Constitution Committee, 'The "Great Repeal Bill" and delegated powers', 2016–2017, 7 March 2017, HL 123.

[108] Lords Constitution Committee, 'European Union (Withdrawal) Bill: interim report', 2017–19, 7 September 2017, HL 19.

[109] Lords Constitution Committee, 'European Union (Withdrawal) Bill', 29 January 2018, HL 89, 2017–19.

[110] M Elliott and S Tierney, 'Political Pragmatism and Constitutional Principle: The European Union (Withdrawal) Act 2018' *Public Law*, 2019 (1), 37–60, 39.

[111] In the 1992–97 Parliament ministers made 405 appearances before departmental select committees – *Griffith and Ryle on Parliament* (n 12 above) para 11-041.

[112] 'From 1979 to 2015 there were 43 instances of judges giving oral evidence, and a further 42 instances of written evidence, on a total of 19 different Bills and draft Bills … Ultimately, we concluded that the practice of

own staff.[113] They can also appoint their own sub-committees. Normally they have eleven members who are backbenchers (as compared with Public Bill Committees on bills where there will always be a minister and a frontbench spokesman for the Opposition). However, party strength in the House determines the numbers of each party on the committee.

As to membership, previously, the names of nominees were put forward by the Select Committee of Selection which is under the control of the party whips.[114] But they had to be approved by the House. Very occasionally a nomination was rejected by the House – as happened in July 2001. The nominations did not include two respected backbenchers (Donald Anderson and Gwyneth Dunwoody) who had respectively chaired the Foreign Affairs Committee and the Transport Sub-Committee in the previous Parliament. To express its resentment, the House rejected the entire list of nominations. The Committee of Selection then came back with a revised list including those two names – and they were later re-elected to chair those two committees.

In 2000, the Liaison Committee, consisting of the chair persons of all Select Committees, recommended that MPs should be nominated to membership of select committees by a body independent of party whips: vacancies would be advertised; names would be chosen by a new Select Committee Panel; and the final decision would remain with the House.[115] This proposal was rejected by the government.[116] The matter became topical again in light of the Anderson/Dunwoody incident and the Leader of the House asked the Modernisation Committee to revisit the issue. It recommended a new Committee of Nomination chaired by the Deputy Speaker.[117] It would operate as a 'fail-safe mechanism to ensure fair play and to provide a court of appeal'. It would only alter party nominations in 'exceptional circumstances where it was clear that a fundamental problem had arisen'. This proposal was rejected by the Commons on 14 May 2002 by 209 to 195.

However, a new system was put in place at the start of the 2010 parliament following recommendations of the Wright Committee.[118] Departmental Select Committee members are now elected in secret ballots in their party groups, and their chairs are elected in a cross-party secret ballot by all MPs with the names still put formally to the chamber for final approval. Hence the Select Committees are not only permanent, and specialist, they now

inviting judges to give evidence on Bills is not just constitutionally defensible, but that it gives rise to clear benefits for both Parliament and the judiciary … [W]e found no clear instance of judicial independence being compromised as a result. Often the reverse was true, since much evidence, especially on the Constitutional Reform Bill, consisted of robustly reminding Parliament of the importance of upholding judicial independence.' (R Hazell and J Wells, 'Judicial Input into Parliamentary Legislation' *Public Law*, 2018, 106–27, 109, 127) See also the earlier article – R Hazell and P O'Brien, 'Meaningful Dialogue: Judicial Engagement with Parliamentary Committees at Westminster' *Public Law*, 2016, 54–73.

[113] The staff typically consists of three to six full-time and several part-time staff.

[114] The Committee of Selection has nine members and is chaired by a senior government backbencher. It includes the Deputy Chief Whip and whips from other parties – though the Liberal Democrat Whip represents the interests of all the other minor parties (*Griffith and Ryle on Parliament* (n 12 above) para 11-087).

[115] *Shifting the Balance: Select Committees and the Executive*, HC 300 of 1999–2000.

[116] Cm 4737, May 2000.

[117] Modernisation Committee, First Report, HC 224 of 2001–02; endorsed by Liaison Committee, Second Report, HC 692 of 2001–02.

[118] The Select Committee on Reform of the House of Commons (the 'Wright Committee') was established in 2009, following the MPs' expenses crisis. It was chaired by Labour MP Dr Tony Wright. The Wright committee proposed the establishment of a new Backbench Business Committee, and a new category of backbench business, in order to give MPs better control over the Commons agenda. With respect to departmental select committees, it recommended limiting membership to 11 MPs (to improve cohesiveness and attendance), enforcing clearer rules about frontbenchers and Parliamentary Private Secretaries (PPSs) not serving on the committees, and introducing secret elections for both committee members and chairs. (Select Committee on Reform of the House of Commons, First Report of Session 2008–09, *Rebuilding the House*, HC 1117, 4 November 2009.)

enjoy significant institutional independence from the whips. This is regarded as a major development.(It did not apply to the selection of chair and members of the Commons Modernisation Committee in 2024. For reasons that were not revealed, the new Starmer Government decided members should be selected by the whips. The chair unusually was a member of the Cabinet – the Leader of the House of Commons no less and one of the opposition members selected was her Shadow opposite.)

In October 2003, the House of Commons voted to recognise the work of Select Committee chairs by paying them an additional salary of £12,500 on top of their standard MPs salary. This followed recommendations from various groups, including the Hansard Society 1992 report on the legislative process (*Making the Law*), in order to create a different career path and set of incentives for MPs.

Departmental Select Committees do not have the adversarial system of the House or of ordinary committees of the House. Moreover they deliberate in private which helps to reduce the party political stance taken by members. They try to produce unanimous reports.[119] Also, unlike Public Bill Committees, Departmental Select Committees build considerable expertise through continuing membership during a Parliament, and even from one Parliament to another. That applies not only to the Committee membership but to their staff:

> While public bill committees rely on a staff team that is drawn together temporarily for the lifetime of the committee (albeit from permanent staff at Westminster), the select committees have a team that remains together from one inquiry to the next. The departmental select committees each have a clerk, second clerk, one or two committee specialists, and normally two committee assistants. Committee specialists are hired for their knowledge on the subject area, and while other staff are more generalist, they will tend to develop subject expertise over their time with the committee. In addition, the select committees are able to appoint specialist advisers to support particular inquiries, who may advise on matters such as the selection of witnesses and drafting of questions, as well as preparing background papers. Like the public bill committees, the select committees can sometimes benefit from additional input from specialists in the House of Commons Library. All of these individuals will not only build up a relationship with each other, and with committee members, but also with other relevant personnel in the field, such as civil servants in the department shadowed by the committee, and outside experts.[120]

Another very significant feature of the work of Select Committees is their nonpartisan character:

> These committees have a nonpartisan character and their reports are almost invariably unanimous. The fact that select committee proceedings are conducted from within a horseshoe seating plan, together with the greater permanence and specialisation of their members, all help to encourage a distinctly consensual method of working.[121]

An assessment of departmental select committees after thirty years began:

> Since their establishment in 1979, departmental select committees in the House of Commons have been one of Parliament's great success stories. Providing for permanent oversight of the executive

[119] See D Englefield, *Select Committees: Catalysts for Progress?* (Longman, 1984). For treatment of dissent in departmental select committees see also *Griffith and Ryle on Parliament* (n 12 above) paras 11-052–053. Dissent did not occur in any of 65 reports issued by the Treasury Committee although many addressed controversial topics. (I Marsh, 'The Commons Select Committee System in the 2015–20 Parliament', 87 *Political Quarterly*, 2016 (1) 97.).

[120] Russell, Morris and Larkin, *Fitting the Bill* (n 32 p 42 above) 16–17.

[121] Ibid, 18.

> their importance in scrutinising and holding the government to account is widely acknowledged. Their influence, direct and indirect, has kept issues alive in the public domain – for example, the conduct of wars in Kosovo, Iraq and Afghanistan, Gulf War syndrome, pit closures, nuclear decommissioning, compensation for Equitable Life policyholders, the operation of the Child Support Act, the blight caused by empty homes and the future of the BBC – resulting, in some cases, in useful legislative and policy changes. Some committees and their chairs have also come to occupy a central place in public debate, as the Treasury Committee in particular has done since 2008 in grilling bankers and regulators about their role in and responsibility for the financial crisis.[122]

See generally *Griffith and Ryle on Parliament*, 2nd edn (Sweet & Maxwell, 2003) paras 11-001–056. For further reading see M Russell, B Morris, P Larkin, *Fitting the Bill – Bringing Commons Legislation Committees into Line with Best Practice*, Constitution Unit, 2013; *The Poodle Bites Back: Select Committees and the Revival of Parliament*, Centre for Policy Studies, 2015, 75pp; *Select Committees under Scrutiny: The Impact of Parliamentary Committee Inquiries on Government*, Institute for Government, 2015, 36pp; L Fisher, 'The Growing Power and Autonomy of the House of Commons Select Committees: Causes and Effects', 86 *Political Quarterly*, 2015 (3), 418–26. The whole of *Parliamentary Affairs* 2019(4) was devoted to the subject of parliamentary select committees.

In 2019, the Liaison Select Committee published *The Effectiveness and Influence of the Select Committee System*, Fourth Report of the Session 2017–19, 9 September 2019, 134pp. The report made a raft of recommendations.

For a critique of machinations by Boris Johnson's government in relation to select committees, see David Judge in 'Walking the dark side: Evading parliamentary scrutiny', 92 *Political Quarterly*, 2021(2), 283–92.

See also the assessment of the role and performance of select committees by Christopher Johnson, 'Select Committees: Powers and Functions' in *Parliament and the Law*, 3rd edn (Hart, 2022) 133–58.

2.2.7. Public Bill Committees – The Case for Reform

The success of departmental select committees stimulated a call in 2013 for reform of Public Bill Committees (PBCs). A report by the Constitution Unit at University College, London identified four main reasons why reform of PBCs was necessary:[123]

Permanence – Departmental select committees remain for a whole parliament. Members of PBCs are chosen to work just on a bill.

> [T]there is little incentive to cooperate, and party barriers are hard to break down. The bonds between members of a given party will always be stronger than the bonds of common interest between members of a temporary committee. In contrast in permanent committees these latter bonds can become important, and come to transcend knee-jerk party differences. We see this in Britain, where long-term working relationships contribute to the select committees' ethos and reputation as effective cross-party bodies.[124]

[122] A Brazier and R Fox, 'Reviewing Select Committee tasks and modes of operation' 64 *Parliamentary Affairs*, 2011, 354, 354.
[123] M Russell, B Morris and P Larkin, *Bringing Commons Legislation Committees into Line with Best Practice* (Constitution Unit, June 2013).
[124] Ibid 32–33.

Specialisation – Members of departmental select committees develop expertise because they serve through a whole parliament. By contrast, members of PBCs serve only for that stage of a bill's progress through the House of Commons. The same applies to their respective staffs. Staff members of select committees not only are, or become, specialists, they can develop a network of contacts with relevant civil servants, academic experts and other significant players in the field.

Selection – As noted, members of select committees are now chosen by MPs by secret ballot. By contrast, members of PBCs are chosen by the Committee on Selection which consists mainly of whips.[125] ('This – rightly or wrongly – feeds suspicions that committee memberships are manipulated in order to block members who might prove awkward to their party leaderships, even including 'expert' members.'[126])

Adverserialism

> The PBCs largely operate along the model of adversarialism that applies to the chamber, rather than the consensual model of the select committees ... Rather than bills being considered by groups of members who know each other well, and must work together again, PBC members have few incentives to behave constructively rather than making party points. This is worsened by the fact that some members may have no particular commitment to the subject area, that they discuss the bill after a high-profile partisan debate has already taken place, and that members whose views diverge from the party line may be intentionally excluded from the committee.[127]

The report made recommendations for pilot studies to address these issues taking into account the fact that departments have very different profiles in terms of the number of bills they promote. For the few heavy legislation departments (eg the Home Office and the Ministry of Justice) there should be new permanent legislation committees. For departments that only had an occasional bill (eg Defence, Foreign Office, Department for Energy) legislation scrutiny could be undertaken by the relevant departmental select committee.[128] For departments with medium heavy legislation (eg Business, Innovation and Skills, Communities and Local Government, Education), PBCs should be reformed through formalising overlap with the relevant select committee and strengthening on the staffing side. There should also be experiments, the report urged, with sending some bills to committees for evidence taking before the Second Reading instead of as now at the start of the Committer stage.

No action was taken in regard to these recommendations.

[125] As was noted above, the rules prohibit ministers and whips from serving as members of departmental select committees.

[126] The report (n 123 above) instanced the case of Sarah Wollaston who had formerly been a GP. Her request to serve on the PBC for the Health and Social Care Bill was rejected by the Conservative whips, which she blamed on her unwillingness to guarantee unconditional support for the bill. (However, on 18 June 2014 she was elected by MPs as chair of the Departmental Select Committee on the NHS!).

[127] Constitution Unit Report (n 123 above) 44.

[128] A House of Commons committee report cited a witness, Andrew Tyrie MP, regarding the role of the Treasury Select Committee in the Financial Services Bill in 2012: 'First, the Committee tabled its own amendment at Report stage in the Commons. This produced a Government concession on the floor of the House.' The Committee then published a Report containing its views on what was still needed to improve the Bill, to coincide with the introduction of the Bill in the Lords. Mr Tyrie continued, 'The Committee's proposals formed the basis for much of the debate in the Lords and a series of Government amendments to the Bill gave effect to some of our most important recommendations. The Bill was improved as a result.' (Political and Constitutional Reform Committee, *Revisiting Rebuilding the House: the impact of the Wright reforms*, HC 82, 18 July 2013, para 31).

2.3. The Role of the Bill Team

The bill team's main work during the legislative process, according to Professor Edward Page in his detailed study of the progress of four bills, was briefing ministers at every stage:[129]

> For civil servants the parliamentary process involves, above all, getting briefings to ministers so they can handle questions and answer points in parliament and the media on both the main policy thrusts of the bill as well as its detail. Bills thus generate huge amounts of paperwork since at this stage the written brief is the basis of all briefing. The dossier for ministers on one of the bills ran to nearly 500 pages. Because the dossiers and briefings are tailored to the particular parliamentary stage of the bill, and are changed as new amendments are proposed, the cumulative volume of paperwork makes its management a substantial part of the parliamentary work of the bill team.[130]

The 'policy work' identified by Professor Page entailed three broad types of activity at the amendments stage: dealing with unfinished business; deciding what amendments need to be taken on board; and developing government amendments.

Dealing with unfinished business Often a bill is published in an incomplete form because the work on some part of it has not been finished in time. The bill team's task of preparing late additions is basically the same as that of preparing the bill itself.

Deciding which amendments proposed by others to accept 'Bill teams and those they work with closely (civil servants, associated with the bill team in an advisory capacity, policy leads and the lawyers) advise on whether governments should accept proposed amendments …'.[131] They also advised on government amendments arising from the government changing its mind, 'or even themselves suggest amendments after coming to realise their original proposals are defective'.[132]

As will be seen (2.6.2 below), amendments are statistically unlikely to succeed unless they are adopted by the Government. Civil servants interviewed by Professor Page suggested that in securing ministerial agreement to amendments, 'the advisory role of the members of the bill team is crucial'.[133] ('One described the advisory role simply: once the amendments come in you have to give advice saying "rotten idea" or "there's something in this"'.) Interest groups lobbying for changes sent their briefing material to the bill team as well as to ministers and the opposition. If the amendments were minor and technical, the bill team could take the decision without ministerial clearance. Occasionally, because of pressure of time, a more significant amendment was accepted by the bill team without ministerial approval.

Responding to government changes of heart

> When ministers themselves accept a political need to change legislation, whether as a result of pressure from government backbenchers, from prominent interest groups, opposition MPs, or

[129] For a similar picture based on interviews with those involved in 12 Bills enacted between 2005 and 2012 see M Russell and D Gover, *Legislation at Westminster* (Oxford, 2017) 63–65.

[130] EC Page, 'The civil servant as legislator: law making in British Administration' 81 *Public Administration*, 2003, 651, 665.

[131] Ibid, 667.

[132] Ibid.

[133] Ibid, 668.

> members of the House of Lords or public opinion, or some combination of them, the advisory role of bill team members changes from one of examining the merits and demerits of amendments to one of exploring how to incorporate the changes in the bill, and how these changes impact on other parts of the proposed legislation.[134]

The bill team's work often continues even after Royal Assent – in drafting implementing regulations in statutory instruments and circulars, codes or other forms of guidance.

Professor Page said that one striking feature of the work of bill teams is the importance of relatively junior civil servants from middle-ranking grades, operating with significant autonomy producing key legislation. While it was usual for a member of the Senior Civil Service (SCS) to head a bill team, this person was from the lowest grade in the SCS, Grade 5.[135] Grade 7s took a leading role in developing major portions of the legislation, as did officials one or two grades below that. Moreover, ministerial control over the process was not guaranteed:

> Ministers typically know little about the law they are bringing in until they receive the submissions and briefings that their officials give them. Perhaps the biggest danger for democracy is not a civil service putting forward proposals which a minister feels forced to accept, but rather that ministers do not notice or fully appreciate what is being proposed in their name although they have the political authority to change it and a civil service which bends over to accommodate them and keep them informed and briefed.[136]

2.4. Interaction between Interested Parties during the Legislative Process

Once a bill has been published, it potentially becomes the focus of lobbying or other forms of bringing pressure or persuasion to bear by all those concerned to get it changed. Lobbying is directed at the minister(s) in charge of the bill, and often also at the lead civil servants on the bill team. Parliamentary Counsel, responsible for drafting the bill, are shielded from this process though they are very much involved in coping with the results of such lobbying in dealing with and drafting government amendments. A rare description of the interaction between ministers, civil servants, MPs and outside interests in the legislative process emerged from an account of the background to the Criminal Justice Act 1972 in a BBC documentary broadcast on 16 September 1972. The presenter was Professor Anthony King of Essex University, who discussed what happened with the then Conservative Minister of State at the Home Office, Mr Mark Carlisle (later Lord Carlisle), with his opposite number in the Labour Opposition, Sir Elwyn Jones (later Lord Elwyn-Jones, Lord Chancellor), with one of the senior civil servants involved, Mr Michael Moriarty of the Home Office, and with a then backbench MP, Mr Edmund Dell. (By sheer coincidence the Act in question was also the subject of the extract in 1.1.1 above from Mr Moriarty's paper. There is

[134] Ibid.

[135] The Senior Civil Service (SCS) runs from Grade 5 to Grade 1 at the top. Outside the SCS, the grades, in descending order, are: Grade 6, Grade 7, Senior Executive Officer (SEO) and Higher Executive Officer (HEO).

[136] Page (n 130 above) 673.

frequent reference to standing committees. Rather than change these references to Public Bill Committees, as they are now known, they have been left.)[137]

MORIARTY: I'm in charge of the small division which has general responsibility for legislation on the powers of the courts and is also the division that looks after the Advisory Council on the Penal System. So it fell to me and to my staff to report to ministers about the two reports of the Advisory Council on reparation and alternatives to imprisonment, and suggest what might be done about them. And this involved, in fact, putting a memorandum together, collecting the views of various other parts of the Office and, indeed, of other governmental departments that were concerned.

KING: It's not generally realised that civil servants brief their ministers not just behind the scenes but while actual debates are going on on the floor or in committee. Michael Moriarty was present during the second reading debate and I asked him, since he's not allowed to sit next to ministers on the front bench, how he went about communicating with them.

MORIARTY: On the whole by rapidly scribbled notes, some of them things that we ourselves realise the minister is going to need from what we hear someone else saying or what we hear him saying, sometimes things that he asks us to produce. The channel of communication is the parliamentary private secretary. These are, on the whole, fairly young MPs, perhaps with a ministerial career before them, who – as it were – learn the trade, and I think you get to know a great deal about what the functions of government ministers are about by understudying in that sort of way.

KING: You do actually sit there, in effect, in the chamber itself? Not technically but in fact?

MORIARTY: That's right, yes. On the right of the Speaker and behind him under the Gallery there is a box, and officials sit there and listen with their papers, scribble their notes, and there's a certain amount of scope for interchange.

KING: Once a Bill's been read a second time – approved in principle that is – it's sent to a committee where amendments can be moved and the various clauses considered in much more detail. In the case of very important pieces of legislation, like the European Communities Bill, the committee may actually consist of the whole House of Commons operating under a somewhat different procedure. But most Bills, including the Criminal Justice Bill, are sent upstairs, as they say, to one of the standing committees. These committees have about two dozen members each and are, in effect, miniature Houses of Commons. The majority party in the whole House also has a majority on the committee and, as in the whole House, there are ministers and Opposition front-bench spokesmen. Standing committees are not specialised: they consider whatever Bills are sent to them and not just ones on particular topics. But, of course, if an MP is interested in a particular Bill, he can usually see to it that he is included on the appropriate standing committee – or at least he can try.

Everyone agrees that the atmosphere of a standing committee is quite different from that on the floor of the House.

CARLISLE: It's usually considerably more intimate. It's more, I think one can say, constructive. It depends a lot on the Bill. For example, on this Bill the atmosphere throughout was that people were wanting to get down and do a careful revision of the details of the Bill in a constructive manner.

KING: Michael Moriarty describes the contrast in more detail.

MORIARTY: It's a good deal easier and less formal. A committee room is I suppose not much larger than a large school classroom. The MPs, of whom in our case there were about twenty in all, sit at desks facing one another, so to that extent it's a sort of mini-chamber. In place of the

[137] The transcript is taken from A King and A Sloman (eds), *Westminster and Beyond* (Macmillan, 1973) ch 12.

Speaker we have a Chairman of the committee, that is an MP, who is on a low dais. On his left he has the House officials and the Hansard people. On the right of the Chairman there is Parliamentary Counsel and then the officials like myself who are there to give advice to the minister on the contents of the Bill.

KING: Let's suppose an MP raises a point and the minister isn't quite sure how he's going to reply: will he in standing committee, actually there and then, turn to you and mutter something to you in order to get some help?

MORIARTY: Yes, because of the geography, which it's slightly difficult to describe. We are, in fact, only a few feet away from the minister, so it's perfectly easy for a minister just to get up from his seat and take a couple of paces so that he can talk quietly to us, or he can even stage whisper from where he's sitting, or he can ask his parliamentary private secretary, sitting just behind him, to turn round and have a word with us. It is all a good deal easier; there's no need for anyone to move to and fro. And, indeed, one occasionally gets a situation where someone from the Opposition or a Government backbencher asks the minister a question and then does a bit of ad-libbing while it's perfectly clear that the minister is getting the answer.

KING: One major advantage a minister has in piloting a Bill through the House of Commons is sheer numbers: despite occasional near-embarrassments, he can normally count on having enough votes to get his Bill carried. But he also has another major advantage: the detailed information and advice supplied by civil servants. Part of the job of civil servants working on a bill is to take all the amendments – on jury service, suspended sentences, and so on and brief the minister on them, as Michael Moriarty explained:

MORIARTY: This is the main task of officials during the committee stage. Each morning the Order Paper is brought down from the Parliamentary Section as early as they can, and one then drops everything else and sets to work looking at the amendments, trying to work out exactly what an MP is getting at – sometimes, of course, it's quite a job – and this may be because he is approaching something in a confused way or because he's just a lot cleverer than we are on a particular matter. And then one goes through the processes of deciding how far the objective is compatible with the objectives of the Government in the Bill, and how far it's a sensible way of achieving it.

KING: How far is it part of the job of a civil servant to warn a minister of unforeseen consequences of an amendment which he might perhaps be about to accept?

MORIARTY: Oh, I think that is really part of the bread-and-butter of briefing on amendments. Of course, this question, I think, raises in turn the question where the initiative lies, and I suppose this is different on different occasions. In our case, the initiative I think lay with us in the first instance. We would usually tender some briefing and advice on an amendment and, if necessary, Mr Carlisle would discuss these with us, tell us if he saw it differently, and so on. But on the whole he let us get on with working out a brief before telling us what his own thoughts were. But one can certainly see if it worked the other way round: that, if it began with the Minister saying what he thought, it would certainly be the task of the civil servant to say: 'Well, but have you considered A, B, and C?'

KING: Backbenchers and Opposition MPs, however, lack that sort of professional assistance. Where do they get help from? How did Edmund Dell inform himself for purposes of taking part in the Committee proceedings?

DELL: Well, here, of course, I have the great good fortune of having a wife who is very deeply acquainted with this whole area and who was therefore able to draw my attention to all the necessary material on every point on which I wanted to speak. So she was of enormous assistance.

KING: So it was then a question of simply going to the library and reading the stuff up?

DELL: It was a matter of going to the library, reading the stuff up, preparing the speech, and putting the available information before the minister and the Committee and saying: 'This is information which has obviously not been considered in preparing this Bill.'

KING: And in addition to what an MP can do on his own, there are also organisations willing to help him, as well as to press their views on him. I asked Sir Elwyn Jones where he and his colleagues got their information from.

JONES: Well, you will remember that there were the reports of committees, which were the foundation of the clauses in the Bill, which we were able to call upon. But then in the background there are a large number of bodies, fortunately, in this country – this is one of our strengths as a democracy – like Justice, the British Section of the International Commission of Jurists, like the National Council for Civil Liberties [now called Liberty(ed)], like the Howard League. There are half a dozen bodies at least who have worked on this sort of problem and whose reports and recommendations are available to us.

2.5. The Time Taken by Parliamentary Debates

The late Professor John Griffith of the London School of Economics studied the time taken by debates on government bills in the Commons in three sessions of Parliament: 1967–68, 1968–69 and 1970–71. In the first session there were sixty bills which took an average of 23 hours each; in the second, fifty bills averaged 20 hours' debate; in the third, 73 bills averaged sixteen hours. The overall average was 19 hours 54 minutes.[138]

Out of the total of 183 bills, no fewer than 74 (40 per cent) were dealt with in less than five hours. At the other end of the spectrum, in each of the three sessions there were seven bills that absorbed over half of the total amount of time. These 21 bills averaged 96 hours of debating time.[139]

The left-hand column of Table 2.1 shows the average distribution of time in the House of Commons for the three sessions studied by Professor Griffith.[140] The right-hand column shows the same for the 2012–13 session.[141] The basic picture is much the same.

Table 2.1 Time spent on parliamentary debate of government bills

	1967–1971	**2012/13**
2nd reading	15%	19%
Committee stage	65%	63%
Report stage	15%	12%
3rd reading	2%	2%
Lords' amendments in Commons	3%	4%
Total	100%	100%

[138] JAG Griffith, *Parliamentary Scrutiny of Government Bills* (Allen and Unwin, 1974) 15–16.

[139] Ibid.

[140] Griffith, *Parliamentary Scrutiny* (n 138 above), derived from Table 1.2, p 17 in *Griffith and Ryle on Parliament*, n 12 above) the authors calculated in respect of debates in the Lords in the sessions 1984–85 and 1985–86, that around a fifth of legislative time was taken with the Second Reading, nearly a half on the Committee Stage, 22 per cent on Report, 7 per cent on Third Reading and a further 3 per cent on proceedings after Third Reading (p 721). The proportions are different from those in Griffith's earlier study but the broad picture is much the same.

[141] Calculated from House of Commons, Sessional Diary 2012–13, 9 May to 25 April 2013, p iii: www.parliament.uk/business/publications/commons/sessional-diary.

In a later study by Griffith and Ryle it was found that there were three main categories of bills.[142] The first was the category of major policy bills of which there might be about ten per session. They were debated on Second Reading on the floor of the House of Commons on one day for six hours, or sometimes over two days for twelve hours. A few were then taken in committee of the full House, but most were sent to Standing Committee where they were debated for fifty or more hours. Most were then further debated on Report, Third Reading and consideration of Lords' amendments.

The second group consisted of fifteen to twenty or so policy bills which took up somewhat less time – say thirty or more hours in committee.

The third group consisted of a further fifteen to twenty or so bills which, for one reason or another, went through very quickly. Some were consolidation bills (see 2.1.8 above). Some small uncontentious bills were debated in Second Reading Committees off the floor of the House under Standing Order No 90 (see 2.2.3 above). The debates averaged some thirty minutes, a few going through virtually 'on the nod'. Most of these bills were introduced in the Lords. Some of the bills in the group were Consolidated Fund and Appropriation bills the function of which is to 'raise supply' (ie, money). Under Standing Order No 54 these are not debated at all.

Thus in the six sessions 1995–96 to 2000–01 there were a total of 231 government bills. Of these, 16 per cent were not debated on the floor of the House of Commons at all; 8 per cent were debated for under an hour; 19 per cent were debated for between one and five hours; 29 per cent were debated for between five and thirteen hours, 10 per cent for between thirteen and twenty hours, and 18 per cent for more than twenty hours.[143]

2.6. The Impact on Bills of the Parliamentary Process

2.6.1. How Often does the Opposition Oppose a Bill?

It is important to appreciate that to a considerable, and perhaps surprising, degree, much legislation is uncontroversial. A study of the years 1970–74, when Mr Edward Heath was Prime Minister, showed that in a high proportion of cases at the Second Reading the Opposition did not oppose the Government's bills.[144] There was bi-partisan support for half the bills (ninety out of 135 or 49 per cent). In another 35 (19 per cent) the Opposition were neutral or critical without however calling any division. In a further 22 (12 per cent) there was either no debate on the floor of the House, or the Second Reading was not reached. In only 38 cases out of 185 (20 per cent) was there a division (ie a vote) on the Second Reading.[145]

The fact that a bill is uncontroversial does not mean that it is unproblematic. Sometimes agreement on the merits of a bill means that it does not get the careful scrutiny that it deserves. A cautionary example given in a study by the Constitution Unit was the Child

[142] JAG Griffith and M Ryle, *Parliament* (Sweet & Maxwell, 1989) 310–13 and 2nd edn (*Griffith and Ryle on Parliament* (n 12 above) paras 8-007–008.

[143] *Griffith and Ryle on Parliament* (n 12 above) para 8-012. (For the broadly similar figures for the 107 government bills in the two sessions 1984–85 and 1985–86 see their 1st edn, Griffith and Ryle, *Parliament* (n 142 above) 313.).

[144] I Burton and G Drewry, *Legislation and Public Policy* (Macmillan, 1981).

[145] Ibid, Table 4.15, p 123.

Support Act 1995: 'Although driven by well-meaning parliamentarians, the cross-party consensus hid some of the bill's flaws. The detail of the legislation was not adequately scrutinised during its passage and it proved to be unworkable when implemented.'[146]

2.6.2. Who Moves and What Happens to Amendments?

If impact is measured by what happens to amendments moved to government bills, John Griffith's 1974 study (see 2.5 above) seems to support the view that parliamentary debates have little impact on bills.

It is true that amendments are not always moved in the hope (let alone the expectation) that they will be adopted. Frequently the Member who speaks to an amendment will say that its purpose is simply 'probing' – to get an explanation from the minister which, when given, enables the mover of the amendment to withdraw it. Often too an amendment is moved simply for the record to indicate a point of disagreement. When the minister has explained the Government's thinking on the matter, the amendment is withdrawn not because the mover of the amendment has been persuaded but because the matter is not sufficiently important to justify pressing the issue to a vote. (In the Lords this is very common.) Sometimes an amendment is withdrawn with a warning that the point will be taken up again at a later stage. An amendment will of course also be withdrawn if the minister gives an assurance that the Government accepts the point and will return at a later stage with its own redrafted version. It will also be withdrawn if the minister indicates that the government is still studying the matter and that it will at a later stage state its position on the issue. In the study by Meg Russell and Daniel Gover of 12 Bills between 2005 and 2012 there were a total of 1,200 amendments considered in the Commons Committee but only 81 divisions.[147]

Sometimes the Minister will say that they will write to the Member, perhaps adding that the letter will be placed in the Library. Normally such a letter would be copied to all members of the Committee and nowadays will be accessible online.[148]

Griffith's 1974 study showed the success rate of amendments by reference to their source. In the Committee stage in the Commons, the great majority (70 per cent) were moved by Opposition Members, one-fifth of amendments (20 per cent) were moved by ministers and 10 per cent by government backbenchers.[149] The number of amendments agreed to in the three categories is shown in Table 2.2.

Table 2.2 The success rate of amendments in Committee

Ministers	906 out of 907 (100%)
Government backbenchers	40 out of 436 (9%)
Opposition Members	131 out of 3,074 (4%)
Total	1,077 out of 4,417 (24%)

(*Source:* JAG Griffith, *Parliamentary Scrutiny of Government Bills* (Allen and Unwin, 1974) Table 3.8, p 93)

[146] G Power, *Parliamentary Scrutiny of Draft Legislation 1997–99*, Constitution Unit, UCL (Hansard Society, 2000), 16 ('G Power').

[147] M Russell and D Gover, *Legislation at Westminster* (Oxford, 2017) 35. Seven of the Bills were from the period of the Labour government 2005–10, five were from the first two-year session of the Coalition government, 2010–12.

[148] Ministerial 'I will write' letters are added to the list of relevant documents relating to the bill `on the parliamentary website. They are also added to the Deposited Papers website.

[149] Griffith, *Parliamentary Scrutiny* (n 138 above) Table 3.6, p 87.

Over three-quarters (77 per cent) of the forty amendments moved by government backbenchers and agreed to, and almost all (90 per cent) of the 131 moved by Opposition Members and agreed to, were agreed without a division. Most were classifiable as drafting, clarificatory or of very minor significance.[150]

On Report Stage, 56 per cent of amendments were moved by ministers, 6 per cent by government backbenchers and 39 per cent by Opposition Members.[151] The number agreed to in each category is shown in Table 2.3.

Table 2.3 The success rate of amendment on Report

Ministers	864 out of 865 (100%)
Government backbenchers	10 out of 89 (11%)
Opposition Members	29 out of 599 (5%)
Total	903 out of 1,553 (58%)

(*Source:* JAG Griffith, *Parliamentary Scrutiny of Government Bills* (Allen and Unwin, 1974) Table 4.3, p 159)

Nine of the ten amendments moved successfully by government backbenchers, and 28 of the 29 moved successfully by Opposition Members, were agreed to without a division.[152]

In the entire three parliamentary sessions there were only 26 substantive matters on which the Government was defeated in Committee. On Report the Government accepted the defeat in nine of these 26 cases. In the other cases the defeat was reversed.[153]

In other words, almost all of the amendments that were moved successfully in the House of Commons were moved by ministers – 94 per cent of those moved successfully in Committee and 96 per cent of those moved successfully on Report. According to Griffith, they were not commonly the result of arguments advanced by Members. 'Usually they reflect later developments in the thinking of civil servants in the department, often reflecting pressures from interest groups'.[154] Of the amendments moved by government backbench and Opposition Members that were agreed to, 'only a very few can be said to be of any real substance'.[155] However, there were a larger number of occasions when government amendments were the result of something said by Members. Griffith concluded:[156]

> Though the direct impact of the House on Government proposals for legislation was unimpressive, the indirect impact shown by the positive response of Government to points made in committee was certainly deeper. On my estimate there were 365 occasions during these three sessions when Government amendments moved on Report were traceable to Committee points made by Government backbenchers and Opposition Members. And of these, I have classed one-third (125 in all) as important in varying degrees. This is not an inconsiderable number.
>
> More significant than the counting of amendments is their weight and their effect on bills. Eleven bills, all of importance, were markedly affected by their passage through the House of Commons. In 1967–8 the Medicines Bill, the Race Relations Bill, and the Gaming Bill were changed in several important particulars; the Town and Country Planning Bill was reshaped and improved; and the Civil Aviation Bill emerged as a better and more coherent measure. In 1968–9 the Finance Bill

[150] Ibid, 93–119.
[151] Ibid, 146.
[152] Ibid.
[153] Ibid, 182–84.
[154] Ibid, 197.
[155] Ibid, 202.
[156] Ibid, 206–07.

> was considerably amended in one important group of provisions, as were the Housing Bill and the Children and Young Persons Bill. In 1970–71, the widest range of amendments was to the Highways Bill while important limited amendments were made to the Finance Bill and to the Immigration Bill.
>
> Against these cases achievements, must be set the long debates, the hundreds of aborted attempts at amendment, the scores of bills, including some of the greatest importance, which remained effectively unchanged despite the efforts of Opposition Members and, to a lesser extent, of Government backbenchers. But even when Members totally fail to persuade the Government to amend its proposals, other purposes of debate may be fulfilled.
>
> When we add the achievements of non-ministerial Members in committee to those on Report we are left with some sense of great effort making for little result and yet with a sense also that some slipshod thinking by ministers, civil servants and draftsmen has been removed or clarified and that some bills look much better on Third Reading than they did on Second, and that a few famous victories have been won. Whether this great effort is justified by those improvements is another matter; as is the question of the ways in which the effort might be made more effective.

Griffith's research was repeated some forty years later by Louise Thompson of Hull University.[157] Whilst Griffith considered every government bill from three parliamentary sessions (a total of 111 bills), Thompson's sample consisted of the bills explicitly listed in the Queen's Speech for the period 2000–10 (a total of 139 bills). There were various differences in the two samples:

- Griffith found that committees spent an average of 18 hours per bill, Thompson found that the average had risen to 24 hours. (para 3.1)
- Griffith found an average of 1,402 non-government amendments in committee per session, an average of 42 per bill; Thompson found 1,747 per session, an average of 128 per bill. (para 3.2)
- In Griffith there were on average 4 government backbench amendments per bill and an average of 26 opposition amendments per bill; in Thompson these two figures doubled to 9 for government backbench amendments but quadrupled to 114 for Opposition amendments. (Table 2)
- In Griffith the Government itself made an average of 8 amendments to their bills in committee. In Thompson the number had risen to 53. Twenty-first century Government was therefore making over six times as many amendments to their own bills as forty years before. (para 3.2)
- By contrast, the Government accepted far fewer opposition amendments in Thompson (an average of 6 per session) than in Griffith (an average of 44 per session). (Table 3)
- In both studies the overwhelming majority of accepted non-government amendments covered simple matters such as correction of drafting or spelling mistakes, or clarification of terms used. Occasionally though non-governments amendments were significant.[158]

An overwhelming number of the MPs interviewed by Thompson highlighted bill committees as just one stage in a very long process if one wished to make an amendment to a

[157] L Thompson, 'More of the same or a period of change? The impact of Bill Committees in the twenty-first century House of Commons' 66 *Parliamentary Affairs*, 2013, 459.

[158] Thompson instanced the Hunting Bill Committee of the 2002–03 session. One-third of all the significant amendments made to a bill in committee between 2000 and 2010 were made during that one committee on a series of unwhipped free votes.

government bill. They cited discussions with ministers outside committee, particularly in the period between the Committee stage and the Report stage, as being important in increasing the pressure or momentum for change. MPs pushed fewer amendments to a division in the whole of the 2000–10 period than during the three sessions analysed by Griffith. The number of government backbenchers pushing their amendments to a division had fallen by two-thirds.

Thompson said that committee members therefore appeared to be adjusting their behaviour in committee as a means of achieving changes to government bills at a *later* stage, outside the committee itself. Examination of the Report stage of those bills demonstrated just how productive this apparent change of strategy had been. In total, government ministers explicitly referred to 1,431 amendments made to legislation at the Report stage as being prompted by discussions in bill committee, an average of over ten amendments for every government bill. By comparison, Griffith noted just 365 government amendments being moved at the Report stage in response to undertakings given in committee in the 1967–71 period; an average of just three per government bill.

Thus it seems that the Committee stage is increasingly becoming just one stage for MPs looking to make changes to government legislation rather than being the primary vehicle for change. Increasingly, the arena for making an impact on legislature was becoming the period after the Committee stage.

Thompson concluded:

> Comparing the work of twenty-first century bill committees with the last comprehensive examination of committee work highlights the key areas of change in modern bill committees. Bill committees appear to be working much harder than before: spending a greater amount of time engaging in the scrutiny of government bills and processing a much higher number of both government and non-government amendments. Yet this extra work seems to be resulting in less material gain in committee itself. Amendments tabled in committee by opposition members and by government backbenchers are much less likely to be successful and the frequency of ministerial assurances and undertakings to reflect upon or redraft opposition amendments has similarly fallen. MPs themselves place the blame for this firmly on the shoulders of government ministers, highlighting the culture of resistance towards the amendment of legislation and of increasingly complex and hastily drafted bills … A much greater number of amendments are introduced by the government at the report stage in response to bill committees. Whilst one could still agree with Griffith that 'the impact of Parliament on government bills is by no means negligible' (p. 256), it is perhaps more negligible in bill committees today than in previous years. Bill committees remain an enduring feature of legislative scrutiny, but are increasingly just one step along the road to achieving changes to government bills.[159]

In the House of Lords the success rate of amendments moved by government backbenchers and Opposition Members in Griffith's 1974 study was somewhat higher than in the Commons. (Their combined success rate in Committee in the Commons was 6 per cent, compared with 12 per cent in the House of Lords. The success rate on Report was 5 per cent in the Commons, compared with 19 per cent in the Lords.) Griffith said:

> When all allowance has been made for the dangers of using such statistics, the difference is not only considerable but also confirms the impression given by reading the debates in the Lords: that Ministers in the Lords are more willing to accept amendments than they are in the Commons. Partly this may be because the details of a House of Commons Bill are much more settled and

[159] Thompson, 'More of the same' (n 157 above) 477.

> firm by the time it arrives in committee in the Lords so that the effect of amendments can be more clearly seen. But partly it may be because the less contentious, less partisan, atmosphere in the Lords makes amendments moved by those who are not Ministers more likely to be accepted …
>
> A case can always be made out for a second, third or fourth look at any proposal, whether legislative or other. And it is no part of my present task to argue the case for unicameral or bicameral legislatures. What is clear is that, with pressures as they are and with the House of Commons and Government Departments functioning as they do, legislation sometimes leaves the Commons in a state unfit to be let loose on the public. Some kind of reviewing is necessary. And the House of Lords is presently the best reviewing body we have.[160]

As has already been noted, the scale of government amendments to bills in the Lords is huge. Griffith and Ryle give figures for the number of such amendments in the five sessions 1997–98 to 2001–02: 2,983, 2,685, 4,740, 440, 649.[161]

Even when the House of Lords does play a revising role it rarely controls the actual text of what goes into the legislation because the text of the crucial amendments is normally drafted by Parliamentary Counsel at the instance of the government.[162]

In 2008, the Hansard Society published a report of a study entitled 'Rubber stamp or cockpit? The impact of Parliament on government legislation'.[163] The study looked at how five, then recent, pieces of legislation[164] came to take the form they did and who or what influenced their final outcome, tracking the consultation stages, pre-legislative scrutiny (if undertaken) and the parliamentary stages. The research drew on interviews with ministers, MPs, peers, government and parliamentary officials, party political staff, journalists and pressure groups.[165]

The study confirmed that most changes to legislation are made in the Lords, usually at report stage. But the case studies showed that arguments raised and assurances given in the Commons were frequently the determining factor in allowing the Lords to extract concessions. As one peer said, 'the Commons outlines the problems, gets the main political issues aired and the Lords then applies the resolution'.[166] One of the five Acts, the Legislative and Regulatory Reform Act, was substantially amended in the Commons. The Government had concluded that there was a real possibility that it would be defeated at Commons report stage and was certain to have the Bill re-written in the Lords, so a pre-emptive move was necessary. One MP said that the Act demonstrated that 'where there is a danger to democracy, people will come together to effect change – and change can be made'.[167]

Surprisingly, only a few of the changes made in the Lords were made in response to government defeats though sometimes it happened in order to avoid anticipated defeat.

The conclusion was that although the Government is the dominant force, the study challenged the view that Parliament was a near-impotent force.

[160] Griffith, *Parliamentary Scrutiny* (n 138 above) 231.

[161] *Griffith and Ryle on Parliament* (n 12 above) 714.

[162] T Millett, 'The House of Lords as a re-writing chamber' 9 *Statute Law Review*, 1988, 70, 74.

[163] S Kalitowski, 'Rubber stamp or cockpit? The impact of Parliament on government legislation' 61 *Parliamentary Affairs*, 2008, 694.

[164] Export Control Act 2002; Equality Act 2006; Immigration, Asylum and Nationality Act 2006; Legislative and Regulatory Reform Act 2006; and Welfare Reform Act 2007.

[165] For the full report of the study see A Brazier, S Kalitowski, G Rosenblatt with K Korris, *Law in the Making: Influence and Change in the Legislative Process* (Hansard Society, 2008).

[166] Kalitowski, 'Rubber stamp or cockpit?' (n 163 above) 706.

[167] Ibid.

> In fact, Parliament, as a whole and through its constituent parts, makes a difference to legislation, sometimes in major ways and more frequently through many minor but significant changes.[168]

A vivid illustration of this observation was the European Union (Withdrawal) Act 2018, described by Professors Mark Elliott and Stephen Tierney:

> Second reading in the Upper House took place on 30–31 January before a protracted committee stage that concluded just before Easter recess, followed by detailed consideration at a report stage that lasted until early May. It was in these lengthy committee and report stages[169] that the most significant amendments were laid. The Lords made 15 amendments to the Bill. While most of these were eventually reversed in the Commons, the Government made some 170 of its own amendments in both houses, making explicit concession on eight of the Lords amendments, but also taking account of numerous parliamentary objections raised throughout the passage of the Bill.[170]

Further important evidence of the substantive role played in legislation by the parliamentary process came in the study of 12 Bills enacted between 2005 and 2012 by Professor Meg Russell and Daniel Gover. Part of the role was by way of amendments. There were a total of 4,361 amendments moved in both Houses. The authors categorised a quarter (25 per cent) as 'technical'; just over a tenth (12 per cent) as 'clarificatory'; and nearly two-thirds (63 per cent) as 'substantive'. Of the amendments moved by government, just over half (55 per cent) were technical, 15 per cent were clarificatory; one-third (32 per cent) were substantive.[171] The great majority of the 2,736 substantive amendments (90 per cent) moved were non-government.[172]

The authors found that some substantive government amendments that were made represented 'a change of heart', that a few were the result of external events, but that well over half (60 per cent) of the substantive government amendments that were made 'responded to pressure from parliament'.[173] In total, 112 distinct changes to the Bills in the study 'were initiated by opposition amendments accounting for over 80 per cent of non-government initiated changes – an apparently similar pattern to that found by Griffith (1974). These concerned both large and small matters.'[174]

But the influence on legislation that can be exerted by parliamentarians is not confined to what occurs during the formal parliamentary proceedings which are on-the-record and therefore visible. The detailed study of 12 Bills by Russell and Gover is a rich source of material on this topic. The book has separate chapters on the role in legislation, visible and invisible, of the Opposition, of government backbenchers, of parliamentarians,

[168] Ibid, 707.

[169] The Committee stage in the Lords lasted 90 hours spread over eleven days; the Report stage in the Lords lasted 42 hours spread over six days.

[170] M Elliott and S Tierney, 'Political Pragmatism and Constitutional Principle: The European Union (Withdrawal) Act 2018', *Public Law* (2019) (1) 37–60, 39.

[171] The Cabinet Office's *Guide to Making Legislation*, 2025, has a whole section (22) on amendments. It begins: 'Every amendment the Government makes to a bill delays its progress. Government amendments to bills after introduction must therefore be kept to a minimum and will only be agreed by the PBL Committee if they are considered essential to ensure that the bill works.'

[172] M Russell and D Gover, *Legislation at Westminster* (Oxford, 2019) Table 3.5, 7; M Russell and D Gover, 'Does the Executive Dominate the Westminster Legislative Process?: Six Reasons to Doubt', 69 *Parliamentary Affairs*,2016, (2) 286–308; M Russell, D Gover, K Wollter and M Benton, 'Actors, Motivations and Outcomes in the Legislative Process: Policy Influence at Westminster', 52 *Government and Opposition* 2017 (1) 1–27.

[173] Russell and Gover, ibid (2019) 77.

[174] Ibid, (2019) 115.

mainly in the Lords, who are independent of any party, of outside pressure groups, and of select committees. In their concluding chapter the authors identified six faces of parliamentary power, only the first of which is visible: (1) Changes made through amendments; (2) Anticipated Reactions or generating fear – often influencing what is put into a Bill; (3) Government Internalising what Parliament will accept; (4) Issue Politicisation and agenda setting – for instance by creating a row that gets media attention; (5) Accountability and Exposure – the mere fact that ministers have to explain and justify their decisions; and (6) Counteractive Pressure and support for the government – in particular from its own MPs and Members in the Lords.[175] They suggest that although the formulation of legislation is indeed overwhelmingly a government-centred activity, 'parliament's influence on government legislation is extensive, and is exercised in various different ways throughout the policy process'.[176] The ideas for policies were frequently put forward by parliamentarians (often working in conjunction with pressure groups). Debates, private members' Bills, Early Day Motions[177] played an important part in setting the policy agenda. So did select committees. Parliamentarians tested the policy arguments. Ministers were careful to consult their own backbenchers. The draftsmen were conscious of what would not get through. If all this failed a Bill would often be amended – usually in a consensual way, via government amendments.

The popular perception was that the lack of visible conflict between Parliament and government indicated parliamentary acquiescence in the face of a dominant executive. But, the authors say, this was to misunderstand the fundamental dynamics in a parliamentary system of government. In such a system the executive depended on parliament for its survival. Parliament was the principal; the executive was its agent. Most decisions were taken by the agent but delegation did not mean that the principal gave up control. 'Parliament is ultimately the decision-maker, whose day-to-day role is to oversee those implementing policy decisions on its behalf.'[178] Much about legislative influence was subtle and immeasurable. Government tended not to admit what influences affected its decision-making. But the role of Parliament was considerable and greater than was often recognised.

See to similar effect Thomas Fleming and Lisa James, 'Parliamentary Influence and Brexit Legislation', 77 *Parliamentary Affairs*, 2023(1), 25–45. The authors examined the parliamentary progress of thirteen Brexit-related government bills introduced to Parliament between the 2017 and 2019 general elections – eleven during Theresa May's period as prime minister and two under Boris Johnson. Only six of the thirteen bills passed into law. Across the thirteen bills, the authors identified and examined what happened in respect of 3,252 amendments. They concluded that parliament exercised considerable influence, not by the passage of non-government amendments but by exerting influence causing the government to make amendments.

[175] Ibid.

[176] Ibid, 282.

[177] 'Early Day Motions (EDMs) are motions tabled by Members, formally for a debate "on an early day", that is, on an unspecified future day. Although rarely debated in practice … EDMs are a mechanism which enable Members to express an opinion on or bring attention to a particular matter and which provide other Members with an opportunity to indicate their support for the sentiments expressed in the motion by adding their name to it, thus demonstrating the extent of parliamentary support for a particular cause or point of view.' (E May, *Parliamentary Practice*, 25th edn (LexisNexis, 2019) 20.17.).

[178] M Russell and D Gover, *Legislation at Westminster* (Oxford, 2019) 283.

An unusual feature of the bills studied was the high number that did not reach the statute book. Partly this was due to government not proceeding with bills that it may have thought would be amended in unacceptable ways. Partly it was due to parliament's success in delaying Brexit.

> Overall, therefore, our findings suggest that parliament played a powerful but nuanced role in the consideration of Brexit legislation. However, any additional parliamentary influence – relative to earlier periods – was largely preventative, rather than constructive, with parliament deterring government legislation rather than getting to actively reshape it.

See also on this topic two chapters in the 3rd edition of *Parliament and the Constitution* (Hart, 2022): Alexander Horne and Jack Simson Chard, 'Parliament and Brexit: scrutiny under pressure' and Louise Thompson, 'Parliament and legislative scrutiny: lessons from Brexit and Covid-19'.

2.7. The Composition and Size of the House of Lords

The 1997 Labour Manifesto promised major reform of the composition of the House of Lords. Phase 1 of that reform addressed the question of the hereditary peers, of whom at that time there were more than seven hundred. Of those who attended the House of Lords, insofar as they belonged to any political party the overwhelming majority were Conservative. (In 1999, 350 Conservative, 19 Labour, 23 Liberal.) The House of Lords Act 1999 did not abolish hereditary peerages but it excluded the great majority from taking part in the proceedings of the House of Lords. Under a compromise settlement, the Act provided for elections by the hereditary peers of 92 of their number. However, Labour's 2024 election manifesto promised legislation to remove the 92 hereditary peers from the House of Lords. The House of Lords (Hereditary Peers) Bill to accomplish that policy was introduced on 5 September 2024. The Bill provided that exclusion of all hereditary peers would take effect at the end of *that* parliamentary session. ('Any writ of summons issued for the present Parliament in right of a hereditary peerage is of no effect after that Session.')

The election manifesto also said that *all* peers would be required to retire at the end of the parliamentary session in which they reached the age of eighty, but this policy was not included in the bill to remove the hereditaries.

Since 1999 there have been various other attempts at reform of the composition of the Upper House, but none have yet come to fruition:

- The Blair Labour Government's White Paper (*Modernising Parliament: Reforming the House of Lords*, 1999, Cm 4183) announced the setting up of a Royal Commission.
- The Report of the Royal Commission (*A House for the Future*, 2000, Cm 4534) recommended that the Lords should consist of some 550 members, a minority of whom would be elected using proportional representation. The majority of members would be appointed by a new appointments commission, which would manage party allocation based on recent general election results. The appointments commission would also ensure a balance in terms of gender, ethnicity, age and region. 20 per cent would be non-political appointees. The Labour Government said it supported the recommendations.

- April 2000, an Independent Appointments Commission was established to take over the nomination of non-party members of the House, reducing the Prime Minister's powers of patronage.
- November 2001, the Blair Government published a White Paper (*House of Lords: Completing the Reform*, Cm 5291) stating that it would implement the Royal Commission's 'broad framework' with membership consisting of up to 332 nominated by political parties, 120 directly elected, 120 independents appointed by an Appointments Commission, plus 16 bishops and 12 Law Lords. This was debated in both Houses 9–10 January 2002. In the Commons, the majority view was that there should be a higher proportion of elected members. In the Lords, the majority supported an appointed House. Virtually no one supported the Government's proposals. The proposals were dropped.
- February 2002, the Commons Public Administration Committee published *The Second Chamber: Continuing the Reform* (HC 494 of 2001–02) recommending a smaller chamber of 350 members, 60 per cent elected and 40 per cent nominated by an Independent Appointments Commission with equal numbers of independent crossbenchers and members from political parties. Bishops, law lords and existing life peers to be phased out.
- May 2002, the Blair government established a Joint Committee of both Houses to achieve the 'broadest possible parliamentary consensus on the way forward'.
- December 2002, the Joint Committee's report[179] proposed that both Houses should be asked to vote on seven options for selection of members – 0, 20, 40, 50, 60, 80 and 100 per cent elected. In the Commons each option was defeated.[180] The Lords voted overwhelmingly for a 100 per cent appointed House.[181]
- September 2003, the Blair government published a Consultation Paper (*Constitutional Reform: Next Steps for the House of Lords*, CP 14/03) with two main proposals: (1) removal of the hereditary peers; (2) putting the Independent Appointments Commission onto a statutory footing.
- 26 November 2003, the Queen's Speech announced that a Lords Reform Bill would be introduced. (That did not happen.)
- 2005 General Election campaign all three parties included statements in their manifestos on proposals to reform the House of Lords. The Conservatives and the Liberal Democrats respectively promised 'substantially' / 'predominantly' elected chambers.
- 8 February 2007, the Blair Labour Government published a new White Paper (*The House of Lords: Reform*, Cm 7027) proposing a half-elected, half-appointed House and a free vote in both Houses on seven options, as in 2003.
- March 2007, this time the Commons voted by a majority of 113 for an all-elected Upper House. One week later, the Lords voted by a majority of 240 for an all-appointed House. No more happened in the life of the Labour government.
- The Conservative–Liberal-Democrat Coalition Government Agreement (2010) outlined a provision for a wholly or mainly elected second chamber.

[179] HL17/HC171(2002–03).
[180] HC *Hansard*, 4 Feb 2003, cols 221–43.
[181] HL *Hansard*, 4 Feb 2003, col 15.

- May 2011, the Coalition government put forward detailed proposals and a draft House of Lords Reform Bill for a 300-member House with 80 per cent elected, 20 per cent appointed. Members would serve single, non-renewable terms of 15 years.
- 27 June 2012, the House of Lords Reform Bill was introduced by Nick Clegg, Deputy Prime-Minister, but on 6 August 2012, Mr Clegg announced that the Government was abandoning the Bill because of opposition by Conservative backbench MPs.[182]

Chris Ballinger in his book *The House of Lords 1911–2011: A Century of Non-Reform* wrote that following the failure of the Clegg bill 'reform looked as far away as ever it had done in 100 years'.[183]

Reforms that *have* taken place in the past 100 years include:

- Parliament Act 1911 – Replaced the Lords' veto on legislation with a power to delay bills for two years.
- Parliament Act 1949 – Reduced the delaying power from two years to one year.
- Life Peerages Act 1958 – Allowed for life peerages and enabled women to join the Chamber.
- Peerages Act 1963 – Allowed hereditary peers to give up their titles and allowed hereditary peeresses and Scottish peers to sit in the Chamber.
- House of Lords Act 1999 – Removed all but 92 hereditary peers elected by the hereditaries. At the same time the House of Lords Appointments Commission (HOLAC) was established, to advise on non-party peer appointments and to vet proposed party nominees.
- Constitutional Reform Act 2005 – Established the Supreme Court removing the judicial function from the House of Lords and Parliament, which resulted in establishment of an elected Lord Speaker to replace the Lord Chancellor as presiding officer of the House of Lords
- House of Lords Reform Act 2014 – Allowed peers to retire and provided for expulsion of peers for non-attendance.[184]
- House of Lords (Expulsion and Suspension) Act 2015 – Extended the grounds on which members could be expelled or suspended.

2.7.1. Reforming the Size of the Membership of the House of Lords – The Report of the Burns Committee

The membership of the House of Lords currently numbers around 800.[185] It is estimated that only some 500 are active members. There has been concern for decades about the size

[182] The government had tried to introduce a programme motion to limit debate on the bill but when it became apparent that it would lose the vote, on 10 July 2012 the motion was withdrawn. On the same day, on the vote as to whether the Bill should have a Second Reading, 91 Conservative MPs voted against the three-line whip and another 19 abstained, in light of which the Government decided that the bill had to be abandoned.

[183] Chris Ballinger, *The House of Lords 1911–2011: A Century of Non-Reform*, Hart Studies in Constitutional Law (Hart Publishing, 2012) 210. See also Meg Russell, *The Contemporary House of Lords: Westminster Bicameralism Revived* (Oxford University Press, 2013).

[184] See M Ryan, 'Bills of Steel: the House of Lords Reform Act 2014', *Public Law*, 2015, 558–70.

[185] It is the second largest second chamber. Only China's National People's Congress is bigger.

and recently there were signs that this issue was finally being addressed. The initiative began after the Lords *unanimously* passed a motion on 5 December 2016 that 'this House believes that its size should be reduced, and methods should be explored by which this could be achieved'. Two weeks later the Lords Speaker announced the establishment of a Committee chaired by Lord Burns to take the matter forward. The Burns Committee reported in under a year.[186]

The problem the committee sought to address was not simply that the current size of the House of Lords was too big, but that there had been a long running tendency for the size of the House of Lords to increase. Since 1997, appointments to the House of Lords averaged 35 per year, and the average life expectancy of new members was 25 years following the date of appointment. At that rate of appointment and deaths, the number of life peers might eventually settle at about 875 which together with 92 hereditary peers and 26 Bishops, would take the size of the House to nearly 1,000. The Report also warned that increasing life expectancy, together with the growing number of members needed for incoming Prime Ministers to rebalance party composition, could well push this number substantially higher.

The Committee proposed:

- The number to be reduced to 600 and be capped at that number.
- The reduction in size to be achieved gradually by a 'two-out, one-in system under which a new appointment could only be made after two members had left through retirement or death.
- Each party group to agree to provide the appropriate number of retirees so that each contributed proportionately.
- New political appointments should be made on a formula based on the most recent general election result.
- The House of Lords Appointments Committee to make new peers aware of the expectation that they be working members.
- New life peers to be required to sign an undertaking that their term would not exceed 15 years.

The 'two-out, one-in' principle would require approximately 450 departures before a target size of 600 was reached. The Burns Report noted that the number of departures in the five years leading up to 2016 was 125 in total. Under the Committee's proposed enhanced rate of departures, it would take 11 years to reach 600.

The Burns Committee report was debated by the Lords on 19 December 2017. 95 peers spoke, almost all in favour of the proposals. The report was also endorsed by the House of Commons Public Administration and Constitutional Affairs Committee.[187] In February 2018, Prime Minister Theresa May wrote to the Lords Speaker promising 'continued restraint over new appointments' to the Lords.[188] The Burns Committee

[186] *Report of the Lord Speakers Committee on the Size of the House*, 31 October 2017.

[187] House of Commons Public Administration and Constitutional Affairs Committee, *A smaller House of Lords: The report of the Lord Speaker's committee on the size of the House*, 13th Report, 2017–19, 19 November 2018, HC 662.

[188] Letter from Lord Fowler, Lords Speaker, *The Times*, 28 June 2019. The letter continued: 'That is the first time a prime minister has made such a commitment. To date Mrs May has appointed 42 new life peers. This is in stark contrast to the policy of Tony Blair, who appointed 374 new life peers, and David Cameron, who appointed a further 245.' She expressed the hope that whoever followed her as Prime Minister would follow the same policy of

published its second Report on 24 October 2018 and its third Report on 8 July 2019.[189] It published benchmark figures for appointments and departures. The third report stated that measured from the date of the June 2017 general election, the proposed 'two-out, one-in' proposal was working. Overall for the five-year Parliament the benchmark called for 150 departures and 75 appointments. To date there had been 62 departures and only 18 appointments.

However, hope that the reforms proposed by the Burns report would achieve significant results has not been realised. The number of prime ministerial appointments has remained very high: Theresa May (2016–19) 43; Johnson (2019–22) 87; Liz Truss (47 days) 29; Rishi Sunak (2022–24) 51; Keir Starmer (2024–) 53.[190]

2.7.2. Party Allegiance in the Lords

Prior to the 1999 reform excluding most hereditaries, the Conservatives were by far the largest party in the Lords. Since 1999, no party has had a majority. The Lord Privy Seal told peers that removing the remaining 92 hereditary peers would have only a small effect on the balance of party allegiance:

> The effect of the change will be that the Conservative share of seats will decrease from about 34% to 32%; the cross-bench share will decrease from around 23% to 21%; the Liberal Democrats will increase from 9.5% to 10% and Labour will increase from around 23% to 25%.[191]

Until 1999 the Conservatives could normally count on a majority unless the cross-benchers voted overwhelmingly with the opposition. This was the more so since more Conservatives attended the House regularly than the members of other parties.[192] Not that a Labour government found it impossible to carry its bills in the Lords. As was seen above, under what is called 'the Salisbury Convention' the Lords traditionally do not wreck or alter beyond recognition bills that derive from manifesto commitments and this convention stands. (The balance between Labour and Conservative was somewhat changed in December 2024 by Keir Starmer's appointment of thirty new Labour peers, as against retiring prime minister Rishi Sunak's appointment of six new Tory peers.)

Since the House of Lords Act 1999, the political balance is held by the Liberal Democrats and the cross-benchers. The result is increased uncertainty for party business managers as to the outcome of votes in the House of Lords. It can also be said that the (partially) reformed and therefore politically more defensible House of Lords appears readier to defeat the government of the day than was the case pre-1999.

As to the relative likelihood of government defeats in the Commons and the Lords, a letter to *The Times* (24 January 2003) from the Liberal Democrat peer, Lord Phillips of Sudbury, stated that in the five parliamentary sessions since Labour came to power in 1997

restraint. However, Boris Johnson who followed her as Prime Minister, in eighteen months appointed 79 new peers, almost twice as many as she had appointed in three years.

[189] The committee reports can be accessed at www.parliament.uk/size-of-the-house-committee.

[190] House of Lords Library, *House of Lords Data Dashboard: Peerage Creations*, 14 April 2025.

[191] HL *Hansard*, 11 December 2024, Baroness Smith of Basildon, col.1723. The actual numbers in the different parties are stated periodically in the House of Lords Data Dashboard which at the time of writing also included: Democratic Unionist Party (DUP) 6; Green Party 2; Ulster Unionist 3; Plaid Cymru 2; Conservative Independent 1; and Non-affiliated 43.

[192] *Griffith and Ryle on Parliament* (n 12 above) para 12-066.

there had been 1,640 whipped divisions (ie, votes) in the House of Commons, of which the Government lost none. Over the same period in the Lords, there were 639 whipped divisions of which it lost 164, or one in four. Since most of the hereditary peers had left the Lords, the proportion of Government defeats had increased to one in three whipped divisions.

The Parliament website gives the number of government defeats in the Lords in each session since 1974–1975:[193]

- Labour Government 1975 to 1979–240 over 4 sessions or 60 per session.
- Conservative Government 1979 to 1997–241 over 18 sessions or 13 per session.
- Labour Government 1997 to 2012–528 over 13 sessions or 41 per session.
- Coalition Government 2012 to 2015–100 over 2 sessions or 25 per session.
- Conservative Government 2015 to 2024–282 over 7 sessions or 40 per session.

2.8. Pre- and Post-Legislative Scrutiny of Bills

The publication of some bills in draft form has become a regular feature. Indeed, the 2017 edition of the Cabinet Office's *Guide to Making Legislation*, 2017 para 22.1 went so far as to state:

> The default position should be that bills will be published in draft prior to formal introduction. There should be a good reason not to publish the bill in draft. The Government is committed to publishing more of its bills in draft before they are formally introduced to Parliament, and to submitting them to a parliamentary committee for parliamentary pre-legislative scrutiny where possible.

That suggested that the majority of bills were published in draft, which is far from the case. The equivalent passage in the 2025 edition of the Cabinet Office's Guide (para 21.1) does not include the first two sentences. It only says 'The Government is committed to publishing more of its bills in draft …'.

The reality is that bills published in draft are a small minority. A 2022 report stated that in the fifteen years since 2007 only just over ten per cent of bills (11.6 per cent) had received pre-legislative scrutiny (PLS). It said:

> Eight select committee reports since 1997 have suggested expanding the use of PLS and making it more of a core part of the legislative process. Indeed, this has been the most common recommendation parliamentary committees have made for improving the legislative process. Nonetheless, PLS remains at the discretion of the government, an infrequently and sporadically used mechanism with untapped potential to improve legislation.[194]

Certainly, some types of bills are not suitable for publication in draft – the annual Finance Bill is an obvious example, as is emergency legislation or legislation to give effect to some form of international obligation. The House of Lords Constitution Committee in its 2017

[193] www.parliament.uk/about/faqs/house-of-lords-faqs/lords-govtdefeats/.

[194] Bennett Institute for Public Policy and Institute for Government, *The Legislative Process: How to Empower Parliament*, Jess Sergeant and Jack Pannell, December 2022, p 25.

report on *Preparing Legislation* said (para 87) that pre-legislative scrutiny 'should be considered an integral part of the … legislative process'. But that is not the case.

When pre-legislation scrutiny does take place it is usually conducted by an existing parliamentary committee.[195] This may be by a standing select committee such as the Joint Human Rights Committee, the House of Commons Home Affairs Committee, the House of Lords Constitution Committee[196] or the relevant departmental select committee. Or it may be an ad hoc select committee (sometimes a joint House of Commons/House of Lords committee) set up for the occasion.

For a proposal that bills would be improved if there were certain agreed standards as recommended by the Lords Constitution Committee see D Oliver, 'Improving the scrutiny of bills: the case for standards and checklists' *Public Law*, 2006, 219.

For proposals arising out of a review of the scrutiny of constitutional bills see R Hazell, 'Time for a new convention: parliamentary scrutiny of constitutional bills 1997–2005' *Public Law*, 2006, 247.

For analysis of the effect of pre-legislative scrutiny on two Bills see J Smookler, 'Making a difference? The effectiveness of pre-legislative scrutiny' 59 *Parliamentary Affairs*, 2006, 522.

The crucial difference between consideration of a draft bill by a parliamentary committee and consideration of an actual bill by a Public Bill Committee is that the former is not under the control of the Government. Also, since the atmosphere is often less politically adversarial than that of Public Bill Committees, it may be easier for a minister to accept suggested amendments. Obviously, though, that depends on the extent and scope of such amendments.

Publishing a bill in draft serves the interests of both government and Parliament – though their interests may conflict. The combination of the consultation outside Whitehall and greater time for deliberation should lead to better legislation. Where a bill is highly technical, the Government is in effect getting free advice from the experts. Also, it will enhance the legitimacy of the legislation, may deal with criticisms or, by drawing potential critics into the process, may diminish their impact. At the least, it will alert the Government to the points of dissension. On the debit side, it involves delay, extra work for officials and it may have the effect of giving time for opposition to build up.

For a detailed account of this constitutional innovation see A Kennon, 'Pre-legislative scrutiny of draft bills' *Public Law*, 2004, 477. A joint report on the legislative process in 2022 by the Bennett Institute for Public Policy and the Institute for Government recommended that *all* government bills should be published in draft. The government and the relevant select committee should agree on the appropriate form of scrutiny. If the select committee indicated that scrutiny was not needed, the government would be free to proceed with introduction of the bill.[197]

[195] In the fourteen sessions 1997–98 to 2010–12, a total of 86 draft bills were published of which 68 (79 per cent) were scrutinised by a parliamentary committee. (Source: House of Commons Library Standard Note, *Pre-legislative Scrutiny*, SN/PC2822; and *Pre-legislative scrutiny under the Coalition Government*, SN/PC5859.

[196] See Constitution Committee, *Pre-Legislative Scrutiny in the 2008–09 and 2009–10 Sessions* (HL 2009–10, 79); *Government Response to a Report on Pre-legislative Scrutiny in 2007–08* (HL 2008–9, 160). See also A Le Sueur and JS Caird, 'The House of Lords Select Committee on the Constitution' in A Horne, G Drewry and D Oliver (eds), *Parliament and the Law* (Hart Publishing, 2013) 289–99. The chapter includes case studies of scrutiny of the Legislative and Regulatory Reform Bill 2006 (which became known as the 'Abolition of Parliament Bill') and the Health and Social Care Bill 2011.

[197] Bennett Institute for Public Policy and Institute for Government, *The Legislative Process: How to Empower Parliament*, Jess Sergeant and Jack Pannell, December 2022.

Post-legislative scrutiny Examination of the *effects* of legislation as to whether the intended policy objectives have been met, and if not, how defects might be remedied, has now been recognised as a topic worthy of serious consideration. In 2004, in a report on the legislative process, the House of Lords Select Committee on the Constitution found that 'There is rarely an attempt and certainly no practice of Parliament regularly reviewing legislation to ensure that it has achieved what was intended'.[198] Most Acts, it thought, should be subject to some form of post-legislative scrutiny. It suggested that government departments should review legislation within three years of commencement and make a report to the relevant select committee. In its response the Government said that it had asked the Law Commission to study options for post-legislative scrutiny.[199]

The Law Commission's report, *Post-Legislative Scrutiny*, was published in October 2006. It said that there was overwhelming support among consultees for the idea of developing more systematic post-legislative scrutiny,[200] though the Commission acknowledged that it involved difficult challenges, namely: how to avoid a replay of policy arguments, how to make it workable within resource constraints and how to foster political will for it.[201] It was better to have effective review of a few pieces of legislation than cursory review of many.[202] Policy objectives that could be tested should be identified in the Regulatory Impact Assessment.[203] The majority of respondents to the Commission's consultation considered that if post-legislative scrutiny was to be effective, 'it should be owned by, and directed by Parliament'.[204] The Government and government departments would not always have the necessary interest in inquiring into the problems generated by legislation. The Law Commission recommended that consideration should be given to setting up a new Joint Select Committee on Post-Legislative Scrutiny.[205]

> 3.47 Select committees would retain the power to undertake post-legislative review, but, if they decided not to exercise that power, the potential for review would then pass to a dedicated committee. The committee, supported by the Scrutiny Unit,[206] could be involved at pre-legislative as well as post-legislative stages in considering what should be reviewed, could undertake the review work itself or commission others to do so and would develop organically within its broad terms of reference.

In March 2008, the Government published its response to the Law Commission's Report.[207] It accepted the desirability of more effort being put into post-legislative scrutiny. It did not accept that there was a need for a new Joint Committee as that would displace the responsibility of the existing departmental select committees. It stated that under its new policy, within 3–5 years of the commencement of new Acts the relevant government department

[198] Constitution Committee, *Parliament and the Legislative Process* (HL, 2003–04, No 173) para 168.

[199] Constitution Committee, *Parliament and the Legislative Process: The Government's Response* (HL 2004–05, No 114) paras 31–32.

[200] Law Commission, *Post-Legislative Scrutiny* (Law Com 302, 2006, Cm 6945) para 2.6.

[201] Ibid, para 2.24.

[202] Ibid, para 3.2.

[203] Ibid, para 3.16.

[204] Ibid, para 3.20.

[205] Ibid, paras 3.32 and 3.47.

[206] The Scrutiny Unit was established as part of the Committee Office of the House of Commons in 2002. The Unit consists of Parliamentary clerks, economists, lawyers and a statistician. The role of the Unit is to assist select committees with pre-legislative scrutiny of draft Bills and to provide advice on matters relating to the scrutiny of expenditure by Government departments (ed).

[207] Office of the Leader of the House of Commons, *Post-Legislative Scrutiny – The Government's Approach* (Cm 7320, 2008).

would be required to produce a memorandum for the relevant Commons departmental select committee. The Memorandum would include:

- information on when and how different provisions of the Act had been brought into operation
- information highlighting any provisions which had not been brought into force, or enabling powers not used, and explaining why not
- a brief description or list of the associated delegated legislation, guidance documents or other relevant material prepared or issued in connection with the Act
- an indication of any specific legal or drafting difficulties which had been matters of public concern (eg issues which had been the subject of actual litigation or of comment from parliamentary committees) and had been addressed
- a summary of any other known post-legislative reviews or assessments of the Act conducted in government, by Parliament, or elsewhere
- a short preliminary assessment of how the Act had worked out in practice, relative to objectives and benchmarks identified at the time of the passage of the Bill.

The Memorandum would thus not in itself be a full post-legislative scrutiny of the Act. This, the Government said, would be unnecessarily burdensome and inflexible and would not be an effective use of resources. But it would be a formal and automatic process whereby the relevant departmental select committee could assess the state of play in relation to the Act and could decide on what further action to take or propose.[208] It might decide to undertake scrutiny itself, or to see whether some other committee or body should do so. The Impact Assessment system already required that departments state when the costs and benefits involved in the legislation would be reviewed, on the basis that after three years would normally be about right. The Memorandum's suggested three to five years after Royal Assent would complement this process.[209]

This is the official approach reflected in the Cabinet Office's *Guide to Making Legislation* (2025, para 40, key points): 'Three to five years (normally) after Royal Assent, the responsible department must submit a memorandum to the relevant Commons departmental select committee (unless it has been agreed with the committee that a memorandum is not required), published as a command paper.'

However, former Law Commissioner Lord Burrows pointed out in his Hamlyn Lectures in 2017:

> Unfortunately, as with pre-legislative scrutiny, the official line on post legislative scrutiny is not being adhered to in practice. Although pinning down what has been happening is not easy, there is a helpful Commons Library Note which points out that in the Commons between May 2010 and January 2013, while there were 58 post-legislative memoranda, only three of those had been the subject of reports by select committees. And while in 2011 the House of Lords Liaison Committee took on an active role in relation to post-legislative scrutiny that appears to have resulted in only six post-legislative reports by a Lords ad hoc select committee in the six years since. The position appears to remain, therefore, one of limited and non-systematic post-legislative scrutiny.[210]

[208] Office of the Leader of the House of Commons, *Post-Legislative Scrutiny: The Government's Approach, Appendix: Detailed Response* (Cm 6945, 2008) paras 17–18.

[209] Ibid, paras 21 and 24.

[210] Andrew Burrows, *Thinking About Statutes*, Cambridge, 2017, 123–25.

A report published in 2022 said publication of these post-legislative memoranda was 'patchy'. While 69 had been published by government departments in the years 2011–14, only 19 were published in the years 2015–19. Also, Departmental select committees were responsible for conducting post-legislative scrutiny, but 'they often prioritise scrutinising new government policy and proactive inquiries, leaving little time for this type of scrutiny'.[211]

2.9. Carrying-Over Legislation from One Session to Another

Governments, as has been seen, normally work on the basis of a one-year-plus cycle for bills. For ordinary bills this may be enough time. But sometimes it is not. Bills are frequently introduced in a half-baked form leading to dozens and sometimes hundreds of government amendments. Also, the deadline of the end of the session leads to an unseemly scramble in the final weeks (sometimes even the final hours) with last-minute horse-trading between the parties to arrive at acceptable compromises before the prorogation.[212] (The House of Commons Modernisation Committee said of this last-minute scramble: 'Bills go to and fro between the Houses, both of which are asked to agree (or disagree), usually with minimal notice, to a large number of amendments. Few, if any, Members are able to know what is going on, and there is potential scope for error. The House has in the past even been asked to debate Lords amendments of which there is no available text.'[213])

The 1992 Hansard Society's Report proposed that governments should move toward the adoption of a two-year cycle. The Future Legislation Committee, it said, should decide on the broad shape of the legislative programme for the next two years. In particular, it should identify the larger more complex bills that required preparation over two years.[214] It also recommended that there should be the possibility of carrying bills over from one session to another.[215] This had been rejected by the Procedure Committee in 1984–85,[216] but the Hansard Society Report said this rejection was based on purely parliamentary considerations. It was able to take a broader view. Carrying a bill on from one session to the next would be especially useful where a bill passed the Commons late in a session. Better to carry it over to the next session than rush it through the Lords or drop it and have to start afresh.

In 1998, the House of Commons Modernisation Committee recommended that in certain circumstances government bills should be carried over (though not more than once) from one parliamentary session to another.[217] The recommendation was that it should be restricted to bills that were considered by some form of select committee scrutiny. This was

[211] Bennet Institute for Public Policy and Institute for Government, *The Legislative Process: How to Empower Parliament*, Jess Sergeant and Jack Pannell, December 2022, p 32.

[212] An example was the Criminal Justice Act 2003. See M Zander, 'The Criminal Justice Bill gets Royal Assent' *New Law Journal*, 28 November 2003, 1778.

[213] *The Legislative Process*, First Report of 1997–98, HC 190, para 12.

[214] Hansard Society, *Making the Law*, 1992, para 485, p 116.

[215] Ibid, para 490, p 117.

[216] HC 49-I of 1984–85, para 24.

[217] Modernisation Committee, Third Report, *Carry-over of Public Bills*, HC 543 of 1997–98.

agreed by the House of Commons. The bill when re-introduced starts exactly where it left off in the previous session.

In September 2002, the Modernisation Committee again recommended that Standing Orders be amended to permit carry-over of a bill by resolution of the House for an experimental period.[218] The recommendation was approved by the Commons on 29 October 2002. The House of Lords also agreed in principle to the carrying-over of Lords bills, subject however to the proviso that the bill has been subjected to pre-legislative scrutiny.

Carrying-over does not mean that more time is spent on the bill as the rule still applies that it should be completed within 12 months of the First Reading unless the House has previously passed an extension motion. But it gives government business managers more flexibility as to when bills are introduced – for instance permitting even quite substantial bills to be introduced later in a session.

The obvious advantage of permitting carry-over is that it avoids the 'sudden death' of legislation which has not completed its passage through Parliament during the session in which it was first introduced. A disadvantage is that it further increases the power of the government of the day to gets its legislation onto the statute book. By the same token it weakens the power of the House of Lords to secure changes in the legislation which can often be achieved in the traditional last-minute bargaining that takes place in the final days and hours of a legislative session. If the government no longer risks losing its legislation by the end of the session, it will be less open to persuasion that the bill should be amended.

For a guidance paper on carrying-over of bills published by the Office of Parliamentary Counsel in November 2013 see – www.gov.uk/government/publications/carrying-over-bills. Carrying-over of bills is dealt with in the Cabinet Office's *Guide to Making Legislation*, 2025, in s 31.

2.10. Control of Business

House of Commons Standing Order No 14 states that 'Save as provided in this order, government business shall have precedence at every sitting'. The exceptions are 13 Fridays when, as noted previously, precedence is given to Private Members' Bills, 20 other days at the disposal of opposition parties and 27 days allocated by the Backbench Business Committee. However, in 2019, during the battle over Brexit, backbenchers twice seized control of business to pass legislation against the wishes of the government. That was unprecedented. The first resulted in the passage of the European Union (Withdrawal) Act 2019[219] which required the Prime Minister, Theresa May, to ask for an extension under Article 50 of the Treaty on European Union to avoid that the UK crash out of the EU on 12 April 2019.[220] In order to achieve their objective the rebels first had to achieve the setting aside of Standing Order 14 and its House of Lords equivalent Standing Order 40. Strong objection was raised

[218] Second Report, HC 1168 of 2001–02.

[219] Originally styled the European Union (Withdrawal) (No 5) Bill.

[220] For consideration see M Zander, 'Brexit: is MPs taking control a good or a bad thing?' *New Law Journal*, 3 May 2019, p 13.

to such innovation by Members in both Houses. An especially powerful speech was made by Lord Norton of Louth, Professor of Government at Hull University:

> Since the emergence of Parliament in the 13th century, Parliament has been a reactive body, responding to demands of the Crown. This Bill marks a departure from that clearly understood position. It confuses the relationship. That relationship has a clear, principled rationale. It means a clear line of accountability, with a Government accountable to Parliament and, through parliamentary elections, accountable to electors. We are in danger of engaging in an exercise that, like referendums, is strictly speaking, irresponsible. With referendums, there is no means by which electors can hold themselves responsible for the outcomes. Similarly, with policy determined by a transient majority of parliamentarians, there is no single coherent body that stands before the electors to be held responsible for the policy.[221]

Many of those who spoke in both Houses warned that MPs taking control of the legislative process set a dangerous precedent. And, only a few months later, it happened a second time when the backbench rebels succeeded in securing the passage of the European Union (Withdrawal) (No 2) Act 2019. The Act required the new Prime Minister, Boris Johnson, to seek an extension under Article 50 unless he had secured a deal with the EU or Parliament had agreed a no-deal Brexit by 19 October.[222] In both instances the Bill was rushed through all its stages in a matter of days.[223]

2.11. Control of the Length of Debates

Parliament has a variety of techniques for controlling or curtailing debates. The 1992 Hansard Society Report *Making the Law* said that timetabling 'is essentially a problem for the Commons; in the Lords informal agreements appear to work well and we have received no evidence in favour of change'. In the Commons, it continued, 'timetabling of debates on bills ranges from none at all, through a considerable measure of voluntary timetabling by agreement between the parties, through the use of the closure (a declining practice) to the imposition of a formal guillotine imposed after lengthy time-wasting debate (a growing practice)'.[224]

But since that date things have moved on considerably and timetabling has become the norm. Agreement between the parties is through 'the usual channels' – a phrase that means the whips and party business managers.[225]

Closure is a procedure (under Commons Standing Order No. 36) whereby any Member may at any time move 'That the question be now put'. The closure motion is then put forthwith unless the Speaker decides that the motion is an 'abuse of the rules of the House' or 'an infringement of the rights of the minority'. But there must be at least one hundred Members in the majority. As previously noted, this is especially relevant in regard to Private

[221] HL, *Hansard*, 4 April 2019, col.341.

[222] See M Zander, 'Brexit: The rebels' Bill to defeat no-deal' *New Law Journal*, 6 September 2019, p 9.

[223] In the first case, the Bill was introduced in the Commons on Wednesday 3 April 2019 and received Royal Assent on Monday 8 April. In the second case, the Bill was introduced and went through all its stages in the Commons on Wednesday 4 September 2019, then went through all its stages in the Lords on the following two days and received Royal Assent on Monday 9 September.

[224] Hansard Society, *Making the Law*, 1992, para 505, p 120.

[225] For further explication see *Griffith and Ryle on Parliament* (n 12 above) paras 7-04–07.

Members' Bills. If the closure is agreed, the question on the motion being closured must then also be put forthwith. Most closures are claimed by the whips.[226]

The basic rule in the Lords is that there is no procedure for closure. It is not the done thing to seek to stop a debate. Erskine May says this:

> The closure (that is "that the question now be put") is not debatable and so requires an immediate conclusion. It is considered a most exceptional procedure. When a Member of the Lords seeks to move the closure the Lord Speaker brings the attention of the House to its exceptional nature and gives the Member of the Lords concerned the opportunity of reconsidering their action by reading the following paragraph before the question is put: "I am instructed by Order of the House to say that the motion 'That the question be now put' is considered to be a most exceptional procedure and the House will not accept it save in circumstances where it is felt to be the only means of ensuring the proper conduct of the business of this House; further, if a Lord who seeks to move it persists in his intentions, the practice of the House is that the question on the motion is put without debate."[227]

If the Member says that they do persist, the question is then put immediately – and voted on.[228]

The *guillotine* is a method, dating back to 1887, of compulsorily timetabling debate on a bill. A guillotine resolution has to be moved in the House of Commons. (There is no such thing as a guillotine in the Lords.) Once granted, subsequent debate follows the terms of the timetable as laid down in the resolution. It was used when the Government found progress on a bill frustrated by Opposition filibustering – usually during the Committee Stage. A guillotine motion can be debated for up to three hours. Such a motion usually generates protest from the Opposition and governments do not like using it. However, guillotine motions have now basically been replaced by programme motions.

2.11.1. Programme Motions

In 1997, the incoming Labour government made timetabling of legislation the first item for consideration by the newly created Modernisation of the House of Commons Committee chaired by the Leader of the House. Reporting a mere eleven weeks after the general election, the Modernisation Committee advocated a system of 'programming' legislation which it said would be 'more formal than the usual channels but more flexible than the guillotine'.[229] The new system, it said, should be introduced initially on a voluntary basis. The bills to which it would apply would be chosen through 'the usual channels'. Immediately after the Second Reading the Government would move an amendable programme motion (debatable for up to 45 minutes) giving the date by which the bill should have completed its Committee Stage and have reported to the House, and the amount of time allowed for the Report Stage and Third Reading. Progress during the Committee Stage would be controlled by a programming sub-committee selected by the Committee on Selection. The Standing

[226] Ibid, paras 6-109–112.
[227] Ibid, paras 576–77.
[228] On 4 April 2019 this happened five times during the accelerated progress of the European Union (Withdrawal) (No 5) Bill introduced by Brexit backbench rebels who had seized control of the Order Paper against the wishes of the government – as to which see 2.10 above. The repeated use of the closure was required to defeat those who wanted to filibuster to prevent the Bill being rushed through to achieve its purpose of requiring the Prime Minister to seek an Article 50 EU extension.
[229] *The Legislative Process*, HC 190 of 1997–98, p xxii.

Committee on the bill would agree the internal 'knives' – the times at which consideration of particular groups of amendments and clauses must be completed – on the basis of proposals made by the programming subcommittee (para 89). This Report was agreed by the Commons in November 1997.[230]

The Modernisation Committee issued a second Report in July 2000. This proposed that new sessional orders were required to regulate all programme motions.[231] The Report was opposed by the Conservative minority on the Committee.[232]

In November 2000, sessional orders to implement the Modernisation Committee's recommendations were approved on a division of the House (296 to 137).[233] They took effect initially on an experimental basis in the session 2000–01.

These arrangements for programming were made permanent from the start of the 2004–05 Session. Debate and argument about the pros and cons of programming have continued, but the Cabinet Office's *Guide to Making Legislation* as revised in 2025 states (para 26.1), 'Most government bills are subject to programme orders in the Commons'. The programme motion is taken immediately after the Second Reading. A programming subcommittee then regulates and adjusts the programme arrangements. The *Guide to Making Legislation* states (at para 26.12):

> Programming sub-committees meet in private and their proceedings are not recorded. Departmental officials, including Private Office, are not permitted to attend the meetings, although Parliamentary Counsel may attend. The programming sub-committee will discuss the resolution drafted by Parliamentary Counsel and may suggest changes including requesting additional witnesses. The whip and the minister will take the lead in the discussion. As long as the overall time allotted or 'out-date' from Committee Stage remains unchanged, there is considerable flexibility. If bill ministers and whips on the committee think changes are needed which would affect the 'out-date', they should discuss this with the Government Whips' Office.

The advantage of programming for the government is that it is assured that the legislation will go through. For the opposition and outside bodies interested in the bill, programming enables them to plan the timing of their interventions. The disadvantage is that it often results in significant parts of a bill receiving no debate at all because the time limit set by the programme has expired. In 2019, the House of Lords Constitution Committee suggested that the Lords Library, in their briefings on Bills brought from the Commons, should highlight the clauses and schedules that were not debated for lack of time at committee and report stages.[234]

The Cabinet Office *Guide to Making Legislation* deals with programming in s 26. The Office of Parliamentary Counsel has its own internal guidance paper on programming – see www.gov.uk./government/publications/programming-bills.

[230] HC, *Hansard*, vol. 300, cols. 1061–129, 13 November 1997.

[231] *Programming of Legislation and Timing of Votes*, July 2000, HC 589, 1999–2000.

[232] For the debate on the report see HC, *Hansard*, vol. 351, col 1084, 13 July 2000. A few days earlier, the report of the Commission to Strengthen Parliament chaired by Lord Norton (*Strengthening Parliament*) had endorsed the case for programming of bills but had proposed that it not be dominated by the government. There should be a Legislative Programme Committee chaired by the Chairman of Ways and Means and including the two other Deputy Speakers, the business managers of the parties and a number of senior backbenchers. The role of the Committee would be to see that a reasonable period was allocated for the Committee and the Report Stages. This proposal was not adopted.

[233] HC, *Hansard*, vol 356, cols 208–88, 7 November 2000.

[234] The Legislative Process: The Passage of Bills Through Parliament, 24th Report, 2017–19, July 2019, HL 393, para 28.

As previously noted, programming does not operate in the House of Lords. The nearest the Lords come to programming is that 'The Government Whips' Office circulates a list of the parts of a bill and related amendments that are anticipated to be debated during each day's sitting, but it is informal guidance for the House rather than the imposition of limits.[235] In its 2019 Report, the Lords Constitution Committee said: 'The system of self-regulation in the House of Lords largely works well in its consideration of bills. We welcome the efforts of the usual channels to arrange business to assist the whole House.'[236]

2.12. The Parliament Acts of 1911 and 1949

The Parliament Act 1911 was passed to limit the ability of the House of Lords to impede the Government's legislative programme. It provided that the Lords could not delay financial provisions,[237] it replaced the Lords' absolute veto on legislation by a delaying power of about two years, and it reduced the maximum length of a Parliament from seven years to five.[238] The Parliament Act 1949 reduced the delaying power from two years to one year.[239]

The reason for both Acts was the same – the dominance of Conservatives in the House of Lords. As has been seen, in 1911, apart from the bishops and Law Lords, the House was composed of hereditary peers, almost all of whom were Conservatives. In 1949, the position was still the same. (The post-war Attlee Labour Government had 16 Labour peers in a House of 789.) Life peerages only became possible through the Life Peerages Act 1959. As has been seen, removal of almost all the hereditary peers took place under the House of Lords Act 1999 and their removal will be completed by the House of Lords (Hereditary Peers) Bill introduced by the Labour Government in 2024.

The Parliament Acts only apply to a bill that was first introduced in the Commons. When re-introduced for the second time it must be the identical bill (though changing the year of the bill and other such changes to reflect the elapse of time is permitted). At least one year must elapse between the Second Reading in the Commons in the first session and the date of passing by the Commons in the second session.

Examples of the use of the Parliaments Act are the War Crimes Act 1991, the European Parliamentary Elections Act 1999, the Sexual Offences (Amendment) Act 2000 and the Hunting Act 2004. The last mentioned Act banning hunting with dogs led to a court challenge by the Countryside Alliance based on the proposition that the Act was not a valid Act of Parliament because the amendment of the 1911 Act by the 1949 Act had been achieved

[235] Lords Constitution Committee, The Legislative Process: The Passage of Bills Through Parliament, 24th Report, 2017–19, July 2019, HL 393, para 29.

[236] Ibid, para 32.

[237] A Money Bill is one providing *exclusively* for taxation, supply, appropriation or the raising or repayment of loans (s 1(2)).

[238] For the historical background see P Norton, 'Parliament Act 1911 in its historical context' in D Feldman (ed), *Law in Politics, Politics in Law* (Hart Publishing, 2013) 155–69. For how it works in practice see D Greenberg, 'The realities of the Parliament Act 1911' in D Feldman (ed), *Law in Politics, Politics in Law* (Hart Publishing, 2013) 187–96; and R Walters, 'The impact of the Parliament Acts 1911 and 1949 on a government's management of its legislative timetable, on parliamentary procedure and on legislative drafting' in D Feldman (ed), *Law in Politics, Politics in Law* (Hart Publishing, 2013) 197–200.

[239] For the story see C Ballinger, 'The Parliament Act 1949' in D Feldman (ed), *Law in Politics, Politics in Law* (Hart Publishing, 2013) 171–86.

only by use of the 1911 Act. The 1911 Act did not include power to amend the 1911 Act and therefore, it was argued, it could only be amended by the sovereign Parliament, comprising the Queen, Commons and Lords. The challenge was rejected first by the Divisional Court,[240] ten days later, by the Court of Appeal[241] and in October 2005 by the House of Lords, sitting with nine judges.[242]

The claimants founded their argument on the proposition that legislation passed under the Parliament Acts was only subordinate or delegated legislation.[243] The Divisional Court held that what emerged from use of the Parliament Acts *was* a proper Act of Parliament. The Court of Appeal arrived at the same result by a different approach. It held that an Act that resulted from use of the Parliament Acts was an Act of Parliament provided that it did not infringe a basic principle of the constitution. It could not, for instance, abolish the House of Lords or extend the life of Parliament. But reducing the period of delay from two years to one year, it held, was not a fundamental constitutional change and was therefore valid.

The nine judges in the House of Lords all agreed on the result but gave eight separate judgments. None supported the reasoning of the Court of Appeal. They preferred the view of the first instance court. Parliament had in effect created a new way of making primary legislation. The only limitations on the power to legislate were those expressed in the Acts.[244] The power could therefore be used even to make major constitutional changes.[245]

2.13. Legislation in Haste

Sometimes the legislature moves with amazing, some would say indecent, haste. The Second Reading of the Commonwealth Immigrants Bill was moved at 4 pm on 27 February 1968 in the House of Commons and the Bill passed all stages in the Commons and the Lords on the same day. Notification of the Royal Assent was received in the Lords at 9.45 am on 1 March 1968. The Northern Ireland Bill transferring power back to Northern Ireland in light of the 'Good Friday Agreement' had its Second Reading in the House of Commons at 10 pm on 23 February 1972 and the Royal Assent only hours later, on 24 February at 2.11 am. The Prevention of Terrorism (Temporary Provisions) Act 1974, passed in the wake of the Birmingham pub bombings, went through all its stages in both Houses of Parliament

[240] *R (Jackson) v Attorney General* [2005] EWHC 94 (Admin).

[241] *R (Jackson) v Attorney General* [2005] EWCA Civ 126, [2005] QB 579.

[242] *R (Jackson) v Attorney General* [2005] UKHL 56, [2006] 1 AC 262.

[243] An argument advanced by Professor HWR Wade in 'The Legal Basis of Sovereignty' *Cambridge Law Journal*, 1955, p 172 and developed by Professor Hood Phillips in O Hood Phillips and Jackson, *Constitutional and Administrative Law*, 8th edn (Sweet & Maxwell, 2001) at pp 79–81.

[244] Though Lord Bingham (at [32]) thought that the Parliament Acts could be used to amend even the provision regarding the duration of Parliament!.

[245] For discussion see, for instance: J Jowell, 'Parliamentary sovereignty under the new constitutional hypothesis' *Public Law*, 2006, 562 (considering dicta that suggest that the rule of law might exceptionally trump parliamentary sovereignty); R Cooke, 'A constitutional retreat' 122 *Law Quarterly Review*, 2006, 224 (regretting and questioning the decision); and R Ekins, 'Acts of Parliament and the Parliament Act' 123 *Law Quarterly Review*, 2007, 91 (approving the decision). (Lord Cooke of Thorndon sat as President of the New Zealand Court of Appeal and was the only Commonwealth judge also to have sat as a Lord of Appeal in Ordinary in the House of Lords.) See also A Bradley, 'The sovereignty of parliament: form or substance' in J Jowell and D Oliver (eds), *The Changing Constitution*, 7th edn (Oxford University Press, 2011) 35–69 and J Goldsworthy, *Parliamentary Sovereignty Contemporary Debates* (Cambridge University Press, 2010).

in seventeen hours. The Imprisonment (Temporary Provisions) Act 1980 passed through all its stages in thirteen hours, twenty minutes. It was introduced on a Tuesday afternoon and completed its parliamentary stages by 5.10 am the following morning. The 348-page Coronavirus Act 2020, with very wide-ranging emergency powers to deal with the pandemic, was introduced and went through all its stages in the Commons on Monday 23 March, went through all its stages in the Lords on Wednesday 25 March and received Royal Assent that day.

The allocation of time motion for the Dangerous Dogs Bill in 1991 provided for the procedural motion and the Second Reading debate to end at 10 pm, with the Committee stage to follow until 3 am, and the Report stage and Third Reading to be completed by 4 am. The Dangerous Dogs Act 1991, introduced in the wake of several savage attacks on small children by pit-bull terriers, is often cited as a prime example of poor legislation resulting from undue haste.

That legislation was at least uncontroversial. A much criticised instance of needlessly rushed legislation was the Data Retention and Investigatory Powers Bill which, following agreement between the three main political parties, went through all its stages in the Commons on 15 July 2014, all its stages in the Lords on the following two days and received Royal Assent on 17 July. The Act required internet and phone companies to store communications data generated by phone calls, email, texts and internet use for up to 12 months and make it accessible to police and security services.

A hundred or so years earlier, the Official Secrets Bill passed all its stages in one day in August 1911. The junior minister responsible for piloting it through the House of Commons later described the event:

> I got up and proposed that the Bill be read a second time, explaining, in two sentences only, that it was considered desirable in the public interest that the measure should be passed. Hardly a word was said and the Bill was read a second time; the Speaker left the Chair. I then moved the Bill in Committee. This was the first critical moment; two men got up to speak, but both were forcibly pulled down by their neighbours after they had uttered a few sentences, and the committee stage was passed. The Speaker walked back to his chair and said: 'The question is, that I report this Bill without amendment to the House.' Again two or three people stood up; again they were pulled down by their neighbours, and the report stage was through. The Speaker turned to me and said: 'The third reading, what day?' 'Now, sir,' I replied. My heart beat fast as the Speaker said: 'The question is that this Bill be read a third time.' It was open to anyone of all the members in the House of Commons to get up and say that no bill had ever yet passed through all its stages in one day without a word of explanation from the minister in charge … But to the eternal honour of those members, to whom I now offer, on behalf of that and all succeeding governments, my most grateful thanks, not one man seriously opposed, and in a little more time than it has taken to write these words that formidable piece of legislation was passed.[246]

In July 2009, the House of Lords Constitution Committee reported on what it called 'fast-track legislation'.[247] Legislation might be expedited for a variety of reasons. The Committee identified some 30 bills that had been fast-tracked in the previous twenty years. The problems created by short notice of legislation also applied to last-minute government amendments to bills that were proceeding at a normal rate. (Government amendments must

[246] JEB Seely, *Adventure* (Heinemman, 1930) 145 – cited by DGT Williams in 'Statute law and administrative law' 5 *Statute Law Review*, 1984, 157, 166.

[247] House of Lords Constitution Committee, *Fast-Track Legislation: Constitutional Implications and Safeguards* (HL 116-I, 15th Report 2008–09).

be tabled no later than three sitting days before the earliest day on which they may be reached in proceedings of a public bill committee or two sittings in committee of the whole House.[248])

The Committee recommended that ministers introducing fast-tracked legislation should be required to make an oral statement to the House of Lords on which there could be a debate. The questions to be addressed in the statement should include: (a) Why was fast-tracking necessary? (b) What was the justification for fast-tracking each element of the bill? (c) What efforts had been made to ensure the amount of time made available for parliamentary scrutiny had been maximised? (d) To what extent had interested parties and outside groups been given an opportunity to influence the policy proposal? (e) Did the bill include a sunset clause for expiry (as well as any appropriate renewal procedure)? If not, why did the Government judge that their inclusion was not appropriate? (f) Were mechanisms for effective post-legislative scrutiny and review within one or two years in place? If not, why did the Government judge that their inclusion was not appropriate? (g) Had an assessment been made as to whether existing legislation was sufficient to deal with any or all of the issues in question? (h) Had relevant parliamentary committees been given the opportunity to scrutinise the legislation?

The government's response accepted that these were legitimate issues that would be taken into account.[249]

In 2019, the Lords Constitution Committee said: 'We welcome the fact that the Cabinet Office's *Guide to Making Legislation* now requires the justification for fast-tracking to be included in a bill's explanatory notes. We note that the Government has observed it in respect of most recent bills that have been fast-tracked.'[250]

In the same report the Constitution Committee regretted that Bills relating to Northern Ireland were especially prone to being fast-tracked. In 2018 no fewer than eight Northern Ireland Bills had been put through an expedited procedure. It said:

> We regret that legislation relating to Northern Ireland has regularly been fast-tracked. This has become common not just for bills which might be required to address urgent or unforeseen problems, but for routine and predictable matters such as budgetary measures. The political stalemate in Northern Ireland has led to an absence of a functioning Executive and a democratic deficit. Fast-tracking bills relating to Northern Ireland reduces further the scrutiny these measures should receive. Routinely fast-tracking in this way is unacceptable, unsustainable and should only be used for urgent matters.[251]

The Government's Response to the Committee's Report said (para 7) that the fast-tracking of Northern Ireland legislation reflected 'the exceptional circumstances currently existing in Northern Ireland' where there was no functioning power-sharing government.

A particular problem arises in the highly unusual situation of fast-track legislation by backbenchers against the wishes of the government which, as previously noted (2.10 above), occurred twice in 2019 in the Brexit crisis. The problem is that although in both cases the rebel backbenchers successfully seized control of the Order Paper to manage the timetabling of the Bill, they could not deal with subsequent micro-management issues that arose. The European Union (Withdrawal) (No 5) Bill went

[248] Cabinet Office, *Guide to Making Legislation, 2025* para 29.44.

[249] HL Constitution Committee, 2nd Report, 2009–10, HL 11.

[250] Lords Constitution Committee, *The Legislative Process: The Passage of Bills Through Parliament*, 24th Report, 2017–19, July 2019, HL 393, para.38.

[251] Ibid, para.39.

through all its stages in the Commons on Wednesday 3 April 2019 between 6.05pm and 11.09pm. It started in the Lords the next day. The intention was that it would conclude all its stages that day but the House spent from 11.37am to 6.55pm debating the desirability of rushing the legislation through. The debate was finally brought to an end when the government's Chief Whip announced that 'the usual channels' had agreed that the Second Reading debate would take place that evening and that the remaining stages would take place on Monday 8 April and would be concluded in time for Commons consideration of Lords amendments and Royal Assent to be given on that day. The backbenchers could not have achieved that themselves. It required the assistance of the 'usual channels'.

2.13.1. Emergency Legislation – The Covid-19 Pandemic

Legislating in an emergency is a sub-set of the larger category of legislating in haste. There are acts that provide for special measures required in an emergency.[252] The worldwide Covid-19 pandemic is an example. (See on this subject especially Adam Wagner, *Emergency State – How We Lost Our Freedoms in the Pandemic and Why it Matters* (Bodley Head, 2022, 221pp – on which this section is largely based.)

On 30 January 2020 the World Health Organization (WHO) declared the novel coronavirus outbreak in China to be a Public Health Emergency. The first UK legislative response was on 10 February with the passing of the Health Protection (Coronavirus) Regulations 2020 (SI 2020/129).The regulations were based on authority created by the Public Health Act 1984 as amended in 2008 after the 2002–04 outbreak of SARS.[253] That Act was the latest of a line of health-related acts of parliament going back centuries.[254]

Amendments passed in 2005 gave ministers the ability to take measures 'for the purpose of preventing, protecting against, controlling or providing a public health response to the incidence or spread of infection or contamination in England', including restrictions on gatherings, travel, children attending school and requirement 'on or in relation to persons, things or premises'. If the minister declared that 'by reason of urgency, it is necessary to make the order without a draft being so laid and approved by Parliament', it would be possible for there to be no Parliamentary scrutiny or approval for 28 days after the law had come into force – and longer if Parliament was in recess.

On 14 February 2020, Matt Hancock, Health Minister, made a 'serious and imminent threat' declaration which meant the start of a state of emergency that was to last for over two years. What became the Corona Virus Act 2020 (325 pages[255]), was debated for a mere six or so hours in the Commons and seven and a half hours in the Lords. It received Royal Assent on 25 March. The Act:

[252] The mass of Second World War regulations were passed under the Emergency Powers (Defence) Act 1939.

[253] Severe Acute Respiratory Syndrome (SARS).

[254] 'Plague Orders' were first enacted in England in 1578 following an outbreak of bubonic plague.

[255] Wagner (op.cit. p 51) explains that the Government was able to produce the bill in those few days because it had been developed – in secret – as the Pandemic Flu Bill between 2016 and 2020. The thinking had been that a future pandemic would be of the 1918 Spanish flu type. This history was revealed to a parliamentary committee in 2022 (*Coronavirus Act 2020 Two Years On*, HC Public Administration and Constitutional Affairs Committee, 7th Report of session 2021–22, 18 March 2022, para 10).

> Would water down the legal duties to meet the care needs of eligible people, grant police stronger powers to quarantine infected people, give the government more power to ban gatherings, change the rules for inquests (investigations into deaths) to make it easier to hold a coronavirus death investigation without a jury, postpone local and mayoral elections for a year, weaken safeguards for detaining people under mental health law, give the Scottish government equivalent powers to those that the Westminster government had under the Public Health Act, and relax judicial safeguards on the power of the Home Secretary to order the interception of communications. This was a vast piece of legislation which demanded full scrutiny and debate not a perfunctory few hours. (Wagner, *Emergency State*, 49)

Of the few amendments made to the bill, the most significant was that instead of the Act automatically being in place for two years, it would have to be re-authorised by Parliament every six months – though parliament could only vote 'yes' or 'no' and could not propose amendments.

> This pattern would be repeated countless times with the coronavirus regulation in the cases of both the Coronavirus Act and the coronavirus regulations. Had the government used the Civil Contingencies Act 2004, which did allow amendments and had far stricter requirements for Parliamentary involvement, it would have led to substantive participation by the legislature, rather than the symbolic but essentially meaningless votes which were held over the next two years, when Parliament would begin to resemble a nodding dog. (Wagner, *Emergency State*, 50)

In his concluding chapter, Wagner writes:

> [O]ut of over one hundred emergency regulations, many of them among the most controversial in history, Parliament could not point to a single one, which was amended by a single word, let along struck down. The voluminous laws which resulted were bloated and inconsistent, and often contradicted by official guidance and ministerial statements. This led to increasing confusion on the part of a public which was just trying to keep up, and to survive the crisis. In the courts, what few challenges were brought against the Covid-19 regulations failed, with judges making clear that the government has a wide discretion when making complex emergency decisions. (Wagner, *Emergency State*, 158)

See also: R Cormacain, R Fox, M Russell and J Tomlinson, *The marginalisation of the House of Commons under Covid has been shocking; a year on, Parliament's role must urgently be restored*, Hansard Society, London, 2021; and D Lock, PG Hidalgo and F de Londras, 'Parliament's One-Year Review of the Coronavirus Act 2020: Another Example of Parliament's Marginalisation in the Covid-19 Pandemic', 92 *Political Quarterly*, 2021(4), 699–706.

2.14. When does a Statute Come into Force?

If the Act says nothing on the matter, a statute comes into force on Royal Assent. But the Act may say otherwise. Commonly the statute specifies that it, or parts, shall come into force on a fixed date or on a date to be appointed by the minister. It was then often a matter of some difficulty to discover whether any particular part of the Act had or had not come into force. A report in 1980 on the problem by the Statute Law Society stated that 64 of the 105 Acts passed between January 1978 and April 1979 postponed commencement in whole or in part and the commencement provisions were of thirteen different kinds. In 34 instances, commencement was on different dates for different sections; in 32 cases, commencement dates were left wholly or partly to be fixed by statutory instrument; and in 28 cases both of these features were present.[256]

Sometimes provisions are not brought into force at all. In 1997 an official report on the problem, *Bringing Acts of Parliament into Force*, stated that of the Acts passed between 1979 and 1992, there were 69 that had not yet been fully brought into effect.[257]

One practical disadvantage of commencement taking place on the day of Royal Assent is that the Act has not yet been published and is therefore not available to be purchased or accessed electronically on the web. The Act will be published on the www.legislation.gov.uk website in pdf format immediately after the approved text has been received from the Lords Public Bill Office and in html format at the same time as the printed copy is made available. Sometimes this takes several weeks. The Cabinet Office, *Guide to Making Legislation* (2025, para 3.45), says that Departments should let Parliamentary Counsel and the Legislation Services Team in the National Archives know if an Act is expected to come into operation immediately. 'This is so that arrangements can be made for early clearance of the approved text, expedited printing and immediate publication of the Act on the www.legislation.gov.uk website.

If commencement takes place on Royal Assent there has been no time to adjust to the new provisions. Dealing with this issue, the Cabinet Office, *Guide to Making Legislation*, states: 'No substantive provision of an Act should be brought into operation earlier than two months after Royal Assent although some sections of the Act can be brought into force on Royal Assent, typically sections setting out how the Act is to be cited and what the procedure is for making regulations or commencing the Act.[258]

It adds: 'Commencement dates should be specified in the Act where possible and appropriate'.[259]

Guidance was issued to government departments in November 1980 that, where there was more than one commencement order, the second and subsequent ones should list earlier orders and the provisions that had already been brought into force.[260] This is now the practice. Looking for that list in the latest Commencement Order statutory instrument on www.bailii.org or other online service is one way of checking whether a provision is in force.

In regard to statutory instruments, there was a provision (Statutory Instruments Act 1946, s 3) that in any proceedings for the contravention of such an instrument it should normally be a defence that, at the date of the offence, it had not been published. The Committee proposed, 'There should be equivalent provisions regarding statutes' (p 51). In fact such provisions should go further, to provide that no statute should be applied so as to affect anyone's rights adversely unless either it had been published or reasonable steps had been taken to bring the purport of the Act and its commencement provisions to the attention of those likely to be affected (p 52). This recommendation has however not been implemented.

Harmonisation of commencement dates The government announced in 2003 that all new legislation regarding domestic employment would in future come into force either

[256] 'Statute Law Society Working Party on Commencement of Acts of Parliament' 1 *Statute Law Review*, 1980, 40, 41.

[257] Cm 3595, 1997.

[258] Cabinet Office, *Guide to Making Legislation* 2025, para 3.44.

[259] Ibid.

[260] See 2 *Statute Law Review*, 1981, 174, 179.

on 6 April or 1 October. This was subsequently extended to all new legislation affecting business and civil society organisations. The Cabinet Office, *Guide to Making Legislation* (2025 para 38.13), states: 'Where the provisions have an impact on business and civil society organisations, they should be commenced on one of the two annual "common commencement dates" (6 April and 1 October)'.

Wrong way to bring it into into force The Government has a choice as to whether and, if so, when to implement a statute but it cannot decide to implement the statutory policy by a completely different prerogative system. The House of Lords held that the Home Secretary could not set up a Criminal Injuries Compensation Scheme by prerogative order when the Criminal Justice Act 1988 set one up under statute – *R v Secretary of State for the Home Department, ex p Fire Brigades Union* [1995] 2 WLR 1, [1995] 2 All ER 244. For comment see A Samuels, '"Is it in force?", Must it be brought into force?' 17 *Statute Law Review*, 1996, 62.

2.15. Statutes Online

The Hansard Society 1992 Report said:

> At present the accessibility of statute law to users and the wider public is slow, inconvenient, complicated and subject to several impediments. To put it bluntly, it is often very difficult to find out what the text of the law is – let alone what it means. Something must be done.[261]

Something has been done. Statutes and statutory instruments are now available free of charge online. The official source is www.legislation.gov.uk[262] which provides access to all UK statutes and their Explanatory Notes since 1988 and to most pre-1988 statutes in force. It also has all UK statutory instruments since 1987 and is loading SIs since 1947. It also has Northern Ireland, Scotland and Wales statutes and statutory instruments. Much of the primary legislation on the website and some of the secondary legislation includes revisions made post-Royal Assent. (The website states what is accessible and whether it is up-to-date.)

Law libraries and lawyers' offices and chambers will also normally have access to subscription services such as those of Westlaw or LexisNexis which *are* brought up-to-date.

A free service giving access to UK, Scotland, Northern Ireland and Wales statutes and statutory instruments is available via the BAILII website (British and Irish Legal Information Institute – www.bailii.org). Legislation on that website is only as originally enacted. It is not brought up to date.

2.16. The Reach of Legislation and Devolution

Most Public Acts apply to the whole of Great Britain: that is to say, England, Scotland and Wales. Some apply to the whole United Kingdom, that is to say, England, Scotland, Wales

[261] Hansard Society, *Making the Law*, para 452, p 108.

[262] The www.legislation.gov.uk website brings together UK legislation formerly held on the OPSI (Office of Public Sector Information) and Statute Law Database websites.

and Northern Ireland. Some Acts apply only to Scotland,[263] some apply only to Wales, some apply only to England and Wales.

Law-making for the constituent parts of the United Kingdom was transformed by the three devolution Acts of 1998: the Scotland Act 1998, the Government of Wales Act 1998 and the Northern Ireland Act 1998.[264] As to the background, James Mitchell, Professor of Politics, in his valuable book *Devolution in the UK*, wrote:

> The new devolved institutions cannot be understood by simply looking at their founding legislation, policy output or the resources available to them. They did not involve a revolution in constitutional design though they represent significant change. They owe far more to past practice and the informal customary constitution than is often appreciated.[265]

The central argument of his book was that devolved government 'was the culmination of processes that had evolved over many decades.[266]

Each of the three devolution acts reflected a different history and employed different methods of transferring power. None, however, altered the principle of parliamentary sovereignty. Each Act states explicitly that Parliament in Westminster can still legislate for all parts of the UK, which means including in relation to devolved policy areas.[267]

The so-called Sewel Convention established the principle that the UK parliament 'will not normally legislate with regard to devolved matters except with the agreement of the devolved legislature',[268] ie the Scottish Parliament, Senedd Cymru (Welsh Parliament) and the Northern Ireland Assembly. The policy expressed by the Sewel Convention held for several decades, but it is not clear whether it still holds today. The principle has been seriously affected by legislation resulting from Brexit and by decisions of the Supreme Court. (See further below.)

When planned UK legislation includes provisions that fall within the scope of the Sewel Convention, the UK must consult with the devolved administrations. After the bill is introduced in parliament, the devolved administrations publish a legislative consent memorandum explaining why the bill requires consent and usually indicating why consent should be granted. Before the bill reaches its final stages, the devolved legislatures vote to either grant or withhold consent, in part or in full. If consent is not granted, the UK government has to decide whether to amend the bill or to pass the legislation despite the refusal of consent.

[263] It was estimated that of 2,258 Acts applying to Scotland enacted between 1945 and 1980, only 249, or slightly more than 10 per cent were Scotland-only Acts (D Van Mechelen and R Rose, *Patterns of Parliamentary Legislation* (Gower, 1986) 71–72).

[264] The Cabinet Office's *Guide to Making Legislation*, 2025 includes a section (pp 131–42) on Devolution. The Cabinet Office has also posted 14 separate Guidance Notes on Devolution.

[265] James Mitchell, *Devolution in the UK*, Manchester University Press, 2009, 268pp at 15.

[266] Ibid, at p 219.

[267] Scotland Act 1998 s. 27(7); Government of Wales Act 2006 s. 107(5); Northern Ireland Act 1998 s. 5(6).

[268] On 21 July 1998, Lord Sewel, speaking in the House of Lords for the Government, said: '[W]e would expect a convention to be established that Westminster would not normally legislate with regard to devolved matters in Scotland without the consent of the Scottish Parliament' (HL, *Hansard*, vol 592, col 791). This became known as the Sewel Convention. It was confirmed by the Memorandum of Understanding with the devolved administration (Cm 4806, 2000, para 13). It is also expressed in the Scotland Act 1998 s 27(8) and in the Wales Act 2006 s 107(6).

It seems that the concept of the legislative consent convention dates back to the 1920s in Northern Ireland. See Adam Evans, 'A Tale as Old as (Devolved) Time? Sewel, Stormont and the Legislative Consent Convention' 91 *Political Quarterly*. 2020 (1) 165–17.

See generally House of Commons Library Briefing Paper 'Devolution: The Sewel Convention', May 2020. (Devolution: The Sewel Convention -https://commonslibrary.parliament.uk/research-briefings/cbp-8883/.

The Supreme Court ruled that the Sewel Convention cannot be enforced by the courts because it is only a convention.[269] An Institute for Government paper ('The Sewel Convention', July 2024) states that in the first 25 years of devolution – from 1999 to July 2024 – some 220 acts were the subject of consent motions. In the great majority of cases consent was given. The Scottish parliament gave consent to 198 acts since 1999, and withheld consent in 15. Senedd Cymru consented to 90 and withheld consent to 20. The Northern Ireland Assembly consented to 90 and withheld consent to 2. In total consent has only been denied, wholly or in part, by at least one of the devolved governments for 28 Acts. 19 of these 28 were during the 2019–24 (Conservative) Government.

In rare instances the devolved authority's dissent led to appropriate application of the Sewel Convention with the UK government making changes to meet the objections. In most cases, however, the UK government proceeded with the legislation unchanged despite the dissent. Theresa May's European Union (Withdrawal) Act 2018 was the first occasion Westminster legislated without Scottish consent. That was then repeated in three further Brexit related Bills.[270] Boris Johnson's European Union (Withdrawal Agreement) Act 2020 was passed despite refusal of consent by all three devolved legislatures.

For pessimistic assessments of the prospects for the devolution project see: K Morgan and R Wyn Jones, 'Brexit and the Death of Devolution';[271] A McHarg, 'The contested boundaries of devolved legislative competence: Securing better devolution settlements';[272] P Thomas, G Cowie and P Larkin, 'The Forward March of Devolution Halted?';[273] P Anderson and CB Swan, 'An unstable union? The Conservative Party, the British political tradition, and devolution in Scotland and Wales 2010–23'.[274]

For the argument that the Supreme Court was playing an important role 'in bringing the devolution project under control' see G Davies, 'The UK Supreme Court and devolution: guardians of the passive revolution'.[275]

2.16.1. Scotland

The Act of Union 1707 abolished and merged the previous English and Scottish Parliaments and created the Parliament of Great Britain in Westminster. The 1707 Act preserved some aspects of Scottish life and culture including its separate legal system. Since Scotland had no legislature, laws for Scotland were made by the Westminster Parliament. In 1885, the Scottish Office was created in the UK Government, headed by a Secretary of State and during the twentieth century separate administrative arrangements for Scotland were increasingly developed.

[269] *R (Miller) v Secretary of State for Exiting the European Union* [2017] UKSC 5 at [148].

[270] The EU (Withdrawal Agreement) Bill; the UK Internal Market Bill and the EU (Future Relationship) Bill.

[271] 94 *Political Quarterly*, 2023 (4), 625–33.

[272] Bennett Institute for Public Policy, May 2023. (The paper was a contribution to the Review of the UK Constitution conducted by the Institute for Government and the Bennett Institute for Public Policy, Cambridge.).

[273] In A Horne, L Thompson and B Yong eds. *Parliament and the Law* 3rd edn (Hart, 2022) 133–58.

[274] 77 *Parliamentary Affairs*, 2024 (4), 790–815.

[275] 2025 *Public Law* 58-80. Davies highlighted *R (on the application of Miller) v Secretary of State for Exiting the European Union* [2017] UKSC 5; *Re UK Withdrawal from the European Union (Legal Continuity) (Scotland) Bill* [2018] UKSC 64; *Re Attorney General's Reference, United Nations Convention on the Rights of the Child (Incorporation) (Scotland) Bill* [2021] UKSC 42.

See also M Elliott and N Kilford, 'The Supreme Court's defence of unqualified law-making power; parliamentary sovereignty, devolution and the Scotland Act 1998' 81 *Cambridge Law Journal*, 2022 (1), 4.

The (Kilbrandon) Royal Commission on the Constitution (1969–73) recommended that legislative competence be devolved to Scotland.[276] In 1978, the then Labour government enacted the Scotland Act to devolve certain specified areas to a Scottish Parliament, but the Act had to be repealed by the incoming Conservative government because the referendum on the Act had failed to obtain approval by the required 40 per cent of the *electorate* (rather than of those who actually voted[277]). The Conservatives were in power from 1979 for the next eighteen years.[278] Devolution for Scotland went into abeyance until the return of the Labour government in 1997.[279]

The groundwork was laid by the Scottish Constitutional Convention, an unofficial body established in 1989 to draw up plans for devolution. Its final report, *Scotland's Parliament, Scotland's Right*, published in 1995, recommended the creation of a strong Scottish devolved government with plenary legislative competence subject to specific exceptions. This became the basis of what was enacted in 1998.

Whereas the 1978 Act listed devolved areas and reserved the rest for Westminster, the Scotland Act 1998 conferred a general legislative power on the Scottish Parliament subject to reserved matters.[280] The parliament is unicameral, elected by proportional representation.

Section 29 provides that an Act of the Scottish Parliament was not law if it purported to have effect outside Scotland, if it related to reserved matters, or if it would have the effect of modifying, inter alia, the Acts of Union, the European Communities Act 1972, the Human Rights Act 1998 or most of the provisions of the Scotland Act itself.

The reserved matters were set out in Sch 5, which is 17 pages long. They are divided into general and specific reservations. The general reservations cover broad areas such as the constitution, political parties, foreign affairs, public service and defence. The specific reservations comprise 12 heads including financial and economic matters, home affairs, trade and industry. Only the specific aspects of the policy areas listed in the Schedule are reserved and s 30(2) provides that Sch 5 can be modified by an Order in Council approved by both the Westminster and the Scottish Parliament.[281]

However, as noted above, s 28(7) expressly preserved the right of the Westminster legislature to legislate for Scotland even in respect of devolved matters.[282] In other words, despite the Sewel Convention, there continued to be a significant pull toward uniformity and the traditional view that the Westminster Parliament dominates.[283]

[276] Cm 5460, 1973.

[277] Of those who cast votes, 56 per cent had approved.

[278] The discordance between political feeling in Scotland compared with the rest of the UK was reflected in the result of the 1987 General Election when the Conservatives secured a 101-seat majority but had their share of seats in Scotland fall from 22 out of 71 in 1979 to 10 out of 72.

[279] The Blair government conducted a Scottish referendum on the topic in September 1997. On a turnout of 60 per cent, 74 per cent voted in favour of the creation of a Scottish Parliament. The Scotland Bill was published in December 1997. It received Royal Assent in November 1998.

[280] For an account of how it works by the Lord Advocate see W James Wolffe, 'Devolution and the Statute Book' 42 *Statute Law Review*, 2021 (2), 121–36.

[281] See further N Burrows, 'Unfinished Business: the Scotland Act 1998', 62 *Modern Law Review*, 1999, 241. For discussion of the respected competence of the Westminster and the Scottish legislature, see especially 248–49.

[282] In 'Unfinished Business' (n 281 above) Burrows said of New Labour's policy on devolution that whilst on the one hand it looked to the decentralisation of power as a means of bringing the United Kingdom constitution into the new millennium, 'on the other hand it remains rooted in a conservative, indeed imperialist, past' (at 249).

[283] For a Supreme Court decision expressing the same philosophy see *Attorney General's Reference United Nations Convention on the Rights of the Child (Incorporation) (Scotland) Bill, Re* [2021] UKSC 42 and commentary on the case by Mark Elliott and Nicholas Kilford, 81 *Cambridge Law Journal* 2022 (1), 4–8.

In the 2007 Scottish Parliamentary election, the Scottish National Party (SNP) for the first time became the largest party.[284] The SNP's aim was independence. In 2008, despite the SNP's opposition, the Scottish Parliament established a Commission[285] to review the operation of devolution. The obvious intention was to head off the independence movement. The Commission on Scottish Devolution, known as the Calman Commission after its Chair, Sir Kenneth Calman, reported in June 2009.[286] It made recommendations seeking to strengthen Scottish devolution, mainly in the area of financing, though it also made recommendations on the re-allocation of responsibilities between the Scottish and UK Parliaments, and on intergovernmental and inter-parliamentary relations.

The Calman Commission's recommendations resulted in the Scotland Act 2012. This amended the Scotland Act 1998 by giving the Scottish Parliament further powers in relation to raising income tax, new borrowing powers and the devolution of stamp duty and landfill tax. It also extended devolution in a number of other areas, including speed limits and drink/drive limits.

In November 2013 the Scottish Parliament unanimously passed the Scottish Independence Referendum Bill, providing for a referendum to be held in September 2014 on whether Scotland should leave the United Kingdom. Just before the referendum, the leaders of the Conservative, Labour and Liberal Democrat parties made a joint commitment in the event of a No vote to deliver extensive new powers to the Scottish Parliament.[287] The referendum resulted in a clear majority (55 per cent to 45 per cent) in favour of remaining in the United Kingdom. On the day after the independence referendum, 19 September 2014, David Cameron, the Prime Minister, announced the establishment of a Commission, chaired by Lord Smith of Kelvin, to facilitate talks on the devolution of further powers to the Scottish Parliament.

The following month, the Government published a Command Paper setting out the three main UK parties' proposals on further devolution in Scotland – *The Parties' Published Proposals on Further Devolution* (Cmnd 8946, October 2014).

The Report of the Smith Commission for further devolution of powers to the Scottish Parliament, agreed by all five of Scotland's political parties – Conservative, Green, Labour, Liberal Democrat and SNP – was published the next month, on 27 November 2014. Its recommendation of further fiscal devolution was implemented in the Scotland Act 2016. The Act also created a new category of 'protected subject- matter' requiring legislation by a two-thirds super-majority.[288] Provided it acts within its areas of competence the Scottish Parliament has full legislative powers, but legislation that is arguably outwith the competence of the devolved legislature can be challenged in the courts – though not by way of judicial review on ordinary common law grounds:

> Acts of the Scottish Parliament are not subject to judicial review at common law on the grounds of irrationality, unreasonabless or arbitrariness ... it would also be quite wrong for the judges to substitute their views on these issues for the considered judgment of a democratically elected legislature ...[289]

[284] The SNP obtained 47 seats, one more than Labour – and its leader, Alex Salmond, became First Minister.

[285] It was proposed by the Labour Opposition supported by the Liberal Democrats and Conservatives. Together they had more votes than the minority SNP government.

[286] Report of the Commission on Scottish Devolution (2009), *Serving Scotland Better: Scotland and the United Kingdom in the 21st Century.*

[287] The so-called 'Vow' was published in the *Daily Record* on 14 September 2014, four days before the referendum.

[288] A super-majority is required to change the Holyrood franchise, the electoral system or the number or territorial distribution of seats.

[289] *Axa General Insurance, Ltd v Lord Advocate* [2012]1 AC 868 at [46].

Successful challenges by way of judicial review have however been brought on the ground of exceeding competence, for instance by reason of breach of ECHR rights.[290] Challenges can also be brought by way of a Law Officer's reference under s 33 of the Scotland Act 199.[291]

See further: Aileen McHarg, Devolution in Scotland' in J Jowell and C O'Cinneide (eds), *The Changing Constitution* 9th edn (Oxford University Press, 2019) 270–95.

2.16.2. Wales

Professor Richard Rawlings described Welsh devolution since 1998 as an extraordinary constitutional journey:

> At the heart of which lies an ongoing series of legislative transformations, a process in which officially labelled 'devolution settlements' quickly prove otherwise by reason of basic defects and limitations and home grown innovation and expansionary pressure. Step by step the path to a reasonable and realistic form of representative government in Wales is travelled, but in arduous, even painful fashion.[292]

Devolution in Wales has so far seen six distinct phases: (1) the Government of Wales Act 1998; (2) the Government of Wales Act 2006; (3) the 2011 Referendum; (4) the Silk Commission; (5) the Wales Act 2014; (6) the Wales Act 2017.[293]

The Government of Wales Act 1998

The Government of Wales Act 1998 created the National Assembly for Wales. The National Assembly had no primary legislative powers. Instead it was given executive powers that allowed it to make secondary legislation in eighteen areas. These areas were broadly based on the administrative powers of the Welsh Office. Powers were transferred to the National Assembly through Transfer of Functions Orders. Between 1999 and 2006, if it wanted primary legislation to be passed in relation to Wales, the National Assembly was dependent on the UK Parliament.

The Government of Wales Act 2006[294]

The Government of Wales Act 2006 formally separated the National Assembly for Wales and the Welsh Assembly Government into legislature and an executive. (The Wales Act 2014 s (1) renamed the Welsh Assembly Government, the 'Welsh Government'.)

The Act also conferred on the National Assembly restricted primary law-making powers. This gave the National Assembly powers to make Assembly Measures on any 'Matter' within the twenty devolved 'Fields' in Schedule 5 of the 1998 Act – which became Schedule 7

[290] See, for instance, *Salvesen v Riddell* [2013] UKSC 236; *Christian Institute v Lord Advocate* [2016] UKSC 59.

[291] See for instance, *The UK Withdrawal from the European Union (Legal Continuity) Scotland Bill – A Reference by the Attorney General and the Advocate General for Scotland (Scotland)* [2018] UKSC 64; *References re the United Nations Rights of the Child (Incorporation) (Scotland) Bill and the European Charter of Local Self-Government (Incorporation) (Scotland) Bill* [2021] UKSC 42; *Draft Independence Referendum Bill Reference* [2022] UKSC 31.

[292] Richard Rawlings, 'The Welsh Way/ Y Ffordd Gymreig' in J Jowell and C O'Cinneide (eds), *The Changing Constitution* 9th edn (Oxford University Press, 2019) 296–322, 296.

[293] See generally D Torrance, *A Process Not an Event: Devolution in Wales 1998–2018* (2018), 46pp, accessible in House of Commons Library, *Twenty Years of Devolution in Wales 1998–2018.*

[294] The 2006 Act was the result of the *Report of the Commission on the Powers and Electoral Arrangements of the National Assembly for Wales* (the 'Richard Commission') 31 March 2004. For commentary see R Rawlings, 'Hastening slowly: the next phase of Welsh devolution' *Public Law*, 2005, 824; TH Jones and JM Williams, 'The legislative future of Wales' *Modern Law Review*, 2005, 642; A Trench, 'The Government of Wales Act 2006: the next steps on devolution for Wales' *Public Law*, 2006, 687. On the proper attitude of the courts to the interpretation of devolution legislation see Lady Justice Arden, 'What is the safeguard for Welsh devolution? *Public Law*, 2014, 189.

of the 2006 Act. Before a Matter could be legislated on, it had to be specifically listed within the Field in Schedule 7 either through provisions in an Act of the UK Parliament or through a complicated procedure known as a 'Legislative Competence Order', requiring the consent of both House of Parliament and of the Secretary of State for Wales. (This was in marked contrast to the devolution system in Scotland where the legislature from the start was given the power to legislate on any topic unless it was 'reserved' to the UK government. It took another decade before the Wales Act 2017 adopted that approach – see below.) The 2006 Act also contained provisions for a process leading to a referendum on the introduction of primary legislative powers in all devolved areas.

The 2011 Referendum

The referendum was held on 3 March 2011. Voters were asked whether the National Assembly should have full law-making powers in the twenty subject areas where it had jurisdiction. A clear majority (63 per cent) voted in favour.

The National Assembly would have power to legislate over the twenty 'Subjects' listed in Schedule 7 of the Government of Wales Act 2006. These Subjects were the same as the Fields listed under Schedule 5 of the 1998 Act. There would no longer be a need to request devolution of specific Matters within a Field. Instead, if a Subject was listed under Schedule 7, the National Assembly had competence to legislate on any issue relating to that Subject as long as it was not listed as an Exception under the Act.

There were a number of areas where the National Assembly could not legislate. Any area that was not listed as a devolved power under Schedule 7 of the Government of Wales Act 2006 was outside the legislative competence of the National Assembly. The main areas that were non-devolved were foreign affairs, defence, policing, immigration and justice, macro-economic policy and the tax and welfare system.

The June 2012 issue of the *Statute Law Review* was a special issue devoted to Welsh devolution at that stage.

The Silk Commission

In October 2011, the Welsh Government established the Commission on Devolution in Wales, chaired by Sir Paul Silk, to review the financial and constitutional arrangements in Wales. The Commission published its first report on the financial arrangements in November 2012.

The Wales Act 2014

The Wales Act 2014 gave the National Assembly and the Welsh Government new powers over taxation and borrowing, including limited power to vary income tax by plus or minus ten per cent. The provisions of the Act were largely based on the recommendations of the Silk Commission's first report.

Recommendations of the Silk Commission's Second Report

The Silk Commission's second report, published in March 2014, recommended, inter alia, that devolution of responsibility to Wales should be extended to several new areas including policing and youth justice, but, more importantly, that the basic system should be fundamentally changed. Devolution in Wales, like that in Scotland and Northern Ireland, should be based on a 'reserved' powers model rather than the existing 'conferred' powers model. Instead of specific powers being referred to Wales with all other powers left to the UK Parliament, all powers to legislate in respect of Wales should be transferred, save for specific powers that would be reserved for the UK Parliament. The reserved topics would be: the constitution, macroeconomic policy, foreign affairs, immigration and defence.

The Wales Act 2017

The Wales Act 2017 introduced the reserved powers system, as recommended by the Silk Commission's second report, subject to a requirement for a Justice Impact Assessment to accompany draft bills. It repealed Schedule 7 of the 2006 Act, which was replaced by new Schedules 7A and 7B of the 2006 Act.

Post-2017

In December 2017, the Welsh Government established a Commission on Justice, chaired by former Lord Chief Justice, Lord Thomas of Cwmgiedd. The Commission's report, published in October 2019, recommended unanimously that justice powers should be wholly devolved to allow the development of Welsh policy on criminal justice, family justice, youth justice and civil and administrative justice. The Commission recommended that Wales should develop a court system entirely separate from England. The Commission considered that the power to legislate on policing, offender management and rehabilitation should follow. (The Silk Commission's second report had recommended that civil and criminal law should be reserved subjects though youth justice should be devolved.) The recommendations of the Thomas Commission have not (yet at least) been implemented.

The Welsh Government's Critique of the Devolution Arrangements

In October 2019, the Welsh Government published *Reforming our Union: Shared Governance in the UK*. Almost two years later, in June 2021, it published *Reforming our Union: Shared Governance in the UK2021*, a revised second edition of the Welsh Government's views on the reforms needed to put the Union on a sustainable footing for the future. Devolution, it said, 'requires consistent, constructive co-operation and collaboration between the governments of the UK, if we are to deliver the best possible outcomes for citizens, and to preserve and strengthen the Union.' It continued: 'Regrettably, this has not been our experience since we published the original "Reforming our Union' in 2019'.

The Government's 2021 second edition offered a series of Propositions. Proposition 1 was that devolution 'must be based on the recognition of popular sovereignty in each part of the UK; Parliamentary sovereignty as traditionally understood no longer provides a sound foundation for this evolving constitution.'

> The powers of the devolved institutions should be founded on a coherent set of responsibilities allocated in accordance with the subsidiarity principle … Central authorities' functions should be subsidiary, being only those which cannot be discharged satisfactorily at local level; the starting assumption should be that responsibilities will be devolved.

Welsh devolution, it said, was based on 'an inappropriately lengthy set of matters reserved to Westminster'.

> In addition, even where matters are not reserved to Westminster, the requirement for UK Ministers' consent to enact certain provisions (within policy areas universally understood to be devolved … is a restriction unique to the Welsh settlement.[295]

It described this 'an opaque and undemocratic clog on the Senedd's powers'.

As to legislation by Westminster on devolved subjects, the Welsh Government saw need for a radical new dispensation:

> In the original *Reforming our Union*, we identified a simple – if radical – solution to this issue. We suggested that, as an element in a new constitutional settlement, the principle should be established

[295] [The report cites s 108A and Sch 7B of the Government of Wales Act 2006. (ed)]

> that the UK Parliament should not be able to legislate on devolved matters, or seek by Parliamentary legislation to modify the competences of the devolved institutions, without the consent of the relevant devolved legislature. In other words, the "not normally" [in the Sewel Convention] qualification, with all its potential for creating uncertainty, misunderstanding and distrust between the UK Parliament and the devolved institutions, would be removed, and a simpler and clearer relationship established between the institutions. The actions taken by the UK government in the time which has elapsed since publication of the original *Reforming our Union* – in particular the United Kingdom Internal Market Act 2020, which has undermined trust in the UK government's commitment to the Sewel convention, as enshrined in the Government of Wales Act 2006 – only add weight to the arguments for this approach. Unless the UK government changes its approach, and demonstrates that it fully respects the Sewel convention, it will become inevitable that a radical safeguard of this sort is the only way to re-establish the integrity of the devolution settlement. This would be a major reform with far-reaching implications, but it will become essential if the UK government persists with the approach it has taken to the Sewel convention since 2019.

It remains to be seen whether what Richard Rawlings described as Wales' 'extraordinry constitutional journey since the advent of democratic devolution in 1998' will realise the hopes expressed by the Welsh government. No UK government has yet shown any inclination to give up the power to legislate for all parts of the United Kingdom.

2.16.3. Northern Ireland

Ireland became divided as a result of the Government of Ireland Act 1920. Southern Ireland, consisting of 26 counties, had its own Parliament and government. Northern Ireland had a bi-cameral legislature (usually referred to as 'Stormont'), with legislative powers over what were called the transferred matters. Section 4(1) of the 1920 Act transferred to the Northern Ireland Parliament power to make laws 'for the peace, order and good government' of the province. The powers so transferred were not described; they were residual. But certain matters were excepted by s 4(1)–(14) for the exclusive competence of Westminster. They included not only the making of peace or war, the armed forces and relations with foreign nations, but submarine cables lighthouses and beacons, coinage and intellectual property. Elections were held under a system of proportional representation.

As a result of the serious civil unrest (known as'The Troubles') that developed in the late 1960s, Stormont was suspended in 1972[296] and direct rule from Westminster was re-introduced. Under the Northern Ireland Constitution Act 1973 there was a Northern Ireland 'Assembly' with limited powers. Most Northern Ireland legislation was proposed by the newly created Secretary of State for Northern Ireland in the form of Orders-in Council passed – after very limited debate – by the Westminster Parliament. There was also delegated legislation called Statutory Rules.

In 1994, the main republican and loyalist paramilitaries declared a ceasefire and, despite several subsequent major breaches, four years later, in April 1998, political negotiations culminated in the Belfast Agreement/ Good Friday Agreement. The Unionists won recognition of the guarantee that the status of Northern Ireland could only be changed with the consent of the majority living in the province. The nationalists won the right to share in government, including joint head of the Executive and several Ministerial posts.

[296] By the Northern Ireland (Temporary Provisions) Act 1972.

In September 1998 a new Northern Ireland Assembly was elected and on 30 November 1998, the Northern Ireland Act transferred power back to Stormont.[297] That began the difficult business of power-sharing.

The Assembly has authority to legislate in all fields of competence, known as 'transferred matters'. These are not explicitly given in the Northern Ireland Act 1998. Rather they include any competence not explicitly retained by the Parliament at Westminster. Powers reserved by Westminster are divided into 'excepted matters', which are to be retained indefinitely and 'reserved matters', which may be transferred to the competence of the Northern Ireland Assembly at a future date. Excepted matters are outlined in Schedule 2 of the Northern Ireland Act 1998.[298] Reserved matters are outlined in Schedule 3.[299]

One of the most difficult issues was devolution of policing. It required the disbandment of the Royal Ulster Constabulary (RUC) and its replacement by a new Northern Ireland Police Service (PSNI). The proportion of police officers coming from the Catholic community was to be increased from 20 to over 40 per cent.[300] A Code of Ethics aligned with the European Convention on Human Rights was introduced. The Office of the Police Ombudsman for Northern Ireland was created to handle complaints against the police. The Hillsborough Castle Agreement in February 2010 set the seal on intra-party talks and devolution took place two months later.

In the quarter of a century since 1998, there have been periods of political tension so great that the Assembly was suspended and Direct Rule from Westminster was re-introduced.[301] One such period lasted from 2002 to 2007.[302] For three years following the collapse of the devolved institutions in 2017, there was neither direct nor indirect rule in Northern Ireland. Devolved government broke down again in 2022 after the Assembly election in which, for the first time, Sinn Féin won the most seats. It was restored in February 2024. In the July 2024 UK General Election, Sinn Féin, also for the first time, won more seats than the Democratic Union Party (DUP).

See Brice Dickson, 'Devolution in Northern Ireland' in J Jowell and C O'Cinneide (eds), *The Changing Constitution*, 9th edn (Oxford University Press, 2019) 239–69 on which this section has drawn heavily.

Common Frameworks and the Internal Markets Act 2020

Common Frameworks

Leaving the EU meant the repatriation of many functions and powers. Insofar as those functions and powers were within devolved competence, how would they transfer as between

[297] See for instance, B Hadfield, 'The Belfast Agreement, Sovereignty and the State of the Union' *Public Law*, 1999, 599; J McGarry and B O'Leary, *The Northern Ireland Conflict: Consociational Engagement* (Oxford University Press, 2004).

[298] The Crown; Parliament; International relations; Defence; Immigration and Nationality; Taxation; National Insurance; Elections; Currency; National security; Nuclear Energy; Outer Space.

[299] Navigation (including merchant shipping); Civil Aviation; the foreshore, sea bed and subsoil and their natural resources; Postal Services; Import and Export Controls, External Trade; National Minimum Wage; Financial Services; Financial Markets; Intellectual Property; Units of Measurement; Telecommunications, Broadcasting, Internet Services; The National Lottery; Xenotransplantation; Surrogacy; Human Fertilisation and Embryology; Human Genetics; Consumer Safety in relation to goods.

[300] The proportion of Catholics in Northern Ireland was 43 per cent. The issue proved problematic. Initially, there was a ten-year affirmative action programme, but when that came to an end, the proportion of police officers from the Catholic community had only increased to 30 per cent.

[301] On Direct Rule see the House of Commons Library Briefing Paper *Northern Ireland: Direct Rule*, March 2022.

[302] The two largest parties following the election, the Democratic Unionist Party (DUP) and Sinn Féin, agreed to enter power-sharing government together, and an administration was established on 10 May 2007 with Ian Paisley as First Minister and Martin McGuinness as Deputy First Minister.

the devolved authorities and the UK Government. The Common Frameworks system was created to develop a consensual intergovernmental approach. There are some 30 Common Frameworks, involving many government departments. Their purpose is to work towards policy coordination, common regulatory standards, common goals and the reduction of policy divergence.

The European Union (Withdrawal) Act 2018, Sch 3, para 4, required the government to report to Parliament every three months on actions taken 'towards implementing any arrangements which are to replace any relevant powers or retained EU law restrictions'. This reporting provision was repealed in March 2022. The last three-monthly report was published that month by the Department for Levelling Up, Housing and Communities:

> Since 2017, the UK government, Scottish Government, Welsh Government and the Northern Ireland Executive have been working together to develop agreements covering a range of policy areas where powers which have returned from the European Union intersect with devolved competence.
>
> The development of UK Common Frameworks is guided by principles agreed at the Joint Ministerial Committee (EU Negotiations) (JMC(EN)) in October 2017 between the UK Government, Scottish Government and Welsh Government, and later, on 15 June 2020, endorsed by the Executive Committee of the Northern Ireland Executive.
>
> **Principles for Common Frameworks**
>
> 1.3. EU laws created common UK-wide approaches even where those policy areas were otherwise within devolved competence. All four governments across the UK have agreed that common approaches will continue to be required in some areas now the UK has left the EU and exited the Transition Period.
>
> 1. Common Frameworks will be established where they are necessary in order to:
>   - enable the functioning of the UK internal market, while acknowledging policy divergence
>   - ensure compliance with international obligations
>   - ensure the UK can negotiate, enter into and implement new trade agreements and international treaties
>   - enable the management of common resources
>   - administer and provide access to justice in cases with a cross-border element
>   - safeguard the security of the UK
> 2. Frameworks will respect the devolution settlements and the democratic accountability of the devolved legislatures, and will therefore:
>   - be based on established conventions and practices, including that the competence of the devolved institutions will not normally be adjusted without their consent;
>   - maintain, as a minimum, equivalent flexibility for tailoring policies to the specific needs of each territory, as is afforded by current EU rules;
>   - lead to a significant increase in decision-making powers for the devolved governments.

The House of Lords Scrutiny Committee

In September 2020, the House of Lords established a Common Frameworks Scrutiny Committee. The Committee was terminated at the end of 2023.[303] It published two

[303] The Committee's website contains a five-page summary letter from Baroness Andrews, Chair, to Michael Gove, the Minister, about the Committee's work, successes and failures.

reports: 'Building a Cooperative Union'[304] in 2021 and 'An Unfulfilled Opportunity?'[305] in 2022. The first report had been optimistic; the second was less so:

> Our first report, published in March 2021, found that common frameworks have unique potential to strengthen the Union and are innovative mechanisms for developing UK-wide policy by collaboration and consensus. Having scrutinised a further 17 frameworks and taken further evidence, we strongly reiterate that conclusion. The success of common frameworks depends on effective cooperation and consensus between the four administrations. However, we are seriously concerned that common frameworks are at risk of becoming a missed opportunity.

The first of several issues identified was Conservative Government legislation:

> Firstly, post-Brexit legislation, including the UK Internal Market Act 2020 and the Subsidy Control Act 2022, has damaged relations between the four administrations. It has also challenged the consensus approach taken in common frameworks.[306]

The Internal Market Act 2020 – 'Undoing Devolution by the Back Door?'

The primary purpose of the Internal Market Act 2020 according to the then Government was to 'guarantee the continued seamless functioning of the UK Internal Market',[307] filling a regulatory gap once the EU ceased to fulfil that function post- Brexit. The Act (UKIMA) introduced two market access principles – mutual recognition and non-discrimination – designed to ensure the flow of goods and services throughout the United Kingdom (with special features for Northern Ireland). The problem was the impact this would have on the devolution project.

'Undoing Devolution by the Back Door: The Implications of the United Kingdom Internal Market Act 2020' was the title of a conference held at Swansea University in July 2020. The conference led to a series of papers published in a special issue of the *Northern Ireland Legal Quarterly* (2024)(1). In the first article in that issue,[308] Thomas Horsley of the University of Liverpool and Jo Hunt of Cardiff University point to the overlap between the role of the legislation and the role played by Common Frameworks:

> As negative harmonisation instruments, the UKIMA's market access principles occupy the same space as the Common Frameworks. Whereas the Frameworks seek to manage diversity by reaching agreement on the coordination of regulatory policies in specific substantive areas, the UKIMA addresses regulatory diversity by scrutinising measures that interfere with the free movement of goods and services within the UK internal market …
>
> In contrast to the Common Frameworks, the market access principles actually prescribe substantive limits on the space for policy divergence in relation to intra-UK trade. Their effect is to impose a set of directly enforceable limits on the exercise of devolved competences.[309]

Scotland, Wales and Northern Ireland had each withheld legislative consent to the Act.

[304] Common Frameworks Scrutiny Committee, *Common frameworks: building a cooperative Union* (1st Report, Session 2019–21, HL Paper 259).

[305] Common Frameworks Scrutiny Committee, *Common Frameworks: an unfulfilled opportunity?* (1st Report, Session 2022–23, HL Paper 41).

[306] The above quotations from the Committee's second report are from the Summary, p 3.

[307] Department for Business, Energy and Industrial Strategy, *UK Internal Market UKIMA 2020* (White Paper CP 278, 2020) 10.

[308] T Horsley and J Hunt, 'Internal market governance by consensus rather than conflict? Common Frameworks and the potential for positive harmonisation', 75 *Northern Ireland Legal Quarterly*, 2024 (1), 7–44.

[309] Ibid at 27 and 29.

> The initial approach under the Frameworks remains the highwater mark in terms of joint agreement on the existence of a functional problem. Signing off the Frameworks programme, the UK and devolved governments recognised a common regulatory challenge arising as a result of the repatriation of competences post-Brexit. The subsequent enactment of the UKIMA disturbed that consensus, with the devolved governments expressly refuting the UK government's diagnosis that further intervention was required in the form of the market access principles to prevent the emergence of future obstacles to intra-UK trade.[310]

By contrast, the authors suggested, the UK Government appeared to favour regulation:

> The UK Government, on the other hand, appears more open, conceptually, to the idea of the UK internal market as a shared regulatory space requiring the introduction of additional directly enforceable legal principles to manage future policy divergence. However, its diagnosis of the regulatory problem (prospective regulatory divergence as an obstacle to intra-UK trade) is not matched by a developed understanding of how shared rule should operate in practice. Its initial attempt through the Common Frameworks represents the clearest attempt to bring together the UK and devolved governments to agree on future policy coordination. But that insight was short-lived. The subsequent approach of the Johnson Government through the UKIMA repudiated the very idea of shared rule by monopolising political authority from the centre.[311]

These principles, the authors suggest, 'are strongly deregulatory, articulating a vision of the UK internal market that prioritises considerations of economic efficiency over the protection of other non-economic values.'[312] Domestic regulatory interactions, they thought, were 'transitioning to a new operational understanding of devolved competences that points to increasing polarisation'.[313]

At the time of writing (late 2024) it remained to be seen how the Labour government, elected in June, might approach the apparent conflict of philosophy behind the Common Frameworks and UKIMA.

See further:

M Dougan, J Hunt, N McEwen and A McHarg, 'Sleeping with an elephant: devolution and the United Kingdom Internal Market Act 2020' 138 *Law Quarterly Review*, 2022, 650–76; J Zglinski, 'The UK internal market: a global outlier?' 82 *Cambridge Law Journal*, 2023 (3), 530–62; C McCorkindale, 'UKIMA as red flag symptom of constitutional ill-health: devolved autonomy and legislative consent' 75 *Northern Ireland Legal Quarterly* 2024 (1), 45–76; N Kilford, 'The market access principle and the subordination of devolved competence' 75 *Northern Ireland Legal Quarterly* 2024 (1), 77–105; and GP Evans, T Hannant, S Hoffman, V Jenkins and K Morrow, 'Beyond UKIMA: challenges for devolved policy-making in the post-Brexit era' 75 *Northern Ireland Legal Quarterly* 2024 (1), 168–84.

[310] Ibid at 34–35.
[311] Ibid at 35–36.
[312] Ibid 36.
[313] Ibid 39.

2.17. Delegated Legislation[314]

Each year several thousand sets of rules and regulations are made by ministers or the Crown in Council[315] or other central rule-making authorities – by comparison with 30 to 60 Acts of Parliament that seems to be the current volume. This form of legislation is under the authority of powers delegated by Parliament. The reason is usually to avoid having too much detail in the main Act and thereby waste the time of parliamentarians in minutiae. In recent years this reasoning has been significantly undermined by the use of delegated legislation when legislation would be more appropriate.

As the Lords Constitution Committee said in a report on delegated legislation: 'Delegated powers are a necessary part of the legislative process. When used appropriately, they allow Parliament to focus on the important policy frameworks and decisions in primary legislation, and to leave the detail of implementation to secondary legislation. They provide the Government with the flexibility to deliver its policy, and adjust its operation as circumstances change, through a less onerous scrutiny process.'[316] The Committee quoted what the then Leader of the House of Commons said were the reasons for delegated legislation:

> In written evidence, the Rt Hon David Lidington MP, then Leader of the House of Commons, set out the various circumstances in which the Government might think it appropriate to use delegated legislation:
>
> – to fill in a level of detail not thought appropriate for primary legislation, possibly as it needs to be updated on a frequent basis;
> – to enable consultation to take place on the detailed implementation of a policy, this may include technical details or levels of fees;
> – to deal with things which it is anticipated may change in future (e.g. uprating for inflation);
> – to provide an acceptable level of flexibility to accommodate small policy changes (e.g. when operating in a novel area, where there may be a desire to retain flexibility to tweak the policy in the light of practical experience);
> – to deal with matters, concerning the technical implementation of a policy, which cannot be known at the point when the primary legislation is being passed;
> – to accommodate the fact that the detailed policy has to work differently for different groups of people, different areas etc.[317]

But there has been a growing concern that delegated powers were being used to make policy. The Lords Delegated Powers and Regulatory Reform Committee said that 'time and again successive governments have attempted to relegate too many important policies to delegated

[314] For the different forms of delegated legislation see S Pywell and T West, *Delegated Legislation: What types are there and how are they made?*, Hansard Society, 2023. See also, S Pywell, 'Something old, something new: busting some myths about Statutory Instruments and Brexit' *Public Law*, 2019, 102–20.

[315] For the procedure used for Orders in Council, see Cyril ES Horsford, 'The Order in Council' *Solicitors' Journal*, 10 April 1987, 462.

[316] Lords Constitution Committee *The Legislative Process: The Delegation of Powers*, 16th Report, 2017–19, November 2018, HL 225, p 2.

[317] Ibid, para.9.

legislation, leaving too little on the face of the bill'.[318] Delegations that provided significant flexibility to the government raised the risk of policy not just being implemented but being amended by secondary legislation. The Secondary Legislation Scrutiny Committee, which scrutinises secondary legislation in the House of Lords, said that while the majority of instruments they scrutinised conformed to the expectation of 'making mundane or technical changes', some 'make major and controversial changes to policy'.[319]

Some Bills, dubbed 'skeleton bills', leave all the policy to be settled by way of delegated legislation. The Lords Constitution Committee has said 'Skeleton bills inhibit parliamentary scrutiny and we find it difficult to envisage any circumstances in which their use is acceptable'.[320]

The Government Response to the Committee's Report (30 January 2019, para.4) said it always explained the reasons for delegated powers in its memorandum to the Delegated Powers and Regulatory Reform Committee and gave the Committee's recommendations serious consideration and provided written responses to each of them, and that this frequently led to government amendments being tabled. In regard to 'skeleton bills' it said (para.17): 'The Government believes that there have been and will continue to be sound reasons for the use of such bills in a limited number of cases.'[321]

The issue festers. During the Covid pandemic, it got significantly worse. In 2021 there were no less than six critical reports: Hansard Society, 'House of Commons Marginalisation under Covid' (21 April 2021); House of Lords, Delegated Powers and Regulatory Reform Committee, 'Democracy Denied? The urgent need to rebalance power between Parliament and the Executive' (24 November 2021);[322] and House of Lords, Secondary Legislation Scrutiny Committee, 'Government by Diktat: A Call to Return Power to Parliament' (also 24 November 2021)[323] and three reports by the Lords Constitution Committee, as to which see 2.19.2 below.

The third edition of *Parliament and the Law* (A Horne, L Thompson and B Yong (eds)) (Hart, 2022) has two relevant chapters: 'Parliament and Legislation: Scrutiny Lessons from Brexit and Covid-19' by Louise Thompson (113–31) and 'Parliament and Brexit: Scrutiny under Pressure' by Alexander Horne and Jack Chard (239–67).

As stated previously, for a vivid account of pandemic related law-making, see also Adam Wagner, *Emergency State How we Lost our Freedoms in the Pandemic and Why It Matters* (Bodley Head, 2022).

In its 2023 report on the Retained EU Law (Revocation and Reform) Bill, the House of Lords Secondary Legislation Scrutiny Committee said it was reporting, unusually, on a piece of *primary* legislation 'because we believe that the Bill is an extreme example of a skeleton bill and, as such, could lead to a significant shift of power not to Parliament but

[318] Ibid, para.18–citing Delegated Powers and Regulatory Reform Committee, *Special Report: Response to the Strathclyde Review* (25th Report 2015–16, HL 119).
[319] Ibid, para.21.
[320] Ibid, para.58.
[321] The Cabinet Office's *Guide to Legislation* (para.5.9) states: 'If it is politically important, a bill may be given a slot in the programme before many of the details have been fully worked out.' But it goes on to state that the Parliamentary Business and Legislation (PBL) Committee should grant a slot 'only if it is confident that the remaining details could be worked out and the bill prepared in good time for introduction, including sufficient time for public consultation where appropriate'.
[322] 12th Report Session 2021–2022, HL 106.
[323] 20th Report Session 2021–2022, HL 105.

to ministers'. Its report, it said, 'identifies the ways in which we believe the Bill runs directly counter to the principles of parliamentary democracy and represents a significant backward step in the narrative highlighted in our report 'Government by Diktat: A call to return power to Parliament' and in the DPRRC's report 'Democracy Denied? The urgent need to rebalance power between Parliament and the Executive.'[324]

It will be of interest to see whether the new Labour Government conducts itself any better. The writer is not optimistic.

2.17.1. Forms of Statutory Instrument (SIs)

The different forms of statutory instrument were described by Stephanie Pywell, Professor of Law at the Open University School of Law.[325] She identified two distinct types – statutory instruments (SIs), of which there were five forms, and byelaws.

> SIs were created by the Statutory Instruments Act 1946. Section 1(1) is entitled 'Definition of "Statutory Instruments"' and provides that there are two ways in which delegated legislation ('orders, rules, regulations or other subordinate legislation') may be made. If the law-making power is conferred on the Crown, it is exercisable by Order in Council; if it is conferred on a Minister, it is exercisable by SI. In either case, the resulting document 'shall be known as a "statutory instrument"'. By definition, therefore, Orders in Council are a form of SI, rather than a separate type of delegated legislation.
>
> The standard reference document used in the drafting of SIs is Statutory Instrument Practice: A Manual for Those Concerned with the Preparation of Statutory Instruments and the Parliamentary Procedures Relating to Them (SIP).[326] SIP identifies one further UK-wide form of SI, an Order of Council, so five distinct forms of SI can be identified: Orders in Council; Orders of Council; Orders; Rules; Regulations.
>
> *Orders in Council*
>
> Orders in Council, which are made by the Queen and Privy Council, can take the form of primary legislation, but most are made as SIs, and should be used when 'an ordinary statutory instrument made by a minister would be inappropriate, as in … an Order which transfers ministerial functions … or where the Order is in effect a constitutional document …' (SIP, paragraph 1.5.2) …
>
> *Orders of Council*
>
> Orders of Council, by contrast, are made by 'the Lords of Her Majesty's Most Honourable Privy Council', and usually involve the regulation of professions or professional bodies … Such SIs amount to little more than a rubber-stamping of detailed rules drafted by the governing bodies of professions; it would clearly be inappropriate to trouble the monarch with such minutiae.
>
> *Orders*
>
> Orders are usually made by government ministers, and serve a specific, closely defined purpose. They should, according to the recommendations of the Donoughmore Report,[327] be used for executive powers and judicial and quasi-judicial decisions …

[324] HL, Secondary Legislation Scrutiny Committee, 'Losing Control?: The Implications for Parliament of the Retained EU Law (Revocation and Reform) Bill', 28th Report of Session 2022–23, 2 February 2023, p.2.

[325] S Pywell, 'Untangling the Law' *New Law Journal* 22 March 2013, 321, later expanded into her 2019 *Public Law* article referenced in fn 314 above.

[326] Office of Public Sector Information, 4th edn, November 2006.

[327] *Report of the Committee on Ministers' Powers*, Cmnd 4060, HMSO, 1932.

Four specific types of order – Commencement Orders, Legislative Reform Orders, Remedial Orders and Public Bodies Orders – are worthy of particular mention:

> *Commencement Orders* (COs) bring into effect one or more sections of an Act of Parliament …
>
> *Legislative Reform Orders* (LROs), created under the Legislative and Regulatory Reform Act 2006 (LRRA 2006), enable Ministers to effect changes to primary legislation … The circumstances in which such orders may be made are specified in the enabling Acts. Section 1 LRRA 2006, for example, permits an LRO to be made in order to reduce a 'legislative burden', which is defined as including the rather nebulous concept of 'an administrative inconvenience'. A Minister proposing an LRO must demonstrate that the proposed legislation: is needed; is proportionate; represents a fair balance of interests; does not remove any necessary protection; does not unreasonably interfere with rights and freedoms; and has no constitutional significance.
>
> Because of concerns that LROs potentially provide a means via which the Government can amend primary legislation without the formal approval of Parliament, LROs may – at the behest of either House of Parliament or of a designated parliamentary committee – be subject to greater-than-usual parliamentary scrutiny via the 'super-affirmative procedure'[328] …
>
> *Remedial Orders* (ROs) are used to correct shortcomings in existing legislation. If a legislative provision is declared by a court to be incompatible with the European Convention on Human Rights, or if the European Court of Human Rights holds that an individual's Convention rights have been infringed, the Human Rights Act 1998, s 10 provides that a Minister may make an RO. ROs can have retrospective effect, and must normally be laid before Parliament. Before they become law, the Joint Select Committee on Human Rights must report on them … [See further below, 2.19.3 (ed)]
>
> *Public Bodies Orders* (PBOs) are made using powers delegated by the Public Bodies Act 2011, which permit Ministers to abolish, merge or modify 285 public bodies as part of an exercise sometimes referred to as 'the bonfire of the quangos' …

Rules

Rules, according to the Donoughmore Report, should be used to make procedural laws: they set out how things should be done, rather than what should be done. The best-known set of rules is probably the Civil Procedure Rules 1998, which govern the running of the civil court system.

Regulations

Regulations are used to make substantive law – often amendments to existing primary or secondary legislation – and are frequently technical in nature …

Byelaws

Byelaws are made under the limited law-making powers conferred on local authorities and statutory bodies, and must be authorised by a Secretary of State. They deal with matters within the jurisdiction of the maker, and may reflect local concerns.

2.17.2. Procedures for Creating Statutory Instruments

There are four different kinds of procedure for creating SIs – affirmative procedure, super-affirmative procedure, negative procedure and 'other' procedure. The procedure that applies in the particular case is specified in the parent primary legislation.

Affirmative procedure[329] A minority of SIs require positive parliamentary approval. There are three different kinds. One requires that the SI be laid before Parliament in draft.[330] It

[328] As to which see p 119 below.

[329] See generally *Griffith and Ryle on Parliament* (n 12 above) paras 8-063–068.

[330] On 'laying' see AI Campbell, 'Statutory instruments. laying and legislation by reference' *Public Law*, 1987, 328.

can then only be made if approved by a resolution in the Commons, or sometimes in both Houses. A second type is when it is laid after it is made, but it cannot come into force until it has been approved. A third kind is when it is made and laid and comes into effect immediately but cannot remain in force after a specified period (28 days, a month, 42 days) unless approved within that time.[331]

For SIs requiring affirmative resolution the government must provide time for debate. During the Committee stage of the Courts and Legal Services Bill 1990, Lord Mackay, the Lord Chancellor, said that in future he would see that the affirmative resolution procedure would be used for all SIs giving effect to 'Henry VIII clauses' (as to which see pp 120–122 below).

In the Commons, debates on affirmative resolutions normally take place not in the Chamber but in Delegated Legislation Committees, assembled ad hoc for each SI. In the House of Lords, affirmative SIs are usually debated in Grand Committee (ie in a committee room rather than the main chamber), but occasionally on the floor of the House. It is exceedingly rare for a statutory instrument requiring affirmative approval not to receive it. In the more than sixty years between 1950 and 2017 only ten statutory instruments subject to the affirmative resolution procedure failed to get that approval.

Super-affirmative procedure A new heightened, 'super-affirmative' procedure was introduced by the Legislative and Regulatory Reform Act 2006. Prior to that Act there was no way a statutory instrument could be amended once it had been laid before Parliament. But if the instrument is laid in draft it can be subjected to comment and criticism which may then lead to amendment. The super-affirmative procedure is designed for especially significant SIs. Governments do not like the extra time involved and try to keep such instruments to the minimum. Under the 2006 Act the appropriate committee of either House has sixty days to make recommendations or resolutions regarding the draft order that has been laid by the minister. At the end of the sixty days the minister has to report to Parliament regarding the recommendations, resolutions or representations that have been made. The minister can choose to go ahead with the draft order without amendment or can lay a revised draft which is then subject to the normal affirmative procedure. If there is still dissatisfaction with the draft, the Act (s 18) provides that the appropriate scrutiny committee in either House can recommend that the order should not proceed. If that happens, the only way it can proceed is for the relevant House to reject that recommendation in the same parliamentary session.

Negative procedures This is the norm. There are two kinds of negative resolution procedure. One is where the SI is laid in draft and cannot be made if within forty days Parliament votes its disapproval. The other is when the SI is made and laid but it cannot remain in effect if within forty days Parliament votes its disapproval. (The Deregulation and Contracting Out Act 1994, s 4 provides for an additional sixty days for parliamentary scrutiny before a final order is laid for formal debate and approval. The Human Rights Act 1998 provides for 120 days.) For SIs that come into force unless negatived, the Opposition registers that it has doubts by 'praying' against it.[332] The government can then give time for the issue to be considered but hardly ever does so, which means that there will only be a debate if the Opposition uses its own allocation of time ('Supply Dates') for a debate. The SI cannot be

[331] See for instance the European Union (Withdrawal) Act 2018, Sch.7, para.5. Para.5 provides that the requirement to lay the instrument does not apply if the Minister 'is of the opinion that by reason of urgency, it is necessary to make the regulation without meeting the requirement'!.

[332] Commenting on the small amount of time given by the House of Lords to considering negative instruments, the Clerk to the House of Lords Delegated Powers and Deregulation Committee, said: 'The late 20th century House of Lords spent more time praying to the Almighty than it did praying against negative instruments' (Tudor, 'Secondary legislation' (n 105 p 63 above) 151).

amended in the course of such debate. It can only be approved, annulled or withdrawn. Since the prospect of success in persuading the Government to withdraw the SI, let alone to defeat it in a vote, is remote, a debate is exceedingly rare.

Statutory instruments not requiring parliamentary approval Some SIs do not need to be laid before Parliament. Other SIs need to be laid but are not then made subject to any form of parliamentary approval. Section 4 of the Statutory Instruments Act 1946 provides that 'if it is essential', instruments which may be made[333] before being laid before Parliament, can come into effect before they are laid.[334] In such a case a notification must be sent to the Speakers of both Houses giving reasons.

An additional committee process for sifting drafts of statutory instruments was created by the European Union (Withdrawal) Act 2018, Sch 7 (Pt 1). Statutory instruments which was proposed to be subject to the negative procedure under the 2018 Act were examined by the European Statutory Instruments Committee (ESIC) in the Commons and the Secondary Legislation Scrutiny Committee (SLSC) in the Lords, either of which could recommend that the instrument be upgraded from the negative to the affirmative procedure. Such recommendations were not binding; but the Government was required to explain why the recommendation for an enhanced form of scrutiny was not being accepted. (Sch.7, Pt.1, para.3(7)) However, the value of this was somewhat reduced when the Government said that the explanation would be given in the Explanatory Memorandum that accompanies regulations – ie after the SI had become law![335]

In 2023–24, a total of 531instruments were laid before the House of Commons. Of these, 32 per cent were subject to the affirmative procedure, 65 per cent were subject to the negative procedure and 2 per cent were made and laid without any parliamentary procedure.[336]

Henry VIII clauses One type of delegated legislative power that attracts especial notice and concern is what are known as 'Henry VIII clauses' – which allow statutes to be amended or even repealed by statutory instrument. The Lords Constitution Committee 2018 report on delegated powers allowed that there were some circumstances where the granting of such powers was acceptable:[337]

[333] A statutory instrument is 'made' when signed by the Minister (or person with authority under the relevant Act). It means that the instrument is not a draft. An instrument is laid before Parliament either in draft form or after it has been made. There is a difference in the procedure used for SIs subject to affirmative resolution compared with that for negative resolution. In 2023–24, in regard to affirmative procedure, 169 were made and 11 were laid in draft, whereas in regard to negative procedure, 342 were made and 12 were laid in draft. (HC, Sessional Returns 2023–2024. HC(2024–2025) s 6A, p 65.) The affirmative resolution SIs come into force when signed by the minister after the parliamentary debate. The negative resolution SIs come into force on the date specified in the SI.

[334] See, for instance, the European Union (Withdrawal) Act 2018, Sch7, para 5. Para 5(2) (provides that the requirement to lay the instrument does not apply if the Minister 'is of the opinion that by reason of urgency, it is necessary to make the regulation without meeting the requirement'!.

[335] Letter from Chris Heaton-Harris MP, Parliamentary Under-Secretary of State for Exiting the EU, to Charles Walker MP, Chair of the House of Commons Procedure Committee, 16 August 2018.

[336] HC, Sessional Returns 2023–2024. HC(2024–2025) s 6A, p 65.

[337] Sebastian Walker, of the Law Faculty of Cambridge University, argues that Ministers should be given the power to alter primary legislation in order to make clear the effect of secondary legislation passed under the Act. This would not change the law, it would only make the law more accessible. Given the difficulty of discovering the law to be found in secondary legislation, this seems both useful and unobjectionable. (S Walker, 'Blurring the divide: clarifying the effect of secondary legislation' *Public Law* 2020, 116–27.).

> First Parliamentary Counsel, said that there was 'a range of situations where it might be entirely sensible to take a Henry VIII power where it is not sensible to come back and expect Parliament to spend time on the sorts of amendments that you might want to make.' She gave as an example a consequential amendment power at the back of a bill where some tidying up might be required, such as amending references across the statute book to a body whose name has been changed: 'So these are not substantive new policies but powers that are just needed to tidy up'.[338]

The Bar Council agreed that 'There will be cases in which it is convenient and appropriate to grant a number of tightly-circumscribed Henry VIII powers, focused on the aspects of a legal regime that may need to be amended in future'.[339] However, the Bingham Centre for the Rule of Law stated that 'Henry VIII clauses should be recognised as constitutionally anomalous'; they were acceptable 'only where there is an exceptional justification and no other realistic way of ensuring effective governance.'[340] The Delegated Powers and Regulatory Reform Committee said 'Henry VIII powers should not be inserted in Bills as a matter of routine, and any that are included should be fully explained and justified.'[341]

The Constitution Committee said:

> Henry VIII clauses are a departure from constitutional principle. Departures from constitutional principle should be contemplated only where a full and clear explanation and justification is provided. Such justification should set out the specific purpose that the Henry VIII power is designed to serve and how the power will be used. Widely drawn delegations of legislative authority cannot be justified solely by the need for speed and flexibility.[342]

> An egregious example of a Henry VIII clause was in the Legislative and Regulatory Reform Bill introduced in January 2006 by the Blair Government.[343] Clause 1 provided that a minister could by order make provision for 'reforming legislation'. The measure was presented as simple streamlining of the Regulatory Reform Act 2001 by which the Government, to help industry, could reduce red tape. The Bill, dubbed the 'Abolition of Parliament bill', produced uproar. Six Cambridge law professors writing to *The Times* (16 February 2006) said that, as drafted, the Government by delegated legislation could curtail or abolish jury trial, allow the Prime Minister to sack judges, rewrite the law on nationality and 'reform' Magna Carta. The Government accepted that the Bill went too far and it was considerably amended to build in safeguards. But the resulting Act still gave Ministers extraordinary powers to amend or repeal legislation.

Henry VIII clauses and the European Union (Withdrawal) Act 2018 Extensive use of Henry VIII clauses was generated by the Brexit legislation following the 2016 referendum. Theresa May's European Union (Withdrawal) Act 2018 was designed to convert all EU law existing at the moment of exit into UK domestic law ('retained EU law') and equally to preserve laws made in the UK to implement EU obligations. (On EU law post- Brexit see pp 422–32 below.) It created temporary powers for Ministers to make secondary legislation to enable corrections to be made to the laws that would otherwise not operate appropriately once the UK had left the EU. Subsection (1) of s 8 began:

[338] Lords Constitution Committee, *The Legislative Process: The Delegation of Powers*, 16th Report, 2017–19, November 2018, HL 225, para 60.

[339] Ibid, para 61.

[340] Ibid, para 62.

[341] Ibid, para 63.

[342] Ibid, para 67.

[343] The Criminal Justice and Courts Bill 2014–15 had a provision giving the Lord Chancellor the power to make 'supplementary' provisions in regard to any provision in the Bill by subordinate legislation. This power would extend to 'amending, repealing or revoking primary legislation' (cl 92(1), (2)).

> A Minister of the Crown may by regulations make such provision as the Minister considers appropriate[344] to prevent or mitigate -
>
> (a) any failure of retained EU law to operate effectively, or
> (b) any other deficiency[345] in retained EU law,
>
> arising from the withdrawal of the United Kingdom from the EU.

Section 8(5) stated:

> Regulations under subsection (1) may make any provision that could be made by an Act of Parliament.

Section 8(7) placed limits on the regulation-making power. Regulations under ss (1) could not: (a) impose or increase taxation or fees, (b) make retrospective provisions, (c) create a relevant criminal offence, (d) establish a public authority, (e) be made to implement the Withdrawal Agreement, (f) amend, repeal or revoke the Human Rights Act 1998 or any subordinate legislation made under it or (g) amend or repeal devolution legislation.

Henry VIII powers can only be used 'to clarify or exemplify but not alter or change'. Statutory police powers to control 'serious' disruption therefore did not justify regulations giving police those powers to deal with 'more than minor' disruption. (*R (NCCL) v Secretary of State for the Home Department* (2025) 571.

2.17.3. Preparation of SIs

The drafting of statutory instruments is usually left to the lawyers and administrators in departments[346] – though in unusual cases of particular importance or difficulty Parliamentary Counsel will be brought in. The policy work on SIs is generally done by quite junior officials[347] under the general supervision of junior ministers.

The process of external consultation is usually fuller than is the case with primary legislation.[348] The need for secrecy is less, since the principles of the new law have already been laid down and the department is therefore less reluctant to take advice on matters of implementation. Sometimes regulations are published in draft for comment. Some Acts of Parliament make consultation on SIs mandatory.

[344] The House of Lords Constitution Committee (9th Report, 2017–19, para 167) had said of this wording: 'The power of ministers to do what they consider "appropriate" is subjective and inappropriately wide. We recommend that the Bill be amended, in line with the Sanctions and Anti-Money Laundering Bill, to provide that, while the power remains available when ministers consider it "appropriate", they must demonstrate that there are "good reasons" for its use and can show that the use of the power is a "reasonable course of action". This will require explanations to be given for the use of the power which can be scrutinised by Parliament. It will also provide a meaningful benchmark against which use of the power may be tested judicially.' (ed).

[345] The word 'deficiency' was defined in ss (2)(a) to (g). The House of Lords Constitution Committee said: 'We are concerned that applying a subjective test of "appropriateness" to a broad term like "deficiency" makes the regulation-making power in [s 8](1) potentially open-ended. However, requiring that ministers set out the "good reasons" to use the power and that it is a "reasonable course of action", ... would ameliorate the subjective nature of 'deficiencies".' The government did not accept the Committee's recommendation to require ministers to justify their decisions with reasons. (ed).

[346] See EC Page, *Governing by Numbers: Delegated Legislation and Everyday Policy-Making* (Hart Publishing, 2001) ch 6.

[347] Page, *Governing by Numbers*, ibid, 180 says that the policy work on the 46 SIs that he examined was mainly done by officials of the rank of HEO to Grade 7s. (For the categories of civil service grades see n 135 above.).

[348] See Page, *Governing by Numbers* (n 346 above) ch 7.

2.18. Rejecting Delegated Legislation

The Lords have the power to veto statutory instruments. In the 65 years between 1950 and 2015 there were only six such cases but the most recent led to strong government reaction. On 25 October 2015 the Lords voted by 289 to 272 to block changes set out in a statutory instrument[349] to cut £4.4 billion from tax credits. Three days later, the Prime Minister, David Cameron, in response to this setback, announced the appointment of Lord Strathclyde, as *The Times* reported, to find ways of ensuring that MPs have 'the decisive role'.

Lord Strathclyde's swiftly completed report[350] suggested three options for restricting the Lords' power over delegated legislation: (1) remove the Lords altogether from scrutiny of statutory instruments; (2) codify the existing convention that the power should be used very rarely; (3) legislate to give the Lords the right to send the statutory instrument back to the Commons – once only – for the Commons to think again. Lord Strathclyde said that he recommended the third option.

The report was criticised by the Commons Public Administration and Constitutional Affairs Committee,[351] by the Lords Constitution Committee[352] and by its Secondary Legislation Scrutiny Committee.[353] In December 2016 the Theresa May Government published its *Response to the Strathclyde Review and the Related Select Committee reports* (Cm 9363). This confirmed an announcement that had already been made by the Leader of the House that the government did not intend to act on any of Lord Strathclyde's three proposed options. But in his Foreword to the Response, the Leader of the House, Mr David Lidington, wrote:

> Whilst recognising the valuable role of the House of Lords in scrutinising SIs, the Government remains concerned that there is no mechanism for the elected chamber to overturn a decision by the unelected chamber on SIs. We do not believe that it is something that can remain unchanged if the House of Lords seeks to vote against SIs approved by the House of Commons when there is no mechanism for the will of the elected House to prevail. We must, therefore, keep the situation under review and remain prepared to act if the primacy of the Commons is further threatened.

The government was understandably apprehensive at the time that the Lords might create difficulties for the progress of Bills and statutory instruments required to implement the result of the June 2016 referendum on withdrawal from the EU.

The Lords Constitution Committee returned robustly to the issue in its 2018 report on delegated powers:[354]

> 110. If the Government uses delegated powers to propose secondary legislation which makes technical provision within the boundaries of the policy that has previously been agreed in primary

[349] The Tax Credits (Income Thresholds and Determination of Rates) Amendment Regulations 2015.
[350] Lord Strathclyde, *Secondary Legislation and the Primacy of the House of Commons*, December 2015, Cm 9177.
[351] 8th Report of Session 2015–16.
[352] 9th Report of Session 2015–16.
[353] 32nd Report of Session 2015–16.
[354] Lords Constitution Committee *The Legislative Process: The Delegation of Powers*, 16th Report, 2017–19, November 2018, HL 225.

legislation, Parliament is unlikely to wish to block statutory instruments. However, we are concerned, and this report has shown, that these boundaries are not always respected and that ministers may seek to use statutory instruments to give effect to significant policy decisions. Without a genuine risk of defeat, and no amendment possible, Parliament is doing little more than rubber-stamping the Government's secondary legislation. This is constitutionally unacceptable.

111. The Government already has a mechanism to remedy faults in statutory instruments which are identified by parliamentary scrutiny. SIs subject to the affirmative procedure are made only when signed by a minister after parliamentary debates have taken place; until they are signed, they can be withdrawn, revised and re-laid. SIs subject to the negative procedure come into force on the date specified on the instrument, but the Government already has the power to lay a second SI to revoke and replace the first.

112. However, for these processes to work, the Government must take account of the scrutiny of statutory instruments and respond promptly to remedy any deficiencies. Where it does not do so, in exceptional circumstances Parliament may use its existing powers to block such instruments. The Government should recognise that parliamentary defeat on a statutory instrument need not be considered momentous nor fatal. It does not prevent the Government subsequently tabling a revised SI having listened to and acted on parliamentarians' concerns.

113. If the Government's current approach to delegated legislation persists, or the situation deteriorates further, the established constitutional restraint shown by the House of Lords towards secondary legislation may not be sustained.

2.19. Scrutiny of Delegated Legislation

2.19.1. Parliamentary Committees

There are different parliamentary committees that are involved in scrutiny of delegated legislation:[355]

Joint Select Committee on Statutory Instruments[356]

Since 1973 there has been a Joint Select Committee on Statutory Instruments of both Houses to consider, inter alia, statutory instruments of a general character and those subject to the negative and affirmative resolution procedure. Its function is to review statutory instruments from a technical, as contrasted with a policy, point of view. To emphasise this, its chairman is a member of the Opposition rather than of the Government.

The function of the Committee is to determine whether the special attention of each House should be drawn to an instrument on any of nine grounds:

(i) that it imposes a tax or a charge;
(ii) that it is made under primary legislation which expressly excludes the instrument from challenge in the courts;
(iii) that it purports to have retrospective effect where the enabling Act does not expressly provide for such effect;

[355] For scrutiny of European Union instruments see 8.1.3 below.

[356] See further Page, *Governing by Numbers* (n 346 p 122 above) 158–68 and *Griffith and Ryle on Parliament* (n 12 p 39 above) paras 11-0071–074.

(iv) that there appears to have been unjustifiable delay in the publication of the instrument or in laying it;
(v) that the instrument has come into operation before being laid and there appears to have been unjustifiable delay in sending notification of this as required by the Statutory Instruments Act 1946, s 4(1);
(vi) that it appears doubtful whether the instrument is *intra vires* the enabling statute, or the instrument appears to make some unusual or unexpected use of the powers in the enabling legislation;
(vii) that for any special reason the form or purport of the instrument calls for elucidation;
(viii) that the drafting of the legislation appears to be defective; or
(ix) any other ground which does not impinge on the merits of the instrument or on the policy behind it.

In determining these matters the Committee has the assistance of Counsel to the Speaker and Counsel to the Lord Chairman of Committees and takes written and oral evidence from the departments responsible for making the regulations. If the Committee raises a question, the department has 14 days to reply (the second stage). In the third stage, the SI comes before the Committee again with the department's reply.

How often does the Committee raise issues? Typically one tenth or less are reported by the Committee as deserving attention, on one or another ground – defective drafting, doubtful vires, unusual use of powers, failure to use the proper procedure etc.[357] That only around 10 per cent of SIs considered by the Committee are the subject of a report does not however adequately reflect the Committee's influence. As Professor Page put it in his empirical study, 'The likely reaction of the Committee is in the minds of those who draft any SI … The impact of the Committee is pervasive despite the fact that it is widely appreciated that the Committee is overworked and some items to which it may want to raise objections are likely to go through unnoticed'.[358]

As has been seen, the Committee does not consider the merits of statutory instruments or of the policies behind them. That is done, if at all, either on the floor of the House or in the case of the House of Commons, in its Standing Select Committee on Statutory Instruments. These procedures are also defective. The debates on the floor of the House usually take place late at night and are poorly attended. Debates in standing Committees are for up to one and a half hours and cannot result in any amendment.[359]

The MPs who are members of the Joint Committee on Statutory Instruments also serve on the House of Commons Committee on Statutory Instruments which performs the same functions as the Joint Committee in relation to statutory instruments that are only laid before the Commons.

The House of Lords Delegated Powers and Regulatory Reform Committee

In 1992, the government established in the House of Lords a Delegated Powers Scrutiny Committee – following a recommendation of the Jellicoe Committee (the Select Committee of the House of Lords on the Committee Work of the House[360]). The Committee was first established on an experimental basis for one session, but in November 1994 the House of

[357] See the annual Sessional Returns, s 6.
[358] Page, *Governing by Numbers* (n 346 above) 161.
[359] T St John Bates, 'Parliament, policy and delegated legislation' *Statute Law Review*, 1986, 117. See also the Report of the Commons Select Committee on Procedure, 1996, HC 152 of 1995–96.
[360] HL 35-1 of 1991–92, para 306.

Lords agreed to give the Committee permanent status.[361] (In 1994, the Committee also took on the additional role of scrutinising deregulation proposals under the Deregulation and Contracting Out Act 1994 – which was then extended under the Regulatory Reform Act 2001 (see below). The Committee is now called the Select Committee on Delegated Powers and Regulatory Reform. There is no equivalent committee in the Commons.[362]

The Committee's function is to report 'whether the provisions of any bill inappropriately delegate legislative power, or whether they subject the exercise of legislative power to an inappropriate degree of parliamentary scrutiny'.

When bills are introduced in the Lords, the Committee aims to report before the Committee stage begins but in practice it often reports before the Second Reading. It will even consider and report on amendments that are moved during the passage of bills. It will also comment on draft bills. Very occasionally it will report on bills that are still in the House of Commons.[363]

The Committee takes evidence in writing from the relevant government department. The sponsoring department provides the Committee with a memorandum identifying any provisions for delegated legislation, briefly stating their purpose and why the matter has been left to delegated legislation and explaining why the affirmative or negative procedure is being used. Departments also on occasion publish a response to the Committee's report. In a Special Report on Sessions 2001–02 and 2002–03 (*The Work of the Committee*) the Committee said: 'We are encouraged to find that the Government almost invariably accepts our recommendations so that the relevant amendment is tabled before the bill is considered on the floor of the House or the Minister is able to announce that such an amendment will be forthcoming.'[364] When the government does not agree with a recommendation and publishes its reasons the Committee on occasion comments on those reasons.

The Committee took a very active part in regard to Theresa May's European Union (Withdrawal) Bill. (See the 23rd and 30th Reports of the 2016–17 Session and the 2nd, 3rd, 10th,12th, 20th, 23rd and 24th Reports of the 2017–19 Session.) In the 3rd Report of the 2017–19 session it wrote (p 5):

> 8. In our 23rd and 30th Reports from the last Session, we set out our expectations for the delegated powers in this Bill.

[361] For the history of the setting up of the Committee see CMG Himsworth, 'The Delegated Powers Scrutiny Committee' *Public Law*, 1995, 34. For a more recent assessment by the Committee's Clerk see Tudor, 'Secondary legislation' (n 105 p 63 above) 149.

[362] The House of Commons Committee on Statutory Instruments only scrutinises the few SIs that deal with financial matters which are therefore subject to proceedings in that House alone.

[363] Three Brexit-related examples were the Committee's reports on the EU (Withdrawal) Bill, 3rd Report, 2017–19, September 2017, HL 22; the Taxation (Cross-Border Trade) Bill, 11th Report 2017–19, January 2018, HL 65; and the Agriculture Bill, 34th Report 2017–19, September 2018, HL194.

[364] First Report for 2003–04, HL 9, December 2003, para 29. The high reputation of this committee was noted by Daniel Greenberg, formerly a member of Parliamentary Counsel's Office: 'It is probably fair to say that the most important proof of the effectiveness and influence of the Committee is that there is a working, although informal, presumption that its recommendations are to be accommodated unless there is a strong reason for resisting them. One could contrast that with the Departmental attitude taken to the Joint Committee on Statutory Instruments (JCSI) … [I]t is not uncommon for Departments simply to ignore express criticisms or recommendations of the JCSI. By contrast, it will be far from easy to persuade a Minister to accept a recommendation simply to ignore a criticism of the Delegated Powers Committee, and he or she will want to be provided with some convincing arguments before going into bat with instructions simply to reject the Committee's report.' (*Laying Down the Law* (Sweet & Maxwell, 2011) 206). A footnote explains that the main reason is that ministers know they will have to face members of the Select Committee in the course of debates on the bill, whereas in the case of negative resolution SIs the instruments on which the JCSI reports is unlikely to be subject to any Parliamentary proceedings and the minister will therefore not have to 'go into bat' on it at all.

- Ministers must not have unfettered delegated powers. In particular, it would be **wholly unacceptable** [(sic)]for the Bill to replicate the European Communities Act 1972 by giving the Government a choice to adopt whichever procedure they liked for statutory instruments made under the Bill.
- Significant Henry VIII powers (the power of Ministers to override Acts of Parliament by statutory instrument) must be fully explained and justified.
- The Bill must not enable major changes to policy or establish new frameworks beyond what is necessary to ensure that UK law continues to work properly on exit day.

Expectations not met [(sic)]

9. The Bill has failed to meet our expectations on all the above points.

The Lords Secondary Legislation Scrutiny ('Merits') Select Committee

On 17 December 2003, the House of Lords agreed to establish a new Select Committee on the Merits of Statutory Instruments. At the start of the 2012–13 session the Committee was renamed the Secondary Legislation Scrutiny Committee to reflect the widening of its responsibilities to include the scrutiny of Orders laid under the Public Bodies Act 2011.[365]

Inevitably dubbed the 'Merits Committee', its remit is 'to consider every instrument which is laid before each House of Parliament and upon which proceedings may be or might have been taken in either House of Parliament, in pursuance of an Act of Parliament' being either an SI or draft SI, or a scheme or draft scheme requiring approval by an SI, or 'any other instrument' involving either an affirmative or negative resolution. Its remit does not, however, cover remedial orders under the Human Rights Act 1998, nor regulatory reform orders under the Regulatory Reform Act 2001, nor Orders in Council under the Northern Ireland Act 2000.

The Committee's task is to determine whether the special attention of the House of Lords should be drawn to the instrument in question on any of the following grounds: '(a) that it is politically or legally important or gives rise to issues of public policy likely to be of interest to the House; (b) that it may be inappropriate in view of the changed circumstances since the passage of the parent Act; (c) that it may inappropriately implement European Union legislation; (d) that it may imperfectly achieve its policy objectives'.

For an influential study of the parliamentary delegated legislation system see the Hansard Society's *The Devil is in the Detail: Parliament and Delegated Legislation*, 2014, which concluded that the parliamentary system for scrutinising delegated legislation was broken.

See also R Fox, J Blackwell and B Fowler, *Taking Back Control for Brexit and Beyond*, (Hansard Society, 2017); E Paterson and Dr Jack Simson Card 'Brexit, Delegated Powers and Delegated Legislation: A Rule of Law Analysis of Parliamentary Scrutiny' (Bingham Centre for the Rule of Law, April 2020); and the Hansard Society's toolkit for scrutinising delegated powers in bills, October 2022, www.hansardsociety.org.uk/publications/delgated-powers-toolkit.

In February 2023, the Hansard Society published a 59-page report entitled 'Proposals for a new System for Delegated legislation'. The proposals included:

[365] The Act (dubbed 'bonfire of the quangos') allows ministers, by order, to abolish, merge or transfer the functions of the public bodies listed in the appropriate schedules to the Act. The Committee reports on draft orders and documents laid before Parliament under s 11(1) of the Public Bodies Act 2011 in accordance with the procedures set out in s 11(5) and (6).

- Government and parliament should conclude a concordat to reset the boundaries between primary and delegated legislation.
- Existing scrutiny procedures ('affirmative', 'negative', 'strengthened') should be replaced by a new process under which Parliament would decide the level of scrutiny (if any) required.
- Other than in exceptional circumstances, all SIs should be laid before parliament in draft.
- The two Houses should have a staff-led joint Parliamentary Office for Delegated Legislation to analyse and produce briefings for MPs and peers.
- A new Joint Secondary Legislation Sifting Committee should be set up to decide the level of scrutiny (if any) that was required.
- MPs should be able to propose amendments.
- Peers should have the power to require the Commons to 'think again'.
- All parliamentarians should have the power within a 30-day 'safety window to table a 'revocation motion' in respect of a made SI.
- There should be a new urgent procedure for use only in exceptional circumstances.

2.19.2. Delegated Legislation during the Covid-19 Pandemic

The House of Lords Constitution Committee published three reports on this subject. These extracts are taken respectively from its second and its third reports:

> 46. At the end of the 2019–21 session, 424 Coronavirus-related statutory instruments had been laid before Parliament since January 2020. These have involved using delegated powers derived from 120 Acts of Parliament, five orders and five EU regulations (which are now retained EU law in the UK) …
>
> 48. It is not simply the volume or frequency of Coronavirus-related statutory instruments which has created challenges for parliamentary scrutiny. There are several other reasons why effective scrutiny has been made more difficult and at times almost impossible, which have been identified by the Secondary Legislation Scrutiny Committee:
>
> (a) Fast-track legislative procedures were frequently used, with the vast majority of statutory instruments (397 of 424) subject to the 'made negative' procedure or 'made affirmative' procedure.[366] This meant these instruments became law prior to being laid before, and scrutinised by, Parliament.
> (b) The policy explanation and justification for each statutory instrument, contained in the accompanying explanatory memoranda, was too often inadequate or unclear.
> (c) A significant number of statutory instruments (including instruments unrelated to COVID-19) were drafted incorrectly and therefore had to be withdrawn and re-introduced …
>
> 50. The high volume of statutory instruments laid in response to the pandemic, and the use of fast-track procedures, have severely limited Parliament's ability to scrutinise significant powers.[367]

***

[366] For definition of these terms see n 333 p 120 above.

[367] Constitution Committee, *COVID-19 and Parliament* (Session 2021–22, HL Paper 4, May 2021).

10. A range of new laws have been introduced to tackle the COVID-19 pandemic. Since March 2020, the law has been changed to implement national lockdowns, limit social contact, and reduce the burden on frontline healthcare staff.

11. The vast majority of these laws, including the most significant and widereaching, have come into effect as secondary legislation and without prior approval from Parliament …

20. Emergency legislation may be necessary in exceptional circumstances, but its use should be limited given its significant constitutional consequences. Fast-tracking legislation in effect results in a transfer of power from the legislature to the executive, enabling governments to take significant policy decisions with limited parliamentary input. Limiting the time available for parliamentary scrutiny also gives rise to an increased risk of legal errors and unintended consequences in legislation. For these reasons, fast-tracking legislation is never a desirable alternative to effective government planning for periods of crisis.

21. All governments should recognise that, however great or sudden an emergency may be, exceptional powers are lent, not granted, by the legislature to the executive, and such powers should be returned as swiftly and completely as possible, avoiding any spill over into permanence. When a government decides to fast-track legislation, it should do so for legitimate and urgent reasons only, limiting parliamentary scrutiny to the extent strictly necessary …

23. Most of the coronavirus-related legal changes have been made through regulations, which is a form of statutory instrument. Regulations are legal rules made by ministers under powers conferred to them by an Act of Parliament. Laws introducing the national lockdowns, limiting the size and location of certain social gatherings, and closing places of work, education and recreation have all been made in the form of public health regulations …[368]

A study of a sample of Covid-related delegated legislation, its authors said, showed a breach of all three of the essential requirements: well-designed parent legislation, the exercise of self-restraint by the executive in the use of delegated authority and the enablement of meaningful scrutiny by Parliament. (D Lock, F de Londras and P Hidalgo, 'Delegated legislation in the pandemic: further limits of a constitutional bargain revealed' 43 *Legal Studies* 2023 (4), 695–733.)

See also R Moosavian et al, 'Coronavirus legislative responses in the UK: regression to panic and disdain of constitutionalism' 72 *Northern Ireland Legal Quarterly* (2021)SI, 1–36 and Hansard Society, *Delegated Legislation: the problems with the process*, 2021.

2.19.3. Remedial Orders under the Human Rights Act 1998

The Human Rights Act 1998 provided for a fast-track method of amending statutes by statutory instrument where the statute has been found to be incompatible with the European Convention on Human Rights (ECHR). The order is called a 'remedial order'.

The Act permits proceedings to be brought on the basis that a public authority has acted in a way that is inconsistent with the ECHR. If it arises in the form of primary legislation, the courts cannot strike the legislation down. Instead, providing the court is of appropriate authority, it has the power to make a declaration of incompatibility, ie, that the legislation is incompatible with the ECHR (s 4(2)). Courts that have the power to make a declaration of incompatibility are the Supreme Court (and previously the House of Lords), the Court of Appeal, the Divisional Court and the High Court (s 4(5)). If the inconsistency (or 'unlawful

[368] Constitution Committee, *COVID-19 and Parliament* (Session 2021–22, HL Paper 15, June 10, 2021).

act') is in the form of subordinate rather than primary legislation, the court *can* itself strike it down or refuse to apply it unless the subordinate legislation is directly required by the parent Act.

A declaration of incompatibility does not invalidate the statutory provision. It simply alerts the Government to the problem. The Government then has to decide whether to change the law to bring it into line with the Convention or to do nothing and wait for the presumably aggrieved litigant to bring proceedings in the European Court of Human Rights in Strasbourg. If the minister considers that there are 'compelling reasons' for speedy action, amendment of the primary legislation does not require primary legislation. Instead it can be done by Order in Council – ie by statutory instrument (s 10(2)). A remedial order can 'contain such incidental, supplemental, consequential or transitional provision as the person making it considers appropriate' (Sch 2, para 1(1)(a)). This phrase, which is typically used in such cases, was criticised by former Law Lord, Lord Oliver of Aylmerton, as 'thoroughly objectionable constitutionally': 'It is unfair to the citizen, who is entitled in a democratic society to have the rules by which his life is to be regulated properly debated and scrutinised by his elected representatives.'[369]

The Order in Council has to be approved by affirmative resolution of both Houses of Parliament. But instead of the usual forty-day period of being 'laid before Parliament', 'remedial orders' are subject to a special procedure (under Sch 2) by which the proposed Order in Council would have to wait normally for 120 days after first being published (sixty days in draft, plus another sixty days) before being approved by resolution in both Houses. (If the matter is urgent it can be done in less time.) If while the Order is in draft, representations are made, the minister must accompany the re-laying of the draft order after the first sixty days with a statement summarising the representations received and, if they have resulted in changes, giving details of the changes. In urgent cases this information must be given after the Order has been made and a replacement Order must be made to give effect to any changes.

As at July 2024, there had been a total of 58 declarations of incompatibility since the Human Rights Act 1998 came into force on 2 October 2000. Twelve had been overturned on appeal and five were still subject to appeal. Sixteen had been remedied by primary or secondary legislation and another five had been remedied by primary legislation passed before the date of the court's declaration. Eleven had been remedied by a Remedial Order and another five were going to be remedied by a Remedial Order. One had been dealt 'by various measures' and three were still under consideration.[370]

For criticism of the House of Lords by a retired member of the Court of Appeal for not issuing declarations of incompatibility in two cases where, he argued, they should have been made see R Buxton, 'The future of declarations of incompatibility', *Public Law*, 2010, 213–22.

2.19.4. Legislation for Northern Ireland

A further example of special methods for implementing SIs relates to Northern Ireland. As has been seen, when Westminster makes law for the Province it does so by Order in Council. Successive governments have made an administrative practice of publishing 'Proposals' for

[369] Lord Oliver, 'A judicial view of modern legislation' 14 *Statute Law Review*, 1993, 1, 3.

[370] Figures taken from the latest annual report, *Responding to Human Rights Judgments, Report to the Joint Committee on Human Rights on the Government Response to Human Rights Judgments 2018–2019*, November 2024, CP 1192, Appendix A.

Draft Orders in Council, together with an Explanatory Memorandum, and allowing a six- to ten-week consultation period. This procedure was put onto a statutory footing in the Northern Ireland Act 1998.

2.19.5. Judicial Scrutiny of Statutory Instruments

With one exception, judicial scrutiny of primary legislation is not possible. The exception has been where it was alleged that a statute conflicted with European Union law. Post-Brexit, under the provisions of the European Union (Withdrawal) Act 2018 and the European Union (Withdrawal Agreement) Act 2020, the same will apply in regard to 'retained EU law' now called 'assimilated law' (as to which see 8.1.2 below). In all other cases the courts must accept a statute as law. As has been seen, even a conflict between a statute and the ECHR can result in no more than a declaration of incompatibility. But delegated legislation *can* be challenged both directly and indirectly before the courts.[371] There have been some striking examples.[372] The subject is a large one and is not dealt with here.

2.20. Delegated Legislation: Anglo-American Comparison

There is an extraordinary difference in the level of interest in delegated legislation in England compared with that in the United States. The topic was the subject of a study by Professor Michael Asimow of the University of California.[373] The study was published many years ago but its findings still seem valid today.

Asimow's point of departure was the observation that 'In the USA the substance of regulations and the procedure by which they are made, present issues which generate enormous controversy in political, judicial and academic circles. In Britain, nearly everyone seems satisfied with (and hardly anyone seems interested in) procedural and substantive aspects of delegated legislation'.

In the United States, delegated legislation was the field of rule-making by regulatory agencies created by Congress to regulate a great variety of fields – airlines, trucking, roads, railways, radio and television, corporate securities, labour relations, energy pricing,

[371] In the 70 or so years from 1914 to 1986 there were only 15 cases in which statutory instruments were challenged successfully in the courts (D Hayhurst and P Wallington, 'The parliamentary scrutiny of delegated legislation' *Public Law*, 1988, 547).

[372] In *R v Secretary of State for the Environment, Transport and the Regions, ex p Spath Holme Ltd* [2000] 3 WLR 141, the Court of Appeal held the Rent Acts (Maximum Fair Rent) Order 1999 to be ultra vires. In *R v Secretary of State for Social Security, ex p Joint Council for the Welfare of Immigrants* [1997] 1 WLR 275 the Court of Appeal held new rules restricting the right of asylum seekers to obtain social security benefits to be ultra vires on the grounds that it was 'so uncompromisingly draconian' that Parliament could not have intended 'a significant number of genuine asylum seekers to be impaled on the horns of so intolerable a dilemma'. In *R v Lord Chancellor, ex p Witham* [1998] QB 575 the Divisional Court ruled that the Lord Chancellor had acted unlawfully in making new regulations regarding court fees for civil cases which did not preserve the traditional special dispensation for poor litigants. In *R (Public Law Project) v Secretary of State for Justice* [2014] EWHC 2365 the Divisional Court held that a statutory instrument establishing a residence test for civil legal aid applications was ultra vires as not within the scope or purpose of the primary legislation.

[373] M Asimow, 'Delegated legislation in the United States and United Kingdom' 3 *Oxford Journal of Legal Studies*, 1983, 253.

business practices, financial institutions, etc. The agencies, in Asimow's phrase, 'generated a huge number of highly controversial regulations which attracted attention to the subject in legal and economic literature as well as in the popular press. A vast number of court decisions have focused on procedural requirements for making rules and clarification of the scope of the court's power to review the rules'. He suggested some reasons why the subject was of such intense interest and controversy in the one country and so uncontroversial and almost uninteresting in the other. Two of those he identified seem especially persuasive:

Importance of delegated legislation Delegated legislation played a more important role in the US, dealing with more significant issues. In the United States the party battles in the Congress and the inability of the administration to have its way in the primary legislation meant that many issues were left to be resolved through subordinate legislation. In Britain by contrast the executive could get its policy enacted in the primary statute and therefore had less need to leave important details to the regulatory process.

Use of different techniques Many matters regulated by agencies in the United States were dealt with in Britain by voluntary codes of practice. Another British technique was the local public inquiry into major planning issues where those who would be affected by a ministerial decision could seek to challenge or at least influence it. But the most important British technique for controlling the private sector was through heavy reliance on official discretion to make individualised orders. Parliament would legislate, giving officials broad discretionary powers. Often the powers were loosely circumscribed by guidelines prepared by the government department concerned. So in the planning field property owners had to ask for planning permission to develop their property. In the United States the same problem would be dealt with more by zoning laws. In Britain, regulation of certain forms of pollution was the task of the alkali inspectorate or regional water authorities who had considerable power to compromise disputes. In the United States, rules regulated permissible levels of air and water pollution and the scope for discretion was less.

Asimow's conclusion was that the difference between the approach of the two systems had its roots in deep cultural differences turning in essence on attitudes to public officials, adversary procedures and judicial interventionism.

2.21. Making Better Law

There are innumerable examples of complaints about statutory law. A leading authority on this subject is the Hansard Society. In 1993, it published *Making the Law: The Report of the Hansard Society Commission on the Legislative Process* which identified a raft of problems. In 2010, it published *Making Better Law: Reform of the Legislative Process from Policy to Act* by Ruth Fox and Matt Korris. Some of the main points of the Hansard Society's report were captured in an article by Matt Korris:

> The quality of law is ultimately shaped by the scrutiny it receives in Parliament. But the tidal wave of often hastily prepared, deficient legislation that the UK Parliament has been asked to scrutinise over the last decade and more has severely stretched the capacity of parliamentarians to perform their constitutional function effectively. There is little incentive for the executive to address this situation and restrain its almost untrammelled power of legislative initiative, and therefore

> Parliament needs to assert its right to receive adequately drafted legislation and the time to scrutinise it thoroughly …
>
> Whether the audience is parliamentarians who make the law, judges who have to apply it or the public who must comply with it, it is not difficult to find vocal critics of the current system. Many are concerned by the sheer volume of new legislation, questioning whether much of it is really justified as an ever-expanding statute book is distorted by an increasing amount of duplicative legal remedies and the introduction of new offences that are never used, or indeed never intended for use. The way that successive governments have legislated in order to meet explicitly political rather than legal imperatives, with ministers treating the legislative programme as a form of extended press release, has also become an increasing source of complaint. In these circumstances, the quality of the statute they are producing is not always uppermost in ministerial minds; their primary objective is to get the law through to Royal Assent to demonstrate that the government has done something.[374]

There was widespread concern, Korris wrote, that the policy development process was 'inadequate and weak', but the Hansard Society's principal focus was the legislative process.

> [T]he torrent of legislation parliamentarians face each session and the increasingly complex and technical nature of many statutes today mean that there is currently a serious mismatch between the scrutiny mission of Parliament and its capacity to carry out that mission. The pressures on scrutiny have grown as a result of the way in which we now make laws, but the resources and expertise in Parliament for this task have not grown in tandem: the scrutiny system is consequently not fit for purpose.

Central to these problems, Korris wrote, was that there was no mechanism within the legislative process to simply evaluate and confirm the necessity of legislation or impose a quality standard on the production of a bill before it was sent to Parliament. Parliament should establish a gateway Legislative Standards Committee 'to assess bills against a set of minimum technical preparation standards that all bills should be required to meet before introduction is permitted'. The standards should be agreed in consultation with the government. Before a bill was presented to the committee the relevant Minister should be required to certify that the bill met the required qualifying standards.

This proposal of the Hansard Society report by Fox and Korris was adopted by the House of Commons Political and Constitutional Reform Committee in its 2013 report, *Ensuring standards in the quality of legislation.*[375] The Committee recommended that there should be a new Code of Legislative Standards[376] and that a Legislative Standards Committee should be created 'to provide oversight of the Cabinet's Parliamentary Business and Legislation Committee's approach to and use of the finalised Code'.[377] The Committee appended a draft Code of Legislative Standards to its report.

The Conservative-Liberal Democrat Coalition Government's Response disagreed with the recommendation that there should be a Code of Legislative Standards:

> The Government does not believe that a Code of Legislative Standards is necessary or would be effective in ensuring quality legislation. It is the responsibility of government to bring forward legislation of a high standard and it has comprehensive and regularly updated guidance to meet this objective. This is publicly available and can be used by parliamentarians in fulfilling their role

[374] M Korris 'Standing up for scrutiny: how and why Parliament should make better law' 64 *Parliamentary Affairs*, 2011 (3), 564–574, 564.

[375] First Report of Session 2013–14, HC 85, 20 May 2013.

[376] Ibid, para 37.

[377] Ibid, para 98.

> of scrutinising legislation. Following a recent review, existing guidance for Parliamentary Counsel will be consolidated in the Cabinet Office's Guide to Making Legislation to further improve accessibility. We undertake annual lessons learned exercises within Government designed to capture best legislative practice and we would be happy to engage with parliamentarians on this exercise if that would be of interest. Ultimately, it is for Ministers to defend both the quality of the legislation they introduce and the supporting material provided to Parliament to aid scrutiny ...[378]

Many of the suggestions in the draft Code, it said, were already included in Explanatory Notes and the Government said it was 'minded to agree' that Impact Statements might usefully also be included so that all the relevant material would be in one document. A Code of Legislative Standards with a list of requirements risked encouraging a tick-box mentality which would do little to support effective scrutiny. Nor could a Code provide the degree of objectivity envisaged to answer proposed questions such as 'Is the bill understandable and accessible?' or 'Is the change politically or legally important?' Similarly, whether purpose clauses or 'sunset clauses'[379] were required would always be a matter for debate on a case-by-case basis.

The Government's Response was equally negative about the proposal that there should be a new Legislative Standards Committee:

> The Government does not believe that a Legislative Standards Committee, as proposed by the Committee, is either necessary or would be effective in improving legislation.[380]

The case for such a Committee to monitor compliance with a Code was significantly weakened, it said, if there was no Code. The proposal that the Committee should monitor the work of the Cabinet Committee on Parliamentary Business and Legislation was not appropriate. Ministers had to be able to debate and stress-test legislation within Government. The process by which the Government arrived at its view, it said, was a matter for Government not for Parliament.

The Hansard Society's report by Ruth Fox and Matt Korris was published in 2010, the year Labour was defeated after thirteen years in office. What followed was fourteen years of Conservative government. Two major reports, published respectively in 2022[381] and 2025,[382] showed that, far from improving, the situation had deteriorated further.

The 2022 report issued jointly by the Bennett Institute for Public Policy in Cambridge and the Institute for Government listed five key cross-cutting problems with the legislative process that limit the extent and effectiveness of parliamentary scrutiny:

1. The legislative process is complex and inaccessible
2. Parliamentarians do not have sufficient time to consider legislation
3. The government introduces bills into parliament before policy is fully developed
4. Parliamentarians do not have the capacity and resources to effectively scrutinise the content of legislation
5. It is difficult for parliament to amend a bill once introduced

[378] Political and Constitutional Committee, *Ensuring standards in the quality of legislation: Government's Response to the Committee's First Report of Session 2013–14*, First Special Report of Session 2013–14, HC 611, 25 July 2013, para 12.

[379] 'Sunset clauses' provide that the legislation expires on a given date unless specifically renewed.

[380] Political and Constitutional Committee, *Ensuring standards in the quality of legislation: Government's Response to the Committee's First Report of Session 2013–14*, First Special Report of Session 2013–14, HC 611, 25 July 2013, para 17.

[381] Bennett Institute for Public Policy and Institute for Government, *The Legislative Process: How to Empower Parliament*, Jess Sergeant and Jack Pannell, December 2022 (56pp).

[382] Meg Russell, 'Should we be worried about the decline of parliamentary scrutiny?' *Public Law* 2025 (1), 31–57.

It looked at the legislative process through its successive stages from policy development in government to post-legislative scrutiny, identifying problem areas. It urged the implementation of recommendations made in reports by others and made recommendations of its own in regard to two areas: Pre-Legislative Scrutiny (see 2.8 at p 87 above) and Public Bill Committees (for these see pp 43–44 above).

The 2025 publication was by Professor Meg Russell, Director of the Constitution Unit at UCL, a leading scholar in this field. Her publication, originally delivered as a lecture, is a masterly, wide ranging and fully documented[383] account of the available data stretching back twenty to 25 years.

Her chief concerns appear from the topics on which she said more and regular information was needed. She called for Parliament and government to publish, and allow monitoring of, annual figures on:

- the number of fast-tracked bills; [too many]
- the days spent on each bill at each stage in the House of Commons; [insufficient]
- the number of government amendments to bills; [too many]
- the use of 'placeholder' clauses;[384] [too many]
- the number of bills published in draft; [too few]
- the number denied an evidence-taking stage; [too many]
- how often intervals set out in the *Cabinet Office Guide to Making Legislation* are breached; [too many]
- the number of 'skeleton' bills … [too many]

Her hope was that having better data would generate better practice. But are there grounds to expect that it will? The 2022 report by the Bennett Institute and the Institute for Government said the authors had analysed 21 parliamentary reports since 1997 on the legislative process, making more than 330 recommendations. 'The vast majority', it said, 'have not been implemented'. Professor Russell quoted Robin Cook, then Leader of the House of Commons: 'Good scrutiny means good government'. History suggests that the unfortunate reality is that, despite fine words to the contrary, governments are actually not all that keen on improving parliamentary scrutiny.

At the time of writing, the Starmer Labour Government was in its first months. It would be surprising if it proved to be different in this respect from its predecessors.[385]

[383] The 121 footnotes are an Open Sesame to the current literature.

[384] 'Placeholder' clauses is a term used for clauses the content of which will be revealed at a later stage.

[385] The Commons Modernisation Select Committee, non-existent during the previous 14 years of Conservative governments, was revived by the Starmer Government. Its chair was the Leader of the Commons and its members included the Conservative Shadow Leader of the House. Unusually, instead of the members being elected by MPs, they were selected by the whips.

3

Statutory Interpretation

3.1. Interpretation is a Necessary Aspect of Communication

Statutory interpretation is a particular form of a general problem – the understanding of meaning or, more broadly still, communication. Like Monsieur Jourdain in Molière's *Le Bourgeois Gentilhomme*, who did not know that he was talking prose, most people are probably unaware of the extent to which the use of language necessarily involves interpretation. Even the simplest statement usually relies on an understanding of habits, knowledge, values and purposes shared between the author and the recipient of the communication. The point was made in a homely example over a hundred years ago.

> Suppose a housekeeper says to a domestic: 'fetch some soup-meat', accompanying the act with giving some money to the latter; they will be unable to execute the order without interpretation, however easy and, consequently, rapid the performance of the process may be. Common sense and good faith tell the domestic, that the housekeeper's meaning was this: 1. They should go immediately, or as soon as their other occupations are finished; or, if they be directed to do so in the evening, that they should go the next day at the usual hour; 2. that the money handed to them by the housekeeper is intended to pay for the meat thus ordered, and not as a present to them; 3. that they should buy such meat and of such parts of the animal, as, to their knowledge, has commonly been used in the house they stay at, for making soup; 4. that they buy the best meat they can obtain, for a fair price; 5. that they go to that butcher who usually provides the family, with whom the domestic resides, with meat, or to some convenient stall, and not to any unnecessarily distant place; 6. that they return the rest of the money; 7. that they bring home the meat in good faith, neither adding anything disagreeable nor injurious; 8. that they fetch the meat for the use of the family and not for themself. Suppose, on the other hand, the housekeeper, afraid of being misunderstood, had mentioned these eight specifications, they would not have obtained their object, if it were to exclude all *possibility* of misunderstanding. For, the various specifications would have required new ones. Where would be the end? We are constrained then, always, to leave a considerable part of our meaning to be found out by interpretation, which, in many cases, must necessarily cause greater or less obscurity with regard to the exact meaning, which our words were intended to convey.[1]

[1] F Lieber, *Legal and Political Hermeneutics*, 3rd edn (FH Thomas, 1880) 18.

Interpretation, in other words, is not something that happens only in cases of doubt or difficulty; it happens whenever anyone tries to understand language used by another person. Usually the process of understanding is instinctive and immediate. It requires no conscious thought and is therefore not even noticed. For the most part we manage in ordinary life without too many difficulties created by misunderstandings. On the other hand, even in family life where the members of the household share broadly common values and common objectives and have a great deal of knowledge about each other's use of language, misunderstandings are far from rare. Interpretation therefore occurs inevitably wherever there is communication; the *problem* of interpretation occurs only when something goes wrong.

Lord Hailsham said that probably as many as 9 out of 10 cases heard on appeal by the Court of Appeal and the House of Lords turned upon or involved the meaning of words contained in statutes or secondary legislation.[2] It is hardly surprising that in legal affairs there are plenty of ways in which things may go wrong. For one thing, legal documents – whether statutes, contracts,[3] leases, mortgages, wills, bills of exchange – tend to be complex. Their subject-matter is difficult. They use a mixture of ordinary language and technical jargon. They are apt to be long-winded. They are frequently the result of drafting by several hands or at least of consultation with a variety of people. The final draft may reflect a compromise between different points of view. Each of these factors militates against simplicity and clarity of expression.

Secondly, a legal document speaks not only to the present but is usually intended to cope with the future. That indeed is normally its chief function. But the draftsman's capacity to anticipate the future is necessarily limited. Even if they provide for 13 possible contingencies, they may overlook the possibility of the fourteenth which happens to be the one that actually occurs. The late Professor Lon Fuller of Harvard posed the example of a statute that provides 'It shall be an offence punishable by a fine of five dollars to sleep in any railway station'. Does the offence cover the case of a passenger waiting for a delayed train who was found at 3 am on a station bench, sitting upright but asleep and even snoring? Equally, does it cover the case of the tramp who was stopped on their way into the station carrying a bed-roll and heading for a bench, apparently with a view to settling down for the night? Neither case is adequately dealt with in the statute. No draftsman, however fertile their imagination, can think of everything.

Moreover, space will not permit them to put down everything that they do think of. In order to avoid the danger of misconstruction of the simple request 'fetch some meat for soup', the careful draftsman/communicator would be best advised to specify that they mean – from the shop at the bottom of the road; before lunch; at the customary price; meat of the kind normally eaten by the family; that the change be returned, etc. In ordinary life, time and patience do not permit such tedious prolixity. Much is left to common sense. But precisely the same is true of legal documents. However pedantic the draftsman there will be much that they will have to leave to common sense. If everything had to be defined, there would be no end to the document. The draftsman must perforce select what they think are the most important matters to be set down. Moreover, there are some things that they cannot foresee simply because later developments are not within the knowledge of

[2] *Hamlyn Revisited: The British Legal System Today* (Stevens, 1983) 65.

[3] For an illuminating discussion of interpretation in the context of statutes and contracts see Justice Michael Kirby, 'Towards a grand theory of interpretation: the case of statutes and contracts' 24 *Statute Law Review*, 2003, 95.

anyone at the time. The draftsman who uses the word 'vehicle' in the days of horse-drawn carriages cannot be blamed for any uncertainty as to whether the word applies to motorcars or aeroplanes.

The third and most important reason for the singular tendency of legal documents to give rise to difficulties is that they commonly reflect attempted solutions to problems affecting different and conflicting interests. A will is the sharing out of property amongst individuals each of whom might prefer to have more than their allotted share; a contract is an agreement between, say, a buyer and a seller who have contrary points of view on the deal; a lease is an allocation of rights and responsibilities between landlord and tenant whose interests diverge at many points. A statute commonly prescribes a new way of dealing with a particular range of problems as between the different groups affected. The problem of drafting language so as to avoid ambiguity and uncertainty is great enough where the relevant parties have broadly the same point of view. It is infinitely greater where they have an incentive to find different meanings in the words used. The English language is richly endowed with words that bear multiple meanings and there is almost no limit to the number of ambiguities that can be found in the ordinary legal document once ingenious and motivated lawyers start picking it over. It is not necessarily a matter of the lawyers being 'bloody-minded'. They may simply be doing their job by looking for ways in which the document can be construed to serve the best interests of their client. Ambiguity here is not the fault of the draftsman nor is it a reflection of the shortcomings of the language; it is simply the result of the obvious fact that where people look at a text from different points of view they are apt to find different meanings in the language used.

If problems of interpretation do occur, they may be resolved in a variety of ways. The opposing parties may come to some accommodation of their dispute without ever calling on their lawyers. Or the lawyers may agree on some formula that is acceptable to the clients. But if the disagreement cannot be solved by negotiation and agreement, the only way to secure an authoritative decision is to take it to the courts. This book is concerned with law-making on a national scale and the remainder of this chapter deals with the way in which the courts approach problems of statutory interpretation. But much of what is said here applies as much to the attitude of the courts to the interpretation of instruments drafted by practising lawyers whether they be contracts, leases, mortgages or any other legal document.

3.2. The Three Basic So-Called 'Rules' of Statutory Interpretation

It is often said that there are three basic rules of statutory interpretation – the literal rule, the golden rule and the mischief rule.[4] As will be seen, it would be better to describe these more as tendencies or approaches than as rules. It is also important to appreciate that this classification is a considerable over-simplification of the process of statutory interpretation.

[4] For the probable origin of this familiar classification see John Willis, 'Statute interpretation in a nutshell' 16 *Canadian Bar Review*, 1938, 1.

But we commence by establishing what the so-called 'rules' mean and then proceed to an examination of each in turn. (Note that there is further consideration of the right approach to interpretation of statutes in 3.11 below.)

3.2.1. The Literal Rule

According to the 'literal rule' it is the task of the court to give the words to be construed their literal meaning regardless of whether the result is sensible or not. Lord Esher put the proposition succinctly in 1892:

> If the words of an Act are clear, you must follow them, even though they lead to a manifest absurdity. The court has nothing to do with the question whether the legislature has committed an absurdity.[5]

In another of the innumerable judicial formulations of the same rule, Lord Bramwell in 1884 similarly reflected the idea that the court should not be concerned whether the construction it gives to a statute is absurd:

> I should like to have a good definition of what is such an absurdity that you are to disregard the plain words of an Act of Parliament. It is to be remembered that what seems absurd to one man does not seem absurd to another … I think it is infinitely better, although an absurdity or an injustice or other objectionable result may be evolved as the consequence of your construction, to adhere to the words of an Act of Parliament and leave the legislature to set it right than to alter those words according to one's notion of an absurdity.[6]

3.2.2. The Golden Rule

The so-called 'golden rule' was attributed by Lord Blackburn to Lord Wensleydale in a case in 1877 in which he said:

> I believe that it is not disputed that what Lord Wensleydale used to call the golden rule is right, viz., that we are to take the whole statute together, and construe it all together, giving the words their ordinary signification, unless when so applied they produce an inconsistency, or an absurdity or inconvenience so great as to convince the Court that the intention could not have been to use them in their ordinary signification, and to justify the Court in putting on them some other signification, which, though less proper, is one which the Court thinks the words will bear.[7]

But the first recorded use of the phrase 'golden rule' seems in fact to have been by Jervis CJ in *Mattison v Hart* (1854) 14 CB 357, 385 ('We must, therefore, in this case have recourse to what is called the golden rule of construction, as applied to acts of parliament, viz. to give the words used by the legislature their plain and natural meaning unless it is manifest from the general scope and intention of the statute injustice and absurdity would result').

In *Grey v Pearson*, Parke B said:

> I have been long and deeply impressed with the wisdom of the rule now, I believe, universally adopted, at least in the courts of law in Westminster Hall, that in construing wills and indeed, statutes, and all written instruments, the grammatical and ordinary sense of the words is to be

[5] *R v Judge of the City of London Court* [1892] 1 QB 273, 290.
[6] *Hill v East and West India Dock Co* (1884) 9 App Cas 448, 464–65.
[7] *River Wear Commissioners v Adamson* (1877) 2 App Cas 743, 764–65.

> adhered to, unless that would lead to some absurdity, or some repugnance or inconsistency with the rest of the instrument, in which case the grammatical and ordinary sense of the words may be modified, so as to avoid the absurdity and inconsistency, but no farther.[8]

According to the golden rule, therefore, the court is supposed to follow the literal approach unless it produces absurdity (and perhaps inconvenience and inconsistency), in which case it should find some other meaning.

3.2.3. The Mischief Rule

The classic statement of the 'mischief rule' is that given by the Barons of the Court of Exchequer in *Heydon's Case* (1584) 3 Co Rep 7a:

> And it was resolved by them, that for the sure and true interpretation of all statutes in general (be they penal or beneficial, restrictive or enlarging of the Common Law), four things are to be discerned and considered:
>
> 1st. What was the Common Law before the making of the Act.
>
> 2nd. What was the mischief and defect for which the Common Law did not provide.
>
> 3rd. What remedy the Parliament hath resolved and appointed to cure the disease of the commonwealth.
>
> And, 4th. The true reason of the remedy; and then the office of all the Judges is always to make such construction as shall suppress the mischief, and advance the remedy and to suppress subtle inventions and evasions for continuance of the mischief, and *pro privato commodo*, and to add force and life to the cure and remedy, according to the true intent of the makers of the Act, *pro bono publico*.

Coke himself later referred to the same approach in his *Institutes*:

> Equity is a construction made by the judges, that cases out of the letter of a statute, yet being within the same mischief, or cause of the making of the same, shall be within the same remedy that the statute provideth; and the reason hereof is, for that the law-makers could not possibly set down all cases in express terms. (I *Inst* 24b)

3.3. The Three Basic Rules Considered

3.3.1. The Dominant Rule was the Literal Rule

There seems to be little dispute that in the nineteenth and for most of the twentieth centuries the literal rule was dominant. In 1969, *Maxwell on Interpretation of Statutes* (12th edn) stated that the literal rule was the primary one – the golden and the mischief rules were merely 'other main principles of interpretation'. The literal rule developed in the early nineteenth century. The first sustained judicial support for it appears to have come from Lord Tenterden in cases decided in the 1820s. According to one authority,[9] the golden

[8] *Grey v Pearson* (1857) 6 HL Cas 61, 106.

[9] JA Corry, 'Administrative law: interpretation of statutes' *University of Toronto Law Journal*, 1935, 286, 299–300.

rule and the literal rule contended for the allegiance of the judges for the next thirty years but by the latter part of the century the literal approach had clearly triumphed.

Lord Evershed considered that the prolixity of statutes emphasised the value of literal interpretation: 'The length and detail of modern legislation has undoubtedly reinforced the claim of literal construction as the only safe rule.' If the statute was long, this suggested that Parliament had expressed its full meaning and that there was no need or scope to imply any additional meanings. Anything omitted was a *casus omissus* which the judge could not supply because that would amount to legislation. But the literal approach was used equally for wills, contracts and other legal documents, so that the philosophy was by no means based exclusively on the constitutional relationship between courts and Parliament nor on the growing length of statutes.

A demonstration of the literal approach in operation is the sequence of events in *Magor and St Mellons v Newport Corporation*:

Magor and St Mellons v Newport Corpn [1950] 2 All ER 1226 (CA) and [1951] 2 All ER 839 (HL)

The Newport Corporation had expanded its boundaries by taking in large parts of two neighbouring rural districts. The parts taken in were mainly the richer parts whose ratepayers paid the highest rates. The Local Government Act 1933, ss 151 and 152, provided for reasonable compensation to the two District Councils by the one that had become enriched through the alteration in the boundaries. But the minister made an order amalgamating the two District Councils into one. The Newport Corporation used this fact to argue that the new council could claim no compensation at all. The statute, it said, provided for compensation only to a surviving council, whereas here the two old councils had been abolished and the claim was therefore invalid.

The trial judge Parker J and the Court of Appeal (Cohen and Somervell LJJ) agreed with the Corporation. Lord Denning, however, dissented. In his view the intention of Parliament and of the minister was obvious. The order dissolving the old councils was not their death but their marriage.

> LORD DENNING: The burdens which each set of ratepayers had previously borne separately became a combined burden to be borne by them all together. So, also, the rights to which the two councils would have been entitled for each set of ratepayers separately became a combined right to which the combined council was entitled for them all together. This was so obviously the intention of the Minister's order that I have no patience with an ultra-legalistic interpretation which would deprive them of their rights altogether … We do not sit here to pull the language of Parliament and of Ministers to pieces and make nonsense of it. That is an easy thing to do, and it is a thing to which lawyers are too often prone. We sit here to find out the intention of Parliament and of ministers and carry it out, and we do this better by filling in the gaps and making sense of the enactment than by opening it up to destructive analysis.
>
> It may be said that these heroics are out of place, and I agree they are, because I think that Parliament has really made its intention plain enough. The Act which conferred the title to compensation conferred it on each of the district councils, not in its own right, but in right of its ratepayers: (see s. 152(1)(*b*) of the Act of 1933). The district council was the hand to receive the compensation, but it only received it so that it might give relief to the ratepayers for the increased burden which the change of boundaries cast on them. The amalgamation changed the legal identity of the two district councils, but it did not change the ratepayers at all, nor did it relieve them of their burdens: and there is no reason whatever why the amalgamated council should not claim the compensation due to the ratepayers.

On appeal, the House of Lords upheld the trial judge and the Court of Appeal. The first judgment was given by Lord Simonds, who said he agreed with the judgment to be given by Lord Morton of Henryton but that he wished to add his reaction to the philosophy expressed by Lord Denning:

> LORD SIMONDS: My Lords, the criticism which I venture to make of the judgment of the learned lord justice is not directed at the conclusion that he reached. It is after all a trite saying that on questions of construction different minds may come to different conclusions and I am content to say that I agree with my noble and learned friend. But it is on the approach of the lord justice to what is a question of construction and nothing else that I think it desirable to make some comment, for at a time when so large a proportion of the cases that are brought before the courts depend on the construction of modern statutes it would not be right for this House to pass unnoticed the propositions which the learned lord justice lays down for the guidance of himself and, presumably, of others. He said ([1950] 2 All E.R. 1236):
>
>> We sit here to find out the intention of Parliament and of Ministers and carry it out, and we do this better by filling in the gaps and making sense of the enactment than by opening it up to destructive analysis.
>
> The first part of this passage appears to be an echo of what was said in *Heydon's* Case three hundred years ago, and so regarded, is not objectionable. But the way in which the learned lord justice summarises the broad rules laid down by Sir Edward Coke in that case may well induce grave misconception of the function of the court. The part which is played in the judicial interpretation of a statute by reference to the circumstances of its passing is too well known to need re-statement. It is sufficient to say that the general proposition that it is the duty of the court to find out the intention of Parliament – and not only of Parliament but of ministers also – cannot by any means be supported. The duty of the court is to interpret the words that the legislature has used. Those words may be ambiguous, but, even if they are, the power and duty of the court to travel outside them on a voyage of discovery are strictly limited: see, for instance, *Assam Railways & Trading Co. Ltd v Inland Revenue Comrs*. and, particularly, the observations of Lord Wright ([1935] A.C. 445, 458).
>
> The second part of the passage that I have cited from the judgment of the learned lord justice is, no doubt, the logical sequence of the first. The court, having discovered the intention of Parliament and of Ministers too, must proceed to fill in the gaps. What the legislature has not written, the court must write. This proposition, which re-states in a new form the view expressed by the lord justice in the earlier case of *Seaford Court Estates Ltd. v Asher* [1950] A.C. 508 (to which the lord justice himself refers), cannot be supported. It appears to me to be a naked usurpation of the legislative function under the thin disguise of interpretation and it is the less justifiable when it is guesswork with what material the legislature would, if it had discovered the gap, have filled it in. If a gap is disclosed, the remedy lies in an amending Act. For the reasons to be given by my noble and learned friend I am of opinion that this appeal should be dismissed with costs.

Lord Morton said that s 151 of the 1933 Act made it clear that the only bodies which could claim a financial adjustment were public bodies affected by an alteration of boundaries. The new amalgamated district council was not such a body since it was not in existence when the boundary change took place.

> The present case is one in which each of two local authorities loses a wealthy portion of its area and is abolished immediately after the loss occurs. It may be that, if the legislature had contemplated such a state of affairs, some special provisions would have been inserted in the Act of 1933. What these provisions would have been can only be a matter of guesswork.[10]

[10] [1951] 2 All ER 839, 845.

He clearly agreed with Lord Simonds' view of Lord Denning's approach.

Lord Morton (with whom Lords Simonds and Goddard agreed) said:

> In so far as the intention of Parliament or of Ministers is revealed in Acts of Parliament or orders, either by the language used or by necessary implication, the court should, of course, carry these intentions out, but it is not the function of any judge to fill in what he conceives to be the gaps in an Act of Parliament. If he does so, he is usurping the function of the legislature [at 846].

Lord Tucker too rejected Lord Denning's approach:

> I think it is clear that the situation which has arisen in the present case was never present to the minds of those responsible for the Local Government Act 1933, and that the language is quite inappropriate to meet it. In these circumstances your Lordships would be acting in a legislative rather than a judicial capacity if the view put forward by Denning L. J. in his dissenting judgment were to prevail.

Lord Radcliffe, without referring to him or to his approach, nevertheless found a way to reach the same result as Lord Denning:

> My Lords, I differ very little from the views expressed by my noble and learned friend, Lord Morton of Henryton, but that small difference has led me to come to an opposite conclusion as to what should be the fate of this appeal …

He thought that s 151 of the 1933 Act was not so narrow as to require that the courts give a result which was unjust to the ratepayers of the new amalgamated district council. The sum to which the ratepayers were entitled was not known when the old councils were abolished, but the right to have the sum ascertained was in existence at the moment that the boundary changes were made.

> Supposing that it has been the right to an ascertained sum, say £1,000 per annum, there would not have been any dispute that the appellants would have been entitled to receive it. Does it make an essential difference that the sum, though its basis was determined, remained to be ascertained by agreement or arbitration? To me the difference appears as one of form, not of substance.

A similar clash between the strict or literal constructionists and a more liberal approach occurred in *Re Rowland*, again featuring Lord Denning as one of the protagonists. The case, which turned on interpretation of the word 'coinciding', happened to concern a will, but the issues raised are again applicable to the interpretation of any legal document:

Re Rowland [1963] Ch 1 (CA)

Before going to the Far East a doctor and his wife made identical wills on printed will forms which provided that each left their property to the other, but in the event of the other's death 'preceding or coinciding' with that of the testator, the property was to go to selected alternative relatives. In the case of the husband, his property would in that event go to his brother and nephew. Both husband and wife were aboard a small ship which disappeared in the South Pacific. The circumstances of the disaster were never discovered. The question for the Court of Appeal was whether the husband's property should go to the wife's relations or, as he intended, to those of the husband. The leading judgment for the majority was given by Lord Justice Russell:

> It was argued that the words 'coinciding with' were not used by this testator in what I have described as their natural meaning. The suggestion is that this testator (in his particular armchair) meant something wider – something which during the hearing was described as 'on the same

> occasion and by the same cause'. It was pointed out that the wills of the spouses were made at a time when they knew they were going in 1956 to employment in the Pacific which would involve such perils or risks as may be inherent in (inter alia) travel between islands and atolls in small ships. Therefore, it was said, this testator should be considered as having had in mind just this kind of episode, and accordingly this phrase in this will should be construed as embracing this event. This appears to me to be a wholly erroneous approach to the problem of construction. One may hazard the guess that if he could now be asked to whom in the events which happened he would wish his property to go, he would say that he would wish it to go to his selected alternates. That would not mean, however, that he has expressed that wish by his will: his answer would be consistent with his having selected language which failed to appreciate all the possible circumstances which would make that outcome desirable. It is an unsound approach to the construction of the will to ask oneself what the testator, if he had thought of an event not covered by the natural and normal meaning of his language, would have wished had he directed his mind to the event. The question is what events does his language cover? To ask more is to desert the source from which his intention is to be gathered, his will as proved …
>
> I am clearly of the opinion that the testator's language does not fit the facts of the case, so far as they are known. To hold otherwise would not in my judgment be to construe the will at all: it would be the result of inserting in the will a phrase which the testator never used by guessing at what a man in his position would have wished had he directed his mind and pen to the facts as they now confront us. There is no jurisdiction in this court to achieve a sensible result by such means.

Lord Justice Harman agreed:

> It is for those claiming under the gift over to prove their case that the deaths of the testator and his wife were coincident. This word in the context in which it appears can in my judgment only be a reference to the time and not the occasion of death. In other words, 'coincident' is equivalent to 'simultaneous'. That was the only event which the testator on the language he used could have contemplated. He had already made the gift to his wife if she survived him and to the defendants if she did not. Can these deaths on the evidence be held to have been simultaneous … I am satisfied that it cannot. Not enough is known. It is not even known at what date, within a week, the ship went down, nor is the whereabouts of either the testator or his wife at that time certain. One or other of them may easily have survived the going down of the ship and the event is too uncertain to infer a simultaneous death, as was possible for COHEN J., in the case of two persons killed in close proximity to each other by the same bomb.
>
> If this meaning of the word be out of the question, it is argued that 'coincident' is a little looser and can mean in this will 'at about the same time and as a result of the same catastrophe'. This in my opinion is an impossible view. The will has provided for both possibilities of survivor-ship and there is no warrant for introducing a reference to something other than time, namely, the same catastrophe. I am, therefore, of the same opinion as the learned judge and would dismiss this appeal.

Lord Denning MR dissented:

> I must confess that, if ever there were an absurdity, I should have thought we have one here … It seems to me that the fallacy in that argument is that it starts from the wrong place. It proceeds on the assumption that, in construing a will, 'It is not what the testator meant, but what is the meaning of his words' that matters. That may have been the nineteenth-century view; but I believe it to be wrong and to have been the cause of many mistakes. I have myself known a judge to say: 'I believe this to be contrary to the true intention of the testator, but nevertheless it is the result of the words he has used'. When a judge goes so far as to say that, the chances are that he has misconstrued the will. For in point of principle the whole object of construing a will is to find out the testator's intentions, so as to see that his property is disposed of in the way he wished. True it

> is that you must discover his intention from the words that he has used; but you must put on his words the meaning which they bore to him. If his words are capable of more than one meaning, or of a wide meaning and a narrow meaning, as they often are, then you must put on them the meaning which he intended them to convey, and not the meaning which a philologist would put on them. In order to discover the meaning which he intended, you will not get much help from a dictionary. It is very unlikely that he used a dictionary, and even less likely that he used the same one as you. What you should do is place yourself as far as possible in his position, taking note of the facts and circumstances known to him at the time, and then say what he meant by his words … I decline, therefore, to ask myself: what do the words mean to a grammarian? I prefer to ask: What did Dr Rowland and his wife mean by the word 'coincide' in their wills? When they came to make their wills it is not difficult to piece together the thoughts that ran through their minds. The doctor might well say: 'We are going off for three years to these far-off places and in case anything happens to either of us we ought to make our wills. If I die before you, I would like everything to go to you, but if you die before me, I should like it to go to my brother and his boy.' She might reply: 'Yes, but what if we both die together? After all, one of those little ships might run on the rocks or something and we might both be drowned: or we might both be killed in an aeroplane crash'. 'To meet that,' he would say, 'I will put in that if your death coincides with mine, it is to go to my brother and his boy just the same'. He would use the words 'coinciding with', not in the narrow meaning of 'simultaneous', but in the wider meaning of which they are equally capable, especially in this context, as denoting death on the same occasion by the same cause. It would not cross Dr Rowland's mind that anyone would think of such niceties as counsel for the first defendant has presented to us. I decline to introduce such fine points into the construction of this will. I would hold that Dr Rowland, when he made his will, intended by these words 'coinciding with' to cover he and his wife dying together in just such a calamity as in fact happened: and that we should give his words the meaning which he plainly intended they should bear. I would allow the appeal accordingly.

Another example of the literal approach to interpretation leading to a foolish decision was the decision of the Divisional Court in *R (Haw) v Secretary of State for the Home Department* [2006] QB 359, [2006] 2 WLR 50. Mr Brian Haw had for years maintained a sizeable demonstration involving many posters in Parliament Square just outside Parliament. He lived there in a tent pitched on the pavement. The Serious Organised Crime and Policing Act 2005 had provisions requiring that demonstration in the vicinity of Parliament required the authorisation of the police. Mr Haw brought proceedings for judicial review to establish that the Act only applied to demonstrations that began after the provisions in the Act were brought into force. His ground was that s 132(1) stated that a person who organised, took part in or carried on a demonstration was guilty of an offence if 'when the demonstration starts' authorisation had not been obtained from the police. He argued that since his demonstration started before the Act came into force that could not apply to him. A divided court upheld his argument – despite the fact that, having looked at the Parliamentary debates, it accepted that the intention had been that the Act should apply to existing demonstrations and especially to Mr Haw! The Court of Appeal, however, came to the opposite conclusion, holding, without recourse to *Hansard*, that Parliament intended that demonstrations that were ongoing when the Act took effect did require authorisation.[11] It found the solution in s 132(6) which dis-applied the Public Order Act to demonstrations in Parliament

[11] [2006] EWCA Civ 552, [2006] QB 780.

Square. The Court said it was inconceivable that Parliament would have contemplated passing that provision if the police were unable to control demonstration in and around Parliament under s 132(1).

The virtues of the classic literal approach were outlined in an article in the *Canadian Bar Review* in 1937:

ER Hopkins, 'The literal canon and the golden rule' 15 *Canadian Bar Review*, 1937, 689

> Literal interpretation means nothing if plain words may be qualified according to common sense and justice as conceived judicially. If the absurdity clause were given free rein, the judicial inquiry would be 'what ought the Act to mean', rather than 'what does the Act mean': the former process has been variously impugned as 'juristic chemistry', 'spurious, interpretation', and 'evasion'.
>
> Then, should the literal canon be dislodged from, or relegated to the position of a presumption in a modern theory of interpretation? ... It is submitted that the formal approach is within its province most consonant with the judicial function. In our constitutional theory, the function of innovation rests primarily with legislative bodies. It is true that the final word in law-making must rest with the courts and that the exercise of any conscious mental process involves an element of discretion: yet, if the assignment of legislative power to parliament is to be otherwise than fictional, the process of interpretation must be divorced so far as may be from that of legislation. What must be sought for by the courts are criteria of meaning as objectivised and impersonal as can be found, so that the initial discretion inherent in legislation will be impaired as little as possible by a supervening discretion in interpretation. From this point of approach, the present attitude of the courts toward the literal canon, namely, that words are to be assigned their plain literal meaning in their context, merits more sympathy than it is currently accorded. Recognising the defects of any theory of statutory construction and without finding in literalness the quality of eternal verity, the judges have proceeded on the basis that the literal canon is founded on truths approximately accurate and criteria sufficiently objectivised for a workaday world and a busy court. The patent meaning is treated as the surest guide to the latent meaning of the statute, and the field of discretion which trenches upon the field of legislation while not eliminated is at any rate reduced to a minimum. If individual hardship, or a socially undesirable result, follows, legislative machinery provides the appropriate corrective, and if, as has been suggested, the literal canon has sometimes been inexpertly applied it must be remembered that to indict a workman is not necessarily to criticize his tools. While it will undoubtedly be necessary where the statutory meaning is obscure to make extensive and important demands upon judicial discretion, hope may be expressed that an improved draftmanship and a more studious regard to the boundaries of literal theory may result in at once an extension of the province and an improvement in the process of formal construction.

However, literalism has been subjected to severe criticism:

(1) The most fundamental objection is that it is based on a false premise, namely that words have plain, ordinary meanings apart from their context. Professor HLA Hart of Oxford argued that a word has a core meaning 'or standard instance in which no doubts are felt about its application' even though at the edges there is a margin of uncertainty.[12] Professor Lon Fuller of Harvard contested this, urging that meaning attaches not to individual words but to sentences and paragraphs, and that 'surely a

[12] H Hart, 'Positivism and the separation of law and morals' 71 *Harvard Law Review*, 1958, 593, 607.

paragraph does not have a "standard instance" that remains constant whatever the context in which it appears'.[13] If a statute seems to have a core meaning, 'this is because we can see that, however one might formulate the precise objective of the statute, *this* case would still come within it'.[14]

(2) Those who apply the literal approach often talk of using the 'dictionary meaning' of the words in question, but dictionaries provide a number of alternative meanings.

(3) The plain-meaning approach cannot be used for general words, which are obviously capable of bearing several meanings.

(4) Not infrequently the courts say that the meaning of the words is 'plain' but then disagree as to their interpretation.[15]

(5) When applying the literal or ordinary meaning approach courts do not allow evidence to be adduced as to the meaning of the word or phrase in question.[16] That means that the outcome of the case will be determined by the particular judge's linguistic understanding based on their knowledge, values and assumptions.

(6) The plain-meaning theory may be acceptable outside the court room since it is no doubt true that a high proportion of statutory materials and other legal documents can in fact be interpreted without recourse to any mischief or golden rule. But in the court room there are, by definition, two parties, usually represented by counsel, arguing over the meaning of the relevant passage. It makes little sense to dispose of the issue between them by reference to the plain meaning when there are at least two meanings in contention. As the late Professor Glanville Williams pointed out, often one party is contending for an 'obvious' meaning of the words while the other argues for a secondary meaning of the words. The choice cannot then be made sensibly without regard to the context.[17]

The most common retort from those who favour the literal approach is that, in spite of some problems, it promotes the certainty which is one of the chief objectives of any legal system. But does it?

If all judges *always* followed the policy of literalism, it may be that there would be some gain in certainty. But in practice they do not. Even the most die-hard advocates of the literal approach sometimes lapse into some alternative method. One commentator has written[18] '[T]he doctrine of literalness can never be applied successfully to general words. For they always include something more than the scope and object of the statute required and so it leads to ridiculous results.' Judges, he said, were torn between a feeling of obligation to

[13] L Fuller, 'Positivism and fidelity to law: a reply to Professor Hart' 71 *Harvard Law Review*, 1958, 630, 663.

[14] Ibid.

[15] See, eg, *London and NE Railway Co v Berriman* [1946] AC 278. In *Ellerman Lines v Murray* [1931] AC 126, all the judges agreed that the meaning was 'plain' but there were at least three different views as to what the plain meaning was. See similarly *Nothman v Barnet London Borough Council* [1979] 1 WLR 67, in which the House of Lords divided three to two; and *Newbury District Council v Secretary of State for the Environment* [1980] 2 WLR 379, where the five judges in the House of Lords unanimously gave a different meaning to the word 'repository' from that given to it by the Secretary of State and the six judges below, including the Lord Chief Justice and the Master of the Rolls. The six thought it clear their way. The five thought it clear the other way.

[16] 'It is the duty of the court to construe a statute according to the ordinary meaning of the words used, necessarily referring to dictionaries or other literature for the sake of informing itself as to the meaning of any words, but any evidence on the question is wholly inadmissible.' *Camden (Marquis) v CIR* [1914] 1 KB 641, 649–50.

[17] Glanville Williams, 'The meaning of literal interpretation' *New Law Journal*, 1981, 1128, 1149.

[18] JA Corry, 'Administrative Law: Interpretation of Statutes', *University of Toronto Law Journal*, 1935, 286, 301–03.

adhere to the doctrine and a feeling of revolt against what they regarded as an absurdity and injustice. So if literalness seemed too ridiculous or threatened things which the judge regarded as fundamental, he exerted himself to escape its conclusions. Even those judges who insisted strongly upon the principle of literal adherence to the words, deserted it in such circumstances.

> Lord Tenterden, who fathered the doctrine, sometimes found that literal meanings could not have been intended.[19] And Lord Bramwell, who affirmed the doctrine with his usual vigour and challenged anyone to show him an absurdity so great as to entitle him to depart from the plain meaning, had some interesting lapses.[20] … Lord Halsbury stated the doctrine of literalness as uncompromisingly as anyone. But in a case before the House of Lords in 1890 he deserted it and appealed to the 'equity of the statute'.[21]

The result of the inevitable inconsistency as to the application of the literal approach is that it loses much of its claim to be the basis of greater certainty. Lord Justices Russell and Harman in *Re Rowland* may have justified their decision on the ground that it would assist in the future by reducing litigation if lawyers were able to predict that the court would adopt the literal approach. But a lawyer advising Dr Rowland's brother and nephew is bound to tell them that there is at least some chance of persuading the court to take a reasonable line. The testator plainly intended to leave his property to the brother and nephew if he and his wife died in the same accident. (Lord Justice Russell himself recognised this when he said 'One may hazard the guess that if he could now be asked to whom in the events which happened he would wish his property to go, he would say that he would wish it go to his selected alternates. That would not mean, however, that he had expressed that wish by his will'.[22]) The chance of succeeding in such a case is good enough to justify litigation. A lawyer would properly tell the client that there are many judges who insist on applying the literal approach but that equally there are others who prefer a more liberal approach and even the literalists can sometimes be persuaded to adopt a broader approach. It is only if judges uniformly applied the literal approach that the lawyer would have to advise that the chances of success were negligible.

If the literal approach does not therefore reduce litigation, does it promote better and more precise draftsmanship? There can be no doubt that the draftsman in the *Rowland* case used the word 'coinciding' inappropriately. Had he thought more carefully about the problem he might have used a phrase such as 'if we die in or as the result of the same accident or incident' or, better still, he might have said, 'if my wife does not survive me by thirty days'. Will draftsmen be frightened into using language more accurately by dreadful warnings such as the *Rowland* case? To imagine that this is likely to be the result of such decisions strains credulity. First, it has to be assumed that the potential drafters become aware of the Court of Appeal's ruling in the *Rowland* case. Most legal drafting is done by solicitors who are busy and have little time to pore over the law reports. Some will notice the case; many will not. Some drafting, especially of wills, is done by laymen. It is obvious that they are highly unlikely to come to hear of the decision. By contrast, if the case concerns a statutory

[19] *Margate Pier Co v Hannam* (1819) 3 B & Ald 266; *Edwards v Dick* (1821) 4 B & Ald 212; *Bennett v Daniel* (1830) 10B&C 500.

[20] For example, *Twycross v Grant* (1877) 46 LJQB 636; *Ex p Walton* (1881) 17 Ch D 746; *Hill v East and West India Dock Co* (1884) 9 App Cas 448.

[21] *Cox v Hakes* (1890) 15 App Cas 506.

[22] [1963] Ch 1, 17.

provision, it is likely that at least some of the small number of parliamentary drafters will see the report and note its significance.

But even assuming that the drafter sees the decision, what difference will it make in practice to the quality of their work in their office? They do not need the Court of Appeal to tell them that they have to take care in drafting to select the right formula and the appropriate words. It is part of the nature of the activity. They have had it dinned into them ever since they came to the office as a trainee, pupil barrister or other junior. It is impossible to draft the simplest document without being all too conscious of the problem of finding the right words to express one's meaning. If they read of the fate of some unfortunate drafter's phrase in a report such as the *Rowland* case, it is improbable that they will do their work better that day as a result. They are already doing their work as well as they can according to their lights. There are far more effective pressures on them to draft well than the remote possibility that their labours will one day fall foul of the High Court or Court of Appeal. Their superiors and colleagues in the office will be reading their work and making suggestions in any event. (As has been seen, parliamentary drafters work in pairs in order to improve the quality of their work.) The probable benefits of the literal approach in terms of improved draftsmanship are at best therefore speculative. When set against the manifest disadvantage of deciding an actual case in a sense contrary to what the judges believe to be the reasonable result for the parties, they appear unimpressive.

The literalist approach makes too little allowance for the natural ambiguities of language, for the frailties of even the most skilled of drafters and for the impossibility of foreseeing future events. In its 1969 report, *The Interpretation of Statutes*, the Law Commission said:

> To place undue emphasis on the literal meaning of the words of a provision is to assume an unattainable perfection in draftsmanship; it presupposes that the draftsmen can always choose words to describe the situations intended to be covered by the provision which will leave no room for a difference of opinion as to their meaning. Such an approach ignores the limitations of language, which is not infrequently demonstrated even at the level of the House of Lords when Law Lords differ as to the so-called 'plain meaning' of words. (para 30)

The literal approach is based on a narrow concentration on the actual words used, to the exclusion of the surrounding circumstances that might explain what the words were actually intended to mean. It is very closely connected with the traditional common law rule that excludes evidence as to the meaning of written documents. Llewellyn Davies wrote of this:

> A very marked feature of the common law rules for the construction of written instruments has been the rigidity with which they excluded all extrinsic evidence, and their insistence that the meaning of a document must be ascertained from its words as they stood. This attitude may well have originated in what Pollock and Maitland call the 'mystical awe' with which the early Common Law regarded the written instrument, and there can be no doubt but that the particular solemnity attributed to the instrument under seal has exercised a great influence on the attitude of the courts towards the written law.[23]

[23] DJ Llewellyn Davies, 'The interpretation of statutes in the light of their policy' 35 *Columbia Law Review*, 1935, 519, 522.

It is a characteristic of some primitive legal systems that they attach excessive weight to the importance of words so that, for instance, the claimant who makes a slip in stating their claim is nonsuited. The literal approach to language by lawyers may be a form of this tradition. The drafter is in effect punished for failing to do their job properly (except that it is their client, or in the case of statutes, the wider community, that bears the cost). The punitive or disciplinarian school of judicial interpretation remains a powerful element in the operation of the English legal system. ('If the drafter has not got it right, let them try again and do better next time.')

At first sight the literal approach to statutory interpretation could be said to be based on a sense of the court's deference to the sovereignty of Parliament. ('It is not for the court to put words into parliament's mouth – we are simply the humble servants who will faithfully implement Parliament's will providing only that we are told clearly what Parliament desires.') But this humble posture is misleading. It conceals an ancient tradition amongst the judges that the common law is a superior form of creation to statutes. The judges have, for instance, often applied the presumption that Parliament does not intend to alter the common law unless it plainly states its intention to do so.[24] The literal approach is part of the same philosophy. ('We cannot be expected to move unless we are given clear marching orders. If we do not consider the marching orders to be clear enough we will refuse to budge and the fault will be parliament's not ours.') This is hardly the attitude of the interpreter that is likely to produce the best results.

A final criticism of the literal approach to interpretation is that it is defeatist and lazy. The judge gives up the attempt to understand the document at the first attempt. Instead of struggling to discover what it means, they simply adopt the most straightforward interpretation of the words in question – without regard to whether this interpretation makes sense in the particular context. It is not that the literal approach necessarily gives the wrong result but rather that the result is purely accidental. It is the intellectual equivalent of deciding the case by tossing a coin. The literal *interpretation* in a particular case may in fact be the best and wisest of the various alternatives, but the literal *approach* is always wrong because it amounts to an abdication of responsibility by the judge. Instead of decisions being based on reason and principle, the literalist bases their decision on one meaning arbitrarily preferred. The limitations of this approach may be seen in a case decided in the nineteenth century.

Whiteley v Chappell (1868–69) 4 LRQB 147

A statute made it an offence for anyone in an election of guardians of the poor 'wilfully, fraudulently and with intent to affect the result of such election … to personate any person entitled to vote at such election'. The defendant was charged with personating someone who was deceased. The full text of the judgments delivered in the case is as follows:

> LUSH J: I do not think we can, without straining them, bring the case within the words of the enactment. The legislature has not used words wide enough to make the personation of a dead person an offence. The words 'a person entitled to vote' can only mean, without a forced construction, a person who is entitled to vote at the time at which the personation takes place; in the present case, therefore, I feel bound to say the offence has not been committed. In the cases of *Rex v Martin*, and *Rex v Cramp* (Russ. & Ry. 324,327), the judges gave no reasons for

[24] 'Few principles of statutory interpretation are applied as frequently' – *Maxwell on the Interpretation of Statutes*, 12th edn (Sweet & Maxwell, 1969) 116.

> their decision; they probably held that 'supposed to be entitled' meant supposed to the person personating.
>
> HANNEN J: I regret that we are obliged to come to the conclusion that the offence charged was not proved; but it would be wrong to strain words to meet the justice of the present case, because it might make a precedent, and lead to dangerous consequences in other cases.
>
> HAYES J concurred.

Since the court applied the literal approach, its failure to discuss the problem was understandable. It gave no attention to the question whether the statute was designed to protect the integrity of the election by preventing voting in the name of *anyone* else or whether it was aimed rather at the protection of the votes of living voters. In another statute it had been made an offence to personate 'a person entitled or supposed to be entitled to any prize money'. In *Rex v Martin* and *Rex v Cramp*, cited by Lush J, the court had held that 'supposed to be entitled' could include the case where the personation was of someone known to be dead. Counsel for the prosecution argued that these cases were in point and that they reflected the policy of trying to stop personation by anyone. 'The gist of the offence', he argued, 'is the fraudulently voting under another's name; the mischief is the same, whether the supposed voter be alive or dead'. Counsel for the defence, on the other hand, drew the court's attention to the Parliamentary Registration Act 1843, s 83 of which made it an offence to personate 'any person whose name appears on the register of voters, whether such person be he alive or dead'. Under the statute being considered by the court there was no express reference to the dead voter – 'the person must be entitled, that is could have voted himself'.

But the court did not do counsel the courtesy of paying any attention to their arguments. The judges looked at the words of the statute and nothing else. A dead person was not entitled to vote, ergo, the prosecution failed. Similarly, in the *Rowland* case, according to the dictionary or the plain meaning, 'coinciding' means two things occurring at the same moment. There being no evidence that Dr and Mrs Rowland died at the same moment, the will was inoperative and the property passed under the provisions of the Law of Property Act 1925. The approach is mechanical, divorced both from the realities of the use of language and from the expectations of the human beings concerned and, in that sense, it is irresponsible.

In the latter part of the twentieth century the courts increasingly moved away from the literal-mindedness seen in cases such as *Rowland* or *Whiteley v Chappell* towards what is nowadays commonly called a 'purposive approach'. But there were still plenty of examples of the literal approach. In *Shah v Barnet London Borough Council* [1983] 2 AC 309, the House of Lords said that overseas students who had been in this country for the purposes of schooling were 'ordinarily resident' in the country and were therefore entitled to mandatory local authority grants for university study. The Law Lords reached this view by analysing the meaning of the words without regard to their context or to legislative intent. (The decision, which had serious public expenditure consequences, was promptly cancelled by legislation.)

In *Griffith v Secretary of State for the Environment* [1983] 2 WLR 172, the plaintiff had to appeal against the Secretary of State's refusal of planning permission within six weeks from the date on which the Secretary of State took action. The House of Lords held by a majority that action was taken when an official put the date stamp on the decision letter even though the letter was never posted and the plaintiff therefore never received it. In *Reynolds* [1981] 73 Cr App R 324, the Court of Appeal, Criminal Division unanimously quashed a conviction where the jury foreman had announced that the conviction was agreed to by ten of the jury but failed to state that two had dissented! (The Juries Act 1974, s 17(3), required that the number voting both for conviction and against should be stated. The House of Lords later overruled the decision in *Pigg* [1983] 1 WLR 6.) In *Lees v Secretary of State for Social Services* [1985] AC 930, the House of Lords held that a blind person who could only go out with a human guide did not qualify for a mobility allowance because his physical disablement did not come within the phrase of being 'unable to walk or virtually unable to do so'. In *Clarke and McDaid* [2008] UKHL 8, [2008] 1 WLR 338 the House of Lords, preferring a literal to a purposive interpretation and reversing the Court of Appeal, held that a conviction had to be quashed because the bill of indictment had not been signed.[25]

Shah, Griffith, Reynolds, Lees, Clarke and McDaid showed that the literal approach was still alive and flourishing.

See further on literal interpretation Glanville Williams, 'The meaning of literal interpretation' *New Law Journal*, 5 and 12 November 1981, 1128 and 1149. Professor Williams argued that the question whether words are plain and unambiguous must always be considered in context. It is futile to ask, first, 'Are the words plain?' and, secondly, 'Can we give effect to the probable interpretation of Parliament?' A court that decides that words are unambiguous is really deciding that the other interpretation suggested is impossible on the wording.

3.3.2. What of the Golden Rule?

If the literal rule is unacceptable, is the golden rule any better? The answer must be that it is not – for the golden rule is based on the literal rule. It tells the judge to follow the literal approach unless that results in absurdity, in which case they should find some other solution. Admittedly, the golden rule does at least have the saving grace that it may protect the court from egregious foolishness. But it does so only in the rare case where the judge is prepared to hold that the result is so absurd or unreasonable as virtually to require that they find some other construction. It is better to have such a rule than not to have it, but it provides an answer to very few cases. Most statutory interpretation problems that come before the courts do not present such easy answers. There is usually a difficult choice to be made between two fairly plausible arguments. (If the matter were clear-cut one would assume that the lawyers would so advise their clients and the case would normally not reach the court.) The golden rule therefore only rescues the court in a tiny number of instances.

Moreover, there is no way of predicting what will strike a court as an absurdity sufficiently clear to justify this exceptional response. The point was made by John Willis in his famous article:

> What is an 'absurdity'? When is the result of a particular interpretation so 'absurd' that a court will feel justified in departing from a 'plain meaning'? There is the difficulty. 'Absurdity' is a concept no less vague and indefinite than 'plain meaning': you cannot reconcile the cases

[25] The statute stated that the proper officer of the court '*shall*' sign the bill of indictment and it shall thereupon become an indictment. The Court of Appeal had based its decision on what it said was the prevailing approach to litigation that cases should be decided on their merits and not on technicalities. The House of Lords decision was the subject of severe criticism – PJT Fields, '*Clarke and McDaid*: a technical triumph' [2008] Crim LR 612–24.

> upon it.[26] It is infinitely more a matter of personal opinion and infinitely more susceptible to the influence of personal prejudice. The result is that in ultimate analysis the 'golden rule' does allow a court to make quite openly exceptions which are based not on the social policy behind the Act, not even on the total effect of the words used by the legislature, but purely on the social and political views of the men who happen to be sitting on the case …
>
> What use do the courts make of the 'golden rule' today? Again the answer is the same – they use it as a device to achieve a desired result, in this case as a very last resort and only after all less blatant methods have failed. In those rare cases where the words in question are (a) narrow and precise, and (b) too 'plain' to be judicially held not plain, and yet to hold them applicable would shock the court's sense of justice, the court will, if it wishes to depart from their plain meaning, declare that to apply them literally to the facts of this case would result in an 'absurdity' of which the legislature could not be held guilty, and, invoking the 'golden rule', will work out an implied exception.[27]

One serious objection to the golden rule is therefore that it is erratic. One can never know whether a particular conclusion will be so offensive to the particular judge to qualify as an absurdity and, if so, whether the court will feel moved to apply the golden rather than the literal rule. As has been seen, there are plenty of decisions in which the courts have preferred to follow the literal approach notwithstanding the fact that it led to absurdity. But a further and equally strong objection is that the rule is silent as to how the court should proceed if it does find an unacceptable absurdity. It must find an answer to the problem, but the rule gives the court no guidance as to how it should set about the task. The Law Commission's report on statutory interpretation said: '[T]he golden rule sets a purely negative standard by reference to absurdity, inconsistency or inconvenience, but provides no clear means to test the existence of these characteristics or to measure their quality or extent.'[28] The golden rule is therefore little more than an unpredictable safety-valve to permit the courts to escape from some of the more unpalatable effects of the literal rule. It cannot be regarded as a sound basis for judicial decision-making.

In *R v McCool* [2018] UKSC 23 the majority of the Supreme Court used the Golden Rule to avoid what they considered would be an absurd literal interpretation of the Proceeds of Crime Act 2002 ('POCA'). Lord Reed dissenting, with whom Lord Mance agreed, said 'I see no absurdity'.[29] Commentators on the decisions wrote: *McCool* is especially worthy of close consideration for how the absurdity principle was deployed. For Lord Kerr, it would be absurd for the pre-POCA confiscation regime to apply to offences that were committed after POCA was commenced. In his dissenting judgment, Lord Reed not only disagreed that such a result would be absurd, but argued that the majority's interpretation would itself lead to absurd results that could not have been intended by Parliament.[30]

[26] Contrast *Vacher v London Society of Compositors* [1913] AC 107, 117, 118 and *Washington v Grand Trunk Railway* 28 SCR 184, where the court refused to find an absurdity, with *Ex p Walton* (1881) 17 Ch D 746 and *The Ruahepu* [1927] P 47, where the court did find an absurdity. See also *The Altrincham Electric Supply Co Ltd v Sale UDC* (1936) 154 LTR 379, in which the arbitrator, the trial judge and a majority of the House of Lords applied the literal interpretation, and the Court of Appeal and a minority of the House of Lords applied the mischief rule.

[27] Willis (n 4 above) 13–14.

[28] Law Commission, *The Interpretation of Statutes* (Law Commission, 1969) para 32.

[29] See [24–26] and [146].

[30] K Laird and S Walker, 'Statutory Interpretation, absurdity and the Proceeds of Crime Act 2002', 135 *Law Quarterly Review* (2019) 390–95, 393.

3.3.3. The Mischief Rule is Now Called the Purposive Approach

The phrase 'the Mischief Rule' is no longer used. For many years the courts have spoken instead of statutory interpretation requiring a purposive or contextual approach.[31] Andrew Burrows, then Professor of Law at Oxford University – now Lord Burrows[32] – noted this in the first of his Hamlyn Lectures given in 2017 under the title *Thinking about Statutes*:[33]

> It is tolerably clear today that our judges have moved from an old literal to a modern contextual and purposive approach. We no longer give words their literal or dictionary meaning in so far as the context and purpose of the statute indicate that that is not the best interpretation of what Parliament has enacted. In *IRC v McGuckian*[34] in 1997 Lord Steyn said: 'During the last 30 years, there has been a shift away from the literalist approach to purposive methods of construction … the modern emphasis is on a contextual approach designed to emphasise the purpose of a statute and to give effect to it. In Lord Bingham's words in *R v Secretary of State for Health ex p Quintavalle*,[35] "The court's task, within the permissible bounds of interpretation, is to give effect to Parliament's purpose, So the controversial provisions should be read in the context of the statute as a whole, and the statute as a whole should be read in the historical context of the statute which led to its enactment".'[36] In the same case Lord Steyn again emphasised that a purposive, rather than a literal, approach was now to be taken. 'The pendulum has swung towards purposive methods of construction … Nowadays the shift toward purposive interpretation is not in doubt'.

A crucial issue is where the court may look to discover the context. As Lord Diplock explained in *Black-Clawson* [1975] AC 591 at 638, when the mischief rule was first propounded, the judges were not supposed to look further than the statute itself:

> LORD DIPLOCK: Statutes in the sixteenth century and for long thereafter in addition to the enacting words contained lengthy preambles reciting the particular mischief or defect in the common law that the enacting words were designed to remedy. So, when it was laid down, the 'mischief' rule did not require the court to travel beyond the actual words of the statute itself to identify 'the mischief and defect for which the common law did not provide', for this would have been stated in the preamble. It was a rule of construction of the actual words appearing in the statute and nothing else. In construing modern statutes which contain no preambles to serve as aids to the construction of enacting words, the 'mischief' rule must be used with caution to justify any reference to extraneous documents for this purpose.

[31] Professor Neil Duxbury makes the historical point that whereas it is generally thought that purposivism is a modern standard of statutory interpretation in fact it pre-dated the plain meaning or literal approach. (N Duxbury, *Elements of Legislation* (Cambridge University Press, 2013) 192.) The so-called 'mischief rule' was the standard convention of statutory construction in the seventeenth century. *Heydon's case* was still being cited regularly by counsel and judges during the eighteenth century when the plain-meaning or literal rule started to come into its own. When Blackstone, in the first volume of his *Commentaries* (1765) set out the main 'rules to be observed with regard to the construction of statutes', the mischief rule was the first to be listed. (1 Bl Comm 87.) Duxbury adds a quote from Blackstone: '[T]he most universal and effectual way of discovering the true meaning of a law when the words are dubious, is by considering the reason and spirit of it; or the cause which moved the legislature to enact it.'

[32] Lord Burrows became a Justice of the Supreme Court in 2020. He was the first person ever to have been appointed to the highest court directly from holding a full-time chair.

[33] Andrew Burrows, *Thinking About Statutes* (Cambridge University Press, 2018) 5–6.

[34] 14 WLR 991 at 999.

[35] [2003] UKHL 13, [2003 AC 687.

[36] [2003] UKHL 13, [2003] AC 687 at [6].

The right to inquire into the background to, and reasons for, legislation was therefore restricted. What then is permitted?

3.4. Understanding the Context: Statutes and Judicial Decisions

3.4.1. The Court Can Read the Whole Statute

There is no doubt, first of all, that a court may read the whole of the statute that has produced the problem. It may also read both *the long and the short title*.[37] Until well into the nineteenth century, the long title could not be considered in construing a statute – on the ground that it was not regarded as part of the statute. But it eventually was accepted that the title of the statute could be consulted for the purpose of ascertaining its meaning.[38]

It may also read *the preamble*. As just noted, old statutes commonly had lengthy preambles setting out the purposes of legislation; today they are rare.[39] But the House of Lords ruled decisively in 1957 that the courts could have regard to the preamble when construing a statute. The case was *Attorney General v Prince Ernest Augustus of Hanover* [1957] AC 436, in which the courts had to consider an application by the Prince to be recognised as a British subject under a statute which granted British nationality to 'all persons lineally descended from the Electoress Sophia of Hanover'. Lord Normand said (467, 468):

> When there is a preamble it is generally in its recitals that the mischief to be remedied and the scope of the Act are described. It is therefore clearly permissible to have recourse to it as an aid to construing the enacting provisions ... The courts are concerned with the practical business of deciding a *lis* [a piece of litigation (ed)], and when the plaintiff puts forward one construction of an enactment and the defendant another, it is the court's business in any case of some difficulty, after informing itself of what I have called the legal and factual context including the preamble, to consider in the light of this knowledge whether the enacting words admit of both the rival constructions put forward. If they admit of only one construction, that construction will receive effect even if it is inconsistent with the preamble, but if the enacting words are capable of either of the constructions offered by the parties, the construction which fits the preamble may be preferred.

In *Prince Ernest*'s case it was found that the enacting words were clear and they could not therefore be affected by contrary indications in a rather vague preamble.

[37] For an article about the significance of titles see BC Jones, 'Do short bill titles matter? Surprising insights from Westminster and Holyrood' 65 *Parliamentary Affairs*, 2012, 448.

[38] For examples see *Fisher v Raven* [1964] AC 210; *Brown v Brown* [1967] P 105, 110; *Haines v Herbert* [1963] 1 WLR 1401, 1404.

[39] Professor Duxbury explains that preambles 'were prevalent in English law in an era when parliament was in the habit of enacting loosely drafted statutes which courts would often interpret, and which parliament knew courts would often interpret, according to their apparent purpose or "spirit". When, in the eighteenth century, legislative drafting became more granular, the value of the preamble waned.' (N Duxbury, *Elements of Legislation* (Cambridge University Press, 2013) 208.)

The *headings* prefixed to sections or sets of sections are regarded as preambles to those sections. They may explain ambiguous words. But clear words in the statute cannot be affected by contrary indications in the heading (*R v Surrey (NE Area) Assessment Committee* [1948] 1 KB 28, 32, 33).[40]

Side notes or marginal notes printed at the side of sections in an Act which purport to summarise their effect have sometimes been used as an aid to construction. There are judicial statements to the effect that they are not part of the statute and should not be considered, on the ground that they are 'inserted not by Parliament nor under the authority of Parliament but by irresponsible persons'.[41] But Bennion, himself formerly a member of Parliamentary Counsel's office, points out that this is not correct. They are inserted by the drafter and are part of the statute when it is approved by Parliament.[42] However, they are no longer used, having been replaced entirely by headings.

Schedules to a statute are treated as fully part of the statute and may be used in construing the Act.

According to some authorities *punctuation* should be disregarded in the construction of statutes on the ground that there was normally no punctuation in ancient statutes. In a 1960 tax case Lord Reid said 'even if punctuation in more modern Acts can be looked at (which is very doubtful), I do not think that one can have any regard to punctuation in older Acts' (*IRC v Hinchy* [1960] AC 748, 765).[43] According to this view punctuation can be ignored or, if the court chooses, it can re-punctuate the words in a way different from that in the text. This view is, however, controversial and some (including three great authorities, Thornton, Dreidger and Bennion), hold that punctuation *is* to be regarded as part of the statute.[44] Bennion rejects the idea that old statutes did not have punctuation. It was true of some but untrue of others.[45] Punctuation in those days was unreliable but to ignore it, he suggests, is 'foreign to the ancient traditions of the law'.[46] In modern times statutes were punctuated by or under the supervision of the person who drafted them. They were unquestionably part of the statute and should be treated as such.

Certainly it is the case that a rule which prohibits reference to any part of a printed statute (be it headings, marginal notes, punctuation) makes nonsense of the notion that a statute is supposed to be accessible to the lay reader. How could the ordinary person be expected to know of such esoteric rules?

[40] See also *Fitzgerald v Hall, Russell & Co Ltd* [1970] AC 984; and *DPP v Schildkamp* [1971] AC 1, 10, 20, 28. But see *Infabrics Ltd v Jaytex Ltd* [1982] AC 1 (HL).

[41] Re Woking Urban Council (Basingstoke Canal) Act 1911 [1914] 1 Ch 300 at 322, per Phillimore LJ. For a learned article of over forty pages on marginal notes see G Stewart, 'Legislative drafting and the marginal note' 16 *Statute Law Review*, 1995, 21. See also BH Simamba, 'Should marginal notes be used in interpretation of statutes?' 26 *Statute Law Review*, 2005, 125.

[42] FAR Bennion, *Bennion on Statutory Interpretation*, 7th edn (LexisNexis, 2017) 638. In *R v Montila* [2004] UKHL 50, [2004] 1 WLR 3141, [33]–[35] the House of Lords cited Bennion's statement approvingly and confirmed that side notes and headings could be used as an aid to construction.

[43] See also *DPP v Schildkamp* (n 40 above) 10; and *Hanlon v The Law Society* [1980] 2 WLR 756, 815, per Lord Lowry.

[44] See VCRAC Crabbe, 'Punctuation in legislation' *Statute Law Review*, 1988, 87.

[45] 'The courts have consistently said that in the original version Acts are not punctuated, and that punctuation forms no part of an Act. However, this is not so. Since the earliest times statutes have in fact been punctuated.' Bennion, *Bennion on Statutory Interpretation*, 7th edn (n 42 above) 640. He cites the legal historian TFT Plucknett who showed that there was punctuation in statutes in the first half of the fourteenth century.

[46] Ibid, 641.

If signposting such as headings, marginal notes and punctuation are to be counted as part of the statute, there remains the further question whether they are to be treated as fully operative or as in some sense of inferior status? Francis Bennion takes the latter view. Of headings and sidenotes, he writes that either 'may be considered in construing any provision of the Act, provided due account is taken of the fact that its function is merely to serve as a brief, and therefore necessarily inaccurate, guide to the material to which it is attached'.[47] So in a conflict between a numbered provision and a descriptive component such as a heading or sidenote, the provision prevails. For the opposite view see Ruth Sullivan, 'Some implications of plain language drafting' 22 *Statute Law Review*, 2001, 175, 201–03:

> I can see no sound basis for treating some parts of a statute as stating the law and other parts as mere commentary or context. What is (or should be) enacted into law is the entire Act. Every part of it, potentially, may serve as evidence of the intended rule that governs particular facts or the disposition of a particular controversy. In the absence of any reason to automatically privilege one type of component over another, what receives the most weight should depend on the circumstances of the case. (p 203)

For a case where reading the whole statute made the difference see *Gibson v Ryan* [1968] 1 QB 250. The question was whether an inflatable rubber dinghy and a fish basket found on the appellant were within the meaning of the word 'instrument' in s 7(1) of the Salmon and Freshwater Fisheries Protection (Scotland) Act 1951. The Divisional Court said they were not. Diplock LJ referred to s 10 of the Act which drew a distinction between instruments on the one hand, boats on the other hand and baskets on the third hand.

In *Oliver Ashworth (Holdings) Ltd v Ballard (Kent) Ltd* [2000] 2 Ch 12 the court had to interpret s 18 of the Rent Act 1737 which, read literally, gave the landlord the right to double rent where a tenant held over after the expiry of his own notice to quit. The Court of Appeal held that the 1737 Act should be read as a whole and together with the Landlord and Tenant Act 1730 with which it was linked. The effect was that the double rent provision only applied if the landlord had treated the tenant as a trespasser after the expiry of the notice to quit, which was not the case there.

3.4.2. The Court Can Read Earlier Statutes

Sometimes, by tracing the history of a particular phrase back through earlier Acts one can throw light on its meaning. If the language changes between one statute and another, inferences can be drawn from the fact; alternatively, sometimes understanding of meaning can be based on a similarity of language in the present Act and some earlier statute when the historical position was different. In *Armah v Government of Ghana* [1968] AC 192 the court had to interpret s 5 of the Fugitive Offenders Act 1891 which required that evidence should raise 'a strong or probable presumption that the fugitive committed the offence'. Lord Reid said that nineteenth-century Acts drew a distinction between two kinds of evidence – that which raised a strong presumption of guilt and that which simply gave reason to inquire into guilt. The distinction, he said, must have been known to those who framed the 1891 Act and indicated that the disputed words must refer to the first kind of evidence. It was therefore not sufficient for the magistrate to be satisfied that there was enough evidence against the fugitive on which a jury might properly convict.

[47] Ibid, 635, 636.

A phrase used in one Act can be construed by reference to the same or a similar phrase used in earlier Acts – at least if the Acts deal with the same subject-matter. But the qualification about the similarity of the subject-matter is not always made. The Betting and Gaming Act 1960, for instance, required an applicant for a betting shop to insert a notice 'in a newspaper circulating in the authority's area'. It was held that an advertisement in *Sporting Life* was sufficient and that the Act did not require an advertisement either in a local paper or in a national paper circulating in the area. The court drew a distinction between the 1960 Act and s 12 of the Highways Act 1959 which specifically referred to 'a local newspaper circulating in the area' (*R v Westminster Betting Licensing Committee, ex p Peabody Donation Fund* [1963] 2 QB 750).

The last case cited is an example of the court inferring that the draftsman of one piece of legislation is aware of the use of similar phrases in earlier Acts and that a difference in wording between one Act and another is conscious and intentional. This theory, based on the omniscience of parliamentary draftsmen, is often carried to improbable lengths. It may be that the draftsman of, say, the latest Rent Act will be aware of the use of language in previous Rent Acts – though given the extreme length and complexity of such legislation even that may be assuming a good deal too much. But it is hardly reasonable to assume that the draftsman has in mind the language used in a mass of other prior statutes which have no direct connection with the one they are presently engaged in drafting.

An example of the court being influenced by the assumption that Parliament must be deemed to have been aware of earlier legislation and non-usage (regarding the meaning of the words 'immoral conduct') was *Crook v Edmondson* [1966] 2 QB 81 (Divisional Court) in which a man, was charged with persistently soliciting for immoral purposes through 'kerb-crawling' in a public place contrary to s 32 of the Sexual Offences Act 1956. The case turned on whether the words 'immoral purposes' included heterosexual advances. The Act was a consolidation measure. Its preamble said it was to 'consolidate … the statute law of England and Wales relating to sexual crimes, to the abduction, procuration and prostitution of women and to kindred offences'. The justices dismissed the case on the ground that although the conduct of the accused was immoral it was not within the meaning of 'immoral purposes' in the 1956 Act. The prosecution appealed. The Divisional Court was divided. Winn LJ said that there was no reported case in which the phrase had been applied to heterosexual conduct. Parliament must be presumed to have been aware of this non-usage as well as the usage of applying the phrase to homosexual advances. Lord Parker CJ said that he entirely agreed and had nothing to add. Sachs J dissented. In his view what was meant by 'immoral purposes'

> should be the responsibility of the jury of the day or of whoever is entrusted with that decision in lieu of a jury. I would, incidentally, be averse to that decision being fettered by the result of any preliminary inquiry into either what were the prevalent sexual vices at the end of the last century or what were then the prevalent views on some aspect of sexual immorality. If on the basis just expressed it were found that the now unfortunately prevalent conduct known as kerb crawling (i.e. a man from a slowly driven car importuning ordinary young women to accompany him for sexual intercourse) fell within the ambit of s 32, that would not seem to me inherently wrong.[48]

[48] In the debates on the Street Offences Act 1959, the Lord Chancellor had said that s 32 of the Sexual Offences Act 1956 covered pestering of women by men and that there was therefore no need for an amendment to cover such solicitation (House of Lords, *Hansard*, vol 216, col 806) (ed).

Farrell v Alexander [1977] AC 59 showed that the assumption that the draftsman knew of the existing statutory precedents or even case law should not *necessarily* be made. The House of Lords was interpreting the meaning of the words 'any person' in the Rent Act 1968, a consolidation measure. In 1972 the Court of Appeal had held that the words in that context meant 'the landlord' and did not include tenants, agents and other middlemen. In its 1972 decision the Court of Appeal had placed emphasis on the fact that in 1921 the Court of Appeal had construed the words 'any person' in a similar provision of an earlier Act in such a way as to limit its meaning to landlords. In 1949 and 1965 there had been further legislation on the same topic and Parliament had used the same phrase. It was contended that this showed that Parliament intended the phrase to mean only landlords. Lord Wilberforce disagreed:

> LORD WILBERFORCE (74): My Lords, I have never been attracted by the doctrine of parliamentary endorsement of decided cases: it seems to me to be based upon a theory of legislative formation which is possibly fictional. But if there are cases in which this doctrine may be applied, and I must respect the opinions of those judges who have so held, any case must be a clear one ... This case is certainly not such a case. It really cannot be said if our reasoning is to have any contact with reality that the draftsman of the Act of 1949 (a) must have had in mind a decision of 1921 [*Remmington v Larchin* [1921] 3 KB 404], whose reported headnote opens with the words 'that section 8(1) was reasonably capable of two constructions' and all of the judgments which underlined the ambiguity and obscurity of the enactment, (b) decided to perpetuate this ambiguity while removing one of the grounds of the decision, (c) should have committed Parliament to the continued existence of a lacuna or loophole which had no merits to commend it. To impute such a process of thought to the architect of the new section and to those who voted it into existence really strains credibility.

Lord Simon of Glaisdale likewise thought the doctrine was sometimes carried too far:

> It is a fact that a parliamentary draftsman (like any draftsman) does acquaint himself thoroughly with the existing law (statutory and judge-made) before starting to draft. Any draftsman of a rent restriction Act after 1921 may be presumed (nor is it an idle presumption) to have had *Remmington v Larchin* in mind. When, then, he used language which had been interpreted in *Remmington v Larchin* he presumptively used it in the sense in which it had there been interpreted. If therefore the object of statutory interpretation were to ascertain what Parliament meant to say, the *Barras* doctrine would indeed be potent and primary. But the object of statutory interpretation is rather to ascertain the meaning of what Parliament has said. On this approach the previous judicial interpretation is merely one of the facts within the knowledge of the draftsman in the light of which he will draft ... If Parliament wishes to endorse the previous interpretation it can do so in terms ... The sovereignty of Parliament is fundamental constitutional law; but courts of law have their own constitutional duties, important amongst which is to declare the meaning of a statutory enactment. To pre-empt a court of construction from performing independently its own constitutional duty of examining the validity of a previous interpretation, the intention of Parliament to endorse the previous judicial decision would have to be expressed or clearly implied. Mere repetition of language which has been the subject of previous judicial interpretation is entirely neutral in this respect – or at most implies merely the truism that the language has been the subject of judicial interpretation, for whatever (and it may be much or little) that is worth. (107)

In this particular case the House of Lords decided to extend the meaning of 'any person' to include a wider range of persons and it was therefore seeking for ways around the argument that Parliament must have been assumed to have meant the same by the phrase as in the cases decided in 1949, 1965 and 1968. The 1968 Act was a consolidation Act and three of the Law Lords (Lord Wilberforce, Lord Simon and Lord Edmund-Davies) said that if the words of a consolidation measure were clear there was no need to refer to the legislative antecedents. Again this is a way for a court to disembarrass itself of the awkward fact that the legislative history suggests a different answer to the problem from the one it had in mind. Given the difference of judicial opinion over the meaning of the words 'any person', it was somewhat disingenuous to argue that they were so clear as not to require elucidation, inter alia, from the previous legislation on the subject.

3.5. Understanding the Context: Evidence Beyond Statutes and Judicial Decisions

In *Attorney-General v Prince Ernest Augustus* [1957] AC 436, Lord Simonds, normally a strict constructionist, stated that in interpreting a statute 'I conceive it to be my right and duty to examine every word of a statute in its context, and I use "context" in its widest sense, which I have already indicated as including not only other enacting provisions of the same statute, but its preamble, the existing state of the law, other statutes *in pari materia*, and the mischief which I can by those *and other legitimate means* discern the statute was intended to remedy' (461, emphasis added).

By this phrase 'and other legitimate means' Lord Simonds suggested that the search for the context might properly go beyond the statute itself, other statutes and the precedents. In 1938 John Willis, in his article 'Statute interpretation in a nutshell', argued that the mischief rule was 'without doubt unworkable' because of the narrow way in which the courts interpreted the nature of the materials that might be consulted: 'You cannot interpret an Act in the light of its policy without knowing what that policy is: that you cannot discover without referring to all the events which led up to the legislation: but a well-settled rule of law forbids reference to any matters extrinsic to the written words of the Act as printed.'[49]

That was then. Since that time, however, there has been considerable development of the law.

3.5.1. International Conventions or Treaties

Already decades previously, the English courts took a more relaxed attitude to the use in interpretation of a statutory provision of an international treaty where it formed the basis for internal legislation – at least if the legislation was ambiguous. In *Salomon v Commissioners of Customs and Excise* [1967] 2 QB 116, the Court of Appeal said it was entitled to resolve ambiguities or obscurities to look at a 1950 international convention, although the 1952 Act did not refer to it, because English law ought to be interpreted in such a way as to be consistent with international law. The terms of the statute and of the convention being virtually identical, the inference was irresistible that the statute was intended to embody the convention. Lord Denning and Lords Justices Diplock and Russell all agreed.

[49] Willis (n 4 above) 15.

In *James Buchanan & Co Ltd v Babco Forwarding and Shipping (UK) Ltd* [1978] AC 141, the House of Lords held that the correct approach in construing a United Kingdom statute which incorporates and gave effect to a European convention was to interpret the English text by the special rules applicable to the interpretation of international conventions unconstrained by technical rules of English law but on broad principles. Where the convention was printed in the statute in both French and English it was legitimate to look at the French text – providing that the English text was ambiguous.

In *Warwick Film Productions Ltd v Eisinger* [1969] 1 Ch 508, by contrast, the Chancery Division refused to permit reference to an international convention on the ground that there was no ambiguity in the English Act. See also *Fothergill v Monarch Airlines* [1980] 3 WLR 209 where the House of Lords preferred the French text of the Warsaw Convention 1955 to the English. The case is also authority for the proposition that English judges interpreting an international convention forming part of English law may take account of the preparatory materials leading up to the convention (the *travaux préparatoires*). The Law Lords were influenced in reaching this conclusion by the fact that in most other countries preparatory materials were admissible in evidence even on the interpretation of internal legislation. It seemed right, therefore, that in this country they should be admissible at least on the interpretation of international agreements – not least because of the desirability of the courts in different countries achieving uniformity in their approach to the same issues.

The special case of international conventions even permitted the court to look at the parliamentary record of debates in *Hansard* before (as will be seen) this was permitted generally. In *Pickstone and Others v Freemans plc* [1989] AC 66, the courts had to interpret the Equal Pay Act 1970 which implemented obligations taken on by the UK under Art 119 of the EEC Treaty and a European Community Council Directive. Three of the judges in the House of Lords referred to the speech of the Secretary of State given in introducing regulations which were made part of the 1970 Act, as a guide to the intention of Parliament. Lord Templeman seemed to place emphasis on the fact that the regulations were not subject to any process of amendment by Parliament. 'In these circumstances the explanations of the government and the criticisms voiced by MPs in the debates which led to approval of the draft regulations provide some indications of the intentions of Parliament' (121–22). The other two (Lords Keith and Oliver) made no reference to this aspect of the case.

3.5.2. General Historical Background

The courts have always been willing to hear counsel state what they understand the general historical setting of legislation to have been, where this is relevant. Counsel may certainly cite earlier cases for this purpose and may also probably refer to legal textbooks. Often the court will refer to such surrounding circumstances in the course of its judgment. But this is not to say that the court would welcome citation by counsel of historical works by learned non-lawyer authors. If this were attempted by counsel, it would be likely to be resisted by the court. For a rare exception see, however, *Mock v Pension Ombudsman* (2000) Times, 7 April, in which Neuberger J (as he then was), said that he had been referred to Anthony Trollope's, *An Autobiography*, published in 1883, to assist in the interpretation of 1834 and 1859 statutes governing superannuation for civil servants. When construing old and obscurely drafted legislation, it was permissible, he said, for the court to have regard to reliable and contemporaneous observations as to how the statute was operated and understood at the time.

3.5.3. Government Publications

There are two categories of relevant official publication. One is the report of a commission or committee – Royal Commission, departmental committee, Law Commission, etc – which precedes and leads to the statute in question. The second is other material. The rule in regard to the latter was supposed to be clear – the courts could not look at any such document either for the purposes of understanding the mischief or of construing the words in question. The courts were not, for instance, permitted to look at the brief explanatory memorandum that used to be attached to all bills before Parliament.[50] (See *Escoigne Properties Ltd v IRC* [1958] AC 549.)

In *Katikiro of Buganda v Attorney-General* [1961] 1 WLR 119, a White Paper containing the recommendations of a constitutional conference held in Uganda was held inadmissible as an aid to the construction of the Buganda Agreement 1955 (Order in Council, 1955).

The *locus classicus* on this topic was the House of Lords' decision in the *Black-Clawson* case.[51] The Law Lords divided as to whether official reports leading to legislation could be consulted in the construction of the disputed words under consideration. Two (Lords Reid and Wilberforce) thought that they could not, even where the legislation corresponded exactly with the draft bill in the report; two (Lords Dilhorne and Simon of Glaisdale) disagreed. Lord Diplock thought they could be used to understand the context, including the construction of an ambiguous phrase, so as to give effect to Parliament's aim. All five, however, held that the reports were admissible for the purpose of understanding the mischief with which the legislation was intended to deal.

Lord Reid said (613):

> The mischief which this Act was intended to remedy may have been common knowledge 40 years ago. I do not think that it is today. But it so happens that a committee including many eminent and highly skilled members made a full investigation of the matter and reported some months before the Act was passed: Foreign Judgments (Reciprocal Enforcement) Committee 1932 (Cmd. 213). I think that we can take this report as accurately stating the 'mischief' and the law as it was then understood to be, and therefore we are fully entitled to look at those parts of the report which deal with those matters.
>
> But the report contains a great deal more than that. It contains recommendations, a draft Bill and other instruments intended to embody those recommendations, and comments on what the committee thought the Bill achieved. The draft Bill corresponds in all material respects with the Act so it is clear that Parliament adopted the recommendations of the committee. But nevertheless I do not think that we are entitled to take any of this into account in construing the Act.
>
> Construction of the provisions of an Act is for the court and for no one else. This may seem technical but it is good sense. Occasionally we can find clear evidence of what was intended; more

[50] These were completely different from the very detailed Explanatory Notes now attached not only to bills but to the Act after Royal Assent, see 3.5.9.

[51] *Black-Clawson International Ltd v Papierwerke Waldhof-Aschaffenburg AG* [1975] AC 591.

> often any such evidence, if there is any, is vague and uncertain. If we are to take into account evidence of Parliament's intention the first thing we must do is to reverse our present practice with regard to consulting Hansard ... [on which see below (ed)].
>
> If we are to refrain from considering expressions of intention in Parliament it appears to me that a fortiori we should disregard expressions of intention by committees or royal commissions which reported before the Bill was introduced. I may add that we did in fact examine the whole of this report – it would have been difficult to avoid that – but I am left in some doubt as to how the committee would have answered some of the questions which we have now to answer, because I do not think that they were ever considered by the committee.

Lord Wilberforce said:

> I only desire to add an observation of my own on one point. In my opinion it is not proper or desirable to make use of such a document as a committee or commission report, or for that matter of anything reported as said in Parliament, or any official notes on clauses, for a direct statement of what a proposed enactment is to mean or of what the committee or commission thought it means – on this point I am in agreement with my noble and learned friend Lord Diplock. To be concrete, in a case where a committee prepared a draft Bill and accompanies that by a clause by clause commentary, it ought not to be permissible, even if the proposed Bill is enacted without variation, to take the meaning of the Bill from the commentary. There are, to my mind, two kinds of reason for this. The first is the practical one, that if this process were allowed the courts would merely have to interpret, as in arguments we were invited to interpret, two documents instead of one – the Bill and the commentary on it, in particular annex V, paragraph 13. The second is one of constitutional principle. Legislation in England is passed by Parliament, and put in the form of written words. This legislation is given legal effect upon subjects by virtue of judicial decision, and it is the function of the courts to say what the application of the words used to particular cases or individuals is to be. This power which has been developed by the judges from the earliest times is an essential part of the constitutional process by which subjects are brought under the rule of law – as distinct from the rule of the King or the rule of Parliament; and it would be a degradation of that process if the courts were to be merely a reflecting mirror of what some other interpretation agency might say.[52]

One problem with the rule laid down by the House of Lords in *Black-Clawson* was that it could never be established whether it had been applied. If the judges read a text for the purpose of understanding the mischief how could one know whether they had been able to exclude from their minds what they read when it came to interpreting the statutory provision in question?[53]

3.5.4. Parliamentary Debates

The rule as to the non-admissibility of parliamentary debates was clear – though its origin is less so.[54] Until 1992 it was accepted that for the purposes of interpretation of a statutory provision it was not permissible to look at the parliamentary debates. (Indeed, until 1980 it was technically not permissible to cite in a court anything said in the House of Commons

[52] Ibid 629–30.

[53] In *Pepper v Hart* [1993] AC 593, 643, Lord Browne-Wilkinson said '... having once looked at what was said in Parliament, it is difficult to put it out of mind'. So too with other material.

[54] It is widely thought to have derived from a case decided in 1769 but it seems that this is not so. See John J Magyar, 'Debunking Millar v Taylor: The History of the Prohibition of Legislative History' 41 *Statute Law Review*, 2020 (1), 32–58.

without prior consent of the House. This rule, which was not always observed, dated back to 1818 but it was abolished in 1980.[55])

The rule that judges should not consult parliamentary debates was first challenged by Lord Denning when Master of the Rolls. In the course of the Court of Appeal's decision in *Davis v Johnson*, Lord Denning confessed that he had been aided in reaching his view by what had been said in Parliament:

Davis v Johnson [1979] AC 264 (CA)

The case concerned the provisions of the Domestic Violence and Matrimonial Proceedings Act 1976 and in particular whether the Act provided protection for cohabitees as well as wives.

> LORD DENNING MR (276–77): Some may say, and indeed have said, that judges should not pay any attention to what is said in Parliament. They should grope about in the dark for the meaning of an Act without switching on the light. I do not accede to this view. In some cases Parliament is assured in the most explicit terms what the effect of a statute will be. It is on that footing that members assent to the clause being agreed to. It is on that understanding that an amendment is not pressed. In such cases I think the court should be able to look at the proceedings. And, as I read the observations of Lord Simon of Glaisdale in *Dockers' Labour Club and Institute Ltd. v. Race Relations Board*,[56] he thought so too. I would give an instance. In the debate on the Race Relations Act 1968 there was, I believe, a ministerial assurance given in Parliament about its application to clubs; and I have a feeling that some of their Lordships looked at it privately and were influenced by it: see *Charter v. Race Relations Board*.[57] I could wish that, in those club cases, we had been referred to it. It might have saved us from the errors which the House afterwards held we had fallen into. And it is obvious that there is nothing to prevent a judge looking at these debates himself privately and getting some guidance from them. Although it may shock the purists, I may as well confess that I have sometimes done it. I have done it in this very case. It has thrown a flood of light on the position. The statements made in committee disposed completely of counsel for the respondent's argument before us.

On appeal, the House of Lords [1979] AC 317 did not, however, look kindly on Lord Denning's approach. All five Lords said expressly that he was wrong. Lord Kilbrandon and Lord Salmon did not elaborate but the other three added some reasons and further thoughts.

> LORD DILHORNE (337): There is one other matter to which I must refer. It is a well and long-established rule that counsel cannot refer to Hansard as an aid to the construction of a statute. What is said by a Minister or by a member sponsoring a bill is not a legitimate aid to the interpretation of an Act. [As Lord Reid said in *Beswick v Beswick* [1968] AC 58 at 73–74:]
>
> In construing any Act of Parliament we are seeking the intention of Parliament, and it is quite true that we must deduce that intention from the words of the Act … For purely practical reasons we do not permit debates in either House to be cited: it would add greatly to the time and expense involved in preparing cases involving the construction of a statute if counsel were expected to read all the debates in Hansard, and it would often be impracticable for counsel to get access to at least the older reports of debates in select committees of the House of Commons; moreover, in a very large proportion of cases such a search, even if practicable, would throw no light on the question before the court …

[55] See Patricia M Leopold, 'References in court to Hansard' *Public Law*, 1981, 316; 'Free speech in Parliament and the courts' 15 *Legal Studies*, 1995, 204; and David Miers, 'Citing Hansard as an aid to interpretation' 4 *Statute Law Review*, 1983, 98.

[56] [1976] AC 285, 299.

[57] [1973] AC 868, 899–901, [1973] 1 All ER 512, 526, 527.

> If it was permissible to refer to Hansard, in every case concerning the construction of a statute counsel might regard it as necessary to search through the Hansards of all the proceedings in each House to see if in the course of them anything relevant to the construction had been said. If it was thought that a particular Hansard had anything relevant in it and the attention of the court was drawn to it, the court might also think it desirable to look at the other Hansards. The result might be that attention was devoted to the interpretation of ministerial and other statements in Parliament at the expense of consideration of the language in which Parliament had thought to express its intention. While, of course, anyone can look at Hansard, I venture to think that it would be improper for a judge to do so before arriving at his decision and before this case I have never known that done. It cannot be right that a judicial decision should be affected by matter which a judge has seen but to which counsel could not refer and on which counsel had no opportunity to comment.

Lord Scarman (349–50) said:

> There are two good reasons why the courts should refuse to have regard to what is said in Parliament or by Ministers as aids to the interpretations of a statute. First, such material is an unreliable guide to the meaning of what is enacted. It promotes confusion, not clarity. The cut and thrust of debate and the pressures of executive responsibility, essential features of open and responsible government, are not always conducive to a clear and unbiased explanation of the meaning of statutory language. And the volume of parliamentary and ministerial utterances can confuse by its very size. Secondly, counsel are not permitted to refer to Hansard in argument. So long as this rule is maintained by Parliament (it is not the creation of the judges),[58] it must be wrong for the judge to make any judicial use of proceedings in Parliament for the purpose of interpreting statutes.

Lord Diplock (329) drew a distinction between consulting parliamentary debates and continental courts or the European Court of Justice looking at *travaux préparatoires*:

> I have had the advantage of reading what my noble and learned friends, Viscount Dilhorne and Lord Scarman, have to say about the use of Hansard as an aid to the construction of a statute. I agree with them entirely and would add a word of warning against drawing too facile an analogy between proceedings in the Parliament of the United Kingdom and those travaux préparatoires which may be looked at by the courts of some of our fellow member states of the European Economic Community to resolve doubts as to the interpretation of national legislation or by the European Court of Justice, and consequently by English courts themselves, to resolve doubts as to the interpretation of community legislation. Community legislation, viz. regulations and directives, are required by the EEC Treaty to state reasons on which they are based, and when submitted to the EEC Council in the form of a proposal by the EEC Commission the practice is for them to be accompanied by an explanatory memorandum by the commission expanding the reasons which appear in more summary form in the draft regulation or directive itself. The explanatory memoranda are published in the Official Journal together with the proposed regulations or directives to which they relate. These are true travaux préparatoires: they are of a very different character from what is said in the passion or lethargy of Parliamentary debate; yet a survey of the judgments of the European Court of Justice will show how rarely that court refers even to these explanatory memoranda for the purpose of interpreting community legislation.

The House of Lords ruling in *Davis v Johnson* seemed to have settled the question of courts looking at Hansard.[59] But thirteen years later in November 1992 the House of Lords changed its mind.

[58] As has been seen (text to n 55 above), this rule was abrogated in 1980 (ed).

[59] See, however, *R v Acton Justices, ex p McMullen* (1990) 92 Cr App R 98 in which the Court of Appeal Criminal Division looked at proceedings in the House of Commons Standing Committee on the Bill; *Criminal Law Review*, 1991, 352–53.

3.5.5. *Pepper v Hart*

In *Pepper v Hart* [1993] AC 593, [1993] 1 All ER 42 heard by seven Law Lords (Lords Mackay, Keith, Bridge, Griffiths, Ackner, Oliver and Browne-Wilkinson),[60] the House of Lords, the Lord Chancellor dissenting, held that judges *could* consult *Hansard*.

As so often in appeals to the House of Lords at that time, it was a tax case.[61] It concerned nine schoolmasters at the well-known public school, Malvern College, who were assessed to tax by the Inland Revenue in respect of the benefit they enjoyed because their sons were educated at the school, for one-fifth of the ordinary fees. The schoolmasters lost in the Court of Appeal but they won in the House of Lords after the Law Lords took notice of a ministerial statement made in Parliament that the purpose of the relevant statutory provision was to tax concessionary education for teachers' children on the marginal cost to the employer and not on the average cost of the benefit.

The leading judgment was given by Lord Browne-Wilkinson. He said that the rule forbidding access to *Hansard* had already been broken in regard to a statutory instrument in *Pickstone v Freemans plc* [1989] AC 66 where the House of Lords had had regard to what was said by the minister in initiating a debate on the regulations.

Lord Browne-Wilkinson set out the reasons for the traditional rule (633):

> Thus the reasons put forward for the present rule are, first, that it preserves the constitutional proprieties, leaving Parliament to legislate in words and the courts (not parliamentary speakers) to construe the meaning of the words finally enacted, second, the practical difficulty of the expense of researching parliamentary material which would arise if the material could be looked at, third, the need for the citizen to have access to a known defined text which regulates his legal rights and, fourth, the improbability of finding helpful guidance from Hansard.

Having put the arguments of counsel (633–34), he said (634):

> My Lords, I have come to the conclusion that, as a matter of law, there are sound reasons for making a limited modification to the existing rule (subject to strict safeguards) unless there are constitutional or practical reasons which outweigh them. In my judgment, subject to the questions of the privileges of the House of Commons, reference to parliamentary material should be permitted as an aid to the construction of legislation which is ambiguous or obscure or the literal meaning of which leads to an absurdity. Even in such cases references in court to parliamentary material should only be permitted where such material clearly discloses the mischief aimed at or the legislative intention lying behind the ambiguous or obscure words. In the case of statements made in Parliament, as at present advised I cannot foresee that any statement other than the statement of the minister or other promoter of the Bill is likely to meet these criteria …
>
> In many, I suspect most, cases references to parliamentary materials will not throw any light on the matter. But in a few cases it may emerge that the very question was considered by Parliament in passing the legislation. Why in such a case should the courts blind themselves to a clear indication of what Parliament intended in using those words? The court cannot attach a meaning to words which they cannot bear, but if the words are capable of bearing more than one meaning why should not Parliament's true intention be enforced rather than thwarted?

[60] The appeal was first heard by five Law Lords. But at the conclusion of the hearing it was relisted for argument before seven judges after one member of the court became aware that there had been a statement relevant to the matter in Parliament and the appellants wanted to challenge the rule that judges could not consult *Hansard*.

[61] In the last twenty or so years tax cases have been a much smaller proportion of appeals to the highest court.

Lord Browne-Wilkinson said that under *Black-Clawson* (p 163 above) the courts were already allowed to look at White Papers and official reports for the purposes of finding the 'mischief – though not at the draft clauses or proposals for remedying the mischief'. There was not much difference between such materials and a ministerial statement in Parliament. Moreover, the distinction between looking at reports to identify the mischief but not to find Parliament's intention was 'highly artificial' (635). It was also now legitimate to look at a draft bill to see that a provision in the draft was not included in the legislation.[62]

> Given the purposive approach to construction now adopted by the courts in order to give effect to the true intentions of the legislature, the fine distinctions between looking for the mischief and looking for the intention in using words to provide the remedy are technical and inappropriate. Clear and unambiguous statements made by ministers in Parliament are as much the background to the enactment of legislation as White Papers and parliamentary reports. (635)

He then dealt with the Attorney-General's objections (636–38). One concerned the practical problems:

> It is said that parliamentary materials are not readily available to, and understandable by, the citizen and his lawyers, who should be entitled to rely on the words of Parliament alone to discover his position. It is undoubtedly true that Hansard and particularly records of committee debates are not widely held by libraries outside London and that the lack of satisfactory indexing of committee stages makes it difficult to trace the passage of a clause after it is redrafted or renumbered. But such practical difficulties can easily be overstated. It is possible to obtain parliamentary materials[63] and it is possible to trace the history. The problem is one of expense and effort in doing so, not the availability of the material …
>
> Next, it is said that lawyers and judges are not familiar with parliamentary procedures and will therefore have difficulty in giving proper weight to the parliamentary materials. Although, of course, lawyers do not have the same experience of these matters as members of the legislature, they are not wholly ignorant of them. If, as I think, significance should only be attached to the clear statements made by a minister or other promoter of the Bill, the difficulty of knowing what weight to attach to such statements is not overwhelming. In the present case, there were numerous statements of view by members in the course of the debate which plainly do not throw any light on the true construction of s. 63. What is persuasive in this case is a consistent series of answers given by the minister, after opportunities for taking advice from his officials, all of which point the same way and which were not withdrawn or varied prior to the enactment of the Bill.
>
> Then it is said that court time will be taken up by considering a mass of parliamentary material and long arguments about its significance, thereby increasing the expense of litigation. In my judgment, though the introduction of further admissible material will inevitably involve some increase in the use of time, this will not be significant as long as courts insist that parliamentary material should only be introduced in the limited cases I have mentioned and where such material contains a clear indication from the minister of the mischief aimed at, or the nature of the cure intended, by the legislation. Attempts to introduce material which does not satisfy those tests should be met by orders for costs made against those who have improperly introduced the material. Experience in the United States of America, where legislative history has for many years been much more generally admissible than I am now suggesting, shows how important it is to maintain strict control over the use of such material. That position is to be contrasted with what has happened in

[62] *Factortame v Secretary of State for Transport* [1990] 2 AC 85.
[63] They are now, of course, accessible online: see 6.3 below (ed).

New Zealand and Australia (which have relaxed the rule to approximately the extent that I favour): there is no evidence of any complaints of this nature coming from those countries.

There is one further practical objection which, in my view, has real substance. If the rule is relaxed legal advisers faced with an ambiguous statutory provision may feel that they have to research the materials to see whether they yield the crock of gold i.e. a clear indication of Parliament's intentions. In very many cases the crock of gold will not be discovered and the expenditure on the research wasted. This is a real objection to changing the rule. However, again it is easy to overestimate the cost of such research: if a reading of Hansard shows that there is nothing of significance said by the minister in relation to the clause in question, further research will become pointless.

In sum, I do not think that the practical difficulties arising from a limited relaxation of the rule are sufficient to outweigh the basic need for the courts to give effect to the words enacted by Parliament in the sense that they were intended by Parliament to bear. Courts are frequently criticised for their failure to do that. This failure is due not to cussedness but to ignorance of what Parliament intended by the obscure words of the legislation. The courts should not deny themselves the light which parliamentary materials may shed on the meaning of the words Parliament has used and thereby risk subjecting the individual to a law which Parliament never intended to enact … (636–38)

He then reached his considered statement as to the new rule:

I therefore reach the conclusion, subject to any question of parliamentary privilege, that the exclusionary rule should be relaxed so as to permit reference to parliamentary materials where: (a) legislation is ambiguous or obscure, or leads to an absurdity; (b) the material relied on consists of one or more statements by a minister or other promoter of the Bill together if necessary with such other parliamentary material as is necessary to understand such statements and their effect; (c) the statements relied on are clear. Further than this, I would not at present go. (640)

Lord Mackay, the Lord Chancellor, the sole dissentient, based himself wholly on his concern about the practical aspects – the concern that it would lead to research in parliamentary materials being undertaken by lawyers at significant cost in a high proportion of cases and often to no purpose:

The principal difficulty I have on this aspect of the case is that in Mr Lester's submission reference to parliamentary material as an aid to interpretation of a statutory provision should be allowed only with leave of the court and where the court is satisfied that such a reference is justifiable (a) to confirm the meaning of a provision as conveyed by the text, its object and purpose, (b) to determine a meaning where the provision is ambiguous or obscure or (c) to determine the meaning where the ordinary meaning is manifestly absurd or unreasonable.I believe that practically every question of statutory construction that comes before the courts will involve an argument that the case falls under one or more of these three heads. It follows that the parties' legal advisers will require to study Hansard in practically every such case to see whether or not there is any help to be gained from it. I believe this is an objection of real substance. It is a practical objection, not one of principle. The submission which Mr Lester makes is not restricted by reference to the type of statute and indeed the only way in which it could be discovered whether help was to be given is by considering Hansard itself. Such an approach appears to me to involve the possibility at least of an immense increase in the cost of litigation in which statutory construction is involved. It is of course easy to overestimate such cost but it is I fear equally easy to underestimate it. Your Lordships have no machinery from which any estimate of such cost could be derived. Two inquiries with such machinery available to them, namely that of the Law Commission and the Scottish Law Commission, in their joint report on *Interpretation of Statutes* (Law Com no 21; Scot Law Com no 11 (1969)), and the Renton Committee report on *Preparation of Legislation* (Cmnd 6053 (1975)) advised against a relaxation on the practical grounds to which I have referred.

> I consider that nothing has been laid before your Lordships to justify the view that their advice based on this objection was incorrect.
>
> In his very helpful and full submissions Mr Lester has pointed out that there is no evidence of practical difficulties in the jurisdictions where relaxations of this kind have already been allowed, but I do not consider that, full as these researches have been, they justify the view that no substantial increase resulted in the cost of litigation as a result of these relaxations, and, in any event, the parliamentary processes in these jurisdictions are different in quite material respects from those in the United Kingdom.
>
> Your Lordships are well aware that the costs of litigation are a subject of general public concern and I personally would not wish to be a party to changing a well-established rule which could have a substantial effect in increasing these costs against the advice of the Law Commissions and the Renton Committee unless and until a new inquiry demonstrated that that advice was no longer valid. (614–15)

It is worth emphasising that, as the Lord Chancellor stated, the same concerns had been expressed by the Law Commission in their 1969 Report, *The Interpretation of Statutes*. They urged adoption of the 'mischief' or 'purposive' approach to statutory interpretation but they did not favour recourse to parliamentary debates. One reason was the lack of clarity of such debates. Another was the fact that practitioners did not have easy access to collections of *Hansard*. That objection no longer applies as Hansard is accessible online. On balance, the Law Commissions thought, the value to be derived from parliamentary debates was likely to be outweighed by the burden of consulting them. The Renton Committee in 1975 took the same view. So too did the Hansard Society in its 1992 *Report on the Legislative Process Making the Law*. Its scepticism was based more on the scope parliamentary debates would give to fresh argument. ('The possibilities for confusion – and for time-wasting argument and counter-argument in the court – are endless' (para 243, pp 61–62).)

As will be seen below, the doubts expressed by the Renton Committee, the Law Commission, the Hansard Society and Lord Mackay are now widely shared – including by several of the judges of the highest court.

3.5.6. *Pepper v Hart* Considered

There are various issues arising from the House of Lords' decision in *Pepper v Hart*.

What is the extent of the decision?

Lord Browne-Wilkinson was at pains to indicate that the relaxation of the rule was intended to be a narrow one applying only where the legislation was ambiguous or obscure or led to an absurdity and a clear ministerial statement made in Parliament would resolve the ambiguity. Lord Oliver expressly agreed with the speech of Lord Browne-Wilkinson, endorsing his narrow conditions. Lords Ackner, Bridge, Griffiths and Keith also said they agreed with the whole of the speech.

But decisions following *Pepper v Hart* showed that these strict conditions were ignored. (As one commentator put it, 'It may be that Lord Browne-Wilkinson's triple locks for the admissibility of parliamentary material are slowly being unpicked by the judiciary and that *Hansard* has become, or is becoming, an open book for guidance on the meaning and purpose of legislative provisions'.[64])

[64] K Mullan, 'The impact of *Pepper v Hart*' in P Carmichael and B Dickson (eds), *The House of Lords: Its Parliamentary and Judicial Roles* (Hart Publishing, 1999) 213, 238.

Thus, in *Warwickshire County Council v Johnson* [1993] AC 583, the House of Lords referred to *Hansard* even though there did not seem to be any ambiguity about the statutory language. Recourse to *Hansard*, Lord Roskill said, merely confirmed the view he had reached independently. Lord Roskill made no mention that the minister's statement resolved an ambiguity, clarified an obscurity or prevented an absurdity. An academic commented, 'the House seems to have authorised recourse to Hansard wherever there is a clear ministerial statement relating directly to the construction of the legislation'.[65]

In several other cases the House of Lords referred to *Hansard* to confirm interpretations that would have been adopted anyway.[66]

Lord Browne-Wilkinson's original formulation was restricted to ministerial statements that *positively* resolved an ambiguity. In *R v JTB* [2009] UKHL 20, 1 AC 1310 the House of Lords used the parliamentary debates to help interpret the statutory provision even though the relevant statements of the Minister in the Commons differed from that of the Minister in the Lords. Sometimes one might wish to produce the parliamentary record to advance an interpretation *negatively* by demonstrating that nothing was said to a particular effect. A Scottish Court allowed such a submission in *Hamilton v Fife Health Board* [1993] SC 369.

Lord Browne-Wilkinson's original formulation was restricted, in terms, to ministerial statements. In *Chief Adjudication Officer v Foster* [1993] 2 WLR 292 at 306, counsel was allowed to refer to the observations of the mover of a successful amendment.

In *Three Rivers District Council v Bank of England (No 2)* [1996] 2 All ER 363 the Commercial Court judge held that where the court was seeking to construe a statute purposively and consistently with any relevant European legislation, or where the purpose of the legislation was to introduce into English law the provisions of an international convention or European directive, the court could adopt a more flexible approach to the admissibility of parliamentary materials than where the court was construing purely domestic legislation.

There is also the question what material is allowed in as 'contextual material' under the heading of Lord Browne-Wilkinson's category of 'such other parliamentary material as is necessary to understand' the ministerial statements and their effect. In *Pepper v Hart* itself Lord Browne-Wilkinson referred to a press statement issued at the same time as a ministerial parliamentary statement.[67]

In *Wilson v First County Trust Ltd* [2003] UKHL 40, [2004] 1 AC 816 the House of Lords considered whether parliamentary material could be introduced in regard to the question whether a statutory provision was compatible with a right under the ECHR. This raised the question, inter alia, of the reasons for the legislation. Counsel instructed by the Speaker of the House of Commons and the Clerk of the Parliaments submitted that it was not appropriate for a court to refer to the proceedings in Parliament in order to decide whether a statute was compatible with the Convention. The policy and objects of a statute must be determined by interpreting its language.

[65] C Scott, 'Consumer sales and credit transactions' *Journal of Business Law*, 1993, 491.

[66] See *Stubbings v Webb* [1993] 2 WLR 120, 128; *Ex p Johnson* [1993] 2 WLR 1, 7, 8; *Chief Adjudication Officer v Foster* [1993] 2 WLR 292, 306.

[67] I was indebted to T St John Bates, 'Judicial application of *Pepper v Hart*' *Journal of Law Society Scotland*, July 1993, 251, for some of the foregoing. See also the same author's 'Parliamentary material and statutory construction: aspects of the practical application of *Pepper v Hart*' 14 *Statute Law Review*, 1993, 46 and 'The contemporary use of legislative history in the United Kingdom' 54 *Cambridge Law Journal*, 1995, 127.

Three of the five Law Lords dealt with the question. Their conclusion was that material by way of background information tending to show, for instance, the likely practical impact of the statute or the extent of the social problem being addressed by the statute (the 'mischief') *could* be consulted by the court in order better to understand the legislation.[68] Lord Nicholls said that the Human Rights Act 1998 required the court to exercise a new role which was fundamentally different from interpreting or applying legislation. The courts were required to evaluate the effect of legislation in terms of Convention rights. They had to compare the effect of the legislation with the Convention right. The legislation had to have a legitimate policy objective and it had to satisfy a proportionality test. If relevant information was provided by a minister – 'or indeed any other member of either House in the course of debate on a bill' (at [64]) – the courts should be able to take it into account. Lord Hope said that proceedings in Parliament were replete with information from a whole variety of sources. Ministers made statements, Members asked questions or proposed amendments based on information which they obtained from their constituencies, answers were given to written questions, issues were explored by select committees by examining witnesses and explanatory notes were provided with bills to assist members. Resort to such information might cast light on what Parliament's aim was when it passed the provision in question (at [118]). Lord Hobhouse, with whom Lords Scott and Rodger agreed, said that judging the 'proportionality' or 'justification in relation to Convention rights' involved 'a sociological assessment – an assessment of what are the needs of society' (at [142]). Useful evidential material might include reports, statistics or oral evidence.

These propositions opened the door very wide indeed.

Conducting Pepper v Hart Research

The cost of researching parliamentary records has been significantly affected by online availability.

Parliamentary debates are accessible online: *Hansard, 1803–present.* But when undertaking *Pepper v Hart* research one needs to know the dates of debates on the successive stages of the Bill. For bills from 2002–03 the information can be found on the parliament website: Parliament Bills – UK Parliament and Bills in Previous Sessions. This information is also provided on the Sessional Returns, which are available online from 1997. Older Sessional Returns are only available in hardcopy or via the subscription service *UK Parliamentary Papers*. If all else fails one can ask the always helpful House of Commons Library which holds hardcopies of bill indexes from 1964.

How Often does Recourse to Hansard *Reveal the Legislative Intent?*

There is no substantial empirical study which shows how often recourse to *Hansard* throws useful light on the statutory interpretation problem before the court. A small-scale study conducted by Vera Sacks before *Pepper v Hart* was decided suggested that it would not be often. The study was based on 34 cases on employment law, land law, family law, criminal law and housing law. There was some positive benefit from looking at *Hansard.* In some cases it threw light on the general legislative purpose. But reference to *Hansard* would very rarely have solved the problem before the court: 'In every case studied the disputed clause was either undebated or received obscure and confusing replies from the Minister'.[69]

[68] See at [51]–[67], per Lord Nicholls; [110]–[118], per Lord Hope; [139]–[145], per Lord Hobhouse.

[69] Vera Sacks, 'Toward discovering parliamentary intent' 3 *Statute Law Review*, 1982, 143, 157. The article did not disclose how the 34 cases were selected and there is therefore no way of knowing to what extent the study was

In preparing this section for the fifth edition of this work, the writer, with the help of an LSE law student, undertook a small follow-up study. We first did a Lexis search of all mentions of *Pepper v Hart* in the six years from the date of the House of Lords decision in November 1992 to October 1998. This produced a total of 232 cases. We started by looking at the reported cases in the first one hundred in the Lexis print-out (excluding those reported only in newspaper law reports) – beginning with the most recent. There were 60 such cases. What we found was so consistent that it seemed pointless to continue the exercise beyond the first one hundred listed cases. The results strikingly confirmed the results of the survey carried out by Vera Sacks.[70] In every case, by definition, *Pepper v Hart* had been cited by counsel in argument as the basis for introducing parliamentary material. But looking for a case in which parliamentary material appeared to have made any difference to the result was looking for the proverbial needle in a haystack. Often the judgment(s) did not even mention *Pepper v Hart* or parliamentary material. Presumably, in the great majority of those cases the court did not permit the material to be introduced. When *Pepper v Hart* argument and/or material were mentioned in the judgment(s), the mention was usually a variation on one or more of the following themes:

(a) The rules laid down in *Pepper v Hart* as to the preconditions for admissibility were not fulfilled. Either there was no ambiguity in the statutory text or the parliamentary materials sought to be introduced were not directed to the specific statutory provision under consideration. (In one case, the House of Lords, in the person of Lord Browne-Wilkinson himself, gave courts a sharp warning against relaxing this rule: 'Judges should be astute to check such misuse of the new rule by making appropriate orders as to costs wasted.'[71]).
(b) We did look at the *Pepper v Hart* material – either because there was ambiguity in the statute, or because we were persuaded to do so *de bene esse*[72] – but it was of no assistance in that it threw no clear light on the matter.
(c) We looked at the *Pepper v Hart* material, there was a clear statement by the minister which was to the point but it only confirmed the court in the view it had already taken of the matter anyway.

Sometimes the court used (b) in combination with (a). (We looked at the material even though there was no ambiguity but it did not advance matters.) There were virtually no cases in which the court appeared actually to have been influenced by reading the parliamentary material.[73] The fact that the court fails to acknowledge that it was influenced by parliamentary material does not prove that it was not. But one suspects that in most cases the failure to acknowledge it reflected the reality.

Thus even in cases where the court agrees to look at *Pepper v Hart* material, it appears to be exceedingly rare that the material affects the outcome. When considering the balance

representative of statutory interpretation cases in the law reports, let alone of statutory interpretation cases that come before the courts.

[70] See to very similar effect K Mullan, 'The impact of *Pepper v Hart*' in P Carmichael and B Dickson (eds), *The House of Lords: Its Parliamentary and Judicial Role* (Hart Publishing, 1999) 213–38.

[71] *Melluish (Inspector of Taxes) v BMI (No 3) Ltd* [1996] AC 454, 482. The Crown had unsuccessfully tried to persuade the Law Lords to consider ministerial statements on another provision and another problem and to argue from those statements by analogy. Lord Browne-Wilkinson said that such 'interpretation' (what one might call 'reading across') of ministerial statements was an improper use of the relaxed rule introduced by *Pepper v Hart*.

[72] Meaning provisionally (ed).

[73] *Thomas Witter Ltd v TBP Industries Ltd* [1996] 2 All ER 573 may have been such a case – see p 590 at *d* to *j*.

of advantage flowing from the decision one also has to put into the scale not only the considerable number of cases where the court refuses even to look at the material, but the presumably much greater number of cases where *Hansard* has been scoured by the lawyers in vain. Their research turns up nothing in the parliamentary debates that could even arguably be made the subject of a *Pepper v Hart* submission to the court.

In short, it seems that the Lord Chancellor, Lord Mackay, who dissented in *Pepper v Hart* mainly out of concern that the costs of the reform would outweigh the likely benefits, was probably right.

The Impact of Pepper v Hart *on Officials and Drafters*

Shortly after the decision in *Pepper v Hart*, Sir Christopher Jenkins, then Second Parliamentary Counsel, speaking at a conference, warned of its effect on the work of his office:

> Departments sponsoring legislation prepare various briefings for their ministers. In future the draftsman may have to take a more active part in vetting this material. This could be very time-consuming. It means looking at notes on clauses, notes on amendments and Ministers' Speaking Notes to check that they accurately and comprehensively explain the provisions of the Bill, and that they include any supplementary material which it is not felt necessary to put in the Bill but which may have to be put on the record in response to questions raised in debate.
>
> In addition the draftsman may in future have to look at other material produced by the Department in connection with the Bill to check its accuracy, in case it is regarded by the courts as 'other parliamentary material … necessary to understand such statements'. I do not know how wide this will go; but in *Pepper v Hart*, Lord Browne-Wilkinson looked at a press release produced by the Inland Revenue.
>
> The draftsmen and the civil servants in the departments will also have to check what was actually said in the House or in Standing Committee to ensure that no additional statements or corrections are needed.

Previously, if a minister gave information during a debate which they later realised was incomplete or inaccurate they would often write to the Member who had requested the information. Now they might feel it necessary also to make the correction on the record. By the same token MPs might be more inclined to ask questions with a view to having explanations on the record for the benefit of later potential judicial interpretation. It had been said that in the United States 'much debate on the floor of Congress takes the form of elaborate, prearranged colloquies in which possible supporters of a particular programme obtain detailed and very technical assurances from its sponsors as to its effects'.

These warnings by Parliamentary Counsel are now reflected in the Cabinet Office *Guide to Making Legislation* (2025, s 23, pp 191–92). The *Guide* says (para 23.2) officials should bear in mind the possibility that parliamentary material may come to be cited in the courts and that accordingly they should 'exercise great care in drafting material for use by Ministers which may find its way into the record of debates in either House (including their committees) and, if necessary, find a satisfactory method for correcting any significant mistakes or ambiguities which appear in such records'. To that end, the Guide says:

- Speeches and speaking notes should be reviewed by the bill team's legal adviser and Parliamentary Counsel.
- The legal adviser should always attend relevant parliamentary proceedings as part of the ministers' official support and clear all speaking notes before they are passed to ministers.

— Officials should take care in providing impromptu advice on interpretation in order to assist a minister to answer a point raised during proceedings on a bill. Where possible, ministers might be invited to offer to reflect on a point and reply on a future occasion.
— The bill team and the legal adviser should always review the *Hansard* record of ministerial contributions and consider whether there was any inaccuracy 'or other hostage to fortune'.
— Ambiguities or inaccuracies in wording of legislation should always be put right by amendments where this is possible.
— References on the record to *Pepper v Hart* itself should be avoided 'as this could be taken to imply that the provision of the Bill being debated is indeed ambiguous'.

If it is considered that the official record cannot be allowed to stand, ministers will need to make a judgment, in the light of the official and legal advice, on whether and how to clarify the record.

Was Pepper v Hart *a Mistake?*

In a lecture in June 1998, Lightman J said that it could be questioned whether use of *Hansard* achieved anything worthwhile.[74] The cost was substantial and beyond the means of many litigants, creating disparities between litigants who could and could not afford such researches. ('I have yet to hear a case where the exercise [of consulting *Hansard*] proved the slightest bit helpful but many when it proved time consuming and wasteful' (ibid).)

In *Robinson v Secretary of State for Northern Ireland*[75] Lord Hoffmann said:

> 39. … The passages in Hansard relied upon in this case are in my experience fairly typical of the material tendered in reliance upon the principle in *Pepper v Hart*. It is now nearly ten years since the case was decided and, as the difference of opinion in that case turned mainly upon predictions of the practical consequences of allowing such material to be used, your Lordships have the advantage of experience in assessing the results. Lord Mackay of Clashfern thought that it would increase the expense of litigation without contributing very much of value to the quality of decision-making. The majority thought that it would occasionally assist in deciding what Parliament intended and, if strictly confined by conditions, would not add greatly to the expense. Speaking for myself, I think that Lord Mackay has turned out to be the better prophet. References to Hansard are now fairly frequently included in argument and beneath those references there must lie a large spoil heap of material which has been mined in the course of research without yielding anything worthy even of a submission.[76]

In a trenchant critique of *Pepper v Hart*, Lord Steyn revealed that, having initially supported it,[77] he had changed his mind. In his view, almost invariably the lawyers' researches amongst the parliamentary materials were fruitless. The decision had 'substantially increased the cost of litigation to very little advantage'. Many appellate judges, he said, shared that opinion.[78]

[74] 'Civil litigation in the 21st century' 17 *Civil Justice Quarterly*, 1998, 373, 383.

[75] [2002] UKHL 32, [2002] NI 390.

[76] Cited with approval in *Campbell v MGN Ltd* [2003] QB 633 at [126] per Lord Phillips, observing that 'resort to parliamentary material under the principle of *Pepper v Hart* should be a last resort'.

[77] For his earlier approving view see 'Does legal formalism hold sway in England?' *Current Legal Problems*, 1996, 43, 50.

[78] '*Pepper v Hart*: A re-examination' 21 *Oxford Journal of Legal Studies*, 2001, 60, 63–64. But for the contrary view see Lord Cooke, 'The road ahead for the common law' 55 *International and Comparative Law Quarterly*, 2004, 273, 282–84.

Quite apart from the poor cost-benefit aspects he doubted whether it was right to invest the statement of a minister in Parliament with such authority.

> The statement of the promoter is treated as canonical. This is also an assumption which seems inherently implausible in respect of the ebb and flow of parliamentary debates. The relevant exchanges sometimes take place late at night in nearly empty chambers. Sometimes it is a party political debate with the whips on … These are not ideal conditions for the making of authoritative statements about the meaning of a clause in a Bill.[79]

The ruling in *Pepper v Hart*, he thought, ignored the constitutional principle that it was Parliament not the executive that legislates.

> To give the executive, which promotes a Bill, the right to put its own gloss on the Bill is a substantial inroad on a constitutional principle, shifting legislative power from Parliament to the executive … The objections are not simply that a minister's view of a clause is irrelevant but that it is in principle profoundly objectionable to treat it as a trump card or even relevant in the interpretative process.[80]

Lord Steyn suggested[81] that perhaps the way out was to treat the Explanatory Notes now attached to the bill and to the statute as a guide to the Government's (as opposed to Parliament's) intention in the legislation. If that were to happen, the disinclination of judges to delve into *Hansard* would increase. Maybe that could one day lead to a reconsideration of the decision in *Pepper v Hart*.

In *Wilson v First County Trust* Lord Hobhouse said,

> Judicial experience has taught me, particularly since I was appointed a member of this House, that the attempt by advocates to use parliamentary material from Hansard as an aid to statutory construction has not proved helpful and the fears of those pessimists who saw it simply as a cause of additional expense in the conduct of litigation have been proved correct.[82]

For the view that *Pepper v Hart* also represents a powerful tool for conservative interpretation of statutes see David Robertson, *Judicial Discretion in the House of Lords* (Clarendon Press, 1998). Robertson devoted a whole chapter of his book to *Pepper v Hart*. He argued that if the words used in Parliament had to be treated as serious evidence of the meaning of the statute the judges lost their capacity to give the law a sensible interpretation in light of changing times. 'The problem is, essentially, that reference to *Hansard* necessarily sets an interpretation within the immediate contemporary understanding of the government of the day' (p 171). 'It risks imposing a literalism in interpretation rather than an interpretation in keeping with the spirit of the law' (p 172).[83]

[79] Lord Steyn, '*Pepper v Hart*: A re-examination' (n 78 above) 65. A former member of Parliamentary Counsel's Office wrote to like effect: '[T]he courts should at least permit themselves to remember that "the Minister said" may mean anything from (a) a considered statement by an expert civil servant who really knew what they were writing about, to (b) a hopeless guess made up by the Minister on the hoof because the questioner sat down before the note from the Official's Box could reach him or her, or (c) a statement misread by way of frantic garble from a crushed handful of last-minute scribble.' (D Greenberg, *Laying Down the Law* (Sweet & Maxwell, 2011) 62–63.).

[80] Lord Steyn, '*Pepper v Hart*: A re-examination' (n 78 above) 70.

[81] Ibid, 71–72.

[82] [2004] 1 AC 816, [140].

[83] Lord Steyn made the same point: '[W]here there has been a qualifying statement under *Pepper v. Hart* it may be said that the position is crystallized as explained by the minister at the time. In the result the reference to *Hansard* settles an interpretation within the contemporary understanding of government and this introduces a new form of literalism. If that is so, a valuable capacity of our system to cope with changing conditions is lost' (n 78 above at p 68).

For the strongly argued view that allowing parliamentary material to be consulted is wrong see also R Summers, 'Interpreting statutes in Great Britain and the United States: Should courts consider materials of legislative history?' in D Butler, V Bogdanor and R Summers (eds), *The Law, Politics and the Constitution* (Oxford University Press, 1999) 222–54. It was a common error, he suggested, to suppose that the main function of authoritative methodology for interpreting statutes is to assist courts resolve issues of interpretation. Rather it is 'to provide guidance to citizens, to corporate and other business entities, and to still other types of statutory addressees, as they act and interact outside of, and far from courts' (p 227).

> This is true of statutes that define private ownership and the rights of owners of property, of statutes specifying criteria of validity for contracts and wills, of statutes providing for the creation of corporations and other business entities, statutes governing the relations of employees with employers, statutes that regulate manufacturing or other economic activities, statutes that specify speed limits on highways, statutes that provide how parties may enter into a lawful marriage, statutes that impose an income tax, statutes that define crime, and on and on. The primary function of these statutes is to provide guidance in daily social, economic or other life. These statutes are not primarily concerned with what may happen by way of dispute resolution in a court of law. (p 227)

These statutes, Summers argues, must be administrable in the first instance not by officials but by citizens acting in real life, often without legal advice. The methodology for interpreting statutes used in court cannot be different from that applicable outside the courtroom. Allowing access to legislative history is not appropriate since it is not reasonable to suppose that ordinary citizens have the ability or the means to research it. Moreover, the material is diffuse and frequently unclear and, even if it were precise and clear, it has not been the object of the focused and intensive deliberation that is given to the text of a bill going through Parliament. It is therefore not a solid basis for interpretation.

For a warning about the dangers of using legislative history based on United States experience, see Reed Dickerson, 'Statutory interpretation in America: dipping into legislative history' 5 *Statute Law Review*, 1984, 76 and 141.

There is a great deal of possible further reading on *Pepper v Hart*: Conference papers presented by opposing counsel in the case, the Attorney-General, Sir Nicholas Lyell and Lord Lester, *Statute Law Review*, 1994, pp 1–9 and 10–22; T St J N Bates, 'The contemporary use of legislative history in the United Kingdom' 54 *Cambridge Law Journal*, 1995, 127–52; D Oliver, '*Pepper v Hart:* a suitable case for reference to *Hansard*?' *Public Law* 1993, 2; FAR Bennion, 'Hansard: a help or hindrance' 14 *Statute Law Review*, 1993, 149 and 'How they got it all wrong in *Pepper v Hart*' *British Tax Review*, 1995, 325; Scott C Styles, 'The rule of Parliament: statutory interpretation after *Pepper v Hart*' 14 *Oxford Journal of Legal Studies*, 1994, 151; R Gordon and C Ward, 'Counting the cost of Hansard' *Local Authority Law*, 27 January 1993, 7; S Vogenauer, 'A retreat from *Pepper v Hart:* a reply to Lord Steyn' 25 *Oxford Journal of Legal Studies*, 2005, 629; A Kavanagh, '*Pepper v Hart* and matters of constitutional principle' 121 *Law Quarterly Review*, 2005, 98; F Bennion, 'Executive estoppel: *Pepper v Hart* revisited' *Public Law*, 2007, 1; KV Krishnaprasad, '*Pepper v Hart*: its continuing implications in the United Kingdom and India' 32 *Statute Law Review*, 2011, 227; JJ Magyar, 'The evolution of Hansard use in the Supreme Court of Canada: a comparative study in statutory interpretation' 33 *Statute Law Review*, 2012, 363.

See generally Bennion, Bailey and Norbury *on Statutory Interpretation*, 8th edn (LexisNexis, 2020) 738–46.

3.5.7. Deriving Intention from Parliamentary Inaction

An argument as to Parliament's intention may be based on its failure to act. The topic was explored by Diggory Bailey.[84] An example was the failure to adopt an amendment.

> The use that may be made of amendments moved but rejected or withdrawn was considered in some detail by the House of Lords in *R. v JTB.*[85] The question in that case was whether section 34 of the Crime and Disorder Act 1998 was intended to abolish the defence of *doli incapax* altogether for children 10–14 years old or merely to reverse the presumption that a child had that defence (leaving the defence available for any child who could prove that they did not know that their action was seriously wrong). During the passage of the Bill through Parliament Lord Goodhart QC had twice moved an amendment designed to reverse the presumption of *doli incapax* rather than abolish it. The amendment was firmly opposed by the Government. On the first occasion the amendment was withdrawn without being pressed to a vote; on the second occasion it was rejected on a division.

Lord Phillips, Lord Carswell and Lord Brown each said that the rejection of Lord Goodhart's amendment and the Minister's reasons for the Government's opposition were clear and strong evidence as to the meaning of the provision. Bailey suggests that this should be regarded as a rare instance where Parliamentary inaction could sensibly be used by the courts as the basis for statutory interpretation. He makes a strong argument that generally such a basis is wholly unsatisfactory:[86]

> While arguments based on Parliament's legislative inaction are deceptively attractive, they are for the most part deeply problematic. Not only are there intrinsic practical difficulties in trying to attach significance to Parliament's failure to do something – silence is by its nature ambiguous – but there are also fundamental conceptual and constitutional problems with seeking to rely on legislative inaction alone as a basis on which to draw inferences as to legislative intent. In short, the absence of law is not law. For this reason, post-enactment legislative inaction is never relevant. That said, in some circumstances it may be possible to derive some support from legislative inaction where it forms part of the contextual background against which legislation is enacted. For example, the failure to pass an amendment during the passage of a Bill through Parliament may be used to strengthen the inferences that may be drawn from other pre-enactment materials such as ministerial statements. Even then it is important to recognise the practical difficulties in trying to attribute meaning to what Parliament has not done and to understand the range of possible causes of inaction.[87]

3.5.8. Legislative Drafting Practice as a Guide to Statutory Interpretation

The Office of Parliamentary Counsel publishes a lengthy (currently 112-page) document of drafting guidance used for training draftsmen.[88] Diggory Bailey, himself a member of the

[84] 'Interpreting Parliamentary Inaction' 79(2) *Cambridge Law Journal*, 2020, 245–59.

[85] *R v JTB* [2009] UKHL 20, [2009] 1 AC 1310.

[86] In *R (ZH and CN) v London Borough of Newham and London Borough of Lewisham*, the Supreme Court criticised it on the ground that the legislative will of Parliament is expressed through its enactments alone.

[87] 'Interpreting Parliamentary inaction' 79(2) *Cambridge Law Journal*, 2020, 258–59.

[88] *Office of the Parliamentary Counsel drafting guidance* (July 2018), www.gov.uk/government/publications/drafting-bills-for-parliament.

Office of Parliamentary Counsel, suggested that use could be made of the guide by judges in interpreting statutes:

> The Office of the Parliamentary Counsel's drafting guidance covers a broad range of topics with a view to making legislation as effective and easy to understand as possible. The guidance is aimed at members of the office but its publication serves the ancillary purpose of sharing knowledge about legislation and how it is drafted and made.
>
> The introduction to the Office of the Parliamentary Counsel's drafting guidance states that it is not intended as a guide to statutory interpretation. But whatever its stated aim, there appears to be nothing in principle to prevent the guidance from being relied on as an external aid to construction. The guidance provides a potentially rich and little utilised source of contextual evidence from which inferences as to legislative intention might legitimately be drawn in an appropriate case.[89]

However, as Lord Halsbury warned over a century ago, the suggestion that there could be value in consulting drafting guidance does not extend to asking the actual drafter what they meant by the words used.

> I have more than once had occasion to say that in construing a statute I believe the worst person to construe it is the person who is responsible for its drafting. He is very much disposed to confuse what he intended to do with the effect of the language which in fact has been employed. At the time he drafted the statute, at all events, he may have been under the impression that he had given full effect to what was intended, but he may be mistaken in construing it afterwards just because what was in his mind was what was intended, though, perhaps, it was not done.[90]

3.5.9. Explanatory Notes

As has been seen, Explanatory Notes are now part of the material available throughout the life of a bill and again when the bill becomes an Act. The history of this important development goes back more than fifty years. In 1969, in their Report *The Interpretation of Statutes*, the English and Scottish Law Commissions urged the use of a *new type of explanatory memorandum* to assist the courts in the search for the context in which statutory provisions should be read. It would be a mixture of three then existing documents: (a) the preamble that used to be a feature of statutes; (b) the Explanatory Memorandum attached to a bill, published for the benefit principally of Members of the two Houses, giving a brief summary of its provisions; (c) notes on clauses prepared by civil servants as a detailed brief to the minister responsible for piloting the legislation through each House.

The Law Commissions proposed that the Explanatory Memorandum would be drafted by the promoters of the bill and the bill to which it related would specifically authorise its use as an aid to interpretation. Ideally the document would be amended as the bill itself was amended and would receive ultimate parliamentary approval. Its status would be like that of a preamble under then existing law and practice. If this took up too much parliamentary time, an alternative would be to give the power to amend and approve to officials.

[89] D Bailey, 'Bridging the Gap: Legislative Drafting Practice and Statutory Interpretation' 2020 *Public Law* 220, 222–23,225. Bailey said that so far there appeared to be only one case in which the drafting guidance had been mentioned – *Ritchie v Revenue and Customs Commissioners* [2017] UKFTT 449 (TC) at [397]. See also the author's postscript in [2021] *Public Law* 2021 687–90.

[90] *Hilder v Dexter* [1902] AC 474 at 477.

Or officials might be required to submit it for parliamentary approval on Third Reading or perhaps by laying it before the House like an Order in Council. But the document would not bind the courts:

> [E]ven if the explanatory statement were amended during the course of the Bill's passage and given some measure of Parliamentary approval, it would be no more binding on the courts than much other contextual material (e.g., other provisions of the statute, earlier legislation dealing with the same subject matter and non statutory material dealing with the mischief) of which under the existing law the courts are entitled to take account. It might however give assistance to the courts in making more explicit the contextual assumptions which at present have to be gleaned, sometimes with great difficulty, from a number of sources of varying reliability. No interpretative device can relieve the courts of their ultimate responsibility for considering the different contexts in which the words of a provision might be read, and in making a choice between the different meanings which emerge from that consideration. The existence of an explanatory statement would not prevent a court from regarding the meaning of the words in an enacting provision in the light of other relevant contexts as so compelling that it must be preferred to a meaning suggested by the statement. (para 70)

The 1992 Hansard Society's Report on the Legislative Process *Making the Law* said: 'We are impressed by the wide desire for more explanation of the meaning and implications of legislation. The practitioners and users need it. The wider public may need it even more' (p 112). It thought that efforts to provide a better explanation might be even more productive than attempts to simplify drafting. Notes on sections (based on the minister's notes on clauses) should be made for every Act of Parliament. The notes on sections would be prepared by government departments with the assistance of Parliamentary Counsel. These notes on sections should be approved by ministers and laid before Parliament but should not require formal parliamentary approval. They should be published at the same time as the Act. There should similarly be Explanatory Notes on statutory instruments to explain their purpose and effect (para 250, p 63). The courts should be allowed to use the notes on sections and the Explanatory Notes on statutory instruments as an aid to interpretation (para 254, pp 63–64).

The First Report of the Select Committee on Modernisation of the House of Commons in July 1997 (HC 190 of 1997–98) recommended greater use of explanatory material to accompany the publication of a bill. The Committee invited Parliamentary Counsel to explore ways in which this might be done.

In December 1997, in its Second Report (HC 389 of 1997–98) the Select Committee said that it had now received the report from First Parliamentary Counsel. He proposed that the existing Explanatory Memorandum and Notes on Clauses should be replaced by a single document entitled 'Explanatory Notes'. The Notes would be revised twice, once to accompany the first print of the bill in the Second House and again on Royal Assent. They should be available on the Internet alongside the bill and then the Act. The Select Committee said 'we wholeheartedly welcome the proposals as the House of Lords Procedure Committee has done in its Second Report, and recommend that the Government implement them as soon as possible'.

Explanatory Notes were first used in the 1998–99 parliamentary session. They are now an established part of the system both during the passage of a bill through Parliament and after Royal Assent.[91] The House of Lords said in a case in 2004, 'It has become common

[91] See C Jenkins, First Parliamentary Counsel, 'Helping the reader of Bills and Act' 149 *New Law Journal*, 1999, 798.

practice for their Lordships to ask to be shown the Explanatory Notes when issues are raised about the meaning of words used in an enactment.'[92] Their length and content obviously depend on the nature of the bill/Act. But they can be very substantial.

As to the status of the Explanatory Notes, Parliamentary Counsel's report, appended to the Select Committee's 1997 report, said:

> The notes will have the same status as the present explanatory memorandum. They are not intended to make law, and so it is not proposed that they should be amendable in either House. Their purpose is to help the reader to get his bearings and to ease the task of assimilating the new law. If the notes are successful in the purpose of helping the reader, they will of course be read by judges as well as by others. However they are not designed to resolve ambiguities in the legislative text – if ambiguities are identified as the Bill progresses, they should be removed by amendment. Occasionally, it may be that the notes are referred to in litigation in the same way that Hansard is, under the rule in *Pepper v Hart*. So it will be important for those producing the notes to achieve a high degree of accuracy, and also to restrict the notes so that they do not seem to take the law further than the Bill or the Act does. (paras 17–18)

They carry a common declaration that their purpose is 'to assist the reader in understanding the Act' and that 'they do not form part of the Act and have not been endorsed by Parliament'.

The *Statute Law Review* suggested editorially that they might come to acquire 'something of the same authority as a statement by the promotor of a Bill for the purpose of resolving a *Pepper v Hart* ambiguity'. There would, it thought, be a certain logic to this. 'After all, a carefully considered written text might be thought to be a surer foundation than an oral statement from a similar text, which is perhaps more likely to include slips, some syntactic ambiguity, and as in reality the politician is likely to be less well informed than the Bill team, simple error.'[93] They are designed as an accurate but less formal means of communicating the meaning of the legislation.

It seems likely that the Explanatory Notes serve many categories of readers – including not only practitioners, journalists, students (and their teachers). MPs and even Ministers and their Shadow opposites.

Richard Crossman in *The Diaries of a Cabinet Minister* (Hamish Hamilton 1975) wrote:

> I never bothered to read any of the bills I got through. I glanced at them and I read the briefs about them and I also knew the policies from the White Papers and therefore knew exactly how the briefs and the White Papers corresponded with the clauses of the bills. But I never bothered to understand the actual clauses, nor did many Members, not even the spokesman for the Opposition. Both sides worked off written briefs to an astonishing extent. (At 628–29)

If that was true then, long before the Explanatory Notes we have today, it is likely they play a significant and valuable role in the actual legislative process itself.

In *R (Westminster City Council) v National Asylum Support Service* [2002] UKHL 38, [2002] 1 WLR 2956, Lord Steyn addressed the question of the status of Explanatory Notes for the courts. In so far as they 'cast light on the objective setting or contextual scene of the statute, and the mischief at which it was aimed, such materials are therefore always admissible aids to construction. They may be admitted for what logical value they have' (at [5]).

[92] *Montilla* [2004] 1 WLR 3141 at [35].
[93] 21 *Statute Law Review*, 2000, 1.

Indeed, Lord Steyn said, they could sometimes be even more useful than Law Commission reports, or the reports of advisory committees, Green or White Papers and the like, all of which were admissible. If, exceptionally, there was to be found in Explanatory Notes 'a clear assurance by the executive to Parliament about the meaning of a clause, or the circumstances in which a power will or will not be used, that assurance may in principle be admitted against the executive in proceedings in which the executive places a contrary contention before a court' (at [6]). What was impermissible, Lord Steyn said, was to treat the wishes and desires of the Government about the scope of the statutory language as reflecting the will of Parliament. 'The aims of the government in respect of the meaning of clauses as revealed in explanatory notes cannot be attributed to Parliament. The object is to see what is the intention expressed by the words enacted' (at [6]).

For an example of the Court of Appeal deriving significant benefit from the Explanatory Notes see *Callery v Gray (No 2)* [2001] EWCA Civ 1246, [2001] 1 WLR 2142. The court there had no doubt that they constituted 'parliamentary material' to which reference could be made under the principle in *Pepper v Hart*. (See at [53], per Lord Phillips MR.)

The Renton Committee (1975) did not think that explanatory materials prepared for the benefit of legislators should be admissible for the purposes of judicial interpretation. To do so, it thought, would risk having a 'split level statute' of which only the primary stage would have been debated in Parliament.[94] The Explanatory Notes for the Criminal Justice Act 2003 occasioned a general denunciation by Dr Roderick Munday of the practice of courts using them as a guide to interpretation. The Government should be estopped from resiling from a clear position adopted in the Explanatory Notes, but otherwise they should not be used by the courts as aids to statutory interpretation. They were not designed for that purpose. They were not always accurate – those for the Criminal Justice Act 2003 being a case in point. ('Let us not be deluded: the Explanatory Notes were not created in order to mediate the legislature's meaning.'[95])

Dr Munday renewed his critique of the use made of Explanatory Notes when considering them and Regulatory Impact Assessments (RIAs or simply, IAs[96]).[97] ('Impact assessments are generally required for all UK Government interventions of a regulatory nature that affect the private sector, civil society organisation and public services. An impact assessment comprises a full assessment of economic, social and environmental impacts.'[98])

> Many would count the courts' systematic resort to purposive interpretation of statutes in recent years a positive development. Paradoxically, however, this approach may induce the judiciary in turn to seek guidance from ever more politically charged materials. Such a step might seem to bring the courts closer into line with one expression of 'the will of Parliament', but it also carries

[94] *The Preparation of Legislation*, Cmnd 6053, 1975, para 19.24.

[95] R Munday, 'Bad character rules and riddles: "Explanatory Notes" and true meanings of s. 103(1) of the Criminal Justice Act 2003' [2005] *Criminal Law Review*, 337, 354. See also Munday, 'Explanatory Notes and Statutory Interpretation' 170 *Justice of the Peace*, 2006, 124, 126, in which he set out instances of significant omissions, structural ambiguity, important questions left unanswered and law misstated from the Explanatory Notes for the Criminal Justice Act 2003. He illustrated his concerns by the use made of Explanatory Notes by the Court of Appeal in *Weir et al* [2005] EWCA Crim 2866. He ended: 'However, just as the hands of a seaside floral clock may happen to coincide with Greenwich Mean Time, telling exact time is not their true function. These shallow, imperfect and not-so-objective writings can only afford the most rough-and-ready guides to courts.'

[96] Regulatory Impact Assessments were first introduced in 1998.

[97] R Munday, 'In the wake of "Good Governance": impact assessments and the politicisation of statutory instruments' 71 *Modern Law Review*, 2008, 386.

[98] Cabinet Office, *Guide to Making Legislation*, 2025, p 125.

a risk: for RIAs, and IAs, are unquestionably the handiwork of the executive arm of government. The ultimate question must be whether it is desirable in a democratic society that, in their efforts to decipher the will of Parliament, the courts should even risk being perceived to be carrying out the bidding of the executive …

Counsel are beginning to incorporate the contents of RIAs routinely into their arguments when seeking to wrest meaning from statutory enactments; and some courts are responding to this stimulus. Throughout the British Isles courts are becoming conversant with the directing role played by RIAs in the legislative process … [I]t is not uncommon for RIAs to be incorporated, without comment or objection, as part of the court's legislative narrative, as part of the story … On occasion, a court will find reasons not to take a particular RIA into account. Yet, the very fact that it has to explain why a particular RIA is of no assistance in the specific case before it may also imply recognition that, given other circumstances, the RIA *could* serve as an authoritative statement on how an enactment is to be viewed or interpreted … On other occasions RIAs arguably play a more decisive role in determining what is found to have been the intention of Parliament.[99] …

RIAs and IAs are not designed to aid judicial interpretation of legislation.[100] That said, they have a certain potential utility: they may provide a very clear statement of governmental objectives. After all, they are now integral to the process whereby departments of government state and refine their legislative policies, passing in review the available options for implementing those policies, and evaluating the respective benefits and costs of pursuing the proposed legislative scheme. They look to furnish a decisive insight into what government is actually thinking. However, we suspect that hitherto the system has not been employed especially rigorously. Elaborating a study, to a formula, to persuade the minister or Cabinet colleagues – and eventually parliamentary colleagues, too – that a particular legislative project is viable, rational and affordable, to present an attractive departmental image of a desirable reform, that will not prove too costly, and that has practical political appeal, is not necessarily the same as supplying a reliable guide to the meaning of the eventual legislation. One needs also to allow for the fact that, as much as anything, RIAs and IAs are employed to satisfy the slippery dictates of 'good governance'. They are instruments witness to the fact that allotted procedures have been followed, that matters have been appropriately weighed at the appropriate level by appropriate entities, and that effective review of contemplated action has taken place. Anyone who has witnessed or participated in such exercises will know that the process is part reality, part window-dressing. Like so much modern administration, one suspects that their function is in no small part presentational. As we know, their veracity is not checked *ex post facto* to see whether their claims ultimately bear relation to reality. One might even wonder whether they ought not to be viewed simply as politically-motivated documents that are just elements in the general political game. Judges, therefore, may need to tread warily before giving them undue credence …

Different drafts of RIAs, and successive versions of the Explanatory Notes, demonstrate how the purpose and content of legislation can mutate during its course through Parliament. The texts of Explanatory Notes sometimes display just how vague even the ministries are about the import of portions of their own legislative texts.[101] We know that the final text of an Act, harried and butchered though it may have been *en route* to the statute book, is the culmination of a complex, collective process, following which not even the participants will be entirely agreed or fully

[99] Cases cited include *International Transport Roth Gmbh* [2002] EWCA Civ 158, [2003] QB 728 at [11]–[12]; *R (Khatun) v Newham LBC* [2004] EWCA Civ 55, [2005] QB 37 at [74]; and *R (Robertson) v Lord Chancellor's Department* [2003] EWHC 1760 (Admin) at [14]–[15] (ed).

[100] This point is endorsed by the fact that, unlike Explanatory Notes, RIAs do not carry any express disclaimer stating that they have not been endorsed by parliament. Who would ever imagine that they were?.

[101] See, eg, R Munday, 'Bad character rules and riddles: "Explanatory Notes" and true meanings of s 103(1) of the Criminal Justice Act 2003' [2005] *Criminal Law Review* 337, 338–40.

> apprehend what they have wrought. To attach weight to one element in preference to all others is chancy. To plump for the promotional propaganda of the executive in such circumstances is of doubtful wisdom.

But Dr Munday's purist *cri de coeur* was always unlikely to be heeded. As Lady Justice (as she then was) Arden said:

> Where the true meaning of a statute is in doubt, and in dispute between the parties, it is the court's function to decide that meaning. In modern theory, the court primarily finds the interpretation of a phrase by examining the words used by Parliament in their particular context. Courts have moved away from a purely literal approach to statutory interpretation ... By 'context', I mean the legislative context, and the policy context, as shown by any admissible material, such as Law Commission reports, explanatory notes accompanying legislation, *travaux préparatoires* and (in certain cases) *Hansard*.[102]

3.6. Presumptions and Subordinate Principles of Interpretation as an Aid to Construction

There are many presumptions that are used by the courts to assist in the construction of statutes. It is not necessary here to do more than give a brief mention of a few of the best known.

(1) Penal statutes should be construed strictly in favour of the citizen.[103]
(2) It is to be presumed that a statutory provision was not intended to change the common law.
(3) Statutes creating criminal offences normally require a blameworthy state of mind (*mens rea*) in the defendant.
(4) It is presumed that Parliament did not intend to oust the jurisdiction of the courts.
(5) It is presumed that a statute does not have retrospective effect.
(6) Words take their meaning from the context:

- *noscitur a sociis*. (Thus in the Refreshment Houses Act 1860 dealing with houses 'for public refreshment, resort and entertainment', the last word was held not to cover theatrical or musical entertainment but to refer rather to refreshment rooms and the reception and accommodation of the public – *Muir v Keay* (1875) LR 10 QB 594 at 597–8.)
- *Expressio unius exclusio alterius* – the express mention of one member of a class by implication excludes other members of the same class. (The word 'land' would

[102] *9 Cornwall Crescent London Ltd* v *Mayor & Burgesses of the Royal Borough of Kensington & Chelsea* [2005] EWCA Civ 324, [2006] 1 WLR 1186 at [50] and [52].

[103] For an example where the presumption gave a remarkable result, see *R v Cuthbertson* [1980] 3 WLR 89, in which the House of Lords held that the Misuse of Drugs Act 1971 did not permit forfeiture of assets in a bank account obtained by the defendants through trafficking in illegal drugs. The Act allowed forfeiture of 'anything shown to the satisfaction of the court to relate to the offence'. The House of Lords said this did not include conspiracy to commit the offence, since this was not specifically mentioned.

normally include mines but a reference to 'lands, houses and coalmines' may mean that no other mines are included in the word 'land'.)

— *Ejusdem generis* – general words at the end of a list of more particular words take their meaning from the foregoing list. (So the statement in the Sunday Observance Act 1677 that 'no tradesman, artificer, workman, labourer or other person whatsoever' shall work on a Sunday was held not to apply to a coach proprietor, farmer, barber or estate agent. The words 'other person whatsoever' were held to be confined to persons in similar occupations to those more specifically defined in the list.)

(7) It is presumed that municipal law is to be interpreted to be in conformity with international law.

Maxims are today not held in the esteem they enjoyed in former times. But in a stout defence of their value it has been rightly said that, properly regarded, they can be of great use:[104]

> The maxims simply describe what drafters *probably* meant through the use of specific patterns of language … maxims can provide creative counsel with a series of highly persuasive arguments that are useful in cases involving legislation.
>
> Used correctly, the maxims of construction are persuasive. They do not provide 'pat answers', or any form of answers for that matter; they raise questions. They force us to acknowledge the unconscious assumptions that are made when we interpret legislation. They draw our attention to important presumptions (such as presumptions concerning extraneous language and consistent expression) and point to logical inferences that flow from these presumptions. The handy Latin phrases in which the maxims are expressed should never *end* an interpretive inquiry, they should add depth to an interpretive inquiry that takes into account all possible sources of legislative meaning. Maxims are neither arbitrary nor whimsical in nature. They were developed over countless generations, reflecting time-honoured arguments concerning the manner in which people write and interpret language.[105]

In *Cusack v Harrow London Borough Council*[106] Lord Neuberger, speaking about principles of construction said:

> With few, if any, exceptions, the canons embody logic or common sense, but that is scarcely a reason for discarding them: on the contrary. Of course there will be many cases, where different canons will point to different answers, but that does not call their value into question. Provided that it is remembered that the canons exist to illuminate and help, but not to constrain or inhibit, they remain of real value.

That 'different canons will point to different answers' is the nub of the point. Books on statutory interpretation provide advocates with ammunition to support contradictory arguments. In the *Cusack* case itself the claimant lost at first instance, won in the Court of Appeal and lost again in the Supreme Court, illustrating the unpredictability of statutory interpretation in general and of the application of the canons of construction in particular.

[104] RN Graham, 'In defence of maxims' 22 *Statute Law Review*, 2001, 46.
[105] Ibid, p 68.
[106] [2013] UKSC 40.

3.7. Are the Rules, Principles, Presumptions and Other Guides to Interpretation Binding on the Courts?

The main principles of statutory interpretation – the literal rule, the golden rule and the mischief rule – are often called rules, but as has been argued above, this is plainly a misnomer. They are not rules in any ordinary sense of the word since they point to different solutions to the same problem. Nor is there any indication, either in the so-called rules or elsewhere, as to which to apply in any given situation. Each of them may be applied but need not be. The same is true of every one of the principles, presumptions, maxims or other guides to interpretation that fill books on interpretation. In other words, there is nothing in any book which tells one how to solve the difficulty that has arisen. For every proposition, there is normally one or more counter-proposition. Each side in litigation will find support in the authorities for whatever principle of interpretation it wants to advance. The rules and principles of interpretation therefore do not solve problems. They suggest arguments that can be advanced and then help to justify conclusions often reached on other grounds.

Professors Hart and Sacks of Harvard Law School gave a helpful example. The bear trainer who comes to the station with their bear sees a notice, 'No dogs allowed on the trains'. By applying the maxim *expressio unius exclusio alterius*, they would claim to be entitled to board the train with the bear. (The express mention of dogs not being allowed may be used as a basis for arguing that other animals, including bears, are allowed.) The competing argument is that if dogs are not allowed on trains, *a fortiori*, by analogy, bears are not either. The solution to the problem does not depend on the deployment of maxims but on some notion as to what the rule is intended to achieve and the application of whatever interpretation best suits this objective.[107] It is the judge and not the rule or principle that determines the outcome.

Justice Frankfurter of the United States Supreme Court said of statutory interpretation 'Though my business throughout most of my professional life has been with statutes, I come to you empty-handed. I bring no answers. I suspect the answers to the problems of an art are in its exercise'.[108] Sir Carleton Allen summarised his lengthy discussion of the problems of statutory interpretation with the words 'we are driven in the end to the unsatisfying conclusion that the whole matter ultimately turns on impalpable and indefinable elements of judicial spirit or attitude.'[109]

3.8. Interpreting the Human Rights Act

Rabinder Singh QC, in a lecture entitled 'Interpreting bills of rights', started by citing some of the famous statements that have been made as to the nature of the exercise:

> [T]here is a great deal of authority, from numerous jurisdictions, emphasising that constitutions and Bills of Rights stand apart from (or above) ordinary statutes. In the US Supreme Court, for

[107] H Hart and A Sacks, *The Legal Process* (1958, unpublished), p 1409.
[108] *The Record of the Association of the Bar of the City of New York* (1947), 213, 216–17.
[109] CK Allen, *Law in the Making*, 7th edn (Clarendon Press, 1964) 526, 529.

> example, Marshall CJ famously declared in *McCulloch v Maryland* that 'we must never forget, that it is a constitution we are expounding'.[110] In *Fisher*, Lord Wilberforce in the Privy Council held that a constitutional instrument, giving effect to fundamental rights, is 'sui generis, calling for principles of interpretation of its own, suitable to its character … without necessary acceptance of all the presumptions that are relevant to legislation or private law'.[111] The Supreme Court of Canada has likewise emphasized that the 'task of expounding a constitution is crucially different from that of construing a statute'[112] … Marshall CJ observed further that a constitution is 'intended to endure for ages to come, and, consequently, to be adapted to the various crises of human affairs'.[113]

What did that mean?

> … The fact that constitutions are enacted in broad terms, meant to be applied to unforeseen scenarios in a distant future, means that judicial adaptation is unavoidable. The European Court of Human Rights has long taken this dynamic approach to interpretation, holding that the European Convention on Human Rights is a living instrument that 'must be interpreted in light of present-day conditions'.[114] The Court must therefore have regard to the 'changing conditions in Contracting States'[115] … A sterile, backward-looking approach to constitutional interpretation would put the entire constitutional project at risk. Justice Kirby of the High Court of Australia reminds us: As one anonymous sage once put it: if you construe a constitution like a last will and testament, that is what it will become.[116] … In the famous words of Lord Wilberforce in *Fisher*, the fact that constitutions deal with basic rights means that they should be given 'a generous interpretation …'[117]

The Human Rights Act 1998 is not a Bill of Rights in the classic form, but it undeniably has some of the main features of a Bill of Rights. Section 1 enumerates the Articles of the ECHR that are 'the Convention rights'[118] and states that they are to have effect and that they are set out in Schedule 1. The Articles set out in Schedule 1 are word for word the text of the Articles in the European Convention. They are precisely those one normally finds in a Bill of Rights: the Right to Life; Prohibition of Torture; the Right to Liberty and Security; the Right to a Fair Trial; the Right to Respect for Private and Family Life; Freedom of Thought, Conscience and Religion; Freedom of Expression etc. Both the rights and the qualifying clauses are couched in broad and open-textured phrases of the kind familiar in Bills of Rights.

In the House of Lords decision of *Brown v Stott*, Lord Bingham described the European Convention as 'an important constitutional instrument':

> The European Convention is an international treaty by which the contracting states mutually undertake to secure to all within their respective jurisdictions certain rights and freedoms. The fundamental nature of these rights and freedoms is clear, not only from the full title and the content of the Convention but from its preamble in which the signatory governments declared: 'their profound belief in those fundamental freedoms which are the foundation of justice and

[110] *McCulloch v Maryland* (1819) 17 US 316, 414.

[111] *Minister of Home Affairs (Bermuda) v Fisher* [1980] AC 319, 328–29.

[112] *Hunter v Southam* (1984) 2 SCR 145, 155.

[113] *McCulloch v Maryland* (1819) 17 US 316, 407.

[114] *Tyrer v United Kingdom* (1979–80) 2 EHRR 1, para 31. [For an eloquent affirmation of that principle see Sir Nicolas Bratza, 'Living Instrument or dead letter: the future of the European Convention on Human Rights' *European Human Rights Law Review*, 2014, 116 (ed)].

[115] *Stafford v United Kingdom* (2002) 35 EHRR 32, para 68.

[116] M Kirby, *Judicial Activism* (Cambridge University Press, 2004) 40.

[117] Rabinder Singh QC, 'Interpreting bills of rights' 29 *Statute Law Review*, 2008, 82.

[118] Arts 2 to 12 and 14 of the Convention; Arts 1 to 3 of the First Protocol; Arts 1 and 2 of the Sixth Protocol. All are set out in Sch 1 of the Act.

> peace in the world and are best maintained on the one hand by an effective political democracy and on the other by a common understanding and observance of the human rights upon which they depend.[119]

What then is its status in domestic law? This statement by Lord Bingham seems to the writer to capture the matter:

> The reason why the Human Rights Act is properly regarded as having a special status in domestic law is ... because, however mundane the drafters made it sound, it is an Act that purports to protect fundamental rights and freedoms, and, moreover, it does so not only by providing a remedy for breaches of human rights and fundamental freedoms, but (and this is crucial) by establishing such rights and freedoms as general norms, that apply to all legislation and all conduct of public authorities.[120]

Section 6(1) of the Act provides that it is unlawful for a public authority (ie a court) to act in a way that is incompatible with a Convention right. Section 6(2) creates an exception where acting compatibly with a Convention right is not possible because of the provisions of, or made under, primary legislation. In that case the court can issue a declaration of incompatibility under s 4, leaving it to the Government to decide whether to cure the incompatibility. To date (as was seen at p 130 above), almost all declarations of incompatibility have been followed by remedial action.

The Human Rights Act s 3 introduced an entirely new concept – a rule of statutory interpretation designed to achieve the maximum possible degree of agreement between human rights law expressed by UK courts and the Strasbourg Court (on this see 3.8.1 below).

For an empirical study of how the Law Lords in the House of Lords and the Justices in the Supreme Court approached the Human Rights Act, see Michael Blackwell, 'Indeterminacy, Disagreement and the Human Rights Act: An Empirical Study of Litigation in the UK House of Lords and Supreme Court, 1997–2017', 83 *Modern Law Review*, 2020 (2) 285–320.)

Would a Conservative Government repeal the Human Rights Act (or withdraw from the ECHR)?

On 3 October 2014, the Conservative Party published an eight-page document, brazenly called *Protecting Human Rights in the UK*. It proposed the repeal of the Human Rights Act and its replacement by a 'British Bill of Rights and Responsibilities'. Despite another ten years of Conservative government, that did not happen.

Since the 2014 pamphlet there have been four general elections and therefore four Conservative Party election manifestos.

What the Conservative Election Manifesto said regarding the Human Rights Act:

— *In May 2015* – 'We will scrap Labour's Human Rights Act and introduce a British Bill of Rights which will restore common sense to the application of human rights in the UK. The Bill will remain faithful to the basic principles of human rights, which we signed up to in the original European Convention on Human Rights It will protect basic rights, like the right to a fair trial, and the right to life, which are an essential part of a modern democratic society. But it will reverse the mission creep that has meant human rights

[119] *Brown v Stott* [2003] 1 AC 681, 703.

[120] T Hickman, *Public Law after the Human Rights Act* (Hart Publishing, 2010) 48.

law being used for more and more purposes, and often with little regard for the rights of wider society Among other things the Bill will stop terrorists and other serious foreign criminals who pose a threat to our society from using spurious human rights arguments to prevent deportation.'

— *In June 2017* – 'We will not bring the European Union's Charter of Fundamental Rights into UK law. We will not repeal or replace the Human Rights Act while the process of Brexit is underway but we will consider our human rights legal framework when the process of leaving the EU concludes. We will remain signatories to the European Convention on Human Rights for the duration of the next parliament.'

— *In December 2019* – 'We will update the Human Rights Act and administrative law to ensure that there is a proper balance between the rights of individuals, our vital national security and effective government.'

— *In July 2024*, the Conservative Party's Election Manifesto did not mention the Human Rights Act. The Strasburg Court was mentioned in one sentence:

> We will run a relentless, continual process of permanently removing illegal migrants to Rwanda with a regular rhythm of flights every month, starting this July, until the boats are stopped. If we are forced to choose between our security and the jurisdiction of a foreign court, including the ECtHR, we will always choose our security.

In other words, the Government would ignore unacceptable decisions by the Strasburg Court blocking or impeding its controversial policy of removing asylum seekers to Rwanda. However, in July 2024 the Conservative Government was removed by the electorate.

The four Tory Party Manifestos – 2015, 2017, 2019, 2024 – reflect the differing approach of Ministers and different pressures created by events.

The Conservative Party's project to replace the Human Rights Act by a British Bill of Rights was first advanced by Dominic Raab before he became an MP in *Assault on Liberty – What Went Wrong with Rights* (Fourth Estate, 2009). He was elected an MP the following year. In June 2022, as Lord Chancellor and Justice Secretary under Boris Johnson, Raab introduced a Bill of Rights Bill to repeal and replace the Human Rights Act. But Raab's Bill made no progress. Boris Johnson's term as Prime Minister ended with his resignation in July 2022. He was succeeded by Liz Truss who did not reappoint Raab. Her premiership lasted only 47 days. She was replaced by Rishi Sunak who did reappoint Raab. But Sunak did not support Raab's Bill of Rights Bill and, despite Raab's position as Lord Chancellor, it never even reached the stage of having a 2nd Reading debate.

In December 2020, Robert Buckland, then Lord Chancellor and Justice Secretary, had set up the Independent Human Rights Act Review, chaired by former Lord Justice Peter Gross. Ironically, the Gross report (518pp) was published by Dominic Raab, who had replaced Buckland – together with Raab's Consultation Paper *Human Rights Act Reform A Modern Bill of Rights.* The contrast between the two was stark. The Gross Report found that, subject to some minor tweaks, the Human Rights Act was fit for purpose. Raab's Consultation Paper called for its repeal. But, in the event, Raab's proposed British Bill of Rights did not get off the launch pad. The Labour Government elected in July 2024 supports the HRA and the ECHR, but at the time of writing (mid-2025) the outlook looked uncertain.

In November 2024, Policy Exchange, a right-leaning think-tank, published *The impact of the Human Rights Act 1998 in twenty-five ca*ses (59pp) by Professor Richard Ekins of Oxford University, Sir Stephen Laws, former First Parliamentary Counsel and Dr Conor

Casey of Surrey University School of Law.[121] Their argument, illustrated by the 25 cases, was that

> The HRA has had a major, negative effect on a wide range of policy questions and has changed the balance of our constitution in ways that wrongly put important constitutional principles in doubt (p 20).

In February 2025, former Supreme Court Justice, Lord (Jonathan) Sumption, added his voice to the view that the UK should leave the ECHR.[122] His objection to the Strasbourg Court was that it had extended the provisions of the Convention beyond acceptable limits. The Court, he wrote had -

> effectively emancipated itself from the text. Its judgments have transformed the Convention from a protection against domestic despotism into a template for most aspects of human life.[123]

Treating the Convention as a 'living instrument', the Strasbourg Court, he suggested, had held a 'vast range of issues' to be covered by Article 8:

> [T]he legal status of illegitimate children, immigration and deportation, extradition, criminal sentencing, the recording of crime, abortion, artificial insemination, homosexuality and same sex unions, child abduction, the policing of public demonstrations, employment and social security rights, legal aid, planning and environmental law, noise abatement, eviction for non-payment of rent and much else besides.[124]

In his view the right course was just to have the provisions of the ECHR enshrined in UK legislation – as it is in Sch.1 of the HRA.[125]

Serious dissatisfaction with the effect of the ECHR had also been expressed from a different, and politically more significant, quarter. On 25 February 2025, the new leader of the Conservative Party, Kemi Badenoch, at an event hosted by Policy Exchange, said: 'Over the last 20 years the ECHR rulings morphed so fundamentally that they now limit our ability to control our borders' and that if the Strasbourg Court stopped us doing what was right for the people of this country 'at some point we will probably have to leave'. Then, on 6 June she announced that she was setting up a commission to consider whether the UK should leave the ECHR.

On 22 May 2025, nine ECHR Member States, including Italy, Denmark, Austria and Belgium, released a joint letter demanding more power over how they combat irregular immigration and the deportation of foreign criminals. ('It is important to assess whether, in some cases, the [ECtHR] has over-extended the scope of the convention compared to its original intentions, thus altering the balance between the interests to be protected').

[121] The authors selected 25 cases, one from each year from 2000 to 2024 – House of Lords (4), Court of Appeal (7), Supreme Court (13) and Northern Ireland High Court (1).

[122] Jonathan Sumption, 'International Tribunals: For and Against' in his *Challenges of Democracy and the Rule of Law* (Profile Books Ltd, 2025) ch 9.

[123] Ibid, p 141.

[124] Ibid, p 140. Lord Sumption suggested (pp 145–48) the most remarkable of the Court's decisions was in the case on climate change – *Verein Klimaseniorinnen Schweiz v Switzerland* (9.04.2024, No.53600/20) in which the Court held that respect for a person's private and family life under Article 8 included a right to require one's government to take effective measures to protect the health of the population against climate change' (ibid at p 146).

[125] 'Britain should withdraw from the Convention but incorporate its text into its statute law, adding such additional protections as seems desirable.' Ibid, p 148.

On 18 June 2025, Labour's Justice Secretary, Shabana Mahmood, expressed a similar view in a speech to the Council of Europe. It was time to consider amending the Convention to restore public confidence which had been fraying. Trust would disintegrate if human rights laws 'appear to protect the rule-breaker over the rule follower'.[126] The UK, she said, would pursue reform of the ECHR both at home and in Strasbourg. Reforming the Convention requires the consent of all 46 Member States. It would take years. The Home Secretary was reported to have set up an enquiry as to how the judges interpret Art. 3 and Art 8 of the Convention – presumably with the objective of looking for a way to affect judicial interpretation of the provisions by 'guidance' or perhaps, legislation.

At the time of writing, this topic was clearly a live political issue.

3.8.1. The Human Rights Act 1998: A New Rule of Statutory Interpretation

Under the Human Rights Act 1998 (HRA), 'So far as it is possible to do so, primary legislation and subordinate legislation must be read and given effect in a way which is compatible with the Convention rights' (s 3(1)). The presumption of interpretation in s 3 applies both to primary and subordinate legislation 'whenever enacted' (s 3(2)(a)).

The critical question raised by s 3 is what is meant by the word 'possible'? Does it mean that a strained interpretation that is consistent with the ECHR must be preferred to a more natural interpretation that is inconsistent with the Convention?

This issue confronted the House of Lords in *R v A (No 2)*.[127] Section 41 of the Youth Justice and Criminal Evidence Act 1999 severely restricts cross-examination of a rape victim about her previous sexual conduct which would otherwise be relevant to a defence based on consent. The House of Lords held unanimously that s 41 had to be read subject to s 3 of the HRA and that the test to be applied was whether admitting such evidence was so relevant to the issue of consent that it would endanger the fairness of the trial in breach of Art 6 of the ECHR. In giving s 41 this interpretation the House of Lords was going against the manifest intention of Parliament. Rather than issue a declaration of incompatibility the Law Lords implied additional words into the statutory provision.

But two different approaches emerged. The leading speech was given by Lord Steyn:

> … the interpretative obligation under section 3 of the 1998 Act is a strong one. It applies even if there is no ambiguity in the language in the sense of the language being capable of two different meanings. It is an emphatic adjuration by the legislature … Under ordinary methods of interpretation a court may depart from the language of the statute to avoid absurd consequences: section 3 goes much further. Undoubtedly, a court must always look for a contextual and purposive interpretation: section 3 is more radical in its effect. It is a general principle of interpretation of legal instruments that the text is a primary source of interpretation: other sources are subordinate to it … Section 3 qualifies this general principle because it requires a court to find an interpretation compatible with Convention rights if it is possible to do so … In accordance with the will of Parliament as reflected in section 3 it will sometimes be necessary to adopt an

[126] See 'ECHR protects criminals and has lost public trust', *The Times*, 19 June 2025, p 7.
[127] [2001] UKHL 25, [2002] 1 AC 45.

> interpretation which linguistically may appear strained. The techniques to be used will not only involve the reading down[128] of express language in a statute but also the implication of provisions. A declaration of incompatibility is a measure of last resort. It must be avoided unless it is plainly impossible to do so. ([44])

In other words, according to Lord Steyn, if necessary, the judges must be prepared even to override clear parliamentary intention in the particular statute in order to give precedence to the requirements of the ECHR.

Lord Hope was not prepared to go quite so far:

> The rule of construction which section 3 lays down is quite unlike any previous rule of statutory interpretation. There is no need to identify an ambiguity or absurdity. Compatibility with Convention rights is the sole guiding principle. That is the paramount object which the rule seeks to achieve. But the rule is only a rule of interpretation. It does not entitle the judges to act as legislators ... The compatibility is to be achieved only so far as this is possible. Plainly this will not be possible if the legislation contains provisions which expressly contradict the meaning which the enactment would have to be given to make it compatible. (at [108])

Lord Hope was not prepared to imply words into s 41 in contradiction of Parliament's intention. His solution was to send the case back for further elucidation of the facts. He elaborated his view in *R v Lambert*:[129]

> Section 3(1) preserves the sovereignty of Parliament. It does not give power to the judges to overrule decisions which the language of the statute shows have been taken on the very point at issue by the legislator. [T]he interpretation of a statute by reading words in to give effect to the presumed intention must always be distinguished carefully from amendment. Amendment is a legislative act. It is an exercise which must be reserved to Parliament. (at [79], [80])

However, even Lord Hope accepted that under s 3 it could be permissible for the courts to arrive at a compatible interpretation by expressing the statutory words in different language 'in order to explain how they are to be read in a way that is compatible'; or even for words to be 'read in', 'to explain the meaning that must be given to the provision if it is to be compatible' (at [81]). But he warned that it ought to be possible for any words that need to be substituted 'to be fitted into the statute as if they had been inserted there by amendment' ([80]).[130]

As was said by one commentator, 'recourse to the precept that judges can engage in interpretation but not legislation does little to illuminate the problem'.[131] The crux of the matter is how far judges are prepared to go in giving expression to ECHR rights that conflict with the express or necessarily implied words of a statute. In the view of that commentator the answer was clear:

> The Human Rights Act is itself a constitutional instrument. Its purpose is to tilt the constitutional balance in favour of fundamental human rights. A refusal to apply a possible section 3 interpretation because it breaches constitutional principle by encroaching into the legislative

[128] 'Reading down' is a term of art meaning to give the words in question a narrow interpretation in order to ensure that the legislation remains valid. It is to be contrasted with 'reading in', which means implying words in the statute (ed).

[129] [2001] 3 WLR 206, [2001] 3 All ER 577: see in particular at [79]–[81].

[130] Given that at [81] Lord Hope said that amendment of statutes by judges was not permissible, his statement at [80] that words substituted by judges in pursuance of the requirements of s 3 should be slotted in as if they were amendments is perhaps not as clear as it might be.

[131] R Clayton, 'The limits of what's "possible": statutory construction under the Human Rights Act', *European Human Rights Law Review*, 2002, 559, 565.

> sphere cannot be justified. That analysis undermines the Parliamentary intention in enacting the Human Rights Act in the first place.[132]

The same commentator accepted, however, that under the guidelines laid down by the House of Lords, s 3 could not be invoked 'if the Convention compliant interpretation is contrary to express statutory words or is by implication *necessarily* contradicted by the statute'.[133] These limitations, he said, are 'very *different* (sic) from rejecting a possible section 3 interpretation because its radical effect would alter Parliament's intention when originally enacting a particular piece of legislation'.[134] But how different are they? Is this not playing with words? If the judge gives precedence to the Convention right over the seemingly conflicting statute, they will do so by stating that their interpretation, however strained, is 'possible' and therefore compatible. If they see the statute as an immoveable block to such an interpretation they will say that such interpretation is not possible and will make a declaration of incompatibility. Section 3 may push the judge harder than any other so-called rule, principle or presumption of interpretation but it still leaves the judge the discretion as to which way to decide the case.

In *Poplar Housing and Regeneration Community Association Limited v Secretary of State for the Environment, Transport and the Regions* [2002] QB 48 Lord Woolf said that finding the boundary between re-interpretation and legislation was not easy. If it was necessary to 'radically alter' the effect of legislation and so defeat Parliament's original objective, then more than interpretation was involved.[135]

Francesca Klug and Claire O'Brien,[136] in 'The first two years of the Human Rights Act', wrote:

> The emerging view is that the 'plain meaning' of statutory language cannot be 'ignored or simply changed in the cause of securing compatibility at all costs'.[137] As Sedley LJ has put it: section 3 is not a 'supplanting mechanism' but a 'strong canon of construction'.[138]

In other words, Lord Hope's position in *R v A* was gaining and that of Lord Steyn seemed to be in retreat. This view was subsequently confirmed by the House of Lords' decisions in *Re S (Minors) (care order: implementation of care plan)*,[139] *R (on the application of Anderson) v Secretary of State for the Home Department*[140] which was decided by a

[132] Ibid, 566.

[133] Ibid, 565. An example, Clayton suggested, was *In Re S (care order: implementation of care plan)* [2002] 2 WLR 720.

[134] Ibid.

[135] At [76], [77].

[136] *Public Law*, 2002, 649, 654.

[137] Citing *R v Daniel* [2002] EWCA Crim 959 [2003] 1 Cr App R 6.

[138] Citing *R (on the application of Wooder) v Forgetters and Mental Health Act Commission* [2002] EWCA Civ 554, [2002] 3 WLR 591.

[139] [2002] UKHL 10, [2002] 2 AC 291. The Court of Appeal had applied s 3 of the HRA to 'read in' a new procedure for ongoing judicial supervision of children in care under the Children Act 1989. The House of Lords held that this was 'judicial innovation' beyond the licence of s 3 of the HRA. A cardinal principle of the Children Act was to entrust local authorities rather than the courts with parental authority under a care order. The Court of Appeal's decision, Lord Nicholls said, amounted to illegitimate 'statutory amendment', as opposed to acceptable 'legislative interpretation' ([43]).

[140] [2002] UKHL 46, [2003] 1 AC 837. The Law Lords declined to read into s 29 of the Criminal (Sentences) Act 1997 a rule that the Home Secretary may not fix a sentence tariff exceeding that recommended by the trial judge. Lord Chief Justice. Lord Bingham (at [30]) said that to do so would not be judicial interpretation but judicial vandalism. It would go well beyond what Parliament intended. Lord Hutton (at [81]) said it would amount to amending the statute.

seven-judge panel; and *Bellinger v Bellinger*.[141] Remarkably, in *Anderson*, Lord Steyn himself accepted this. Contradicting what he had so powerfully said in *R v A*, s 3(1), he said,[142] was not available where the suggested interpretation was contrary to express statutory words or was by necessary implication contradicted by the statute. He emphasised the importance of parliamentary sovereignty. ('[T]he supremacy of Parliament is the paramount principle of our constitution.'[143]) It followed that there had to be a declaration of incompatibility.

As one commentator suggested, the emphatic rejection of 'over-zealous' interpretation in these three cases showed that the House of Lords had made up its mind in favour of restricting its use of s 3 and correspondingly availing itself more readily of s 4 declarations of incompatibility. This, he argued, was the preferable approach. The judges raised the question but government and Parliament had the task of determining the solution. 'In a society which increasingly recognises that fundamental rights are matters on which reasonable people disagree, this constitutes a more attractive vision of the HRA than the assertion of a judicial monopoly of wisdom underlying *R v A*.'[144]

The Independent Review of the Human Rights Act chaired by Sir Peter Gross, published in October 2021, said (p 203): 'The leading statement on the approach to be taken to the use of section 3 is now *Ghaidan v Godin-Mendoza*' [2004] UKHL 30, [2004] 2 AC 557. The House of Lords by a majority held that the survivor of a same-sex partnership had the same status as the spouse of a protected tenant entitled to succeed on the tenant's death as a statutory tenant.[145] Lord Steyn attached to his speech an appendix detailing all the cases in which a breach of the ECHR had been found where the court went on to consider whether to apply s 3 or whether instead to make a declaration of incompatibility under s 4. The appendix showed that there were ten cases in which the court had proceeded under s 3 and 15 in which it issued a declaration of incompatibility. In five of the latter cases, the decision was reversed. In four of the five the appeal court held that there was no incompatibility, in the fifth case the basis of the decision was unclear. Lord Steyn said that given that s 3 was supposed to be the 'principal remedial measure' and that s 4 was supposed to be 'a last resort' the statistics raised the question whether s 3 was being properly applied. A study of the cases, he said, 'reinforces the need to pose the question whether the law has taken a wrong turning' (at [39]). The speeches of the four members of the majority suggest that the pendulum was moving slightly back

[141] [2003] UKHL 21, [2003] 2 AC 467. The Law Lords refused to apply Arts 8 and 14 of the ECHR so as to hold that Mrs B, a male-to-female transsexual could validly marry Mr B. Such an act of interpretation would constitute a legislative exercise of law reform that should be undertaken if at all by Parliament. It made a declaration of incompatibility.

[142] At [59].

[143] At [39].

[144] D Nicol, 'Statutory interpretation and human rights after *Anderson*' *Public Law*, 2004, 274. See also the same author's comment on *Bellinger* – 'Gender reassignment and the transformation of Section 3 of the Human Rights Act 1998' 120 *Law Quarterly Review*, 2004, 194. For a critique of Nicol's view see A Kavanagh, 'Statutory interpretation and human rights after *Anderson*: a more contextual approach' *Public Law*, 2004, 537.

[145] S 3 as interpreted by the Supreme Court in that case, Lord Neuberger said in a lecture, permitted courts 'to interpret statutes in a way which some may say amounts not so much to construction as to demolition and reconstruction' (Lord Neuberger, 'The role of judges in human rights jurisprudence: a comparison of the Australian and the British experience' 8 August 2014, Conference at the Supreme Court, Melbourne – accessed on www.supremecourt.uk). See also J Van Zyl Smit, 'New purposive interpretation of statutes: HRA section 3 after *Ghaidan v Godin-Mendoza*' 70 *Modern Law Review*, 2007, 294.

toward the approach adopted in *R v A* – but it seems likely that for the foreseeable future, it will oscillate unpredictably.

The Gross Review concluded (para 64, p 207): 'The principles articulated in *Ghaidan* provide clear and sensible guidance to UK Courts to apply section 3's interpretative duty. Since they were set out it is difficult to identify cases where UK Courts have strayed beyond Parliament's intention in enacting section 3'.

Lord Neuberger, President of the Supreme Court, spoke in a lecture of the effect of ss 3 and 4 on the relationship between judges and Parliament:

> [S]ection 3 of the HRA enables judges to give a statutory provision a meaning which it does not naturally bear and which Parliament never intended it to bear. It is true that this power was bestowed by Parliament, and it can therefore be said that when judges rewrite statutes under section 3, they are giving effect to Parliament's will, but Parliament has written us judges something of a blank cheque in this connection. The way in which section 3 of the HRA has been interpreted by judges is not a case of the UK courts making their own grab for power. Although it was intended by Parliament, this new judicial power of quasi-interpretation can be said to involve a subtle but significant adjustment to the balance of power between the legislature and the judiciary of the UK … [T]he UK approach can be seen as effectively conferring a law making function on the judiciary. The UK courts have developed new rules which control the way in which this power can be exercised. For instance, the section 3 power cannot be used in a way which would involve an apparently incompatible statutory provision having a meaning which was inconsistent with the scheme of the Statute concerned, or if it is not clear how an apparently incompatible statutory provision would have been rewritten.
>
> Even the power to make a declaration of incompatibility represents an important shift in the balance of power in a country whose institutions have such a deep respect for the rule of law such as the UK … [A]common law judge's power to make a declaration of incompatibility is revolutionary, as it does not affect the rights of the parties to the relevant case, and it is ultimately advisory. Unlike a normal declaration which binds the parties to the litigation, a declaration of incompatibility binds nobody. In that sense it can be said to represent a role for the judiciary which is subordinate to that of parliament, but, as I have mentioned, in a parliamentary democracy without a constitution, the judiciary can in other ways fairly be seen as ultimately subordinate to the legislature. In more practical terms, however, the power now given to judges in the UK by section 4 of the HRA is demonstrated by the fact that, with one exception, Parliament has always acted on every such and cured any incompatibility. The one exception is prisoners' right to vote which is a very contentious political issue in some quarters in the UK.[146]

See also Lady Justice Arden, 'The interpretation of UK domestic legislation in the light of European Convention jurisprudence' 25 *Statute Law Review*, 2004, 165.

For earlier writings see for instance: Anthony Lester, 'The art of the possible: interpreting statutes under the Human Rights Act' in *The Human Rights Act and the Criminal Justice and Regulatory Process* (Hart Publishing, 1999), 29; Francis Bennion, 'What interpretation is "possible" under section 3(10) of the Human Rights Act 1998?' *Public Law*, 2000, 77; Geoffrey Marshall, 'Two kinds of compatability: more about section 3 of the Human Rights Act 1998' *Public Law*, 1999, 377 and 'The lynchpin of parliamentary intention: lost, stolen or strained' *Public Law*, 2003, 236.

[146] Lord Neuberger, 'The role of judges in human rights jurisprudence: a comparison of the Australian and the British experience' 8 August 2014, Conference at the Supreme Court, Melbourne, paras 14, 15 accessible at www.supremecourt.uk.

3.8.2. The Gross Independent Review Recommended only Minor Changes in Regard to Section 3

The Gross Review recommended:

- Setting out an order of priority in which courts should approach resort to Convention rights. Look first at the normal ways of interpreting legislation whether the legislation can be interpreted compatibly with the Convention and apply section 3 only if that is not possible. That was already the approach but it would be strengthened by statutory statement.
- Strengthening Parliament's role. Parliament should consider how the role of the Joint Human Rights Select Committee could improve its scrutiny of section 3 judgments and how parliamentary consideration of such judgments and JCHR reports concerning them, could also properly be improved. (paras 200–01, p 256)

Research conducted by JUSTICE[147] to test the belief that s 3 was a radical instrument that authorised judicial lawmaking contrary to the will of Parliament, examined the 593 cases shown by Westlaw to involve reference to the section between 1 January 2013 and 31 December 2020. The authors excluded the cases where the decision was later overturned and those where the court was simply following precedent. The study found:

- Over the eight years there were only 25 cases in which s 3 was used to interpret legislation that would otherwise have been incompatible with Convention rights. The other cases fell into one of three categories: the legislation did not breach Convention law; a Convention compliant interpretation could be reached without using s 3; the court did not use s 3 but issued a declaration of incompatibility.
- When s 3 was used, the decision was rarely contrary to Parliament's intention. It was often used 'to address unforeseen drafting issues or factual situations that clearly fell within the overall intention of the legislative scheme'. Some decisions were to address technicalities with legislative wording. Some used s 3 to interpret legislation in accordance with other equivalent legislation (eg the Equality Act 2010).

The authors conclude:

> [T]he cases we identified where s 3 has been used demonstrate that it is not a radical judicial law-making tool that poses a threat to the rule of law. Instead, s 3 is a well-crafted interpretative tool that is rarely relied on by the courts, but when it is used, the courts have done so to protect Convention rights in a way which maintains the constitutional separation of power.

3.9. What (if any) is the Function of General Statutory Rules on Statutory Interpretation?

In most countries there is some form of Interpretation Act, defining common terms or stating that, for instance, the male shall include the female unless the context indicates

[147] F Powell and S Needleman, 'How radical an instrument is Section 3 of the Human Rights Act 1998' UK Const L Blog (24 March 2021 (available at https://uk.constitutionallaw.org/).

otherwise. In England there has been such an Act since 1889. A modern version was enacted in 1978.[148]

But some countries have gone beyond guidance on such matters to attempt to guide the judges on the main problems of interpretation. The New Zealand Interpretation Act 1888 provided that –

> Every Act, and every provision or enactment thereof, shall be deemed remedial, whether its immediate purport is to direct the doing of anything Parliament deems to be for the public good, or to prevent or punish the doing of anything it deems contrary to the public good, and shall accordingly receive such fair, large, and liberal construction and interpretation as will best ensure the attainment of the object of the Act and of such provision or enactment according to its true intent, meaning, and spirit.[149]

Obviously the purpose behind the New Zealand provision was to deter the judges from applying a narrow, literal approach to interpretation. It was a modern restatement of the mischief rule in *Heydon's* case – cast in mandatory form.

How has it worked? The answer was given by Mr Denzil Ward who for 24 years was a parliamentary drafter in New Zealand. The Act, he said, had been invoked occasionally but for every case in which it had been applied there were many others in which it had been ignored. The courts in fact had continued to apply the 'heterogeneous collection of canons of construction developed by the English courts over a period of several hundred years'.

DAS Ward, 'A criticism of the interpretation of statutes in the New Zealand courts' *New Zealand Law Journal*, 1963, 293

> Sometimes it is difficult to discover just which approach has been favoured by the court. Usually no reason is given for preferring one approach to any other. The most that can be said is that some judges at some periods have been fairly consistent in using the approach that they prefer.
>
> Thus we occasionally find a court applying the 'mischief rule' laid down in *Heydon's* case …
>
> Sometimes it is clear that the court, by its concentration on the actual words it is construing, is applying the 'literal rule' which in the nineteenth century dominated the judicial approach to a spate of legislation in general terms.
>
> Sometimes … it applies one of the presumptions (such as the presumption that a statute is not intended to alter the common law or the presumption of *mens rea*) which developed mainly during the eighteenth century when the courts regarded themselves more as standing between parliament and the people than as interpreters of authoritative texts. Alternatively a presumption may be brought into play to reinforce one of the other rules.
>
> There are other cases where a court applies one of the maxims (such as the '*ejusdem generis* rule') which are really no more than condensed statements of the ordinary use of English; or decides the case on any one of a number of subsidiary and technical 'rules' secreted in the judgments of the past.

[148] See WA Leitch, 'Interpretation and the Interpretation Act 1978' 1 *Statute Law Review*, 1980, 5.

[149] The provision is now to be found in the Acts Interpretation Act 1924, s 5(*j*). A similar provision was inserted in 1981 into the Australian Acts Interpretation Act 1901: '15AA.(1) In the interpretation of a provision of an Act, a construction that would promote the purpose or object underlying the Act (whether that purpose or object is expressly stated in the Act or not) shall be preferred to a construction that would not promote that purpose or object.' S 11 of the Canadian Interpretation Act 1967–68 stated that 'every enactment shall be deemed remedial, and shall be given such fair, large and liberal construction and interpretation as best ensures the attainment of those objects'. See to like effect s 12 of the Canadian Federal Interpretation Act, RSC 1985, c 1–21.

> These 'rules' and presumptions and maxims are inconsistent, and often flatly contradict each other, but they are treated in the textbooks and in judgments as having equal validity today, regardless of the differing social, political, and constitutional conditions in which they arose. The 'literal rule' cannot be reconciled with the 'mischief rule'. Many of the presumptions have become unreal in these days when legislation invades so many aspects of life with its administrative machinery for the Welfare State, its taxes, its controls, and its innumerable minor offences. Some of them cannot be reconciled with the statement in s. 5(*j*) that every enactment shall be deemed remedial.
>
> The result is chaos. It is impossible to predict what approach any court will make to any case. The field of statutory interpretation has become a judicial jungle. It is only fair to say that the jungle has been inherited; but our courts have been so busy cultivating the trees that they have lost sight of the pathway provided by parliament in the Acts Interpretation Act.

It seems from this account that a statutory enactment of the mischief rule had not been successful in New Zealand.[150] The Law Commission in their 1969 Report on Statutory Interpretation were surely right in offering the possible explanation of the New Zealand history that 'exhortations to the courts to adopt "large and liberal" interpretations beg the question as to what is the real intention of the legislature, which may require in the circumstances either a broad or a narrow construction of language' (para 33).[151] But the Law Commission did nevertheless propose that it should be provided by statute that among the principles to be applied in the interpretation of statutes was that 'a construction which would promote the general legislative purpose underlying the provision in question is to be preferred to a construction which would not'. The Renton Committee supported this proposal (*The Preparation of Legislation*, Cmnd 6053, 1975, para 19.28).

In February 1980 Lord Scarman, introduced a bill in the Lords to implement some of the recommendations of the Law Commission in its 1969 Report on Statutory Interpretation (when he had been its chairman). Its purpose was to make available to the courts a wider range of aids to construction. It would have permitted reference to the reports of any Royal Commission, committee or other body moved or laid before Parliament or any document declared by the Act to be relevant. It also specified that among the principles to be applied in the interpretation of statutes was that a construction 'which would promote the general legislative purpose underlying the provision in question is to be preferred to a construction which would not'. The Law Lords gave the bill an extremely frosty reception and it was withdrawn.[152]

Nothing daunted, a year later Lord Scarman returned to the subject and introduced another, slightly amended, version of the original bill. This time it received a rather warmer welcome, and in fact went through all its stages in the House of Lords.[153] But the bill went no further and was not even debated in the House of Commons. That was the end of that attempt at reform.

[150] The New Zealand 1924 Acts Interpretation Act, s 5(j) was replaced by the Interpretation Act 1999, s 5(1) which provides: 'The meaning of an enactment must be ascertained from its text and in the light of its purpose.' For the background see S Glazebrook, 'From "Curious Provision" to "Cardinal Rule" – The Purposive Approach to Statutory Interpretation in New Zealand' in C Hunt, L Neudorf and M Rankin (eds), *Legislating Statutory Interpretation: Perspectives from the Common Law World* (Thomson Reuters, 2018), 293–319. The author concludes (at 319): 'The purposive interpretation of statutes is now mainstream in New Zealand. However, the text remains paramount.'

[151] The Canadian provision requiring a 'fair, large and liberal' construction of every enactment was held in 1981 not to override the principle that penal statutes must be given a narrow construction – *R v Philips Electronics Ltd* (1981) 116 DLR (3d) 298, noted in 2 *Statute Law Review*, 1981, 111.

[152] See House of Lords, *Hansard* vol 405, cols 276–306, 13 February 1980.

[153] See House of Lords, *Hansard*, vol 418, cols 64–83 9 March 1981, and vol 418, cols 1341–47 26 March 1981.

For a commentary on the history of this abortive attempt to reform statutory interpretation see Francis Bennion, 'Another reverse for the Law Commission's Interpretation Bill', *New Law Journal*, 13 August 1981, 840.

As previously noted, official reports such as reports of the Law Commission are now commonly cited in the courts.

Note – interpretation of a criminal code

During the work done for the Law Commission toward the production of a draft Criminal Code (as to which see p 473 below) the drafting team was asked to draft 'rules which should govern its interpretation'. In its report to the Law Commission in 1985 the drafting team included a clause dealing with interpretation. The draft Code was then sent out for comment. Comments on the interpretation clause were mixed and included so many adverse comments that the Law Commission decided to drop it altogether from the next draft, seemingly on the ground that there was no need for such a clause since the general rules of interpretation would apply. See A Ashworth, 'Interpreting criminal statutes: a crisis of legality' 107 *Law Quarterly Review*, 1991, 419, 425–26. Professor Ashworth suggested that there may be a constitutional principle that statutory interpretation is for the courts rather than for Parliament.

For a valuable collection of essays see *Legislating Statutory Interpretation: Perspectives from the Common Law World* (eds C Hunt, L Neudorf and M Rankin) Thomson Reuters, 2018.

3.10. Do Statements of General Principle Assist?

One of the recommendations of the Renton Committee was that the use in statutes of statements of principle should be encouraged (*The Preparation of Legislation*, 1975, Cmnd 6053, para 10.13).

Mr IML Turnbull, First Parliamentary Counsel in Canberra, commented critically on this suggestion, and similar suggestions, at a conference in 1983:

IML Turnbull, 'Problems of legislative drafting' 7 *Statute Law Review*, 1986, 72–73

> Although it sounds like a good idea in theory, it is very different in practice. If the clause is to cover the scope of the whole Bill, it must necessarily be drafted in very general terms. Yet its very generality will render it redundant and it will be little more than what Professor Reed Dickerson, the American draftsman and author, has described as a 'pious incantation'. The general purpose of a Bill will be apparent on the reading of its clauses: the problems of interpretation do not arise from the main body of cases that fall within the scope of a Bill, but from the cases that are on the borderline, requiring a consideration of the details of the legislation.
>
> For example, section 2 of the Conciliation and Arbitration Act 1904 sets forth the chief objects of the Act as being: (a) 'to promote goodwill in industry; (b) to encourage, and provide means for, conciliation with a view to amicable agreement, thereby preventing and settling industrial disputes; (c) to provide means for preventing and settling industrial disputes not resolved by amicable agreement, including threatened, impending and probable industrial disputes, with the maximum of expedition and the minimum of legal form and technicality; (d) to provide for the observance and enforcement of agreements and awards made for the prevention or settlement of industrial disputes; (e) to encourage the organisation of representative bodies of employers and employees and their registration under this Act; and (f) to encourage the democratic control of organisations so registered and the full participation by members of such an organisation in the affairs of the organisation.'

> I suggest, first, that there is nothing in section 2 that is not apparent on the reading of the 200 sections of the Act, and secondly, that section 2 is of very little assistance, if at all, in the interpretation of the details of those sections. It is interesting to note that, notwithstanding the hundreds of amendments that have been made to different provisions of the Act since it was first enacted, section 2 has been remade once and amended twice. If the terms of the section have been wide enough to encompass so many alterations made by the legislature, they are wide enough to encompass an equal number of different interpretations made by the judiciary.

The Renton Committee (para 11.B) recognised the problem of the generality of such clauses:

> A distinction should, however, be drawn between a statement of purpose which is designed to delimit and illuminate the legal effects of the Bill and a statement of purpose which is a mere manifesto. Statements of purpose of the latter kind should in our view be firmly discouraged.
>
> Yet it is difficult to conceive of an objects clause that can 'delimit and illuminate' the legal effects of the Bill with sufficient accuracy to be of any use unless it is comparable in length with the clauses of the Bill.

The Hansard Society's 1992 Report on *The Legislative Process: Making the Law* also said it disagreed with the Renton Committee's suggestion that there should generally be a statement of principle and purpose:

> We firmly believe that certainty in the law must be the paramount aim in the drafting of statutes, and we do not believe that the automatic inclusion of statements of principle or purpose in the body of the Act would help to that end … In the first place, statements of principle or purpose would still have to be interpreted by the courts, even if other detail remained in the Act, and their very generality would leave open the possibility of differing interpretations … Secondly, 'we see considerable problems in including in an Act two different formulations of what must be intended to be the same law on a single point – one in the form of a statement of principle or purpose (in some cases perhaps both) and the other in the form of detailed provisions'. That would be a recipe for confusion. (paras 239, 240, 241 pp 60–61)

In short, it considered that it would not be helpful to have statements of principle or purpose in statutes.

3.11. What is the Court's Proper Function in Interpreting a Statute?

3.11.1. Is it to Seek Out Parliament's Intention or is it to Seek Out the Purpose of the Statute?

There are innumerable statements in judicial decisions that the chief duty of a court faced with a problem of statutory interpretation is to discover the intention of Parliament.[154]

[154] See on this issue M Radin, 'Statutory interpretation' 43 *Harvard Law Review*, 1930, 863; Douglas Payne, 'The intention of the legislature in the interpretation of statutes' *Current Legal Problems*, 1956, 96; R Ekins, 'The intention of Parliament' *Public Law*, 1970, 709–26, Ekins' book, *The Nature of Legislative Intent* (Oxford University Press, 2012) and the review article by J Goldsworthy, 'Legislative intention vindicated?' 33 *Oxford Journal of Legal Studies*, 2013, 821. See also Mary Arden, 'The changing judicial role: human rights, community law and the intention of Parliament' 67 *Cambridge Law Journal*, 2008, 487; and D Greenberg, 'The nature of legislative intention and its implications for legislative drafting' 27 *Statute Law Review*, 2006, 15.

But such statements have also been criticised. To speak of the legislature's intention, it has been objected, is a fiction – an abstraction that can have no intention. In most cases only a few people drafted the statute, only some spoke in the debates, many voted against it and many more had little notion of what they were voting about when they voted in favour. Whose intention represents that of the legislature? It is often clear that the draftsmen did not anticipate the problem that has occurred or, in other cases, that the statute did not provide any clear solution. For such reasons the concept of legislative intention is today somewhat discredited.

These points can be met.[155] An amorphous group can have an intention even though it cannot be linked to any particular individuals. Those who voted against it obviously did not share the intent – but under the ordinary principles of democracy the majority prevails and the minority can for this purpose be disregarded. Those who voted without fully understanding the subject are deemed to have accepted the intention that emerges from the document. Those who were actively involved in formulating and promoting the statute could be said to be those who had a subjective intent which may or may not have been reflected in the ultimate language of the document. Matters that were not anticipated could still be said to be covered by the legislative intent in the sense that the statute may show how such problems should be solved. The authors of the statute may not have foreseen the particular problem, but they may nevertheless have had an intention which covers the situation that occurs – through reasoned elaboration of their text or by way of analogy.

Of course, the fact that there is some generalised intent implicit in a statute does not mean that there will have been something approaching a specific intent in regard to the problem under consideration. If the concept of intention is required to mean detailed answers to the problem in hand, it must be conceded that often no such intention can be said to have existed. But if the concept of intention is defined in a broader and more realistic way, it does have genuine application to the situation. Certainly in the layman's sense the legislators had an intention and the layman's common-sense approach seems sufficiently close to the real situation to make the word 'intention' not as inappropriate as has often been suggested.

Those who have objected to the phrase 'legislative intention' have tended to prefer the seemingly more objective phrase 'legislative purpose'. This phrase, it is said, avoids most of the difficulties associated with the word 'intention'. It has been argued that some of these objections have been exaggerated, but perhaps the more telling argument is that, on analysis, 'legislative purpose' is perhaps only a different way of stating the same concept as 'legislative intent'. Both are ways of stating that the function of the interpreter is to give the words, to the best of their ability, a meaning that reflects the objectives of those responsible for the statute, insofar as this has been expressed in the language used.

In his discussion of this issue in his 2017 Hamlyn Lectures, Andrew (then Professor, now Lord) Burrows, does not agree that 'intention' and 'purpose' are essentially the same. He rejects Parliamentary intention but accepts the concept of purpose of a statute:

> When we talk of 'purpose', we are looking for the policy behind the statute or statutory provisions. Identifying the policy behind is not dependent on identifying any person's

[155] This discussion is based largely on Reed Dickerson, *The Interpretation and Application of Statutes* (Little Brown, 1975) 67. See also S Vogenauer, 'What is the proper role of legislative intention in judicial interpretation?' 18 *Statute Law Review*, 1997, 235; R French, 'The Principle of Legality and Legislative Intention', 40 *Statute Law Review*, 2019, 40–52 and P Sales, 'Legislative Intention, Interpretation and the Principle of Legality', 40 *Statute Law Review*, 2019, 53–63.

> intention. It may be said to be analogous to identifying the principle behind a common law precedent.[156]

In a footnote, he added: 'Even if it were correct that at a high level there is a link between intention and purpose, at a practical level it is the purpose that matters.' We were concerned 'with the meaning of the statute, ascertained by considering *the statute's* words, context and purpose'.[157]

For a strongly argued riposte see Jeffrey Goldsworthy, 'Lord Burrows and Legislative Intention, Statutory Purpose and the "Always Speaking" Principle', 43 *Statute Law Review*, 2022 (1), 79–102. Concluding, he summarised his argument:

> It is inconsistent to deny the relevance of legislative intention, while endorsing reliance on statutory purpose and context. Purpose is a kind of intention, and context is relevant because it is evidence of purpose and other more particular intentions. Relying on statutory purpose and context is therefore not an alternative to enquiring into legislative intention; they are one and the same.

For a challenging critique of both the purposivist and the intentionalist position see Tim Sayer, 'Statutory interpretation and the administrative state: refocusing the purposivist and the intentionalist debate', 44 *Legal Studies*, 2024 (3), 437–57. Sayer argues that in hard cases of genuine ambiguity, judges should permit intervention by the executive to offer the view of those who crafted the text – and should regard that as determinative!

When applying the purposive approach it is of course to be hoped that the court's statement of the purpose is correct. In *Yemshaw v Hounslow LBC* [2011] UKSC 3 the Supreme Court, reversing the Court of Appeal, decided that the word 'violence' for the purposes of the Housing Act 1996 extended to non-physical harm – with the result that the local authority was under a duty to rehouse the applicant. Examination of the background to the 1996 Act suggested it was improbable that the legislature intended any such charitable intention.[158] Another such case is *R v Central Criminal Court, ex p Francis & Francis* [1988] 2 WLR 627. Writing about the problems of the purposive approach, Lord Oliver said that the House of Lords gave the statutory words in that case an interpretation that both ignored their literal meaning and conflicted with the minister's statement as to the purpose of the provision.[159]

3.11.2. To Give Effect to What Parliament Said, Rather than What it Meant to Say?

The school of thought which insists on focusing prime attention on the words used regardless of context has a fundamental point of great importance. 'The primacy of the text is the first rule of interpretation for the judge considering a point of interpretation'.[160] The intellectual integrity of the process demands that there be some limit to the process of 'interpretation'. The point may be made by reference to the will in *Re Rowland* p 144 above) where the question was whether the two deaths coincided. If the evidence had shown that

[156] Andrew Burrows, *Thinking About Statutes* (Cambridge University Press, 2018) 19.
[157] Ibid, 20.
[158] C Bevan, 'Interpreting Statutory Purpose – Lessons from *Yemshaw v Hounslow LBC*' 76 *Modern Law Review*, 2013, 742–56.
[159] Lord Oliver, 'A Judicial View of Modern Legislation' 14 *Statute Law Review*, 1993, 5–11.
[160] Lord Steyn, '*Pepper v Hart*: a re-examination' 21 *Oxford Journal of Legal Studies*, 2001, 59 at 60.

Dr Rowland survived his wife by, say, 48 hours by clinging on to a raft which eventually sank, it would be straining the meaning of words to have held that their deaths coincided. On the other hand, if it had appeared that they died within half an hour of each other – he in New York, she in Melbourne – *in the context* it would arguably have been within the legitimate elaboration of the word 'coinciding' to have held that it covered the event. In both cases it would have been obvious that the testator would have wished his property to go to his own relatives rather than to his wife's, but in the one case it would have been reasonable and in the other case unreasonable to have given effect to his intention.

The literalists are therefore not wrong to focus attention on the text. Their error is rather to focus exclusive attention on the text, and to deny the importance of seeing and comprehending the context. Clearly there must be some limit to the amount of context that the court can consider. But to apply the literal approach is unnecessarily to put on blinkers.

However, sometimes the question whether there *is* an ambiguity can only be answered when at least some context has been considered. It may appear that the words are clear but when seen in the light of the background they may take on a quite different shading. ('I leave all my property to mother' seems clear. But what if the testator always referred to his wife as 'mother'?) The court should be willing to receive sufficient material to establish the nature of the issue raised between the parties – so that it can give an informed decision. The point was made by Lord Wilberforce. Speaking of contracts, he said that there is always a setting in which they have to be placed. The court, he said, is always entitled to be informed of the contextual scene of the contract.[161]

When deciding whether to give the text a narrow ('literal') or a broader ('liberal' or 'strained') interpretation the court needs to take into account all relevant factors. Having considered the context, the court may come to the conclusion that the literal interpretation is the best (ie the 'right') answer to the problem because it reflects the purpose of the authors of the text. Or, if the court is unable to discover the purpose of the enactment and has no other material to guide it as to the likely meaning it may have no basis for departing from the literal meaning. But the crux of the matter is that it should consider the context.

The 'Literal' and the 'Ordinary' Meaning are Distinguishable

It is common to treat the words 'literal meaning', 'plain meaning' and 'ordinary meaning' as if they were interchangeable. It may be that 'literal' and 'plain' in this context are indeed so similar as not to make any difference. But 'ordinary' *is* different. The point was made by the United States scholar, Professor Robert Summers:

> An ordinary meaning of a word in the context of its use is frequently not the same as its literal meaning. In discussing the interpretation of law, Cicero put the case of a 'salvage' law that prescribed that those who in a storm forsook a ship should forfeit all property in it and the ship should belong entirely to those who 'stayed' with it. One such passenger, who was by reason of illness unable to escape with the rest, claimed the ship as a salvor after it by chance came safely to port. Literal usage might suggest that the sick passenger in a literal sense 'stayed' with the ship and that he might claim the benefit of the law. But it is highly doubtful whether an informed, competent, and purposive user of the English language, knowing the facts of the case, would feel compelled to say the sick man was someone who had 'stayed' with the ship. Such a person would almost certainly understand from the words that any reward for salvage should go only to a person who *by choice stayed* with the ship. After all the reward is a *reward for salvage*.

[161] *Reardon Smith Line v Yrgrar Hansen-Tangen (trading as Hansen-Tangen)* [1976] 1 WLR 989, 995.

A sick person who is unable to do anything other than remain on board could not save the ship or its contents and so is not deserving of such a reward, anyway. Thus, in this context, the ordinary or common usage of 'stayed' – stayed by choice – can be seen to differ from the literal meaning – stayed in the sense merely of remaining on board. Also, the literal sense is not necessarily a narrower meaning. In fact, the literal sense in this instance, embraces a wider class of persons than the ordinary sense that the informed, competent, and purposive user of English would, without more, take the word to mean.[162]

Interpretation to Correct Drafting Errors

In *Inco Europe Ltd v First Choice Distribution*[163] the House of Lords, agreeing with the Court of Appeal, added words to a statute to cure what it held to be a manifest drafting error.[164] It held that this was permissible where the court was sure of three matters: (1) the intended purpose of the statute or provision in question; (2) an inadvertent error by the draftsman in giving effect to that intended purpose; (3) the substance of the provision that Parliament would have made if the error had been noticed.[165]

Even when all three conditions are fulfilled, sometimes the court will decide that the required alteration in language would be too great – 'before our courts can imply words into an Act the statutory intention must be plain and the insertion not too big, or too much at variance with the language in fact used by the legislature'.[166]

3.11.3. Should Interpretation Reflect Changing Times?

It is a familiar principle of statutory interpretation that 'the words of an Act will generally be understood in the sense they bore when it was passed'.[167] The statute should be construed, it has been said, 'as if we had read it the day after it was passed'.[168] But another familiar principle is that interpretation changes with the times. Statutes, it is said, are deemed to be 'always speaking'.[169]

An obvious instance of the adaptability of statutes is when the statutory words are later interpreted to apply to a concept that was unknown at the time when the statute was passed. In *Barker v Wilson* [1980] 1 WLR 884, Caulfield J said he had no doubt that the Bankers' Books Evidence Act 1879, s 9, could be interpreted so as to include microfilm in

[162] R Summers, 'Interpreting statutes in Great Britain and the United States: should courts consider materials of legislative history?' in D Butler, V Bogdanor and R Summers (eds), *The Law, Politics and the Constitution* (Oxford University Press, 1999) 222, 247.

[163] [2000] 1 WLR 586 (HL).

[164] The phrase in the statute 'from any decision of the High Court under that Part' was to be read as 'from any decision of the High Court under a section in that Part which provides for an appeal from such decision'. In the result a right of appeal was allowed which according to the strict terms of the statute would have been denied.

[165] For an application of the principle see *R (Secretary of State for the Home Department) v Southwark Crown Court* [2013] EWHC 4366 (Admin), [2014] 1 WLR 2529 where the Divisional Court inserted the words 'or order' into the statute so as to allow a production order to be made for the purposes of a criminal investigation in the US. See also *OB v Director of Serious Fraud Office* [2012] EWCA Crim 901, [2012] 1 WLR 3188 adding words to the statute so as to restore the possibility of appeal to the Supreme Court in a case involving contempt as it could not have been Parliament's intention to remove that right.

[166] *Western Bank Ltd v Schindler* [1977] Ch.1 at 18(CA) per Scarman LJ.

[167] *Maxwell on Interpretation of Statutes*, 12th edn (Tripathi, 1969) 85.

[168] *Sharpe v Wakefield* (1888) 22 QBD 239.

[169] See on this subject DJ Hurst, 'The problem of the elderly statute' 3 *Legal Studies*, 1983, 21, from which some of the examples that follow are drawn. See also the valuable article by MD Kelly, 'Applying Laws Across Time: Disentangling the "Always Speaking" Principle' 44 *Oxford Journal of Legal Studies*, 2024 (3), 563–90.

the definition of bankers' books as 'ledgers, day books, cash books, account books and all other books used in the ordinary business of the bank'.

Some phrases have been held by the courts to be mobile – changing in content as society changes. This is true of words like 'insulting' in s 5 of the Public Order Act 1936, or 'obscene' in the Obscene Publications Act 1959.[170] The phrase 'actual bodily harm' in the Offences against the Person Act 1861 has been held to include psychiatric injury, which was unheard of when the statute was passed.[171]

In *Quintavalle* [2003] UKHL 13 involving a new fertility technique, Lord Bingham said:

> There is, I think, no inconsistency between the rule that statutory language retains the meaning it had when Parliament used it and the rule that a statute is always speaking. If Parliament, however long ago, passed an Act applicable to dogs, it could not properly be interpreted to apply to cats; but it could properly be held to apply to animals which were not regarded as dogs when the Act was passed but are so regarded now. The meaning of 'cruel and unusual punishments' has not changed over the years since 1689, but many punishments which were not then thought to fall within that category would now be held to do so. ([9])

Lord Bingham cited with approval views expressed by Lord Wilberforce in a dissenting speech in *Royal College of Nursing of the United Kingdom v Department of Health and Social Security* [1981] AC 800 as to whether nurses could lawfully take part in a pregnancy termination procedure not known when the Abortion Act 1967 was passed.

> [W]hen a new state of affairs, or a fresh set of facts bearing on policy, comes into existence, the courts have to consider whether they fall within the Parliamentary intention. They may be held to do so, if they fall within the same genus of facts as those to which the expressed policy has been formulated. They may also be held to do so if there can be detected a clear purpose in the legislation which can only be fulfilled if the extension is made. How liberally these principles may be applied must depend upon the nature of the enactment, and the strictness or otherwise of the words in which it has been expressed. The courts should be less willing to extend expressed meanings if it is clear that the Act in question was designed to be restrictive or circumscribed in its operation rather than liberal or permissive. They will be much less willing to do so where the subject matter is different in kind or dimension from that for which the legislation was passed. (at 822)

Lord Wilberforce had also made clear what was *not* permissible:

> In any event there is one course which the courts cannot take, under the law of this country; they cannot fill gaps; they cannot by asking the question 'What would Parliament have done in this current case – not being one in contemplation – if the facts had been before it?' attempt themselves to supply the answer, if the answer is not to be found in the terms of the Act itself. (at 822)

In his speech in *Quintaville*, Lord Steyn (at [23]) said that Lord Wilberforce's statement had been approved by the Lords[172] and was now to be treated as authoritative. On the question whether a statute was an 'always speaking' statute or one tied to the circumstances existing when it was passed, he cited *R v Burstow*[173] in which the House of Lords had said

[170] See *Brutus v Cozens* [1973] AC 854, 861; *DPP v Jordan* [1977] AC 699, 719.
[171] *R v Chan-Fook* [1994] 1 WLR 689 (CA).
[172] In *Fitzpatrick v Sterling Housing Association Ltd* [2001] 1 AC 27.
[173] Sub nom *R v Ireland* [1998] AC 147, 158.

that it was a matter of interpretation, but that generally they should be regarded as 'always speaking'.[174]

Lord Hoffmann in his speech (at [36]) said that a decision about whether a statute applies to unforeseen circumstances did not involve speculating about what Parliament would have done – which was not permissible. It was a decision about what best gave effect to the policy of the statute as enacted.

Sometimes the courts will give statutory words a fresh interpretation based on changes in society. In *Dyson Holdings Ltd v Fox* [1976] QB 503 the Court of Appeal had to decide whether Miss Fox could succeed as a statutory tenant to a rent-protected house after the death of the tenant, Mr Wright, with whom she had been living for 21 years. In order to qualify she had to be a member of his family. In 1950 in *Gammans v Ekins* [1950] 2 KB 328 the Court of Appeal had held that the phrase 'member of the tenant's family' could not extend to a man who had been living for some years with a lady who was not his wife – even though she had taken his name. Lord Evershed said there that it 'was indeed difficult to imagine any context in which by the proper use of the English language a man living in such a relationship with her could be described as of the tenant's family'. But in the case of Miss Fox a different view prevailed. Lord Justice James, commenting on the changed circumstances since the 1950 decision, said (at 511):

> Between 1950 and 1975 there have been many changes in the law effected by statute and decisions of the courts. Many changes have their foundations in the changed needs and views of society. Such changes have occurred in the field of family law and equitable interests in property. The popular meaning given to the word 'family' is not fixed once and for all time. I have no doubt that with the passage of years it has changed. The popular meaning of 'family' in 1975 would, according to the answer of the ordinary man, include the defendant as a member of Mr Wright's family. It is not so easy to decide whether in 1961 [the date when Mr Wright had died] the ordinary man would have regarded the defendant as a member of Mr Wright's family. The changes of attitude which have taken place cannot be ascribed to any particular year. Had we to consider the position as at 1955 I would not be satisfied that the attitude reflected in the words of Asquith LJ in *Gammans v Ekins* [1950] 2 KB 328, 331 had changed. I am confident that by 1970 the changes had taken place. There is no magic date in 1961. I think that, having regard to the radical change which has by 1975 taken place, it would be a harsh and somewhat ossified approach to the present case to hold that in 1961 the defendant was not in the popular sense a member of the family.

Lord Justice Bridge went even further (at 513):

> … if language can change its meaning to accord with changing social attitudes, then a decision on the meaning of a word in a statute before such a change should not continue to bind thereafter, at all events in a case when the courts have consistently affirmed that the word is to be understood in its ordinary accepted meaning … When the modern meaning is plain, we should, I think, be prepared to apply it retrospectively to any date, unless plainly satisfied that, at that date, the modern meaning would have been unacceptable.

[174] In a lecture Lord Steyn cited two House of Lords decisions for the same principle: *R v Ireland* [1998] AC 147 and *McCarten Turkington Breen (A Firm) v Times Newspapers Ltd* [2001] 2 AC 277. In *Ireland* the Law Lords held that 'bodily harm' in an 1861 Act covered psychiatric harm done to a victim by a stalker even though that would not have been recognised in 1861. In *McCarten* the Law Lords held qualified privilege for things said at a public meeting under an 1888 statute included things said at a press conference, even though press conferences did not exist in 1888. (Lord Steyn, 'Dynamic interpretation amidst an orgy of statutes' 24 *European Human Rights Law Review*, 2004, 245.).

In *Fitzpatrick v Sterling Housing Association* [2001] 1 AC 27 the issue was whether a homosexual partner of a tenant could enjoy rights under the Rent Act 1977 as a 'member of … the tenant's family'. By a majority of three to two the House of Lords held that he could (and in that case, did).[175] Changing social attitudes had brought a same-sex partner within the intention that Parliament had when using the word 'family'.

The obvious problem with this approach is that it creates a degree of uncertainty. In *Helby v Rafferty* [1979] 1 WLR 13, Lord Justice Cumming Bruce commenting on the decision in *Dyson* (above) said that it 'gave rise to many difficult problems'. He continued (at 25):

> Where a word is used in a succession of Acts of Parliament … and … is an ordinary English word … I have the greatest difficulty in following how the meaning of that word … changes over a period of 25 years. I still find it difficult to see how the change in social habit, to which James and Bridge LJJ referred in the *Dyson* case, has the effect of changing the meaning of the word enacted and re-enacted in successive Acts of Parliament – the word being an ordinary word – and, to my mind, the judges in the majority judgments in the *Dyson* case formulated a canon of construction which is novel to me and for which I know no previous authority.

One imagines that the decision in *Fitzpatrick* would have been even less to the liking of Lord Justice Cumming Bruce.

Albie Sachs[176] and Joan Hoff Wilson showed how in the nineteenth century the courts in both England and America consistently interpreted the statutory words 'any person' in such a way as to deprive women of the right to participate in public life – by voting, being elected to office or becoming a member of a profession. Finally, in 1929 the Privy Council in an appeal from Canada[177] held that women were persons. ('The exclusion of women from all public offices is a relic of days more barbarous than ours …') Lord Sankey swept away nearly fifty years of judicial history with the brief statement, 'The word "person" may include members of both sexes, and to those who ask why the word should include females, the obvious answer is why not. In these circumstances the burden is upon those who deny that the word includes women to make out their case' (at 138). What had changed was not the statutory formula but the approach of the judges. The climate of the times had altered and what was unthinkable in the latter part of the nineteenth century had become tolerable and indeed unexceptionable in the late 1920s.[178]

An equally clear if less dramatic example was the change between 1876 and 1928 in judicial attitudes to the problem of liability without fault. In 1876 the House of Lords decided *River Wear Comrs v Adamson*.[179] The Harbour Clauses Act 1847 provided that the owner of every vessel 'shall be answerable to the undertakers [the harbour authority] for any damage done by such vessel or by any person employed about the same to the harbour dock …' A ship which had been abandoned was blown by a gale into a harbour and crashed into the dock, causing considerable damage. In spite of the clear words of the statute, both the Court of Appeal and the House of Lords (though for different reasons)

[175] See to like effect *Ghaidan v Godin-Mendoza* [2004] UKHL 30. But in *Fitzpatrick* (above) the House of Lords, unanimously rejected the argument that the tenant's male homosexual partner could qualify as a 'spouse' – as to which see further p 228 below.

[176] Then a Lecturer in Southampton University Law Department, later a Justice of the South African Constitutional Court.

[177] *Edwards v Attorney-General, Canada* [1930] AC 124.

[178] Albie Sachs and Joan Hoff Wilson, *Sexism and the Law* (Martin Robertson, 1978) 4–66.

[179] (1876) 1 QBD 546 (Ct of App); (1877) 2 App Cas 742 (HL).

held that the shipowner was not liable. The notion of liability without fault was clearly so offensive to the judges that they found that Parliament could not have intended such a result. Almost fifty years later, in 1928, the House of Lords on similar facts took the exactly opposite view of the same section.[180] What had changed was the judges' attitude to allocation of losses in the light of insurance – Lord Haldane actually referred to the fact. It is inevitable and proper that the courts should reflect changing attitudes in their approach to statutes.

DJ Hurst showed[181] how the same kind of development took place in the judicial attitude to the word 'cruelty' used in matrimonial legislation. Conduct that would never have been recognised as within the concept in the mid-nineteenth century was accepted as being cruelty in the mid-twentieth century. Indeed, the word which for decades was treated by the judges as having a technical legal sense, was reinterpreted in modern times on the basis that it should be read in an ordinary and popular sense. Hurst suggested that the same was true of the phrase 'actual occupation' as used in dozens of statutes before the Land Registration Act 1925 and in the 1925 Act itself. Until the decision of *Williams and Glyn's Bank Ltd v Boland* [1981] AC 487, the phrase was a term of art. In that case the House of Lords held that a popular meaning for the phrase was to be preferred. 'As a result', Hurst said, 'a substantial part of both land law textbooks and building society mortgage deeds [was] having to be rewritten' (p 41).

Hurst (pp 41–42) suggested that this was basically a dishonest way of proceeding. The judges felt a pressure, notably from politicians and the press, to state the law in a modern way. But a much better way was to have a modern statute: '[J]udge-made novelty … which by a fiction declares the new rule always to have existed at a stroke revokes or nullifies established and well-founded interests. It is a crude and harsh weapon. But the most sinister effect of the rewriting of statutes by judges is that it wholly unsettles the law; nowhere is any principle in any judgment reliable if it derives from more than a few decades ago.'

In other words if the process of pouring contemporary attitudes into old statutes is carried too far, the judges will be exceeding their proper role. Here again they must find the right balance between adherence to precedent and continuity on the one hand, and a necessary flexibility and creativity on the other.

Randall Graham, a Canadian scholar, suggests that the interpreter's approach should be determined after scrutiny of the nature of the language used in the text to be interpreted. He distinguished two approaches – 'originalism' where the interpreter attempts to give effect to what appears to have been the original intention and 'dynamic interpretation' where the interpreter is concerned to give a sensible interpretation in light of later developments. In his proposed 'unified theory of statutory interpretation' if the interpretative problem is the result of vague language, the interpreter can invoke 'dynamic' construction because vague language implies either a lack of specific legislative intention or a specific intention to leave the development of the enactment to the judiciary. By contrast, if the problem is the result of ambiguity, the interpreter should respect the drafters' intention.[182]

As noted above (p 176), David Robertson in his book *Judicial Discretion in the House of Lords* (Clarendon Press, 1998) argued that the effect of the decision in *Pepper v Hart* was to freeze interpretation of statutes in the meaning that was given contemporaneously. In his discussion of the problem of interpreting 'elderly statutes' he says (170) that in Code

[180] *The Mostyn* [1927] P 25.
[181] Hurst, 'The problem of the elderly statute' (n 169 above) 39–40.
[182] Randall A Graham, 'A unified theory of statutory interpretation' 23 *Statute Law Review*, 2002, 91.

Law countries the legislative history is 'simply disregarded' where legislation is too old for it to be apposite. He was correct in saying that in the United States the problem is a serious one – 'sticking to the original intent of the framers of the constitution, as evidenced by the history of the constitutional convention, has become a prime methodological tool for ideologically conservative judges' (171).

Two contrasting cases that illustrate the way the courts have dealt with the problem of trying to reconcile statutory words with changing times are *Ex p Adedigba* and *Re Bravda*, both decided by the Court of Appeal in February 1968 and both of which required interpretation of statutory provisions that were more than a hundred years old and that had been interpreted judicially on many occasions.

R v Bow Road Domestic Proceedings Court, ex p Adedigba [1968] 2 QB 572 (CA) An unmarried Nigerian woman applied for maintenance against the putative father of her two children both of whom were born abroad. The court considered the effect of *R v Blane* (1849) 13 QB 769, which had held that no maintenance could be awarded under the statute to a woman whose children were born abroad and which had been applied many times.

> LORD DENNING MR (at 578): None of those cases is binding on this court: and I think that the time has come when we should say that *R. v Blane* in 1849 was wrongly decided and also the two cases which followed it. It seems plain to me that if the mother and father are both here and the child is here, the words of the statute are satisfied. I can see no possible reason for denying the court's jurisdiction to order maintenance; and every reason for giving them jurisdiction. The father ought to be made to pay for the child …
>
> I know that since *R. v Blane* the statutory provisions have been reenacted in virtually the same words; but that does not trouble me. I venture to quote some words that I used in *Royal Crown Derby Porcelain Co. Ltd v Russell* [1949] 2 K.B. 417, 429:
>
>> I do not believe that whenever Parliament re-enacts a provision of a statute it thereby gives statutory authority to every erroneous interpretation which has been put on it. The true view is that the court will be slow to overrule a previous decision on the interpretation of a statute when it has long been acted on, and it will be more than usually slow to do so when Parliament has, since the decision, re-enacted the statute in the same terms, but if a decision is, in fact, shown to be erroneous, there is no rule of law which prevents it being overruled.
>
> Nor am I troubled by the fact that *R. v Blane* has stood for 118 years. It is not a property or commercial case. It has not formed the basis of titles or commercial dealings. It is the sort of precedent which we can and should overrule when it is seen to be wrong. Only yesterday in *Conway v Rimmer* [1968] AC 910 Lord Morris of Borth-y-gest used words appropriate to the situation:
>
>> Though precedent is an indispensable foundation on which to decide what is the law, there may be times when a departure from precedent is in the interests of justice and the proper development of the law.
>
> If we were to affirm today *R. v Blane* as being the law of this land, the only consequence would be a reference to the Law Commission; then a report by them, and eventually a Bill before Parliament. It would be quite a long time before the law could be set right. Even then the law would only be set right for future cases. Nothing could be done to set right this present case. The mother here would not get maintenance for the child which she needs now. So I would overrule *R. v Blane* now. In the days of 1849 the question may not have been of any particular social significance; but now there are many illegitimate children here in England who were born abroad. It is only right and just that the mothers of those children should be able to take out proceedings against the fathers, and that the fathers should be ordered to pay reasonable maintenance for their own children. Otherwise what is the position? The children will be left to the care of the State. The national

> assistance fund will have to pay – the father will get out of his just responsibilities. That would be a most undesirable state of affairs.

Lord Justices Salmon and Edmund-Davies delivered concurring judgments.

In the second case the court was again unanimous but its decision went the other way. (Lord Justice Salmon was a member of the court on both occasions.)

In the *Estate of Bravda* [1968] 1 WLR 479 (CA)

A testator made a will on one side of a piece of notepaper. Evidence showed that two independent witnesses signed first but that his two daughters, who were the chief beneficiaries under the will, then signed above them 'to make it stronger'. The gift to the daughters was challenged on the ground that under s 15 of the Wills Act 1837 a beneficiary who signed the will as attesting witnesses could not take a gift. (The Wills Act, s 15 stated that 'if any person shall attest the execution of any will … to whom … any beneficial devise … shall be given, such devise … shall so far only as concerns such person … be utterly null and void'.) All three judges refused to adjust the traditional interpretation of s 15:

> WILMER LJ (at 488): The suggestion is made that s. 15 of the Wills Act, 1837, was never intended to apply in a case where there was already a valid execution by two unimpeachable witnesses. It has been suggested that the object of the section was merely to ensure that a will would not fail altogether if one or both of the two witnesses required were named as beneficiaries, as had been the case earlier. In other words, what is said is that the object of the section was merely to ensure that both those witnesses would be 'credible' witnesses. That result was achieved by requiring that they should forgo any benefits they would otherwise derive, but that the will would be left unimpaired. That is a point which does not appear to have been argued in the court below. It is not, of course, raised in the notice of appeal. There has been no cross-notice on behalf of the plaintiffs; and I do not think, in those circumstances, that the point is strictly open in this court. If it were open, I should merely say that, in my judgment, it is a point of no substance, for two reasons. One is that I think the words of the section are much too plain to admit of this rather tortuous construction. Secondly, I think that, after 130 years, it is now much too late to endeavour to put this entirely new construction on the well-known words of this section.
>
> RUSSELL LJ (at 491):
>
> I would welcome a change in the law in this regard. I would expect most people to regard the outcome of this case as monstrously unfair to the testator and to his daughters. I do myself; but every time a beneficiary is an attesting witness, s. 15 of the Wills Act 1837 deprives him of his benefit and defeats the testator's intention. This is considered necessary to ensure reliable unbiased witnesses of due execution; but why it was thought necessary to interfere in cases where there are the requisite number of unbiased witnesses, I cannot imagine. I regretfully agree that the appeal succeeds.
>
> SALMON LJ (at 492): With very great regret, I also agree that this appeal succeeds. I was at an early stage struck by the force of the argument on the part of the defendant. I confess that I tried very hard to find some way round it – some ground on which in conscience I could find in favour of the plaintiffs; but I have failed. The words of s. 15 of the Wills Act 1837, are too plain, and the evidence filed on behalf of the plaintiffs is wholly inadequate. Section 15 makes it clear that, if any person attests the execution of any will to whom or to whose wife or husband any benefit is given under the will, then that part of the will which gives the benefit shall be null and void, but such person shall be a competent witness to prove the validity or invalidity of the will.
>
> That statutory provision makes it impossible for the intentions of the testator to be carried out in the case of a beneficiary signing the will as a witness. That is the very object of the statutory provision. So, when the court is faced with the kind of problem which arises in this case, it is not open to the beneficiary to urge that the intention of the testator must not be defeated. Parliament has clearly laid down that, when the testator intends to benefit a person who signs the will as a witness, the testator's intention shall be defeated. I wholly agree with RUSSELL L. J., for the reasons which

> he gives, that it is high time that this provision of the Wills Act 1837, should be amended, so that, when there are two independent credible witnesses, the mere fact that a beneficiary has also signed as a witness should not operate (as it now does) to defeat the intention of the testator.

Why was the court prepared to move in *Adedigba* but not in *R v Blane*? One of the chief reasons given for the decision in *Adedigba* was that no one could reasonably be said to have arranged their affairs in reliance on the decision in *R v Blane*. But would the reasonable expectations of testators have been upset if the court had interpreted s 15 of the 1837 Wills Act in such a way as to discount the signatures of beneficiaries if there were already two independent witnesses?[183]

Note

In this instance Parliament moved with remarkable speed to correct the defect in the law revealed by *Re Bravda*. The Court of Appeal's decision was handed down on 2 February 1968. On 14 February a Private Members' Bill was introduced to deal with the problem. It was reintroduced under a new title (the Wills Bill) on 21 February. It received the Royal Assent in May, only three months after the Court of Appeal had asked for legislative action!

Such speed is very rare. Another example was the County Court (Penalties for Contempt) Act which received the Royal Assent on 13 May 1983, only two months after the House of Lords held, in *Peart v Stewart* [1983] 2 AC 109, that a county court's power to punish for contempt of court was limited to one month's imprisonment.

3.11.4. The Principles of Statutory Interpretation when Dealing with EU Law

Membership of the European Union (on which see 8.1 below), had an effect on many aspects of English law. As long ago as the 1970s it was predicted by Lord Denning that one of the areas in which such impact might be felt was statutory interpretation. In *Bulmer v Bollinger* he described the differences between the English and the European approach to statutory interpretation:

HP Bulmer Ltd v J Bollinger SA [1974] Ch 401, 425 (CA)

Action was brought over use of the word 'champagne' in champagne cider and champagne perry. There was a request for the case to be transferred to the European Court for a ruling as to whether such use infringed Community regulations. The court refused to make a reference and this point was then appealed. In the course of refusing the appeal, Lord Denning spoke of the nature of Community Law:

> *10. The principles of interpretation*
>
> It is apparent that in very many cases the English courts will interpret the Treaty themselves. They will not refer the question to the European Court at Luxembourg. What then are the principles of interpretation to be applied? Beyond doubt the English courts must follow the same principles as the European Court. Otherwise there would be differences between the countries of the nine. That would never do. All the courts of all nine countries should interpret the Treaty in the same way. They should all apply the same principles. It is enjoined on the English courts by section 3 of the European Communities Act 1972, which I have read.

[183] Cf *Beswick v Beswick* [1966] Ch 538 (CA), [1968] AC 58 (HL), in which the Court of Appeal gave a statutory provision a startling interpretation in order to reform the law but the House of Lords reversed the decision on this point.

> What a task is thus set before us! The Treaty is quite unlike any of the enactments to which we have become accustomed. The draftsmen of our statutes have striven to express themselves with the utmost exactness. They have tried to foresee all possible circumstances that may arise and to provide for them. They have sacrificed style and simplicity. They have forgone brevity. They have become long and involved. In consequence, the judges have followed suit. They interpret a statute as applying only to the circumstances covered by the very words. They give them a literal interpretation. If the words of the statute do not cover a new situation which was not foreseen – the judges hold that they have no power to fill the gap. To do so would be a 'naked usurpation of the legislative function': see *Magor and St Mellons Rural District Council v Newport Corporation* [1952] A.C. 189, 191. The gap must remain open until Parliament finds time to fill it.
>
> How different is this Treaty! It lays down general principles. It expresses its aims and purposes. All in sentences of moderate length and commendable style. But it lacks precision. It uses words and phrases without defining what they mean. An English lawyer would look for an interpretation clause, but he would look in vain. There is none. All the way through the Treaty there are gaps and lacunae. These have to be filled in by the judges, or by Regulations or Directives. It is the European way. That appears from the decision of the Hamburg court in *In re Tax on Imported Lemons* [1968] C.M.L.R. 1.
>
> Likewise the Regulations and Directives. They are enacted by the Council sitting in Brussels for everyone to obey. They are quite unlike our statutory instruments. They have to give the reasons on which they are based: article 190. So they start off with pages of preambles, 'whereas' and 'whereas' and 'whereas'. These show the purpose and intent of the Regulations and Directives. Then follow the provisions which are to be obeyed. Here again words and phrases are used without defining their import … In case of difficulty, recourse is had to the preambles. These are useful to show the purpose and intent behind it all. But much is left to the judges. The enactments give only an outline plan. The details are to be filled in by the judges.
>
> Seeing these differences, what are the English courts to do when they are faced with a problem of interpretation? They must follow the European pattern. No longer must they examine the words in meticulous detail. No longer must they argue about the precise grammatical sense. They must look to the purpose or intent. To quote the words of the European court in the *Da Costa* case [1963] C.M.L.R. 224, 237, they must deduce 'from the wording and the spirit of the Treaty the meaning of the community rules.' They must not confine themselves to the English text. They must consider, if need be, all the authentic texts, of which there are now six: see *Bestuur der Sociale Verzekeringsbank v Van der Vecht* [1968] C.M.L.R. 151. They must divine the spirit of the Treaty and gain inspiration from it. If they find a gap, they must fill it as best they can. They must do what the framers of the instrument would have done if they had thought about it. So we must do the same. Those are the principles, as I understand it, on which the European Court acts.

Lord Denning returned to the theme in 1977:

Buchanan and Co Ltd v Babco Forwarding and Shipping (UK) Ltd [1977] 2 WLR 107 (CA)

Defendants agreed to carry 1,000 cases of the plaintiffs' whisky to Iran. The contract was subject to the terms and conditions of the Convention on the Contract for the International Carriage of Goods by Road, set out in the Schedule to the Carriage of Goods by Road Act 1965. The whisky was stolen from the defendants. The plaintiffs had to pay the excise duty and claimed this sum from the defendants. Judgment was given for the plaintiffs and the Court of Appeal dismissed the appeal. In the course of giving judgment, attention was given to the interpretation of an international convention scheduled to a United Kingdom statute:

> LORD DENNING: This article 23, paragraph 4, is an agreed clause in an international convention. As such it should be given the same interpretation in all the countries who were parties

to the convention. It would be absurd that the courts of England should interpret it differently from the courts of France, or Holland, or Germany. Compensation for loss should be assessed on the same basis, no matter in which country the claim is brought. We must, therefore, put on one side our traditional rules of interpretation. We have for years tended to stick too closely to the letter – to the literal interpretation of the words. We ought, in interpreting this convention, to adopt the European method. I tried to describe it in *H. P. Bulmer Ltd v J. Bollinger S.A.* [1974] Ch. 401, 425–6. Some of us recently spent a couple of days in Luxembourg discussing it with the members of the European Court, and our colleagues in the other countries of the nine.

We had a valuable paper on it by the President of the court (Judge H. Kutscher) which is well worth study: 'Methods of interpretation as seen by a judge at the Court of Justice, Luxembourg 1976.' They adopt a method which they call in English by strange words – at any rate they were strange to me – the 'schematic and teleological' method of interpretation. It is not really so alarming as it sounds. All it means is that the judges do not go by the literal meaning of the words or by the grammatical structure of the sentence. They go by the design or purpose which lies behind it. When they come upon a situation which is to their minds within the spirit – but not the letter – of the legislation, they solve the problem by looking at the design and purpose of the legislature – at the effect which it was sought to achieve. They then interpret the legislation so as to produce the desired effect. This means that they fill in gaps, quite unashamedly, without hesitation. They ask simply: what is the sensible way of dealing with this situation so as to give effect to the presumed purpose of the legislation? They lay down the law accordingly. If you study the decisions of the European Court, you will see that they do it every day. To our eyes – shortsighted by tradition – it is legislation, pure and simple. But, to their eyes, it is fulfilling the true role of the courts. They are giving effect to what the legislature intended, or may be presumed to have intended. I see nothing wrong in this. Quite the contrary. It is a method of interpretation which I advocated long ago in *Seaford Court Estates Ltd v Asher* [1949] 2 K.B. 481, 498–9. It did not gain acceptance at that time. It was condemned by Lord Simonds in the House of Lords in *Magor and St. Mellons Rural District Council v Newport Corporation* [1952] A.C. 189, 191, as a 'naked usurpation of the legislative power'. But the time has now come when we should think again. In interpreting the Treaty of Rome (which is part of our law) we must certainly adopt the new approach. Just as in Rome you should do as Rome does, so in the European Community, you should do as the European Court does.

Lord Justice Russell agreed:

I would like to support what Lord Denning M. R. has said and what Lawton L. J. will say regarding the need to alter the traditional English method of approach to questions of construction of statutes such as the Act of 1965 which give effect on a matter of municipal law to international conventions. Some such conventions are drafted in languages other than English. The English language, though used, may in other cases not be the predominant language of the convention, or in yet other cases may at the most be only of equal force with one or more other European languages. Now that this country has joined the European Community our courts are likely to be increasingly concerned with the interpretation of legislation of one kind or another of which English is not the original or the dominant language. Such legislation is likely also to fall for interpretation in the courts of other members of the community. It would be disastrous if our courts were to adopt constructions of such legislation different from those of other courts whose method of approach is different and far less narrow than ours merely because of over-rigid adherence to traditional – some might call them chauvinist – English methods. Conflict would arise between courts in different jurisdictions within the European Community with the untoward consequences to which Lord Denning M. R. and Lawton L. J. refer and if it became known that if a party sued in one country one result would follow, but if in another country another – a state of affairs which has arisen in other branches of the law between, for example, this country and the United States – what is sometimes known as forum-shopping would be encouraged, whereas within the

> Community it should be discouraged. I think in the future our courts should be far more ready, in cases where international conventions, especially those affecting the members of the European Community, are under judicial consideration, to assimilate their approach to questions of the construction of our legislation giving effect to those conventions to that which the courts of other members of the Community are likely to adopt. The doctrine once proclaimed in the phrase 'Athanasius contra mundum' caused much trouble many centuries ago. That attitude of mind has no place in our courts in the latter part of the 20th century.

For other cases in which decisions regarding the meaning of statutes introduced to give effect to Community law was influenced by continental rather than customary English standards of statutory interpretation see for instance: *Pickstone v Freeman's Plc*,[184] and *Litster v Forth Dry Dock & Engineering Co Ltd.*[185] In *Pfeiffer* the European Court stated that the duty to interpret national legislation so as to be consistent with a directive applies especially when the legislation was passed to give effect to the directive.[186]

The effect of membership of the European Community/European Union on the canons of statutory interpretation has been seen mainly in relation to European Union law. It does not seem to have had a direct effect on interpretation of English statutes.

See further Vera Sacks and Carol Harlow, 'Interpretation European style' 40 *Modern Law Review*, 1977, 578. See also Shael Herman, 'Quot judices tot sententiae: a study of the English reaction to continental interpretative techniques' 1 *Legal Studies*, 1981, 165; Lord Slynn, 'Looking at European Community texts' 14 *Statute Law Review*, 1993, 12; T Millett, 'Rules of interpretation of EEC legislation' 10 *Statute Law Review*, 1989, 163; T Rensen, 'British statutory interpretation in the light of community and other international obligations' 14 *Statute Law Review*, 1993, 186. See also Professor John Bell's review essay comparing common law with the continental approach to statutory interpretation, 22 *Legal Studies*, 2002, 473.

For how English courts should approach interpretation of 'assimilated' (previously 'retained') EU law see Lord Sales, 'Retained EU law: purposive interpretation when the constitutional architecture changes' 49 *European Law Review*, 2024 (1), 3–14.

3.11.5. Is Statutory Interpretation a Form of Legislation?

There are few today who deny that the interpreter of legislation exercises some creative role. In recent years this has become conventional wisdom even amongst the judges themselves. But generally they claim that interpretation is something less than legislation. In a revealing lecture given 40 years ago at Birmingham University, Lord Diplock, however, had no doubt that statutory interpretation could amount to legislation:

Lord Diplock, *The Courts as Legislators* (Holdsworth Club of the University of Birmingham, 1965) 5–6

> … there are also cases – many more than one would expect – where there is room for dispute as to what the rule of conduct really is. This is so as much with rules laid down by Act of Parliament as with those which have evolved at common law …

[184] [1989] AC 66, [1988] 3 WLR 265. The House of Lords held that it could not have been Parliament's intention that the regulation in question should be interpreted in a way that rendered them inconsistent with Community law even though this required reading in words that were not there.

[185] [1990] 1 AC 546, [1989] 2 WLR 634. Again the House of Lords was prepared to imply words into a statute passed to implement a directive in order to make it conform to the directive.

[186] Cases C-397–403/01, [2004] ECR I-8835.

> [E]very revenue appeal that comes before the court – generally after any dispute of fact there may have been has already been decided by the Commissioners – involves a dispute as to whether a particular kind of gain is taxable, whether a particular kind of document attracts stamp duty. Whenever the Court decides that kind of dispute it legislates about taxation. It makes a law taxing all gains of the same kind or all documents of the same kind. Do not let us deceive ourselves with the legal fiction that the court is only ascertaining and giving effect to what Parliament meant. Anyone who has decided tax appeals knows that most of them concern transactions which Members of Parliament and the draftsman of the Act had not anticipated, about which they had never thought at all. Some of the transactions are of a kind which had never taken place before the Act was passed: they were devised as a result of it. The court may describe what it is doing in tax appeals as interpretation. So did the priestess of the Delphic oracle. But whoever has final authority to explain what Parliament meant by the words that it used makes law as much as if the explanation it has given were contained in a new Act of Parliament.

Lord Diplock was of course fully aware of the many ways in which judicial decisions are different from legislation but his last sentence recognises the important truth that, within its limits, interpretation is a form of legislation. It reminds us uncomfortably of the famous words of Lewis Carroll's *Alice in Wonderland.*

> 'When I use a word', Humpty Dumpty said, in a rather scornful tone, 'it means what I choose it to mean – neither more nor less.'
>
> 'The question is', said Alice, 'whether you can make words mean so many different things.'
>
> 'The question is', said Humpty Dumpty, 'which is to be master – that's all.'

A chapter in *Being a Judge in the Modern World* (OUP, 2017, ed Jeremy Cooper) by former Court of Appeal judge, Sir John Laws, was devoted to law-making in the interpretation of statutes: 'Time and again', he wrote (at p 202), 'there will be a choice how a text is to be interpreted – how it is to be given life, how its words are to have effect in the world. And time and again the choice will not be concluded by the language of the text.' His particular examples were drawn from cases in which interpretation had been based on constitutional principles. In *Anisminic v Foreign Compensation Commission* [1969]2 AC 147, for instance, the statutory provision requiring interpretation was that decisions of the Commission 'shall not be called in question in any court of law'. The House of Lords held that such a clause aimed at ousting the jurisdiction of the courts did not apply to a decision that it described as 'a nullity'.[187] In *R v Lord Chancellor ex p Witham* (1998) QB 575 the Divisional Court (Rose and Laws LJJ) had to interpret a statute which gave the Lord Chancellor the power to prescribe the fees charged to litigants. The Court held that the fees charged were unlawful in that they were so high 'as to bar absolutely many persons from seeking justice from the courts.'[188] Access to the courts, was a constitutional right that could only be denied by express provision. In his chapter Sir John Laws wrote (p 209): '[W]here an Act of Parliament touches a constitutional fundamental … the judicial act of statutory construction makes law, because it insists that the statute complies with the applicable constitutional principle.' There was the danger, he admitted, that the judges might 'step too far, or be thought to step too far, onto territory that properly belongs to the elected arms of government'. In considerable measure that danger had been 'foisted on the judges' by the

[187] On the Courts' attitude to different forms of ouster clauses see, ie, M Elliott, 'Through the Looking-Glass? Ouster Clauses, Statutory Interpretation and the British Constitution' in C Hunt, L Neudorf and M Rankin (eds) *Legislating Statutory Interpretation, Perspectives from the Common Law World* (Carswell, 2018). (The chapter can be accessed on Professor Mark Elliott's blog: Public Law for Everyone.) (ed).

[188] See to like effect *R (on the application of Unison) v Lord Chancellor* [2017] 3 WLR 409 – employment tribunal fees held to be unlawful because too high (ed).

Human Rights Act 1998' (p 210). Too muscular a vindication of human rights exposed the judges to the claim that they were making political decisions.

On the creative aspect of the judicial role see Lord Radcliffe, p 323 below; Justice Cardozo, p 325 below; Lord Devlin, pp 393–5 below; Lord Edmund-Davies, p 354 below; Lord Pearson, p 355 below.

But how can one describe the extent of judicial creativity in statutory interpretation? A helpful image was used by Reed Dickerson in his book, *The Interpretation and Application of Statutes* (Little Brown, 1975). Dickerson used the simile of the restorer of an ancient vase. Everything depends on how much of the original vase was available to him. Sometimes he was simply making a substitute for a small piece missing from the body of the vase. 'Here he is guided by the adjacent contours, and, if he is skilful, the result blends well enough to attract little or no attention … His job is harder if the vase has been decorated, but the difficulty is small if the decoration follows a discernible pattern' (p 26). In this activity there was some creativity but it was of the lowest order. It still fell within the general heading of 'ascertainment of meaning' in the sense of discovering something that is in a real sense latent in the material.

The position was plainly very different if the craftsman had only a single piece and the decoration was free and non-recurring. Here by imaginative speculation they must attempt to produce something 'in the general style' of the original without being able to pretend that their effort would necessarily approximate to it very closely. Here the element of creativity was very considerable. The greater the range of choice open to the judge, the greater their law-making as opposed to their law-finding function. If the statute was a Bill of Rights with broad, open-textured provisions, the scope for judicial legislation would be vast compared with the opportunities offered by the tight provisions of, say, an income tax Act. There was, however, no general way that the proper limit of the creative function of judges in statutory interpretation could usefully be defined. The judge should be open and sensitive to the subtleties and complexity of language, to the fallibility of draftsmen and to the variety of interests that may be reflected in legal documents. On the other hand, they must respect the limits of language and not place on the disputed words a meaning they would not fairly bear. The judges must not threaten to compete with the legislature, but they should recognise that intelligent interpretation necessarily involved a creative function.

For an example of the judge refusing to accept an 'imaginative' argument as to the meaning of words, see *Bourne (Inspector of Taxes) v Norwich Crematorium* [1967] 1 WLR 691, in which the question was whether the activities of a crematorium could be said to be within the statutory phrase 'the subjection of goods or materials to any process'. Stamp J declined to accept the suggestion (at 696):

> I can only say that, although the human body is no doubt material in the same sense that all things visible are material, there is in my judgment something in the word 'materials', in the plural, which forbids the construction of the phrase 'goods and materials' that is urged on me. In my judgment it would be a distortion of the English language to describe the living or the dead as goods or materials …
>
> [H]aving given the matter the best attention that I can, I conclude that the consumption by fire of the mortal remains of homo sapiens is not the subjection of goods or materials to a process within the definition of 'industrial building or structure' contained in s 271 (1) (*c*) of the Income Tax Act 1952.

On statutory interpretation generally, see especially: Bennion, Bailey and Norbury *on Statutory Interpretation*, 8th edn (LexisNexis, 2020) and *Craies on Legislation*, 11th edn, ed by Greenberg (Sweet & Maxwell, 2017). For two major contributions on this subject by Michael Kirby, former Justice of the High Court of Australia, see his article 'Towards a grand theory of interpretation: the case of statutes and contracts' 24 *Statute Law Review*, 2003, 95 and his 2003 Hamlyn Lectures published as *Judicial Activism: Authority, Principle and Policy in the Judicial Method* (Sweet & Maxwell, 2004), especially pp 31–41. See also Lord Justice Sales, 'Modern Statutory Interpretation' (2017) 38 *Statute Law Review* (2) 125–32.

See also N Duxbury, *Elements of Legislation* (Cambridge University Press, 2013) especially ch 4 (Legislatures and intentions), ch 5 (Fidelity to texts) and ch 6 (Purposivism).

Drafting Legislation, Art and Technology of Rules for Regulation (Hart Publishing, 2014) by Helen Xanthaki, Professor of Law and Legislative Drafting at the Institute of Advanced Legal Studies, London is a book aimed at academics and practitioners.

4

Binding Precedent: The Doctrine of Stare Decisis

One of the fundamental characteristics of law is the objective that like cases should be treated alike. It is therefore natural that, other things being equal, one court should follow the decision of another where the facts appear to be similar. In the common law systems precedents have a greater potency than simply as models for imitation. The rules *require* that in certain circumstances a decision be followed whether the second court approves of the precedent or not. Thus in *Re Schweppes Ltd's Agreement* [1965] 1 WLR 157, the Court of Appeal, with Willmer LJ dissenting, ordered discovery of documents in a case involving restrictive trade practices. On the same day the same three judges gave judgment in a second case involving the same point – *Re Automatic Telephone and Electric Co Ltd's Agreement* [1965] 1 WLR 174. Judgment in the second case was delivered by Lord Justice Willmer who simply said: 'If the matter were res integra, I should have been disposed to dismiss the appeal in this case for the same reasons as those which I gave in my judgment in the previous case. It seems to me, however, that I am now bound by the decision of the majority in the previous case. In these circumstances, I have no alternative but to concur in saying that the appeal in the present case should be allowed.' The second decision was therefore unanimous. The example illustrates not only the impact of binding precedent but also the fact that under the English system the effect is instantaneous. In civil law countries based on Roman law, by contrast, precedents may be followed and commonly are, but there is no rule requiring that they be followed.

However, it took centuries before the concept of binding precedent was established:

> Precedent emerges late in the history of the common law – it would take until the nineteenth century for the courts to become properly equipped to develop the common law according to the principle that like cases should be treated alike.[1] Before then, a case (or line of cases) would typically be treated as persuasive rather than as binding authority – as something which judges might recognise as venerable legal opinion, and which a lawyer might rely on in court because it provided evidence of what the common law was rather than because it was itself common law.[2]

The doctrine of binding precedent is called *stare decisis* (more precisely *stare rationibus decidendis*, keep to the decisions of past cases). It must be distinguished from the very different doctrine of *res judicata.* Res judicata signifies that the parties to a litigated dispute cannot reopen it after the normal period for an appeal has lapsed or after they have exhausted their

[1] See N Duxbury, *The Nature and Authority of Precedent* (Cambridge University Press, 2008) 53–57.
[2] N Duxbury, 'Custom as law in English law', 76 *Cambridge Law Journal*, 2017 (2), 341–42.

right to appeal. The parties are bound by the result of the case once it is finally concluded. Stare decisis is a doctrine that affects not the parties but everyone else – it concerns the impact of the decision in future cases.

The first essential element of the doctrine of binding precedent is a hierarchy of courts and rules that indicate the interrelationship of the different courts.

4.1. The Hierarchy of Courts and the Doctrine of Binding Precedent

4.1.1. The House of Lords and Supreme Court

Until 2009, the final court of appeal was the Appellate Committee of the House of Lords.[3] The judges were the Lords of Appeal in Ordinary, known as the Law Lords. It is now the Supreme Court. The judges are Justices of the Supreme Court.

On 12 June 2003, Tony Blair, the Prime Minister, with no warning and no official consultation, announced that the Appellate Committee of the House of Lords was to be abolished and replaced by a Supreme Court separate from Parliament. He announced at the same time that the office of Lord Chancellor was to be abolished and replaced by the Secretary of State for Constitutional Affairs, that the Lord Chancellor's Department would be renamed the Department for Constitutional Affairs and that the appointment of judges, save those for the Supreme Court would be made in future by a Judicial Appointments Commission. The Justices of the Supreme Court would be appointed by a new separate procedure.[4]

Implementation took time and was controversial.[5] The Supreme Court met in its fine new premises for the first time on 1 October 2009.[6] The first Justices were the then Law Lords. So far as concerns the doctrine of precedent, however, there was no change.

The basic rule is that the decisions of the Supreme Court are binding on all lower courts. From the end of the nineteenth century to 1966 the rule was that the decisions of the House of Lords were binding also on itself. The House of Lords ruled in *London Tramways v London County Council* [1898] AC 375 that it was bound by its own decisions. In fact this

[3] It heard appeals in both civil and criminal cases from the Court of Appeal, in civil matters from the Court of Session in Scotland and in both civil and criminal matters from the Court of Appeal in Northern Ireland.

[4] See 7.3.1 below.

[5] The detailed story of the legislation is told in Lord Windlesham, 'The Constitutional Reform Act 2005: the politics of constitutional reform' *Public Law*, 2005, 806 and 2006, 35 and by A Le Sueur, 'From Appellate Committee to Supreme Court: a narrative' in L Blom-Cooper, B Dickson and G Drewry (eds), *The Judicial House of Lords 1876–2009* (Oxford University Press, 2009) 64–94. See also Lord Steyn, 'The case for a Supreme Court' 118 *Law Quarterly Review*, 382; Lord Bingham of Cornhill, 'The old order changeth' 122 *Law Quarterly Review*, 2006, 211. For a sceptical or pessimistic view see Lord Hope, 'A phoenix from the ashes? Accommodating a new Supreme Court' 121, *Law Quarterly Review*, 2005, 253. For a celebration of the House of Lords as an appellate body before which he had appeared more than a hundred times see D Pannick, '"Better that a horse should have a voice in the House [of Lords] than that a judge should" (Jeremy Bentham): replacing the Law Lords by a Supreme Court' *Public Law*, 2009, 723. See also generally: L Blom-Cooper, B Dickson and G Drewry (eds), *The Judicial House of Lords 1876–2009* (Oxford University Press, 2009); J Lee (ed), *From House of Lords to Supreme Court* (Hart Publishing, 2011); A Le Sueur (ed), *Building the UK's New Supreme Court: National and Comparative Perspectives* (Oxford University Press, 2004).

[6] Opposite Parliament.

rule had been virtually settled nearly forty years earlier in *Beamish v Beamish* (1861) 9 HL Cases 274, but the *London Tramways* case finally decided the matter.[7] Lord Halsbury said:

> Of course I do not deny that cases of individual hardship may arise, and there may be a current of opinion in the profession that such and such a judgment was erroneous; but what is that occasional interference with what is perhaps abstract justice, as compared with the inconvenience – the disastrous inconvenience – of having each question subject to being reargued and the dealings of mankind rendered doubtful by reason of different decisions, so that in truth and in fact there would be no real final court of appeal. My lords, 'interest rei publicae' is that there should be 'finis litium' sometime and there can be no 'finis litium' if it were possible to suggest in each case that it might be reargued because it is 'not an ordinary case' whatever that may mean. (380)

In the decades that followed, the doctrine that the House of Lords was bound by its own decisions seemed solidly established even though from time to time it was criticised.[8] However, on 26 July 1966, Lord Gardiner, the Lord Chancellor, read a statement on behalf of himself and all the other Lords of Appeal in Ordinary announcing that the House of Lords would in future regard itself as free to depart from its own previous decisions:[9]

Practice Statement (Judicial Precedent) [1966] 1 WLR 1234

> Their Lordships regard the use of precedent as an indispensable foundation upon which to decide what is the law and its application to individual cases. It provides at least some degree of certainty upon which individuals can rely in the conduct of their affairs, as well as a basis for orderly development of legal rules.
>
> Their Lordships nevertheless recognise that too rigid adherence to precedent may lead to injustice in a particular case and also unduly restrict the proper development of the law. They propose therefore to modify their present practice and, while treating former decisions of this House as normally binding, to depart from a decision when it appears right to do so.
>
> In this connection they will bear in mind the danger of disturbing retrospectively the basis on which contracts, settlements of property and fiscal arrangements have been entered into and also the especial need for certainty as to the criminal law.
>
> This announcement is not intended to affect the use of precedent elsewhere than in this House.

The above is the statement that appeared in the law reports. It was issued to the press with the following additional explanatory note:

> Since the House of Lords decided the English case of *London Street Tramways* v. *London County Council* in 1898, the House have considered themselves bound to follow their own decisions, except where a decision has been given per incuriam in disregard of a statutory provision or another decision binding on them.
>
> The statement made is one of great importance, although it should not be supposed that there will frequently be cases in which the House thinks it right not to follow their own precedent. An example of a case in which the House might think it right to depart from a precedent is where they consider that the earlier decision was influenced by the existence of conditions which no longer prevail, and that in modern conditions the law ought to be different.
>
> One consequence of this change is of major importance. The relaxation of the rule of judicial precedent will enable the House of Lords to pay greater attention to judicial decisions reached in

[7] For the history see D Pugsley, 'London Tramways' 17 *Journal of Legal History*, 1996, 172.

[8] See especially Lord Wright's famous article, 'Precedent' *Cambridge Law Journal*, 1944, 118.

[9] See A Paterson, *The Law Lords* (Macmillan, 1982) 146–51 and L Blom-Cooper, '1966 and all that: the story of the practice statement' in L Blom-Cooper, B Dickson and G Drewry (eds), *The Judicial House of Lords 1876–2009* (Oxford University Press, 2009) 128–44. For a discussion of the 1966 Practice Statement as a source of law see John Bell, 'Sources of Law' 77 *Cambridge Law Journal*, 2018 (40), 64–71.

> the superior courts of the Commonwealth, where they differ from earlier decisions of the House of Lords. That could be of great help in the development of our own law. The superior courts of many other countries are not rigidly bound by their own decisions and the change in the practice of the House of Lords will bring us more into line with them.

In 2010, the Supreme Court was asked to depart from a rule confirmed in two decisions of the House of Lords. Applying the 1966 Practice Statement, it declined to do so. Lord Hope, Deputy President, said:

> The Supreme Court has not thought it necessary to reissue the Practice Statement as a fresh statement of practice in the court's own name. This is because it has as much effect in this court as it did before the Appellate Committee of the House of Lords.[10]

The House of Lords' 1966 Practice Statement was hailed as an event of great consequence.[11] According to Professor Alan Paterson, the most influential judge in formulating the principles on which the House ought to exercise its new discretion under the Practice Statement was Lord Reid:

Alan Paterson, *The Law Lords* (Macmillan, 1982) 156–57

> In a series of cases between 1966 and 1975 Lord Reid articulated at least seven criteria relating to the use of the new freedom:
>
> - The freedom granted by the 1966 Practice Statement ought to be exercised sparingly (the 'use sparingly' criterion).[12]
> - A decision ought not to be overruled if to do so would upset the legitimate expectations of people who have entered into contracts or settlements or otherwise regulated their affairs in reliance on the validity of that decision (the 'legitimate expectations' criterion).[13]
> - A decision concerning questions of construction of statutes or other documents ought not to be overruled except in rare and exceptional cases (the 'construction criterion').[14]
> - A decision ought not to be overruled if it would be impracticable for the Lords to foresee the consequences of departing from it (the 'unforeseeable consequences' criterion).[15] A decision ought not to be overruled also if to do so would involve a change that ought to be part of a comprehensive reform of the law. Such changes are best done 'by legislation following on a wide survey of the whole field' (the 'need for comprehensive reform' criterion).[16]
> - In the interest of certainty, a decision ought not to be overruled merely because the Law Lords consider that it was wrongly decided. There must be some additional reasons to justify such a step (the 'precedent merely wrong' criterion).[17]
> - A decision ought to be overruled if it causes such great uncertainty in practice that the parties advisers are unable to give any clear indication as to what the courts will hold the law to be (the 'rectification of uncertainty' criterion).[18]

[10] *Austin v Southwark LBC* [2010] UKSC 28 (at[25].

[11] However, one brave commentator, a distinguished practising solicitor, doubted whether the Practice Statement was sound in law! (FA Mann, 'Reflections on English civil justice and the rule of law' *Civil Justice Quarterly*, 1983, 320, 330–32.).

[12] *Jones v Secretary of State for Social Services* [1972] AC 944, 966.

[13] *Ross-Smith v Ross-Smith* [1963] 1 AC 280, 303; *Indyka v Indyka* [1969] 1 AC 33, 69.

[14] *Jones* (n 12 above) 966.

[15] *Steadman v Steadman* [1976] AC 536, 542.

[16] *Myers v DPP* [1965] AC 1001, 1022; *Cassell v Broome* [1972] AC 1027, 1086; *Haughton v Smith* [1975] AC 476, 500.

[17] *Knuller v DPP* [1973] AC 435, 455.

[18] *Jones* (n 12 above) 966; *Oldendorff & Co v. Tradex Export SA* [1974] AC 479, 533, 535.

- A decision ought to be overruled if in relation to some broad issue or principle it is not considered just or in keeping with contemporary social conditions or modern conceptions of public policy (the 'unjust or outmoded' criterion).[19]

Paterson found that in the fourteen years 1966 to 1980 there were 29 cases in which the House of Lords was invited to overrule one of its own precedents (or in which the question was raised by the Law Lords themselves without any prompting from counsel). The success rate was 28 per cent (eight out of the 29), but in a further ten cases at least one of the Law Lords was willing to overrule the previous House of Lords precedent. Paterson also argued that in a considerable number of other cases the Law Lords seemed to have a preference for getting round earlier decisions by distinguishing them rather than directly overruling them.

For a magisterial review of the issues involved in overruling see the article by the late Professor JW Harris of Oxford University, 'Towards principles of overruling: when should a final court of appeal second guess?'[20] Professor Harris favoured the view that absent new reasons, in the interests of certainty and finality the precedents should be followed 'unless … the issue at stake is so fundamental that it is [the appellate judge's] duty to enforce his own view'.[21] For a different view, see the riposte by Professor BV Harris of Auckland University, 'Final appellate courts overruling their own "wrong" precedents: the ongoing search for principle'[22] – doing justice in the particular case should be given greater weight than the values embodied in stare decisis. In making that determination Harris suggested eight considerations that the court should weigh:

- If the precedent can be distinguished, the question of whether it should be overruled is avoided.
- If the precedent was given per incuriam (on which see pp 237–38 below), it need not be followed.
- A precedent that has proved unworkable may be overruled.
- Were any reasons advanced on the present appeal that were not considered when the precedent was decided?
- If none of the above apply, does different weighting of reasons justify departing from the precedent?
- Do the merits of changing the rule outweigh the merits of sticking with the existing rule? Contrary to what is often said, the presumption should be that a precedent that is thought to have been wrongly decided should be overruled unless the stare decisis considerations warrant its maintenance.
- Is there reason to suppose that the problem will be cured by the legislature?
- Does the issue raise fundamental principles?

For a striking example of the Supreme Court abandoning a line of cases approved by both the House of Lords and the Judicial Committee of the Privy Council see *R v Jogee* [2016]

[19] *Jones* (n 12 above) 966; *Conway v Rimmer* [1968] AC 910, 938.

[20] JW Harris, 'Towards principles of overruling: when should a final court of appeal second guess?' 10 *Oxford Journal of Legal Studies*, 1990, 135.

[21] Ibid, 162, 184, 189 and 198.

[22] BV Harris, 'Final appellate courts overruling their own "wrong" precedents: the ongoing search for principle' 118 *Law Quarterly Review*, 2002, 408.

UKSC 8 and [2016] UKPC 7. In *Chan Wing-Siu* [1985] AC 168 the Privy Council had held that if two people set out to commit an offence (crime A), and in the course of it one of them commits another offence (crime B), the second person is guilty as an accessory to crime B if they foresaw it as a possibility, even though they did not necessarily intend it. In *Jogee* the Supreme Court held that that was too broad a ruling. Under its ruling the secondary party to murder can only be convicted if they participated with the intention to encourage or assist the principal offender commit the offence with the intent to kill or cause GBH. The Court gave several reasons (at [80–86]) for its conclusion that the principle stated in *Chan Wing-Siu* was wrong:

- The Supreme Court had had the benefit of fuller argument and citation of relevant authorities that had not been cited in that case.
- The law stated in the Privy Council decision was controversial and caused difficulties for the courts.
- If a wrong turning had been taken on an important matter as a result of a court decision it should be corrected – and the correction should be by the courts rather than by the legislature.
- Foresight of a possibility was an insufficient basis as the test.

For another example of the Supreme Court departing from House of Lords decisions see *Knauer v Ministry of Justice* [2016] UKSC – especially [23].

For a suggested philosophy for not following precedent see Sebastian Lewis, 'Precedent and the Rule of Law' 41 *Oxford Journal of Legal Studies*, 2021(4), 873–98.

Number of Judges Sitting

The House of Lords normally sat with five judges but occasionally sat with seven. The Supreme Court usually sits with five but occasionally sits with seven, nine or even eleven. In the two great Brexit cases brought by Mrs Gina Miller it sat with eleven of the twelve justices.[23] (The statute requires that it always sits with an odd number.[24]) Technically, from the point of view of the doctrine of precedent, it makes no difference how many judges sat. However when the court sits with more than the usual number of five it is obvious that it regards the decision as being of more than usual importance and it is unavoidable that if the judges agreed, the decision will be treated as having even more weight by virtue of the court's composition.

4.1.2. The Court of Appeal, Civil Division

There are two main issues: the relationship between the Court of Appeal and decisions of the House of Lords or the Supreme Court; and the relationship of the Court of Appeal towards its own previous decisions.

Is the Court of Appeal Bound by the Decisions of the House of Lords and the Supreme Court?

Until the 1970s there was never any doubt that the Court of Appeal was bound by the decisions of the House of Lords. But in *Broome v Cassell* [1971] 2 QB 354 the Court of Appeal had the temerity to hold (unanimously) that the House of Lords had been wrong in its view

[23] *R (Miller) v Secretary of State for Exiting the European Union* [2017] UKSC 5 and *R (Miller) v The Prime Minister* [2019] UKSC 41.

[24] Constitutional Reform Act 2005, s 42(1).

in *Rookes v Barnard* [1964] AC 1129, 1221–31, per Lord Devlin, on the circumstances in which exemplary damages could be awarded. In *Rookes v Barnard* Lord Devlin, with the unanimous approval of his brethren, had laid down that exemplary damages could only be awarded in three types of circumstances. The trial judge in *Cassell v Broome* regarded himself as bound by this ruling. But the Court of Appeal (Lord Denning MR, Salmon and Phillimore LJJ) held that the House of Lords decision was not binding because it ignored two other House of Lords cases, *Hulton v Jones* decided in 1910 and *Ley v Hamilton* decided in 1935. They therefore invoked the doctrine that the House of Lords in *Rookes v Barnard* had acted per incuriam (in ignorance!). This suggestion was not well received. When the case went on appeal to the House of Lords, Lord Hailsham delivered a sharp rebuke to Lord Denning and his brethren.

> I am driven to the conclusion that when the Court of Appeal described the decision in *Rookes* v. *Barnard* as decided 'per incuriam' or 'unworkable' they really only meant that they did not agree with it. But, in my view, even if this were not so, it is not open to the Court of Appeal to give gratuitous advice to judges of first instance to ignore decisions of the House of Lords in this way … The fact is, and I hope it will never be necessary to say so again, that, in the hierarchical system of courts which exists in this country, it is necessary for each lower tier, including the Court of Appeal, to accept loyally the decisions of the higher tiers. ([1972] AC 1027, 1054)

Lords Reid, Wilberforce, Diplock and Kilbrandon all agreed with Lord Hailsham that it was not open to the Court of Appeal to advise judges to ignore decisions of the House of Lords on the ground that they were decided per incuriam, or were unworkable.

Despite this the issue came up again only two years later. In *Schorsch Meier GmbH v Hennin* [1975] QB 416 the Court of Appeal held by two to one (Lord Denning and Foster J, Lawton LJ dissenting) that judgment in an English court could be given in a currency other than sterling notwithstanding a clear decision to the contrary by the House of Lords in 1961 in the *Havana Railways* case. Lord Denning based his view on the maxim *cessante ratione cessat ipsa lex* (when the reason for the rule goes the rule lapses):

> LORD DENNING (at 424–5): Why have we in England insisted on a judgment in sterling and nothing else? It is, I think, because of our faith in sterling. It was a stable currency which had no equal. Things are different now. Sterling floats in the wind. It changes like a weathercock with every gust that blows. So do other currencies. This change compels us to think again about our rules. I ask myself: Why do we say that an English court can only pronounce judgment in sterling? Lord Reid thought that it was 'primarily procedural': see the *Havana* case [1961] A.C. 1007, 1052. I think so too. It arises from the form in which we used to give judgment for money. From time immemorial the courts of common law used to give judgment in these words: 'It is adjudged that the plaintiff *do recover* against the defendant £x' in sterling. On getting such a judgment the plaintiff could at once issue out a writ of execution for £x. If it was not in sterling, the sheriff would not be able to execute it. It was therefore essential that the judgment should be for a sum of money in sterling: for otherwise it could not be enforced …
>
> Those reasons for the rule have now ceased to exist …
>
> Seeing that the reasons no longer exist, we are at liberty to discard the rule itself. Cessante ratione legis cessat ipsa lex. The rule has no support amongst the juridical writers. It has been criticised by many. Dicey[25] says:
>
>> Such an encroachment of the law of procedure upon substantive rights is difficult to justify from the point of view of justice, convenience or logic.

[25] Dicey and Morris, *The Conflict of Laws*, 9th edn (Stevens, 1973) 883.

Foster J simply said he agreed with the judgment of Lord Denning and with his reasons. Lord Justice Lawton did not agree. He was, he said, a timorous member of the court. 'I stand in awe of the House of Lords.' He regarded himself bound by the *Havana Railways* decision. It was disturbing to find that a rule which did injustice to a foreign trader was based, as he thought it was, on archaic legalistic nonsense. 'It is however my duty to apply the law, not to reform it' (430).

The case did not go to the House of Lords, but the issue did, only a year later, in *Miliangos v George Frank (Textiles) Ltd* [1976] AC 443 which raised precisely the same issue. In *Miliangos* the trial judge, Bristow J, had to choose between the 1961 House of Lords decision in the *Havana Railways* case that judgment could only be given in sterling and the Court of Appeal's decision in *Schorsch Meier* holding that this was no longer the case. He chose the House of Lords decision on the ground that it was still binding on him – Parliament had not altered it nor had the House of Lords itself. It represented the view of the law held in this country for some 350 years – [1975] 1 QB 487, 492. On appeal to the Court of Appeal, Lord Denning, Stephenson and Geoffrey Lane LJJ held unanimously that they were bound by the Court of Appeal's decision in *Schorsch Meier* [1975] QB 416.

The House of Lords held that the Court of Appeal had been wrong – though it agreed that the rule regarding the currency of judgments should be changed.

Miliangos v George Frank (Textiles) Ltd [1976] AC 443

> LORD SIMON OF GLAISDALE (472): Since the Court of Appeal is absolutely bound by a decision of the House of Lords and (at least on its civil side) by a previous decision of the Court of Appeal itself, it would be surprising if the meaning and application of the maxim 'cessante ratione' were really that accepted by the majority of the Court of Appeal in *Schorsch Meier* and again by the learned Master of the Rolls in the instant case. For as such it would enable any court in the land to disclaim any authority of any higher court on the ground that the reason which had led to such higher court's formulation of the rule of law was no longer relevant. A rule rooted in history could be reversed because history is the bunk of the past. Indeed, taken literally, there is no ground for limiting 'lex' to judge-made law. Coke, apparently the originator of the tag (Co. Litt. 70b), was quite prepared to say that a statute which conflicted with reason could be declared invalid by the courts (*Dr Bonham's Case* (1610) 8 C.Rep 107a, 118a) ... It would be easy to compile a bulky anthology of authoritative citations to show that those courts of law which are bound by the rule of precedent are not free to disregard an established rule of law because they conceive that another of their own devising might be more reasonable ...
>
> To sum up on this part of the case: (1) the maxim in the form 'cessante ratione cessat ipsa lex' reflects one of the considerations which your Lordships will weigh in deciding whether to overrule, by virtue of the 1966 declaration, a previous decision of your Lordships' House; (2) in relation to courts bound by the rule of precedent the maxim 'cessante ratione cessat ipsa lex,' in its literal and widest sense, is misleading and erroneous; (3) specifically, courts which are bound by the rule of precedent are not free to disregard an otherwise binding precedent on the ground that the reason which led to the formulation of the rule embodied in such precedent seems to the court to have lost cogency; (4) the maxim in reality reflects the process of legal reasoning whereby a previous authority is judicially distinguished or an exception is made to a principal legal rule; (5) an otherwise binding precedent or rule may, on proper analysis, be held to have been impliedly overruled by a subsequent decision of a higher court or impliedly abrogated by an Act of Parliament; but this doctrine is not accurately reflected by citation of the maxim 'cessante ratione cessat ipsa lex.'

Lord Simon dissented on the question whether the rule should now be changed; Lords Wilberforce and Fraser expressly agreed with Lord Simon on the maxim *cessante ratione*. Lord Cross went even further and thought that although normally the Court of Appeal was bound to follow its own previous decisions, it should not have done so in *Miliangos* – since the Court of Appeal was wrong in *Schorsch Meier* to have departed from the *Havana* decision of the House of Lords:

The Court of Appeal accepted the very strong indications from the House of Lords, first in *Broome v Cassell* and then in *Miliangos*, that the Court of Appeal *was* absolutely bound by the decisions of the House of Lords – whatever it might think of them. But in his autobiographical book *The Discipline of Law* (Butterworth, 1979), Lord Denning made it clear (p 308) that *he* did not regard the Court of Appeal's *lèse-majesté* in *Schorsch Meier* as having been wrong:

> If in the *Schorsch Gmb. H.* v. *Henning* case we had held ourselves bound by the *Havana* case, we would have given judgment in sterling. In that event, in the *Miliangos* case the Swiss firm [the plaintiffs] would automatically have taken judgment in sterling also … The Swiss firm would not have appealed. The House of Lords would never have had the opportunity of overruling the *Havana* case. The law would still have been that an English court could only give judgment in sterling. That would have been a disaster for our trade with countries overseas.

A surprising echo of Lord Denning s approach emerged in a unanimous decision of the Court of Appeal in 1989 in which it was held that a decision of the House of Lords should not be followed because it had become obsolete![26] The House of Lords had held in *Smith v Baker* in 1891 that an appeal could not be brought from the county court to the Court of Appeal on a point of law not raised below. The Court of Appeal in 1989 held that the Lords' 1891 decision was not binding:

> For these reasons we hold that the rule in *Smith* v. *Baker & Sons* ought no longer to be applied. We are conscious that it may seem a strong thing for this court to hold thus of a rule established by the House of Lords, albeit one enfeebled by exceptions, the statutory support which gave it life at last turned off. But, where it can see that the decision of the higher court has become obsolete, the lower court, if it is not to deny justice to the parties in the suit, is bound to say so and to act accordingly.

The case was not appealed. (The Court of Appeal in fact refused the losing party leave to appeal!)

In *D v East Berkshire Community NHS Trust* [2003] EWCA Civ 1151, [2004] QB 558 at [83], a tort case involving child abuse, the Court of Appeal held that in so far as the position of a child is concerned the decision of the House of Lords in *X (Minors) v Bedfordshire County Council*[27] could not survive the introduction of the Human Rights Act 1998. In a later case Lord Bingham accepted that the Court of Appeal had been right, exceptionally, not to follow the House of Lords decision. When the case 'reached the Lords, no criticism of the Court of Appeal's bold course was expressed, the House agreed that the policy considerations which had founded its decision in *X v Bedfordshire* had been very largely eroded and it was accepted that that decision was no longer good law'.[28] The other Law Lords expressed their full agreement with Lord Bingham's observations.

A different reason for the Court of Appeal to ignore an otherwise binding decision of the House of Lords was given in *R v James, R v Karimi* [2006] EWCA Crim 14 – namely that the decision had effectively been overruled by a decision of the Judicial Committee of the Privy Council. In *R v Holley* [2005] 2 AC 580 the Judicial Committee had sat with nine members to

[26] See *Pittalis v Grant* [1989] QB 605, per Slade, Nourse and Stuart-Smith LJJ.
[27] [1995] 2 AC 633.
[28] *Kay v London Borough of Lambeth* [2006] UKHL 10 [45].

consider the decision in *R v Smith (Morgan James)* [2001] 1 AC 146 on the law of provocation in murder. In *James and Karimi*, the Court of Appeal, sitting with five judges including Lord Phillips, the then Lord Chief Justice, and Sir Igor Judge, the then President of the Queen's Bench Division, said that the Privy Council decision was clearly intended to declare the law of England and the Court of Appeal should accept that it had done so. However, in 2016 in *Willers v Joyce*[29] the Supreme Court held that an English court is only permitted to follow a Privy Council decision that conflicts with a decision of the House of Lords or the Supreme Court if the Privy Council in its decision expressly stated that that was to be the effect of its decision.

For an example of the Court of Appeal essentially ignoring a House of Lords decision, see *Ghaidan v Godin-Mendoza* [2002] EWCA Civ 1533. In *Fitzpatrick v Sterling Housing Association Ltd* [2001] 1 AC 27 the House of Lords held that the survivor of a long-standing homosexual partnership could qualify as a member of the 'family' of his deceased partner but that he could not qualify as the 'spouse' within the meaning of the phrase 'his or her wife or husband'.[30] In *Ghaidan*, a unanimous Court of Appeal (Kennedy, Buxton, Keene LJJ), held that the survivor of a same-sex relationship was within the meaning of the statutory phrase on the basis that that phrase should be read as 'as *if they* were his or her wife or husband'. The Court of Appeal said it was applying s 3 of the Human Rights Act 1998 which, as has been seen (3.8.1 above), requires the courts to read down a statutory provision 'so far as it is possible' to make it compatible with the ECHR. The judgments did not specifically address the problem created by the decision in *Fitzpatrick*.[31] The House of Lords in *Ghaidan v Godin-Mendoza* [2004] UKHL 30, [2004] 2 AC 557 upheld the Court of Appeal's decision by a majority of four to one. None of the judges referred in their speeches to the issue of the Court of Appeal's attitude to precedent.

Is the Court of Appeal Bound by its Own Decisions?

The basic rule is that the Court of Appeal, Civil Division is bound by its own decisions. The court has ruled that it makes no difference whether the decision is that of a two-judge, three-judge or five-judge court.[32] (For the probably different position regarding the Criminal Division see 4.1.3 below.)

The classic statement of the basic rule is in *Young v Bristol Aeroplane Co Ltd*:[33]

Young v Bristol Aeroplane Company Ltd [1944] KB 718 (CA)

Plaintiff claimed damages for injuries at work. The defendant argued that his claim was bad since according to a Court of Appeal decision, *Perkins v Hugh Stevenson & Sons, Ltd* [1940] 1 KB 56, a claim for common law damages was barred where the injured workman had received compensation under the Workmen s Compensation Acts. The plaintiff appealed.

Lord Greene MR, in the course of giving judgment for a full court of six judges, said (at 723, 725):

> The question thus raised as to the jurisdiction of this court to refuse to follow decisions of its own was obviously one of great general importance and directions were given for the appeal to be

[29] [2016] UKSC 44 – a unanimous decision of all nine Justices who sat on the appeal. The judgment, most unusually, was devoted solely to the question of precedent and technically was therefore all obiter dicta.

[30] Under para 2(2) of Sch 1 to the Rent Act 1977.

[31] For sharply critical comment see B Hewson, 'Usurping Parliament?' *Solicitors' Journal*, 13 December 2002, 1127.

[32] *Limb v Union Jack Removals Ltd* [1998] 1 WLR 1354, 1364 para 34 (CA). The dictum did not refer to the possibility of a decision by more than five judges.

[33] The rule that the Court of Appeal is bound by its own decisions in fact appears to date back to its origin – see D Pugsley, 'Precedent in the Court of Appeal' *Civil Justice Quarterly*, 1983, 48, 54–57.

argued before the full court. It is surprising that so fundamental a matter should at this date still remain in doubt. To anyone unacquainted with the rare cases in which it has been suggested or asserted that this court is not bound to follow its own decisions or those of a court of co-ordinate jurisdiction the question would, we think, appear to be beyond controversy. Cases in which this court has expressed its regret at finding itself bound by previous decisions of its own and has stated in the clearest terms that the only remedy of the unsuccessful party is to appeal to the House of Lords are within the recollection of all of us and numerous examples are to be found in the reports. When in such cases the matter has been carried to the House of Lords it has never, so far as we know, been suggested by the House that this view was wrong and that this court could itself have done justice by declining to follow a previous decision of its own which it considered to be erroneous. On the contrary, the House has, so far as we are aware, invariably assumed and in many cases expressly stated that this court was bound by its own previous decision to act as it did.

… The Court of Appeal is a creature of statute and its powers are statutory. It is one court though it usually sits in two or three divisions.[34] Each division has co-ordinate jurisdiction, but the full court has no greater powers or jurisdiction than any division of the court. Its jurisdiction is mainly appellate, but it has some original jurisdiction … Neither in the statute itself nor (save in two cases mentioned hereafter) in decided cases is there any suggestion that the powers of the Court of Appeal sitting with six or nine or more members are greater than those which it possesses when sitting as a division with three members. In this respect, although we are unable to agree with certain views expressed by Greer L. J.[35] as will presently appear, we think that he was right in saying that what can be done by a full court can equally well be done by a division of the court. The corollary of this is, we think, clearly true, namely, that what cannot be done by a division of the court cannot be done by the full court …

On a careful examination of the whole matter we have come to the clear conclusion that this court is bound to follow previous decisions of its own as well as those of courts of co-ordinate jurisdiction. The only exceptions to this rule (two of them apparent only) are those already mentioned which for convenience we here summarise: (1) The court is entitled and bound to decide which of two conflicting decisions of its own it will follow. (2) The court is bound to refuse to follow a decision of its own which, though not expressly overruled, cannot, in its opinion, stand with a decision of the House of Lords. (3) The court is not bound to follow a decision of its own if it is satisfied that the decision was given per incuriam.

Two main issues have arisen since the decision in *Young*'s case in 1944. One is whether the House of Lords Practice Statement in July 1966 could be invoked by the Court of Appeal to release it from the rule that it was generally bound by its own decisions and, if not, what is the extent of the exceptions to the rule in *Young*'s case?

Is the Court of Appeal Bound to Follow Young v Bristol Aeroplane?

For many years after 1966 Lord Denning led a campaign to establish the principle that the House of Lords' Practice Statement should apply to the Court of Appeal as well. The culmination of this campaign came in *Davis v Johnson*:

Davis v Johnson [1979] AC 264

The appellant and the respondent were cohabiting as man and wife in a council flat. The respondent was the father of the applicant's daughter. After much violence the applicant fled to a refuge for battered women. She applied under the Domestic Violence and Matrimonial Proceedings Act 1976 for an injunction to restrain him from using violence and ordering him to vacate the flat. At the hearing the respondent argued that the Court of Appeal was bound to follow its own two previous and very recent decisions given on the

[34] Today it sits in many more divisions (ed).

[35] *In re Shoesmith* [1938] 2 KB 637, 644.

interpretation of the 1976 Act – which had ruled that a person with a proprietary interest in property could not be excluded by an injunction granted under the 1976 Act. The case was heard by five judges. Three (Lord Denning, Sir George Baker P, and Shaw LJ) held that the Court of Appeal was free to depart from its previous decisions. Two (Goff and Cumming-Bruce LJJ) disagreed:

Lord Denning MR (at 278–83):

> *Departure from previous decisions*
>
> I turn to the second important point: can we depart from those two cases? Although convinced that they are wrong, are we at liberty to depart from them? What is the correct practice for this court to follow?
>
> On principle, it seems to me that, whilst this court should regard itself as normally bound by a previous decision of the court, nevertheless it should be at liberty to depart from it if it is convinced that the previous decision was wrong. What is the argument to the contrary? It is said that, if an error has been made, this court has no option but to continue the error and leave it to be corrected by the House of Lords. The answer is this: the House of Lords may never have an opportunity to correct the error; and thus it may be perpetuated indefinitely, perhaps for ever. That often happened in the old days when there was no legal aid. A poor person had to accept the decision of this court because he had not the means to take it to the House of Lords. It took 60 years before the erroneous decision in *Carlisle and Cumberland Banking Co.* v. *Bragg*[36] was overruled by the House of Lords in *Gallie* v. *Lee* ([1971] A.C. 1004). Even today a person of moderate means may be outside the legal aid scheme, and not be able to take his case higher, especially with the risk of failure attaching to it. That looked as if it would have been the fate of Mrs Farrell when the case was decided in this court,[37] but she afterwards did manage to collect enough money together, and by means of it to get the decision of this court reversed by the House of Lords. Apart from monetary considerations, there have been many instances where cases have been settled pending an appeal to the House of Lords; or, for one reason or another, not taken there, especially with claims against insurance companies or big employers. When such a body has obtained a decision of this court in its favour, it will buy off an appeal to the House of Lords by paying ample compensation to the appellant. By so doing, it will have a legal precedent on its side which it can use with effect in later cases. I fancy that such may have happened in cases following *Oliver* v. *Ashman*. By such means an erroneous decision on a point of law can again be perpetuated forever. Even if all those objections are put on one side and there is an appeal to the House of Lords, it usually takes 12 months or more for the House to reach its decision. What then is the position of the lower courts meanwhile? They are in a dilemma. Either they have to apply the erroneous decision of the Court of Appeal, or they have to adjourn all fresh cases or await the decision of the House of Lords. That has often happened. So justice is delayed, and often denied, by the lapse of time before the error is corrected. The present case is a crying instance. If it took the ordinary course of appeals to the House, it would take some months before it was decided. Meanwhile many women would be denied the protection which Parliament intended they should have. They would be subjected to violence without redress; because the county court judges would have to say to them: 'We are sorry but the Court of Appeal says we have no jurisdiction to help you.' We were told that, in this very case, because of the urgency, the House might take special measures to hear it before Christmas. But, even so, I doubt whether they would be able to give their decision until well on in the New Year. In order to avoid all the delay, and the injustice consequent on it, it seems to me that this court, being convinced that the two previous decisions were wrong, should have the power to correct them and give these women the protection which Parliament intended they should have.

[36] [1911] 1 KB 489.
[37] *Farrell v Alexander* [1976] QB 345, 359.

It was suggested that, if we did this, the county court judges would be in a dilemma. They would not know whether to follow the two previous decisions or the later decision of this court. There would be no such dilemma. They should follow this later decision. Such a position always arises whenever the House of Lords corrects an error made by a previous decision. The lower courts, of course, follow the latest decision. The general rule is that, where there are conflicting decisions of courts of co-ordinate jurisdiction, the later decision is to be preferred, if it is reached after full consideration of the earlier decision: see *Minister of Pensions v Higham* ([1948] 2 K.B. 153, 155).

So much for principle. But what about our precedents? What about *Young* v. *Bristol Aeroplane Co Ltd*?

The position before 1944

I will first state the position as it was before the year 1944. The Court of Appeal in its present form was established in 1873. It was then the final court of appeal. Appeals to the House of Lords were abolished by that Act and only restored a year or two later. The Court of Appeal inherited the jurisdiction of the previous courts of appeal such as the Court of Exchequer Chamber and the Court of Appeal in Chancery. Those earlier courts had always had power to reconsider and renew the law as laid down in previous decisions; and, if that law was found to be wrong, to correct it; but without disturbing the actual decision. I take this from the statements of eminent judges of those days who knew the position. In particular in 1852 Lord St Leonards LC in *Bright v. Hutton, Hutton v. Bright*[38] said in the House of Lords:

> … you are not bound by any rule of law which you may lay down, if upon a subsequent occasion, you should find reason to differ from that rule; that is, that this House, like every Court of Justice, possesses an inherent power to correct an error into which it may have fallen …

Young v Bristol Aeroplane Co. Ltd[39]

The change came about in 1944. In *Young v Bristol Aeroplane Co. Ltd* the court overruled the practice of a century. Lord Greene MR,[40] sitting with a court of five, laid down that this court is bound to follow its previous decision as well as those of co-ordinate jurisdiction, subject to only three exceptions: (i) where there are two conflicting decisions, (ii) where a previous decision cannot stand with a decision of the House of Lords, (iii) if a previous decision was given per incuriam.

It is to be noticed that the court laid down that proposition as a rule of law. That was quite the contrary of what Brett MR had declared in *The Vera Cruz (No 2)*[41] in 1884. He said it arose only as a matter of judicial comity. Events have proved that in this respect that Brett MR was right and Lord Greene MR was wrong. I say this because the House of Lords in 1898 had held itself bound by its own previous decisions as a rule of law: see *London Street Tramways Co Ltd v London County Council.*[42] But yet in 1966 it discarded that rule. In a statement it was said:[43]

> Their Lordships nevertheless recognise that too rigid adherence to precedent may lead to injustice in a particular case and also unduly restrict the proper development of the law. They propose, therefore, to modify their present practice, and while treating former decisions of this House as normally binding, to depart from a previous decision when it appears right to do so.

That shows conclusively that a rule as to precedent (which any court lays down for itself) is not a rule of law at all. It is simply a practice or usage laid down by the court itself for its own guidance; and, as such, the successors of that court can alter that practice or amend it or set up other guidelines, just as the House of Lords did in 1966. Even as the judges in *Young v Bristol Aeroplane Co. Ltd* thought fit to discard the practice of a century and declare a new practice or usage, so we in 1977 can discard the guidelines of 1944 and set up new guidelines of our own or revert to the

[38] (1852) 3 HL Cas 341, 388.
[39] [1944] KB 718.
[40] [1944] KB 718, 729, 730.
[41] (1884) 9 PD 96, 98.
[42] [1898] AC 375.
[43] [1966] 1 WLR 1234.

old practice laid down by Brett MR. Nothing said in the House of Lords, before or since, can stop us from doing so. Anything said about it there must needs be obiter dicta.[44] This was emphasised by Salmon LJ. in this court in *Gallie v Lee*.[45]

The point about the authority of this court has never been decided by the House of Lords. In the nature of things it is not a point that could ever come before the House for decision. Nor does it depend on any statutory or common law rule. This practice of ours apparently rests solely on a concept of judicial comity laid down many years ago and automatically followed ever since … Surely today judicial comity would be amply satisfied if we were to adopt the same principle in relation to our own decisions as the House of Lords has recently laid down for itself by pronouncement of the whole House.

The new guidelines

So I suggest that we are entitled to lay down new guidelines. To my mind, this court should apply similar guidelines to those adopted by the House of Lords in 1966. Whenever it appears to this court that a previous decision was wrong, we should be at liberty to depart from it if we think it right to do so. Normally, in nearly every case of course, we would adhere to it. But in an exceptional case we are at liberty to depart from it.

Alternatively, in my opinion, we should extend the exceptions in *Young v Bristol Aeroplane Co. Ltd*[46] when it appears to be a proper case to do so. I realise that this comes virtually to the same thing, but such new exceptions have been created since *Young v Bristol Aeroplane Co. Ltd.* For instance, this court can depart from a previous decision of its own when sitting on a criminal cause or matter: see the recent cases of *R. v Gould*,[47] *R. v Newsome* and *Browne*.[48] Likewise by analogy it can depart from a previous decision in regard to contempt of court. Similarly in the numerous cases when this court is sitting as a court of last resort. There are many statutes which make this court the final court of appeal. In every jurisdiction throughout the world a court of last resort has, and always has had, jurisdiction to correct the errors of a previous decision: see *Webster v Ashton-under-Lyne Overseers, Hadfield's Case*.[49] In the recent case of *Tiverton Estates Ltd* v. *Wearwell Ltd*,[50] we extended the exceptions by holding that we could depart from a previous decision where there were conflicting principles as distinct from conflicting decisions, of this court: likewise we extended the notion of per incuriam in *Industrial Properties (Barton Hill) Ltd v Associated Electrical Industries* Ltd.[51] In the more recent cases of *Re K (minors) (wardship: care and control)*,[52] and *Re S (BB) v S (BI) (infants: care and control)*,[53] this court in its jurisdiction over children did not follow the earlier decision of *Re L (infants)*.[54] I would also add that when the words of the statute are plain, then it is not open to any decision of any court to contradict the statute; because the statute is the final authority on what the law is. No court can depart from the plain words of a statute. On this ground may be rested the decisions in *W and J B Eastwood Ltd v Herrod (Valuation Officer)*,[55] and *Hanning v Maitland (No 2)*,[56] where this court departed from previous interpretations of a statute. In *Schorsch Meier GmbH v Henning*,[57] we introduced

[44] As regards obiter dicta see 5.1.1 below (ed).
[45] [1969] 2 Ch 17, 49.
[46] [1944] KB 718.
[47] [1968] 2 QB 65.
[48] [1970] 2 QB 711.
[49] [1873] LR 8 CP 306.
[50] [1975] Ch 146.
[51] [1977] QB 580.
[52] [1977] Fam 179.
[53] [1977] Fam 109.
[54] [1962] 1 WLR 886.
[55] [1968] 2 QB 923.
[56] [1970] 1 QB 580.
[57] [1975] QB 416, 425.

> another exception on the principle 'cessante ratione legis cessat ipsa lex'. This step of ours was criticised by the House of Lords in *Miliangos v George Frank (Textiles) Ltd*;[58] but I venture to suggest that, unless we had done so, the House of Lords would never have had the opportunity to reform the law. Every court would have held that judgments could only be given in sterling. No one would have taken the point to the House of Lords, believing that it was covered by *Re United Railways of the Havana and Regla Warehouses.*[59] In this present case the applicant, Miss Davis, was at first refused legal aid for an appeal, because the point was covered by the two previous decisions. She was only granted it afterwards when it was realised by the legal aid committee that this court of five had been specially convened to reconsider and review those decisions. So, except for this action of ours, the law would have been regarded as settled by *B v B* and *Cantliff v Jenkins*; and the House of Lords would not have had the opportunity of pronouncing on it. So instead of rebuking us, the House of Lords should be grateful to us for giving them the opportunity of considering these decisions.
>
> The truth is that the list of exceptions from *Young v Bristol Aeroplane Co. Ltd* is now getting so large that they are in process of eating up the rule itself; and we would do well simply to follow the same practice as the House of Lords.

Sir George Baker P, sitting with Lord Denning, agreed, but he put his principle rather differently (at 290–91):

> I listened with care to counsel for the applicant's careful argument that *Young's* case does not bind this court. I cannot agree with that, but I am prepared to accept that there should be, and must be, a further carefully limited exception which is in part founded on an extension of, or gloss on, the second exception in *Young*'s case that the court is bound to refuse to follow a decision of its own which though not expressly overruled cannot in its opinion stand with a decision of the House of Lords.
>
> I would attempt to define the exception thus: 'The court is not bound to follow a previous decision of its own if satisfied that that decision was clearly wrong and cannot stand in the face of the will and intention of Parliament expressed in simple language in a recent Act passed to remedy a serious mischief or abuse, and further adherence to the previous decision must lead to injustice in the particular case and unduly restrict proper development of the law with injustice to others.' My reasons, briefly, are (1) the practice statement in the House of Lords which recognises the danger of injustice, (2) that there is a conflict between a statutory provision and a decision which has completely misinterpreted the recent statute and failed to understand its purpose, (3) and to me the most compelling, by his judicial oath a judge binds himself to do 'right to all manner of people after the laws and usages of this Realm'. Here, by refusing the injunction, I would be doing a great wrong to the applicant, her child, and many others by following a decision which I firmly believe is not the law. The statute is the law, the final authority. It is said that the proper course for this court is to be bound by the precedent of *B* v. *B*, whatever we may think of it, give leave to appeal and grant an injunction until the hearing which can be expedited. If one learns anything in the Family Division it is that the unexpected always happens in family affairs. There is no certainty that this case will ever reach the House of Lords. The respondent may end his tenancy. The applicant may decide to go and stay elsewhere. There are many possibilities which could lead to the withdrawal of legal aid which is not normally given in order that an important point of law may be decided where the decision will not benefit the immediate parties.
>
> For the rest, I agree with the judgment of Lord Denning M. R.

[58] [1976] AC 443.
[59] [1961] AC 1007.

Shaw LJ put his exception to *Young*'s case even more narrowly (at 308):

> For my part I venture to think that if in 1944 a situation like the present had been in contemplation a further exception might have found a place in the judgment in *Young v Bristol Aeroplane Co Ltd*. It would be in some such terms as that the principle of stare decisis should be relaxed where its application would have the effect of depriving actual and potential victims of violence of a vital protection which an Act of Parliament was plainly designed to afford to them, especially where, as in the context of domestic violence, that deprivation must inevitably give rise to an irremediable detriment to such victims and create in regard to them an injustice irreversible by a later decision of the House of Lords.

Neither of the other two judges, however, would go along with the majority:

> GOFF LJ (at 292): In my judgment, with the greatest respect to those who think otherwise, this court when exercising its civil jurisdiction is bound by the general rule in *Young's* case, save possibly where it is the final court of appeal, and further the class of exceptions is closed. My reasons for this conclusion are the necessity for preserving certainty in our law, which has great value in enabling persons to obtain definite advice on which they can order their affairs, the care which should always be taken to see that hard cases do not make bad law and the oft repeated occasions on which *Young's* case has been approved on the highest authority …
>
> CUMMING-BRUCE LJ (at 311) agreed: It seems to me that in any system of law the undoubted public advantages of certainty in civil proceedings must be purchased at the price of the risk of injustice in difficult individual situations. I would think that the present practice holds the balance just about right. The temptation to depart from it would be much less seductive if there could be readier access to the House of Lords. The highest tribunal is within the reach of those whose modest means enable them to qualify for legal aid, and of the extremely rich. Its doors are closed, for practical purposes, to everyone else. The injustice which today is liable to flow from the fact that unsatisfactory old cases are so seldom capable of review in the House of Lords would be mitigated or removed if Parliament decided to give this court and the House of Lords power to order that costs in the House of Lords should be paid by the Exchequer in those cases in which this court or the House of Lords on an application for leave to appeal certified that an appeal to the House of Lords was desirable in order to enable that House to review a decision regarded as mistaken but binding on the Court of Appeal. The expense to the public and any resulting inconvenience would be infinitely less than that which would flow from a relaxation of the present practice in respect of stare decisis as declared in *Young's* case. I consider that we are bound to act in accordance with the practice as stated in *Young's* case and the *Morelle Ltd* case.[60] This is because I consider that the constitutional functions of their Lordships sitting in their judicial capacity include the function of declaring with authority the extent to which the Court of Appeal is bound by its previous decisions, and the function of defining with authority the exceptional situations in which it is open to this court to depart from a previous decision. So I hold that this court is bound by the declaration made by Viscount Dilhorne, Lord Simon of Glaisdale and Lord Russell of Killowen in *Farrell v Alexander*,[61] that this court is bound by precedent exactly as stated by Scarman L. J.[62] in his judgment in the Court of Appeal in that case affirming the declaration made by Lord Hailsham of St Marylebone L. C. in *Cassell & Co. Ltd v Broome*,[63] a declaration again which commanded the express assent of a majority of their Lordships' House.

[60] [1955] 2 QB 379.
[61] [1977] AC 59.
[62] [1976] QB 345, 371.
[63] [1972] AC 1027, 1055.

On appeal, the House of Lords [1979] AC 317 rejected the view of the majority and admonished the Court of Appeal to abide by its own previous decisions save to the extent allowed by *Young*'s case:

> LORD DIPLOCK (at 326, 328): In an appellate court of last resort a balance must be struck between the need on the one side for the legal certainty resulting from the binding effect of previous decisions and on the other side the avoidance of undue restriction on the proper development of the law. In the case of an intermediate court, however, the second desideratum can be taken care of by appeal to a superior appellate court, if reasonable means of access to it are available; while the risk to the first desideratum, legal certainty, if the court is not bound by its own previous decisions grows ever greater with increasing membership and the number of three-judge divisions in which it sits, as the arithmetic which I have earlier mentioned shows. So the balance does not lie in the same place as in the case of a court of last resort. That is why Lord Gardiner L. C.'s announcement about the future attitude towards precedent of the House of Lords in its judicial capacity concluded with the words: 'This announcement is not intended to affect the use of precedent elsewhere than in this House.' … In my opinion, this House should take this occasion to re-affirm expressly, unequivocally and unanimously that the rule laid down in the *Bristol Aeroplane* case as to stare decisis is still binding on the Court of Appeal.
>
> LORD SALMON (at 344): I am afraid that I disagree with Lord Denning M. R. when he says that the Court of Appeal is not absolutely bound by its own decisions and may depart from them just as your Lordships may depart from yours. As my noble and learned friend, Lord Diplock, has pointed out, the announcement made in 1966 by Lord Gardiner L. C. about the future attitude of this House towards precedent ended with the words: 'This announcement is not intended to affect the use of precedents elsewhere than in this House.' I would also point out that that announcement was made with the unanimous approval of all the Law Lords, and that, by contrast, the overwhelming majority of the present Lords Justices have expressed the view that the principle of stare decisis still prevails and should continue to prevail in the Court of Appeal. I do not understand how, in these circumstances, it is even arguable that it does not. I sympathise with the views expressed on this topic by Lord Denning M. R., but until such time, if ever, as all his colleagues in the Court of Appeal agree with those views, stare decisis must still hold the field. I think that this may be no bad thing. There are now as many as 17 Lords Justices in the Court of Appeal,[64] and I fear that if stare decisis disappears from that court there is a real risk that there might be a plethora of conflicting decisions which would create a state of irremediable confusion and uncertainty in the law. This would do far more harm than the occasional unjust result which stare decisis sometimes produces but which can be remedied by an appeal to your Lordships' House. I recognise, as Cumming-Bruce L. J. points out, that only those who qualify for legal aid or the very rich can afford to bring such an appeal. This difficulty could however be surmounted if when the Court of Appeal gave leave to appeal from a decision it has felt bound to make by an authority with which it disagreed, it had a power conferred on it by Parliament to order the appellants' and/or the respondents' costs of the appeal to be paid out of public funds. This would be a very rare occurrence and the consequent expenditure of public funds would be minimal.

Lord Dilhorne (at 336), Lord Kilbrandon (at 340) and Lord Scarman (at 349) all expressly agreed. There can therefore be no doubt that in the view of the House of Lords the Court of Appeal was bound by its own decisions – subject to the exceptions admitted in *Young*'s case. Technically, it is true that anything said by the House of Lords as regards precedent in the Court of Appeal would be obiter and therefore not binding. (See 5.1.1 below.) But this is to ignore the reality of how the English judges operate the doctrine of precedent. Even Lord Denning, writing in *The Discipline of Law* (Butterworth, 1979) 300, described the House of

[64] In April 2024 there were 36 (ed).

Lords' decision as a 'crushing rebuff'. 'My arguments were rejected by the House of Lords. So my plea failed.' But he remained unrepentant:

> I am consoled to find that there are many intermediate Courts of Appeal in the Commonwealth which adopt the course which I have advocated. So this has made my dissent worthwhile. There are the Courts of Appeal in New South Wales, Victoria, South Australia and New Zealand. In particular, in *Bennett* v. *Orange City Council* [1967] 1 N.S.W. 502 Wallace P. said: 'Giving full credit to the desirability of certainty in the law (which occasionally appears to be a pious aspiration) I consider that even an intermediate Court of Appeal may, on special occasions and in the absence of higher authority on the subject in hand, play its part in the development of the law and in ensuring that it keeps pace with modern conditions and modern thought, and accordingly, in an appropriate case, I do not think that an earlier decision of the Court (including this Court) should be allowed to stand when justice seems to require otherwise'.

Lord Denning said that these words from New Zealand prompted the question whether the Court of Appeal should always simply cut short parties who wished to re-argue points already settled by the Court of Appeal. Should they apply the leap-frog procedure under the Administration of Justice Act 1969, s 12, for sending cases direct to the House of Lords? In either case the House of Lords would then not have the benefit of the views of the Court of Appeal.

The exceptions in Young v Bristol Aeroplane Company Limited

Lord Greene in *Young*'s case stated three exceptions to the general rule that the Court of Appeal was bound by its own decisions:

Prior conflicting decisions The first was where there were two conflicting prior decisions and it had to decide between them. This could happen in two possible ways. One is where the two conflicting decisions were both reached before *Young*'s case in 1944 established that the court was bound by its own decisions. The second possibility is that the court discovers a conflict where previously it had thought that none existed. This happened in a series of cases relating to annulment of marriage. In *Casey v Casey* [1949] P 420, the Court of Appeal held that English courts had no jurisdiction to hear a petition for nullity when the marriage was voidable and the only links with this country were that the marriage was celebrated in England and the petitioner resided in England. In *Ramsay Fairfax v Ramsay Fairfax* [1956] P 115, this case was distinguished by the Court of Appeal, which held that English courts did have jurisdiction to annul a marriage wherever it had been celebrated and whether or not it was voidable, provided both parties were resident in England. In *Ross-Smith v Ross-Smith* [1961] P 39, the Court of Appeal treated the two cases as irreconcilable and chose to follow the former. That is no longer correct. Where there are two irreconcilable decisions of the Court, provided that the issue was properly considered in the second case, that decision should be followed. That was the view of the Court of Appeal in *Patel v Secretary of State for the Home Department* [2013] EWCA Civ 741, [2013] 1 WLR 63 at [59]:

> In *Minister of Pensions v Higham* [1948] 2 KB 153, 168, Denning J referred to 'the general rule that where there are conflicting decisions of courts of co-ordinate jurisdiction, the later decision is to be preferred, if it is reached after full consideration of the earlier decision' – a principle applied by Nourse J in *Colchester Estates (Cardiff) v Carlton plc* [1986] Ch 80, 85. Although that referred to first instance decisions, I consider that it also has force in relation to decisions of this court.)

(The Supreme Court referred to that statement in *Patel* with approval in *Willers v Joyce (Re Gubay (Deceased) No.2)* [2016] UKSC 44 at [9] when referring to a lower court faced with conflicting decisions. The later decision should be followed unless there were cogent reasons to the contrary.)

A variant of this first exception is where a Court of Appeal decision which is in point has wrongly been distinguished in a later Court of Appeal case. In a third case raising the same issue the court can return to the first decision – see *Starmark Enterprises Ltd v CPL Distribution Ltd* [2001] EWCA Civ 1252, [2002] Ch 306.

Inconsistent House of Lords' decision The second exception was where a Court of Appeal decision, though not expressly overruled, could not stand with a decision of the House of Lords. Where the House of Lords' decision is subsequent to that of the Court of Appeal this exception creates no problem. This is simply a case of implied overruling. But does the doctrine also cover the case of inconsistency with a *prior* decision of the House of Lords? This would happen where the Court of Appeal held that one of its decisions had been wrongly decided because it had ignored a then-existing House of Lords' decision. This is precisely what did happen in *Fitzsimmons v Ford Motor Co Ltd* [1946] 1 All ER 429, where the Court of Appeal refused to follow two earlier decisions of its own because they were inconsistent with a previous decision of the House of Lords. This was in spite of the fact that in both cases the Court of Appeal had actually discussed the House of Lords' decision.

In *Miliangos* [1976] AC 443 two Law Lords disagreed as to whether the Court of Appeal could disregard one of its own decisions because it conflicted with a prior decision of the House of Lords. As has been seen, the Court of Appeal in *Schorsch Meier* had refused to follow the earlier House of Lords' decision in the *Havana Railways* case. Lord Denning in *Miliangos* said that Lord Greene's second exception did not permit it to reopen the question. It had simply to follow its own decision in *Schorsch Meier* since the House of Lords' decision had been prior to and not after *Schorsch Meier* ([1975] QB 416, 502). Lord Simon in the House of Lords agreed ([1976] AC 443, 479); whilst Lord Cross, to the contrary, thought that the Court of Appeal in *Miliangos* should have followed the *Havana Railways* case and not its own erroneous decision in *Schorsch Meier* (496).

In *McGoldrick & Co v CPS* [1990] 2 QB 261, the Lord Chief Justice on behalf of a unanimous Court of Appeal, Criminal Division, said that it was not bound to follow its own previous decision in which a previous House of Lords' decision had been wrongly distinguished. The report states that 'His Lordship inclined to the view that the court's duty was to follow the law as it believed it to have been laid down in the previous decision of the House of Lords. (The case concerned the circumstances when solicitors can be made liable for costs as a result of serious dereliction of duty. The question was whether the Court of Appeal had to follow the previous decision of the Civil Division of the Court of Appeal in *Sinclair-Jones v Kay* [1989] 1 WLR 114 which had distinguished the House of Lords' decision of *Myers v Elman* [1940] AC 282.)

A variant of the second exception is where the first case decided by the Court of Appeal goes on appeal to the House of Lords which rules that the point decided by the Court of Appeal did not arise for decision. If the issue then comes up again, the Court of Appeal is not bound by its own previous decision – see *R v Secretary of State for the Home Department, ex p Al-Mehdavi* [1989] 2 WLR 603.

Per incuriam The third and most problematic exception is where the earlier decision was given per incuriam (in ignorance). In ignorance of what?

The leading statement of the principle of per incuriam is by Lord Evershed in *Morelle v Wakeling*:

Morelle v Wakeling [1955] 2 QB 379 (CA)

The Court of Appeal had to decide whether to follow its own previous decision given the same year. It was contended that the previous decision was given per incuriam, in that the arguments were brief (counsel for one side having only been instructed the afternoon before the hearing) and the law was highly specialised.

The Court of Appeal sat with five judges. Lord Evershed MR gave the judgment of the court (at 406):

> As a general rule the only cases in which decisions should be held to have been given per incuriam are those of decisions given in ignorance or forgetfulness of some inconsistent statutory provision or of some authority binding on the court concerned: so that in such cases some part of the decision or some step in the reasoning on which it is based is found, on that account, to be demonstrably wrong. This definition is not necessarily exhaustive, but cases not strictly within it which can properly be held to have been decided per incuriam must, in our judgment, consistently with the stare decisis rule which is an essential feature of our law, be, in the language of Lord Greene M. R., of the rarest occurrence. In the present case it is not shown that any statutory provision or binding authority was overlooked, and while not excluding the possibility that in rare and exceptional cases a decision may properly be held to have been per incuriam on other grounds, we cannot regard this as such a case. As we have already said, it is, in our judgment, impossible to fasten upon any part of the decision under consideration or upon any step in the reasoning upon which the judgments were based and to say of it: 'Here was a manifest slip or error'. In our judgment, acceptance of the Attorney-General s argument would necessarily involve the proposition that it is open to this court to disregard an earlier decision of its own or of a court of co-ordinate jurisdiction (at least in any case of significance or complexity) whenever it is made to appear that the court had not upon the earlier occasion had the benefit of the best argument that the researches and industry of counsel could provide. Such a proposition would, as it seems to us, open the way to numerous and costly attempts to re-open questions now held to be authoritatively decided. Although as was pointed out in *Young* v. *Bristol Aeroplane Co. Ltd*, a 'full court' of five judges of the Court of Appeal has no greater jurisdiction or higher authority than a normal division of the court consisting of three judges, we cannot help thinking that, if the Attorney-General's argument were accepted, there would be a strong tendency in cases of public interest and importance, to invite a 'full court' in effect to usurp the function of the House of Lords and to reverse a previous decision of the Court of Appeal. Such a result would plainly be inconsistent with the maintenance of the principle of stare decisis in our courts.

In *Miliangos* [1975] QB 487 (at 503) Lord Denning gave guidance as to when 'per incuriam' did *not* arise:

> Another exception is where a previous decision has been given per incuriam. 'Such cases,' said Lord Greene M. R. in *Young* v. *Bristol Aeroplane Co. Ltd* [1944] K.B. 718, 729 – 'would obviously be of the rarest occurrence and must be dealt with in accordance with their special facts.' So it has been held that a decision is not given per incuriam because the argument was not 'fully or carefully formulated': see *Morelle Ltd* v. *Wakeling* [1955] 2 Q.B. 379, 399, or was 'only weakly or inexpertly put forward': *Joscelyne* v. *Nissen* [1970] 2 Q.B. 86, 99; nor that the reasoning was faulty: *Barrington* v. *Lee* [1972] 1 Q.B. 326, 345 by Stephenson L. J. To these I would add that a case is not decided per incuriam because counsel have not cited all the relevant authorities or referred to this or that rule of court or statutory provision. The court does its own researches itself and consults authorities; and these may never receive mention in the judgments. Likewise a case is not decided per incuriam because it is argued on one side only and the other side does not appear. The duty of counsel, in those circumstances, as we all know, is to put the case on both sides to the best of his ability: and the court itself always examines it with the utmost care, to protect the interests of the one who is not represented. That was done in the *Schorsch Meier* case itself. (at 503)

> The cases in which we have interfered are limited. One outstanding case is *Tiverton Estates Ltd* v. *Wearwell Ltd* [1975] Ch. 146, where this court in effect overruled *Law* v. *Jones* [1974] Ch. 112, on the ground that a material line of authority was not before the court and that the point called for immediate remedy.

The Court of Appeal applied the per incuriam rule in *Williams v Fawcett* [1986] QB 604. It discarded four previous Court of Appeal decisions on the formalities necessary for a notice to commit someone to prison for contempt on the ground that they were based on error. Sir John Donaldson said there were special features that justified this extension of the per incuriam doctrine. One was the 'clearness with which the growth of the error can be detected if the decisions are read consecutively'. Secondly, the cases concerned the liberty of the subject (committal for contempt of court). Thirdly, the cases were very unlikely to go on appeal to the House of Lords.

But in *Duke v Reliance Systems Ltd* [1988] QB 108 the Court of Appeal refused to apply the per incuriam doctrine to avoid one of its own decisions which it accepted was probably wrong in the light of an EEC Directive. Sir John Donaldson MR said that per incuriam only applied where another division of the Court of Appeal had 'reached a decision in the absence of knowledge of a decision binding on it or a statute, and that in either case it has to be shown that, had the court had this material, it must have reached a contrary decision. That is per incuriam. I do not understand the doctrine to extend to a case where, if different arguments had been placed before it or if different material had been placed before it, it *might* have reached a different conclusion' (at 860).

In *Rickards v Rickards* [1990] Fam 194, Lord Donaldson said previous decisions 'show that this court is justified in refusing to follow one of its own previous decisions not only where that decision is given in ignorance or forgetfulness of some inconsistent statutory provision or some authority binding upon it, but also, in rare and exceptional cases, if it is satisfied that the decision involved a manifest slip or error' (at 199). Usually it would be preferable to refuse the appeal and grant leave to appeal to the House of Lords. Certainty in relation to substantive law was usually to be preferred to correctness since that allowed the public to order their affairs with confidence. But in questions of procedure a change from established procedure affected only the parties and was therefore less objectionable.

In *Rakhit v Carty* [1990] 2 QB 315 which concerned the fixing of rent in premises covered by the Rent Acts, the Court of Appeal applied *Rickards v Rickards* in holding that it was not bound to follow a previous decision which was based solely on the authority of an earlier Court of Appeal decision which was itself given per incuriam in that the court had not been referred to a crucial statutory provision.

It is not clear whether a court is permitted to apply the per incuriam doctrine to decisions of higher courts – ie, whether the Court of Appeal can refuse on the ground of the per incuriam rule to regard itself bound by the decision of the House of Lords or the Divisional Court or a High Court judge can refuse to apply a decision of the Court of Appeal.

It happened in *Hughes v Kingston Upon Hull City Council*,[65] where the Divisional Court declined to follow the Court of Appeal's decision in *Thai Trading Co v Taylor* [1998] QB 781 on the ground that the Court of Appeal had not been asked to consider the House of Lords decision in *Swain v Law Society* [1983]1 AC 598. The propriety of this has not been

[65] [1999] 2 QB 1193.

considered by a higher court. But in *Awwad v Geraghty* [2001] QB 570, the Court of Appeal accepted that *Thai Trading* was not binding on it because it had been decided in ignorance of *Swain v The Law Society.*

Other Exceptions to Stare Decisis in the Court of Appeal

Although only three exceptions were mentioned in *Young*'s case and although the House of Lords in *Miliangos* urged the Court of Appeal to follow its own decisions unless one of the three exceptions mentioned in *Young* applied, a large number of other exceptions appear in fact to have been created. As has been seen, Lord Denning set out a list in the section of his judgment in *Davis v Johnson* headed 'The new guidelines' (p 232 above). And there are quite a few others.

In *Actavis UK Ltd v Merck and Co Inc* [2008] EWCA Civ 444, [2009] 1 WLR 1186, Lord Justice Jacob said one reason for the Court of Appeal not being bound by an earlier decision was if there was no ratio decidendi or at least no ratio of sufficient clarity. (For definition and discussion of the ratio decidendi see 5.1.1 below.) Another reason, in a patent case, was where the court was satisfied that the European Patent Office Boards of Appeal had formed a settled view of European patent law that was inconsistent with the earlier decision. But, he noted, the same did not apply to decisions of the European Court of Human Rights. The House of Lords had ruled in *Kay v Lambeth Borough Council* [2006] 2 AC 465 that where there was a conflict between a decision of the Court of Appeal and a later decision of the Strasbourg Court the matter should be dealt with only by an appeal to the House of Lords and not by the Court of Appeal departing from its previous decision.

Another exception is that a proposition decided in a previous decision of the Court of Appeal is not binding if it was adopted without consideration, on the basis of an assumption, without argument, that it was correct. This may be seen as a variant of the per incuriam rule. Surprisingly, it applies even when the assumed proposition formed part of the ratio (*Kadhim v Brent London Borough Council* [2001] 2 WLR 1674 (CA)).

There is also the question of the impact of decisions of the Privy Council. In *Worcester Works Finance Ltd v Cooden Engineering Co Ltd* [1972] 1 QB 210 at 217 Lord Denning said that 'although decisions of the Privy Council are not binding on this Court, nevertheless when the Privy Council disapproves of a previous decision of this Court or casts doubt upon it, we are at liberty to depart from the previous decision'. For an example of the Court of Appeal preferring a later decision of the Privy Council to its own prior decision see, for instance, *Doughty v Turner Manufacturing Co Ltd* [1964] 1 QB 518 in which the Court of Appeal followed the Privy Council's decision in the *Wagon Mound (No 1)* [1961] AC 388 rather than its own decision in *Re Polemis* [1921] 3 KB 560.

In *Boys v Chaplin* [1968] 2 QB 1 it was held that the court need not follow its own decision where it was an interlocutory (preliminary) one given by a two-judge court. The distinction between interlocutory and final appeals was abolished by the Civil Procedure Rules so the proposition in the terms stated in *Boys* is no longer relevant. The equivalent distinction today is rulings on substantive appeals as opposed to rulings in the course of an application for leave to appeal.

In *Limb v Union Jack Removals Ltd* [1998] 1 WLR 1354 Lord Justice Brooke giving the judgment of the court enunciated five propositions regarding precedent that could be distilled from the cases. The fifth proposition was this: 'Any departure from a previous decision of the court is in principle undesirable *and should only be considered if the previous decision is manifestly wrong*' (at [34]), emphasis added, based on *Langley v North West Water Authority* [1991] 3 All ER 610 at 622, per Donaldson MR giving the court's unanimous judgment.

The proposition that the court may decline to follow decisions which it regards as 'manifestly wrong' would obviously drive a coach and four through the rule in *Young*'s case. The proposition was repeated by all three judges in *Cave v Robinson Jarvis & Rolf* [2002] 1 WLR 581 (CA).

Deploring this development, Professor T Prime and G Scanlan have argued: 'The "manifestly wrong" exception to the doctrine of stare decisis is unacceptable because it is impossible to define when the concept is satisfied with any degree of certainty. ... [W]hat is manifestly wrong to one judge or court is "manifestly right" to another judge or court'.[66] This, they suggested, was in effect the resurrection of the previously rejected 'one-man crusade' of Lord Denning to get his fellow judges to apply the 1966 Practice Statement to the Court of Appeal. It would make it impossible to predict with any degree of certainty whether the Court of Appeal would or would not depart from the doctrine of precedent. The situation called for urgent action which, they suggested, should take the form of a new Practice Statement issued on behalf of both the Court of Appeal and the House of Lords setting out the circumstances in which the Court of Appeal may depart from its previous decisions in clearly defined and precise terms. This call for urgent action was, however, not heeded.

4.1.3. The Court of Appeal, Criminal Division

The Court of Appeal, Criminal Division is the successor of the Court of Criminal Appeal which was set up in 1907 and which existed until it became one of the divisions of the Court of Appeal in 1966. The Court of Criminal Appeal had in turn been the successor of the old Court of Crown Cases Reserved.

In principle, in all three stages of its existence – as Court of Crown Cases Reserved, Court of Criminal Appeal and Court of Appeal, Criminal Division – the basic rule has been that stare decisis applied. But it has always been true that the doctrine has not been rigidly endorsed and there are examples where the court has refused to follow an earlier decision.[67] The greater flexibility on the criminal side was formally recognised in *R. v Taylor* in 1950 and was confirmed and extended in *R v Simpson* in 2003:

R v Taylor [1950] 2 KB 368 (CCA)

The appellant pleaded guilty to a charge of bigamy. He had been advised to do so because the facts of the case were virtually identical to those of *R v Treanor*, a previous decision given by three judges of the Court of Criminal Appeal. Judgment was given by Lord Goddard CJ on behalf of himself and the other six members of the court:

> I desire to say a word about the reconsideration of a case by this court. The Court of Appeal in civil matters usually considers itself bound by its own decisions or by decisions of a court of co-ordinate jurisdiction. For instance, it considers itself bound by its own decisions and by those of the Exchequer Chamber; and, as is well known, the House of Lords also always considers

[66] '*Stare decisis* and the Court of Appeal: judicial confusion and judicial reform?' 23 *Civil Justice Quarterly*, 2004, 212, 224.

[67] See, ie, *Ring* (1892) 61 LJMC 116; *Power* [1919] 1 KB 572; *Norman* [1924] 2 KB 315; and *Newsome and Browne* [1970] 2 QB 711. For a more recent example see the sequence of cases on identification parades culminating in *Popat* (1998) 2 Cr App R 208; *Forbes* (1999) 2 Cr App R 501; and *Popat (No 2)* (2001) 2 Cr App R 387.

> itself bound by its own decisions.[68] In civil matters this is essential in order to preserve the rule of stare decisis.
>
> This court, however, has to deal with questions involving the liberty of the subject, and if it finds, on reconsideration, that, in the opinion of a full court assembled for that purpose, the law has been either misapplied or misunderstood in a decision which it has previously given, and that, on the strength of that decision, an accused person has been sentenced and imprisoned it is the bounden duty of the court to reconsider the earlier decision with a view to seeing whether that person had been properly convicted. The exceptions which apply in civil cases ought not to be the only ones applied in such a case as the present, and in this particular instance the full court of seven judges is unanimously of opinion that the decision in *Rex v Treanor* was wrong.

See to somewhat the same effect *Gould* [1968] 2 QB 65, 68 where Lord Justice Diplock said:

> In its criminal jurisdiction, which it has inherited from the Court of Criminal Appeal, the Court of Appeal does not apply the doctrine of stare decisis with the same rigidity as in its civil jurisdiction. If on due consideration we were to be of the opinion that the law has been either misapplied or misunderstood in an earlier decision of this court, or its predecessor the Court of Criminal Appeal, we should be entitled to depart from the view as to the law expressed in the earlier decision notwithstanding that the case could not be brought within any of the exceptions laid down in *Young v Bristol Aeroplane Co. Ltd.*

For discussion see in particular G. Zellick, 'Precedent in the Court of Appeal, Criminal Division' *Criminal Law Review*, 1974, 222; and Rosemary Pattenden, 'The power of the Criminal Division of the Court of Appeal to depart from its own precedents' *Criminal Law Review*, 1984, 592.

As has been noted, it is established in regard to the Court of Appeal, Civil Division (and in the Divisional Court) that a full court has no more authority than a court of three, or indeed two. The late Professor Glanville Williams objected that there was no basis for taking a different view in regard to the Court of Appeal, Criminal Division.[69] But Professor Zellick argued that the case of *Newsome and Browne* [1970] QB 711 established that a full court of five of the Criminal Division can depart from an earlier decision on grounds not covered by the exceptions in *Young v Bristol Aeroplane* where the law has been 'misapplied or misunderstood'. Zellick contended that the difference between the Civil and the Criminal Divisions of the Court of Appeal could be justified by the rarity of appeals in criminal cases to the House of Lords and the consequential greater importance of appeals at the Court of Appeal level.

In *Spencer* [1985] QB 771, the Criminal Division said that there was no difference between it and the Civil Division in regard to precedent save that when the liberty of the subject was at stake it might decline to follow one of its own decisions. That was in effect a restatement of the ruling in *Taylor.*

In *Simpson* [2003] EWCA Crim 1499, [2003], [2004] QB 118 the question posed for the court was whether it was bound by its own very recent decision in *Palmer (No 1)*, The Times, 5 November 2002. The case concerned the procedural rules regarding the giving notice of confiscation orders.[70]

[68] This was, of course, before the House of Lords Practice Statement of July 1966.

[69] *Salmond on Jurisprudence*, 11th edn (Sweet & Maxwell, 1957) 193–94, quoted by G Zellick in his 1974 *Criminal Law Review* article at 226.

[70] The same issue had arisen in *Sekhon* [2002] EWCA Crim 2954, [2003] 1 WLR 1655 in which judgment was also given by Lord Woolf in basically the same terms.

Lord Woolf began by saying the question of precedent was of considerable significance which explained why it had been thought appropriate to convene a court of five instead of the usual three judges.

Counsel for the defendant/appellant argued that the court should not follow *Palmer.* He cited in support a passage from *Halsbury's Laws*, 4th edn reissue (Butterworth, 1986), para 1242 as to the situations in which it was appropriate for the Court of Appeal to depart from its own decisions. This set out the three basic exceptions stated in *Young v Bristol Aeroplane Co Ltd* (see above) – plus a fourth: 'where in exceptional and rare cases, the court is satisfied that there has been a manifest slip or error and there is no prospect of an appeal to the House of Lords.' He also cited two further passages from *Halsbury.* One was that a full court of five has no greater powers than the usual court of three. The other said:

> In its criminal jurisdiction the Court of Appeal applies the same principles as on the civil side, but recognises that there are exceptions (a) where the applicant is in prison and in the full court's opinion wrongly so; (b) where the court thinks the law was misunderstood or misapplied; and (c) where the full court is carrying out its duty to lay down principles and guidelines in relation to sentencing.

Lord Woolf continued:

> These statements from *Halsbury's Laws* are unexceptional and are soundly based upon the authorities to which they refer. Prominent among them are the decision in *Young v the Bristol Aeroplane Co. Ltd.* However the paragraphs in *Halsbury's Laws* should not be read as if they are contained in a statute. The rules as to precedent reflect the practice of the courts and have to be applied bearing in mind that their objective is to assist in the administration of justice. They are of considerable importance because of their role in achieving the appropriate degree of certainty as to the law. This is an important requirement of any system of justice. The principles should not, however, be regarded as so rigid that they cannot develop in order to meet contemporary needs. (at [27])

Lord Woolf could see that there might be a case for not interpreting the law contrary to a previous authority in such a way that a defendant who would not have otherwise committed an offence, would be held to have committed one. But he did not see why that principle should apply to a situation 'where a defendant, as here, wishes to rely upon a wrongly decided case to provide a technical defence' (at [34]). ('While justice for a defendant is extremely important, justice for the public at large is also important. So is the maintenance of confidence in the criminal justice system.')

In the view of the court, Lord Woolf said, the law had been misunderstood and misapplied in *Palmer.* It had not considered all the relevant authorities and it had had before it conflicting authorities. 'The combination of these features provided in our judgment ample grounds for this court to regard the decision in *Palmer* as being irregular and therefore not binding on this court' (at [37]). It was also, Lord Woolf said, 'not wholly without significance' that the court in *Simpson* was a full court of five. In exercising its residual discretion to decide whether a decision should be treated as a binding precedent, the constitution of the court was relevant. The court agreed with the view (expressed in 1974 by Professor Graham Zellick) that the decision of a five-judge court in *Newsome, Browne* was relevant. He also put forward the argument that appeals to the House of Lords in criminal cases were more restricted than in civil matters. There had to be not only leave to appeal but a certificate from the Court of Appeal that a point of law of general public importance was at stake. Also, there could be no appeal after an acquittal.

One conclusion to emerge from the court's judgment in *Simpson* (to adapt a well-known saying) is that while all decisions of the Court of Appeal, Criminal Division are equal, some are more equal than others. The decision of a full court *does* carry more weight. Secondly, the court is prepared to regard itself as free to depart from one of its own previous decisions to the disadvantage of the defendant where that would deprive the defendant of a technical defence. Thirdly, the criteria for holding a prior decision as not binding include the fact that the court in the previous case had not had all the relevant authorities before it or had conflicting decisions before it – even though having had them available would not necessarily have been decisive. Fourthly, the doctrine of per incuriam covers declining to follow a previous decision because the result of following would not be in the public interest. This fourth proposition amounts to a generous expansion of the concept of declining to follow on the grounds that the precedent was decided per incuriam.

This view was confirmed in the later case of *Rowe* [2007] EWCA 635, [2007] QB 975 in which the Court of Appeal suggested that *Simpson* stood for a very wide proposition:

> The court [in *Simpson*] concluded that the law was misunderstood and misapplied in *Palmer*. Because the court in *Palmer* had not been referred to all the relevant authorities and some of these were in conflict, Lord Woolf held that there were ample grounds for regarding the decision as irregular and not binding. It seems to us, however, that the dominant reason why the court did not follow *Palmer* was not any procedural irregularity but the firm conviction on the part of the court of five that the decision in *Palmer* was manifestly unsound and its consequences manifestly unsatisfactory. (per Lord Phillips CJ at [26])

If precedents can be ignored if the decision is 'manifestly unsound' and their consequences are 'manifestly unsatisfactory' the concept of binding precedent must be regarded as significantly dented. Lord Denning would certainly have approved.

4.1.4. Divisional Courts

The leading authority on whether a Divisional Court is bound by its own decisions is that of *Police Authority for Huddersfield v Watson*, in which Lord Goddard CJ made it clear that the rule was the same as that applied in *Young v Bristol Aeroplane Co Ltd* to the Court of Appeal (Civil Division):

Police Authority for Huddersfield v Watson [1947] KB 842 (Divisional Court, QBD) The Divisional Court had to consider whether it was bound by its own prior decision in *Garvin v Police Authority for City of London* [1944] KB 358.

> LORD GODDARD CJ (at 846–48): Mr Streatfield has argued that it is open to us to depart from *Garvin's* case if we think it was wrongly decided. As we have not heard his full argument, I prefer only to say this: Nothing that I have heard in this case, as far as the argument has gone, satisfies me that Garvin's case was wrongly decided; but whether it was rightly decided or not I am clearly of opinion that we ought to follow it. This court is made a final court of appeal in these matters, and I can imagine nothing more disastrous than that where the court has given a decision upon the construction or application of this Act another court should give a decision contrary to the decision already given, because there then would be two conflicting cases. You might get a court consisting perhaps of different judges choosing one of those decisions, and another court choosing the other decision, and there would be no finality in the matter at all. For myself, I think we ought to hold that we are bound by this decision. [Lord Goddard referred to the rule laid down in *Young* v. *Bristol Aeroplane Co. Ltd* for the guidance of the Court of Appeal.]

> If that is the rule which is applicable in the Court of Appeal – it is to be remembered that Court of Appeal judgments are reviewable in the House of Lords, at any rate by leave – and the Master of the Rolls pointed out in the course of his judgment that in some cases Court of Appeal judgments are final, as in bankruptcy, and in others are reviewable by the House of Lords and yet he draws no distinction – and if, therefore, in a court most of whose decisions are reviewable, although it may be only by leave, in the House of Lords, those decisions are binding on the court, how much more important is it that this court, which is a final court, should follow its own decisions and consider that it ought to give full force and effect to them. Otherwise, as I have said, a great deal of uncertainty would be introduced into the law.
>
> I know that in the writings of various eminent people the doctrine of stare decisis has been canvassed from time to time. In my opinion, if one thing is certain it is that stare decisis is part of the law of England, and in a system of law such as ours, where the common law, and equity largely, are based on decisions, it seems to me it would be very unfortunate if a court of final appeal has given a decision and has laid down a definite principle and it cannot be said the court has been misled in any way by not being referred to authorities, statutory or judicial, which bear on the question, that it should then be said that that decision was not to be a binding authority. [Atkinson and Lewis JJ agreed.]

This meant that the exceptions recognised in *Young*'s case were equally accepted as exceptions in the Divisional Court but that the basic rule was that the Divisional Court was bound by its own decisions. See also *Nicholas v Penny* [1950] 2 KB 466.

However, a decision in 1984 threw doubt on this proposition. In *Ex p Tal* the Divisional Court decided that, although it would normally follow one of its own decisions, it could depart from it if it was convinced that the previous decision was wrong (*R. v Greater Manchester Coroner, ex p Tal* [1985] QB 67). The court distinguished the *Huddersfield Police Authority* case on the ground that the foundation of that decision was that the Divisional Court was sitting as a final court of appeal – because at that time there was no appeal to the House of Lords in criminal cases. This had become possible since 1960 just as it was from the Court of Appeal, Criminal Division. Robert Goff LJ for the court said that the position of the Divisional Court in criminal cases was the same as that of the Court of Appeal, Criminal Division under *R v Taylor* and *R v Gould* [1968] 2 QB 65. But the case before the court was not an appeal but a case of judicial review in which the court was exercising a first instance jurisdiction. It would only be in a rare case that a Divisional Court would depart from a decision of another Divisional Court but it could do so if convinced that the decision was wrong.

The decision in *Ex p Tal* was considered in *Hornigold v Chief Constable of Lancashire* [1985] *Criminal Law Review* 792, where the appellant had sought to re-argue a point regarding the admissibility of evidence of excess alcohol in a driving case which had been decided by the Divisional Court earlier the same year. Lords Justices Goff and Beldam held that, although the decision in *Tal* was right in stating that the Divisional Court was not absolutely bound by a previous decision of a previous Divisional Court, it was plain from what was said in *Tal* that there would be a departure from a previous decision only where the court was convinced that the earlier decision was wrong. The case could not be used as the basis for having a point reargued simply because the later court might reach a different conclusion.

In *R v Stafford Justices, ex p Customs and Excise Commissioners* [1991] 2 QB 339 the Divisional Court declined to follow its own previous decision in *R v Ealing Magistrates' Court, ex p Dixon* [1990] 2 QB 91 because it was persuaded that the previous decision was 'wrongly decided'. The case concerned the question as to whether the Customs and Excise could conduct criminal proceedings. One ground of justification for not following the earlier decision was that the court in *Dixon*'s case had not had before it 'the wide-ranging arguments which have been urged upon us'.

In the earlier case of *Re Osman* [1988] *Criminal Law Review* 611 the Divisional Court declined to follow its own decision in *Tomsett* because the prosecution in that case had declined to argue the point. (Lloyd LJ said: 'The law of England cannot be made or unmade by the willingness of counsel to argue a point. The ratio of *Tomsett* stands. It was not per incuriam. But the present point was left undecided.') Commenting on the decision (ibid, 614), Professor Sir John Smith agreed this could not properly be an application of the per incuriam rule.

In *Shaw v DPP*, The Times, 23 November 1992, 142 *New Law Journal* (1992) 1683, the Divisional Court declined to follow its own decision in *DPP v Corcoran* [1992] RTR 289, [1993] *Criminal Law Review* 139 on the ground that it had been reached per incuriam, or if not per incuriam, was simply wrong. Professor Sir John Smith's commentary in the *Criminal Law Review* argued that this left the law in the unsatisfactory state of two conflicting decisions of the Divisional Court.

A Divisional Court exercising civil jurisdiction is bound by the decisions not only of the House of Lords and Supreme Court but also of the Court of Appeal, Civil Division – see *Read v Joannou* (1890) 25 QBD 300, 302–3. Equally a Divisional Court exercising criminal jurisdiction is bound by decisions of the Court of Criminal Appeal and is bound by its successor, the Court of Appeal, Criminal Division – see *Ruse v Read* [1949] 1 KB 377, 384. See also *Carr v Mercantile Products Ltd* [1949] 2 KB 601, 605 per Goddard CJ, holding that a Divisional Court exercising criminal jurisdiction was bound by a decision of the civil Court of Appeal.

In *R v Northumberland Compensation Appeal Tribunal* [1951] 1 KB 711 the Divisional Court, per Goddard CJ, refused to follow one of its own decisions on the ground that it was inconsistent with an earlier decision of the House of Lords. But this was implicitly disapproved of by the House of Lords in *Cassell v Broome* [1972] AC 1027, when the Lords held that the Court of Appeal had been wrong to treat one of the House of Lords earlier decisions *(Rookes v Barnard)* as mistaken. By the same token presumably the Divisional Court should follow its own decisions rather than an earlier decision of the House of Lords, even if it concludes that the earlier House of Lords' decision is inconsistent with its own later decision.

4.1.5. Trial Courts

The basic rule is that decisions of trial courts are not binding on that court. Thus the decisions of the High Court are not binding on any High Court judge, and the decisions of the county court and of magistrates' courts are not binding on those courts. But magistrates' courts and county courts are bound by the decisions of the High Court and of all the appellate courts. That applies even when the county court and the High Court are applying precisely the same jurisdiction. The county court is inferior to the High Court and is therefore bound by its decision – *Howard de Walden Estates Ltd v Aggio, Earl Cadogan Square Ltd* [2007] EWCA Civ 499, [2008] Ch 26. However, in 2014, a Deputy Master said that Masters were not bound by the decisions of the High Court.[71] There were then three other decisions to the same effect, though in 2018, David Foxton QC, sitting as a Deputy High Court judge, said a High Court judge's decision did bind a Master. This matter is unresolved.[72]

Given that there are around one hundred High Court judges and that they are not bound by their own decisions, there are obvious problems regarding this doctrine. Since High Court judges can reach different decisions on the same point, how is a county court judge supposed to decide which to follow? The position is made worse by the fact that the High Court judge in the second case may not even have been told about the previous High Court decision. Since one High Court judge is not bound by another, the second decision cannot be dismissed as having been given per incuriam. The county court judge may be bound to follow two contradictory decisions with no guidance as to how to proceed.

In *Uganda Co (Holdings) Ltd v Government of Uganda* (1979) 1 Lloyds Rep 481 it was submitted that a judge of first instance should always follow the latest decision of the Court of Appeal in preference to an earlier decision of that court. This was rejected by Donaldson J (as he then was) who stated that if a conflict arose, the first instance judge should 'seek to anticipate how the Court of Appeal itself, would, or more accurately should resolve the conflict on any appeal from his decision' (485).[73]

But this view was rejected in the later case of *Colchester Estates (Cardiff) v Carlton Industries plc* [1984] 2 All ER 601, 604–05 by Nourse J (as he then was) who held that when a decision of the High Court has been fully considered and not followed, the second decision should be regarded as having settled the issue and in a later case the High Court judge should therefore follow the second of the two conflicting decisions.

The High Court is bound by the decisions of higher courts, but a problem arises where these conflict. Should the High Court judge, for instance, follow the Court of Appeal or an inconsistent House of Lords' decision? As has been seen (p 226 above), this dilemma faced Bristow J in *Miliangos v George Frank (Textiles) Ltd* [1975] QB 487 and he chose to follow the House of Lords' decision in *Havana Railways* (holding that damages had to be awarded in sterling), rather than the Court of Appeal's decision in *Schorsch Meier* (holding that this ancient rule had lapsed). But when the case went to the House of Lords, one of the Law Lords criticised the trial judge:

> LORD SIMON OF GLAISDALE (at 477, 478): Greatly as I sympathise with Bristow J. in his predicament, I feel bound to say, with all respect, that I think he was wrong … It is the duty of a subordinate court to give credence and effect to the decision of the immediately higher court, notwithstanding that it may appear to conflict with the decision of a still higher court. The decision of the still higher court must be assumed to have been correctly distinguished (or otherwise interpreted) in the decision of the immediately higher court. For example, in the instant case, in my respectful opinion, Bristow J. should have assumed that the Court of Appeal in *Schorsch Meier* had correctly interpreted and applied the maxim 'cessante ratione …' and had in consequence correctly held that it was not bound to apply the *Havana* decision [1961] A.C. 1007 to the facts

[71] *Randall v Randall* [2016] EWCA 494 (Civ). The case was only reported when it reached the Court of Appeal, but the court said nothing about the Deputy Master's view of precedent.

[72] For very helpful discussion of the cases and the issue see Kwan Ho Lau, 'Precedent within the High Court' 40 *Legal Studies*, 2020, 40, 397–418. See also P Morgan, 'Doublethink and district judges – High Court precedent in the county court' 2012, 32(3) *Legal Studies* 421.

[73] For a helpful, long article on this issue see Morgan, ibid. Morgan suggests that county courts should not be bound by decisions of the High Court.

> judicially ascertained in *Schorsch Meier*. Any other course is not only an invitation to legal chaos but in effect involves a subordinate court sitting in judgment on a decision of its superior court. That is contrary to law. Moreover, in this respect, as so often, the law is a distillation of practical experience, even though all knowledge of the experience may be lost. Here, however, the experience is recoverable. If a subordinate court fails to abide loyally by the judgment of its superior court, the decision of the subordinate court is likely to be appealed to the superior court, which is in turn likely to vindicate its previous decision.

Lords Wilberforce and Cross both said simply that no one except the House of Lords could review decisions of the House of Lords. They did not, however, express any views on whether a trial judge faced with the dilemma of Bristow J should do as he did.

In *Amanuel v Alexandros Shipping Co, The Alexandros P* [1986] QB 464, Webster J had to consider whether he was bound by an ex parte Court of Appeal decision. He held that a High Court judge was bound by a Court of Appeal decision whether ex parte or inter partes unless that decision had been overruled by a subsequent decision of the House of Lords or there was a subsequent inconsistent decision of the Court of Appeal or the decision was per incuriam.

The case of crown courts is different in that the judge does not decide the case in the same way that they do in the High Court, or as the county court or the magistrates decide it. The judge in the crown court sums up the law for the jury and they may give rulings on points of law that come up during the trial. Very occasionally the summing-up or the gist of a ruling may be reported (for instance, in the *Criminal Law Review*). The better view is that rulings of the crown court do not bind other crown courts or magistrates' courts.[74]

4.1.6. Precedents of Common Law Courts that are not Binding

The decisions of lower courts are never binding. Thus the Supreme Court could not be bound by a decision of the Court of Appeal nor the Court of Appeal by a decision of the High Court. The decisions of the Judicial Committee of the Privy Council are not binding on any of the courts in the United Kingdom, though the Privy Council ruled in 1986 that if the matter in issue was a point of English law, it would regard itself as bound by a decision on the point of the House of Lords.[75] There are two exceptions to the general rule. One exception is if it is a devolution case given between 1998 and 2005 – as to which see 4.4 below.[76] The other exception is if the Privy Council decision itself states expressly that it is to be followed rather than a contrary decision of an English court. That exception was formulated by the Supreme Court sitting with nine justices in *Willers v Joyce (Re Gubay (Deceased) No.2)* [2016] UKSC 44. As previously noted, the whole of that judgment given by Lord Neuberger on behalf of himself and the other eight justices was devoted to the doctrine of precedent.)[77]

[74] R Cross and JW Harris, *Precedent in English Law*, 4th edn (Clarendon Press, 1991) 123; and also [1980] Crim LR 402.

[75] *Tai Hing Cotton Mill Ltd v Liu Chong Hing Bank Ltd* [1986] AC 80 per Lord Scarman at [108].

[76] Under the 1998 devolution legislation the Judicial Committee of the Privy Council was the final court of appeal but the Constitutional Reform Act 2005 transferred that jurisdiction to the Supreme Court.

[77] *Willers v Joyce (Re Gubay (Deceased No.2)* [2016] UKSC 44, [2016] 3WLR 534. The decision was the subject of an approving eight-page Editor's Note in *Civil Justice Quarterly* (2017) (3) 265–72. But see also the strongly critical comment by Peter Mirfield, 'A Novel Theory of Privy Council Precedent' (2017) 133 *Law Quarterly Review* 1–6.

An applicant for leave to appeal to the Judicial Committee is required to state whether the appeal would involve re-consideration of earlier House of Lords or Supreme Court decision so that that can be taken into consideration when a decision is made as to the constitution of the court for the hearing of the appeal.

The decisions of courts in other countries are not binding. Citation of precedents from other common law jurisdictions is very common; use of precedents from civil law countries much less so.[78] None are binding.

A non-binding precedent may of course be of very great persuasive power. The precise extent of its persuasive power will depend on all the circumstances. Precedents, as will be seen, are minutely weighed and measured for their proper impact and effect. But a precedent that does not bind the court considering it cannot by some mysterious process create law that is in some way binding. If a decision is not binding on the court it means that the court ultimately is free to accept or reject the rule for which the case stands. The issue is explored in the next chapter.

4.1.7. Courts of Co-ordinate Jurisdiction Operate Informal Rules

Lewis Graham of Wadham College, Oxford, examined the impact on the ordinary rules of precedent applied by courts of co-ordinate jurisdiction of five different factors: the rank of the judge(s) involved in a case; the expertise or experience of the judge(s) involved in a case; the function of the court or the reason for which it is sitting; and the number of judges deciding the case; the level of unanimity on the bench. He concluded his article 'Strong Decisions and Stare Decisis in co-ordinate Courts':[79]

> This article has shown that the operation of precedent in courts of co-ordinate jurisdiction is not as straightforward as it may at first seem. Formal rules of practice apply in each court; these rules generally stipulate that earlier decisions of the same court are to be followed, unless certain conditions are met (these conditions differ from one court to another). But these formal rules operate only as a starting point, to be modified depending on other factors in play. Which of these factors are relevant and what effect do they have?
>
> Although rare, it seems that the presence of certain factors can transform a relationship between judges of two co-ordinate courts into one which is *governed by strict precedent* – a second court will consider the decision of the first court binding, and as such even the ordinary rules allowing departure under some circumstances cannot apply. At the High Court level, this seemingly applies to decisions of Masters (when considering decisions of High Court judge), but even if this is not the case, it certainly applies to decisions of Masters when considering those decisions of High Court Judges which were themselves appeals from Masters. There are also some authorities suggesting that this relationship applies to decisions of single judges on the High Court (when considering decisions of multi-judge panels) although this has been disputed. Finally, there is evidence that

[78] A study of 110 tort cases decided by the House of Lords and Supreme Court between 1990 and 2013 showed that there was reference to common law cases in other countries in two-thirds (66 per cent). Australia (53), the United States (39), Canada (34) and New Zealand (29) dominated. Material from other major common law jurisdictions was rarely used. There were six references to South Africa, five to the Republic of Ireland, two to Hong Kong and a single reference to decisions from India and Singapore. By contrast, there were only 12 cases (11 per cent) in which there was reference to civil law – and in the decisions of very few judges, notably Lords Goff and Bingham. (K Stanton, 'Comparative law in the House of Lords and Supreme Court' 42 *Common Law World Review*, 2013, 269, 286.).

[79] *King's Law Journal* 2023; published online: https://doi.org/10.1080/09615768/2023.2236733.

> this applies to certain decisions by the UKSC [UK Supreme Court], in that a 'regular' panel of five judges will consider itself bound by precedent to follow the decision of an enlarged panel (and as such only a second enlarged panel of the UKSC can depart from an earlier decision decided by an enlarged panel).
>
> There are other circumstances where, should a certain factor be present, a kind of *heightened comity* applies – a second court will treat the decision of the first court with particular respect, beyond that which is required by the ordinary rules applicable to that court, but will not be strictly bound to follow it as a matter of precedent. This applies to decisions of Deputy High Court judges (when considering decisions of 'full' High Court judges), as well as (possibly) decisions of single judges in the High Court (when considering decisions of a panel of judges). More doubtful, but still backed with some evidence, is that this also applies to judges exercising an appellate function on the High Court (when considering decisions of the court in exercise of its first-instance or supervisory jurisdiction). In some cases it may also apply to when it comes to judges considering earlier decisions of judges with expertise and experience in a particular area. There may also be some greater reluctance, across different courts, to depart from a precedent set by judicial leaders (Presidents of a court, the Master of the Rolls, etc.) and, in the Court of Appeal, there is some evidence that enlarged panels may have some greater leeway to depart from decisions compared to regular panels of three. All of these situations may be described as being *governed by heightened comity.*
>
> In most circumstances, however, it was found that the *ordinary rules* will apply: that is, the factor in question does not change the application of the ordinary rules applicable in that court. There is seemingly no evidence, for example, that any great weight is afforded by a second judge to the presence of a judge from a higher court sitting in a case in a lower court, or whether a decision being considered happened to be unanimous or not. Concerning the Court of Appeal, it seems to make no difference whether a decision was handed down by two judges or three judges, nor whether it was handed down by an enlarged panel of five (or more) judges. Similarly, the UKSC seems not to need an enlarged panel in order to depart from its own case law (unless that earlier case law was itself handed down by an enlarged panel of judges) …
>
> For now, however, the position sketched in this article presents a useful picture of how horizontal stare decisis operates in practice. It shows that, when it comes to reviewing and applying earlier decisions of co-ordinate courts, even if the formal rules suggest that all cases should be considered as equals, some cases are more equal than others in practice.

4.1.8. The Effect of the Human Rights Act 1998 on Precedent

The Human Rights Act 1998 (HRA) marked a major and completely novel development in regard to precedent. The Act makes it unlawful for a public authority 'to act in a way which is incompatible with a Convention right' (s 6(1)). The section states that a public authority includes a court or tribunal (s 6(3)). A 'Convention right' under the Act is defined to mean a right set out in the provisions of the European Convention on Human Rights (ECHR) which are stated in Sch 2 to the Act (s 1(1)). A court therefore acts unlawfully if it gives a decision that is inconsistent with the ECHR. Section 2 provides that in determining any question concerning a Convention right a court 'must take into account' the full range of judgments, decisions and opinions of the relevant organs of the ECHR – namely, the European Court of Human Rights, the Commission and the Committee of Ministers. All Strasbourg jurisprudence is thereby available as a source for legal argument by anyone arguing in a United Kingdom court about the meaning or application of the ECHR.

But what is meant by the requirement in s 2 that the United Kingdom courts must take Strasbourg case law into account? Are the Strasbourg decisions binding on UK courts and what are UK courts to do when there is disagreement between a domestic decision by which they would normally be bound and a later decision of the Strasbourg Court?

In June 2009 in *Secretary of State for the Home Department v AF*[80] the House of Lords in a nine-judge decision unanimously held that it was bound to follow the decision of the Grand Chamber of the Strasbourg Court in *A v United Kingdom.*[81] The Strasbourg Court had decided that a person subject to a control order had to be given sufficient information regarding the case against him to enable him to give his lawyers effective instructions. The statements about the binding effect of the Strasbourg Court were strong and clear. Lord Phillips said (at [64]) 'the Human Rights Act requires the courts to act compatibly with Convention rights, in so far as Parliament permits, and to take into account the Strasbourg jurisprudence. That is why the clear terms of the judgment in *A v United Kingdom* resolve the issue raised in these appeals.' Lord Hoffmann said (at [70]) 'I do so with very considerable regret, because I think that the decision of the ECtHR was wrong and that it may well destroy the system of control orders which is a significant part of this country's defences against terrorism. Nevertheless, I think that your Lordships have no choice but to submit.' Lord Rodger said (at [98]), 'Even though we are dealing with rights under a United Kingdom statute, in reality, we have no choice: *Argentoratum locutum, iudicium finitum* – Strasbourg has spoken, the case is closed. Lord Carswell said (at [108]), 'the authority of a considered statement of the Grand Chamber is such that our courts have no option but to accept and apply it.'[82]

But only six months later in *R v Horncastle*[83] the Supreme Court held that it was *not* bound to follow a decision of the Strasbourg Court. In *Al-Khawaja and Tahery v United Kingdom*[84] the Strasbourg Court had held that a defendant could not receive a fair trial if the only or main ('sole or decisive') evidence against him was hearsay evidence. The Court of Appeal, in a five-judge decision, rejected that view, holding that the Criminal Justice Act 2003 provided sufficient safeguards to ensure a fair trial.[85] The United Kingdom applied for the *Al-Khawaja* decision to be referred to the Grand Chamber. The Grand Chamber decided to adjourn the hearing until the Supreme Court had decided the appeal in *Horncastle.* In December 2009, a unanimous seven-judge Supreme Court upheld the Court of Appeal.[86] In a 75-page judgment, Lord Phillips said,

> [T]he requirement to 'take into account' the Strasbourg jurisprudence will normally result in the domestic court applying principles that are clearly established by the Strasbourg court. There will, however, be rare occasions where the domestic court has concerns as to whether a decision of the Strasbourg court sufficiently appreciates or accommodates particular aspects of our domestic process. In such circumstances it is open to the domestic court to decline to follow the Strasbourg decision, giving reasons for adopting this course. This is likely to give the Strasbourg court the opportunity to reconsider the particular aspect of the decision that is in issue, so that there takes place what may prove to be a valuable dialogue between the domestic court and the Strasbourg court. This is such a case. (at [11])

[80] [2009] UKHL28, [2010] 2 AC 269.

[81] (2009) 49 EHRR 625.

[82] In *Cadder v HM Advocate* [2010] UKSC 43, [2010] 1 WLR 2601 the Supreme Court followed the decision of the Grand Chamber of the ECHR in *Salduz v Turkey* (2009) 49 EHRR 19 – which it said (at [48]) had been followed in several other cases and had become firmly established in the Court's jurisprudence. The decision caused a major upheaval in the system in Scotland for giving legal advice to suspects in police stations.

[83] [2009] UKSC 14, [2010] 2 AC 373.

[84] (2009) 49 EHRR 1.

[85] [2009] EWCA Crim 964.

[86] [2009] UKSC 14 [2010] 2 AC 373.

That leaves the English court with a significant measure of freedom to decide whether a decision is binding or not.[87]

The question was how would the Strasbourg Court react? No doubt having in mind the delicate situation, it backed off. It held that the 'sole or decisive' principle was not an inflexible rule. Its admission would therefore not necessarily result in a breach of the Convention.[88] As the commentary in the *Criminal Law Review* put it, 'the sighs of relief in Parliament Square and the Strand when this judgment was handed down can be imagined'.[89] In his concurring opinion, Judge Bratza, the British judge, said that the Grand Chamber had recognised the necessity for dialogue between the Strasbourg Court and national courts. That is exactly what Lord Irvine, the architect of the Human Rights Act, had had in mind. Lord Kingsland moved an amendment during the Committee stage of the Bill in the House of Lords to replace the words 'must take account of' by 'shall be bound by'. Opposing the amendment, Lord Irvine, the Lord Chancellor, said,

> [t]he Bill would of course permit United Kingdom courts to depart from existing Strasbourg decisions and upon occasion it might well be appropriate to do so, and it is possible they might give a successful lead to Strasbourg.[90]

The *Independent Human Rights Act Review* conducted by Sir Peter (former Lord Justice) Gross (October 2021 at p 49), identified three categories of case where the English courts had over the years not followed decisions of the Strasburg Court:[91]

> *Where there is no clear and constant line of ECtHR case law*[92]
>
> UK Courts have decided not to follow the approach of the ECtHR to Convention rights where its approach does not form part of a clear and constant line of ECtHR case law. They have done so, for instance, where there is only one ECtHR decision or there are a limited number of decisions. They have also done so where an ECtHR decision stems from an early period of its development and where a decision was criticised at the time it was made. They have further done so where later cases are inconsistent with a specific decision, or where they have concluded that the ECtHR was likely to depart from its own decision today.

[87] In *Manchester City Council v Pinnock (Secretary of State for Communities and Local Government intervening)* [2011] 2 AC 104 [48] Lord Neuberger said: 'Where, however, there is a clear and constant line of decisions whose effect is not inconsistent with some fundamental substantive or procedural aspect of our law, and whose reasoning does not appear to overlook or misunderstand some argument or point of principle, we consider that it would be wrong for this court not to follow that line.' In *R v Secretary of State for the Home Department, Ex p Anderson* [2002] UKHL, [2003] 1 AC 837 at [18], Lord Bingham said: '[T]he House will not without good reason depart from the principles laid down in a carefully considered judgment of the court sitting as a Grand Chamber. In *R v Abdurahman (Ismail)* [2019] EWCA Crim 2239; 2020 Crim LR (5) 453–58 the Court of Appeal refused to quash a terrorism conviction that had been held unlawful by the Grand Chamber of the ECHR. For the powerfully argued view that it is not open to domestic courts to refuse to follow the Strasbourg Court see C Draghici, 'The Human Rights Act in the shadow of the European Convention: are copyist's errors allowed ?' *European Human Rights Law Review*, 2014, 154.

[88] *Al-Khawaja and Tahery v United Kingdom* [2012] EHRR 23.

[89] *Criminal Law Review*, 2012, 376. However the Strasbourg Court did not accept the reasoning of the Supreme Court's decision. In the later case of *R v Ibrahim(Dahir)* [2012] EWCA Crim 837 the Court of Appeal criticised the Grand Chamber's approach.

[90] HL Deb, 18 November 1997, col 514.

[91] See C Gearty, 'The HRA Comes of Age', 2022 *European Human Rights Law Review* 117–26.

[92] *R (Quila) v Secretary of State for the Home Department* [2011] UKSC 45; [2012] 1 AC 621 at [43]; *R (Chester) v Secretary of State for Justice* (Rev 1) [2013] UKSC 63; [2014] 1 AC 271 at [27]).

Where an ECtHR decision is based on a misunderstanding of UK law[93]

UK Courts have decided not to follow the approach of the ECtHR to Convention rights where its approach has, for instance, failed to understand properly UK domestic criminal procedure or the operation of the law relating to sentencing for criminal offences.

Where there is a fundamental principle of UK law or a failure to properly consider UK law[94]

UK Courts have decided not to follow the approach of the ECtHR to Convention rights where its case law, including that of its Grand Chamber, involves a failure to take proper account of a fundamental principle of UK law or its case law is based on significant oversight.

If there are differences between the Supreme Court and the Strasbourg Court, lower English courts must ordinarily follow the Supreme Court. Lord Bingham, quoting a well-known adage, set out the position in terms to which the other six justices agreed:

> [I]n legal matters, some degree of certainty is at least as valuable a part of justice as perfection. That degree of certainty is best achieved by adhering, even in the Convention context, to our rules of precedent. It will of course be the duty of judges to review Convention arguments addressed to them, and if they consider a binding precedent to be, or possibly to be, inconsistent with Strasbourg authority, they may express their views and give leave to appeal, as the Court of Appeal did here. Leap-frog appeals may be appropriate. In this way, in my opinion, they discharge their duty under the 1998 Act. But they should follow the binding precedent …[95]

Lord Bingham gave a second reason:

> There is a more fundamental reason for adhering to our domestic rule. The effective implementation of the Convention depends on constructive collaboration between the Strasbourg court and the national courts of member states. The Strasbourg court authoritatively expounds the interpretation of the rights embodied in the Convention and its protocols, as it must if the Convention is to be uniformly understood by all member states. But in its decisions on particular cases the Strasbourg court accords a margin of appreciation, often generous, to the decisions of national authorities and attaches much importance to the peculiar facts of the case. Thus it is for national authorities, including national courts particularly, to decide in the first instance how the principles expounded in Strasbourg should be applied in the special context of national legislation, law, practice and social and other conditions. It is by the decisions of national courts that the domestic standard must be initially set, and to those decisions the ordinary rules of precedent should apply. (at [44])

Are there any exceptions? In *R (RJM) v Secretary of State for Work and Pensions (Equality and Human Rights Commissioner intervening)* in the speech of Lord Neuberger of Abbotsbury with whom the other law lords agreed, the House of Lords stated that where the Court of Appeal considers that an earlier decision of the House of Lords, which would

[93] *R v Horncastle* [2009] UKSC 14; [2010] 2 WLR 47, where (as seen above), the court refused to follow a decision of the ECtHR on the basis that it failed to understand domestic criminal process. This decision resulted in the ECtHR altering its approach in *Al-Khawaja v UK* 26766/05 [2011] ECHR 2127, (2012) 54 EHRR 23 and thus also illustrates the importance of judicial dialogue between UK courts and the ECtHR. See also *Attorney-General Ref No. 69 of 2013* [2014] EWCA Crim 188, [2014] 1 WLR 396; *R (Hallam) v Secretary of State for Justice* [2019] UKSC 2; [2020] AC 279.

[94] *R (Chester) v Secretary of State for Justice* (Rev 1) [2013] UKSC 63; [2014] 1 AC 271 at [27]; also see *R (Alconbury Developments Ltd) at [26]; Manchester City Council v Pinnock* [2010] UKSC 45, [2011] 2 AC 104 at [48]. Also see *Ali v Birmingham City Council* [2010] UKSC 8; [2010] 2 AC 39 and *Poshteh v Kensington and Chelsea Royal London Borough Council* [2017] UKSC 36, [2017] AC 624, esp. at [32]–[37].

[95] *Kay and Others and Another (FC) v London Borough of Lambeth and Others and Leeds City Council v Price and Others and Others (FC)* [2006] UKHL 10 [44].

otherwise be binding on the Court of Appeal, may be, or even is clearly, inconsistent with a subsequent decision of the ECtHR, then, *other than in wholly exceptional circumstances*, the Court of Appeal must faithfully follow the decision of the House of Lords.[96] An exception for 'wholly exceptional circumstances' provides some degree of freedom.[97]

Lord Neuberger for his part seemed clear that the courts should not be unduly subservient to Strasbourg. Speaking at a judicial conference in Australia he said:

> [W]e UK judges have, I suspect, sometimes been too ready to assume that a decision, even a single decision of a section of that court, represents the law according to Strasbourg, and accordingly to follow it. That approach is attributable to our common law attitude to precedent and to our relatively recent involvement with Strasbourg. I think we may sometimes have been too ready to treat Strasbourg court decisions as if they were determinations by a UK court whose decisions were binding on us. It is a civilian court under enormous pressure, which sits in chambers far more often than in banc, and whose judgments are often initially prepared by staffers, and who have produced a number of inconsistent decisions over the years. I think that we are beginning to see that the traditional common law approach may not be appropriate, at least to the extent that we should be more ready not to follow Strasbourg chamber decisions.

Not that he welcomed the prospect of many cases in which UK judges disagreed with decisions of the Strasbourg Court.

On the other hand, if a UK judge is considering not following Strasbourg jurisprudence, he or she should bear in mind that one of the purposes of introducing the HRA was to prevent litigants whose human rights were not recognised domestically having to go to Strasbourg to vindicate their rights against the UK government. If UK judges are too ready to depart from Strasbourg, we get back where we were before the HRA came into force.[98]

4.2. A Comparison with Some Other Countries

The English doctrine of precedent is unlike that followed in civil law countries and is not even identical to that operating in other common law jurisdictions. The late Professor Sir Rupert Cross, in his book *Precedent in English Law*, described some of the differences between our system and others. There follow some extracts:

Rupert Cross and JW Harris, *Precedent in English Law*, 4th edn (Clarendon Press, 1991) 10–23

Comparison with France

> Although there are important differences between them, the French legal system may be taken as typical of those of Western Europe for the purposes of the present discussion.

[96] [2009] 1 AC 311 at [64] (emphasis supplied).

[97] Draghici, The Human Rights Act in the shadow of the European Convention' (n 87 above) 167 suggests that requiring a lower court to follow a domestic precedent in conflict with Strasbourg jurisprudence is contrary to HRA 1998, s 6 which makes it unlawful for a court or tribunal to act in a way that is incompatible with a Convention right. For the argument that lower courts should feel freer not to follow precedents that conflict with later decisions of the Strasbourg Court see equally Shaun D Pattinson, 'The Human Rights Act and the Doctrine of Precedent', 35 *Legal Studies*, 2015 (5), 142–64.

[98] Lord Neuberger, 'The role of judges in human rights jurisprudence: a comparison of the Australian and the British experience', 8 August 2014, Conference at the Supreme Court, Melbourne – accessed on www.supremecourt.uk.

From the practical point of view one of the most significant differences between English and French case law lies in the fact that the French judge does not regard himself as absolutely bound by the decision of any court in a single previous instance. He endeavours to ascertain the trend of recent decisions on a particular point. To quote a distinguished French legal writer: 'The practice of the courts does not become a source of law until it is definitely fixed by the repetition of precedents which are in agreement on a single point.'[99]

… Allowance must also be made for the difference in the structure of the judgments of English and French courts and for the vast number of cases decided by the *Cour de Cassation*. A rule that a single precedent should be binding would be unlikely to develop when it was difficult to discover a precise *ratio decidendi* and it is not always easy to extract a precise *ratio* from a French judgment. A rule that one single decision of an appellate court should suffice to constitute a binding precedent is hardly likely to develop in a jurisdiction in which there are numerous appeals. The House of Lords only hears some 30 appeals from the English courts each year, but some 10,000 cases are dealt with annually by the different chambers of the *Cour de Cassation* …

Contrast with the USA

Although the North American practice of giving judgment in the form of elaborate discussions of previous cases is more like the English than the continental, the United States Supreme Court and the appellate courts in the different states do not regard themselves as absolutely bound by their past decisions. There are many instances, some American lawyers would say too many, in which the Supreme Court has overruled a previous decision.

Thanks to the change of practice in the House of Lords, the English rules of precedent may come to approximate more closely to the North American, but two reasons why the North American rules should remain more lax suggest themselves. These are the number of separate State jurisdictions and the comparative frequency with which the North American courts have to deal with momentous constitutional issues.

Numerous jurisdictions

A multiplicity of jurisdictions produces a multiplicity of law reports which has, in its turn, influenced the teaching of law and led to the production of 'restatements' on various topics. The 'case method' of instruction which, in one form or another, prevails in most North American law schools, aims at finding the best solution of a problem on the footing of examples from many jurisdictions, and few schools confine their instruction to the law of any one State. The restatements are concise formulations and illustrations of legal principles based on the case-law of the entire United States and, from time to time, model codes and sets of uniform rules relating to various branches of the law are produced in a form fit for immediate adoption by the legislature. Judges who have been trained by the case method and who are familiar with the restatement and kindred documents will tend to concentrate on recent trends after the fashion of the French courts.

Constitutional issues

When a court is construing a written constitution the terms of that document are the governing factor and the case-law on the meaning of those terms is only a secondary consideration.

[99] R Lambert and MJ Wassernan, 'Case-method in Canada' 39 *Yale Law Journal*, 1929, 1, 14. A helpful account of the operation of precedent in France together with examples of the judgments of French courts was given by FH Lawson, *Negligence in Civil Law* (Clarendon Press, 1950) 231–35. See also O Kahn-Freund, C Lévy and B Rudden, *A source-book of French Law*, 2nd edn (Clarendon Press, 1979) 98–140. In Spain it seems that two decisions of the Supreme Court constitute a 'doctrina' binding on inferior courts, though the Supreme Court may later alter the 'doctrina' (Neville Brown, 'The sources of Spanish law' 5 *International and Comparative Law Quarterly*, 1956, 367).

This point was put very clearly by Frankfurter J. when he was giving judgment in the Supreme Court. He said:

> The ultimate touchstone of constitutionality is the Constitution itself, and not what we do about it.[100]

A further reason why North American courts in general, and the United States' Supreme Court in particular, should not apply our rule of the absolute binding effect of a single decision to constitutional matters is provided by the momentous nature of the issues involved in such cases. To quote Lord Wright:

> It seems clear that, generally speaking, a rigid method of precedent is inappropriate to the construction of a constitution which has to be applied to changing conditions of national life and public policy. An application of words which might be reasonable and just at some time, might be wrong and mischievous at another time.[101]

When the difficulty of amending the Constitution of the United States is borne in mind, it is scarcely surprising that the Supreme Court has become less and less rigorous in its adherence to the principle of *stare decisis.*

Contrast with Scotland

The following remarks made by a Scottish court in 1950 certainly suggest that the Scottish doctrine of precedent is less strict than our own.

> 'If it is manifest that the *ratio decidendi* upon which a previous decision has rested has been superseded and invalidated by subsequent legislation or from other like cause, that *ratio decidendi* ceases to be binding.'[102]

No doubt it would be quite incorrect to represent the English judiciary as a body which pays no attention to the maxim *cessante ratione cessat ipsa lex*, but the House of Lords considers that it should be treated as a ground for creating an exception to a binding rule when that is possible, not as a ground for disregarding it. The maxim also indicates a fact to be taken into account by an English court when deciding whether to overrule a case which it has power to overrule ...[103]

Contrast with Parts of the Commonwealth

The Judicial Committee of the Privy Council used to be the final court of appeal for all Commonwealth countries outside the United Kingdom. The Judicial Committee has never considered itself to be absolutely bound by its own previous decisions on any appeal. The form in which the decisions are expressed is often said to militate against the adoption of a rigid rule of precedent, for the judgment of the Committee consists of advice tendered to the Sovereign together with the reasons upon which such advice is based ...

The Judicial Committee is, however, strongly disposed to adhere to its previous decisions.[104] The decisions of the Privy Council are only of strong persuasive authority in the English courts.

[100] *Graves v New York*, 306 US 466, 491 (1939). The importance of the fact that the United States' Supreme Court is frequently concerned with constitutional problems was stressed by AL Goodhart in 'Case law in England and America' in *Essays in Jurisprudence and the Common Law.* See also AL Goodhart, 'Some American interpretations of law' in his *Modern Theories of Law* (Oxford University Press, 1933) 1.

[101] 'Precedents', 8 *Cambridge Law Journal*, 1944, 118, 135.

[102] *Beith's Trustees v Beith* 1950 SC 66, 70; see also *Douglas-Hamilton v Duke and Duchess of Hamilton's antenuptial marriage contract trustees* 1961 SLT 305, 309.

[103] *Miliangos v George Frank (Textiles) Ltd* [1976] AC 443, 472–76.

[104] *Fatuma Binti Mohamed Bin Salim v Mohamed Bin Salim* [1952] AC 1. But on occasion it will overrule itself. For discussion of three such cases, decided respectively in 2001, 2004 and 2007, see D O'Brien, 'The Privy Council overrules itself – again' *Public Law*, 2008, 28.

The right of appeal to the Privy Council has been abolished in some Commonwealth countries, including Canada, and Australia.[105] In the days when there was still an appeal to the Privy Council, the Supreme Court of Canada regarded itself as bound by its own past decisions although there was a saving clause relating to 'exceptional circumstances'.[106] Since the abolition of the right of appeal to the Privy Council, the Supreme Court of Canada has claimed the power of declining to follow its own past decisions as it is the successor to the final appellate jurisdiction of the Privy Council which is not bound by its own past decisions.[107]

The High Court of Australia has never regarded itself as absolutely bound by its own past decisions.[108] As long ago as 1879 it was said to be of the utmost importance that in all parts of the Empire where English law prevails, the interpretation of that law by the courts should be as nearly as possible the same.[109] It is for this reason that, in the absence of some special local consideration to justify a deviation, the Australian and Canadian courts would be loath to differ from decisions of the House of Lords, but there does not appear to be any question of the decisions of the House being binding in either country. The High Court of Australia in fact stated that a leading decision on the English criminal law (since largely overruled by an English statute) was to be treated as no authority in Australia,[110] and the Judicial Committee of the Privy Council has held in a civil case that the Australian High Court was right not to follow a decision of the House of Lords on exemplary damages.[111]

4.3. The European Court of Justice

The European Court of Justice (ECJ) in Luxembourg is not bound by its own decisions though in practice it tends to follow them:[112]

> It might be said that the general approach of the Court of Justice is not dissimilar to that which, following the 1966 Practice Statement now prevails in the House of Lords. However, that would be to underestimate the influence on the Court's practice of its civil law origins. In the civilian tradition, the judge is merely the mouthpiece of the law: judicial decisions are not a formal source of law and judges do not feel compelled to analyse or reconcile earlier judgments in the manner of the common law judge. Indeed, for many years the Court rarely referred in its judgments to its previous decisions, even when repeating a passage verbatim. Perhaps under the influence of the common law, where it has been acknowledged at least since the time of Dicey that judges do make law, the Court of Justice now deals more fully with previous cases in its judgments. But by

[105] And in 2003, New Zealand The establishment of the Carribean Court of Justice in 2005 has meant the ending of the Judicial Committee's jurisdiction, so far, for Barbados (2005) and Belize (2010). Appeals to the Judicial Committee still lie from some 30 Crown dependencies, commonwealth countries and independent republics. (For the list see the Appendix at the end of the Supreme Court's annual report.) From 1 April 2013 to 31 March 2014 the Judicial Committee heard 51 appeals and gave 32 judgments (*Supreme Court Annual Report 2013–14*, p 35.) The Judicial Committee now sits in the Supreme Court building – see www.supremecourt.uk. For the Judicial Committee's website see www.jcpc.uk (ed).

[106] *Stuart v Bank of Montreal* (1909) 41 SCR 516, 535. See Andrew Joanes '*Stare decisis* in the Supreme Court of Canada' 36 *Canadian Bar Review*, 1958, 174.

[107] *Re Farm Products, Marketing Act* (1957), 7 DLR (2nd) 257, 271.

[108] *A-G for NSW v Perpetual Trustees Co* (1952), 85 CLR 189.

[109] *Trimble v Hill* (1879) 5 App Cas 342, 345.

[110] *Parker v R* [1963] ALR 524.

[111] *Australian Consolidated Press Ltd v Uren* [1967] 3 All ER 523.

[112] Anthony Arnull, 'Interpretation and precedent in European Community Law' in M Andenas and F Jacobs (eds), *European Community Law in the English Courts* (Clarendon Press, 1998) 115, 127–28.

> the standards of English courts the analysis remains superficial and selective. The reader of its judgments will be struck by the fact that previous decisions are frequently only cited by the Court where they support its argument …

In *HAG II*[113] the court for the first time expressly overruled one of its own previous decisions. Again in *Cabanis-Issarte*[114] the court made it clear that an earlier ruling was to be regarded as confined to its own facts and that a series of later cases based on it were no longer good law. The decision 'represented a courageous attempt by the Court to correct what it saw as a wrong turning in its earlier case law'.[115]

4.4. Precedent in Devolution Cases

Under the 1998 devolution legislation for Scotland, Wales and Northern Ireland, the Judicial Committee of the Privy Council was given a new role as the final court of appeal whose decisions would be binding on all courts in the United Kingdom – though not on the Privy Council itself.[116] The Privy Council rather than the House of Lords was made the final court of appeal for devolution issues because it was felt inappropriate that a part of the Westminster Parliament should be the arbiter of devolution matters, including decisions as to the competence of the devolved assemblies.

Under the three devolution Acts the Privy Council could take references on devolution issues arising in the course of litigation, it could hear appeals against determination of a devolution issue from the High Court, the Court of Appeal, the Inner House of the Court of Session in Scotland, or the Court of Appeal in Northern Ireland.[117]

However, the Privy Council's role in UK devolution matters was short-lived. The Constitutional Reform Act 2005 transferred jurisdiction over devolution matters to the Supreme Court.[118] In a challenging article, Gregory Davies of Liverpool University argues that this gave the Supreme Court a crucial role in controlling the development of devolution, a role it had played to the advantage of the central state.[119]

Further reading on precedent

On the history of the doctrine of precedent, see T Ellis Lewis, 'The history of judicial precedent' 46 *Law Quarterly Review*, 1930, 207, 341; vol 47, 1931, 411; vol 48, 1932, 230.

On the differences between common law and civil law techniques of law-making, see: Joseph Dainow, 'The civil and the common law: some points of comparison' 15 *American Journal of Comparative Law*, 1967, 419; Bernard Rudden, 'Courts and codes in England, France and Russia' 48 *Tulane Law Review*, 1973–74, 1010–28; Jean Louis Goutal, 'Characteristics of judicial style in France, Britain and the USA' 24 *American Journal of*

[113] Case C-10/89 *CNL-Sucal v HAG GF* [1990] ECR I3711.
[114] Case C-308/93 [1996] CMLR 729.
[115] Arnull, 'Interpretation and precedent' (n 112 above) 129.
[116] See Scotland Act 1998, s 103; Government of Wales Act 1998, Sch 8, para 32; and Northern Ireland Act 1998, s 82.
[117] Scotland Act, ss 32, 33, 98 and Sch 6; Government of Wales Act 1998, s 109 and Sch 8; Northern Ireland Act 1998, ss 11, 79 and 82 and Sch 10.
[118] Constitutional Reform Act 2005, s 40(4)(b) and Sch 9.
[119] Gregory Davies, 'The UK Supreme Court and devolution: guardians of the passive revolution' *Public Law*, 2025 (1), 58–80.

Comparative Law, 1976, 43; FH Lawson, 'Comparative judicial style' 25 *American Journal of Comparative Law*, 1977, 364; B Markesinis, 'Conceptualism, pragmatism and courage: a common lawyer looks at some judgments of the German Federal Court' 34 *American Journal of Comparative Law*, 1986, 3, 49–67; B Markesinis, 'A matter of style' 110 *Law Quarterly Review*, 1994, 607; K Zweigert and H Kötz, *An Introduction to Comparative Law*, 3rd edn (Oxford University Press, 1998) ch 18.

For an assessment of the role of the Judicial Committee of the Privy Council in common law jurisdictions generally see JW Harris, 'The Privy Council and the common law' 106 *Law Quarterly Review*, 1990, 574.

See generally Neil Duxbury, *The Nature and Authority of Precedent* (Cambridge University Press, 2009).

5

How Precedent Works

Precedents are the raw material from which lawyers and judges in the common law world distil rules of law. Anyone wishing to state the law on a matter not governed by statute – whether they be a judge, a practitioner, an academic or a student – must look at the decided cases. But how do they use the raw material?

The first principle is that anything relevant may be grist to the mill. If there is a clear decision of the House of Lords or Supreme Court which is precisely in point, one need usually search no further. If in that case all the judges agreed that the rule of law is X, then for all practical purposes one may assume that it is X. One may still argue that Y would be a better rule and, if one is advising a client prepared to litigate all the way up to the highest court, one may consider with them the practical prospects of persuading the judges to change the rule. But, subject to that rather remote possibility, lawyers are likely to agree that the rule on that point is X.

At the opposite extreme, search for relevant precedents may reveal nothing more than a decision on the point by a county court judge reported briefly only in the *Solicitors' Journal*, and a remark to the same effect made in the course of giving judgment on a related point in a decision of the High Court of Australia. Anyone wishing to propound the rule in England would be likely to say that there was virtually no authority on the matter. They would cite the county court decision and the remark of the Australian court and would then speculate as to whether the rule on which they appeared to agree would be likely to commend itself to a court somewhat higher in the hierarchy than the county court. Little confidence could be placed in the precedents as giving authoritative guidance as to the prevailing rule, but for what they are worth they are the best available. In other words, even the slenderest of authorities are some evidence of the law.

Usually, the relevant precedents will be a mixed bag of decisions of different levels of court, different degrees of relevance to the facts under consideration, coming from different periods and, quite often, appearing to state conflicting rules. The lawyer's task then is to organise the available material in the most coherent fashion depending on their purpose. A lawyer advising a client will start with the bias that they wish, if possible, to provide advice that the client will find constructive and encouraging. They will therefore seek to marshal the material in such a way as to enable them to tell the client that they can do what they wish to do – subject, however, to the important caveat that they will not want to lose the client through incompetence. The better they are as a lawyer the more likely it is that they will draw the client's attention to the weaknesses and doubts about their analysis of the state of the law.

If they are preparing a legal argument to be presented on behalf of their client in court, they will try to present the precedents in the most attractive form with as few concessions to their opponent as possible. It is a rule of professional conduct that an advocate must cite to a court all the relevant precedents whether they help their client's case or not. But this is also common sense. Far better to draw the court's attention to an awkward precedent and so have the first opportunity of dealing with it oneself – by showing that it can be explained satisfactorily or distinguished – than to have it produced as a trump card by one's opponent.

If the person in question is a scholar writing a book or article they will present their material as objectively as they can. But they too may have a bias in the sense that they favour one approach to the problem under consideration rather than another, and may be seeking to persuade the reader that their approach is justified by the state of the authorities. In the case of the practitioner who is paid to represent the interests of a client, everyone understands and forgives a little stretching of the argument to favour the client's point of view. If the authorities do not quite go all the way for their client, they are permitted to push them to their utmost limits and then a little further in the hope of persuading the court to adopt their argument. Providing the arguments are not far-fetched, the lawyer's reputation will not suffer from such imaginative working of the precedents. The case of the scholar, however, is different. When presenting an analysis of what the law is, they are expected to remain severely within the limits of straightforward analysis. As will be seen, this may still offer a good deal of scope but it will not normally give as much licence for 'interpretation' as is available to the practitioner.

The case of the judge is different again. In a sense their position is somewhere between that of the practitioner and of the scholar. They will normally have heard argument from opposing counsel each seeking to persuade the judge to adopt their view of the precedents and to reject that offered by their learned friend. Having made up their mind as to which argument they prefer they will present it in their judgment as representing the law. They will wish to be 'right' in the sense of not being the subject of a successful appeal by the disappointed loser. Judges, until they become members of the highest court, are accustomed to the, hopefully, minor irritation of being told by a superior court that their view of the law was wrong. It is simply an occupational hazard. (They may still on occasion harbour the distinct feeling that it was the appeal court rather than themselves that got the law wrong but such feelings would be veiled in decent silence. Only Lord Denning permitted himself the luxury of sometimes informing the world that he preferred his own solution to the problem to that offered by his 'superiors' in the House of Lords.) But, however case-hardened or thick-skinned they may be, a judge would normally prefer to be upheld than reversed on appeal and they will therefore have some concern for the likely opinion of other judges when formulating their decision. They will also wish, if possible, to avoid merited criticism from writers in the professional and scholarly journals. The more unpredictable their decision, the more likely that they will be subjected to waspish attack by some academic. Also their sense of the dignity of their office will tend to incline the judge to construct their decision in such a way as to conform with professional expectations.

On the other hand, a judge is not a machine. Some attention will be given later in this book to the vexed question of whether judges do, or should, allow their personal views to obtrude into their decision-making, but it is obvious that where two arguments are presented by the advocates there will usually be enough merit in both to make a decision either way a real possibility. If one side is so weak as to make its success highly improbable, the client will normally accept the advice of their lawyers and withdraw or settle the dispute. Litigated cases, whether they raise issues of law or of fact, can often be decided respectably either way. Much may then depend on the particular way the judge sees the question. Their view of the precedents may be affected by some feeling about the respective merits of the two parties before them or by some sense that the law on the point 'ought to be' X rather than Y. In a marginal case such impressions can have an effect. But such feelings are subject to the discipline of appropriate use of precedent.

This sense of the primacy of the precedents was expressed by Lord Justice Goff (as he then was) in a case concerning the definition of the word 'reckless' in the Criminal Damage Act 1971. The judge said that he agreed with his brother judge most reluctantly:

> GOFF LJ: I agree with the conclusion reached by Glidewell J., but I do so simply because I believe myself constrained to do so by authority. I feel moreover that I would be lacking in candour if I were to conceal my unhappiness about the conclusion which I feel compelled to reach. In my opinion, although of course the courts of this country are bound by the doctrine of precedent, sensibly interpreted, nevertheless it would be irresponsible for judges to act as automatons, rigidly applying authorities without regard to consequences. Where therefore it appears at first sight that authority compels a judge to reach a conclusion which he senses to be unjust or inappropriate, he is, I consider, under a positive duty to examine the relevant authorities with scrupulous care to ascertain whether he can, within the limits imposed by the doctrine of precedent (always sensibly interpreted), legitimately interpret or qualify the principle expressed in the authorities to achieve the result which he perceives to be just or appropriate in the particular case. I do not disguise the fact that I have sought to perform this function in the present case.[1]

In spite of careful and anxious consideration of the precedents, he felt himself unable to reinterpret them, and especially the words of Lord Diplock in *Caldwell* in such a way as to give the result that he favoured. (*Caldwell* was eventually disposed of by the House of Lords in 2003 in *R v G* [2003] UKHL 50.)

The person most likely to bring a dispassionate and 'objective' approach to the process of reading the precedents may be the law student. They have no client; the facts of the problem with which they are dealing are usually stated in so arid a way as to denude it of emotional impact; and they will probably lack the self-confidence to have any strong opinion as to what the law on the point ought to be. They will be likely to come to the question of what the law on that point is with the belief that there is a 'right' answer which they want to discover. The judge, the practitioner and the scholar all know that there are no right answers – there are only better or worse answers, answers that are more or less likely to find acceptance in the courts or in the eyes of the client, the profession or the community. There are answers that will solve the particular problem and stand the test of time, and others that will not. But whatever the particular vantage point or perspective of the person concerned, the raw material with which they are dealing will be the same precedents and the methods they use will be the same professional techniques.

5.1. Professional Techniques for Using Precedents

5.1.1. Ratio, Dictum or Obiter Dictum

The first thing a lawyer wants to know when inspecting a precedent is whether the proposition of law in which they are interested forms the ratio decidendi of the case, or whether it is only something said which is dictum or obiter dictum.

[1] *Elliott v C* [1983] 1 WLR 939, 947–48.

The ratio (in England pronounced rayshio) of a case is its central core of meaning, its sharpest cutting edge. It is the ratio and only the ratio that is capable of being binding. Whether it *is* binding will depend on the position in the hierarchy of the court that decided the case and of the court that is now considering it. Thus, as has been seen, the ratio of a decision of the House of Lords or Supreme Court binds all lower courts; the ratio of a High Court decision binds only the county courts; the ratio of a county court decision binds no one; the ratio of a Court of Appeal case binds the Court of Appeal and all lower courts but does not bind the Supreme Court.

If the proposition of law does not form part of the ratio it is by definition either dictum or obiter dictum. (Dicta or judicial dicta is the term used when they relate to a matter in issue in the case; obiter dicta are dicta that are more peripheral. Obiter dicta is, however, also commonly used to cover both meanings.)

Dicta may be of very great persuasive weight but they cannot under any circumstances be binding on anyone. The most carefully considered and deliberate statement of law by all five Law Lords or Supreme Court Justices which is dictum cannot bind even the lowliest judge in the land. Technically they are free to go their own way. In practice, of course, weighty obiter pronouncements from higher courts are likely to be followed and will certainly be given the greatest attention, but in strictest theory they are not binding. (For an example of a decision of the House of Lords with immense implications for the future of that branch of the law that was almost entirely obiter, see *Hedley Byrne v Heller Bros*, as to which see p 362 below.) This is the reason that technically the Court of Appeal is not bound by statements in the House of Lords or Supreme Court that the Court of Appeal should follow its own decisions. Such a statement cannot form part of the ratio of the House of Lords decision, since a case in the highest court does not require a decision as to the handling of precedents by the Court of Appeal and therefore anything said on the subject is necessarily obiter.[2]

Being bound, therefore, is a function of three different elements – the precedents must have been pronounced by a court that stands in the hierarchy in a position to bind the present court, the proposition of the law must have formed the ratio of that decision and, thirdly, it must be relevant to the facts of the present case. (The issue of relevance is considered below.) An obiter dictum does not qualify, since it fails to meet the second test.

Other things being equal, a statement of law that is the ratio of the case even if it is not binding ranks higher than the same statement of law that is only an obiter dictum. Thus if the Supreme Court, for instance, is evaluating a proposition of law emanating from the Court of Appeal, it will regard it as weightier if it proves to be the ratio of the case than if it turns out to have been said obiter. So the distinction between ratio and obiter dicta is of importance whether or not the case is capable of being binding in the particular situation.

There have been many definitions of the ratio decidendi. My own is – a proposition of law which decides the case, in the light or in the context of the material facts. If there appear to be more than one proposition of law which decides the case, it has more than one ratio and both are binding – see *Jacobs v LCC* [1950] AC 361, 369. Any statement of law, however carefully considered, which was not the basis of the decision is obiter.

[2] For differing views on this issue see PJ Evans, 'The status of rules of precedent' 41 *Cambridge Law Journal*, 1982, 162; L Goldstein, 'Some problems about precedent' 43 *Cambridge Law Journal*, 1984, 88; PJ Evans, 'A brief reply', ibid, 108.

The crucial problem in ascertaining the ratio of a case is usually to determine how widely or narrowly the principle of law should be stated. Another way of putting this is, at what level of abstraction should the facts be stated? The law report will state a mass of facts, some of which will be properly part of the ratio and others of which will be ignored. The judge in the concluding part of their judgment may indicate what they conceive the ratio to be – but normally judges do not do this explicitly. They know that whatever they say, later courts have the right to interpret and re-interpret the ratio of their case. The ratio of each case must take into account the facts of that particular case and then generalise from those facts as far as the statement of the court and the circumstances indicate is desirable.

Thus the case may have concerned an action brought by a blind purchaser of a defective car. The fact that the purchaser was blind would not be part of the ratio of the case unless the fact of blindness was relevant to the rule of law. This would only be the case if the rule formulated by the court depended in some way on the purchaser's capacity to inspect the car visually. The rule might then be different for a purchaser who was blind. But if the defect in the car would have been equally obvious to, or equally hidden from, a sighted and a blind purchaser, then the rule for both situations would be framed without reference to the fact of blindness. Equally, the fact of blindness would not be part of the ratio if the rule were framed without regard to the purchaser's ability or otherwise to inspect the car.

The greater the number of facts in the ratio, the narrower its scope; conversely, the fewer, or the higher the level of abstraction, the broader the reach of the ratio – the more fact situations it covers.

Karl Llewellyn's famous book *The Bramble Bush*, based on lectures first given at Columbia Law School, has a passage which helps to elucidate the meaning of the ratio decidendi:

KN Llewellyn, *The Bramble Bush* (1930; Oceana, 1975) 42, 43

> … 3) The court can decide the particular dispute only according to a general rule which covers a whole class of like disputes. Our legal theory does not admit of single decisions standing on their own … But how wide, or how narrow, is the general rule in this particular case? … That is a troublesome matter. The practice of our case-law, however, is I think fairly stated thus: it pays to be suspicious of general rules which look too wide; it pays to go slow in feeling *certain* that a wide rule has been laid down at all, or that, if seemingly laid down, it will be followed. For there is a fourth accepted canon:
>
> 4) *Everything, everything, everything, big or small, a judge may say in an opinion, is to be read with primary reference to the particular dispute, the particular question before him.* You are not to think that the words mean what they might if they stood alone. You are to have your eye on the case in hand, and to learn how to interpret all that has been said merely as a reason for deciding *that* case *that* way.
>
> … I do believe, gentlemen, that here we have as fine a deposit of slow-growing wisdom as ever has been laid down through the centuries by the unthinking social sea. Here, hardened into institutions, carved out and given line by rationale. What is this wisdom? Look to your own discussion, look to any argument. You know where you would go. You reach, at random if hurried, more carefully if not, for a foundation, for a major premise. But never for itself. Its interest lies in leading to the conclusion you are headed for. You shape its words, its content, to an end decreed. More, with your mind upon your object you use words, you bring in illustrations, you deploy and advance and concentrate again. When you have done, you have said much you did not mean. You did not mean, that is, *except* in reference to your point. You have brought generalisation after generalisation up, and discharged it at your goal; all, in the heat of argument, were over-stated. None would you stand to, if your opponent should urge them to *another* issue.

So with the judge. Nay, more so with the judge. He is not merely human, as are you. He is, as well, a lawyer; which you, yet, are not. A lawyer, and as such skilled in manipulating the resources of persuasion at his hand. A lawyer, and as such prone without thought to twist analogies, and rules, and instances, to his conclusion. A lawyer, and as such peculiarly prone to disregard the implications which do not bear directly on his case.

More, as a practiced campaigner in the art of exposition, he has learned that one must prepare the way for argument. You set the mood, the tone, you lay the intellectual foundation – all with the case in mind, with the conclusion – all, because those who hear you also have the case in mind, without the niggling criticism which may later follow. You wind up, as a baseball pitcher will wind up – and as in the pitcher's case, the wind-up often is superfluous. As in the pitcher's case, it has been known to be intentionally misleading.

With this it should be clear, then, why our canons thunder. Why we create a class of dicta, of unnecessary words, which later readers, their minds now on quite other cases, can mark off as not quite essential to the argument. Why we create a class of *obiter dicta*, the wilder failings of the pitcher's arms, the wilder motions of his gum-ruminant jaws. Why we set about, as our job, to crack the kernel from the nut, to find the true rule the case in fact decides: the *rule of the case*.

Now for a while I am going to risk confusion for the sake of talking simply. I am going to treat as the rule of the case the *ratio decidendi*, the rule *the court tells you* is the rule of the case, the ground, as the phrase goes, upon which the court itself has rested its decision. For there is where you must begin, and such refinements as are needed may come after.

The court, I will assume, has talked for five pages, only one of which portrayed the facts assumed. The rest has been discussion. And judgment has been given for the party who won below: judgment affirmed. We seek the rule …

Perhaps in this, as in judging how far to trust a broadly stated rule, we may find guidance in the facts the court assumes. Surely this much is certain: the actual dispute before the court is limited as straitly by the facts as by the form which the procedural issue has assumed. What is not in the facts cannot be present for decision. Rules which proceed an inch beyond the facts must be suspect.

But how far does that help us out? What are *the* facts? The plaintiff's name is Atkinson and the defendant's Walpole. The defendant, despite his name, is an Italian by extraction, but the plaintiff's ancestors came over with the Pilgrims. The defendant has a schnauzer-dog named Walter, red hair, and $30,000 worth of life insurance. All these are facts. The case, however, does not deal with life insurance. It is about an auto accident. The defendant's auto was a Buick painted pale magenta. He is married. His wife was in the backseat, an irritable, some what faded blonde. She was attempting backseat driving when the accident occurred. He had turned around to make objection. In the process the car swerved and hit the plaintiff. The sun was shining; there was a rather lovely dappled sky low to the West. The time was late October on a Tuesday. The road was smooth, concrete. It had been put in by the McCarthy Road Works Company. How many of these facts are important to the decision? How many of these facts are, as we say, legally relevant? Is it relevant that the road was in the country or the city; that it was concrete or tarmac or of dirt; that it was a private or a public way? Is it relevant that the defendant was driving a Buick, or a motor car, or a vehicle? Is it important that he looked around as the car swerved? Is it crucial? Would it have been the same if he had been drunk, or had swerved for fun, to see how close he could run by the plaintiff, but had missed his guess?

Is it not obvious that as soon as you pick up this statement of the facts to find its legal bearings you must discard some as of no interest whatsoever, discard others as dramatic but as legal nothings? and is it not clear, further, that when you pick up the facts which are left and which do seem relevant, you suddenly cease to deal with them in the concrete and deal with them instead in *categories* which you, for one reason or another, deem significant? It is not the road between Pottsville and Arlington; it is 'a highway'. It is not a particular pale magenta Buick eight, by number 732507, but 'a motor car', and perhaps even 'a vehicle'. It is not a turning around to look at Adorée Walpole, but a lapse from the supposedly proper procedure of careful drivers, with which you are concerned. Each concrete fact of the case arranges itself, I say, as the *representative* of a much wider abstract *category* of facts, and it is not in itself but as a member of the category that you attribute significance to it. But what is to tell you whether to make your category 'Buicks' or 'motor cars' or 'vehicles'? What is to tell you to make your category 'road' or 'public highway'? The court may tell you. But the precise point that you have up for study is how far it is safe to trust what the court says. The precise issue which you are attempting to solve is whether the court's language can be taken as it stands, or must be amplified, or must be whittled down.

This brings us at last to the case system. For the truth of the matter is a truth so obvious and trite that it is somewhat regularly overlooked by students. *That no case can have a meaning by itself!* Standing alone it gives you no guidance. It can give you no guidance as to how far it carries, as to how much of its language will hold water later. What counts, what gives you leads, what gives you sureness, *that is the background of the other cases* in relation to which you must read the one. They colour the language, the technical terms used in the opinion. But above all they give you the wherewithal to find which of the facts are significant, and in what aspect they are significant, and how far the rules laid down are to be trusted.

Here, I say, is the foundation of the case system. For what, in a case class, do we do? We have set before you, at either the editor's selection or our own, a *series* of opinions which in some manner are related. They may or may not be exactly alike in their outcome. They are always supposedly somewhat similar on their legally relevant facts. Indeed, it is *the aspects in which their facts are similar* which give you your first guidance as to what *classes* of fact will be found legally relevant, that is, will be found *to operate* alike, or to operate *at all*, upon the court. On the other hand, the states of fact are rarely, if ever, quite alike. And one of the most striking problems before you is: when you find two cases side by side which show a difference in result, then to determine *what* difference in their facts, or *what* difference in the procedural set-up, has produced that difference in result.

This, then, is the case system game, the game of matching cases. We proceed by a rough application of the logical method of comparison and difference.

And here there are three things that need saying. The first is that by this matching of facts and issues in the different cases we get, to come back to where we started, some indication of when the court in a given case has over-generalised; of when, on the other hand, it has meant all the ratio decidendi that it said. 'The Supreme Court of the United States,' remarks the sage Professor T. R. Powell, 'are by no means such fools as they talk, or as the people are who think them so.' We go into the matter expecting a certain amount of inconsistency in the broader language of the cases. We go into the matter set in advance to find distinctions by means of which we can reconcile and harmonise the outcomes of the cases, even though the rules that the courts seem to lay down in their deciding may be inconsistent. We are prepared to whittle down the categories of the facts, to limit the rule of one case to its new whittled narrow category, to limit the rule of the other to its new other narrow category – and thus to make two cases stand together. The first case involves a man who makes an offer and gets in his revocation before his offer is accepted. The court decides that he cannot be sued upon his promise, and says that no contract can be made unless the minds of both parties are at one at once. The second case involves a man who has made a similar offer and has mailed a revocation, but to whom a letter of acceptance has been sent before his revocation was received. The court holds that he can be sued upon his promise, and says that his offer was being repeated every moment from the time that it arrived until the letter of acceptance was duly mailed. Here are two rules which are a little difficult to put together, and to square with sense, and which are, too, a little hard to square with the two holdings in the cases. We set to work to seek a way out which will do justice to the holdings. We arrive perhaps at this, that it is not necessary for the two minds to be at one at once, if the person who has received an offer thinks, and thinks reasonably, as he takes the last step of acceptance, that the offeror is standing by the offer. And to test the rule laid down in either case, as also to test our tentative formulation which we have built to cover both, we do two things. First and easiest is to play variations on the facts, making the case gradually more and more extreme until we find the place beyond which it does not seem sense to go.

Suppose, for example, our man does think the offeror still stands to his offer, and thinks it reasonably, on all his information; but yet a revocation has arrived, which his own clerk has failed to bring to his attention? We may find the stopping-place much sooner than we had expected, and thus be forced to recast and narrow the generalisation we have made, or to recast it even on wholly different lines. The second and more difficult way of testing is to go to the books and find further cases in which variations on the facts occur, and in which the importance of such variations has been put to the proof. The first way is the intuitional correction of hypothesis; the second way is the experimental test of whether an hypothesis is sound. Both are needed. The first to save time. The second, to make sure … Not the least important feature in the cases you are comparing will be their dates. For you must assume that the law, like any other human institution, has undergone, still undergoes development, clarification, change, as time goes on, as experience accumulates, as conditions vary. The earlier cases in a series, therefore, while they *may* stand unchanged today, are yet more likely to be forerunners, to be indications of the first gropings with a problem, rather than to present its final solution even in the state from which they come. That holds particularly for cases prior to 1800. It holds in many fields of law for cases of much more recent date. But in any event you will be concerned to place the case in time as well as in space, if putting it together with the others makes for difficulty.

The third thing that needs saying as you set to matching cases is that on your materials, often indeed on all the materials that there are, a perfect working out of comparison and difference cannot be had. In the first case you have facts *a* and *b* and *c*, procedural set-up *m*, and outcome *x*. In the second case you have, *if* you are lucky, procedural set-up *m* again, but this time with facts *a* and *b* and *d*, and outcome *y*. How, now, are you to know with any certainty whether the changed result is due in the second instance to the absence of fact *c* or to the presence of the new fact *d*? The court may tell you. But I repeat: your object is to *test* the telling of the court. You turn to your third case. Here once more is the outcome *x*, and the facts are *b* and *c* and *e*, but fact *a* is missing, and the procedural set-up this time is not *m* but *n*. This strengthens somewhat your suspicion that fact *c* is the lad who works the changed result. But an experimentum crucis still is lacking. Cases in life are not made to our hand. A scientific *approach* to prediction we may have, and we may use it as far as our materials will permit. An exact science *in result* we have not now. Carry this in your minds: a scientific approach, no more. Onto the green, with luck, your science takes you. But when it comes to putting you will work by art and hunch …

But if you arrive at the conclusion that a given court did not mean all it said in the express ratio decidendi it laid down, that the case must really be confined to facts narrower than the court itself assumed to be its measure, then you are ready for the distinction that I hinted at earlier in this lecture, the distinction between the ratio decidendi, the court's own version of the rule of the case, and the *true* rule of the case, to wit, what *it will be made to stand for by another later court*. For one of the vital elements of our doctrine of precedent is this: that any later court can always re-examine a prior case, and under the principle that the court could decide only what was before it, and that the older case must now be read with that in view, can arrive at the conclusion that the dispute before the earlier court was much narrower than that court thought it was, called therefore for the application of a much narrower rule. Indeed, the argument goes further. It goes on to state that no broader rule *could* have been laid down ex-cathedra, because to do that would have transcended the powers of the earlier court.

You have seen further that out of the matching of a number of related cases it is your job to formulate a rule that covers them all in harmony, if that can be done, and to test your formulation against possible variants on the facts. Finally, to test it, if there is time, against what writers on the subject have to say, and against other cases.

The ratio is therefore something that can be ascertained tentatively as soon as the case has been decided. The law reporter in preparing his account of the case will attempt a formulation of the ratio which he will state in his headnote. He will base this partly on the facts of the case, partly on what the judge has said in his judgment and partly on his sense of the proper limits of the doctrine formulated in the case. Thereafter the ratio may be widened in later cases (by reducing the facts stated in it thus raising the level of abstraction), or, conversely, it may be narrowed by the opposite process. The ratio is therefore not fixed but a formula that is capable of adjustment according to the force of later developments.

The process has been described in another classic American book:

Benjamin N Cardozo, *The Nature of the Judicial Process* (Yale University Press, 1921) 48–50

[48] The implications of a decision may in the beginning be equivocal. New cases by commentary and exposition extract the essence. At last there emerges a rule or principle which becomes a datum, a point of departure, from which new lines will be run, from which new courses will be measured. [49] Sometimes the rule or principle is found to have been formulated too narrowly or too broadly and has to be reframed. Sometimes it is accepted as a postulate of later reasoning, its origins are forgotten, it becomes a new stock of descent, its issue unite with other strains, and persisting, permeate the law. You may call the process one of analogy or of logic or philosophy as you please. Its essence in any event is the derivation of a consequence from a rule or principle or a precedent which, accepted as a datum, contains implicitly within itself the germ of the conclusion. In all this, I do not use the word philosophy in any strict or formal sense. The method tapers down from the syllogism at one end to mere analogy at the other. Sometimes the extension of a precedent goes to the limit of its logic. Sometimes it does not go so far. Sometimes by a process of analogy it is carried even farther. That is a tool which no system of jurisprudence has been able to discard. A rule which has worked well in one field, or which, in any event, is there whether its workings have been revealed or not, is carried over into another. Instances of such a process I group [50] under the same heading as those where the nexus of logic is closer and more binding. At bottom and in their underlying motives, they are phases of the same method. They are inspired by the same yearning for consistency, for certainty, for uniformity of plan and structure. They have their roots in the constant striving of the mind for larger and more inclusive unity, in which differences will be reconciled, and abnormalities will vanish.

It is of course desirable that there should always be a ratio. Giving a lecture on the Rule of Law, Lord Bingham said:

[W]hatever the diversity of opinion, the Judges should recognise a duty, not always observed, to try to ensure that there is a clear majority ratio. 'Without that, no one can know what the law is.'[3]

But, as Lord Bingham allowed, it does not always happen – a point made by Lord Justice Jacob giving the Court of Appeal's judgment in *Activas UK Ltd v Merck & Co Inc* [2008] EWCA Civ 444, [2009] 1 WLR 1186:

79 Moreover there are cases where there is simply no *ratio*. It is wrong to assume that every decision must have a *ratio* if only it can be found. A clear example of a no- *ratio* decision would be where three judges in the Court of Appeal each reached the same ultimate conclusion for

[3] Lord Bingham, 'The rule of law' 66 *Cambridge Law Review*, 2007, 67, 71.

> different reasons, and, *a fortiori*, if they are inconsistent reasons.[4] In such cases there is simply no *ratio* which can be followed.
>
> 80 As for an individual judgment, although we suppose every judge who writes his or her own decision tries to articulate a *ratio* it would be an article of faith and contrary to reality to say that every judge has succeeded or that a *ratio* (or *rationes*) can readily be distilled from every judgment.
>
> For an example see Aaron Taylor, 'In search of the ratio decidendi' 2019 *Law Quarterly Review*, 135, 556–61.

5.1.2. Is the Precedent Distinguishable?

Having assigned the statement of law to one or other of the two categories of ratio or dictum, the lawyer will wish to determine its relevance to the facts in issue. If one side can marshal a precedent that is binding and in point, that will conclude the debate. The only way for the opponent to avoid losing the case is by showing that the case is *distinguishable*. The process of distinguishing is important, however, not simply as the only means of avoiding a precedent that if applicable would be binding, but equally as a means of avoiding one that is merely of persuasive authority. Very commonly the lawyers on one side of an argument will produce one or more precedents that they claim are in point and which their opponents claim are distinguishable, whilst in turn their opponents rely on a different line of authorities which the first side maintain have no relevance. Distinguishing between factual situations and applying the appropriate rule of law is one of the lawyer's and judge's most crucial functions. It is the business of drawing lines, or seeing how far to take a particular rule and of expanding or contracting the scope of rules to meet new circumstances. The question is always the same – are there any material differences between the facts of the present case and the facts of the precedents to warrant the rule being different?

Sometimes the court distinguishes the indistinguishable – as the only way to escape from the clutches of an unwelcome precedent which would otherwise be binding. This process brings the law into disrepute, for it abuses the integrity of the process and cheapens the intellectual tools of the trade. This cannot be said, however, of the two Divisional Court decisions that follow because, although they give opposite answers to virtually identical facts, they were decided by the same three judges (Brabin and Ashworth JJ and Lord Parker CJ) on the same day. Brabin J gave the judgment of the court in both cases.

Whitton v Garner [1965] 1 WLR 313 (Divisional Court, QBD)

> BRABIN J: This is an appeal by way of Case Stated from a decision by the justices for the county of Lancaster sitting at Bolton. They heard a summons under the Affiliation Proceedings Act, 1957, by the respondent, who maintained that the appellant was the putative father of her child. The respondent is, and at all material times was, a married woman, and the point that arises is whether a married woman can be a single woman within the meaning of s. 1 of the Affiliation Proceedings Act, 1957 [which provided for claims for maintenance to be made by a single woman against the putative father of her child]. That is a matter which has been decided many times in

[4] This happened in the House of Lords decision in *R (on the application of Bapio Action Ltd) v Secretary of State for the Home Department* [2008] UKHL 27. Two of the Law Lords decided the case on the ground that guidance given by the Secretary of State was not in accordance with the relevant law. Another two gave as their ground the fact that relevant persons had been deprived by the guidance, of a legitimate expectation. The fifth dissented.

the affirmative. In this particular case, at the time when the summons was taken out the respondent was living in the same house as her husband. She gave evidence before the justices, and the justices found as a fact on that evidence, that for four years she had occupied a separate bedroom in the house in which both parties lived and that she and her husband had lived separate and apart during the whole of that time. The respondent gave further evidence, and a finding of fact was made by the justices in respect of it, that the child had been registered by the respondent's husband as his child, but that such registration was made without the respondent's consent, approval or knowledge.

It is submitted on behalf of the appellant that the justices could not come to the finding that the respondent was a single woman within the meaning of s. 1, because she and her husband were both living in the same house. It is urged further that there is a rule of law that the magistrates cannot, in such circumstances, act on the evidence of the respondent complainant unless that part of her evidence is corroborated. I know of no such rule of law. The rule of law in respect of corroboration is by statute laid down in s. 4(2) of the Act of 1957. There is no rule of law specifically relating to s. 1 of the Act. Clearly, when a husband and wife are living in the same house, it is much more difficult for a wife in those circumstances to establish that she is a single woman within the meaning of s. 1 of the Act of 1957. This matter was dealt with by this court in *Watson* v. *Tuckwell* (1947) 63 T.L.R. at p. 635, when Lord Goddard C. J. said:

> I agree that if a husband and wife are found living under the same roof, it is prima facie evidence that the parties are living together; but it is no more than prima facie evidence. It is evidence that can be rebutted, and if the justices are satisfied that it has been rebutted they are justified in finding that there was a de facto separation. It is clearly a question of fact, and, in my opinion, there is evidence upon which they could find that fact.

Applying that direction to this particular appeal, the evidence of the respondent that she lived separate and apart from her husband over this period of four years and that, during that time, there had been no access to her by her husband, was evidence which the justices could accept or reject. The justices accepted that evidence, and it appears from the Case Stated that, on these material matters in the respondent's evidence, no cross-examination was addressed to the respondent in respect of them. The prima facie presumption that exists when husband and wife are living in the same house was rebutted in this case to the satisfaction of the justices and, in my judgment, the justices were right in holding that, on the evidence called before them, the respondent was a single woman within the meaning of s. 1 of the Act of 1957. I, therefore, consider that this appeal should be dismissed.

Giltrow v Day [1965] 1 WLR 317 (Divisional Court, QBD)

CASE STATED.

This was a Case Stated by justices of the county of Middlesex Quarter Sessions in respect of their adjudication on an appeal sitting at The Guildhall, Westminster, London, on 20 March 1964. On that day the respondent, Ivor Day, appeared before the justices of the county of Middlesex Quarter Sessions as appellant against an order made by the magistrates' court sitting at Ealing on 6 February 1964, whereby the respondent was adjudged to be the putative father of a male child born to the appellant, Maureen Margaret Giltrow, on 8 May 1963, and the magistrates' court ordered that he pay to the appellant the weekly sum of £1 5s. towards the maintenance of the child until he reached the age of sixteen years. The general grounds of the appeal were stated to be that the order was made against the weight of evidence in that the respondent, on the evidence, could not have been held to be the putative father of the child, and that the order was wrong in law in that the appellant was not a single woman within the meaning of the Affiliation Proceedings Act, 1957. At the hearing of the appeal the first ground was not proceeded with, and the appeal was heard only on the preliminary issue of law before the justices, who allowed the appeal.

BRABIN J: The justices who heard this appeal have carefully set out the facts as they find them in the case as stated. It is quite clear from their findings that the appellant and her husband had ceased to have sexual intercourse together or to occupy the same bedroom since August, 1961, and that, from that date, the appellant had not visited her husband's bedroom. The husband and wife lived together in a flat, and the flat was occupied by reason of an arrangement by which the appellant supplied services in respect of, no doubt, the main building. There were two children of the marriage, one who slept with the father and one who slept with the mother, and, when the mother became pregnant, the child who slept with her then moved into the husband's bedroom. The finances of the household were provided by the husband, as they had always been, and the appellant bought the food and cooked the meal which the husband ate daily in the house. The husband always prepared his own breakfast, and his mid-day meal was eaten away from home. These arrangements existed before, and were continued after, the parties occupied separate bedrooms. There is no doubt that the appellant and her husband were not living in amity; they each went their separate ways. The one manifestation of that after August, 1961, when the marriage in the normal circumstances might be said to have broken down, was that the appellant ceased to do the mending of the husband's clothes or to clean his bedroom, but a cleaner was provided who did the latter. There was further evidence as found by the justices that, on one occasion and one only at Christmas, 1963, when the appellant was entertaining some friends, the husband unexpectedly insinuated himself into the party and dispensed the drinks. This method of living, which continued after August, 1961, was found to have so continued because both parties acquiesced in it … On the facts found by the justices, I consider that the justices hearing the appeal were wholly justified in finding that the presumption existing in these circumstances [that a husband and wife living under the same roof are living together] was not rebutted, and that, therefore, the appellant was not a single woman within the meaning of the Affiliation Proceedings Act, 1957.

What appear to have been the critical differences between this and the previous case that explain the different result arrived at?

5.1.3. What Weight should be Given to the Precedent?

Having determined the status of the precedent as ratio or dictum and whether, and if so to what extent, it is in point, the lawyer will now wish to scrutinise the precedent minutely for its true worth. The process is similar to that of assaying precious metals. They will take into account a number of different considerations:

Which court decided the case?

Other things being equal, the higher the court in the hierarchy the greater its authority.

Which judges were involved?

There are judges who are regarded as being of special eminence – Lord Atkin, Lord Justice Scrutton, Lord Reid, Lord Bingham are examples. Apart from such luminaries, counsel is usually wise to avoid making invidious distinctions between the reputations of individual judges.

A recent new practice is that an appeal may be heard by a court consisting of the three heads of division – the Master of the Rolls, the Lord Chief Justice and the Vice Chancellor.[5] Such decisions are likely to be regarded as carrying additional weight.

[5] *Locabail Ltd v Bayfield Properties* [2000] QB 451 on what bias is sufficient to disqualify a judge was an example of this development.

Although, as has been seen, the number of judges involved in a decision supposedly does not affect its authority it is difficult to believe that judges do not treat with even greater respect decisions given by a larger than usual number of judges. When a specially large panel is assembled to hear an important issue it is obvious that the decision is being invested with more weight than it would otherwise have. As has been seen above, this has been acknowledged in respect of the Court of Appeal, Criminal Division and it surely applies to the Civil Division and to the highest court as well.

Was there a dissent?

The existence of any dissenting opinions would affect the weight of a decision, especially if the dissenting judge was thought of as being of particular eminence, such, for instance, as Lord Reid or Lord Bingham. A dissent, it has been said, is 'an appeal to the brooding spirit of the law, to the intelligence of another day'.[6] Dissents do not occur in the Court of Appeal, Criminal Division nor traditionally did they occur in the Judicial Committee of the Privy Council. In the case of the former the reason was the importance attached to clarity in criminal cases; in the case of the latter the reason was that technically the Judicial Committee is giving advice to the monarch and it is inappropriate that advice be proferred subject to dissent. In 1996 an Order in Council for the first time recognised the possibility of a dissent in the Judicial Committee.[7] Dissents in devolution cases heard by the Judicial Committee however were quite frequent.[8] (On dissents see further pp 278–79 and pp 400–01 below.)

When was the case decided?

If the precedent is old, one side will argue that it reflects well-settled law, whilst the other will contend that it is no longer apt for modern conditions. Something may then turn on whether or not it has been challenged in previous cases. Every time that a precedent is put to the test of argument and emerges unscathed it develops new roots and accordingly, to that extent, becomes harder to dislodge. If, on the other hand, it has stood unchallenged, one side will suggest that this shows that its roots are shallow and flimsy whilst the other will argue that the fact of no challenge over a long period demonstrates the strength of the rule – it was so clear and so deeply rooted that no one even thought to contest the point.[9]

How does the precedent fit with the surrounding law?

Sometimes it can be argued that the precedent is based on faulty reasoning, or illogically drawn analogies, or that it is at odds with other, better established principles.

How has the decision been dealt with in later cases?

There are various possibilities:

(a) It may have been *overruled* by the decision of a higher court that it was wrongly decided. Overruling can be explicit or implicit. The former is clear and has the effect of removing the precedent entirely from the field of play – subject only to the possibility of it being brought back into play if a still higher court decides that it was, after all, rightly decided. Implied overruling occurs where it is arguable that the decision cannot stand with a later decision of a higher court. But this contention often meets determined counter-argument.

[6] CE Hughes, *The Supreme Court of the United States* (Columbia University Press, 1928) 68.

[7] Judicial Committee (Dissenting Opinions) Order 1996. The Order did not permit assenting judgments.

[8] For discussion of this development see R Munday, 'Judicial configurations' 61 *Cambridge Law Journal,* 2002, 612, 619, 622–26.

[9] For discussion of relevant authorities see 'The aged precedent' *Scots Law Times Reports*, 1965, 53.

(b) The precedent, whilst not being overruled, may nevertheless have been undermined either by direct aspersions cast upon it by judges in later cases or because it was not applied to factual situations that appeared to be well within the scope of the principle for which it stands (not following or restrictive distinguishing).
(c) On the other hand, it may have been approved and followed in later cases and expanded by being applied to new factual situations not apparently within the contemplation or the scope of the principle as first framed.

What reputation does the precedent enjoy generally?

Any published comment on the case or the principle of law for which it stands could be significant in either strengthening or weakening its authority. The case may have been the subject of discussion in scholarly writings. It may have given rise to problems in the community of which the courts could be made aware. Suggestions may have been made for the reform of the rule by law-reform bodies. Any such indications may create a climate of opinion about a precedent which can be turned to advantage by one or other side in litigation.

An academic study attempted to assess the influences that are likely to weigh most heavily with the judges in the House of Lords. Interviews with the Law Lords themselves suggested that the source of critical evaluations which were most influential were the views of other Law Lords, very much more than either those of academic writers or those expressed by counsel.[10]

5.1.4. Inconvenience and Injustice

Counsel arguing a case are permitted to assert that a precedent has had unhappy consequences or, alternatively, that such consequences would ensue if the court adopted the rule proposed by the opponent. But counsel is not permitted to call evidence in the form of witnesses as to the predictable consequences of any existing or proposed formulation of law. The only exception to the rule that the courts will not receive evidence as to what the law is, is foreign law. Expert witnesses, normally practitioners in the foreign system, are permitted to testify on oath as to the prevailing state of the law on the matter in contention in the foreign country concerned. Foreign law, therefore, is treated as a matter of fact to be proved by evidence. English law by contrast is something of which the court takes judicial notice.

5.1.5. The 'Brandeis Brief'

What, however, of evidence in the form of citation of non-legal material with arguably relevant information about the present or likely future effects of rules of law? This technique of argument is often referred to as a 'Brandeis brief' – after the later US Supreme Court Justice, Louis Brandeis, who first introduced it as an advocate in the case of *Muller v Oregon* in 1908. The circumstances were described by his biographer:

[10] Alan Paterson, *The Law Lords* (Macmillan, 1982) 33.

Alpheus Thomas Mason, *Brandeis* (Viking Press, 1956) 248–51

> … in 1907, Mrs Florence Kelly and Miss Josephine Goldmark learned that the Oregon ten-hour law for women was to be contested before the United States Supreme Court. To defend the law, these women wanted the most competent legal talent in the land … The next day they asked Brandeis, who accepted at once …
>
> The invitation was gladly extended. Brandeis then outlined the material needed for his brief. The legal part he would himself cover in a few pages. For the economic and social data showing the evil of long hours and the possible benefits from legislative limitation, he would look to his sister-in-law. It was on these materials, not on the legal argument, that he would base his case.
>
> This was a bold innovation … Many years earlier he had recorded in his *Index Rerum*: 'A judge is presumed to know the elements of law, but there is no presumption that he knows the facts.' In this spirit he drew up his revolutionary social and economic brief …
>
> Brandeis's brief-making enormously extended the bounds of common knowledge and compelled the court to 'take judicial notice' of this extension. In the *Muller* brief only two scant pages were given to conventional legal arguments. Over one hundred pages were devoted to the new kind of evidence drawn from hundreds of reports, both domestic and foreign, of committees, statistical bureaux, commissioners of hygiene, and factory inspectors – all proving that, long hours are *as a matter of fact* dangerous to women's health, safety and morals, that short hours result in social and economic benefits.
>
> Brandeis appeared in oral argument in January 1908, before a court dominated by superannuated legalists, including Chief Justice Fuller, Justices Peckham, Brewer, and Day. The 'dry bones of legalism rattled' as opposing counsel argued that women were endowed, equally with men, with the fundamental right of free contract, that woman's 'freedom' to bargain with employers must not be impaired. This time, however, the court could not be screened from all knowledge of the living world …
>
> The Oregon ten-hour law was upheld, and the court, speaking through Justice Brewer, approved Brandeis's technique and, most unusually, mentioned him by name. The court's spokesman, Justice Brewer, said:
>
> > 'In the brief filed by Mr Louis D. Brandeis … is a very copious collection of all these matters …
> >
> > 'The legislation and opinions referred to in the margin may not be, technically speaking, authorities, and in them is little or no discussion of the constitutional question presented to us for determination, yet they are significant of a widespread belief that woman's physical structure, and the functions she performs in consequence thereof, justify special legislation restricting or qualifying the conditions under which she should be permitted to toil.
>
> Here for the first time the Supreme Court was recognising the need for facts to establish the reasonableness or unreasonableness of social legislation. For the time being the court had rejected its own freedom-of-contract fiction as regards working women. Brandeis followed up this advantage immediately. After the Muller case he appeared for oral argument in defence of other labour laws and sent briefs to some fourteen different courts.

This form of argument used to be very uncommon in English courts. A rare early example was *Nowotnik v Nowotnik* [1967] P 83. The Court of Appeal had given an extremely narrow interpretation to a provision in the Legal Aid Act 1964 designed to compensate the successful defendant who had the misfortune to be sued by a legally aided plaintiff. The section provided that such a person could ask to have their costs paid out of the legal aid fund if they could show that they would otherwise suffer 'severe financial hardship'. N, the husband, was the successful respondent in divorce proceedings. He claimed under the Act. His costs had been £345. His capital was £5 17s 9d; he earned £24 a week as a manual labourer; he had a car and had had two holidays in Germany. The court

(Lord Denning and four other Lords Justices) held that there was insufficient evidence of severe financial hardship. The husband's capital admittedly was very low but he had not had to restrict his activities. They rejected his claim. Three years later precisely the same issue came up in *Hanning v Maitland (No 2)* [1970] 1 QB 580. The successful defendant there had an earned income of £18 or £19 gross, and savings of between £2,500 and £3,000. The costs he was claiming from the fund were £325. Lord Denning, delivering judgment as he had in *Nowotnik*, said that the court had been given some figures by counsel for the Law Society who appeared as *amicus curiae* (friend of the court – see 7.8 below). These showed the sums set aside each year in the legal aid accounts, for payments expected to be made out of the fund under the 1964 Act. In the first three years the Law Society had estimated the expected payments and the government had paid into the fund the sum of £40,000 a year against this liability. The payments out in the three years were respectively, £74, £838 and £24. (*Nowotnik* was decided in the middle of the second year.) Lord Denning (at 587) said: 'Those figures show one of two things: either that the Act itself was badly worded so that it did not give effect to the intention of the makers of it; or the courts have interpreted it wrongly so as to defeat the intention of Parliament. I am afraid that it is the second. We can and should learn by experience. In the light of it, I must confess that this court in *Nowotnik v Nowotnik* interpreted the Act wrongly.' The court gave the defendant his costs, and changed the interpretation of the phrase 'severe financial hardship' to such an extent that in 1972 an insurance company was able to claim successfully under the Act – see *General Accident Fire and Life Assurance Ltd v Foster* [1973] QB 50.

In *Haley v London Electricity Board* [1965] AC 778 involving the duty of care owed to a blind person, the House of Lords referred to evidence that one in five hundred persons in London were blind in support of the proposition that it was reasonably foreseeable that a blind person would be affected by an obstacle in the street.

In *R v Preston Supplementary Benefits Appeal Tribunal, ex p Moore* [1975] 1 WLR 624 information concerning the working of the supplementary benefit system was presented to the Court of Appeal. In *R v Lord Chancellor, ex p Witham* [1998] QB 575 the Public Law Project was permitted to submit a supporting affidavit which read 'more like a Brandeis brief than evidence in support of the individual application'.[11]

An example of a trial (as opposed to appeal) judge admitting a Brandeis brief occurred in the case of the two Leeds footballers Lee Bowyer and Jonathan Woodgate who were charged with affray and causing grievous bodily harm. The judge stopped the trial close to its end on the ground that a newspaper article which framed the case as racially motivated was 'seriously prejudicial'. In hearings regarding a stay of a second trial, the judge received a scientific report on the impact of pre-trial publicity and heard legal argument based on its contents. The report consisted of analysis of 369 pages of newspaper reports of the first trial.[12]

Lord Woolf, Lord Chief Justice, writing in 2000, predicted that the Human Rights Act 1998 would generate a need for Brandeis briefs: 'The type of issues which will arise under the Human Rights Act will mean that appellate courts will need to have to adjust to many more individuals and organisations wishing to intervene or place before the court

[11] Rosalind English, 'Wrong footing the Lord Chancellor: access to justice in the High Court' 61 *Modern Law Review*, 1998, 245, 251.

[12] For an account by the authors of the report see TM Honess, S Barker, EA Charman and M Levi, 'Empirical and legal perspectives on the impact of pre-trial publicity' *Criminal Law Review*, 2002, 719, 724–27.

Brandeis style briefs ...'[13] Even more strikingly, he said there was a need for 'more effective decision making by the courts'. This, he said, had three dimensions:

> The first is the research which should be undertaken as to what have been the consequences of decisions of the courts and the remedies which have been provided. The second is the material which should be placed before the courts so that they can anticipate more accurately what is likely to happen as a result of their decisions ...[14]

Both – and especially the second – sounded like a call for Brandeis brief material. Lord Woolf was prescient. Brandeis brief type material is now commonly produced by parties and interveners – and is received by the courts.

(See further, 7.8 below for consideration of the United States practice of intervention by third parties to litigation, and 7.10 for the United States practice of having written briefs to supplement oral argument.)

5.2. Preparation and Delivery of Judgments

5.2.1. Judgments in the House of Lords and the Supreme Court

In the early part of the nineteenth century the judgments of the Law Lords were proper speeches delivered extempore.[15] But since then the final product of a case in the Lords was written 'speeches' prepared after completion of the oral argument. Little was known in this country about the processes that take place behind the scenes in the preparation of reserved judgments by the Law Lords. Some knowledge of the matter first became available from Professor Alan Paterson's book *The Law Lords* (Macmillan, 1982). The Law Lords generally had a first conference about the case immediately it had finished. If the argument finished before one of the times when the judges adjourned – for example, before 1 pm or 4 pm – they would normally meet in the same room where the argument was heard. The presiding judge asked each of their brethren (starting with the most junior) to state their preliminary views. (By contrast, in the Supreme Court of the United States the Chief Justice traditionally speaks first.) It was rare for these to be a surprise to their colleagues because usually their views had become plain during the course of the oral argument – either in the court room itself or in the corridors or retiring room where the judges commonly chatted about cases as they developed.

Forty years later Professor Paterson published a second book (*Final Judgment – The Last Law Lords and the Supreme Court* (Hart, 2013). It seems that the Supreme Court justices operate in much the same way as the Law Lords, with a meeting at the conclusion of the oral argument. The difference is that after that first meeting whereas the Law Lords did not generally engage in much interaction, Supreme Court Justices did.

If they were not unanimous the presiding judge asked whether anyone wished to change their mind, and debate often ensued. There was then discussion as to who should write an opinion. Sometimes it was agreed that one judgment should be written on behalf of

[13] Lord Woolf, 'The additional responsibilities of the judiciary in the new millenium' in B Markesinis (ed), *The Clifford Chance Millenium Lectures* (Hart Publishing, 2000) 132, 138.
[14] Ibid, 139. The third dimension was 'the need for precision remedies'.
[15] Lord Rodger, 'The form and language of judicial opinions' 118 *Law Quarterly Review*, 2002, 226, 232.

all – though agreement to this effect did not then prevent any judge from changing their mind and writing a separate opinion. The decision as to who should write the single or the leading opinion emerged from discussion. It was not the tradition, according to Paterson (*The Law Lords*, p 92), that the presiding judge should allocate the task – though obviously, depending on their personality, they might have considerable influence on the outcome of this decision.

Obviously, a judge can only write an opinion which will be concurred in by their brethren if they agree with their reasons. If they agree with the result but for different reasons, they will normally write their own speeches and if they disagree with the result they will write a dissent. Sometimes judges write concurring speeches even when they wholly or mainly agree with both the result and reasons.

Paterson said that the first conference tended to last about half an hour, 'though some may be over in ten minutes, while others ... may go on for up to two hours' (*The Law Lords*, p 93). There was then the drafting stage which tended to last about six weeks. (In the Supreme Court of the United States it commonly takes many months.) Nowadays, even the most senior – ie older – judges will use word processors, which did not exist when Paterson conducted that research. When ready, the speeches were circulated to the others who had taken part in the case – never to anyone else. Sometimes one judge (or more) who had written an opinion decided that what they wanted to say had been said better by someone else and withdrew their own opinion. Sometimes, on the contrary, a judge who thought that they would not need to write a separate opinion decided that after all they should do so.

The opinions were eventually printed in order of seniority of the judges, but this did not necessarily mean that the order in which they were produced was the same.

The judges interviewed by Professor Paterson for the *The Law Lords* were divided as to whether it was good or not to have multiple opinions. But a large majority at that time favoured having several speeches in common law hard cases while there was considerable support for a norm of single speeches in criminal appeals – especially those based on points of statutory construction (p 98).[16] Paterson's second book shows that the proportion of cases ending with single judgments fluctuated markedly over the years. In the years 1981 to 1992 it was relatively high – ranging from a low of 40 per cent to a high of 70 per cent. Between 1992 and 2008 it was on a downward trajectory – reaching 13 per cent in 2008. From 2009, the first year of the Supreme Court it was basically on an upward trajectory, reaching 53 per cent in 2013.[17] In recent years it has been even higher – see 523 below.

The judges vary as to whether or not to make public a dissenting view. Sometimes they did not do so in the belief that it was better that the court should speak with one voice. The dissent was written with the objective of persuading the other judges; that having failed, the dissenting judge gave up the struggle. About half of the sample of Law Lords interviewed by Paterson agreed at least to some extent with the view that judges should exercise a measure of self-restraint in publishing their dissents – that resorting too frequently to the right to dissent created uncertainty in the law. Even Lord Denning said, 'I don't think any of us

[16] For a different view expressed in relation to the Court of Appeal Criminal Division see G Drewry, L Blom-Cooper and C Blake, *The Court of Appeal* (Hart Publishing, 2007) 183. ('Other than appeals against sentence, there is no more compelling reason for a unified voice in criminal as in civil law, particularly now that the Court of Appeal in its Civil Division is resorting to composite judgments ...').

[17] A Paterson, *Final Judgment: The Last Law Lords and the Supreme Court* (Hart, 2013) Table 3.5, 106.

would want to dissent unless we felt strongly about it … I don't dissent unless I feel sufficiently strongly in a sense' (p 102).

Lord Radcliffe thought that attitudes had changed somewhat. When he first went to the Lords in 1949, 'there was a bit of an olde-worlde feeling, you know, that we all ought to hang together and you oughtn't to expose the differences in the House of Lords because it weakened its authority' (p 103). But by the time he retired in 1964 that view no longer prevailed. Many of the judges agreed that the right to individual expression was more important than any pressure to present a united front.

The role of the presiding judge in the US Supreme Court has often been described as being of critical importance. Commentators speak of 'the Warren court' or 'the Burger court'. There was never any equivalent in the House of Lords. The Senior Law Lord (at the time of Paterson's first book (1982), Lord Bingham of Cornhill) presided every time he sat but, according to Paterson, he played no equivalent role to that in the United States Supreme Court. He did not provide intellectual leadership; he did not seek to impose his views; he did not regard it as his responsibility to reconcile differences between the judges or to achieve any particular result. Occasionally, of course, any of these things might occur, but it was not a normal part of the business of being the senior judge. Paterson concluded: '[T]he prevailing ethos on these matters in the House of Lords is that of laissez faire. By and large it is up to the individual Law Lord whether he writes or not, and whether he dissents or not. Except in a small minority of appeals the support for unity in the court is only tentative; there is little resistance to dissents on the ground that they are detrimental to the authority of the court and attempts to reconcile differences in the court are the exception rather than the rule' (pp 108–09).

Bargaining between the justices of the United States Supreme Court is common.[18] They bargain, sometimes passionately, over their votes and the content of their judgments.[19] In the House of Lords each judge tended much more to go their own way.

For a similar verdict on decision-making by the Law Lords see David Robertson, *Judicial Discretion in the House of Lords* (Clarendon Press, 1998). Robertson said that it was rare for there to be a second meeting after the initial discussion at the close of the oral argument for reconsideration or discussion of drafts. Opinions, he suggested, were circulated 'for information, not for discussion'. It was rare for draft opinions to be altered. 'To an extent vastly greater than seems to be the case in equivalent courts, the Law Lords make their law as individuals' (pp 15–16). 'In a real sense the Lords seldom argue, because they do not address each other's points. Only relatively rarely will a dissenting opinion actually take on the logic of the majority and try to rebuff it' (p 77).

As will be seen, the way the UK Supreme Court operates is not the same. (See especially 7.12 below.)

Selection of Judges for the Particular Case

Robertson's book also raised the delicate question as to which particular judges at that time sat in the House of Lords and the process by which they were selected for the actual case. This issue had surfaced dramatically in the context of the appeal in December 1998 over the

[18] For a vivid description of the process see B Woodward and S Armstrong, *The Brethren* (Coronet Books, Hodder and Stoughton, 1979).

[19] A study of the work of eight of the court's Justices concluded: 'Supreme Court decisions are an intricate and shifting composite of law, politics, policy, principle, efficiency, expedience, pragmatism, dogmatism, reason, passion, detachment, individual personality, group mythology, institutional forces and external pressures' (D Dickson (ed), *The Supreme Court in Conference (1940–1985): The Discussions Behind Nearly 300 Supreme Court Decisions* (Oxford University Press, 2001)).

extradition to Spain of the former Chilean dictator, General Pinochet. The first decision of the House of Lords[20] had to be set aside by the House of Lords and a new hearing ordered when it emerged that Lord Hoffmann had failed to reveal his involvement with Amnesty International which was an intervener in the case. (Lord Hoffmann was a Director and Chairman of Amnesty International Charity Limited, an Amnesty fund-raising company.) Since the first decision that General Pinochet did not have immunity from extradition as a former Head of State had been by a bare majority of three to two the case threw into high relief the significance of the identity of individual judges in a case.[21] In the second decision the Law Lords by six to one confirmed the view of the majority in the first decision that General Pinochet did not have immunity ([2000] 1 AC 147).

In former times it was the Lord Chancellor's prerogative, as Head of the Judiciary, not only to preside when sitting but also to decide which judges would sit on cases. Normally selection depended on who was available, who was sick, the fact that newly appointed Law Lords could not sit on cases in which they had given judgment below, the need to have a Scot to hear a Scottish appeal, special expertise and such like. But the choice might be influenced by other, more policy related, considerations. In 1999, Lord Irvine, the then Lord Chancellor, was asked by Lord Lester QC whether there was any constitutional convention governing the Lord Chancellor's power to decide the composition of Appellate Committees to hear appeals. In a Written Answer, Lord Irvine said that there was no such convention. The Lord Chancellor, he said, chaired both the Appeal Committee which decided whether to grant leave to appeal and the Appellate Committee which heard the appeal but 'in practice he does not attend the Appeal Committee and delegates to the Senior Law Lord the day-to-day management of judicial business *including the composition of the committees*'.[22]

In 2002, Lord Bingham, in a lecture at University College, London, revealed details of how it really worked. Forthcoming appeals, he said, were allotted dates by the Judicial Office of the House of Lords and the Registrar of the Judicial Committee of the Privy Council according to time estimates given by counsel. This draft programme was then given to the two most senior Law Lords 'with enough material to enable them to understand the nature of the cases listed'.

> A meeting is then held attended by these two law lords, the head of the Judicial Office and the Registrar (but no one else) to review the draft programme. The object of this meeting is to match horses to courses, that is, to try and ensure that so far as possible every committee includes members with specialised expertise and experience in the field to which the appeal relates, in addition of course to members with more general experience. There are a number of other matters which affect the outcome: the desirability of including Scottish and Northern Irish law lords in committees hearing appeals from those jurisdictions respectively; unavailability; any conflict to which any law lord may be subject; the desirability of achieving some balance, for individual law lords, between sittings in the House and the Privy Council; the work loads of individual law lords; and so on. The likely outcome of any appeal, or the possible effect of it, is not considered. Neither in its draft nor in its revised form is the programme the subject of consultation with or approval by anyone I have not mentioned. Inevitably, the programme, in its final form, may have

[20] *R v Bow Street Metropolitan Stipendiary Magistrate, ex p Pinochet Ugarte No 1* [2000] 1 AC 61.

[21] The five judges in the first *Pinochet* hearing were chosen because they were due to hear an appeal starting on that day which was postponed on account of the urgency of the *Pinochet* case. They were simply moved from one case to the other.

[22] House of Lords, *Hansard*, vol 602, WA, cols 77–78, 22 June 1999 (emphasis added).

> to be changed, sometimes at short notice, for a variety of reasons of which illness is the most obvious.[23]

Professor Paterson in *Final Judgment* (Hart Publishing, 2013) gave a slightly different gloss on the meeting described by Lord Bingham:

> Although, by convention, the final say lay with the two most senior Law Lords, since the proposals of the Principal Clerk would be put to them in a meeting once a term, dubbed the 'horses for courses' meeting, in practice neither of the Law Lords made many changes to the Clerk's proposals.[24]

That had not changed in the Supreme Court:

> The panels to hear appeals are largely selected by the Registrar, in practice, using the same criteria as in the last years of the House.[25]

The possible significance of the selection of the individual judges for the case was confirmed in David Robertson's book, the main purpose of which was to develop the thesis that the judges in the House of Lords had almost unlimited freedom in their decision-making. Basing himself on a statistical analysis of decisions by fifteen judges in the years from 1986 to 1995 he suggested (p 70) that it was predictable which way a case would be decided by reference simply to what combination of judges was sitting on the appeal – though the degree of predictability varied somewhat from subject area to subject area. (It was highest in constitutional cases.)

For interaction between the Justices of the UK Supreme Court see 7.12 below.

5.2.2. Oral (Extempore) and Written (Reserved or Handed Down) Judgments

One of the unusual traditional features of English judicial method by comparison with that of most other countries is the high proportion of cases in which the judges deliver judgment 'off-the-cuff' immediately after the case is over. In modern times the House of Lords always reserved judgment and the Supreme Court always does so. But until quite recently the Court of Appeal, Civil Division frequently delivered oral extempore judgments and the Criminal Division still does so in most cases. In 1977, Professor H Lawson wrote that reserved judgments in the Civil Division of the Court of Appeal were something between one-tenth and one-twentieth of the whole. ('Oral judgment is the rule.'[26]). In 1997, the Bowman *Review of the Court of Appeal (Civil Division)* said that the percentage of Court of Appeal judgments that were reserved had fluctuated between about one-quarter and one-third. (para 47, p 90). By 2013, the proportion of reserved judgments had risen to around two-thirds[27] and today it is much higher still – probably closer to 90 per cent.[28] In the High Court, however, extempore judgments are still common.

[23] 'A new Supreme Court for the United Kingdom' (2002, published by the Constitution Unit, UCL) 13.

[24] Paterson, *Final Judgment* (n 17 above) 71.

[25] Ibid, 72.

[26] 'Comparative judicial style' 25 *American Journal of Comparative Law,* 1977, 364.

[27] In the three years July 2011 to July 2014 the percentage of reserved judgments respectively was 65 per cent, 68 per cent and 70 per cent. (HM Courts and Tribunals Service, information provided to the writer under a Freedom of Information Request, 22 August 2014.)

[28] There seem to be no current figures but that was the view of a senior member of the Court expressed to the writer in January 2025.

In a speech in August 2014 Lord Neuberger suggested two reasons for the growth in reserved (or handed down) judgments:

> I think that the increase in reserved judgments has two connected causes. First, with the advent of written arguments and pressure of work, cases are argued much more quickly than they were, and so judges have much less time to prepare judgments during argument. The second reason is that there is such a wealth of material these days of the word processer and professional liability: neither solicitors nor barristers want to leave anything out, whether it is a document, a witness, an argument or an authority. That makes an ex tempore judgment much more challenging.[29]

Another reason is that a reserved judgment is guaranteed to be uploaded on BAILII and other online systems whereas that may or may not be the case with a judgment given extempore. (See further on this issue 6.4 below.)

Giving extempore judgment is no mean feat.[30] Lord Rodger of Earlsferry, a Scottish Law Lord said:

> The Scottish judges have always looked with unfeigned admiration on the skill of their English colleagues in giving judgment extempore. To give a good judgment of that kind requires a very special skill which even the most distinguished judges may not possess ... To do this day after day, like Lord Denning, is an astonishing feat that requires not only extremely hard work, but intellectual attainments of the highest order.[31]

As Lord Neuberger has explained, however, the judge does have an opportunity to edit the text:

> Of course, one of the secrets of the ex tempore judgment, at least in England, is that the judge gets the opportunity to 'approve' the transcript of the judgment before it goes to the parties. I use inverted commas because, while some judges just improve the punctuation and the syntax, many judges use the opportunity to effect a fairly comprehensive rewriting. I have rewritten sentences even paragraphs. I have transposed paragraphs or even whole sections. I have even deleted sentences or paragraphs – sometimes because I simply could not understand what I had been trying to say.[32]

When a court reserves judgment this is indicated in the law reports by the phrase *Cur adv vult*. It is rare for practitioners or academics to make anything of this point as a factor in evaluating the weight of a precedent, but a revealing lecture by Lord Justice Russell suggests that more attention might well be paid to it:

Sir Charles Russell, *Behind the Appellate Curtain* (Holdsworth Club of the University of Birmingham, 1969) 3–8

> It is important in considering appellate judgments to differentiate between reserved judgments and unreserved judgments. The quality of the former is, or should be, better than that of the latter. Many may think that in the Court of Appeal judgment should be more often reserved, since in I suppose 95% of cases it is in fact a judgment of the court of final decision. I would not dissent from that view. Some appellate judges have a great ability for stating the relevant facts without significant omission or error, and I think those with a background of summing up to juries in

[29] Speech of Lord Neuberger, President of the Supreme Court, entitled 'Sausages and the judicial process: the limits of transparency' Annual Conference of the Supreme Court of New South Wales, Sydney 1 August 2014, para 22 – accessible on the Supreme Court's website – www.supremecourt.uk.).

[30] It may however be aided by a bench memo setting out the basic facts of the case prepared by judicial assistants – as to which see 7.11 below.

[31] Lord Rodger, 'The form and language of judicial opinions' 118 *Law Quarterly Review*, 2002, 226, 231.

[32] Neuberger, 'Sausages and the judicial process' (n 29 above) para 23.

criminal cases have an advantage in this respect. Others – among whom I number myself – find some difficulty in giving judgment off the cuff, and would prefer reservation of judgments more frequently. But it must be recognised that the pressure of civil appellate business discourages the practice of reservation of judgments.

Accordingly I take, first, academic consideration by academic lawyers and others of reserved judgments of the Court of Appeal. The production of these may involve different combinations of events. Suppose that in general terms all three judges are at the end in agreement on the outcome. Away they go and write their judgments in draft and circulate them. Here sometimes is the crunch. Lord Justice Frog does not altogether approve of a particular ratiocination of Lord Justice Toad. What does he do? This is apt to depend upon the state of Frog LJ's work. If he is busy – and he may now be sitting in a different division of the C.A. with its own problems – he may be content to leave his judgment to stand without arguing the toss or trying to persuade Toad, LJ to amend his judgment. Or he may add to his judgment words of doubt of the proposition of Toad LJ. Now what happens? In the latter case lawyers – and not only academic lawyers – hasten to point out that Frog LJ took the opposite view. But in fact Frog LJ in his mind has done no more than *suspect* the proposition. He has not had the time to discuss the proposition with Toad LJ – one or other has had a committee meeting at 4.30 pm every evening for a fortnight, and Frog LJ lives in West Sussex. In effect the apparent dissent of Frog LJ should not be regarded as anything except an undigested reservation that has no persuasive value in the formation of legal principles. It should do no more than encourage a critical approach to the views of Toad LJ. If he leaves it alone, this should not be taken as wholehearted agreement. Take another case of reserved judgments. There maybe a full scale battle behind the scenes between Frog LJ and Toad LJ on some matter of principle, with Slug LJ a trifle out of his depth and relatively disinterested, but on the whole prepared to march with Toad LJ in the decision. Now in such a case Frog and Toad read each other's drafts. Frog observes in Toad what he considers to be gross heresy and amends his draft in a manner calculated to expose it as such, hoping that thus he will bring Toad to his senses. Undeterred, Toad fortifies his draft by analogy with other branches of the law. Frog is drawn unwillingly into this new field, and by postponing his first gin and catching the late train to West Sussex works hard at it for his third draft. Toad LJ – who lives in London and never touches gin – produces an amendment digging into ancient authorities including a resounding declaration about the turn of the century that has in fact (unknown to him because this tangential approach to the problem was never discussed by counsel) been later roundly disapproved. Frog LJ reads the amended judgment of Toad and is too busy to trouble further. What happens? Slug LJ agrees in general terms with Toad LJ. Frog LJ has not objected to the reliance on the turn of the century declaration. And, lo and behold! it has apparently been reinstated as the law. This is an example that should warn us all that when in search of the law as authoritatively propounded by an appellate court (1) it is important to stick to what was necessarily said for the decision of the particular case, and (2) silence does not necessarily mean consent.

The latter point is even more relevant in the case of *unreserved judgments* in the Court of Appeal, and most particular caution is to be recommended in such cases. It must be realised that when the shorthand writer circulates transcripts of such judgments for correction he sends only the individual transcript to the individual Lord Justice. It is true that reported cases are entire: but speaking for myself I only check my own judgments in proof, being sufficiently hard put to remember what I had said.

Envisage, please, the production of unreserved judgments in the C.A. Ordinarily the first judgment is delivered by the presiding Lord Justice. Of course in many cases the way the minds are working on the bench has been to a greater or lesser extent displayed in the course of exchanges during the argument. If there has been an adjournment during the case no doubt the members of the Court have discussed the progress of the case and have exchanged tentative views on the points emerging. But in the end the moment arrives when judgment is to be given. Often a short huddle is to be observed in the face of the public. Sometimes – and I think with more dignity – the Court adjourns for a few minutes. But, whatever the discussion, in many cases Frog LJ is never quite sure how Toad LJ will express himself; and Slug LJ is unsure about both, however much they may all be agreed on dismissing or allowing the appeal. Toad LJ leads off. Slug LJ as the junior has decided to say nothing of his own. Frog LJ has decided to say a little piece of his own. Consider the situation of Frog LJ who prefers to jot down his thoughts. With his right hand and most of his brain he is doing this. With his left ear and the rest of his brain he is at the same time trying to follow what Toad LJ is saying – not really an easy exercise. All too often Frog LJ is rash enough to start his judgment with the words 'I agree'. Really he means by this that he agrees with the order proposed and that he has not been able to detect in what he has grasped of the judgment of Toad, LJ any errors, or any error that he is able at such short notice to denounce as such or refute. But what happens? Other lawyers – and I do not confine them to the writers of text books or articles or the teachers of youth – pick upon those two introductory words and claim for some proposition the weighty authority of not only Toad LJ but also Frog LJ Whereas in truth Toad LJ had a brilliant notion half way through a sentence, a notion that he much later rather regretted, and Frog LJ never heard the notion, or having heard assumed that he had misheard or was unwilling to produce an undigested disclaimer. Moreover, even if Frog LJ follows the cautious practice – one that I approve myself – of never starting with 'I agree', but if anything at all with the phrase 'I agree that this appeal fails/succeeds', what happens? It is said by others that Frog LJ did not dissent from or disagree with what was said by Toad LJ therefore he must be taken to have agreed. And what of Slug LJ who had decided to say nothing original? He was as a result able to listen to everything that was said by the other two. But suppose that he heard from them or one of them something with which he was not altogether happy? Poor Slug is in rather a fix. Is he to recite his objections, which anyway he finds it difficult to formulate at short notice, and add 'otherwise I agree'? Or suppose he prefers the way in which Frog LJ has put it to that of Toad LJ? Does he say that for the reasons given by Frog LJ he agrees with the order proposed by Toad LJ? Even more delicate is his position if he happens to be Slug LJ standing in for Grub LJ who has been taken away from his proper task in order to conduct an enquiry on a subject on which he has no expertise, because the government is anxious not to carry the burden of decision? In the end Slug contents himself with saying tersely 'I agree' – though he may, frequently with every justification, continue 'and there is nothing I can usefully add', an addendum that denies its own function …

Now what is the moral of all this? For my address, so far, though based upon the principle that a light touch sometimes illuminates, is intended to seek a moral. As I see it, it is one not only for the teacher and text book writer but also for the practitioner. In particular in the case of unreserved judgments weight should be attributed only to pronouncements that in express terms approve of other pronouncements, and with particularity rather than generality. All else should be suspect in point of value …

5.2.3. The Trend Toward Composite Judgments

In 2002, Dr Roderick Munday of Peterhouse College, University of Cambridge, wrote that 'in comparatively recent times English courts, to a surprising degree, have espoused something resembling a civilian judicial procedure'.[33] By 'civilian judicial procedure' Dr Munday meant the practice of continental judges of handing down collegial or collective judgments – as contrasted with the common law system where judges traditionally delivers their own individual judgment. A single collective judgment, Munday suggested, was likely to be the product of behind-the-scenes compromise 'and in likelihood, would lack the

[33] R Munday, '"All for one and one for all": The rise to prominence of the composite judgment within the Civil Division of the Court of Appeal' 61 *Cambridge Law Journal*, 2002, 321, 322.

detailed sinewed argument that was the embodiment of the common law'.[34] Although the practice of the collective judgment, he thought, went entirely against the English legal grain, it had attracted no comment. He was not sure that it had even been noticed.

Munday referred to a dozen or so well-known cases but said that it would be a mistake to assume that this phenomenon only occurred in high-profile cases. A 'veritable multitude of lesser appellate fry' had received this treatment. His 'rough-and-ready' initial research conducted 'within the midden mounds' of Lexis and BAILII (see below), had unearthed a couple of hundred instances in the previous five years where the English courts, and especially the Court of Appeal, Civil Division had delivered single composite judgments. A more orderly trawl of reported Court of Appeal cases for the four years 1999 to 2002 confirmed this picture. In summary, 'The simple fact is that within a very short space of time the composite judgment has established itself as a standard means whereby the Civil Division of the Court of Appeal now despatches between 10% and 15% of its business'.[35] What was more, in a much larger proportion of cases, only one judge gave judgment whilst the other one or two judges merely assented. (In 1999, 44 per cent, in 2000, 49 per cent and in 2001, 37 per cent of all judgments fell into this category.[36]) In aggregate therefore only one judgment was given in something like half of the Court of Appeal's non-criminal cases.[37]

Dr Munday suggests that from slow beginnings in the 1980s, the story of the composite judgment had been much affected by the identity of the presiding judge in the case. During the 21 years when Lord Denning presided over the Court of Appeal, composite judgments were virtually unknown. Slade LJ seemed to have a predilection for composite judgments. He communicated this taste to Woolf and Bingham LJJ who often sat with him when Slade delivered composite judgments. In the 1990s there was a high incidence of cases in which these two judges, often joined by Lord Phillips, continued and developed the tradition.[38] The fact that Lord Woolf was Master of the Rolls and then Lord Chief Justice; that Lord Bingham was successively Master of the Rolls, Lord Chief Justice and Senior Law Lord; and that Lord Phillips was Master of the Rolls (and later first President of the Supreme Court) legitimated the practice.

By the early 2000s, Munday said, the composite judgment had become an established part of the system – 'just one more tool at the judges' disposal serving the utilitarian ends of economy, clear judicial pronouncements on matters of law, and generally adroit case management'.[39] Reasons for giving composite judgments varied. Some were cases in which a single, authoritative statement of the law seemed to be indicated.[40] Some were cases

[34] Ibid, 321.

[35] Ibid, 323. And the proportion has since increased – see n 36 below.

[36] Ibid, 325. The difference between the composite judgment and the single judgment is that in the case of the former it is overtly the work of all the judges, whereas in the case of the latter, the judgment is presented as the work only of the judge who delivers it. In 2002 and 2003 the number of single judgments with the other judge or judges merely assenting decreased – to 19 per cent and 24 per cent. The reason was a dramatic rise in the proportion of composite judgments – 32 per cent in 2002 and 29 per cent in 2003. (R Munday, 'Reasoning without dissent; dissent without reasoning' 168 *Justice of the Peace*, 2004, 968–75, 991–1000. See also Munday, 'Suppressing dissent' 172 *Justice of the Peace Notes*, 2008, 830.).

[37] According to Dr Munday's later figures, the proportion of single judgments in the Court of Appeal Civil Division was then closer to two-thirds.

[38] Others such as Lord Justices Henry, Brooke and Stuart-Smith had also played a role.

[39] Munday, 'All for one, one for all' (n 33 above) 330.

[40] For instance, *Greig Middleton & Co. Ltd v Denderowitz* [1998] 1 WLR 1164; *Bannister v SGB plc* [1997] 4 All ER 129; and *Callery v Gray* [2001] EWCA Civ 1117, [2001] 1 WLR2112. For further examples see Munday, 'All for one, one for all' (n 33 above) 332–33.

calling into question the conduct of lawyers or of law enforcement agencies where there was a 'closing of ranks and a strong desire either to cleanse or to vindicate the system'.[41] Some were big cases, or cases that involved the fate of many potential litigants.

Sometimes it was stated that one or other of the judges had prepared (or had largely prepared) the judgment. Sometimes, 'improbably', all the judges were said to have contributed equally.

More recently there had been examples of composite majority decisions. Munday said that this development seemed to align the Court of Appeal with the practices of courts such as the United States Supreme Court, the High Court of Australia or the European Court of Human Rights 'with individual members of the bench forming into judicial clusters'.[42]

Professor Paterson's *Final Judgment* published in 2013 stated that in the Supreme Court composite judgments of the whole court were extremely rare[43] but that single majority judgments in the name of one Justice were very common – 60 per cent of cases in the first third of 2013 were single majority judgments. ('Nevertheless, such judgments are almost always a collective work product of most of the Justices in the case'.[44])

Lord Neuberger, President of the Supreme Court, discouraged unnecessary concurring judgments:

> I do think that what I have called a 'vanity judgment' should be avoided. By that I mean a judgment which is intended to agree with the lead judgment, but not to add anything other than saying 'I have understood this case' or 'I think I can express it better' or 'I am interested in this point' or simply 'I am here too'. Such judgments, of which virtually every appellate judge, not least myself, has been guilty, are at best a waste of time and space, and, at worst, confusion and uncertainty – although they are popular with academics. Further, in some cases, such as judgments giving guidance to courts below, it is positively undesirable to have more than one judgment. However, if you do not agree with all the reasoning in a judgment, it may be your duty to write – at least on the point or points you disagree with. And in some cases, eg where one is extending the scope of tort law in an area, it is often positively helpful to have more than one judgment to take the debate forward.[45]

Lord Reid, by contrast, considered that if the matter raised issues of principle, concurring judgments were very valuable:

> With the passage of time I have come more and more firmly to the conclusion that it is never wise to have only one speech in this House dealing with an important question of law. My main reason is that experience has shown that those who have to apply the decision to other cases … find it difficult to avoid treating sentences and phrases in a single speech as if they were provisions in an Act of Parliament. They do not seem to realise that it is not the function of noble and learned Lords, or indeed of any judges to frame definitions or to lay down hard and fast rules. It is their function to enunciate principles and much that they say is intended to be illustrative or explanatory and not to be definitive. Where there are two or more speeches they must be read together and often it is generally much easier to see what are the principles involved and what are merely illustrations of it.[46]

[41] For examples see Munday, 'All for one, one for all' (n 33 above) 333–36.

[42] Ibid, 339.

[43] For an example see *Horncastle* [2010] 2 AC 373, the decision of seven Justices. For details of why that case was important see p 253.

[44] Paterson, *Final judgment* (n 17 above) 11.

[45] Lord Neuberger speech (n 29 above) para 32.

[46] *Broome v Cassell* [1972] AC 1027, 1085.

The Court of Appeal, Criminal Division *always* delivers a single, unanimous judgment.[47] 'In most instances, by prior allocation, one member of the Court will have been deputed to deliver judgment, normally orally, after the three judges have gone into a huddle on the bench and settled that they are still agreed on the outcome.'[48] This obviously reflects the view that in criminal cases it is better that the court speaks with one voice. (Curiously, in the Divisional Court which hears appeals from magistrates' courts, concurring and dissenting judgments are not unknown.) A phenomenon noted by Dr Munday is that occasionally the Court of Appeal specifically stated that the judgment represents the united view of the court. Examples were cases in which the court had to criticise a judge or a practitioner, especially high-profile cases or unusually difficult cases.[49]

In his concluding observations Dr Munday expressed his disquiet at the development of the composite or single judgment. He quoted the view of Justice Patricia Wald of the United States Federal Court of Appeal:

> Predictably … most judges will compromise their preferred *rationale* and rhetoric to gain a full concurrence from other members of the panel. In an appellate court composed of strong-minded men and women of different political and personal philosophies, consensus is a formidable constraint on what an opinion writer says and how he says it. Her best lines are often left on the cutting-room floor.[50]

Judges, Justice Wald suggested, became more absorbed in doctrines than in individual cases – they liked to see their favourite doctrinal flowers grow and flourish and conversely, they rejoiced 'when doctrinal weeds or aberrant strains wither and die'.[51] Much of the individual character of a judgment could be excised during the process of trying to achieve consensus.

In Dr Munday's view, the Court of Appeal's growing attachment to composite judgments reflected a desire on the part of the court 'to be more *dirigiste*'. The common law had often been distinguished from continental systems for its more particularist and less systematic approach. ('The instinct of the civilian is to systematise. The working rule of the common lawyer is *solvitur ambulando.*'[52]) If the Court of Appeal was beginning to address English law's supposed intellectual disorderliness, then it was plainly moving away from the orthodox common law posture as exemplified in Lord Macmillan's celebrated speech in *Read v J Lyons & Co*:

> Your Lordships' task in this House is to decide particular cases between litigants and your Lordships are not called on to rationalise the law of England. That attractive if perilous field may well be left to other hands to cultivate … Arguments based on legal consistency are apt to mislead for the common law is a practical code adapted to deal with the manifold diversities of human life and as a great American judge has reminded us, 'the life of the law has not been logic; it has been experience'.[53]

[47] The Supreme Court Act 1981, s 59 goes so far as to prohibit separate judgments in the Criminal Division of the Court of Appeal – unless the presiding judge states that separate judgments would be appropriate. Munday said that the last example of which he was aware was a case in 1967.

[48] Munday, '"All for one and one for all"' (n 33 above) 340.

[49] Ibid, 343–44.

[50] 'The rhetoric of results and the results of rhetoric: judicial writings' 62 *University of Chicago Law Review,* 1995, 1371, 1377.

[51] Ibid, 1378.

[52] TM Cooper, 'The common law and the civil law – a Scot's view' 63 *Harvard Law Review,* 1950, 468, 470.

[53] [1947] AC 156, 175, quoting Oliver Wendell Holmes.

It was difficult to predict the longer-term consequences of such a sea-change, he thought, but it was possible that the substance and the texture of the English judgment might well alter. Dr Munday ended with a warning:

> Collaboration between members of the court has not yet fulfilled its destiny. Intuitively, one senses, were the practice to become settled, and were composite preparation of judgments to become a matter of judicial routine, the likely result would be a more formulaic product. The composite judgment is fast becoming a secure fixture within our legal system. To the outsider this development, introduced without noticeable consultation or – so far as one can see – any philosophic forethought, looks something of a bow at a venture. English appellate legal method is being surreptitiously reconstructed. For what?[54]

See further on composite judgments pp 385–86 below.

5.2.4. The Form of Judgments

In a subsequent article Dr Munday analysed what had been happening in regard to the form of judgments.[55] He suggested that the shape of the English judgment was metamorphosing:

> Some judgments are now accompanied by a summary and index, the latter normally stated not to be part of the judgment itself. This almost gives them the semblance of reports of a departmental committee rather than traditional English judicial utterances. Some judgments now come with subtitles, and even postscripts are appended. Meanwhile neutral citation with numbered paragraphs that occasionally read more like bullet points than connected prose, compound this impression. One could add that many judgments today are unquestionably more concerned to take in the broad picture and set out to regulate entire classes of case rather than simply settling the *lis* before the courts, as has hitherto been English law's normal practice. Plainly, we have entered an era of active judicial experimentation.[56]

Another 'ominous' feature illustrated in a then recent case,[57] he thought, was relegation of the full analysis of the facts to an appendix.

> It is commonly said that one of the pre-eminent features of the common law judgment, which differentiates it sharply from its Continental counterparts, is the court's almost obsessive attention to the facts. The facts are inextricably woven into the law. The common law judge's judgment is grounded in and grows out of fact. Pierre Legrand has suggested that in the common law 'it would not be excessive to observe that the facts take the place of the system: their enhanced role is the result of an absence, that of a conceptual system; in sum the facts occupy the empty square' … As Legrand points out whilst 'the common-law judge persistently operates at the level of the messy facts (and) is concerned with disorder', the civilian is preoccupied with order and inhabits a legal world where debate is conducted at the level of posited law, not of fact.[58] If the courts are growing ever more directorial, indulging themselves with the fantasy that they are the architects of a grand, overarching monument of handsomely proportioned, interlocking legal principles, facts would naturally become an encumbrance.[59]

[54] R Munday, '"All for one and one for all"' (n 33 above) 350.

[55] R Munday, 'Judicial configurations: permutations of the court and properties of judgment' 61 *Cambridge Law Journal*, 2002, 612, 612.

[56] Ibid, 612–13.

[57] *Sutherland v Hatton* [2002] EWCA Civ 76, [2002] 2 All ER 1.

[58] P Legrand, 'What Borges can teach us' in his *Fragments on Law-as-Culture* (Tjeenk Willink, 1999) 76.

[59] R Munday, 'Judicial configurations' (n 55 above) 614.

The move from an essentially oral to a written system, Munday suggested, was of fundamental significance. It was facilitated by word-processing and the speed and ease with which drafts of judgments could now be circulated amongst the judges. It might also reflect convergence with European systems. Another strand was the concern about economy of effort and efficiency. ('Composite judgments, clipped numbered paragraphs, indexes, moral lessons spelled out in *post scripta*, the subordination of fact to principle, all these features combine to create an impression that the law is coherent and readily intelligible even to those who dwell outside the legal conventicle.'[60]) Munday suggested that the changes reflected drift rather than any thought-out, coherent strategy.

Lord Rodger of Earlsferry, in 'The form and language of judicial opinions',[61] equally saw great significance in the move from extempore to written decisions. An opinion delivered extempore in court was addressed to those present in court, the parties and their advisers who were familiar with the case and had just heard it argued. When they went off and considered the issue in their chambers, the judge would tend to address their judgment to the wider world. The introduction of cross-referencing, tables, appendices and footnotes[62] signified that judges were increasingly preparing 'what to all intents and purposes amount to academic articles, mini-treatises'.[63]

What then are the distinguishing features of a traditional English common law judgment? Dr Munday suggested that one might be the highly individual way in which judgments were expressed. The most celebrated examples were Lord Denning's:[64]

> It happened on April 19, 1964. It was bluebell time in Kent. Mr and Mrs Hinz had been married some ten years, and they had four children, all aged nine and under. The youngest was one. Mrs Hinz was a remarkable woman. In addition to her own four, she was foster-mother to four other children. To add to it, she was two-months pregnant with her fifth child. On this day they drove out in a Bedford Dormobile van from Tonbridge to Canvey Island ... etc[65]

But as Dr Munday observed, the colourful and highly personal style of a Lord Denning was hardly typical. ('The system permits these judicial extravagances, but they are far from

[60] Ibid, 616.

[61] Lord Rodger, 'The form and language of judicial opinions' 118 *Law Quarterly Review,* 2002, 226.

[62] In 2001, when Lord Rodger wrote and delivered his lecture he was able to say that Britain had thus far (rightly, he thought) resisted the onward march of the footnote. Five years later, however, Dr Munday, ever vigilant, marked what he thought might be the first appearance of a footnote in an English judgment with an excoriating critique of this development: R Munday, 'Fish with feathers: English judgments with footnotes' 170 *Justice of the Peace,* 2006, 444–48.

[63] Rodger, 'The form and language of judicial opinions' (n 61 above) 237. Lord Rodger added that one waited with fascinated horror for the moment when judges choose to follow another 'nauseating academic habit of thanking their partners and kids for tolerating their absence during the long hours needed to produce the opinion. ('Most self-respecting children would, I believe, regard such sentiments as good grounds for leaving home. One can only imagine what Maitland's wife, Florence Fisher and his daughters, the formidably named Fredigond and Ermengard, would have thought if he had written such self-indulgent nonsense in a preface (ibid).)

[64] Lord Denning s famous openings were not to Lord Rodger's taste. ('They strike me as *faux naif* – something like the literary equivalent of the primitive paintings of Grandma Moses. But Grandma Moses was not an educated woman, whereas Lord Denning was a clever and highly educated man. No one ever spoke as Lord Denning wrote in those passages and no one ever wrote in that way except in fairy stories and tales for children (Rodger, 'The form and language of judicial opinions' (n 61 above) 244–45).).

[65] *Hinz v Berry* [1970] 2 QB 40, 42. Munday quoted as another example the opening of Megarry J's judgment in *Re Flynn* – 'Errol Flynn was a film actor whose performance gave pleasure to many millions ... When he was 17, he was expelled from school in Sydney; and in the next thirty-three years he lived a life that was full, lusty, restless and colourful. In his career, in his three marriages, in his friendships, in his quarrels, and in bed with the many women he took there, he lived with zest and irregularity' ([1968] 1 WLR 103, 105).

being the staple. They are the province of a relatively small number of hardy souls whose desire to cut a dash … cannot always be held in check.'[66])

Another, very different distinctive characteristic was the common-law judge's candour in revealing their difficulties in reaching their decision. ('A German or French judge would rather swallow his tongue than … say that he found the case difficult …'.[67])

> They are not unanimous dooms handed down by a monolithic bench whose real thoughts cannot be guessed at. The strength of the common-law method then is its humanity and the evidence that each member of the court has fully met his or her responsibilities and given the arguments presented scrupulous attention.[68]

The litigant who appeals to the Court of Appeal would tend to assume that their contentions will receive more intense attention from all three members of the court than they were given by the single trial judge. Confronted with a single judgment, the litigant cannot know to what extent that was actually the case.

The most obvious form of the individual judge speaking their mind was in the right to dissent.[69] Munday suggested a variety of justifications for the right to dissent: (1) The majority may not have the better of the argument. (2) Dissent exposes more of the pros and cons of the issues. (3) Knowing that other judges may disagree will inspire 'more muscular' construction of one's own judgments. (4) The dissent may stimulate a debate and eventually become the majority view. (5) The dissent reflects the common law's assumption that the law is subject to perpetual reappraisal. (On dissents see further pp 400–01 below.)

Delivery of concurring judgments was another example. The concurring judge 'has reached an identical conclusion by a different route, feels the duty or desire to set out matters in his own words, perhaps wishes to add a personal gloss to the other judgments or to address a point passed over in his colleagues' judgments'.[70] They feel prompted to make a personal contribution. The arguments favouring concurring judgment were similar: (1) There is not just one approach to the problem. The concurring judgment 'is part of the unremitting search for the correct formulation of the principle'.[71] (2) Like the dissent, it may help to move opinion on a given point. (3) Like the possibility of dissent, it will help to sharpen the faculties of the judges. (4) It demonstrates that all the judges have indeed given the case their careful attention.

Dissenting and concurring judgments were to a great extent cut from the same cloth:

> Together, they guarantee a high measure of openness in the system, as well as conferring on English judgments a pronounced personalised stamp that, in likelihood, contributes to making them more acceptable to litigants than impersonal, bureaucratic collective dooms. Concurring judgments play their part in keeping the system honest; and transparently honest, at that.[72]

Of course, concurring judgments did not promote clarity. They could make the search for the ratio decidendi of the case like *The Hunting of the Snark*. The single judgment avoided

[66] Munday, '"All for one and one for all"' (n 33 above) 630.

[67] H Kötz, 'The role of the judge in the court-room: the common law and the civil law compared' 1 *Tydskrif vir die Suid-Afrikaanse Reg,* 1987, 35, 41.

[68] Munday, '"All for one and one for all"' (n 33 above) 634.

[69] See generally J Alder, 'Dissents in courts of last resort: tragic choices?' 20 *Oxford Journal of Legal Studies,* 2000, 221.

[70] Munday, 'Judicial configurations' (n 55 above) 639.

[71] Munday, 'Judicial configurations' (n 55 above) 640.

[72] Munday, 'Judicial configurations' (n 55 above) 641. See also J Lee, 'A defence of concurring speeches' *Public Law*, 2009, 305.

such confusion. But there was a cost. It made the law-making role of the court more evident. It concealed the likely differences of approach of the judges. It traded the openness of the system for 'a smidgen of certainty'.[73] We no longer knew what the judges were really thinking. The composite judgment was not a vehicle that would produce strong phrases or ringing prose. Three judges could not credibly share a doubt, admit to having oscillated in their opinions or to having changed their minds. 'The composite judgment may lack elements that mean something in the context of English law and may discard an important component, its freedom and hence, its humanity.'[74]

Worse, this method of proceeding, Munday suggested, was almost bound to generate a working practice whereby one member of the court was assigned the task of writing the judgment and the others decided whether they could go along with it. Given that we lived in an era of increasing specialisation, the tendency naturally would be for the member of the court with the requisite expertise to be allocated this task. Any such development would exacerbate the suspicion that the composite judgment was 'a hollow device that economises judicial effort under colour of enhancing legal certainty'.[75]

Already it was common for one or more of a three-man court simply to say, 'I agree'.[76] Full concurring judgments occurred in only roughly half the cases heard by the Court of Appeal.

Dr Munday referred to empirical research conducted in France by a judge of the Montpellier Court of Appeal to test the relative merits of decisions arrived at singly or in a collegiate framework. One hundred and sixty-five students at the Ecole Nationale de la Magistrature in Bordeaux were given a problem to solve either singly or in teams. The judge reported that the single-judge judgments were better constructed, better referenced and better argued.[77]

Dr Munday feared that the attractions of the composite judgment were such that it might become *the* accepted mode of handing down judgments – thereby losing something of real significance in the English common law tradition.

5.2.5. Putting a Judgment Together

It is obvious that when it comes to give judgment the judge will make use of material provided by the lawyers for the successful party. In fact, now that so much is readily transmitted electronically, the judge could prepare their judgment by wholesale adoption of counsel's submissions. But just as a student must be careful in writing an essay to avoid giving evidence of plagiarism, so too the judge must be careful. The point came up in *Crinion v IG Markets Ltd* [2013] EWCA Civ 587, [2013] CP Rep 41. Lord Justice Underhill said:

> The present appeals, for which permission was given by Ward LJ at a hearing, have nothing to do with the merits of the underlying claims. They are based solely on the fact that almost all of

[73] Munday, 'Judicial configurations' (n 55 above) 645.

[74] Ibid.

[75] Ibid.

[76] It seems that in the United States, it is not unknown for a dissenting judge to say simply 'I dissent'. (See Munday, '"All for one and one for all"' (n 33 above).

[77] Munday, 'Judicial configurations' (n 55 above) 650–52 reporting an experiment conducted by M Jean-Marie Baudouin, described in 'La collegialité est-elle une garantie de la sureté des jugements?' *Revue trimestrelle de droit civil*, 1992, 532–38.

> the Judge's judgment is taken word-for-word from Mr Chirnside's closing submissions. Ward LJ referred to them being 'cut-and-pasted' into the judgment, but that does not quite accurately describe what happened. It is in fact apparent that the Judge proceeded by taking Mr Chirnside's submissions – that is, the Word file that he had been sent – as, in effect, his first draft and revising it to include some, though not much, material of his own drafting. ([4])

The Court of Appeal made it clear that that would not do. Counsel's submissions had run to 63 pages of text. It appeared that 94 per cent of the judgment and the whole of its structure was derived from those submissions. The appellants objected that for the judge to base their judgment to such an extent on the other side's submissions 'creates the impression that he had abdicated his core judicial responsibility to think through for himself the issues which it was his job to decide'. What mattered was the impression that the judgment gave. A litigant who saw the other party's submissions adopted in the wholesale way which occurred here would justifiably not believe that their own side of the case had received any attention. Moreover the judgment had failed to address the appellants' arguments. There were no quotations from their written submissions. The judge should at the least address the losing side's central argument and explain why they had been rejected. The appellants' contention was that whatever its substantive merits, because of the serious procedural irregularity, the judgment could not stand.

The Court of Appeal agreed that there had been a serious procedural irregularity:

> In my opinion it was indeed thoroughly bad practice for the Judge to construct his judgment in the way that he did, essentially for the reasons given by Mr Cherry. Mr Bob Moxon Browne QC, for the Respondent, submitted that if the Judge accepted the entirety of Mr Chirnside's submissions, as he evidently did, and believed that they were well expressed, there could be nothing objectionable in his adopting them as the basis of his judgment; to set out to paraphrase them would be a wasted labour. I do not accept that submission. I agree with Mr Cherry that appearances matter. For the Judge to rely as heavily as he did on Mr Chirnside's written submissions did indeed risk giving the impression that he had not performed his task of considering both parties' cases independently and even-handedly. I accept of course that a judge will often derive great assistance from counsel's written submissions, and there is nothing inherently wrong in his making extensive use of them, with proper acknowledgement, whether in setting out the facts or in analysing the issues or the applicable legal principles or indeed in the actual dispositive reasoning. But where that occurs the judge should take care to make it clear that he or she has fully considered such contrary submissions as have been made and has brought their own independent judgment to bear. The more extensive the reliance on material supplied by only one party, the greater the risk that the judge will in fact fail to do justice to the other party's case – and in any event that that will appear to have been the case. (per Underhill LJ at [16])

Lord Justice Sedley added his own concurring words:

> Information technology has made it seductively easy to do what the judge did in this case. It has also made it embarrassingly easy to demonstrate what he has done. In principle, no doubt, it differs little from the modus operandi of the occasional judge, familiar to an earlier generation of counsel, who would pick up his pen (sometimes for the first time) and require the favoured advocate to address him at dictation speed. But in practice, for reasons which Lord Justice Underhill has described, the possibility of something approaching electronic plagiarism is new, and it needs to be said and understood that it is unacceptable. Even if it reflects no more than the judge's true thinking, it reflects poorly on the administration of justice: for, as Lord Justice Underhill says, appearances matter. ([39])

However, despite the judge's handling of the judgment, the Court of Appeal held that the decision should stand and dismissed the appeal.

Length of judgments

> English judges do tend to 'go on a bit'. There may be a variety of reasons for this 'culture'. They may be meticulous and thorough; they may have ingenious and inquiring and constructive and creative minds; they may be very knowledgeable in the law; they may be stimulated by good and challenging advocacy, and feel the need to deal with each and every point raised; they may be stimulated by reading the cited judgments of the great judges of the past, and indeed the present; they may be of a scholarly disposition, with academic pretensions; they may be trying to score points off their brethren; they may wish to make a significant and lasting contribution to the jurisprudence of English law; they may be self-important, arrogant, vain, loquacious, verbose, unrestrained – though luckily few justify such harsh adjectives. The current practice is a matter of the collective tradition and culture of the appellate bench.[78]

A major cause of the length of judgments not mentioned in that passage is the inordinate quantity of material nowadays produced by the parties both on the facts and on the law. Sir Louis Blom-Cooper QC had these general words of advice:

> Einstein is recorded as having stated as a golden rule that 'everything should be made as simple as possible, but not simpler'. Simplicity is best achieved by pruning the content of the judgment. Reciting the arguments of counsel is unnecessary. They tend to complicate the subject matter in hand … Recitation of the facts at length is rarely necessary … Even the exposition of case law can be annexed to the judgment, with only the conclusion of chunks of cited passages from past authorities in the body of the reasoned decision … Citation of the case law is often overdone. It is all too easy to quote large chunks of earlier judgments, easier than to summarise them … If necessary, the parade of case law can be put into an annex, where it does not clutter up the judgment or deflect the reader from the thrust of the judicial reasoning.[79]

One doubts, however, whether hand-wringing, complaint or admonition make any impact on the problem of the length of judgments.

5.2.6. Making Draft Judgments Available to the Lawyers

In former times, reserved judgments were read aloud in open court. Nowadays, in order to save time and costs, the court hands down reserved judgments in written form. They are referred to as 'handed down' judgments.[80] When judgment is reserved, it is quite usual for the judge to provide the lawyers in the case a draft before it is handed down. In 1998, a Practice Statement said that the purpose was

> to enable them to submit any written suggestions to the judge about typing errors, wrong references and other minor corrections of that kind in good time, so that, if the judge thinks fit, the judgment can be corrected before it is handed down formally in court. The parties' legal advisers are therefore being requested to submit a written list of corrections of this kind to the judge's clerk … Lawyers are not being asked to carry out proof-reading for the judiciary, but a significant cause of the significant delays is the fact that minor corrections of this type are being mentioned

[78] A Samuels, 'Those multiple long judgments' 24 *Civil Justice Quarterly*, 2005, 279, 280–81.

[79] L Blom-Cooper, 'Style of judgments' in L Blom-Cooper, B Dickson and G Drewry (eds), *The Judicial House of Lords 1876–2009* (Oxford University Press, 2009) 162–63.

[80] For the arrangements for handed-down judgments see Practice Note (Court of Appeal: Handed Down Judgments) [2002] 1 WLR 344.

to the judge for the first time in court, when there is no time to make any necessary corrections to the text.[81]

The statement about the procedure in the Civil Procedure Rules[82] emphasises the obligation of confidentiality but allows that the lawyers can show the draft judgment to their clients. Any proposed corrections should be sent to the other party. A study of the issue[83] said that there were cases illustrating four types of request going beyond the accepted uses:

— Counsel seeks to reargue a point of law[84]
— Counsel seeks to introduce new evidence[85]
— Counsel seeks to argue a new point of law[86]
— Counsel seeks to amend judicial opinion[87]

The courts had allowed substantive submissions in 'exceptional circumstances' but it was not clear what was and what was not permitted – though the *Condron* case[88] ruled out the introduction of new evidence. Ms Hughes suggested that the apparently open-ended possibility of asking for changes conflicted with the need for finality in litigation. It introduced an unwelcome new dimension into the process almost amounting to negotiation over the content of a judgment. It had implications for the independence of the judiciary and for the principle of open justice.

5.3. Are Precedents Law or only Evidence of the Law?

There is an important jurisprudential debate as to whether judges make law or whether they simply declare the law, and whether precedents are law or only evidence of the law. The two issues are closely related.

In the eighteenth century, Blackstone said: 'the decisions of courts of justice are the evidence of what is common law'.[89] In 1892 Lord Esher stated: 'There is in fact no such thing as judge-made law, for the judges do not make the law though they frequently have to apply existing law to circumstances as to which it has not previously been authoritatively

[81] Practice Statement (Supreme Court: Judgments [1998] 1 WLR 825, para 2. See also Practice Note (Court of Appeal: Handed Down Judgments [2002] 1 WLR 344, para 6.

[82] The procedure is now dealt with in the Civil Procedure Rules – Practice Direction (Reserved Judgments) Part 40E.

[83] K Hughes, 'The uses and implications of the draft judgment procedure' 127 *Law Quarterly Review*, 2011, 565–88. This section is based on her article.

[84] *Robinson v Bird* [2003] EWCA Civ 1820, [2004] WTLR 257; *Gravgaard v Aldridge & Brownlee* [2004] EWCA Civ 1529, Times December 2, 2004; *Egan v Motor Services (Bath) Ltd* [2007] EWCA Civ 1002, [2008 1 WLR 1589; and *R (Edwards) v Environment Agency* [2008] UKHL 22, [2008] 1 WLR 1587.

[85] *R (on the application of Condron) v National Assembly for Wales (Application to adduce evidence)* [2005] EWHC 3316 (Admin), [2006] JPL 1512 (QB).

[86] *Sanderson v Hull* [2008] EWCA Civ 1211, [2009] CP Re 12; and *R (Edwards)* (n 84 above).

[87] *R (on the application of Binyam Mohamed) v Secretary of State for Foreign and Commonwealth Affairs* [2010] EWCA Civ 158. The issue became national news when it became known that counsel had asked the court to remove criticism of the Foreign Service and the Security Service in a case arising out of alleged torture of Mohamed in Guantanamo Bay.

[88] Hughes, 'The uses and implications of the draft judgment procedure' (n 83 above).

[89] *Commentaries* (13th edn), vol i, p 88–89.

laid down that such law is applicable.'[90] According to Professor Rupert Cross a rule stated in a precedent 'is law properly so called and law because it was made by the judges, not because it originated in common usage, or the judge's idea of justice and public convenience'.[91] So far as Lord Esher's statement was concerned, the application of existing law to new circumstances could never clearly be distinguished from the creation of a new rule of law. If there were no such thing as judge-made law, it would be impossible to account for the evolution of much legal doctrine which had been formulated by the judges and no one but the judges.[92] If a previous decision was only evidence of what the law is, no judge could ever be absolutely bound to follow it, and it could never be effectively overruled because a subsequent judge might always treat it as having some evidential value.[93] There cannot be any cavil with Cross's statement that 'the fact that our judges can and do make law is now universally recognised by writers on the British Constitution'.[94] Lord Reid painted a fanciful picture of the traditional view:

> There was a time when it was thought almost indecent to suggest that judges make law – they only declared it. Those with a taste for fairy tales seem to have thought that in some Aladdin's cave there is hidden the common law in all its splendour and that on a judge's appointment there descends on him knowledge of the magic word 'open sesame'. Bad decisions are given when the judge has muddled the password and the wrong door opens. But we do not believe in fairy tales any more.[95]

As Lord Radcliffe said: '... there was never a more sterile controversy than that upon the question whether a judge makes law. Of course he does. How can he help it?'[96] But there is also merit in the view that precedents are evidence of law rather than law itself.

When a judge decides a point of law, they are declaring what they find the law on that point to be. They are not saying what they think it ought to be but what they believe it is. In giving voice to their opinion as to what the law is, they may have added something new to the existing corpus of the law. In fact, unless they have simply restated an existing principle or applied it in a totally predictable way to new facts, they *will* have done so. Many decisions on points of law add something new in this sense and can therefore be said to be 'making law'. From the judge's point of view, their function is to declare the law; from the point of view of the observer, they may in declaring it have added something new or even changed the law. The 'declaratory theory' and the 'judges-do-make-law theory' therefore appear both to be right.[97]

But there is a further dimension. It is possible that the judge, having stated what they think the law to be, proves to be in error. They may be reversed almost immediately on appeal or the ratio of their decision may be overruled in a later case by a higher court. This shows that inspection of a precedent at the time when it is handed down does not necessarily reveal whether the precedent reflects 'good law'. This will only emerge later when, with the advantage of hindsight, one will be able to say that the judge in 1986 stated what judges

[90] *Willis v Baddeley* [1892] 2 QB 324, 326.
[91] R Cross and JW Harris, *Precedent in English Law*, 4th edn (Clarendon Press, 1991) 28.
[92] Ibid, 29.
[93] Ibid, 30.
[94] Ibid.
[95] Lord Reid, 'The Judge as Law-Maker' (1972) 12 *Journal of the Society of Public Teachers of Law* (N.S.).
[96] Lord Radcliffe, *Not in Feather Beds* (Hamish Hamilton, 1968) 215.
[97] For an article defending the declaratory theory – with full acceptance that the judges make law – see A Beevor, 'The declaratory theory of law' 33 *Oxford Journal of Legal Studies*, 2013, 421–44.

in the succeeding decades agreed was the law on that point. Even then, fifty years later a different view may prevail.

The theory that precedents are no more than evidence of the law has the advantage that it seems to fit the facts. It explains one of the most fundamental and important aspects of the doctrine of precedent – that every principle that emerges from a judicial decision is capable of being changed. However well settled a principle of law may appear to be, it can be challenged and changed at any time. Even if the Supreme Court itself has enunciated the rule, it can be altered by the Supreme Court. In other words, it is possible to look at the rule of law that seems to emerge from a precedent and say 'That cannot be right and to prove it I shall litigate the point up to a higher court to get the rule changed'.

Lord Goff put it even more strongly:

> Seen in the perspective of time all statements of the law, whether by the legislature, or by judges, or by jurists, are no more than working hypotheses. They are quite simply, temporary approximations which some people in their wisdom have found to be convincing at certain points of time. To the layman, this may appear a startling proposition. The layman thinks of the law as inherently predictable, clear, precise, certain, even rock-like in quality. It is in fact nothing of the sort.[98]

Moreover, when a rule of law is enunciated by a court, its effect is retrospective. The newly enunciated rule is now the law and in theory always has been. Any different previous formulations of the rule have now been held to have been mistaken. The retrospective effect of the new rule is in one sense obviously a fiction, but it has the concretely practical result that a person may bring an action based on an injury suffered before the new rule and claim the benefit of the new formulation. The only exceptions are where the case has already been litigated (in which case the doctrine of *res judicata* prevents the issue being reopened), and where the Statute of Limitations operates to bar the action through the lapse of time. (An action for personal injuries, for instance, cannot normally be brought more than three years after the injury has been suffered.) The theory that precedents are only evidence of the law is consistent with the reality that what is thought to be the law at one time may turn out to be wrong.

The doctrine of precedent can be said to operate something like the best-evidence rule in the law of evidence – that the court wishes always to have the best evidence on any issue. The doctrine of precedent lays down rules as to how the courts should approach precedents. A decision of the House of Lords or the Supreme Court, other things being equal, is better evidence than one of the Court of Appeal, etc. Moreover, so far as the Court of Appeal is concerned, a decision of the House of Lords or the Supreme Court is not only the best evidence of what the law is, but creates an irrebuttable presumption that it is correct. On the other hand, the Supreme Court reviewing its own prior decision will treat the precedent as the best extant evidence of the rule, but the presumption that it is right is rebuttable since it is free to depart from its own prior decisions. Equally there is no difficulty with the problem of overruling. Again, the doctrine of precedent acts, in effect, to prohibit a court from receiving as evidence a decision that has been overruled. The exclusion of otherwise relevant evidence is a familiar principle of the law of evidence.

The view that precedents are evidence of the law and not the law itself is not only consistent with the innate flexibility and fluidity of the common law system, but also reflects the actual practice of the courts. Argument in a court as to what the law is, is based on marshalling by each side of its proofs – counsel comes armed with their precedents or their

[98] Lord Goff, 'Judge, jurist and legislature' *Denning Law Journal*, 1997, 79, 80.

reinterpretation of their opponent's precedents and submits that their view of the law is the correct one. Having heard each side, the judge decides between them. To say that the precedents *are* the law is the equivalent of saying that the witnesses to a question of fact are the truth. Whether the precedents reflect the law cannot emerge authoritatively until after the judge has spoken and even then only in the partial and qualified sense that at most the decision reflects the best evidence available at that moment as to what the law is.

There is a somewhat similar dispute as to whether the rules of precedent are 'law' or 'rules of practice'. See on this issue, for instance, L Goldstein, 'Four alleged paradoxes in legal reasoning' *Cambridge Law Journal*, 1979, 373; PJ Evans, 'The status of rules of precedent' *Cambridge Law Journal*, 1982, 162; CEF Rickett, 'Precedent in the court of appeal' *Modern Law Review*, 1980, 136; P Aldridge, 'Precedent in the Court of Appeal – another view' *Modern Law Review*, 1984, 187.

It is a nice question whether our doctrine of precedent promotes law-making in too rapid a way by over-emphasising the importance of individual decisions. Whilst it is true that the ultimate shape of a rule cannot be fully discerned until it has had time to mature, there is nevertheless a tendency to dramatise the significance of the latest case. Lord Radcliffe reflected on the dangers of this tendency:

Lord Radcliffe, *Not in Feather Beds* (Hamish Hamilton, 1968) 216–17

> I cannot help thinking that there is a tendency today to give too much importance to particular decisions, and by so doing to discover leading cases before they have proved that they have in them the quality to lead. There is too much forcing of unripe growth. Seen from the inside hardly any decision comes out ready made as of general authority; nor, I believe, do those who participate in it think of it in that way. One learns the vast difficulty of generalising on any matter of principle, just because, short of genius, there are very few minds that have the imaginative grasp to see the full implications of a generalisation and to pass in review its effect upon the interconnected strands of our body of law. It is not a question of playing safe: it is rather that a sensitive, not a blinkered, concentration upon the direct issue that has to be resolved makes for sounder construction of that legal body. And, perhaps, only their successors who have to work upon them appreciate how flashy have been the gnomic utterances of some of our best known judicial sages.
>
> I do not regret this counsel of reticence. It accords well with the methodology of our law-making. Just as under our system a court decision is formed out of the work of those who prepare a case, those who argue it before the court and those who ultimately explain and record their view, so a decision of even a final court, when pronounced, has only begun its life as a constituent of the full corpus of the law. It is a mistake, just because it is final, to think that the matter is then closed. On the contrary, it has been handed over to the care of the profession. It will be chewed over by barristers and solicitors, commented on in law journals, made the subject of moots and law lectures, reviewed by the writers of the legal text books. It will be read in the light of previous decisions, upon which it is itself a commentary: and it will be read in the light of later decisions, to which itself it forms a text. In the end, but only in the end, general legal opinion will come to assign to it a more or less determined place in the whole compendium of law, important or unimportant, formative or a dead end, malleable or rigid. Until a decision has been subjected to a process of this kind, in the course of which indeed it may come out wearing a very different air from that with which it entered and serving a purpose hardly intended by its authors, I should be reluctant to class it as a leading authority. We must not declare a vintage before it is made.
>
> If you happen to share the rather sober view I am putting forward you may share too my strong feeling that contemporary comment tends to attach far too much weight to particular phrases or passages in the body of a decision. Analysis of this order is almost morbid in its intensity, and it can, so often, be only sterile skill and ingenuity. A man must work according to his material. The English language is peculiarly ill-adapted to such elaborate analysis, being, as we know, though

copious and expressive, a pliable and shifting medium, in which even key words and phrases take shape and colour from their context and have no rigid internal structure of fixed meaning. The difficulty becomes that much the greater when the decision of a final court is conveyed not by a single pronouncement but in the separate deliveries of several judges. Then indeed a baffling task awaits the reader. Is one deliverance more leading than another, and, if so, how do you identify it? In course of time, no doubt, there will be selection through the operation of the kind of winnowing process that I have been describing. We all know how one particular speech or judgment comes to be regarded as the critical one, the one which is turned to as the core of the decisions. But time is needed for that.

5.4. The Values Promoted by the System of Precedent

A catalogue of the values promoted by the common law system of precedent was drawn up by Professors Hart and Sacks of the Harvard Law School in their widely known but unpublished set of materials on the legal process:

Henry Hart and Albert M Sacks, *The Legal Process* (tentative edition, 1958, mimeographed) 587–88

In furtherance of private ordering

(a) The desirability of enabling people to plan their affairs at the stage of primary private activity with the maximum attainable confidence that if they comply with the law as it has theretofore been announced, or can fairly be expected to be announced thereafter, they will not become entangled in litigation.
(b) The desirability of providing private counsel so far as possible with stable bases of reasoning. Think about this factor, in particular, from the point of view of efficient social engineering. The potential contribution of the legal profession in the avoidance of social friction is very large, is it not? A lawyer must have tools with which to work if he is to make this contribution.
(c) The desirability of encouraging the remedial processes of private settlement by minimising the incentives of the parties to try to secure from a different judge a different decision than has been given by the same or other judges in the past.

In furtherance of fair and efficient adjudication

(a) The desirability, from the point of view of the litigants, of expediting litigation and minimising its costs by sparing them the necessity of relitigating every relevant proposition in every case.
(b) The need, from the point of view of the judicial system, of facilitating the dispatch of business – indeed, the sheer impossibility of re-examining *de novo* every relevant proposition in every case.
(c) The need of discouraging a rush of litigation wherever there is a change of personnel on the bench.
(d) The desirability, from the point of view of fairness to the litigants, of securing a reasonable uniformity of decision throughout the judicial system, both at any given time and from one time to another.
(e) The desirability of promoting genuine impersonality of decision by minimising the elements of personal discretion, and of facilitating the operation of the check of professional criticism.
(f) The propriety of according respect to the conclusions of predecessor judges.

(g) The injustice of disappointing expectations fairly generated at the stage of primary private activity.

In furtherance of public confidence in the judiciary

(a) The desirability of maximising the acceptability of decisions, and the importance to this end of popular and professional confidence in (1) the impersonality of decisions and (2) their reasoned foundation, as manifested both by the respect accorded to them by successor judges and by their staying power.
(b) The necessity, considering the amorphous nature of the limits upon judicial power and the usual absence of an effective political check at the ballot box, that judges be subject to the discipline and the restraint of an obligation to build upon the prior law in a fashion which can withstand the test of professional criticism.

There are, however, various problems associated with law-making by judges and the doctrine of precedent, which have to be set against the positive aspects of the system:

(1) It over-emphasises the importance of individual decisions.
(2) It creates law which may upset expectations with no advance notice to those likely to be affected.
(3) The system depends on the accidents of litigation. A bad decision may stand for many years.
(4) It tends to be backward-looking and conservative, and therefore to be slow to respond to changing needs.
(5) Once a point has been decided at the level of the Court of Appeal or the House of Lords, it tends to remain the law whether or not it is apt for the situation.
(6) There are often technical problems associated with the fact that the judges give separate decisions so that it is difficult to ascertain what is the ratio. Or a judge may give several reasons for his decision so that again the ratio is obscure. Also the proliferation of precedents makes it difficult for lawyers to discover what the law is.
(7) The doctrine of precedent focuses attention on minute differences of fact between cases at the expense of consideration of principle and policy.

5.5. Flexibility and Stability in the Common Law System

It is not the system but the judges that create the balance between flexibility and stability. Whether it is a good balance is for judgment in each country where the common law system operates. (More discussion of the problems posed by this question is presented in chapter 7.) But the system itself does permit both flexibility and stability.

Inevitably with a system of precedent there is a strong tendency to follow the precedents whether they are binding or not and whether or not the precedent seems a wise one. A doctrine of precedent that progressed on the basis that precedents would only be followed when the court agreed with the decision reached in the earlier case, would be a weak doctrine. Equally it would dissipate much of the benefit of stability to which the system of precedent aspires. Professor Julius Stone expressed this tendency of the common law in memorable form in an article in 1959:

> The doctrine *of stare decisis*, in addition to whatever it may enjoin upon the intellect, certainly evokes an atmosphere and a mood to abide by ancient decisions, to follow the old ways, and conform to existing precedents. It suggests a condition of rest, even of stasis, a system of law

> whose content is more or less settled, the past content by past decisions, and the present and future content because they too are controlled by those past decisions. It implies the stability of the legal system along the stream of time, that despite all the vast social, economic and technological changes of the last eight or nine hundred years, society remains nevertheless in some meaningful sense under the governance of the same system of law.[99]

On the other hand, there is no doubt that the doctrine does lead to the perpetuation, sometimes for long periods, of bad decisions. Not infrequently they are even widely recognised to be bad decisions, and yet the courts somehow lack the energy to change them.

However, the doctrine of precedent has many gaps to permit judges wishing to avail themselves of the opportunity to refuse to be crabbed by it:

(a) The Supreme Court, like the House of Lords before it, is not bound by its own decisions, nor is the High Court, and the Court of Appeal (Criminal Division) is only lightly bound.
(b) There is a long list of exceptions to the rule that the Court of Appeal is bound by its own decisions (see p 232 above).
(c) The Judicial Committee of the Privy Council is not bound by its own decisions and the English courts sometimes prefer to follow its decisions in preference to inconsistent decisions from within the system by which they are technically bound.
(d) An unwelcome precedent can in the last resort be distinguished and thus be avoided.
(e) The appeal system allows *any* principle of common law to be challenged and thus changed by a court high enough in the hierarchy.
(f) If a decision is not binding it *need* not be followed.

Obviously, individual judges vary in their instincts – some are keener on stability, others prefer to emphasise the objective of keeping the law abreast of changing times. But each type of judge usually can find the means to achieve their purpose within the common law system.

A quite different source of flexibility in the system is that judges can manipulate precedents, logic, social policy and all the other bases of arguments presented to them by counsel in any way they please. This is not something that is usually acknowledged. But it is familiar to practitioners and it emerged with great force from an important article by two then young lecturers (both later distinguished professors) at the London School of Economics. The article was based on close textual analysis of speeches by House of Lords judges in all the 58 cases decided by the Law Lords in the twelve months from October 1979. Their paper demonstrated a startling state of affairs. Frequently the judges dealt with precedent by simply asserting that it was or was not relevant, with no explanation or reasoning to justify the assertion. Case law was sometimes described and discussed at length and at other times was simply rejected as being 'unhelpful' without discussion. In general the quality of reasoning in their lordships' judgments proved to be less impressive than one would have expected. If this was true of judgments in the House of Lords, how much more is it likely to be true of judgments in lower courts?[100]

[99] J Stone, 'The ratio of the ratio decidendi' 22 *Modern Law Review*, 1959, 597–98.

[100] See WT Murphy and RW Rawlings, 'After the ancien regime: the writing of judgments in the House of Lords 1979/80' *Modern Law Review*, 1981, 617; 1982, 34.

For an especially fine addition to the literature on the way of the common law see Sir Philip (now Lord) Sales, 'The common law: context and method', 135 *Law Quarterly Review* (2019) 47–66.

Further reading on precedent:

N Duxbury, *The Nature and Authority of Precedent* (Cambridge University Press, 2008); R Cross and JW Harris, *Precedent in English Law*, 4th edn (Clarendon Press, 1991); CK Allen, *Law in the Making*, 7th edn (Clarendon Press, 1964); Benjamin Cardozo, *The Nature of the Judicial Process* (Yale University Press, 1925); Karl Llewellyn, *The Bramble Bush* (Oceana Press, 1930); Jerome Frank, *Law and the Modern Mind* (Coward-McCann, 1930). There is also much of value on precedent in Peter Goodrich, *Reading the Law* (Blackwell, 1986). For further, advanced, reading see RA Wasserstrom, *The Judicial Decision* (Stanford University Press, 1961); and LJ Goldstein (ed), *Precedent in Law* (Clarendon Press, 1987).

6

Law Reporting

One of the essential elements in a system based on precedent is some tolerably efficient method for making the precedents available to those wishing to discover the law. It is through law reporting that the common law is available to the profession and anyone else wishing to know the law. An unreported decision is technically of precisely the same authority as one that is reported, but until the advent of online systems, decisions that were unreported were more or less inaccessible to all but scholars. Now they are accessible online in great profusion.

Law reporting in England goes back to the earliest days of the system.

6.1. The History of Law Reporting

There have been five distinct periods in the history of law reporting. The first, lasting for some two hundred and fifty years from 1282 to 1537, was the period of the Year Books. They were not law reports in the full modern sense, since they appear to have been designed more as guides to pleadings and procedure for advocates than as accounts of the decisions of the courts. They were written originally in Norman French and later in law French – a mixture of Norman French, English and Latin. In modern times they have been published in two editions – the Rolls Series (RS) and the Selden Society Series (SS). They are mainly of historical and antiquarian interest. Practitioners would rarely, if ever, have occasion to consult or cite the Year Books.

The second period, lasting three hundred and fifty years, was from 1537 to 1865. When the Year Books ceased around 1537, private sets of reports started to appear. They began to include summaries of counsel's argument and of the judge's decisions. The citation of reports in court became more common as the reports improved in quality. Some were excellent – the best is probably Coke, whose reports were published between 1600 and 1658. Coke was also a judge, as was Dyer (Chief Justice of the Common Pleas) and Saunders (Chief Justice of the King's Bench). But contemporaneous reports were rare until the end of the eighteenth century. The private reports are now collected in one great series – the English Reports. These are occasionally cited in the courts.

The third period dates from 1865, when the profession established the Incorporated Council of Law Reporting for England and Wales. The Council produces a series called the Law Reports, which are the most authoritative reports. But this is a private sector not a public sector enterprise. (As to what makes them the most authoritative and whether they are 'official' see 6.7 below). In addition to the *Law Reports* there are a great variety of other series, some general, some specialised – the *Weekly Law Reports* produced by the Incorporated Council of Law Reporting, the *All England Law Reports* originally published by Butterworths and now by LexisNexis, *Lloyd's Law Reports*, *Criminal Appeal Reports*, etc.

The fourth period dates from 1980 when for the first time a computerised database, Lexis, provided access to decisions on subscription via dedicated terminals which was then in turn superseded by subscription based online systems – see further 6.3 below.

The fifth period from the start of this century began a true revolution in access to law reports when they became accessible online free of charge – see further p 310 below.

In 1940 an official committee published a report on law reporting which gives the historical background:

Report of the Law Reporting Committee (1940)

> 4. It is a commonplace to lawyers at least that the law of this country consists substantially of legislative enactments and judicial decisions. The former are made known to the public in the most solemn form, printed at the public expense and preserved under conditions which ensure that they shall be permanently and authentically recorded. With the latter it always has been and still is far otherwise. Yet the importance of accurate and permanent reports of judicial decisions is and always has been obvious. We need not discuss at what stage in our legal history the theory of the binding force of precedent first appeared. In its present form it would have received little favour from the judges of the 14th and 15th centuries but already it was plain, as the pages of the Year Books testify, that uniformity and certainty of the law, the essentials of its just administration, cannot be attained without some measure of judicial consistency. As late as the latter half of the 18th century, on the one hand, Blackstone wrote 'For it is an established rule to abide by former precedents, where the same points come again in litigation; as well to keep the scale of justice even and steady, and not liable to waver with every new judge's opinion; as also because the law in that case being solemnly declared and determined, what before was uncertain, and perhaps indifferent, is now become a permanent rule, which it is not in the breast of any subsequent judge to alter or vary from, according to his private sentiments: he being sworn to determine, not according to his own private judgments, but according to the known laws and customs of the land; not delegated to pronounce a new law, but to maintain and expound the old one'.[1] On the other hand Lord Mansfield took a more elastic view of the relation of precedent to principle. 'The law of England', he said, 'would be a strange science indeed if it were decided upon precedents only. Precedents serve to illustrate principles, and to give them a fixed certainty. But the law of England, which is exclusive of positive law, enacted by statute, depends upon principles; and these principles run through all the cases according as the particular circumstances of each have been found to fall within the one or other of them'.[2] To-day, whatever the reasons may be, the theory of the binding force of precedents is firmly established, if not unreservedly, at least only with some such reservation as that a decision need not be followed if it appears to have been given *per incuriam* e.g. by reason of a relevant statute not having been called to the attention of the court.
>
> 6. … It may seem strange but it is true that, except for a brief interlude in the reign of King James I, the State has taken no part in, and made no financial contribution to, the publication of law reports … Apart from this single instance of State aid or interference the task of law reporting has been, as it still is, left wholly to private enterprise. Nor do we find any record of supervision by the State of an enterprise so vitally affecting the common welfare except that by a Statute of Charles II in 1662 (14 Car. II C. 33. S.2) it was enacted that 'All Books concerning the Common

[1] Comm 69.
[2] *Jones v Randall* (1774) Cowper 37, 39.

Lawes of this Realm shall be printed by the special allowance of the Lord Chancellor or Lord Keeper of the Great Seal of England for the time being the Lords Chiefe Justices and Lord Chiefe Baron for the time being or one or more of them or by theire or one or more of theire appointments' …

It was left, as we have said, to private enterprise to preserve in law reports that part of our law which consists of judicial decisions. How was this task performed? It is at this stage necessary to recall that at an early date in our legal history the right was established to cite as an authority before any tribunal a law report which had annexed to it the name of a barrister.[3] It is probable that this right arose from a still earlier privilege of a member of the Bar as amicus curiae to inform the court of a relevant decision of which he was aware. It was his right and perhaps his duty to give oral evidence of the law by stating that such and such a decision had been given. Thence followed the right to cite his written report of decisions which he personally vouched as a member of the Bar. Nor must it be forgotten that if it was the privilege of a barrister to write reports that might be cited to the courts, it was his privilege alone except so far as His Majesty's Judges from time to time might for the public benefit and perhaps their private profit devote a part of their leisure to the compilation of reports.

Here then was a field for private enterprise, for profit and for abuse. In earlier times, as now, the barrister must rely both on reason and authority, and if he must choose between them, would choose the latter. To the law-reporter the opportunity was given and he took advantage of it. It had been calculated that in the period between 1535 (when the Year Books ceased) and 1765 (when Burrow's Reports began to appear) more than one hundred persons were responsible for volumes of reports. Great names are among them – Dyer, Plowden, Coke, Saunders – and their reports have at all times been of high authority. But there are many others to whom perhaps a higher degree of authority is likely to-day to be given than was by their contemporaries. Some indeed were of such ill repute that, rule or no rule, privilege or no privilege, the judges would not listen to quotations from them. Of them Sir Harbottle Grimson wrote in 1657: 'A multitude of flying reports (whose authors are as uncertain as the times when taken …) have of late surreptitiously crept forth … we have been entertained with barren and unwanted products; which not only tend to the depraving the first grounds and reason of our students at the common law, and the young practitioners thereof, who by such false lights are misled; but also to the contempt of our common law itself, and of divers our former grave and learned justices and professors thereof; whose honoured and revered names have, in some of the said books, been abused and invocated to patronise the indigested crudities of these plagiaries.'

The last third of the eighteenth century saw an improvement which the first half of the nineteenth century maintained. Douglas, who in the Preface to his report showed the high purpose that he meant to serve, Burrows with his introduction of headnote and scientific division of his report, Durnford and East with their Term Reports, which for the first time aimed at a timely and regular publication – these and other reporters at least set a standard which had not been reached in earlier times. Moreover, at some date which we cannot discover, but which the late Sir Frederick Pollock put as at least later than 1782, the Judges or some of them were willing to revise reports of their judgment or even to supply written copies of them to the reporter, and a custom grew up whereby as a matter of professional etiquette some one reporter in each Court was supposed to have a monopoly of this assistance from the Judge. This reporter was thus in a sense 'authorised' and his reports were known as 'authorised' or 'regular' reports as distinguished from other reports, which were 'irregular' or 'unauthorised'. This did not, however, prevent all reports, whether regular or irregular, from being cited if they satisfied the single condition of being vouched by the name of a barrister. And so the flood of reports did not subside but, on the contrary, was increased by a new kind of publication which, anonymous in title and originally disclaiming any intention of

[3] The Bar's monopoly was enlarged to include solicitors by the Courts and Legal Services Act 1990, s 115.

competing with the regular reports, became in due course a serious rival and by its merits and in particular by its speedier publication commanded a larger sale than any of the regular reports. Such was the Law Journal first published in 1822 as a weekly and in 1830 as a monthly series. It was natural that its immediate success should provoke competition and it was in due course followed by the Jurist, established in 1837, the Law Times in 1843, the Weekly Reporter, established in 1852 and united in 1858 with the already established Solicitors Journal …

7. This was the condition of affairs when in 1863 certain members of the Bar inspired and led by the late W. T. S. Daniel, Q.C., commenced the agitation which led to the establishment of the series of reports known to us all as 'The Law Reports' … The objective which Mr Daniel had from the outset was to establish a series of reports under the control of the profession. It was still to be private enterprise in the sense that it received no State aid and was subject to no State interference. But it was not to be profit-making except so far as was necessary to render it self-supporting. No other purpose was to be served than to produce the best possible reports at the lowest possible price for the benefit of the profession and of the public at large. Inaugurated with such aims and under such auspices such a series, it was confidently hoped, would drive all competitors from the field and thus there would be established a single series of reports, accurate and scientific, reporting all cases that ought to be reported and none that ought not to be reported.

…

11. In the face of no little difficulty Mr Daniel and his friends carried the day. A council representative of the profession was established consisting of two *ex officio* members, the Attorney-General and the Solicitor-General for the time being, eight barristers, two of whom were chosen by each of the four Inns of Court, two serjeants chosen by Serjeants' Inn and two solicitors chosen by the Incorporated Law Society. This council, whose constitution remains substantially unchanged except that Serjeants' Inn has ceased to exist and therefore is not represented, was in 1870 incorporated under the Companies' Acts with the title 'The Incorporated Council of Law Reporting for England and Wales.' Its first object as stated in its Memorandum of Association was 'the preparation and publication in a convenient form, at a moderate price, and under gratuitous professional control of Reports of Judicial Decisions of the Superior & Appellate Courts of England.'

12. With the issue of the 'Law Reports' the old authorised Reports disappeared except that Best and Smith and Beavan and a few others for a very short time continued their publications. In 1867 the Jurist, one of the Reports, also ceased. The other Reports, the Law Journal, the Law Times, the Weekly Reporter and Solicitors Journal, continued and still continue, the last-named series under the name of the Solicitors' Journal, and to them there have been added two more publications, the 'Times Law Reports' first published in 1884 and the 'All England Reports' first published in 1936.

6.2. Criticisms of the System

The 1940 Report then referred to a number of criticisms made of the system – cost, repetition of the same case in different sets of reports and the problem of tracing cases.

14(e) The next criticism is of a far-reaching and very different character. Its substance really is not so much that the Reports are numerous, as that, being numerous, they are what they are. The 'Law Reports' are recognised as accurate: against them the criticism is made that they are incomplete in that they omit to report cases which ought to be reported, not merely cases of a

> special character which are properly relegated to special Reports, but cases in which light is thrown upon general legal principles or the construction of Acts of Parliament. Against other general Reports it is said that, while they may to some extent make good the deficiencies of the Law Reports by reporting cases not reported there, yet their accuracy is not beyond challenge and it is a grave matter if, as has more than once happened in recent years, the profession and the public are misled by an inaccurate Report. In our opinion it is impossible to emphasise too strongly the seriousness of this criticism. Further it is said that even the number of Reports does not ensure safety, but on the contrary decisions of importance may be unreported and at some future date be disinterred from their grave in forgotten shorthand notes. The complaint is echoed of an old editor of a text-book well known in its day, 'Watkins' Principles of Conveyancing': 'Is the law of England to depend upon the private notes of an individual and to which an individual only can have access? … Is a paper evidencing the law of England to be buttoned up in the side pocket of a judge or to serve for a mouse to sit upon in the dusty corner of a private library? If the Law of England is to be deduced from adjudged cases, let the reports of those adjudged cases be certain, known and authenticated.'
>
> (f) Finally, the criticism is heard that far too many cases are reported. It is said that the hearing of suits is protracted and the time of the court wasted by the citation of authorities of doubtful relevance, and that, if counsel is not darkened, at least first principles are apt to be obscured by the introduction of exceptions and refinements which had better be forgotten.

The Committee considered but rejected the idea that there should be any form of monopoly for a single official set of reports:

> To such a proposal or anything like it we are unanimously opposed. It ignores, as we think, the fundamental fact that the law of England is what it is not because it has been so reported but because it has been so decided. Thus, as we have said before in this report, it is the privilege, if not the duty, of a member of the Bar to inform the court, whether as counsel engaged in the case or as *amicus curiae*, of a relevant decision whether it had been reported or not. So it is the duty of a Judge to follow the decision of a competent court whether reported or not: it may well be that there has not been time to report it. The basis of the rule of precedent is the need for certainty and uniformity – suppose that a decision has been given on a question of (say) banking or insurance law or some other topic of professional interest which is likely to be quickly disseminated amongst a large circle of interested persons, and suppose that it be reported by a barrister in a Journal, whether devoted exclusively to law reports or not, is a judge to approach that question of law unaware of the previous decision, unless it has been reported in the Law Reports or other official Reports? Is a lawyer to advise his client: 'This is the law according to Mr Justice A, but his decision has not been reported in the Law Reports: if then your case comes, not before him, but before Mr Justice B, the latter may come to a different decision, for he may not be told what Mr Justice A has decided?' And what of a text-book writer? Is he to ignore decisions except those reported in the Law Reports? It appears to us that it is only necessary to ask these questions to show that a monopoly of citation would run counter to the spirit in which English law has been administered these many centuries.

Nor would it be right if some reporters were specially licensed – to put a check on the multiplicity of reports:

> In our view such proposals are fundamentally wrong. They strike, as we think, at the base of a principle which is one of the pillars of freedom, that the administration of justice must be public. The decision of the court must be open for publication, discussion and criticism. It is not consistent with this principle that a licence to report should be given to one man and withheld from another. If a case is once reported, then, as we have already pointed out, it is proper that it should be cited in order that the law may be interpreted and administered in the same way for all

> men. Nor can a Judge by any means deny the right to publish as laws that which he has decided to be law. Technical competence of the reporter there ought to be, and it exists to some extent in the requirements that a report should be vouched by a barrister-at-law; but that is a very different thing from monopolistic reporting …
>
> 19. We repeat, and it cannot be said too often, that the first essential of a Report is accuracy. In that lies its value as a precedent. In this respect the Law Reports maintain a remarkably high standard and they are assisted by the fact that judges themselves read and approve the reports of their decisions before they are published. We have been told that the same privilege is sometimes given to the Reports of patents, etc., cases, and to the Law Journal Reports, but to no other Reports. For this reason it has been generally but not universally the custom in the courts to demand that, if a case is reported in the Law Reports, it should be cited from those Reports and no other. We venture to hope that this practice may except in very special circumstances be rigidly enforced. We were indeed told that by some persons other reports were preferred for the very reason that it was supposed that they contained judgments as actually delivered and not as the judges, on second thoughts, would like to have delivered them. We need perhaps say no more about this point of view than that it appears to us a somewhat unscientific way of regarding an exposition of law.

The Committee considered whether it should recommend that a shorthand writer take down the exact text of every judgment, that this should be sent to the judge for correction and that a copy should be filed with the office of the Records of the Court. This would avoid the occasional instance of faulty reporting. It would also ensure a full record of all decisions. The Committee said the proposal would obviously cost money and it would impose an additional burden on the judges. It thought on the whole that most decisions that ought to be reported, were. ('What remains is less likely to be a treasure house than a rubbish heap in which a jewel will rarely, if ever, be discovered' p 20). On the whole it did not think there was a need to record all judgments.

A strong dissenting report from Professor AL Goodhart dealt with the fact that large numbers of reports were uncorrected by the judges and many more were not reported at all. Yet an unreported decision was nevertheless authoritative law.

Goodhart dealt in turn with the three problems mentioned by the Committee. The cost of having each judgment recorded, he thought, would not be great. The burden on the judges revising them would equally, he thought, not be serious. Nor need it add greatly to delays in getting publication. The advantage would be to reduce inaccurate reports. Judges would be able to delete phrases which did not accord with their considered opinions. He hoped that shorthand writers would be attached to each court and that judgments would be placed after revision in an official library.

What cases find their way into the pages of the law reports is determined by the editors of each series. A study of the reports for 1985, stated that almost all the decisions of the House of Lords were reported, as were something over 70 per cent of those of the Court of Appeal, Civil Division. A little over a third of the decisions of the Family Division of the High Court, 29 per cent of the Queen's Bench Division and 22 per cent of the Chancery Division decisions were reported. But under 10 per cent of the decisions of the Court of Appeal, Criminal Division appeared in the law reports. Only a handful of county court decisions are reported.[4]

[4] P Clinch, *Using a Law Library*, 2nd edn (Oxford University Press, 2001) 102–03.

The question whether it is satisfactory to leave the decision as to the reporting of cases to the decisions of law reporters[5] was addressed by the late Dr Olive Stone, of the London School of Economics:

Olive Stone, 'Knowing the law' 24 *Modern Law Review*, 1961, 475, 476–77

> Even if proper reports or transcripts were available of all cases, it seems very doubtful if the final decision on whether a case is reportable should lie with an editor responsible to no one but those who employ him. Surely this is pre-eminently a decision to be taken by a committee, which should have the fullest information about all cases decided, and should not be drawn exclusively from practising members of the Bar. Solicitors, law teachers and magistrates should obviously be represented, and in the field of family law (which suffers greatly from meagre reporting), there is also a case for representation of the social services to counterbalance the excessive stress on the types of litigation most profitable to the legal profession.

Dr Roderick Munday of the Cambridge Law Faculty made the subject of law reports one of his special fields of interest and over thirty or more years published important articles on the subject. In 1978 he dwelt on the proliferation of reports, on the role of overseas' authorities in stimulating law reform by the judges and on the problem of the unreported decision:

RJC Munday, 'New dimensions of precedent' *Journal of the Society of Public Teachers of Law*, 1978, 201

> Three recent developments in the field of precedent have added considerably to the volume of authorities upon which the legal profession has a tendency to draw …
>
> A NEW GENERATION OF LAW REPORTS
>
> Complaints concerning the bulk of English case-law are perennial. No one recently has troubled to calculate just how many reported cases our system possesses. But in 1951 it was estimated that in common law and equity there existed more than 312,000 reported decisions. Such statistics on their own mean little. However, the clear trend today is for an increasing number of cases to be reported, either in complete or abbreviated form, in an expanding range of law reports …
>
> In themselves, new series of law reports may be quite innocuous, if not desirable additions to the lawyer's armoury. Even if they do add appreciably to the volume of reported cases, there exist digests which compile and list all the decided authorities and these are perfectly capable of coping with any fresh additions. The bulk of case-law is tolerated by the common lawyer as an occupational hazard. Our rules of practice of course conspire to this result in as much as counsel are under a duty to the court to cite all relevant authorities, and an authority is probably still taken to mean an account of a case, whether written or oral, attested to by a member of the Bar present at the decision. The existence of a published report of a case does at least ensure that there is a permanent and reliable record of the judgment. However, the proliferation of series of reports raises a number of serious practical problems which were diagnosed by the Law Reporting Committee in 1940: namely, those of expense and accommodation, not to mention needless duplication, the difficulty of tracing authorities, the danger of textual variants and inaccuracies, and the fact that important cases can still be over-looked …
>
> UNREPORTED CASES
>
> Before turning to consider broader questions of policy affecting our methods of law reporting, it remains to examine one further development in the realm of precedent: namely, the rise to prominence of the unreported case. That the citation of unreported cases is on the increase scarcely requires a statistical proof.

[5] See further Burton M Atkins, 'Communication of appellate decisions: a multivariate model for understanding the selection of cases for publication' 24 *Law & Society Review*, 1990, 1171.

Munday's concern was that the growing mass of inaccessible unreported decisions created difficulties not only for lay people but for lawyers.[6] Today, the problem of unreported decisions is not their inaccessibility but their undue accessibility.

6.3. The Advent of Online Access to Law Reports

In 1978 when Dr Munday wrote his comments he was able to say that a computerised system of data retrieval for law reports would be 'totally undesirable' since it would result in the availability of far too much material. Only two years later this revolution had started to take place.

In 1980, Butterworths introduced into the English market the American system known as Lexis providing access to the main law reports and many specialist series of reports as well as transcripts of unreported decisions. (The company is now called LexisNexis.) Initially provision was via dedicated terminals which were soon replaced by online access. Lawtel, another subscription provider also started in 1980. In 2000, Sweet & Maxwell together with the American company Westlaw, started Westlaw UK.

The Incorporated Council of Law Reporting, the official provider of the Law Reports, has its own website with all its reported decisions from 1865 (www.iclr.com). Other subscription services include Casetrack[7] and Justis.[8]

These developments are of immense importance. Of perhaps equal importance has been the establishment of online access to law reports (as well as statutory materials) *free of charge*.

Until 1999 the official court shorthand writers had been allowed to charge fees for the work they did in helping to prepare reserved judgments for publication. (That help, it has been said, did not amount to very much. The main work was done by the judges and their clerks. As Lord Justice Brooke said in a speech in 2003, the shorthand writers basically just 'tidied them up (if they needed tidying) and placed their name on the title sheet.'[9] They were also allowed to assert a copyright entitlement over re-publication.) But in 1999 a new contract came into effect which changed all that. The Court Service became entitled to publish judgments of the Court of Appeal and the High Court free from any copyright.[10]

In 2000, the British and Irish Legal Information Institute (BAILII), a charitable trust, started its free of charge website www.bailii.org. Its main objective is to put on the website as much as possible of the legislation and caselaw of the United Kingdom and the

[6] 'Such is the ingratitude of man that the resultant headaches for practitioners, teachers and reporters have led some to sigh again for the old days when the obscurity surrounding the unreported decision was usually impenetrable'. RE Megarry, *Miscellany-at-Law*.

[7] Casetrack, owned by Merrill Corporation, has the monopoly, previously enjoyed by Smith Bernal Ltd, of being the only official transcriber for the judgments of the Court of Appeal, Civil Division and Criminal Divisions, and of the Administrative Division of the High Court. It is an official transcriber in competition with other commercial providers for judgments of other Divisions of the High Court. In 2014 it had some 80,000 judgments on its database.

[8] For a very useful listing by the Bodleian Library of what is provided by the many legal databases go to Bodleian Library: Legal Databases.

[9] Lord Justice Brooke, 'The use of technology in the courts', speech given at Leeds University, 23 May 2003.

[10] Lord Justice Brooke, ibid.

Republic of Ireland. (It also includes the decisions of the Court of Justice of the European Union and of the European Court of Human Rights.) It simply uploads the judgments. As a small charity, it does not have the resources to add headnotes, annotations, citation services and other features offered by commercial suppliers nor is its coverage as comprehensive as the subscription services. The website has some 50,000 visits per day. Its expanding database draws on over 100 different databases and holds over a million documents.

Transcripts of the decisions of the Supreme Court and of the Privy Council were accessible from their respective websites – www.supremecourt.uk and www.jcpc.uk. However, access to these decisions has changed. As from 4 December 2024, the text is on the new Find Cases Law service managed by the National Archives online service (as to which see below).

Decisions of the House of Lords from 1996 to 2009 are accessible from the parliament website: www.publications.parliament.uk/pa/ld/ldjudgmt.htm. Earlier decisions of the House of Lords and of the Privy Council may be available on the Parliamentary Archive website. They will likely also be available on BAILII.

The entire series of the English Reports from 1457 to 1873 is accessible free of charge on www.CommonLII, the amalgamated site of BAILII and other legal information institutes from the common law jurisdictions. (The English Reports are also accessible by subscription via Westlaw, Lexis and HeinOnline.)

The online services can upload transcripts of judgments within hours of the decision, though if the judgment is given extempore (orally), it first has to be transcribed. In the Criminal Division of the Court of Appeal the overwhelming majority of decisions are given extempore.[11] In the Civil Division, the proportion is much lower.[12] (In former times transcription would be based on recording by stenographers. They were largely replaced by voice recognition audio recording, which is now largely replaced by digital recording.[13] Decisions of the Court of Appeal, Criminal Division are still recorded by human stenographers, but only a minority are subsequently transcribed.

6.3.1. National Archives Provides New Case Law Website

In June 2021 it was announced that selected court and tribunal judgments would be held on a new website to be managed by The National Archives. The website went live in April 2022. New court and tribunal decisions from the Supreme Court, Court of Appeal, High Court and Upper Tribunals became available – free of charge – on the National Archives Find Case Law site (https://caselaw.nationalarchives.gov.uk). There is a page on the website explaining its coverage. The advent of this new free facility does not affect what is accessible via BAILII.

The initial collection of judgments and decisions totalled 50,000, dating back to 2003 for court judgments and 2015 for Tribunal decisions. Users can search by neutral citation,

[11] In 2014, Master Egan QC, Registrar of the Court of Appeal, Criminal Division, said that although there were no statistics, the proportion of extempore decisions was around 85 per cent (email to the writer 29 July 2014).

[12] As previously noted, most Court of Appeal, Civil Division decisions are now 'handed down', as compared with delivered extempore. They would certainly include the decisions that justify inclusion in the law reports. The judges are very aware that such judgments should be reserved and handed down.

[13] Run by the Courts Transcription and Recording Unit in the Royal Courts of Justice.

party name, judge's name, court/chamber and date.There are two free licences allowing re-use of content from the service:

> The Open Justice Licence allows members of the public to continue to use, quote and publish judgments or extracts from judgments. There are some limits to protect the proper administration of justice, around computational analysis of judgments as data.
> For data users, there is a separate free licence, which one needs to apply for. This allows users such as legal publishers, LawTech companies or academic researchers to process judgments as data, to provide a website search services, compute statistics or computationally analyse the law.
> More information can be found on the Find Case Law website.

6.4. What Decisions are Reported in the Law Reports?

In modern times, virtually all decisions of the House of Lords and the Supreme Court have been reserved and then reported in the *Law Reports* and the *All England Law Reports* but the proportion of decisions of the other courts reported in the law reports has been much lower. (There are no available statistics.) What is certain is that the online uploading of judgments has meant a massive and rapidly increasing number of accessible unreported decisions. (As to this issue see 6.5 below.)

Lord Neuberger, then President of the Supreme Court, made law reporting the focus of his contribution to the volume published in 2007 to celebrate the centenary of *Halsbury's Laws of England.*[14] He described law reporters as 'the unsung heroes and heroines of our legal system'. The skills needed for law reporting, he wrote, included selecting the right cases to be reported – decisions introducing a new principle, or modifying an old principle or which decided disputed or uncertain issues or which were in some way 'peculiarly instructive'. Another necessary skill was that of editing of the judgments which included correction of errors made by the judges in their judgments. Lord Neuberger said: '[A] good law reporter will find mistakes, sometimes quite serious ones, in judgments as approved or handed down. Throughout my judicial career, I have had frequent cause to be grateful to a number of law reporters for saving my blushes in this connection.' Finally there was the preparation of the other parts of the report:

> Depending on the report, these can include (a) identification of catchwords (for indexing), (b) writing the headnote, (c) identifying cases which are followed, applied, distinguished, disapproved, overruled or explained (d) listing cases referred to in argument and in the judgment, (e) explaining the procedural history including the essential features of court documents, and (f) a summary of the arguments. These all require skill and patience. The headnote is of particular importance as advocates' arguments on cases often go no further than the headnote. Even if they go further, the assessment of the judgment concerned is often coloured by the headnote, which tends to be fuller than 50 years ago. Headnotes now set out the facts (albeit in summary form) and often explain the *ratio* in some detail.

[14] Lord Neuberger, 'Law reporting and the doctrine of precedent: the past, the present and the future' in *Halsbury's Laws of England Centenary Essays* (LexisNexis, 2007) 69–83: www.lexisnexis.co.uk/en-uk/products/halsburys-laws-of-england.page.

Lord Neuberger went on to consider some more recent developments:

> Over the past few decades, it appears to me to be increasingly true that (a) many more cases are being decided, (b) a higher proportion of decided cases are being reported, and (c) a higher proportion of reported cases are being cited in subsequent cases. The combined effect of these changes is to effect a substantial alteration to legal advice, hearings and judgments.
>
> In 1957, there were about 45 High Court Judges and ten (including the Lord Chief Justice) who sat regularly in the Court of Appeal. By 2007, the figures were about 108 High Court Judges and 40 in the Court of Appeal. The increase in judicial manpower is nearly three-fold; indeed, once one takes into account the substantial number of Circuit Judges and senior practitioners now sitting every day as Deputy High Court Judges, the number of sitting days in courts of record must have more than tripled since 1957.
>
> It is true that hearings, especially at first instance, now last, at least on average, significantly longer than they used to last, partly because so many more cases are now cited. Even allowing for this, the substantial increase in judges sitting in courts of record must result in many more decisions. This is attributable to the fact that, while few, if any, areas of law have died off, many new areas have been appearing for the first time and many established areas have grown substantially. There has been a considerable increase in the volume of primary and secondary legislation, as examination of the bound annual volumes of statutes and of statutory instruments demonstrates. There has been an explosion in the quantity of regulation. Administrative law has grown out of all recognition in the past 50 years. EU law only came on the scene in the early 1970s, and has been on the march since then. Human rights came onto the domestic agenda less than ten years ago. The so-called culture of complaint, or blame culture, has had a marked and expanding influence on the law.
>
> The increase in the number of reported cases is also plain to see. Over the past 35 years or so, Butterworths have vastly expanded their repertoire to include at least 12 sets of specialist law reports, starting with Industrial Relations Law Reports in 1972. It is interesting to note that of these twelve new sets of reports, eight began in or after 1995. The total number of cases these twelve new sets have reported to date exceeds 15,000; by comparison, since 1936, the All ER have published just under 25,000 decisions. Since 1970 or so, the vastly improved Estates Gazette Law Reports have published, on average, two full reports a week. Over that period, other companies also have started to publish specialist reports; examples notably include well-established legal publishers such as Thomson's Sweet & Maxwell (who publish, for instance, Common Market Law Reports and Housing Law Reports) and Jordans (whose publications include UK Human Rights Reports and Family Law Reports). Additionally, there has been the very significant development of the overnight reports (such as the Daily Law Notes, All ER (D) and Lawtel), consisting of electronically transmitted decisions (often of verbatim judgments) given the previous day.
>
> Having said that, it is interesting to note that the number of cases reported in the leading established non-specialist law reports has actually fallen. The number of cases reported in [1937], [1957], [1987], [1997], and (up to 10 August) [2007] All ER were, respectively, 495, 382, 333, 227 and 163. As for the Council, the figures for [1907], [1977], [1997] and (up to 10 August) [2007] are 468 (the Full Reports, as that was all the Council published then), and 333, 281, and 190 (the WLR). I think that the fall in these numbers is attributable to three factors. First, more careful, even ruthless, editing; with the knowledge that most cases of any interest will be reported somewhere, the WLR and All ER reporters are trying, quite rightly, to ensure that they only report cases which really do fall into one or more of Lindley LJ.s four categories.[15] Secondly, judgments

[15] In a Paper in 1863, Nathaniel Lindley QC (as he then was) established four categories of cases that justified reporting: '(a) decisions which introduce a new principle, (b) decisions which modify an old principle, (c) decisions which settle disputed or uncertain issues, and (d) decisions which are "peculiarly instructive".' (Lord Neuberger, 'Law reporting and the doctrine of precedent' (n 14 above) 71–72).

are increasingly long, as judges explain with greater particularity the reasons for their decisions, and have to deal with the increasing number of authorities raised in argument. Thirdly, there is the evergrowing number of specialist law reports, which make it easier for the general reports to eschew reporting cases, however important, if they are or may be largely of specialist interest.

There had been a considerable increase in the number of cases cited.

In [1907] AC, the average number of cases cited in argument was five, and in [1957] and [1987] it was 23 and 20 respectively; by [2007] the average had increased to 41. Interestingly, these figures were roughly reflected in the average length of the Law Lords' speeches: six pages in [1907], 16 and 17 respectively in [1957] and [1987], increasing to 25 pages in [2007].

The increase in the number of cited cases is, of course, in part due to the increase in the number of reported cases and the increase in the number of published unreported cases: the more decisions that are reported or otherwise available, the more potentially relevant reported decisions there are to be cited. Other reasons for the large increase in unreported cases are, I think, perhaps not surprisingly, the same as those which explain the increase in reported cases. I also suspect that the decision of the House of Lords in *Saif Ali v Sidney Mitchell and Co*[16] has had an effect. In that case, effectively taking advantage of the 1966 *Practice Statement*,[17] the House departed from its previous view that an advocate could not be sued for negligence in relation to the conduct of a case in court. If my suspicion is right, this would be a case of a change in the common law having an effect on law reporting, rather than the converse.

The increase in the number of available decisions created considerable problems:

The large number of judicial decisions reported or otherwise available gives rise to significant challenges to the law reporters, legal advisers, advocates, judges, and academics, and thus to the common law itself …

For the law reporters, the large number of judgments, particularly with many being given *ex tempore*, and therefore being unpredictable as to timing, renders covering the courts a difficult and expensive exercise. Although the rising proportion of reserved judgments mitigates the problem, it by no means neutralises the effect of the large increases in the number of judges and, hence, of judgments. As to the selection of the cases for reporting, the total number of cases reported in the All ER, the WLR and the Full Reports should not cause (and has not caused) the number of reported cases to increase. Accordingly, the growing tide of cases produces increasing challenges on selection.

The increase in the number of decisions, and, in particular, the introduction of overnight reporting, has resulted in editing of judgments being either more challenging or (in the case of many of the websites and the overnight verbatim reports) effectively abandoned. The contents of the report other than the judgment (for instance the headnote represent a challenge which can only increase with the growth in both the number of decisions given, and the proportion getting reported.

For all those who wish to rely on case law, whether practising lawyers, academics, judges or students, there is a potential trade-off between speed and reliability. If a case is properly reported, it will be reliable, but, with the exception of House of Lords decisions (which are proof-read by reporters before they are given, and are reported normally within two weeks), there is a significant delay between the judgment and its reporting. Further, substantial number of cases are never reported, and therefore never have the benefit of professional editing or a headnote … [B]ecause of the absence of editing or a headnote (or other information provided in a proper law report), an unreported judgment may well be less reliable and much more cumbersome to consider. Apart

[16] [1980] AC 198.

[17] *Practice Note (Judicial Precedent)* [1966] 3 All ER 77, sub.nom. *Practice Statement* [1966] 1 WLR 1234, HL.

from giving a clear summary of the facts, issues and *ratio* of a case, a headnote enables one quickly to contextualise the judgment or judgments to which it relates. Particularly if there is more than one judgment, or there is a long judgment, the provision of a headnote acts like a road map, saving a lot of time and minimising the risk of misunderstanding. Overnight reports present an additional difficulty in the case of *ex tempore* decisions: in contrast to reported decisions, the judge is given no opportunity to approve (ie to edit and correct) what he is recorded as having said.

As to practising lawyers, the concern about being sued for professional negligence is reinforced and facilitated by an increase in the number of decisions which are reported, and also in the speed with which decisions are notified. Indeed, as mentioned, it encourages the proliferation of published decisions, reported and unreported. The inevitable consequence for clients is, of course, increased costs. The same point applies to argument in court: more reported cases and the possibility of a negligence suit result in fuller submissions and much more citation of authority, which produces longer and more expensive hearings. This in turn results in longer judgments, and has contributed to the increase in the proportion of reserved judgments. This produces an increased number of long judgments, which in turn feeds back into rendering legal advice and legal argument at hearings longer and more expensive.

Additionally, the welter of available case law leads to an increased risk of lawyers, whether advising or advocating, losing sight of the wood for the trees. With a morass of authorities, one risks becoming bogged down in other cases, when one should be concentrating on identifying the basic principles which apply to the case in hand.

The problems for the judiciary mirror those for the advocates. The increased citation of cases means more pre-reading, longer hearings, and longer judgments, and more reserved judgments, all of which mean more pressure and more work. There is also an increased risk of losing sight of the central issues.

6.5. Too Many Unreported Decisions

Vast quantities of unreported decisions are now easily available to lawyers preparing their legal arguments, and, not surprisingly, the citation of unreported decisions has risen very significantly.

In 1983, the House of Lords, responding to this development, attempted to deal with it by laying down a rule as to the circumstances in which it would be prepared to allow unreported decisions to be cited. The relevant passage, to which the other four judges expressly agreed, was delivered by Lord Diplock:

> My Lords, in my opinion, the time has come when your Lordships should adopt the practice of declining to allow transcripts of unreported judgments of the civil division of the Court of Appeal to be cited upon the hearing of appeals to this House unless leave is given to do so; and that such leave should only be granted upon counsel's giving an assurance that the transcript contains a statement of some principle of law, relevant to an issue in the appeal to this House, that is binding upon the Court of Appeal and of which the substance, as distinct from the mere choice of phraseology, is not to be found in any judgment of that court that has appeared in one of the generalised or specialised series of reports.[18]

In 1996 the Court of Appeal, Civil Division laid down a similar rule that 'leave to cite unreported cases will not usually be granted unless counsel are able to assure the court that the

[18] *Roberts Petroleum Ltd v Bernard Kenny Ltd* [1983] 2 AC 192, 200.

transcript in question contains a relevant statement of legal principle not found in reported authority' (Practice Note [1996] 1 WLR 854).

The House of Lords' edict in *Roberts Petroleum* provoked strong critical comment. See, in particular, GW Bartholomew, 'Unreported judgments in the House of Lords' *New Law Journal*, 2 September 1983, 781. First, there was no need to ban unreported decisions. If counsel was citing an authority which was not useful, the remedy was to stop counsel. They did this with reported decisions and could presumably do so just as much with unreported cases. Secondly, most of the points made by Lord Diplock as to the shortcomings of unreported judgments applied equally to those that were reported. Both were dependent on the facts of the case in question, both were liable to include statements of principle that might be wider or narrower than the facts required. He continued:

> It is surely still true that it is the judges who make the law (to the extent that they do so) and not the editors of either the generalised or specialised law reports. If that remains true then the publication of a judgment should have little or nothing to do with its citability …
>
> For transcripts of unreported judgments of the Civil Division of the Court of Appeal to be citable in the House of Lords then, in Lord Diplock's view, two conditions must be satisfied. First, the principle of law for which the transcript is being cited must (*a*) be binding on the Court of Appeal, and (*b*) not be found in any reported judgment of that court. Second, counsel must give an assurance that both limbs of the first condition are satisfied. Now the first limb of the first condition is part and parcel of the traditional doctrine of precedent, and needs no further comment in this context. It is the second law of the first condition, with its implicit distinction between principles of law on the one hand, and the circumstances of their application and the form in which they are stated, on the other, which will surely prove difficult to apply.
>
> The somewhat amoeboid principles of the common law grow or are restrained by their application, re-application or non-application to varying fact situations. They are re-phrased, re-stated and re-iterated over and over again, and what eventually emerges is often startlingly different from that from which one started. The great principle of the common law in this context is that 'great oaks from little acorns grow' – this is the *leitmotif* of the judicial process. It is of the essence of the common law system that freedom, and all other principles of law, broaden down from precedent to precedent.

Similar objections were made in 1998 to the extension of the restrictive approach to unreported decisions of the Court of Appeal – see FAR Bennion, 'Citation of unreported cases – a challenge' *New Law Journal*, 16 October 1998, 1520. Mr Bennion stated that in the 1997 edition of his textbook there were no fewer than 1,463 citations of unreported decisions. He argued that the courts had no right to abridge the citizen's basic right to conduct legal proceedings as they see fit – subject to the court's power to control repetitious, irrelevant or improper argument.

Other problems identified by commentators in response to the House of Lords' ruling in *Roberts Petroleum* included the following:

(1) Decisions of the courts are the law in the sense that they may contain the articulation of a legal rule and must in any event amount to the application of a rule.[19]
(2) In an adversary system, counsel should be left to make their case as best they can. Lexis provided full-text access to decisions and was therefore to be preferred to the many forms of edited reports.[20]

[19] Colin Tapper, *Law Society's Gazette*, 29 June 1983, 1636.
[20] Ibid.

(3) Lord Diplock described the role of the Court of Appeal in terms that were more suitable to that of a trial court in a provincial town. He seemed to discount its vital role in the law-making process.[21]

(4) Lord Diplock seemed to downgrade the role of courts generally by complaining that facts constrained him to qualify the principles of law. But law is about facts – the facts define the categories of situations that are covered by the rule. The function of the court is to generalise from the facts.[22]

(5) The effect of Lord Diplock's ruling was to make the law reporters, rather than the judges, the arbiters of what is the law.[23]

(6) In some areas the law suffered from under-reporting of decisions, not over-reporting. This was true, for instance, in the company law field.[24]

A different attack on the House of Lords ruling in *Roberts Petroleum* was made by the managing director of Butterworths (Tele publishing) Ltd – the company that marketed Lexis. His main point was that in reality there was little evidence of a great upsurge of irrelevant unreported decisions being cited. In *Roberts Petroleum* itself, although Lord Diplock said that three out of four transcripts cited were unreported, in fact all four had been referred to in traditional legal sources. None was to be found in any computer database! Moreover, he argued, the House of Lords ruling was based on an unworthy view that counsel could not be relied on to do their duty efficiently.[25]

In *Michaels v Taylor Woodrow Developments Ltd*,[26] Mr Justice Laddie devoted the last three pages of a judgment to the problem of the excessive number of unreported cases being cited as authorities. Until recently that had not been a serious problem. Even in the 1970s there had been no readily available and cheap means for copying unpublished reports, even if they could be found. The growth of computerised databases made it an ever more frequent and extensive occurrence.

> Large numbers of decisions, good and bad, reserved and unreserved, can be accessed. Lawyers frequently feel that they have an obligation to search this material. Anything which supports their client's case must be drawn to the attention of the court. ([79])

The extra costs incurred had to be paid for by the litigants. Another consequence was that weak or poor decisions that previously would have been quietly buried by being ignored were now liable to be 'dug up' and used to bolster cases that previously would not have been pursued. In *Roberts Petroleum* Lord Diplock had suggested that citing unreported decisions should require leave. But the requirement of leave could itself involve additional costs. (In the State of Victoria such a rule had become a dead letter since it was usually easier to let counsel cite the case rather than argue over whether it should be cited.) Moreover, it was difficult to see how judges of first instance or the Court of Appeal could refuse leave to cite an unreported decision of the Court of Appeal when the decision, if applicable, would be binding on them. Nor would Lord Diplock's suggestion reduce the lawyers' task of undertaking research.

[21] Francis Bennion, *New Law Journal*, 30 September 1983, p 874.
[22] Ibid.
[23] WH Goodhart, *New Law Journal*, 1 April 1983, p 296.
[24] Ibid.
[25] See N Harrison, 'Unreported cases: myth and reality' *Law Society's Gazette*, 1 February 1984, 257. See also Bennion (n 21 above), 29 June 1983, 1635; NH Andrews, 'Reporting case law: unreported cases, the definition of a *ratio* and the criteria for reporting decisions' 5 *Legal Studies*, 1985, 205.
[26] [2001] Ch 493, [2000] 4 All ER 645.

6.6. Restricting the Citation of Authorities

Since 1995 there have been a series of Practice Directions in regard to citation of authorities in the Court of Appeal.[27] In April 2001, the Lord Chief Justice, Lord Woolf, with the concurrence of the Master of the Rolls, the President of the Family Division and the Vice-Chancellor, issued a new Practice Direction[28] regarding the citation of authorities in all civil courts. It began:

> In recent years, there has been a substantial growth in the number of readily available reports of judgments in this and other jurisdictions, such reports being available either in published reports or in transcript form. Widespread knowledge of the work and decisions of the courts is to be welcomed. At the same time, however, the current weight of material causes problems both for advocates and for courts in properly limiting the nature and amount of material that is used in the argument of subsequent cases.

With a view to limiting the citation of authorities to cases that were 'relevant and useful to the court' the Practice Note laid down a series of new rules:

1. A judgment in certain categories[29] could only be cited if it 'clearly indicates that it purports to establish a new principle or to extend the present law'. In regard to judgments delivered after the Practice Note, that indication must be expressly stated. In regard to earlier judgments 'that indication must be present in or clearly deducible from the language used in the judgment' (para 6.1).
2. When it was sought to cite other categories of judgments, the courts would in future 'pay particular attention, to any indication given by the court delivering the judgment that it was seen by that court as only applying decided law to the facts of the particular case; or otherwise as not extending or adding to the existing law'. Advocates seeking to cite a judgment containing indications of that type would be required 'to justify their decision to cite the case' (paras 7.1–2).
3. Advocates citing any authority (including any from another jurisdiction) would be required to state in respect of each authority the proposition of law for which it was being cited and the parts of the judgment that supported that proposition (para 8.1).
4. If it was sought to cite more than one authority in support of a given proposition, the reasons must be stated (para 8.1).
5. In regard to authorities from another jurisdiction the advocate would have to say also what that authority added that was not to be found in an authority from this jurisdiction or why it was appropriate to add to such domestic authority.

[27] *Practice Direction (Court of Appeal: Citation of Authority)* [1995] 1 WLR 1096; *Practice Statement (Court of Appeal: Authorities)* [1996] 1 WLR 854; Practice Statement (Supreme Court: Judgments) [1998] 1 WLR 825; *Practice Direction: Form and Citation* [2001] 1 WLR 194; *Practice Direction: Citation of Authorities* [2012] 1 WLR 780.

[28] [2001] 1 WLR 194.

[29] These categories were: applications attended by one party only; applications for permission to appeal; decisions on applications that only decide that the application is arguable; and county court cases unless cited to illustrate the measure of damages in personal injury cases or to demonstrate a proposition for which there is no better authority (para 6.2).

The Practice Direction stated that it would remain the duty of advocates to draw the court's attention to any authority not cited by an opponent which is adverse to the case being advanced (para 4).

Dr Roderick Munday was critical of this Practice Direction.[30] The requirement in para 8 (item 3 above) that counsel had to state the proposition underlying each authority to be cited, he suggested, 'paints a curiously unsophisticated picture of legal argument'.[31] It seemed to pre-suppose that each and every proposition was supported by a single case, and that 'arguments are assembled rather like a child let loose on a box of Lego bricks'. ('Authorities with slightly differing facts afford the means whereby we identify the limit of our rules. Very often, it is the clusters of cases, rather than the isolated authorities, which most frequently enable us to define and apply the rules … Not even an undergraduate with the limpest grasp of his subject would imagine that the unfailing pattern of the legal world is one authority per legal proposition.'[32])

The importance given by the Practice Direction (item 2 above) to 'indications' by a court that its decision was not intended to be a precedent, underlined and extended, he suggested, the lawmaking role of the courts. Hitherto such indications were non-binding 'obiter dicta'. Now it seemed they were to be treated as presumptively binding unless counsel could justify the decision to cite the case.

Dr Munday suggested that the Practice Direction also made a further inroad into what used to be regarded as counsel's right and duty to cite what he conceived to be all relevant cases. However it appeared that in practice the judges were not being heavy handed in their approach to this issue. Dr Munday wrote that at a then recent conference on law reporting attended by many practitioners he had asked the audience whether they had ever been prevented by the court from citing unreported authorities. Apparently, no one had.[33]

The 2012 Practice Direction was issued 'to clarify the practice and procedure governing the citation of authorities throughout the Senior Courts of England and Wales, including the Crown Court, in county courts and in magistrates' courts'. In regard to unreported decisions the Practice Direction said:

> 10. Where a judgment has not been reported, reference may be made to the official transcript if that is available, not the handed-down text of the judgment, as this may have been subject to late revision after the text was handed down. Official transcripts may be obtained from, for instance, BAILII (*http://www.bailii.org/*). An unreported case should not usually be cited unless it contains a relevant statement of legal principle not found in reported authority.

In July 2009, the Court of Appeal, Criminal Division added its voice to the complaint that the judges were having to cope with the citation of many too many authorities. Lord Judge, the Lord Chief Justice, giving judgment in *R v Erskine and R v Williams*,[34] said that reference should not be made to authorities which merely illustrated a principle or which

[30] His criticisms were expressed in the first of three articles entitled 'Over-citation: stemming the tide' *Justice of the Peace*, 5 January 2002, 6.

[31] Ibid, 8.

[32] Ibid, 8.

[33] Ibid, p 9, fn 18.

[34] [2009] EWCA Crim 1425, [2010] 1 WLR 183.

merely restated it. Only an authority that established a principle should be cited. He cited what Lord Bingham had said, speaking extra judicially:

> 'The quick, effortless and relatively inexpensive availability of vast new swathes of material hitherto inaccessible, unorganised, unfiltered, unedited, presents a very real risk to the system which may … simply succumb to the weight of the materials presented.'

Lord Judge continued:

> 74. There is no doubting the problem. It is not confined to this particular type of case, but is a feature of all types of appeal against conviction and sentence. Repeating that we imply no criticism of counsel in either case, these appeals illustrate it. The question is whether this judgment will merely be one more plaintive lament against what has become an irreversible process, or whether action should be taken to avoid the impending crisis identified by Lord Bingham. If that is the choice, the answer is self-evident. We must do more than complain. Even if, long term, this issue must be examined again and the various differing views considered, there can be little doubt that firm measures are immediately required, at least in this court, to ensure that appeals can be heard without an excessive citation of or reference to many of its earlier, largely factual decisions.
>
> 75. The essential starting point, relevant to any appeal against conviction or sentence, is that, adapting the well known aphorism of Viscount Falkland in 1641: if it is not *necessary* to refer to a previous decision of the court, it is *necessary* not to refer to it. Similarly, if it is not *necessary* to include a previous decision in the bundle of authorities, it is *necessary* to exclude it. That approach will be rigidly enforced.

Lord Judge did not specify how such enforcement would (or could) be implemented.

Fake precedents

On 6 June 2025, the Divisional Court, exercising its disciplinary jurisdiction, gave judgment in two cases involving fake precedents.[35] In one, a pupil barrister had cited five fake cases. In the other, the solicitor had submitted written legal argument in pre-trial proceedings that included a large number of fake precedents and fake quotations. The court referred the lawyer in both cases to their respective regulator and said it was also sending its decision to the Bar Council, the Law Society and the Council of the Inns of Court for them to consider what further steps should be taken to address the problem of fake precedents generated by AI. In an appendix to the decision the court listed a number of other cases that raised the same issue.

6.7. The Hierarchy of Reports

When a case is reported in the *Law Reports* published by the Incorporated Council of Law Reporting for England and Wales that is the report that should be cited as authority. If a case is not, or is not yet, reported in the *Law Reports*, a report in the *Weekly Law Reports* or the *All England Law Reports* should be cited.

If a judgment is not reported in any of those, but is reported 'in any of the authoritative specialist series of reports which contain a headnote and are made by individuals holding a

[35] *R (Frederick Ayinde v London Borough of Haringey)* and *Hamad Al-Haroun v Qatar National Bank)* [2025] EWHC 1383 (Admin).

Senior Courts qualification [as law reporter] (as to which see p 322 below) a report in any of the specialist series of reports may be cited.[36] (It is estimated that there are now some fifty series of law reports.) The Practice Direction says that where a judgment is not reported in any of such reports but is reported in other reports, 'they may be cited'.[37]

The 2001 Practice Statement referred to the *Law Reports* published by the Incorporated Council of Law Reporting as the 'official' reports. It said: 'These are the most authoritative reports; they contain a summary of arguments and they are the most readily available.'[38] The use of the word 'official', which is recent,[39] was queried by Dr Roderick Munday.

> The simple truth is that in one sense there never have been any 'official' law reports. Law reporting has always been left to private enterprise. Anyone can publish reports of cases and, traditionally, a court would accept as authentic any report of a case attested to by a member of the Bar.[40]

The special attributes of the *Law Reports* were that the judges checked the text of the judgments for this series but not for the others;[41] the reports listed not only the cases referred to in the judgments but also other authorities cited by the advocates; and the reports usually summarised the arguments addressed to the court. An Assistant Editor of the *Weekly Law Reports*, writing about the 'added value' of law reports over unreported decisions,[42] suggested those were not the only factors:

- The assessment that a case is worth reporting will have been made by a legally qualified reporter.
- The addition of catchwords enables the reader to see instantly what the case is about.
- The headnote will set out the ratio of each reportable point along with the parts of the factual background necessary to makes sense of the court's conclusion. It will also show the court's treatment of earlier authorities.
- When viewed through an online database, authorities listed will be hyperlinked so that they can be accessed by a click.
- The report will include the procedural history of the case.

Despite the advantages, Dr Munday wrote:

> The simple fact is that there are no 'official' law reports in our jurisdiction. The expression 'official law reports' merely denotes those series, published normally under the aegis of the Incorporated Council of Law Reporting, and thus the creature of the Bar, which can invariably be relied upon to produce reports of superior quality ...[43]

It might be better, he suggested, to refer to them as 'semi-official'.

[36] Practice Statement [1998] 1 WLR 825 at [8].

[37] Practice Direction: Citation of Authorities [2012] 1 WLR 780, para 9.

[38] Ibid. For obvious reasons, the 2012 Practice Statement did not include the words 'and they are the most readily available'.

[39] The 1998 Practice Statement repeated and extended to all courts what was originally pronounced for the Court of Appeal – [1995] 1 WLR 1096, [1996] 3 All ER 382. Its 1990 direct forbear, *Practice Direction (Law Reports: Citation)* [1991] 1 WLR 1, [1991] 1 All ER 352, proclaimed the same hierarchy but the Incorporated Council's reports were not referred to as 'official'.

[40] R Munday, 'The "official" law reports' 165 *Justice of the Peace*, 3 March 2001, 162, 164.

[41] However, nowadays the judges prepare, and presumably check, 'handed down' (ie reserved) judgments and are given the transcript of extempore judgments for checking.

[42] G D'Avola, 'Anatomy of a law report', *Counsel*, April 2024, p 36.

[43] Munday, 'The "official" law reports' (n 39 above) 167–68.

Even given the recognised authority of the Law Reports, it is important to appreciate that they cover only a tiny proportion of published cases. It was estimated that the number of cases published annually was of the order of some 2,500.[44] The number included in the Law Reports was a mere 175 to 200.

6.8. The Form of Law Reports

6.8.1. Neutral Citation

In 2001, the Lord Chief Justice, Lord Woolf, with the concurrence of the Master of the Rolls, the Vice Chancellor and the President of the Family Division, issued a Practice Note to alter the way that judgments are presented and cited in the Court of Appeal and the Administrative Court of the High Court.[45] In 2002 this was extended to the other parts of the High Court.[46] The current Practice Direction (Citation of Authorities) is at [2012] 1 WLR 780. All judgments now have paragraph numbers in square brackets.

Abbreviations for 'neutral' citation: House of Lords – UKHL; UK Supreme Court – UKSC; Court of Appeal, Civil Division – EWCA (Civ); Court of Appeal, Criminal Division – EWCA (Crim); High Court, King's Bench Division – EWHC (KB); High Court, Chancery Division – EWHC (Ch); High Court Family Court – EWHC (Fam); High Court, Administrative Court – EWHC (Admin); Patent Court – (Pat); Commercial Court – (Comm); Admiralty Court – (Admlty); Technology and Construction Court – (TCC); Judicial Committee of the Privy Council – UKPC.

Note – Law Reporters

The Courts and Legal Services Act 1990, s 115 provided that a law report by a person who is a solicitor or who has a '[Senior Courts] qualification' within the meaning of s 71 of the Act has the same authority as a report by a member of the bar. (A [Senior Courts] qualification is having a right of audience in relation to all proceedings in the Senior Courts.[47])

Fake precedents generated by AI

Deciding two cases in June 2025, the Divisional Court referred to their respective regulators a pupil barrister and a solicitor for including fake precedents in their legal arguments. The court asked the authorities to consider what further steps should be taken to address this serious new problem.[48]

[44] P Clinch, *Using a Law Library*, 2nd edn (Oxford University Press, 2001) 100.

[45] [2001] 1 WLR 194, [2001] 1 All ER 193.

[46] [2002] 1 WLR 346. The Practice Note said it would not automatically apply to judgments given outside London 'because they appear much less frequently in published reports' ([4]).

[47] The Constitutional Reform Acts 2005 which established the Supreme Court provided in s 59 that all references to 'Supreme Court' in previous legislation should be read as 'Senior Courts'.

[48] *(R (Frederick Ayinde v London Borough of Haringey)* and *Hamad Al-Haroun v Qatar National Bank)* [2025] EWHC 1383 (Admin).

7

The Nature of the Judicial Role in Law-Making

A great deal has been written about the judicial role and no attempt can be made here to cover all aspects of this topic. The issues addressed are only a few of those that affect the law-making process but they are some of the most important. The first is what role is played by the judge himself in the process.

7.1. The Personal Element in Judicial Law-Making

The first extract is from the writings of one of Britain's most distinguished post-war judges.

Lord Radcliffe, *Not in Feather Beds* (Hamish Hamilton, 1968) 212–16

> More and more I am impressed by the inescapable personal element in the judicial decision. We are fond of saying, approvingly, that a judge should be objective, but is it perhaps the wrong metaphor, an idea borrowed, like so much else that obscures our thinking on general topics, from an analogy between the physical sciences and things incommensurable with them? Say indeed that a judge must be fair, or that he must be impartial: that is essential. He must strip himself of all prejudices, certainly; except, I ought to add, those prejudices which on consideration he is prepared to stand by as his sincere convictions. You see how quickly, just because he is not a machine, one begins to tie oneself in words and qualifications of words. He has no right to be biased; but then no human mind is constructed with perfect balance. He must give an honest hearing to all points of view and to arguments that do not even introduce themselves to him as plausible; but it is unreal to think of a judge of experience as if he were a mere hearing aid. It was said of the late Lord Bryce that to him all facts were born free and equal. That may be all right for facts, before the work of evaluation begins, but a judge is a mature man, of long and professional experience, with prepared approaches and formed attitudes of mind, and it would be, I think, almost hypocritical to speak of him as if each case presented itself to his eye in the light of the first dawn of creation. To me fairness of mind cannot involve such innocence as that.
>
> The trust is, I believe, that the law must not be mistaken for a scientific pursuit. Much contemporary analysis and criticism seem to be based on this false analogy. Let me put the contrasting points of view. At the back of your mind you may think of the law on some particular questions as being a given fact, an absolute, which it is the judge's duty to discover. It is all there already, hidden in the ground and needing only excavation, or shrouded in a veil which requires no more

than to be drawn apart. To excavate or to unveil, neatly and accurately, calls for the exercise of no minor talents, and to do the work well there should be a solid apparatus of equipment, a detailed knowledge of the formulae of law (statutes, authorities and commentaries) and an ability to use the reasoning power with strict regard to its own inherent rules. The legal answer, you may say, is written out in close print or even in archaic language on some distant tablet. To read it off, you should choose for your judge the man with unusual length of sight or one who has had the skill to construct a powerful telescope or, for that matter, one who has made a study of the ancient tongues. Then he will read it off and announce to you what is there.

I would not deny that, in a legal system such as that which we operate in this country, a great deal of a judge's work involves no more than the practice of this science or skill of 'reading off'. But the essence of that curious activity, the judicial decision, does not consist in that. The law has to be interpreted before it can be applied, and interpretation is a creative activity. The law was not there until that particular decision was given. Once it has been given, the whole enormous component, which is the body of the law, has changed its composition by the addition of a new element, significant or insignificant, which in some degree modifies the whole.

There are two things that have impressed themselves on me when I have thought in this way. One is that, if the judge is not a machine, however ingeniously constructed, that is to work a mechanical system, it does very much matter what personal quality he brings to his work, because it is not going to be only his command of the reasoning process or his knowledge and learning that will determine his interpretation, but, in the end, his experience of life and the structure of thought and belief that he has built upon it. Most questions are debatable, just as most arguments can be made plausible: but what will incline him to one side or the other is what I called his whole structure of thought. I hope that you do not think that I am putting forward the judge as a sort of prophet or seer, making his pronouncements by some uncriticisable right of divination. Perhaps a few of the great ones have been something of that order, and for better or worse, sometimes for the worse, we take them as such. I do not see them that way at all, but I do think that it is of some importance in the society of today that the judge's function should not be confused with that of a reading clerk and that it should be realised that judicial decisions, no matter who gives them, must always be related to certain basic beliefs about the nature and purpose of a human being which are held by another human being. In that sense he may not be 'objective'; but he can be honest and fair. Of the two it is much the more valuable achievement.

It has been a pity, I think, that so much of judicial opinion in this country has been conveyed by the method of logical deduction. It was natural enough that this should be the preferred route, since the deductive method based on the syllogism was the favoured weapon of Western Europe thinkers in the Middle Ages, and the judges probably inherited its use from them. But, as we know, syllogistic reasoning is only conclusive if you first import your chosen meaning into the words of the premise you start with. It is only a demonstration of a truth if you have already been converted to the truth. In our history of judgment-making too many decisions have begun by insisting that particular words have one particular meaning and then deducing that, if they have, certain consequences must necessarily follow. That is to put the icing on the cake, not to bake it. I am afraid that what I am saying is that the making of law is not a subject which is capable of anything like scientific demonstration, and there are some disadvantages in dressing it up to look as if it were. It is the unexpressed assumptions, which are nevertheless very much present, that are often the real hinges of decision. After all, what a judgment seeks to do is to persuade or convince, and there are sometimes cogent considerations that achieve this without having any resort to deductive reasoning. Arrangement, by which an illuminating spark is generated from the skilful combination of certain facts and considerations, is one of them. Anyone who makes a careful study of the judgments of a great master of exposition, such as was Lord Macnaghten, for instance, will see how much conviction he can bring from nothing more than his skill of arrangement.

In this context there was never a more sterile controversy than that upon the question whether a judge makes law. Of course he does. How can he help it? The legislature and the judicial process respectively are two complementary sources of law-making, and in a well ordered state each has to understand its respective functions and limitations. Judicial law is always a reinterpretation of principles in the light of new combinations of facts, of which very relevant ones, unprovable by evidence, are the current beliefs of the society in which those facts occur. True, judges do not reverse principles, once well established, but they do modify them, extend them, restrict them or even deny their applicability to the combination in hand. But does Parliament do anything very different in its law-making, except in some revolutionary context to which no ordinary rule can be referred? I doubt it. It is not that the well known phrase, 'That is not for us, it is for the legislature' does not carry plenty of significant meaning. What it means is, I think, that, while it is an illusion to suppose that the legislature is attending or can possibly attend all the time to all aspects of the law, there are certain areas of public interest which at any one time can be seen to be a matter of its current concern. It has recently legislated on that subject according to certain principles (if they can be detected) or it regularly legislates on the whole field covered by that subject (as, for instance, the law of taxation). In those areas I think that the judge needs to be particularly circumspect in the use of his power to declare the law, not because the principles adopted by Parliament are more satisfactory or more enlightened than those which would commend themselves to his mind, but because it is unacceptable constitutionally that there should be two independent sources of law-making at work at the same time.

The next extracts are from the pen of one of the United States greatest and most eloquent judges:

Benjamin N Cardozo, *The Nature of the Judicial Process* (Yale University Press, 1921) 12–13, 112–15, 167–68

[12] There is in each of us a stream of tendency, whether you choose to call it philosophy or not, which gives coherence and direction to thought and action. Judges cannot escape that current any more than other mortals. All their lives, forces which they do not recognise and cannot name, have been tugging at them – inherited instincts, traditional beliefs, acquired convictions; and the result is an outlook on life, a conception of social needs, a sense in James's phrase of 'the total push and pressure of the cosmos,' which, when reasons are nicely balanced, must determine where choice shall fall. [13]In this mental background every problem finds its setting. We may try to see things as objectively as we please. None the less, we can never see them with any eyes except our own. To that test they are all brought – a form of pleading or an act of parliament, the wrongs of paupers or the rights of princes, a village ordinance or a nation's charter …

[112] My analysis of the judicial process comes then to this, and little more: logic, and history, and custom, and utility, and the accepted standards of right conduct, are the forces which singly or in combination shape the progress of the law. Which of these forces shall dominate in any case must depend largely upon the comparative importance or value of the social interests that will be thereby promoted. One of the most fundamental social interests is that law shall be uniform and impartial. There must be nothing in its action that savors of prejudice or favor or even arbitrary whim or fitfulness. Therefore in the main there shall be adherence to precedent. There shall be symmetrical development, consistently with history or custom when history or custom has been the motive force, or the chief one, in giving shape to existing rules, and with logic or philosophy when the motive power has been theirs. But symmetrical development may be bought at too high a price. Uniformity ceases to be a good when it becomes uniformity of oppression. The social interests served by symmetry or certainty must then be balanced against the social interest served by equity and fairness or other elements of social welfare. These may enjoin upon the judge the duty of drawing the line at another angle, of staking the path along new courses, of marking a new point of departure from which others who come after him will set out upon their journey. If you ask how he is to know when one interest outweighs another, I can only answer that he must get his knowledge just as the legislator gets it, from experience and study and reflection; in brief, from life itself. Here, indeed, is the point of contact between the legislators' work and his. The choice of methods, the appraisement of values, must in the end be guided by like considerations for the one as for the other. Each indeed is legislating within the limits of his competence. No doubt the

> limits for the judge are narrower. He legislates only between gaps. He fills the open spaces in the law. How far he may go without travelling beyond the walls of the interstices cannot be staked out for him upon a chart. He must learn it for himself as he gains the sense of fitness and proportion that comes with years of habitude in the practice of an art. Even within the gaps, restrictions not easy to define, but felt, however impalpable they may be, by every judge and lawyer, hedge and circumscribe his action. They are established by the traditions of the centuries, by the example of other judges, his predecessors and his colleagues, by the collective judgment of the profession, and by the duty of adherence to the pervading spirit of the law … Nonetheless, within the confines of these open spaces and those of precedent and tradition, choice moves with a freedom which stamps its action as creative …
>
> [167] I have spoken of the forces of which judges avowedly avail to shape the form and content of their judgments. Even these forces are seldom fully in consciousness. They lie so near the surface, however, that their existence and influence are not likely to be disclaimed. But the subject is not exhausted with the recognition of their power. Deep below consciousness are other forces, the likes and dislikes, the predilections and the prejudices, the complex of instincts and emotions and habits and convictions, which make the man, whether he be litigant or judge … There has been a certain lack of [168] candor in much of the discussion of the theme, or rather perhaps in the refusal to discuss it, as if judges must lose respect and confidence by the reminder that they are subject to human limitations. I do not doubt the grandeur of the conception which lifts them into the realm of pure reason, above and beyond the sweep of perturbing and deflecting forces. None the less, if there is anything of reality in my analysis of the judicial process, they do not stand aloof on these chill and distant heights; and we shall not help the cause of truth by acting and speaking as if they do. The great tides and currents which engulf the rest of men do not turn aside in their course and pass the judges by.

For the view that the personal element in judicial decision-making is crucial, see further, in particular, Jerome Frank, *Law and the Modern Mind* (Coward-McCann, 1930).

The question was addressed also in a major article by an Australian jurist:

HK Lücke, 'The common law: judicial impartiality and judge-made law' 98 *Law Quarterly Review*, 1982, 29, 60–61, 74–76, 88

> [T]he common law possesses a great deal of historical and contemporary colour: it is lively, realistic and, incidentally, eminently teachable. The student of the common law rubs shoulders with Indian princes, fishwives, conjurors, shopkeepers and sea-captains of the East India Company. Translated into statutory language, only the pale shadows of this colourful assembly would remain, they would become plaintiffs, traffic accident witnesses, promisors of rewards, hire-purchasers and applicants for public office. The common law is a storehouse for worm tubs, ornamental broughams, snails in ginger beer bottles and fancy waistcoats, all of which would long since have turned to rust and rubbish had the cases which brought them into prominence been governed by some statute.
>
> This element of colour may be thought a trivial advantage in itself, but it helps to create and keep alive a keen sense of reality and respect for the special circumstances of each case. The facts of precedents are always vividly remembered as the background against which all proposed general formulae must be understood. Facts are like safe, dry ground: when judges venture on to the sea of abstraction, they try at least to remain within sight of the coast. This primacy of the facts, this preference for the concrete, this reluctance to use general concepts and abstract legal ideas is one of the main characteristics of the common law. Without a full understanding of the reasons for this stylistic element and of its consequences no critical evaluation of the common law can be worthwhile.
>
> Proximity breeds engagement. Being so close to the conflict, to the interests and aspirations, needs and fears which have given rise to it, will engage the judge's direct sympathetic (or antipathetic) understanding of the parties' roles in the situation which he is called upon to judge. Although

he has no personal stake in the case, he will nevertheless find his feelings invoked vicariously, on behalf of the various *dramatis personae*. He will experience sentiments ranging from approval to disapproval, from warm appreciation to indignation. What is at work here is a kind of emphatic 'sense of touch' to which any case involving real conflict must be exposed before it can be fully understood. A feeling human being is needed for such understanding: no computer would ever be able to perform the task.

It might be argued that a judge should act 'purely rationally' and that he can no longer do so once he allows his feelings to play any part in his decision-making. Undeniably, the judge's empathic responses to the case are deeply suspect: they seek to predispose him in favour of one party or the other. If uncontrolled, they would be quite irreconcilable with the necessary attitude of impartiality. However, emotion is not incompatible with justice. If the judge's empathic responses are to work impartially, they must, to adapt Cardozo's famous words, be 'informed by tradition, methodised by analogy, disciplined by system.' So controlled, they are the essence of the judge's sense of justice.

Professor Lücke considered the reaction to a judicial decision on a point of law that might have gone either way:

> The most critical of all observers, the losing party, might respond:
>
> > No rule such as the one you have stated was to be found in the law before you chose to announce it. You are a skilful lawyer and master rationaliser: hence it was easy enough for you to formulate such a proposition and to act as if it were a rule of general application. To me it is only window dressing, intended to conceal your real motive: to vent your prejudice against me and people like me. Even if you have tried to be sincere, your attitudes and prejudices have still had a decisive, though perhaps subconscious, impact upon your judgment.
>
> To such a charge the judge appears to have three answers: his first line of defence is to invoke the great reputation of the judiciary to which he belongs, for independence and impartiality. He may refer to great constitutional battles for the independence of the judiciary, the purpose of which was to gain for judges the freedom to be impartial. He may point to his professional ethos and to his judicial oath. All this is impressive evidence of impartiality; but the more loudly it is invoked, the more suspect it must seem to an already suspicious mind. Even the greatest traditions are sometimes broken, or may, indeed, cease to be a living reality.
>
> The judge's second line of defence lies in the quality, as a 'socio-moral norm', of the ratio he has stated. His credibility will be enhanced if his ratio balances fairly the interests of the disputants in this and in similar disputes, and if it thus seeks to order the affairs of the community in a rational, fair and sensible way. If, on the other hand, it appears forced, unjust or obscure it will be less likely to quell suspicion that the judge's real motives had nothing to do with his alleged ratio and were incompatible with impartiality. However, the 'socio-moral' quality of the ratio, without more, will not overcome the argument that the ratio is just 'window-dressing', used ad hoc to camouflage the judge's bias and likely soon to be discarded.
>
> To rebut this charge of 'window-dressing', the judge's third and final argument will be to show the strength of his commitment to his ratio. He will reply to his critics as follows:
>
> > Don't see the ratio I have provided solely in the context of the present dispute. Under the rule of precedent, the law offers you the following assurance. Should your and your adversary's roles ever be reversed in a future, but otherwise identical dispute, I (or any other judge) will give judgment for you and against the other side, acting in accordance with the very same rule which I have just formulated and applied against you. The rule will also be applied to all other substantially identical future disputes, whoever the parties may be, for the legal system places confidence in the ratio I have stated and regards it as a strongly persuasive or even (depending upon my place in the judicial hierarchy) as a binding rule. If the law accepts it, why should you not accept it also?

The rule of precedent is an essential chain in the argument which establishes the judge's impartiality, and is therefore an instrument of effective and convincing adjudication. To know that his decision will be treated by the law as setting a persuasive, or even a binding, standard adds to the burden of responsibility felt by the judge. It is a powerful reminder that the judge's duty is to base his decisions upon rules fit for general application rather than upon factors which may raise doubts as to his impartiality. The rule of precedent offers reassurance to the parties and to the public that judges will continue to act in a principled and impartial way. If the rule of precedent is seen in this light, judicial impartiality no longer depends upon adherence to declaratory theories.

> If *rationes decidendi* are to play their role effectively as instruments of adjudication, they must be formulated in concrete and specific terms ... In fact, this has been the practice among common law judges for so long that it is rightly seen as one of the most characteristic style elements of the common law. Only when *rationes decidendi* are stated in this way can the 'reversal test' be applied with complete confidence: broad and abstract premises do not dictate results in the same way as specific premises do ...
>
> The judge's task is to reconcile and, if necessary, to adjust conflicting interests. Before he can do so fairly and with true understanding, he must strain his powers of empathic identification with both parties so as to gain a full appreciation of their personalities, their interests and positions in the particular dispute. His exposure to the detailed facts gives him a unique advantage as he seeks to gain such understanding. As he 'identifies' with each party in turn, he must maintain an attitude of impartiality. That is a deeply problematic commitment, for it is contrary to man's innate tendency which is (if not to take flight) to adopt a partisan role in any conflict to which he is exposed at close quarters. A studied attitude which combines continuing involvement in the conflict with continuing impartiality seems a highly civilised, if not an artificial form of conduct. There is no such thing as a basic human urge or instinct to remain impartial in the face of conflict. This may explain why the reality of impartiality is denied by many critics of the legal system and why its value as an element of government is so often grossly underrated.

The role of discretion available to the judge in deciding cases may vary according to the level of court. This is one of the points made in the extract from Browne-Wilkinson that follows.

In his book, *Judicial Discretion in the House of Lords* (Clarendon Press, 1998), David Robertson, an Oxford political scientist, argued that, at least in the House of Lords, the personal views of the judges dominate decision-making. His thesis was radical: that 'law in almost any case that comes before the Lords turns out to be whatever their Lordships feel it ought to be' (108). Robertson presented statistical evidence to support the proposition that 'a good prediction can be made of case resolution by knowing who is on the panel, which hears the appeal' (70). He also made his point through analysis of decisions in a variety of fields.

Unexpected support for Robertson's view came in a pronouncement by Lord Browne-Wilkinson, then the Senior Law Lord, in a brief chapter he contributed to a series of lectures on the Human Rights Act 1998. Lord Browne-Wilkinson started his lecture with the following remarkable words:

> When I was first made a judge, a wily old judge advised me – 'just remember, Nick, dirty dogs don't win'. That is a principle which lies at the heart of the common law. It is the basis on which the overwhelming majority of cases are decided. The judge looks for what are called 'the merits' and having found them seeks to reach a result, consistent with legal reasoning, whereby the deserving win and the undeserving lose.
>
> Unfortunately, this judicial method is seldom reflected in judicial behaviour or in the reasons given by judges for their decisions ... The outward presentation of the process of adjudication on questions of law is that the blind goddess rules, and that, willy-nilly, the judge is forced to the

> conclusion which he reaches. When we get to the judgment, we very seldom find any reference to 'the merits'. The articulated reasoning purports to be based on a process of compelling legal argument leading inexorably to the result achieved …
>
> In the case of statutory interpretation, the courts have acted in much the same way.

The features of judicial reasoning, Lord Browne-Wilkinson said, consisted of three elements:

> First, the actual decision is primarily based on moral, not legal factors. Second, those moral reasons are not normally articulated in the judgment. Third, the morality applied in any given case is the morality of the individual judge: although this will, to an extent, reflect the values of contemporary society …[1]

Professor Alan C Hutchinson of Osgoode Hall Law School in Toronto, argues that the judges are unavoidably engaged in policy choices:

> Despite the denials and resistance of traditional judges and jurists, the common law is awash in the roiling and mucky waters of political power. While judges and lawyers claim to keep relatively clean and dry by wearing their institutional wet-suits of abstract neutrality and disinterested fairness, they are up to their necks in ideological muck. And this is no bad thing. Because it is only when judges come clean, as it were, and admit that they have political dirt on their hands that they will appreciate that adjudication generally and constitutional adjudication particularly amount to an organic and messy process that has a similarly organic and messy connection to those social needs which it claims both to reflect and shape. So enlightened, judges might begin to accept that they are involved in a political enterprise whose success and legitimacy are best evaluated not by the courts' formal dexterity and technical competence, but by their substantive contribution to the local advancement of social justice.[2]

One aspect of judicial decision-making that is unavoidably based on the judge's own subjective judgment, is applying familiar concepts such as 'the reasonable' landlord, tenant, consumer, motorist, man, woman. Professor Mark Pawlowski has rightly pointed out that the reasonable man, the honest person and such concepts are:

> no more than a personification of the court's own subjective judgment of what is right or wrong; in other words, they are mere contrivances designed to hide the fact that the judge is actually imposing his (or her) own sense of what is rational or reasonable in the given circumstances of the case … While the standard itself is objective and impersonal, it does not eliminate the personality or idiosyncrasies of the individual judge. Like wizards, our judges make legal magic by converting the subjective into the objective with the sleight of the hand.[3]

There are of course many other aspects of the personal element in law-making.[4]

[1] Basil Markesinis (ed), *The Impact of the Human Rights Bills on English Law* (Oxford University Press, 1998) 22–23. On an earlier occasion Lord Browne-Wilkinson said that the common law method was inclined to concentrate on the 'merits' of the parties in the case 'and to shape the law in such a case so that the meritorious win and the undeserving lose'. In cases involving, say, the freedom of the press or the rights of prisoners, 'this leads English courts to concentrate unduly on the often disreputable behaviour of those who are asserting their human rights to the detriment of the underlying principles'. He hoped that because of the Human Rights Act 1998 'the more principled approach in the [European] Convention and the Strasbourg jurisprudence will lead the English courts to give greater emphasis to the importance of protecting the basic human rights regardless of the merits of the person who is seeking to rely on them'. It was easy, he said, to afford a saint their human rights: but a sinner has the same rights. ('Some comparative reflection' in BS Markensis (ed), *The Gradual Convergence* (Clarendon Press, 1994) 203–04.

[2] 'Judges and politics: an essay from Canada' 24 *Legal Studies*, 2004, 275, 284–85.

[3] M Pawlowski, 'Judges as wizards – the making of legal magic', *New Law Journal*, 13 September 2019, 22.

[4] See further R Hunter and E Rackley, 'Judicial leadership on the UK Supreme Court' 38 *Legal Studies*, 2018, 191–220; Sir Ernest Ryder and S Hardy, *Judicial Leadership* (OUP, 2019); Alan Paterson, 'Presidency and the Supreme Court: Lord Neuberger's Legacy' www.ucl.ac.uk/judicial-institute/2019-events.

7.2. The Background of Judges

The legal profession has traditionally been drawn overwhelmingly from the upper and upper middle classes.[5] (It would not be surprising if the same was true in many, or even most other countries.) Most High Court judges and above are former barristers.[6]

As regards the university education of senior judges, Oxford and Cambridge (Oxbridge) still dominate. All the judges who reached the House of Lords and some 80 per cent of those who between 1965 and 2009 sat in the Court of Appeal or the High Court were from Oxbridge. Of the QCs appointed between 1965 and 2009, 66 per cent were from Oxbridge.[7]

Michael Blackwell's study showed that the great majority also come from a narrow range of schools. He investigated the educational background of all Queen's Counsel appointed from 1965 to 2010 and of all judges appointed to or retired from the High Court, Court of Appeal or House of Lords between 1965 and 2009. He found that the proportion of High Court and Court of Appeal judges educated at schools in the state sector was consistently under 32 per cent for the entire period, compared with the at least 93 per cent of the British population educated in the state sector throughout that period.

Moreover, in the highest levels a small group of elite schools (the so-called Clarendon schools[8]) dominated.[9] The proportion of Court of Appeal judges from the nine Clarendon Schools was consistently greater than the proportion educated in the whole state sector.[10] But in the High Court, judges educated in the state sector sometimes outnumbered those who had been to the nine Clarendon schools.[11] Of the QCs appointed since 1965, 16 per cent had attended a Clarendon school and 37 per cent attended other independent schools.[12]

The question of the background of the judges had been addressed by the House of Commons Home Affairs Select Committee in 1996.[13] The Committee's Report, whilst admitting that it was 'certainly remarkable' that the proportion of Oxbridge graduates in the higher judiciary was so high, did not think that it was evidence of bias. Rather it thought

[5] A study by the College of Law showed that 84 per cent of its barrister students were from the professional, managerial, executive or administrative class – and that the same was true of no less than 77 per cent of the solicitor students. (Evidence to the Royal Commission on Legal Services of the College of Law, 1977, p 5.)

[6] Of the 386 judges appointed to the High Court from 1965 to 2009, only 31 were not QCs prior to their appointment – and of the 31, 8 were Junior Counsel to the Crown who traditionally go to the bench as juniors and 19 were promoted from lower levels of the judiciary. (M Blackwell, 'Old boys' networks, family connections and the English legal profession' *Public Law*, 2012, 426, 431.)

[7] Blackwell, 'Old boys' networks' (n 6 above) 435.

[8] Charterhouse, Eton, Harrow, Merchant Taylors', Rugby, St Paul's, Shrewsbury, Westminster and Winchester. The name derives from the fact that these schools were the subject of the Clarendon Royal Commission in 1861.

[9] 'Among High Court and Court of Appeal judges and Lords of Appeal in Ordinary who sat since 1965 and for whom it has been possible to identify their schooling (96 per cent of them), eight of the nine schools that educated the most such judges are Clarendon Schools, Marlborough and Oundle (joint ninth) replacing Merchant Taylors. Among QCs appointed since 1965 for whom it has been possible to identify their schooling (79 per cent of them), seven of the nine schools that educated the most QCs are Clarendon schools Marlborough and Downside (respectively eighth and ninth) replacing Merchant Taylors' and Shrewsbury.' (Blackwell, 'Old boys' networks' (n 6 above) 434.

[10] Blackwell, 'Old boys' networks' (n 6 above) 434.

[11] Ibid.

[12] Blackwell, 'Old boys' networks' (n 6 above) 435.

[13] *Judicial Appointments Procedures*, Third Report, HC 52-I of 1995–96.

that it reflected the background of those entering the Bar 30 years previously. The Report stated that the proportion of Oxbridge entrants from state schools was then more or less equal to that from public schools.[14] The Committee concluded (para 117) 'we are confident that decisions on judicial appointments are not guided by information on where candidates were educated'.

The Labour minority on the Committee disagreed. ('We find it hard to think of a good reason why four-fifths of the senior judges should come from the same two universities.') It thought this situation was an indictment of the present system of appointments. It suggested that there was a glass ceiling between the middle and the higher judiciary beyond which those of the 'wrong' background or gender found it difficult to progress. Reform of the system was needed. The minority thought that matters would be improved by the setting up of a broadly based judicial appointments commission to advise the Lord Chancellor on appointments. The majority disagreed. ('From the evidence we have taken, we have not been persuaded that the quality of appointees would necessarily improve if a Judicial Appointments Commission were to be established' (para 142).)

7.3. The Appointment of Judges

7.3.1. The Lord Chancellor Replaced by a Judicial Appointments Commission

Judicial appointments used to be basically in the hands of the Lord Chancellor and their officials. Up to the level of the Court of Appeal, appointments were made by the monarch 'on the advice of the Lord Chancellor'. Appointments of Lords Justices of Appeal and of the Law Lords were made by the Queen 'on the advice of the Prime Minister', which in reality again meant on the advice of the Lord Chancellor. There was little wrong with the results in terms of the quality of the bench. The English judiciary enjoys a very high reputation worldwide. But the system had obvious problems. In his 2010 Hamlyn Lectures, Professor Alan Paterson said:

> The old system of the Lord Chancellor or the Lord Advocate in Scotland appointing someone after consultation with the senior judiciary and others had certain advantages and it produced many excellent judges. However, it was wholly lacking in transparency, was not equal opportunities compliant, had no input from the non-lawyer community and was open to the accusation of cronyism. It was 'chaps appointing chaps'.[15]

In July 1999, the Lord Chancellor, Lord Irvine, asked Sir Leonard Peach, a former Commissioner for Public Appointments, to examine the selection procedures for appointing both Queen's Counsel and judges. In his report, Peach stated that after a review of procedures in 1993 the appointments system had become 'more orthodox in personnel terms with the creation of job descriptions and personal specifications, open advertisements,

[14] The proportion of state school students at both Oxford and Cambridge has risen from around half in 1990 to around two-thirds. In 2020, the proportion of state school student acceptances at Oxford was 67 per cent and at Cambridge was 68 per cent. (Paul Bolton 'Oxbridge Elitism' House of Commons Library Briefing Paper No.0616, 25 May 2021, p 18.) In 2023, it was 67.6 per cent at Oxford and 71 per cent at Cambridge. (UniAdmissions, 2025)

[15] A Paterson, *Lawyers and the Public Good* (Cambridge University Press, 2012) 146.

application forms, a shortlisting scrutiny and interviews'.[16] Since then further changes had been made. Basically the system compared favourably with that of other organisations, both in the private and in the public sector, though it had one unique feature, consultation, which was controversial. The consultation process, Peach said, could be improved by redesign of the form used to obtain views from consultees. The application form could be restructured to provide more self-appraisal and so more information and material for the short-listing and interviewing panels.[17]

Peach also recommended that confidence in the system would be increased by the appointment of a Commissioner for Judicial Appointments. This recommendation was implemented. The Judicial Appointments Order in Council 2001, which came into effect in March 2001, required the Commissioners 'to promote economy, efficiency, effectiveness and fairness in appointment procedures' and to exercise their functions 'with the object of maintaining the principle of selection on merit'. A university Vice Chancellor was appointed the first Commissioner. Seven others were appointed as Deputy Commissioners. None was either a practising lawyer or judge.

The Commission's first annual report (for 2002) stated that the high quality of the judiciary was widely recognised and that changes to the appointments process 'should not compromise this enviable reputation' (para 8.1). But it thought that there were a number of significant respects in which the current judicial appointments system should be improved. There was no reason to believe that the system resulted in the appointment of persons who did not have the required qualities. The issue was 'whether others, who also have the required qualities, are not being fairly considered or selected due to flaws in the processes and systems and how this impacts on confidence in judicial appointments and consequently the whole legal process' (para 8.3). In particular the Commission said that the audit trail for processing applications had not always been sufficient 'to provide assurance that the Lord Chancellor's policies and procedures have been followed in every case and to provide confidence that individual applications have received equal treatment'.[18]

On 12 June 2003, the Prime Minister, Tony Blair, made the famous announcement that the office of Lord Chancellor was to be abolished, that the Law Lords would be transferred to a new Supreme Court and that a Judicial Appointments Commission would be established. The Judicial Appointments Commission (JAC) was created by the Constitutional Reform Act 2005. Despite the title, its job is to select not to appoint.

The 2005 Act (Sch 12) specified that the JAC consisted of a lay chairman and 14 others, five of whom had to be judges, five lay persons, two members of the legal profession, one lay magistrate and one tribunal member. The Crime and Courts Act 2013, Sch 13, Pt 3 changed this by providing that the JAC has such number of members as the Lord Chancellor specifies with the agreement of the Lord Chief Justice;[19] that judges must be fewer in number on the Commission than non-judges; and that the members must include judges, practitioners

[16] *An Independent Scrutiny of the Appointment Process of Judges and Queen's Counsel*, December 1999, p 3.

[17] *An Independent Scrutiny of the Appointment Process of Judges and Queen's Counsel*, December 1999.

[18] In July 2004 a damning report by the Commission, carried these criticisms much further. It made no criticism of the quality of those appointed who it said were of the highest quality but, having studied the process of appointing High Court judges in close detail, the Commission concluded that it was 'opaque, outdated and not demonstrably based on merit'. It reached the astonishing conclusion that the selection of High Court judges should be altogether halted pending an overhaul! ('We would be concerned to see any further High Court judges' selection processes take place on the basis of the present system, which we have found to be seriously lacking in transparency and accountability' (*Audit of High Court 2003 Competition*, para E.10.2).

[19] In 2020, the number was still a lay chairman and 14 Commissioners.

and lay persons. (For the Commission's website see www.jac.judiciary.gov.uk.) The JAC began work in April 2006.

The first Justices of the Supreme Court were the existing Law Lords.[20] New Justices of the Supreme Court are not selected by the Judicial Appointments Commission. The Constitutional Reform Act 2005, Sch 8 provided that they are appointed by an ad hoc body that exists only when a vacancy occurs, consisting of the President and Deputy President of the Supreme Court and one person from each of the judicial appointments commissions for England and Wales, Scotland and Northern Ireland. This too was changed by the Crime and Courts Act 2013, Sch 13. The commission must now have at least five members, must always be an odd number, and must include one member of the Court and a lay person. In practice the President would usually be a member unless the vacancy was of the post of President or Deputy President. If the vacancy is that of President, or Deputy President, the outgoing holder of that office cannot be a member. If the vacancy is that of President, the selection commission must be chaired by a lay person.[21]

The Constitutional Reform Act provided that for any appointment, only one name is put forward.[22] The Lord Chancellor (or as the case may be, the Lord Chief Justice) can reject the nominated name only if they have reason to believe that the person is not fit for the office. If they believe that one or more better qualified person has not been selected, they can ask for the appointment to be reconsidered.[23]

Judges are now appointed by the Queen on the advice of the Prime Minister (the Supreme Court), of the Lord Chancellor (High Court and above) or of the Lord Chief Justice (below the High Court).[24]

The retirement age for judges was set at 70 by the Judicial Pensions and Retirement Act 1993, though judges appointed before April 1995 could serve to age 75.[25] In 2022, the retirement age for all judges was raised to 75.[26]

Lay magistrates were previously appointed by the Lord Chancellor on the advice of local panels. Under the Crime and Courts Act 2013, the Lord Chancellor's role was transferred to the Lord Chief Justice.[27]

The Lord Chancellor is the Minister with overall responsibility and accountability to Parliament for the appointment of judges.

[20] Every Justice of the Supreme Court is automatically styled Lord or Lady but this is a courtesy title which does not include a peerage. Those who were Law Lords retained their peerages but they became unable to sit or vote in the House of Lords until they retired from judicial service. It remains to be seen whether a convention will develop of appointing non-peer Justices to a peerage after retirement. (For more information and discussion see G Zellick, 'Judicial titles and dress in the Supreme Court and below' IALS, 95 *Amicus Curiae*, Autumn 2013, 2–5.)

[21] Crime and Courts Act 2013, sch 13, para 4(1). For commentary see P O'Brien, 'Changes to judicial appointments in the Crime and Courts Act 2013' *Public Law*, 2014, 179–88.

[22] Constitutional Reform Act 2005, s 70(3) (Lord Chief Justice and Heads of Divisions); s 79(3) (Lords Justices of Appeal); s 88(4) (puisne judges etc).

[23] Constitutional Reform Act 2005, ss 73–75 (Lord Chief Justice and Heads of Divisions); ss 82–84 (Lords Justices of Appeal); ss 90–93 (puisne judges etc).

[24] The Lord Chancellor's functions in regard to the appointment of judges below the rank of High Court were transferred to the Lord Chief Justice by the Crime and Courts Act 2013, Sch 13, Pt 4.

[25] Retirement at 75 was fixed by the Judicial Pensions Act 1959. Prior to that Act there was no retirement age. (The last judge not subject to a retiring age was Lord Denning who retired at the age of 83 – having held high judicial office for 38 years.) The House of Lords Constitution Committee recommended in 2012 that the retirement age for judges of the Court of Appeal and the Supreme Court should be 75. (*Judicial Appointments*, 25th Report of the Session 2010–12, HL 272, March 2012, para 197.) But this has not yet been adopted. See generally, A Blackham, 'Judicial Retirement Ages in the United Kingdom – Legitimate Aims and Proportionate Means' *Public Law*, 2017, 196–214.

[26] Public Service Pensions and Judicial Offices Act 2022 s 121 and Sch 1.

[27] Crime and Courts Act 2013, Sch 13, para 39.

7.3.2. Diversity on the Bench

For many years there has been an issue over diversity on the bench – namely, the low proportion of women and ethnic minority judges, especially at the higher levels. Table 7.1 shows the current position:

The figures show that the gender imbalance, while considerable at all levels, is greatest in the higher reaches of the judiciary. As at April 2024, of the 148 posts held by the senior judiciary (Supreme Court, Court of Appeal and High Court), women held just 38, amounting to 26 per cent. Ten years earlier, in 2014, the proportion of women at that level was 17 per cent. For 13 years Dame Brenda Hale was the sole woman in the highest court. She was appointed to the House of Lords in 2004. The next ten appointments to the highest court were all men. It was not until 2017 that Dame Brenda was joined on the Supreme Court by Lady Black and a year later by Lady Arden. In 2024, after all three had retired, the number of female Supreme Court justices fell to two – Lady Rose and Lady Simler. However, in October 2023 Dame Sue Carr became the first Lady Chief Justice. The gender diversity of the judiciary has been a major issue for many years.

Table 7.1 Diversity on the bench

	No	**Women**	**Ethnic minorities**
		%	%
Justices of the Supreme Court	12	16	0
Lords Justices	36	25	3
High Court judges	108	31	2
Circuit judges	738	36	9
Recorders	989	31	9
District judges	453	47	12
Deputy District judges	888	48	11
District judges (Magistrates' Courts)	127	39	14
Deputy District judges (Magistrates' Courts)	100	43	10
Lay Magistrates	14,576	57	13

(As at April 2024 Source: Diversity of the Judiciary: Legal professions, new appointments and current postholders – 2024 Statistics.)

The issue has received a great deal of attention. In its first annual report in 2002, the Judicial Appointments Commission (JAC) said:

> The current judiciary is overwhelmingly white, male and from a narrow social and educational background. It is not unexpected that the make-up of the judiciary does not mirror that of society at large, given that the judges are drawn from a narrow section of society i.e. lawyers. However, statistics suggest that the make-up of the judiciary does not reflect that of the potential pool of applicants from which it could be drawn which raises questions about equality of opportunity. It is also argued that, if the judiciary was more diverse in its composition, this would positively affect public perceptions of its fairness, and the degree to which it is in touch with issues of concern to society as a whole.[28]

[28] JAC, *Annual Report*, 2002, para 6.10.

The JAC said that the Lord Chancellor had made significant efforts to encourage applications from a wider range of qualified applicants – by publicising the process, publishing annual statistics on gender and ethnic diversity and making clear statements of policy ('Don't be shy, apply') in regard to the desirability of appointing women, ethnic minority candidates, candidates with disabilities, and lesbian and gay candidates. The question of how best to promote diversity in the judiciary was 'an immensely complex one'. Differing views had been expressed in particular as to whether the under-representation of women and ethnic minorities would be resolved in due course by a 'trickle up' effect as their numbers increased in the more senior levels of the profession or whether some form of active intervention was required to achieve it.

In its annual report for 2003, the JAC said it had reached the view that 'trickle up' could not be relied on to redress the gender and ethnic imbalance in the judiciary (para 5.43).[29] Procedures needed to be reviewed to ensure that they did not operate in a way that failed to promote diversity. So, for instance, there should be a review of the selection criteria/competencies to ensure that they were justified – especially where some of these (for example, age or length of experience) might indirectly discriminate by gender or ethnicity; less reliance on consultation; better training for sift panels and interview panel members.

The Commission said that there were a variety of wider systemic biases in the way the profession and the judiciary operated. There was a disproportionately high rate of women dropping out of the profession. Women were affected by working practices at the Bar which were not 'family friendly' such as long working hours, requirements to travel long distances and work away from home. They were affected by partnership requirements for solicitors which might cause them to delay having a family. In both branches there were problems in re-starting a career after having a family. Ethnic minorities were affected by lack of role models and suitable mentors, by the concentration of many ethnic minority practitioners in chambers without a culture of judicial appointments, by lack of access to high-quality work which had implications for visibility to influential consultees. Both women and ethnic minority practitioners tended to gravitate toward the Government Legal Service and the Crown Prosecution Service which were excluded from judicial appointments.[30] Solicitors were affected by the negative attitude of partners to those seeking judicial office and by reliance on consultees in higher judicial appointments since most solicitors were not exposed regularly to influential consultees (paras 5.49–54). There was also a problem in the traditional pattern of entry to the judiciary and the limited scope for promotion within the judiciary. ('We believe that more needs to be done to encourage suitable applicants to seek part-time or full-time judicial offices at an earlier stage of their careers and to use these positions as opportunities to identify and develop suitable candidates for higher judicial offices' (para 5.56).)[31]

> An identifiable career path, open to both barristers and solicitors, which enabled them to apply for a first judicial appointment after a number of years in practice, say, eight to ten, and offered realistic prospects of further progression thereafter to higher office, would provide an alternative route alongside the traditional route of remaining in practice and entering the judiciary at the higher level (para 5.57).

[29] For Lord Sumption's, pessimistic assessment see pp 341–42 below.

[30] In June 2003 it was announced that CPS and Government Legal Service lawyers could become Recorders in civil matters and that CPS lawyers could become Deputy District Judges sitting in criminal cases not brought by the CPS.

[31] The Crime and Courts Act 2013, Sch 13, Pt 2 provides for judges to be appointed on a part-time basis.

In 2009 the Lord Chancellor asked Baroness Julia Neuberger to chair an Advisory Panel on Judicial Diversity. The Advisory Panel's report published in February 2010[32] made 53 recommendations.[33] One of the 53 recommendations was that a Judicial Diversity Taskforce, comprising the Ministry of Justice, senior members of the judiciary, the Judicial Appointments Commission, the Bar Council, the Law Society and Chartered Institute of Legal Executives (formerly Institute of Legal Executives), be established to oversee implementation of the recommendations. This recommendation was accepted.

In 2015, the Judicial Diversity Taskforce became the Judicial Diversity Forum (JDF). The website says:

> JDF provides strategic direction in the areas of challenging structural barriers to appointment, analysing and addressing the reasons behind how people's careers progress, and the gathering and use of data and evidence. The Forum's objective is to resolve issues of common concern, and coordinating agreed activities aimed at encouraging greater judicial diversity.[34]

JDF's annual report provides a very wide range of relevant statistics. The fifth annual report, dated 11 July 2024,[35] stated:

> **Sex** The female population is generally well represented in the legal professions. 40% of barristers, 53% of solicitors, 77% of Chartered Legal Executives, and 43% of all judges were female.
>
> There is no disparity between female and male candidates in their selection to judicial posts. Female candidates represented 49% of the eligible pool and 53% of recommendations in legal judicial selection exercises. (*Main Points*, para 1.1)
>
> [A]s at 1 April 2024, female representation among all court judges (38%) was 14 percentage points higher than in 2014. (s 5.3)
>
> [A]s at 1 April 2024, in the courts, female judges held 30% of the more senior posts (High Court and above). The highest level of female representation was among the Deputy District Judges (County Court) at 48%.
>
> In tribunals, female judges accounted for nearly two-thirds (62%) of the most senior roles (Presidents) (s 5.3)
>
> **Ethnicity** Since 2014, the ethnic minority proportion of barristers increased from 13% to 17%, of solicitors from 15% to 19%, of Chartered Legal Executives from 5% to 11%, and from 7% to 11% for all judges … Ethnic minority representation amongst the legal professions is in line with the general population of working age (25–74). Representation within the judiciary is lower compared to the general working age population but is comparable to older ages of this working population (50–74). (*Main Points*, para 1.2)

The proportion of black judges (1 per cent) had not changed in the ten years since 2014. There was no black judge in the Court of Appeal or on the full-time High Court bench. There were two black Deputy High Court judges (down from five in 2018–19).

What has become clear, however, is that the various efforts to make an impact on the problem have not been very successful. Professor Kate Malleson, a leading scholar in the field, wrote in 2013:

[32] www.judiciary.gov.uk/publications/advisory-panel-recommendations/.

[33] For another list of 20 recommendations see the report for the Labour Party by Sir Geoffrey Bindman QC and Karon Monaghan QC, *Judicial Diversity – Accelerating Change*, October 2014, accessible on the JAC website.

[34] https://judicialappointments.gov.uk/equality-and-diversity/diversity-and-equality-measures/judicial-diversity-forum/.

[35] *Diversity of the judiciary: Legal professions, new appointments and current office holders – 2024 statistics*, available at ibid.

> Increasingly, academic and policy work on diversity has concluded that despite concerted official efforts to develop and implement a range of policies to increase the diversity of decision-making bodies, 30 years of equal opportunity policies have not produced the results which policymakers had hoped for.[36]

If significant change is to be achieved it seems that new approaches will be needed. One such would be a change in the approach to the definition of merit.[37]

Merit as the basis of appointment

In its first report the JAC said that everyone agreed that it was vital that appointments be made on merit 'and that it would be wrong to seek to lower standards in order to produce a more diverse judiciary'.[38] The Constitutional Reform Act 2005 Act does not define 'merit'.[39] Sections 27(5) (the Supreme Court) and 63(2) (appointments generally) both state simply and without definition: 'Selection must be solely on merit'. Section 64(1), under the heading 'Encouragement of diversity', stated: 'The Commission, in performing its functions under this Part, must have regard to the need to encourage diversity in the range of persons available for selection for appointments.' But ss (2) adds that the section is subject to s 63 – the requirement that selection must be solely on merit.

The Crime and Courts Act 2013 extended the duty to encourage diversity to the Lord Chancellor and the Lord Chief Justice.[40] The Equality Act 2010, s 149 requires all public authorities to have due regard to the need to eliminate discrimination and to advance equality of opportunity.

The Equality Act 2010 s 159 also introduced what has been called a 'tie-breaker' or 'tipping point' provision. Where two candidates are equally qualified, preference may be given to the one whose appointment would contribute to rectifying under-representation of some disadvantaged category. The same tie-breaker concept is now included also in the Constitutional Reform Act 2005 by virtue of amendments providing that where two candidates are of equal merit, the Equality Act does not prevent the Judicial Appointments Commission from preferring one of them over the other if the purpose is increasing diversity.[41]

Lord Sumption, who before he became a Supreme Court Justice served for five years on the Judicial Appointments Commission, has doubted whether the tie-breaker provision could have much effect because it was only rarely the case that two candidates were considered to be equally qualified. ('[A]t the upper end of the ability range, there is usually clear water between every candidate once one looks at them in detail.'[42]) Christopher Stephens, Chair of the JAC, made the same point when he told the House of Lords Select Committee on the Constitution that in 500 appointment recommendations by the JAC there had not

[36] K Malleson, 'Gender quotas for the judiciary in England and Wales' in U Shultz and G Shaw (eds), *Gender and the Judiciary* (Hart Publishing, 2013) 481–99, at 483 and 498. See further L Barmes and K Malleson, 'The legal profession as gatekeepers to the judiciary: design faults in measures to enhance Diversity' 74 *Modern Law Review*, 2010, 245 and K Malleson, 'Diversity in the judiciary: the case for Positive Action' 36 *Journal of Law and Society*, 2009, 376.

[37] For discussion of the 'merit principle' see K Malleson, 'Re-thinking the merit principle in judicial selection' 33 *Journal of Law and Society*, 2006, 126.

[38] JAC, *Annual Report*, 2002, para 6.11.

[39] The JAC assesses applicants on six Qualities and Abilities: intellectual capacity; personal qualities; ability to understand and to deal fairly; authority and communication skills; efficiency; leadership and management skills.

[40] Crime and Courts Act 2013, Sch 13, para 11 inserting new s 137A into the Constitutional Reform Act 2005.

[41] For appointments to the Supreme Court, s 27 (5A) inserted by the Crime and Courts Act 2013, Sch 13, para 9; for other judicial appointments, s 63(4) inserted by the Crime and Courts Act 2013, Sch 13, para 10.

[42] Sumption, 'Home truths about judicial diversity' (n 29 above) 6.

been a single case of a discussion 'of the tipping point between two indistinguishable candidates'.[43]

The JAC takes the view that the tie-breaker provision has to be applied at the final selection stage.[44] But it could be applied at the earlier sift for shortlisting stage. The 2014 report on Judicial Diversity for the Labour Party by Sir Geoffrey Bindman and Karon Monaghan QC urged that that would have more impact because 'At sift or short-list stage, it is less easy to distinguish between the best candidates'.[45] Whatever its potential, it is improbable that the tie-breaker concept can bring about significant change.

The central question is whether in making a selection the appointment body can look beyond the qualities of the individual applicants to consider the overall composition of the court in question and of the judiciary as a whole? This question was addressed in 2004 by Sir Thomas Legg, former Permanent Secretary at the Lord Chancellor's Department, who had been involved in judicial appointments over more than twenty years. Selection on merit, he wrote, could have two quite different meanings. One was what he called 'maximal merit'. On this approach there was only one candidate fit for appointment, namely the strongest. This approach left no flexibility in decision making for supplementary policies about the make-up of the judiciary. That was the approach that had been adopted until then. The second ('minimal merit') approach was where all the candidates who reached an agreed minimal standard as appointable were treated as equally qualified for appointment. The appointing authority could then select among the qualified candidates in accordance with any relevant supplementary principle, for instance, that there should be more women or ethnic minority judges.

The 'maximal method is problematic because of the difficulty of ranking and because it does not promote diversity. The second method arguably could give an acceptable level of merit and could promote diversity but there is no present indication that it would be adopted – unless legislation required it. In that regard it may be relevant that the first recommendation made by Sir Geoffrey Bindman and Karon Monaghan QC in their October 2014 report to the Labour Party was:

> In assessing the 'merit' of candidates for judicial appointment, the ability of the candidate to contribute to a diverse judiciary should be included as a factor to be taken into account.[46]

A more radical proposal is that the discredited 'tap on the shoulder', formerly deployed by the Lord Chancellor's Department, be reinvented as a 'tap on the *under-represented* shoulder' through which talented and potentially well-qualified candidates from under-represented groups could be approached and encouraged to apply. Professor Kate Malleson argues that it would turn the advantages of the earlier practices which perpetuated homogeneity to work instead for the promotion of diversity.

> By co-opting judges, lawyers and other insiders to identify, counsel, encourage and persuade the most able lawyers they know from under-represented groups to apply for judicial office, the benefits of the network-based consultations system are used to encourage diversity.[47]

[43] Select Committee on the Constitution, *Judicial Appointments Process Oral and Written Evidence*, www.parliament.uk/documents/lordscommittees/constitution/JAP/JAPCompiledevidence28032012.pdf.

[44] Judicial Appointments Commission, 'Equal Merit Provision: JAC Policy' (2014) http://jac.judiciary.govuk/static/documents/EMP_policy.pdf.

[45] *Judicial Diversity – Accelerating Change* (n 33 above) para 4.9.

[46] *Judicial Diversity – Accelerating Change*. The authors had been asked by Sadiq Khan, Shadow Secretary of State for Justice, 'to suggest what a future Labour Government could do to ensure our judges better reflect wider society'.

[47] Malleson, 'Diversity in the judiciary' (n 36 above) 388.

Bindman and Monaghan – as well as Malleson – also recommend adoption of the even more radical solution of quotas.[48]

> The most compelling argument for quotas, therefore, is that they work and they work quickly … [W]e consider that the time has come to introduce quotas for both gender and ethnicity.[49]
>
> Quotas can operate at the application stage of a selection process, the short-listing stage, the appointment stage or all three. The potential advantage of their operation at the application stage is that they increase the size of the underrepresented group in pool.[50]
>
> The level at which the quota is set for women need not be 50:50. Many quota systems employ lower proportions. Austria, for example, set a gender quota for High Court judges at 30 per cent and the new gender quota for the Belgian Supreme Court requires the Court to be composed of at least a third of judges of each sex.[51]
>
> Quotas could also be set initially at a lower level but increased over time as the candidate pool widens.[52]

Professor Malleson, supporting quotas, said that there had been a reluctance to consider positive action because of a fear that it would undermine selection on merit:

> Yet, despite the growing awareness of the entrenched problem of the lack of diversity in the judiciary, the dominant view in the debate in England and Wales has been that policies based on positive action are a potential threat to selection on merit. Official support for positive action has been limited to a number of modest initiatives designed to widen the recruitment pool. These include 'road shows' by the Judicial Appointments Commission directed at women and black and minority ethnic lawyers and judicial job shadowing targeted at those who are not from traditional recruitment groups or career paths.
>
> The case against quotas rests largely on the misconception that the judicial appointments process is and can be a ranking merit system. In reality, such a model is not applicable given the particular nature of the judiciary and the candidate pools from which it is selected. Marginal decisions will always need to be made between well-qualified candidates drawn from an increasingly diverse recruitment pool. Such decisions must inevitably prioritise different qualities which cannot be numerically quantified one against the other. In the past, the characteristics which were prioritised often led to self-replication at best and discrimination at worst. By contrast, a selection system which has an open commitment to the values of equality and diversity can quite legitimately apply quotas within a threshold merit system. This ensures that only well-qualified candidates are selected while allowing space for the promotion of gender balance in the judiciary.[53]

Why is diversity of the judiciary considered to be important?

The desirability that the judiciary be diverse has in recent years become sanctified dogma subscribed to by most right-thinking members of society. Just about everyone seems to agree that although the English judiciary has the highest of high reputations worldwide, there is something seriously amiss in the fact that it is not sufficiently diverse.

Dame Brenda Hale, the first and for many years the only woman Law Lord or Justice of the Supreme Court, set out three possible justifications for improving diversity. First, equal opportunities, so 'all properly qualified and suitable candidates should have a fair crack

[48] For consideration of quotas as against targets see Malleson, 'Diversity in the judiciary' (n 36 above) 393–97.

[49] *Judicial Diversity – Accelerating Change* (n 33 above) paras 8.8 and 8.19.

[50] Ibid, para 8.21.

[51] Ibid, para 8.24.

[52] Ibid, para 8.25.

[53] Malleson, 'Gender quotas' (n 36 above) 498. See Barmes and Malleson, 'The legal profession as gatekeepers' (n 36).

of the whip and an equal chance of appointment',[54] meaning both that the appointment process is transparent and fair and that the appointment criteria are appropriate. Secondly, to 'make a difference'[55] to decision making, both in style and substance. Thirdly, democratic legitimacy because 'it is wrong in principle for that authority to be wielded by such a very unrepresentative selection of the population … not only mainly male, overwhelmingly white, but also largely the product of a limited range of educational institutions and social backgrounds.'[56]

As to whether women judges made different decisions on law than their male colleagues, Dame Brenda Hale quoted Justice Bertha Wilson of the Canadian Supreme Court:

> … there are probably whole areas of the law on which there is no uniquely feminine perspective … the principles and underlying premises are so firmly entrenched and so fundamentally sound that no good would be achieved by attempting to reinvent the wheel … [She cited contract, real property and company law as examples]. In some other areas of the law, however, a distinctly male perspective is clearly discernible. It has resulted in principles that are not fundamentally sound and that should be revisited when the opportunity presents itself. [She cited some aspects of the criminal law.][57]

Justice Ruth Bader Ginsburg of the United States Supreme Court at her inauguration had said that a wise old man and a wise old woman would probably reach the same decision but she also had no doubt that women, like persons of different racial groups and ethnic origins, contribute what had been described as 'a distinctive medley of views influenced by differences in biology, cultural impact and life experience'.

A system of justice, Dame Brenda Hale said, would be the richer for diversity of background and experience and would be the poorer, in terms of appreciating what is at stake and the impact of its judgments, if all its members were cast in the same mould.[58]

In a later lecture, Dame Brenda said that although in some cases women judges had a different voice from that of their male colleagues, the main reason for wanting greater diversity was democratic legitimacy:

> In a democracy governed by the people and not by an absolute monarch or even an aristocratic ruling class, the judiciary should reflect the whole community, not just a small section of it. The public should be able to feel that the courts are their courts; that their cases are being decided and the law is being made by people like them …[59]

Professor Kate Malleson has suggested that the reason for seeking a more diverse judiciary is certainly not to create a body which is representative in the sense used in relation to elected politicians. ('The idea that a judge can represent the interests of a group from which he or she is drawn is clearly incompatible with the notion of impartial justice.'[60]) The assumption that women judges would represent the interests of women more effectively than their male counterparts was 'theoretically weak and empirically questionable'.[61]

[54] B Hale, 'Equality and the judiciary: why should we want more women judges?' *Public Law*, 2001, 489, 490. See also Lady Hale, *How Diverse are Judges in Being a Judge in the Modern World?* (Oxford University Press, 2017) 183–98.

[55] Hale, 'Equality and the judiciary' (n 54 above) 496–500.

[56] Ibid, 502.

[57] B Wilson, 'Will women judges really make a difference?' 28 *Osgoode Hall Law Journal*, 1990, 507, 515.

[58] Hale, 'Equality and the judiciary' (n 54 above) 504.

[59] Hale, 'Women in the judiciary', Fiona Woolf Lecture, 27 June 2014, p 3.

[60] K Malleson, 'Creating a Judicial Appointments Commission: which model works best?' *Public Law*, 2004, 102, 106.

[61] Ibid.

Her primary rationale for having a more diverse judiciary, like Dame Brenda Hale, was to strengthen the legitimacy of the judiciary. ('Irrespective of whether or not the inclusion on the bench of members of under-represented groups, such as solicitors, women, minority lawyers and disabled lawyers will have a significant effect on the decision-making of the courts, the corrosive impact of their absence on the legitimacy of the judiciary is now too great to ignore.'[62])

But dissident voices have been raised – notably that of Lord Sumption in his Bar Council Law Reform Lecture in November 2012 under the title 'Home truths about judicial diversity'. Lord Sumption first suggested that the entire enterprise of increasing diversity was based on the belief that

> there was a large untapped reserve of potential talent among women and ethnic minorities, comprising people who were at least as good as those who were actually being appointed, but who had been overlooked or devalued by the Lord Chancellor's Department. It followed that this had only to be corrected for the benefits to become apparent.[63]

This he suggested was 'a desperately crude analysis of a complicated situation'. Worse,

> [I]t was unintentionally encouraged by the assertion, constantly reiterated by politicians, senior judges and even occasionally by spokesmen for the Commission itself, that the achievement of a fully diverse judiciary was entirely compatible with selection on merit.[64]

The reality was that judges, at least at the senior level, were drawn from successful practitioners. There were only a limited number of women and ethnic minority lawyers in that pool. Without some form of positive discrimination the judiciary would never be more diverse than the pool from which it was drawn, namely the legal profession.

> In England, the recruitment of judges from the higher ranks of the legal profession has, on the whole, served us well. It has generated a culture in which many of the ablest lawyers of their generation have come to regard judicial appointment as the culmination of a successful professional career. It has produced a judiciary of outstanding intellectual calibre and broad legal experience. It is a significant contributory cause of the highly developed sense of judicial independence among English judges. These are particularly important considerations in a system such as ours in which judges have a higher public profile and a larger role in the making of law than their civil law counterparts.
>
> However, the price that we have paid for these advantages is a less diverse judiciary than most of Europe. We are simply deluding ourselves if we try to pretend that selection from that pool on merit alone will produce a fully diverse, or even a reasonably diverse judiciary quickly. It will happen, but it will take a long time. The average judicial career lasts for more than twenty years. It follows that even if a rigid quota system were to be introduced tomorrow morning requiring the appointment of women and ethnic minority candidates in proportions exactly matching their presence in the population at large, something which no one is suggesting, it would still take fifteen or twenty years to achieve a fully diverse judiciary. As it is, it seems certain to take much longer. Professor Alan Paterson offers the gloomy forecast that under the current system and on current trends it will take more than a hundred years. Personally, I think that it may take fifty. But we are both guessing. By any measure, this is a long haul.[65]

[62] Ibid.

[63] Lord Sumption, 'Home truths about judicial diversity' 12th Annual Bar Council Law Reform Lecture, November 2012, 9.

[64] Ibid.

[65] Ibid, 14.

If society wished to achieve a swifter route to a diverse judiciary it would require amendment of the criteria for appointment to permit some form of positive discrimination.

He suggested there were three possible reasons for reform. One was that the selection process was defective. In his view the system operated by the JAC was 'careful, fair and meritocratic'.[66] A second argument was that justice was better delivered by a diverse judiciary. He suggested that the research evidence, most of which was American, was unconvincing.

> Broadly speaking, most of it seeks to establish a statistically significant connection between the presence of one or more women or non-whites on a multi-member panel of judges, and the likelihood of a 'liberal' or a 'conservative' outcome. The criteria used for identifying any particular outcome as 'liberal' or 'conservative' seem to me to be rather crude, even as applied to the areas of civil rights, discrimination and penal policy on which most of the research has concentrated. Moreover, most of it makes no, or very little allowance, for the possibility that the outcome, however classified, may actually be attributable to the facts of individual cases or the state of the law, rather than to the gender or ethnic balance of the tribunal. Even so, most of this substantial body of work is inconclusive.[67]

A more persuasive line of argument, he thought, was that of the then current Chief Justice of Canada, Beverley McLachlin. She did not believe that male and female judges necessarily approached cases differently. ('We are all trained jurists, and when we apply the law and common sense, we are likely to come to the same conclusions irrespective of gender.'[68]) But Chief Justice McLachlin argued that a diverse judiciary was able to draw on a wider range of collective experience:

> Jurists [she says] are human beings and, as such, are informed and influenced by their backgrounds, communities and experiences. For cultural, biological, social and historic reasons, women do have different experiences than men. In this respect women can make a unique contribution to the deliberations of our courts. Women are capable of infusing the law with the unique reality of their life.[69]

Similar views had been expressed by Chief Justice Elias in New Zealand.

Lord Sumption said he had the strongest doubts about that argument. In the first place it could only apply to multi-member courts. Most judicial decision were given by single judge courts. But secondly it overstated the importance of personal as opposed to vicarious experience. Most fact situations that judges confronted were outside their direct personal experience. Judicial experience derived from 'intelligent social observation, and a sensitive empathy with those who find themselves in situations that the judge is unlikely to have experienced himself'.[70] Courts consisting only of male judges were perfectly capable of dealing sensitively with issues confronting women just as courts consisting only of female judges were capable of dealing sensitively with issues confronting men. Moreover, if experience of a relevant group was important, there were countless sub-groups each with their own particular experiences, starting with the great variety of ethnic minorities and religious groupings. Emphasis on the personal judicial experience of different groups led to the fragmentation of the judicial function.

[66] Ibid, 16.
[67] Ibid, 17.
[68] Ibid, 18.
[69] Ibid, 18.
[70] Ibid, 19.

> It leads to an attitude of mind which treats appellate courts as a sort of congress of ambassadors from different interest groups. I cannot be alone in regarding this as a travesty of the judge's role.[71]

The other argument for positive discrimination, Lord Sumption suggested, was concern that an undiverse judiciary lacked legitimacy in the eyes of the wider public. He accepted that that was so but he deplored it.

> The call for more members of particular groups on the bench is a symptom of the fragmentation of our society. It is influenced by a widespread belief that judicial decisions are vitiated by the social ignorance of judges, or by their tacit loyalty to their class, gender, race or other constituency, or by inescapable social conditioning. I regard this belief as profoundly mistaken. I think that it is also unrealistic. Whoever they are and however recruited, judges as a group will never be representative of the public at large. Even in a fully diversified system, we would continue to expect our judges to have outstanding intellectual and personal qualities which will necessarily mark them out from the average.[72]

If diversity were made a criterion in the selection of judges Lord Sumption believes that there would be a loss in the quality of the bench.

> Outstanding candidates will not apply in significant numbers for judicial appointments if they believe that the appointment process is designed to favour ethnic or gender groups to which they do not belong. They will not walk away out of pique. They will do it because the qualification of the principle of appointment on merit will have undermined much that makes judicial office attractive to outstandingly able people. Judicial appointments which are not made 'solely on merit' will lack the prestige in their eyes that was previously due to the assumption that only the best people get appointed.[73]

This would be true as much for women and ethnic minorities as for men.

> Positive discrimination is patronising. Those women and ethnic minority candidates who have been appointed under the current system are justifiably proud of having achieved this under a system based exclusively on individual merit. Many, probably most of those who are not judges but aspire to be appointed, do so because the principle of selection on individual merit makes it an ambition worth achieving. A partial abandonment of that principle would therefore be likely to make judicial office a great deal less attractive to the very people that its proponents are trying to help.[74]

The contrast with the position in France, he suggested, was instructive. The position there was as unsatisfactory as here, but for different reasons. Being a judge in France was a career choice made as a young person. Over half the judges in France now were women. In civil first instance courts and family courts the proportion was around three-quarters. The proportions were bound to rise even higher because the pool from which judges were drawn was dominated by women. Currently 83 per cent of new graduates emerging from the Ecole Nationale de la Magistrature were women.

> The major factor behind the rising proportion of women embarking on a judicial career in France has been the increasing reluctance of men to contemplate a judicial career. Only about 16% of those sitting the final examinations of the Ecole Nationale de la Magistrature last year were men.

[71] Ibid, 20.
[72] Ibid, 21.
[73] Ibid, 23.
[74] Ibid, 24.

> The evidence is that in a world where professional and judicial careers are separate streams with very little in the way of transfer between them, men will opt disproportionately for professional practice. This is because it is perceived to bring higher financial rewards, greater independence, and more status than the judiciary, at a cost in terms of hours and working conditions which men are more willing to pay than women are.[75]

Fifty years ago, 93 per cent of French judges were men.

> [T]he current situation results from an artificial reduction in the pool from which judges are chosen, by the wholesale withdrawal of men. This hardly seems to be in the public interest and is no more compatible with a diverse judiciary than our own situation.[76]

The implication suggested by Lord Sumption was that moving away from selection of the best to selection by some other criteria threatened the quality of the bench. He concluded his lecture with these words:

> What I hope I may have persuaded you to accept is that the whole subject of judicial diversity is an exceptionally complex and delicate issue, in which crude slogans, easy clichés and simple policy prescriptions are likely to have unintended and damaging side effects. They are likely to undermine much that is good about our current system, without necessarily curing what is bad about it. In this area, as in life generally, we just cannot have everything that we want. We have to make choices and to accept impure compromises. We may even have to learn patience. The alternative is to do serious harm to the quality and standing of the judiciary, undermining an institution which however imperfect has been one of the more successful areas of English public life.[77]

A report by JUSTICE, *Increasing judicial diversity*, 2017[78] made further recommendations:

— Creating a 'Senior Selections Committee' dedicated to appointments to the Court of Appeal, Heads of Divisions and UK Supreme Court.
— Introducing targets for selection bodies with monitoring, transparency and reporting to the House of Commons Justice Select Committee.
— Introducing 'appointable pools', ie talent pools for each court which would require a rolling proactive programme of recruitment.
— External review of selection processes.
— Creating an upward judicial career path, where junior lawyers can take up an 'entry-level' position and work their way to the top.
— A 'Talent Management Programme' to enable talented judges to progress their career.
— Making flexible working the default.

A different take on the diversity issue is to look beyond its overt manifestations of gender and race to personal values. For an ambitious attempt to delve into that elusive topic see RJ Cahill-O'Callaghan, 'Reframing the judicial diversity debate: personal values and tacit diversity', 35 *Legal Studies*, 2015(1), 1–29, based on a study of UK Supreme Court decisions. The author concludes (at 29):

[75] Ibid, 13.
[76] Ibid, 14.
[77] Ibid, 25.
[78] In January 2020 JUSTICE published *Increasing Judicial Diversity: an Update* making further recommendations. Both reports are accessible on the JUSTICE website: www.justice.org.uk.

> The study of personal values suggests that gender alone cannot be used as a proxy for the many life experiences that influence personal values. A focus on gender alone should therefore be approached with caution: male and female Supreme Court Justices may have a range of life experiences that have a profound effect on their values. These experiences extend beyond overt demographic characteristics … The study of personal values highlights the limits of arguments that centre on the explicit characteristics of the judiciary and lose sight of the judge as an individual.

See also G Gee and E Rackley (eds), *Debating Judicial Appointments in an Age of Diversity* (Routledge, London 2018).[79] R Hunter, 'More than just a different face? Judicial diversity and decision-making' *Current Legal Problems*, 2015, 68; and E Rackley, 'A short history of judicial diversity' 76 *Current Legal Problems*, 2023(1), 265–96.

7.3.3. Should Parliament have a Role in the Selection of Judges?

The question whether Parliament should have a role in the selection at least of the most senior judges was considered by the House of Lords Constitution Committee in 2012 in the course of an enquiry into the appointment of judges. The Committee was against any such involvement: 'Parliamentarians should not hold pre- or post-appointment hearings of judicial candidates, nor should they sit on selection panels. Political considerations would undoubtedly inform both the selection of parliamentarians to sit on the relevant committees or panels and the choice of questions to be asked.'[80]

This extract from the Committee's report shows the arguments and evidence pro and con:[81]

> PRE- OR POST-APPOINTMENT HEARINGS
>
> 39. We received evidence arguing that candidates for some senior judicial posts should be subject to a pre-appointment hearing before a parliamentary committee. Professor Robert Hazell, Director of the Constitution Unit, University College London, and Professor Kate Malleson, Professor of Law, Queen Mary, University of London, set out the arguments in favour of such hearings as follows:
>
> - hearings act as a check on political patronage, help to ensure that independent and robust candidates are appointed and add to the appointee's legitimacy;
> - Parliament has the power to scrutinise all acts of the executive – appointments of senior judges are an important exercise of ministerial discretion and should be subject to parliamentary scrutiny which is a useful check against political bias;
> - Parliament nowadays has little contact with the judges: the senior judges are largely unknown to MPs; Supreme Court Justices will be unknown to the Lords now that the law lords have departed – through dialogue, political and judicial actors can better understand the constraints under which the other operates;[82] and
> - the judges should meet the body vested with the constitutional power to dismiss them.
>
> 40. A number of witnesses focused the case for some form of pre-appointment hearing on the increasingly complex role of the senior judiciary and the legitimate role for Parliament to consider candidates' competing judicial philosophies. Individual decisions made by judges impact on policy and determine the interpretation of legislation enacted by Parliament. Some witnesses argued that

[79] The book was awarded the 2013 Birks Books Prize by the Society of Legal Scholars.

[80] Lords Constitution Committee, 'Judicial Appointments', 25th Report, 2011–12, 28 March 2012, HL 272.

[81] The paragraphs in bold are in bold in the original (ed).

[82] But see p 63 n 182 above about the participation of judges in the work of select committee (ed).

in respect of legislation such as the Human Rights Act 1998, and in the development of judicial review, the judiciary has a wide margin in which to develop the law and that Parliament has a legitimate interest in the manner in which this is done. Professor Alan Paterson, Professor of Law at the University of Strathclyde, argued that:

> 'We already have committees to ask Supreme Court nominees what they think the role of a Supreme Court justice is in a democracy. I see no reason why the appointments panel could not ask that and I see no reason why a parliamentarian could not ... Indeed, it could ask about the judge's views on parliamentary sovereignty. We know that there is a split among some judges in their views on this. I do not see why one could not elicit views in general terms on that sort of thing.'

41. Jack Straw MP, a former Lord Chancellor, stressed the need to address the 'lack of mutual confidence between the senior judiciary and this place [Parliament] in respect of the role of the senior judiciary and its broadening authority into areas that are inevitably political'. Sir Thomas Legg, former Permanent Secretary in the Lord Chancellor's Department, considered it to be 'more and more desirable that our most senior judges should be able to ground their mandate on the authority, not only of the executive, still less of the judges themselves and a few laymen alone, but of Parliament itself'.

42. A number of witnesses on both sides of the argument referred to the system of confirmation hearings in the United States. However, Professor Cheryl Thomas, Professor of Judicial Studies, University College London, noting the more extensive powers of US judges and their appointment by the President, argued that there were 'extremely good reasons for there to be a legislative hearing process for those judges that do not apply to judges in this country.'

43. The weight of our evidence was against pre-appointment hearings for UK judges. Professor Brice Dickson, Professor of International and Comparative Law at Queen's University, Belfast, stressed the ability of Parliament to overturn individual judicial decisions, whilst Lord Kerr, Justice of the Supreme Court, described such hearings as 'the complete antithesis of the preservation of judicial independence'. The benefits of pre-appointment hearings in respect of senior public appointments are many, but the relationship between Parliament and the judiciary is a unique one. Parliament is best placed to protect the independence of, for example, ombudsmen from the executive. Judges must be independent of both the executive and Parliament: it is imperative that they remain one step removed from the political process.

44. Our witnesses also raised more immediate concerns about pre-appointment hearings. It would be difficult to limit the questioning of candidates to matters of general judicial philosophy and approach. There is a real danger that questions might touch on specific issues that could come before the courts or on candidates' individual political positions. Even if parliamentarians did limit themselves, the answers would either be at a level of such generality as to be effectively meaningless or be sufficiently detailed as to risk politicising the process. Some witnesses were concerned that hearings would act as a disincentive to many potential candidates. There is a further question of what impact criticism of a candidate, explicit or implicit, might have on his or her future public standing.

45. Pre-appointment hearings 'would also risk undermining the public's confidence that the senior judiciary is appointed strictly on merit and having regard to integrity and independence.' Roger Smith, Director of JUSTICE, thus described the proposal as 'a quagmire into which no one would want to go.'

46. **We are against any proposal to introduce pre-appointment hearings for senior members of the judiciary. However limited the questioning, such hearings could not have any meaningful impact without undermining the independence of those subsequently appointed or appearing to pre-judge their future decisions. In the United Kingdom, judges' legitimacy depends on their independent status and appointment on merit, not on any democratic mandate.**

47. One alternative to pre-appointment hearings which we examined was the idea that senior members of the judiciary should appear before a parliamentary committee following their appointment. This would enable a dialogue to take place between those judges and parliamentarians with less risk of politicising the appointment. Our witnesses demonstrated little support for this idea. Baroness Hale, Justice of the Supreme Court, stressed that post-appointment hearings would not improve the accountability of the system. Lord Judge CJ, noting that most senior judges are not responsible for administrative issues, argued that there was no purpose in parliamentarians simply meeting a Justice of the Supreme Court for the sake of it: 'I think the idea of beauty parades is not a good one.'

48. **We agree that post-appointment hearings of senior judges would serve no useful purpose. There may be an exception in the case of the Lord Chief Justice and the President of the Supreme Court who undertake leadership roles for which they can properly be held to account.**

PARLIAMENTARY PARTICIPATION IN SELECTION PANELS

49. A number of witnesses, including some of those who disagreed with the concept of pre-appointment hearings, proposed that parliamentarians should in future sit as members of selection panels, in particular for the Supreme Court. Lord Justice Etherton and Baroness Hale both argued strongly in favour of this proposal on the grounds that 'politicians have the legitimacy of being elected' and that it would be 'a small step towards increasing the democratic accountability of the process'. Baroness Hale further argued that it would 'reduce the potential for "cloning"', an argument reflected in the evidence of Lord Mance who considered that this could be one way of ensuring that candidates were assessed 'from different angles'.

50. Lord Phillips, President of the Supreme Court, disagreed with this analysis. He argued:

> 'Once you start introducing some kind of parliamentary choice of who is appointed, one asks what the criteria are that Parliament is going to be adopting in making the choice. If it is simply to appoint the best person, well, I do not think Parliament is best placed to do that. If it is, alternatively, to have regard to political considerations, I do not myself think that is desirable.'

This concern was shared by a number of other witnesses, including Lady Justice Hallett and Lord Neuberger MR.

51. We accept the concern raised by Baroness Hale and others that selection panels must not simply contain judges who might seek, subconsciously or otherwise, to appoint others in their own image. But we disagree that the involvement of parliamentarians is the means to prevent this. The first question, to which none of our witnesses suggested a convincing answer, is how would these parliamentarians be chosen, and on what basis? Whilst there is no objection to lay persons who happen also to be parliamentarians sitting on panels – indeed, the first Chair of the JAC [Judicial Appointments Commission], Baroness Prashar, is a cross-bench member of this House – and emphasising that there is a strong case for more lay representation on selection panels to increase diversity, we do not see what additional questions a parliamentarian might sensibly ask which could not be asked by a lay person.

52. **Parliamentarians, acting in that capacity, should not sit on selection panels for judicial appointments. There is no useful role that parliamentarians could play that could not be played by lay members on selection panels. It would not be possible to choose one or two parliamentarians without recourse to political considerations and in so doing it would be difficult to maintain the appearance of an independent judicial appointments process.**

The question of parliamentary involvement in judicial appointments came up again during the Brexit saga, especially after the Supreme Court's unanimous 11-0 decision that Prime Minister Boris Johnson's decision to prorogue Parliament for five weeks was unlawful.[83]

[83] *R (Miller) v The Prime Minister* [2019] UKSC 41.

The decision was given on 24 September 2019. On 3 October, the Attorney-General, Sir Geoffrey Cox, was asked in the House of Commons 'What recent discussions he has had with the Secretary of State for Justice on the judicial appointments process.' Cox answered that while the Supreme Court judgment 'undoubtedly represents a significant development in our constitutional arrangements', it was 'important to take stock of the implications of that judgment not in the immediate aftermath of a ruling, but deliberately, carefully and thoughtfully'. He was asked 'whether he would categorically rule out any changes that could result in a political appointment system'. He answered: 'The Government have no plans to introduce any such appointment system. The only thing I would say is that this House must have the right to determine the constitutional arrangements of this country, and of course parts of that will have to reflect on the role of the Supreme Court and its constitutional functions. But I agree with him that a US-style appointment system would be a wholly retrograde step.'[84]

Shortly after that, Parliament was (lawfully) prorogued for preparation of the new session of Parliament. During that prorogation, Lord Keen of Elie QC, Advocate General for Scotland, gave a written ministerial answer to a question put by Baroness Taylor on the appointment of Supreme Court judges:

> We have no plans to alter the process for making judicial appointments. Our judges are selected following a rigorous, independent, merit based system which is key to maintaining their quality, integrity and independence. The Government agrees with the conclusion of the Lords Constitution Committee 2012 report into judicial appointments, that a judges' legitimacy depends on their independence and appointment on merit, rather than a parliamentary mandate.[85]

There was nothing directly about the appointment of judges in the Conservative Party's December 2019 Election Manifesto, but some thought that the promise (p 48) 'In our first year we will set up a Constitution, Democracy & Rights Commission that will … come up with proposals to restore trust in our institutions and in how our democracy operates' might presage proposals on this topic.

In December 2019, Policy Exchange, a right-leaning think-tank, published a short pamphlet, entitled *Protecting the Constitution* by Richard Ekins.[86] Ekins was strongly critical of the Supreme Court's unanimous decision holding Boris Johnson's prorogation of Parliament by Prime Minister to be unlawful:[87]

> In quashing the Prime Minister's advice to Her Majesty and the prorogation that followed, the Supreme Court breached Article 9 of the Bill of Rights 1689.[88] The Court evaded this statutory prohibition by reasoning that prorogation was not a proceeding in Parliament – despite it literally being a proceeding carried out in Parliament, which each House of Parliament records. The Supreme Court's intervention was a landmark victory for political litigation in which the Court

[84] HC, *Hansard*, 3 October 2019, col 1361.

[85] The letter, written from the Ministry of Justice, dated 'October 2019'– without indication of the actual day – was posted on the House of Lords Constitution Committee's website.

[86] Professor of Law and Constitutional Government, University of Oxford.

[87] *R (Miller) v The Prime Minister* [2019] UKSC 41.

[88] This is not the view of Lord Lisvane who before he retired and became a peer was Clerk of the House of Commons. Speaking in the Lords on the Queen's Speech after the December 2019 General Election he said: 'As the Supreme Court quite rightly pointed out, the Bill of Rights is statute law and so falls to the courts to interpret but, of course, there is room for more than one opinion on the matter. It is a close call but, on balance, I think the court, in paragraph 69 of the judgment, was right to conclude that it was not precluded by Article 9 from considering the validity of the prorogation' (HL, *Hansard*, 8 January 2020, col 253).

> yielded to the temptation to superintend the political process, to make new law to quash what was otherwise a perfectly lawful – if politically controversial – action on the part of the Government.

One of the ways of addressing the problem he suggested was for Ministers to take a more active role in the appointment of the most senior judges:

> It would be a bad mistake to politicise judicial appointments. The answer to the expansion of judicial power is to restore principled limits not tacitly to legitimate and encourage that expansion by selecting judges on overtly political grounds. However, the Government, accountable to Parliament, has a responsibility to attempt to secure sound appointments to senior judicial office. There is now too much judicial influence over senior judicial appointments – it is only a slight exaggeration to say that senior judges are appointing other senior judges. The Lord Chancellor should be more actively involved in judicial appointments: meaningful ministerial involvement in the selection of senior judges will inject – or rather, restore – an important measure of accountability and legitimacy. The Lord Chancellor has the final say over whether to appoint the candidate for a top senior vacancy recommended to him by a selection commission. Previous Lord Chancellors have been reluctant to exercise their right to reject or request reconsideration of a candidate where there have been doubts about whether that person is the best for the post.
>
> The Government should:
>
> - Stand by a Lord Chancellor who is confident in exercising his or her right to reject or request reconsideration of candidates recommended by a commission.
> - Introduce legislation requiring the relevant selection commissions to provide the Lord Chancellor with a short-list of three names for senior judicial vacancies. (p 18)

Boris Johnson never did set up the Constitution, Democracy and Rights Commission promised in the 2019 Election Manifesto. For comment regretting this and suggesting topics that might have been addressed see Tom Fleming and Petra Schleiter 'What Happened to the Constitution, Democracy and Rights Commission?' (Constitution Unit blog, UCL, April 12 2022).

7.3.4. A New Way of Selecting the Senior Judiciary?

Paterson and Paterson proposed that what was needed was both a different selection process and different selection criteria for the senior judiciary.[89] Even more serious than the diversity deficit, they argued, was the issue of constitutional legitimacy:

> [T]the process of Supreme Court appointments 'currently lacks any democratic accountability'[90] – it involves no input whatsoever from the legislature, minimal input from the executive and actually requires no participant with a substantive role to be an elected office-holder.[91]

It was estimated that around half the cases heard by the Supreme Court were public law cases which usually turned on evaluation of policy questions. Because of the role they played, appointment of the senior judiciary was a political act. The selection process should

[89] A Paterson and C Paterson, *Guarding the Guardians? Towards an Independent, Accountable and Diverse Senior Judiciary, 2012*– accessible at www.centreforum.org/assets/pubs/guarding-the-guardians.pdf.

[90] Quoting Lady Hale's written evidence to the House of Lords Constitution Committee's 2011 inquiry into Judicial Appointments, HL 272, 25th Report 2010–12. (The Constitution Committee's report said: 'We support the current appointments model and believe that no fundamental changes should be made.').

[91] Paterson and Paterson, *Guarding the Guardians?* (n 89 above) 32.

take into consideration not only the qualities of the individual judge but what was needed for the court as a collective:

> What is instead required is a more fundamental reconsideration of the manner in which 'merit' is determined in relation to judicial appointments, particularly at a senior level. The relentless focus on one (flawed) construction of perceived individual merit must move towards a process in which the needs of the judiciary as a collective institution are central. It is in relation to this that the consideration of the constitutional rationale for a diverse judiciary becomes crucial …
>
> The Supreme Court and the Court of Appeal are *collegiate courts* that make binding legal (and increasingly, 'small p political') decisions *as a collective*. The competence of these courts is therefore a *corporate competence*, not simply an aggregation of the individual competences of their individual members. This collective competence – the institutional 'merit' of such a court – must therefore play a much more central role in the process of appointments to it.[92]

The existing selection criteria required 'that between them the Judges will have knowledge of, and experience of practice in, the law of each part of the United Kingdom'.[93] But this was the only recognition given to the importance of representativeness.

> To explicitly recognise the impact of geographical representation on institutional 'merit' and yet to ignore this idea of collective competence completely in relation to everything else is fundamentally flawed.[94]

A wider definition of 'merit' would permit a more effective approach to both the diversity deficit and constitutional legitimacy.[95]

> The understanding of merit for appointments to the Supreme Court (and also the Court of Appeal) should therefore be altered to reflect the need to give primacy to the collective competence of the court. With this, a person will – importantly – only be appointed when they are the *best* candidate. They will be the best candidate because they *best reflect what would be most beneficial to the court* (and, as a direct result, the society it serves). Surely this is what 'merit' in this context should actually mean?[96]

The selection of the senior judiciary should not be done, the Patersons said, by ad hoc selection commissions but by a new *standing* commission responsible for selecting judges of the Supreme Court and Court of Appeal, the Lord Chief Justice and the Heads of Divisions.

> [T]he membership of the appointing commissions for the senior judiciary should be expanded and altered in a manner that reduces the scope for self-perpetuation and introduces a greater degree of democratic legitimacy. Rather than a system of ad-hoc panels convened as and when a vacancy arises, a more permanent senior judiciary JAC should be established … This JAC should be composed of 9 individuals: 3 senior judicial members,[97] 3 parliamentary members[98] and 3 lay members[99] …

[92] Ibid, 48.

[93] Constitutional Reform Act 2005, s 27(8).

[94] Paterson and Paterson, *Guarding the Guardians?* (n 89 above) 49.

[95] In September 2014 the Chief Executive of the Supreme Court sent a questionnaire to 50 senior judges and public officials under the heading 'Appointments Review – Possible Questions' asking 19 different questions about the selection process. For a report of the results of the exercise (*Review of process supporting independent selection commissions for Supreme Court*) see: www.supremecourt.uk/docs/review-of-selection-commission-process-july-2015.pdf.

[96] Paterson and Paterson, *Guarding the Guardians?* (n 89 above) 51.

[97] The President and Deputy President of the Supreme Court and the Lord Chief Justice.

[98] One from each of the main parties, members of the Commons Justice Committee or the Lords Constitution Committee.

[99] One from each of the three regional Judicial Appointment Commissions.

> The political members of this commission would be in a position to drive the application of the broader understanding of merit, emphasising its impact on collective competence and therefore its important role as a factor in the appointments process. This would perhaps particularly involve an emphasis on the possibility of appointing to the highest court members from a wider range of career backgrounds …[100]

7.4. Can Judges Undertake their Own Researches into the Law?

In continental countries the theory is that the court knows the law – *curia novit legem.* This has never been the position in England. The common law proceeds on the basis that judges know no law. They are basically supposed to take the law from the submissions put to them by the advocates, though this tradition has been somewhat affected by skeleton arguments and the appointment of judicial assistants.[101] If the judges study the skeleton arguments exchanged by the parties before the hearing there is nothing to prevent them undertaking their own research on the relevant law, though in practice it would be rare for judges to do so.[102] But in the Supreme Court and to a lesser extent in the Court of Appeal, Civil Division it is quite common for the judicial assistants to be asked to conduct legal research with a view to helping the judges both to prepare for the oral hearing and later to write their judgments. In former times counsel were permitted to devote a great deal of time in reading to the court lengthy passages from precedents that were completely familiar to the judges.[103] This happens much less today. But can the judge undertake and utilise their own research in the process of hearing or deciding cases? During the hearing the answer is Yes. A judge may ask counsel to respond to a point – whether as a result of their own prior knowledge, or their study of the case, including study in the library. But when it comes to giving judgment the position is different. There have been instances when judges have taken points in their judgments or have referred to precedents that were not discussed by counsel during argument. But this is extremely rare. In *Rahimtoola v Nizam of Hyderabad* [1958] AC 379, 398, Lord Simonds said that he did not assent to Lord Denning's views on questions and authorities 'in regard to which the House has not had the benefit of the arguments of counsel or of the judgment of the courts below'.[104] Lords Reid, Cohen and Somervell said they entirely agreed with Lord Simonds' observations.[105] Professor Alan Paterson reported in 1982 that his interviews with judges and counsel showed that amongst the majority 'there was a shared expectation that a Law Lord in giving his reasons for deciding for or against

[100] Paterson and Paterson, *Guarding the Guardians?* (n 89 above) 65, 77.

[101] For more information about judicial assistants see 7.11 below.

[102] 'Judges are in my experience, divided into Pre-Raphaelites and Impressionists. Judicial Pre-Raphaelites read everything, whereas Judicial Impressionists read very little – often just skimming the skeleton arguments' (Lord Neuberger in his lecture 'Sausages and the judicial process: the limits of transparency' 1 August 2014 – accessible www.supremecourt.uk. He said he was an Impressionist.).

[103] One of the reasons for Lord Devlin's early retirement as a Law Lord – 'It was boredom and boredom of the way in which time was wasted reading judgments' – Lady Devlin, cited by RFV Heuston, 'Patrick Arthur Devlin' 84 *Proceedings of the British Academy,* 1994, 247, 256.

[104] Lord Denning had spent a considerable part of his summer vacation researching points of law not raised by counsel in the appeal.

[105] See also *Hadmor Productions Ltd v Hamilton* [1982] 1 All ER 1042.

the appeal ought to confine his propositions of law to matters covered by the arguments of counsel'.[106] There had been some who doubted the rule. Lord Hailsham, for instance, said that it applied 'usually but not necessarily'. The quality of counsel's arguments varied, he said, and it was 'sometimes necessary to break new ground'. Lord Simon said that a court which did its own research 'should proceed with special caution', but he did not rule it out altogether.[107]

The judicial self-denying ordinance applies not only in regard to precedents which might be discovered by the judges but also to propositions of law. In general judges seem to accept the view that in their judgments they should not advance points not put to them by counsel – except that sometimes they do. The practice in such cases seems to be to ask counsel to submit written arguments on the new matter or, occasionally, to restore the case for further argument. Sometimes, however, the rule is ignored.[108] (In the high profile case of Julian Assange, concerning extradition of the founder of Wikileaks to Sweden, when judgment was being handed down his counsel objected that it was based on a point that had not been argued. She backed her argument with an 18-page submission. The Supreme Court rejected the submission without having a further hearing.) There may nowadays be a greater readiness to ignore the general rule than in the past.[109]

For an argument that courts should be permitted to require counsel to argue points of law that seem relevant even if counsel does not wish to do so see NH Andrews, 'The passive court and legal argument' 7 *Civil Justice Quarterly*, 1988, 125. Andrews reviewed the then existing case law as to the judge doing private research into the law.

7.5. What the Law is and What it Ought to be

Is there a danger that through focusing more openly on policy issues the courts will come to decide cases on the basis of what the law ought to be rather than what the law is? This question lies at the heart of one of the most vital debates about the nature of the judicial process. It reflects the anxieties of the many judges and lawyers who deprecate the efforts made by 'reformist' judges to improve the quality of justice by looking beyond the form to the substance below.

Any young counsel unwise enough to argue in court that their submission represents what the law ought to be will immediately be interrupted by the court – 'Mr Smith', they will be told, 'we are here to decide what the law is, not what it ought to be'. The statement, in one sense, is of course true. The court, in deciding the question of law before it, must decide on the basis of what it thinks the law is. (The only exception is if the court could say 'we think the law in the past was X and that is the law we are applying to the present case, but in future we will decide that it is Y'. This technique, known as prospective overruling,

[106] Alan Paterson, *The Law Lords* (Macmillan, 1982) 38.

[107] Ibid, 40.

[108] Ibid, 42, cited as examples: *R v Hyam* [1975] AC 55, per Lords Diplock and Dilhorne; *Miliangos v George Frank (Textiles) Ltd* [1976] AC 443 at 478, per Lord Simon; and *DPP v Humphreys* [1977] AC 1, per Lords Salmon and Edmund-Davies. In *Final Judgment: The Last Law Lords and the Supreme Court* (Hart Publishing, 2013), Paterson (p 22) cited *Walumba Lumba (Congo) v Secretary of State for the Home Department* [2011] UKSC 12 [25] per Lord Dyson criticising Lord Phillips for breaching the convention; and *McDonald v Royal Borough of Kensington and Chelsea* [2011] UKSC 33 [28] per Lord Walker criticising Baroness Hale for the same reason.

[109] Paterson, *Final Judgment* (Hart, 2013) 20–29.

is discussed 7.7 below.) But the statement that the court is only interested in what the law is, misrepresents the position. It is based on the false premise that, in determining the issue before it, the court is exercising no choice or discretion. This view is the classic formalistic position actually adopted by countless English judges. An example was the reply given in 1951 by Lord Jowitt, the Lord Chancellor, when he was asked at an Australian conference what the House of Lords would do if there was an appeal in the then recently decided case of *Candler v Crane, Christmas*:

> We should regard it as our duty to expound what we believe the law to be and we should loyally follow the decisions of the House of Lords if we found there was some decision which we thought was in point. It is not really a question of being a bold or a timorous soul; it is a much simpler question than that. You know there was a time when the earth was void and without form, but after these hundreds of years the law of England, the common law, has at any rate got some measure of form to it. We are really no longer in the position of Lord Mansfield who used to consider a problem and expound it ex aequa et bona–what the law ought to be … I do most humbly suggest to some of the speakers today that the problem is not to consider what social and political conditions do today require; that is to confuse the task of the lawyer with the task of the legislator. It is quite possible that the law has produced a result which does not accord with the requirements of today. If so, put it right by legislation, but do not expect every lawyer, in addition to all his other problems, to act as Lord Mansfield did, and decide what the law ought to be. He is far better employed if he puts himself to the much simpler task of deciding what the law is.[110]

Lord Jowitt's response would have accurately reflected the view of generations of English lawyers and judges. However, it would have been difficult to find many American practitioners or judges at that time who would have accepted the proposition in that form. The difference in the two countries was that American legal culture had by then absorbed the insights of the so-called Realist School, which flourished from the 1930s and whose leading exponents were writers such as Jerome Frank in *Law and the Modern Mind*. The chief contribution of the Realists was to expose the role of the judge himself in deciding the outcome of cases raising points of law. Some of the claims of the Realists no doubt went too far (a caricature of their view is that the decision is ultimately determined by the state of the judge's digestion). But their central claim had become fully accepted by virtually all American lawyers – and by the beginning of the twenty-first century it was also accepted by most English judges and lawyers.

The validity of the Realist view seems readily demonstrable. The judge hears argument from two parties, each of whom is normally represented by a professional lawyer. Each side advances argument as to why their position represents the law. The court must decide between them. Sometimes it may be that the question virtually decides itself. There are, let us say, six precedents each of which says that the law on the point is X. The proposition has been unchallenged for 150 years. Every textbook confirms it. X seems a reasonable rule – no one has criticised it. The party that seeks to show that the law on that point is Y obviously has an extremely uphill task. Indeed, few lawyers would undertake it. The great majority would advise the client that the prospects of success were nil and would urge the client to spend their money on something more promising. That case is therefore most unlikely ever to reach the courts.

[110] Cited by WK Fullagar, 25 *Australian Law Journal*, 1951, 278, and referred to by Robert Stevens, *Law and Politics: The House of Lords as a Judicial Body, 1800–1976* (Weidenfeld and Nicolson, 1969) 338.

In any case before the courts where both parties are professionally represented (where one can therefore rule out the possibility of cranks and vexatious litigants), the court is almost always required to decide between two arguments that have some substance. One side may come with stronger precedents but the other side will perhaps have greater merits on the facts. Or the strength of the precedents may be fairly evenly matched and the real battle will be to capture the sympathy of the court for the client's position. Of course, in some cases the lawyers on both sides will accurately predict the outcome and to that extent it may be that there was little scope for the judge's individual discretion. He was 'forced' by the strength of the precedents and the lack of any solid argument to the contrary to decide in favour of one of the two litigants. But, again, those cases tend not to come to court and when they do the decision is often only predictable after the event – before it is handed down, there appears to be the possibility that it might go the other way. Moreover, after the decision there remains the chance of an appeal. The higher one goes in the appeal system, the greater the chance of getting free of the clutches of the precedents – one climbs above the clouds and can survey the mountain peaks. At the level of the highest court the judges are absolutely free to decide either way.

In this context the House of Lords' 1966 Practice Statement was highly significant. If the House of Lords was free to depart from its own previous decisions, it meant *by definition* that their decisions do not always reflect the law. When the House first enunciated the principle it thought the law was X. Later it might conclude that the rule was Y – not because that conclusion was revealed by the precedents but because of a conscious decision by the judges. But this is only a particularly clear demonstration of something that occurs each time a court reaches a view of the law which is different from what the existing precedents appear to establish – for instance through the ordinary process of overruling. The very possibility that the Court of Appeal can overrule the decisions of the High Court means, again by definition, that it need not follow even the clearest precedents established by the High Court. Precisely the same is true even of the High Court. Since the High Court is not bound by its own decisions, it too can look at the precedents and reject them – in the name of some other better argument. In other words, whenever a court is faced with precedents that are not binding, it has the choice of following or not following them. Even if there are ten previous precedents all saying that the law is X, providing none is binding, the court is free to reject them and find the law to be Y. (Where the precedent is binding there is, of course, also a choice, since ultimately it is the court and not the precedent that decides that the precedent is apposite and not distinguishable.) Obviously, the court will be slow to reject a relevant precedent. It will need to have strong reasons for doing so. In some fields it will be most reluctant to upset settled rules. This is especially true in areas of the law where people can be assumed to have arranged their affairs in reliance on the existing state of the law, such as in commercial, tax or property matters. But in the final analysis, not being bound by a decision means that one can depart from it. Ten non-binding precedents still do not add up to a binding rule – ten times nothing remains nothing. Of course, ten non-binding precedents present more of an obstacle than one, but it remains an obstacle that a determined court can surmount if it is persuaded that it should do so.

By the 1970s it had become respectable in England to recognise that judges made law. Even conservative judges affirmed as much. Lord Edmund-Davies said in 1975: 'The simple and certain fact is that judges inevitably act as legislators … The inevitable interim between the discovery of social needs and demands and the provision of legislative remedies to meet them presents judges with the opportunity (indeed, it imposes upon them the *duty*) of filling the need and meeting the demand in accordance with their notions of what is just. Nolens volens they thereby act as law-makers.'[111] Lord Pearson, another judge who could hardly be described as a radical, said in *Herrington v British Railways Board* [1972] 2 WLR 537 of *Addie v Dumbreck*, the House of Lords' decision that stood in the plaintiff's way: 'It seems to me that the rule of *Addie's* case has been rendered obsolete by changes in physical and social conditions and has become an incumbrance impeding the proper development of the law … In my opinion the *Addie v Dumbreck* formulation of the duty of occupiers to trespassers … has become an anomaly and should be discarded.'

But it has not become respectable to talk in courts of law of what the law ought to be. Lawyers are still constrained to talk there only of what the law is, with insufficient recognition of the fact that for the court the question what the law is necessarily *includes* the question what the law ought to be. To discuss what the law ought to be is only another way of defining the proposition that a court is inevitably and properly involved in law-making. As Lord Edmund-Davies put it – *nolens volens* they act as law-makers.

If they are law-makers, should the judges not only recognise the fact but permit and even encourage debate before them of what law they should make, or should they, rather, conceal the fact as recommended for instance by Lord Devlin (pp 363–64 below) and Lord Radcliffe (p 395–96)?

For an illuminating systems theory discussion of the impossibility of judges being honest as to how and why they reach a decision involving making new law see R Nobles and D Schiff, 'Why do judges talk the way they do?' 5 *International Journal of Law in Context*, 2009, 25, esp 40–46.

7.6. The Practical Effect of the Retrospective Impact of Common Law Decisions

When a court delivers a ruling which is perceived to change the law the effect is not only for the future. It also affects the past. This is because of the fiction that when it states the law a court is stating the law as it always has been. To use a familiar metaphor, the law is a seamless web. The jagged edges when the law changes should not be seen. If the judges were thought to be engaged in law-making it might generate unease. The best way to cover up the fact of judicial creativity is to pretend that it does not happen. The new rule is the law and always has been.

Of course, if the case has already been litigated it cannot be reopened. It is subject to the principle expressed in the phrase *res judicata*. Equally, if the time allowed under the Statute of Limitations for bringing proceedings of that kind has expired, no case can now be brought on the basis of the changed rule. But if neither *res judicata* nor the Statute of Limitations applies, an action can be brought based on circumstances that occurred before the new decision.

The effect of this rule was the nub of a disagreement between the Law Lords in a case in 1991. Local authorities had invested millions of pounds in what were called 'interest rate swap transactions'. A district auditor challenged the lawfulness of such investments by a local authority on the grounds that they amounted to speculative trading for profit.

[111] 'Judicial Activism' 28 *Current Legal Problems*, 1975, 1.

The House of Lords upheld that view.[112] The decision led to much further litigation. In one such action, a bank sought to recover moneys paid to local authorities under interest swap agreements. The money had been paid by the bank more than six years previously and action for its recovery would therefore normally have been barred by lapse of time. But the Limitation Act 1980 states that where money is paid under a mistake, time should only run when the mistake has been discovered or could with reasonable diligence have been discovered. In the High Court the bank lost on the basis of binding Court of Appeal authority that no action lay for the recovery of money paid under a mistake of law. The case went on appeal directly to the House of Lords.[113]

The House of Lords by three to two held that that rule, which had been established for over a century, should no longer form part of English law. It was inconsistent with a modern approach to the principle of unjust enrichment. The law should recognise a general right to recover money paid under a mistake regardless of whether it was a mistake of fact or a mistake of law. The payer had to be regarded as having been mistaken as to what the law was at the time of payment because the declaratory theory of judicial decision-making means that the law is regarded as always having been what the most recent decision states it to be. Time only started to run when the mistake was discovered which was the date of the new judicial decision. So, the bank could recover its money.

This ruling has remarkable implications. The lengthy leading judgment was given by Lord Goff. In the course of his magisterial review of the subject he accepted that this decision was one of those rare cases where judicial development of the law was of an unusually radical nature. If the change in the law had been made by legislation instead of by judicial decision there would have been no question of retrospective effect.

Lord Browne-Wilkinson, dissenting, said he did not agree that the money should be recoverable since when it was paid the payer was not labouring under a mistake. At the time of the payment, on the basis of the law as it was then understood, the bank correctly thought that local authorities could lawfully enter into swap transactions. The majority's view meant that payments which when made and for years after were irrecoverable could become recoverable if the courts changed the rule.

> This result would be subversive of the great public interest in the security of receipts and the closure of transactions. The position is even worse because all your Lordships consider that the claims to recover money paid under a mistake of law are subject to s. 32(1) of the Limitation Act 1980, i.e. that in such a case time will not begin to run until the 'mistake' is discovered. A subsequent overruling of a Court of Appeal decision by the House of Lords could occur many decades after payments have been made on the faith of the Court of Appeal decision: in such a case 'the mistake' would not be discovered until the later overruling. All payments made pursuant to the Court of Appeal ruling would be recoverable.[114]

Lord Browne-Wilkinson urged that instead the law should be changed by Parliament on the advice of the Law Commission and that a satisfactory way be found to limit the impact of the change in the law by regulating the limitation period. Lord Lloyd agreed. He said that he viewed with alarm the possibility that whenever the House of Lords overruled a Court of Appeal decision it would be open to those who had entered into transactions in reliance on the previous decision to seek to reopen their transaction.[115]

[112] *Hazell v Hammersmith and Fulham London Borough Council* [1992] 2 AC 1.

[113] *Kleinwort Benson Ltd v Lincoln City Council* [1998] 2 AC 349.

[114] At 359–60.

[115] For a critique of the majority's approach see J Beatson, 'The role of statute in the development of common law doctrine' 117 *Law Quarterly Review*, 2001, 247, 271.

What is the retrospective effect of changes in the law in criminal cases? Is a person who was convicted and sentenced to a prison term on the basis of one judicial view of the law entitled to be freed from prison if that view of the law is overruled in a later case? Curiously, the answer is not clear.

The first question is whether the Court of Appeal will regard the change in the law as a reason for giving leave to appeal out of time. In *Hawkins* (1997) 1 Cr App Rep 234 at 239 Lord Bingham, Lord Chief Justice, cited a dictum from *Mitchell* (1977) 65 Cr App Rep 185 where Lord Lane had said: 'It should be clearly understood … that the fact that there has been an apparent change in the law or, to put it more precisely, that previous misconceptions about the meaning of a statute have been put right, does not afford a proper ground for allowing an extension of time in which to appeal against conviction.' But in a previous case *Ramsden* [1972] Crim LR 547, (CA), Lord Lane had said that in such a situation the court might grant leave to appeal out of time. In the last analysis, he said, 'this must in every case be a matter of discretion'. In *Hawkins* Lord Bingham said, 'If such convictions were to be readily reopened it would be difficult to know where to draw the line or how far to go back'. The general practice of the court he said was to set its face against the reopening of convictions in these circumstances, but the court should 'eschew undue technicality and ask whether any substantial injustice has been done'.[116] Hawkins, the court found, could have been successfully prosecuted for other criminal acts, so leave to appeal out of time after a change in the relevant principle of law was refused. But in *David Cooke* (2 December 1996, unreported, CA No 9604988) the decision went the other way. Leave to appeal out of time was granted because the appellant was serving a prison sentence – though, in the event, convictions for different offences were substituted.

In *Percy v Hall* [1997] QB 924 the Court of Appeal considered a civil action for damages against Ministry of Defence constables who had arrested the plaintiffs on over 150 occasions on or near military premises. The plaintiffs, surprisingly, had been acquitted of criminal charges. On an appeal by the DPP, the Divisional Court held that the byelaws under which they had been arrested were void for uncertainty. The plaintiffs thereupon sued for damages. The Court of Appeal, dealing with a preliminary issue, held (a) that the byelaws were not sufficiently unclear as to be invalid; but (b) that even if they had been void for uncertainty, the constables would still have had a defence of lawful justification to allegations of wrongful arrest and false imprisonment provided they could show they acted in the reasonable belief that the plaintiffs were committing a byelaw offence. A declaration that the byelaws were invalid would entitle a person who had been convicted to have the conviction set aside but that could not convert conduct which at the time had been regarded as the lawful discharge of the constables' duty into actionable tortious conduct.

The decision in *R v Governor of Brockhill Prison, ex p Evans (No 2)* [2001] 2 AC 19 went the other way. The House of Lords was considering a claim for damages for false imprisonment brought by a convicted prisoner. Under a line of judicial authority as to the meaning of the Criminal Justice Act 1967, s 67(1) known as the *Gaffney* approach, her date of release had been calculated to be 18 November 1996. However, the *Gaffney* approach had been overruled by *R v Secretary of State for the Home Department, ex p Naughton* [1997]

[116] In *Budimir* [2010] EWCA Crim 1486, [2011] QB 744, the Court of Appeal dismissed an appeal against conviction even though the statute under which B was convicted ought to have been held unenforceable because it had not been notified under an EU Directive to the European Commission. The House of Lords and the Court of Appeal had consistently held that where a conviction was based on the law as it was understood at the time, a change in the law would only be the basis for an application to appeal out of time where substantial injustice had been done.

1 WLR 118. If the new ruling were applied to Evans' case, she should have been released two months earlier, on 17 September. The House of Lords held that the ordinary principle of retrospectivity applied and she was therefore entitled to compensation in respect of false imprisonment for those two months. See to similar effect, a decision by Silber J in January 2004 holding that a prisoner could take advantage of the retrospective effect of a decision of the European Court of Human Rights in Strasbourg to claim damages for wrongful detention. There was no such remedy in English law but the court upheld his claim that Art 5(5) of the Convention required Member States to give victims of wrongful detention an enforceable claim to compensation – though on the facts the judge decided that an award of damages was not required.[117]

Commenting on *Ex p Evans* (above), Francis Bennion said that the case showed that no general answer could be given to the question what is the effect on previous transactions when a ruling on the law changes: 'it depends on the nature of the law in question.'[118] The issue was posed dramatically by the joint decision of the Supreme Court and the Privy Council in *Jogee, Ruddock v The Queen* [2016] UKSC 8, [2016] UKPC 7 greatly narrowing the rule as to what constitutes culpable mens rea in secondary liability for murder. (See p 224 above.) The ruling could in theory have rendered a very large number of convictions unsafe. In order to manage hopes and fears generated by the decision the Supreme Court said, however, that the Court of Appeal would give leave to appeal out of time only 'if substantial injustice be demonstrated, but it will not do so simply because the law applied has now been declared to have been mistaken'.[119]

For a rare case where a person was convicted on the basis of the retrospective effect of a judicial decision see *R v C* [2004] EWCA Crim 292, [2004] 1 WLR 2098. In April 2002 the appellant had been convicted of rape over thirty years previously of his then wife. Rape of a wife during marriage only became punishable after the decision in *R v R* [1992] 1 AC 599. On appeal he argued that his trial contravened Art 7.1 of the ECHR which expressed the common law presumption against the retrospective effect of penal statutes. The Court of Appeal held that the husband could not rely on Art 7 because the wife was entitled to protection from inhuman and degrading treatment under the Convention.

What happens when a case is referred back to the Court of Appeal, Criminal Division under the Criminal Appeal Act 1995, by the Criminal Cases Review Commission? Often the reference comes years after the original conviction. In such a case the court is not restricted to consider the law as it stood at the time of the conviction. It can take later developments into account. In the case of Judith Ward it was able to overturn the conviction on the basis of non-disclosure by the prosecution to the defence even though at the time of the trial the prosecution's conduct had not been in breach of the rules (*Ward* [1993] 1 WLR 619). The common law rules had changed. In the Carl Bridgwater murder appeal (*Molloy*, 23 July 1997, unreported, CA No 96/5131/SI) the court took into account then

[117] *R (on the application of Richards) v Secretary of State for the Home Department* [2004] EWHC 93 (Admin), 28 January 2004; *New Law Journal*, 6 February 2004, 176.

[118] 'Consequences of an overrule' *Public Law*, 2001, 450, 451.

[119] At [100]. See also *Johnson, Garwood, Green and others* [2017] 4 WLR 104. For discussion of the difficulty of interpreting the phrase 'substantial injustice' in this context see D Ormerod and K Laird, '*Jogee*: Not the End of a Legal Saga but the Start of One?' [2016] *Criminal Law Review* (8) 539–52, 549–52. The article stated (at p 551) that the problem affected thousands of convicted persons. In 2012–13 alone, 659 defendants were jointly charged with murder. For the first case that did satisfy the 'substantial injustice' test see *R v Crilly* [2018] EWCA Crim 168, [2018] Crim LR (12) 1009.

recent decisions on relevant points of law as a ground contributing to the unsafeness of the conviction.[120]

In *Bentley* [2001] 1 Cr App Rep 307, the appeal related to a homicide 45 years earlier. Giving the court's judgment, Lord Bingham said that the statutory law of homicide had to be taken as it was at the time of the trial but that the relevant common law was that current at the time of the review. The conduct of the trial and the judge's direction of the jury should likewise be judged by the standards that would currently apply. This approach would open a large number of convictions to challenge. It was strongly criticised.[121] The Court of Appeal appeared to have taken the point as in *Hanratty (decd)* [2002] EWCA Crim 1141, concerning a murder 40 years earlier, it put the matter very differently: 'If certain of the current requirements of, for example, a summing up are not complied with at a trial which takes place today this can almost automatically result in a conviction being set aside but this approach should not be adopted in relation to trials which took place before the rule was established.' It upheld the conviction even though it found that much material that would be required to be disclosed then had not been disclosed (at [98]).

If the change in the law occurs whilst the convicted defendant is in the process of seeking leave to appeal, the defendant is entitled to have the benefit of the change – *Chapman (Helen)* [2013] EWCA Crim 1370.

For a review of the authorities resulting in refusal of two applications for extension of time on account of a change in the law and the allowing of one application see *Bestel* [2013] EWCA Crim 1305, [2014] 1 WLR 457.

7.7. Prospective Overruling as an Aid to Creative Law-Making

A technique used occasionally in the United States is prospective overruling, whereby the court announces that it will change the relevant rule but only for future cases. In *Jones v Secretary of State for Social Services* [1972] AC 944, Lord Simon of Glaisdale suggested that the technique had some advantages but that it should be introduced, if at all, by legislation (at 1026):

> I am left with the feeling that, theoretically, in some ways the most satisfactory outcome of these appeals would have been to have allowed them on the basis that they were governed by the decision in *Dowling*'s case, but to have overruled that decision prospectively. Such a power – to overrule prospectively a previous decision, but so as not necessarily to affect the parties before the court – is exercisable by the Supreme Court of the United States, which has held it to be based on the common law: see *Linkletter v Walker* (1965) 381 U.S. 618.
>
> In this country it was long considered that judges were not makers of law but merely its discoverers and expounders. The theory was that every case was governed by a relevant rule of law, existing somewhere and discoverable somehow, provided sufficient learning and intellectual rigour were

[120] See generally H Blaxland, 'Developments in the common law since conviction: the approach of the Court of Appeal' *Archbold News*, issue 8, 10 October 1997, 6.

[121] See Professor Sir John Smith, *Criminal Law Review*, 1999, 330, 332; and F Bennion, 'Rewriting history in the Court of Appeal' *New Law Journal*, 14 August 1998, 1228. See also DC Ormerod, *Criminal Law Review* 2000, 835, 838–41.

> brought to bear. But once such a rule had been discovered, frequently the pretence was tacitly dropped that the rule was preexisting: for example, cases like *Shelley's Case* (1581) 1 Co. Rep. 93b, *Merryweather v Nizan* (1799) 8 Term Rep. 186 or *Priestley v Fowler* (1837) 3 M. & W. 1 were (rightly) regarded as new departures in the law. Nevertheless, the theory, however unreal, had its value – in limiting the sphere of lawmaking by the judiciary (inevitably at some disadvantage in assessing the potential repercussions of any decision, and increasingly so in a complex modern industrial society), and thus also in emphasising that central feature of our constitution, the sovereignty of Parliament. But the true, even if limited, nature of judicial lawmaking has been more widely acknowledged of recent years; and the [Practice Statement] of July 20, 1966, may be partly regarded as of a piece with that process. It might be argued that a further step to invest your Lordships with the ampler and more flexible powers of the Supreme Court of the United States would be no more than a logical extension of present realities and of powers already claimed without evoking objection from other organs of the constitution. But my own view is that, though such extension should be seriously considered, it would preferably be the subject-matter of parliamentary enactment. In the first place, informed professional opinion is probably to the effect that your Lordships have no power to overrule decisions with prospective effect only; such opinion is itself a source of law; and your Lordships, sitting judicially, are bound by any rule of law arising extra-judicially. Secondly, to proceed by Act of Parliament would obviate any suspicion of endeavouring to upset one-sidedly the constitutional balance between executive, legislature and judiciary. Thirdly, concomitant problems could receive consideration – for example, whether other courts supreme within their own jurisdictions should have similar powers as regards the rule of precedent; whether machinery could and should be devised to apprise the courts of the potential repercussions of any particular decision; and whether any court (including an Appellate Committee in your Lordships' House) should sit in banc when invited to review a previous decision.

Lord Diplock lent his powerful support to consideration of prospective overruling. In a lecture, he referred to the fact that the retrospective impact of judicial decisions was one of the reasons that judges were reluctant to correct previous errors or to adapt an established rule to changed circumstances. Yet the retrospective effect of judicial decisions was simply a reflection of the legal fiction that the courts merely expounded the law as it always had been. The time had come, he thought, 'to reflect whether we should discard this fiction', and he thought that the development of prospective overruling in appellate courts in the United States deserved consideration.[122]

In *Hall v Simons* [2002] 1 AC 615 in which the House of Lords overruled its decision in *Rondel v Worsley* [1969] 1 AC 191 giving advocates immunity from negligence actions, Lord Hope said, 'I consider that this is a change in the law which should take effect only from the date of the judgment in this case' (726). None of the other judges said anything regarding this proposition.

Prospective overruling was again referred to in *Ex p Evans* (p 358 above) in which the House of Lords held that E was entitled to damages on account of the retrospective effect of a decision on the calculation of prisoners' release dates. Lord Slynn said, 'I consider that there may be situations in which it would be desirable, and in no way unjust, that the effect of judicial rulings should be prospective or limited to certain claimants'.[123] The European Court of Justice had sometimes restricted the effect of its ruling to the particular claimant and to those who had begun proceedings before its judgment. 'Such a course avoided

[122] *The Courts as Legislators* (Holdsworth Club of the University of Birmingham, 1965) 17–18. However, in *Kleinwort Benson v Lincoln City Council* [1999] 2 AC 349, in which the House of Lords abolished the rule against recovery of money paid under a mistake of law, Lord Goff said that a system of prospective overruling 'has no place in our legal system'.

[123] [2001] 2 AC 19, 26–27.

unscrambling transactions perhaps long since over and doing injustice to defendants.'[124] Lord Hobhouse disagreed with Lord Slynn's suggestion: 'It is a denial of the constitutional role of the courts for courts to say that the party challenging the *status quo* is right, that the previous decision is overruled, but that the decision will not affect the parties and apply only subsequently. They would be declining to exercise their constitutional role and adopting a legislative role deciding what the law shall be for others in the future.'[125] Moreover, he pointed out, such a decision would by definition not be part of the ratio decidendi of the case and therefore would not constitute an authoritative decision.

The pros and cons of prospective overruling were considered by an LSE lecturer who became a High Court judge:

Andrew Nicol, 'Prospective overruling: a new device for English courts?' 39 *Modern Law Review*, 1976, 542

> Prospective overruling is used by several [American] states and by the United States Supreme Court ... The justification most often advanced has been reliance. Several states, for instance, have been taking a fresh look at various immunities from tort suit.[126] A court may believe that the decision on which a particular immunity was based ought to be overruled, but it may also have to recognise that institutions which benefit from this immunity have not taken out insurance in reliance on it. Prospective overruling of the case granting the immunity has been used to break the *impasse* ... A somewhat different reliance has been claimed by prosecutors and police when faced with a court determined to tighten the procedures which must be followed in a criminal investigation. It is unfair, they say, to penalise the prosecution for failing to observe standards which were not set down until after the investigation has taken place.[127] The United States Supreme Court accepted this argument as one ground for limiting the effect of *Miranda v Arizona*.[128]
>
> Another justification for the use of prospective overruling has been that the desire which impels the court to overrule is the desire to implement a new policy, but a policy which need not be retroactive to be effective. In *Mapp v Ohio*,[129] the United States Supreme Court held that evidence which was discovered in an unlawful search could not be used at trial. In *Linkletter v Walker*,[130] the court held that the *Mapp* rule was to be prospective only. The new rule, the court said, was intended to discourage unlawful searches. It was too late to discourage those searches which had already taken place. Therefore nothing could be gained by giving *Mapp* retroactive effect ...
>
> *Objections to prospective overruling*
>
> ... (3) *It allows a court to make new law without applying it to the case before the court*: There are few lawyers now who would agree with Montesquieu that 'the judges are the mere mouthpieces of the law.'[131] The opportunity for creativity in choosing 'the' relevant statutes or precedents, in favouring one of a pair of antagonistic canons of construction,[132] in distinguishing a case on its facts or following it on principle, is apparent on both sides of the Atlantic.

[124] Ibid, 27.

[125] Ibid, 48.

[126] Units of government, *Molitor v Kaneland Community School Dist* No 32 163 NE 2d 89 (1959) Ill; charities, *Kojis v Doctor's Hospital*, 107 NW 2d 131 (1961) Wis; intra-family, *Goller v White*, 122 NW 2d 193 (1963) Wis; religious institution, *Widell v Holy Trinity Catholic Church*, 121 NW 2d 249 (1963) Wis. Plaintiff in this case had tripped over a negligently placed prayer kneeler.

[127] *Johnston v New Jersey*, 384 US 719 (1966).

[128] 384 US 436 (1966). This case required the police to issue a caution before questioning a suspect, on pain of having the statement excluded from the trial. The caution informs the suspect of their right of silence.

[129] 367 US 643 (1961).

[130] 381 US 618 (1965).

[131] *Esprit de Lois*, XI 6.

[132] See K Llewellyn, 'Remarks on the theory of appellate decision and the rules or canons of how statutes are to be construed' 3 *Vanderbilt Law Review*, 1950, 395, 401.

However, a traditional restraint on this law-making power has been that courts are limited to expounding the law on the facts to dispose of the instant case and then add an unnecessary post-script as to how they will act in the future. Another version of the same argument is to say that the new rule is *obiter*, and therefore a waste of time.

Yet a similar practice is already used by the courts. In *Hedley Byrne v Heller Partners*,[133] the House of Lords stated a new principle of liability for negligent misrepresentors, but the defendant, who came within the general description, was not held liable. The court added a rider, absolving from liability a representor who had expressly excluded his liability at the time he made his statement. An announcement by the court, as it prospectively overrules, that it will apply a new and different rule in other situations, is no more *obiter* than the House of Lords saying that in other cases it would hold negligent misrepresentors liable. In both situations, the court lays down a principle, argues that there is an exception, and finds that the parties to the suit come without the exception. While the principle is not conclusive, it is applied in the instant case, and it is difficult to see how it can be said to form no central part of the reasoning of the court.

(4) The Hedley Byrne technique referred to in (3) is prospective overruling in disguise. A naked use of prospective overruling is therefore unnecessary:[134] This is not so. In Hedley Byrne, the court was able to declare a new rule without applying it to the party in the instant case, but it achieved this result by qualifying substantively the new rule. If, the following day, a similar case had come up for judgment, but where the representor could not bring himself within the qualification, the representor would have been held liable, even though the representation may have been made many years previously. On the other hand, if Candler v Crane, Christmas[135] had been prospectively overruled, the temporal qualification would have protected all persons (not liable under some other doctrine) who had made negligent misrepresentations before the date of the overruling. The Hedley Byrne technique goes some way, but not far enough, in protecting those who relied on a prior statement of the law.

(5) *A judge who uses prospective overruling has too much the appearance of a legislator*: It is argued[136] that however much judges are innovators in practice, in popular belief they are still the 'finders' of law, not its 'makers'. This belief, the argument runs, could not be sustained if judicial opinions read: 'this precedent is out-of-date and ought to be changed, but the change will only be effective from today.'

This writer has serious doubts as to whether the public would have greater respect for a court that slavishly followed precedent, than for one that tried to reconcile the competing claims of change and reliance. However, for the sake of appearances, there is another formula that the court might use: 'the rule that we announce today is and always was the correct view of the law. However, recognising the reliance which was placed on the old view, we will not apply the true view to events happening before today.'

This form was used in *Golak Nath v State of Punjab*,[137] when the Supreme Court of India prospectively overruled the Land Reform Statutes. The court held that these statutes violated fundamental rights, guaranteed by the constitution, but because of the property interests which had been transferred and settled in reliance on them, they should be struck down with prospective effect only …

[133] [1964] AC 465.

[134] W Friedmann, 'Limits of judicial law-making and prospective overruling' 29 *Modern Law Review*, 1966, 593, 605.

[135] [1951] 2 KB 164, the Court of Appeal decision in effect (though not technically) overruled in *Hedley Byrne*.

[136] Lord Devlin, 'Judges and lawmakers' 39 *Modern Law Review*, 1976, 1.

[137] [1967] 2 SCR (India) 762; and see Pillai, 'Precedent in the House of Lords and the doctrine of prospective overruling in the U.S.A. and India' 1 *Supreme Court Journal*, 1967, 79; Rajput, 'The doctrine of *stare decisis* and prospective overruling' II *Supreme Court Journal*, 1968, 51.

(7) If prospective overruling were available, it would make overruling more common and upset the certainty which results from a strict doctrine of stare decisis: However, 'for the most part, certainty is an illusion.'[138] The discovery of old cases, the power to distinguish, the uncertainty of which facts will be believed in court[139] mean the outcome of a particular dispute is not necessarily certain, even in a system where overruling is rarely used. It is appreciated that a sense of proportion is necessary. Many disputes are within the 'core application'[140] of a rule. Most rules would be affirmed on challenge, even by a court with the power to overrule prospectively. Nevertheless, one must ask, as Goodhart did,[141] whether, if the rule is unjust, certainty is not bought at too high a price. To add a gloss to Goodhart's comment; if through prospective overruling, we take away the element of individual reliance, then although stability and predictability are important, can it always be said that they will be more important than the removing of injustice or correcting the anomaly.

(8) Prospective overruling is undesirable because it encourages judicial law reform. The principal thrust of law reform should come from a democratically elected Parliament, rather than an appointed judiciary: ... In 1953, the Evershed Committee considered a proposal for financing litigation on points of law of general public interest. In its conclusion it stated:[142]

> We do not think this method of a law reform committee fully meets the public need. Legislation is slow and cumbersome. Parliamentary time is notoriously limited, and may in future become even more precious. Clarification of the law by judicial decision is a swifter and surer process which can go forward at all times, without regard to parliamentary time and quite independent of the political process.

Judicially developed law also has the advantage that it can be more cautious and developed according to experience. A judgment need not, indeed it is probably better if it does not, set out the whole ambit of the rule, complete with all qualifications. The courts are bound by the words of a statute, but only by the *ratio decidendi* of a decision. Statutory law has been scorned in the past for disturbing the growth of the common law. The scorn is often a reflection of the conservatism of the speaker, but it is true that the words of a statute have a rigidity which is not always desirable ...

Thus I conclude that judicial law-making is inevitable. Parliament and the courts, in the words of Jaffé, are in the law business together and should be continually at work on the legal fabric of our society.[143] The establishment of the Law Commission has reduced, but not abolished the part which the courts should play in law reform. They will always be the junior partner in the partnership, but even so their methods enjoy some advantages over statute. Prospective overruling gives the courts more scope for reforming judicially developed law, but does not deny the superior weight which must be given to the words of the senior partner.

By contrast, Lord Devlin expressed himself unpersuaded by the arguments for prospective overruling:

Lord Devlin, 'Judges and Lawmakers' 39 *Modern Law Review*, 1976, 11

Courts in the United States have begun to circumvent retroactivity by the device of deciding the case before them according to the old law while declaring that in future the new law will prevail: or they may determine with what measure of retroactivity a new rule is to be enforced. This device has attracted the cautious attention of the House of Lords. I do not like it. It crosses the Rubicon

[138] OW Holmes, 'The path of the law' 10 *Harvard Law Review*, 1897, 457, 465.
[139] Jerome Frank, *Courts on Trial* (Princeton University Press, 1949) passim.
[140] HLA Hart, *The Concept of Law* (Oxford University Press, 1961), chapter VII and pp 120 ff.
[141] 'Precedent in English and Continental law' 50 *Law Quarterly Review*, 1934, 934.
[142] *Final Report of the Committee on Supreme Court Practice and Procedure* (Cmd 8878, 1953).
[143] LL Jaffé, *English and United States Judges and Lawmakers* (Clarendon Press, 1969).

> that divides the judicial and the legislative powers. It turns judges into undisguised legislators. It is facile to think that it is always better to throw off disguises. The need for disguise hampers activity and so restricts the power. Paddling across the Rubicon by individuals in disguise who will be sent back if they proclaim themselves is very different from the bridging of the river by an army in uniform and with bands playing. If judges can make law otherwise than by a decision in the case at Bar, why do they wait for a case? Prevention is better than cure, so why should they not, when they see a troublesome point looming up, meet and decide how best to deal with it? Judicial lawmaking is at present, as Professor Jaffé phrases it,[144] 'a by-product of an *ad hoc* decision or process.' That this is so is of course in itself one of the objections to judicial lawmaking. Dependent as it is upon the willingness of individuals to litigate, it is casual and spasmodic. But to remove the tie with the *ad hoc* process would be to make a profound constitutional change with incalculable consequences. What is the business of a court of law? To make law or to do justice according to law? This question should be given a clean answer. If the law and justice of the case require the court to give a decision which its members think will not make good law for the future, I think that the court should give the just decision and refer the future to a lawmaking body.

The High Court of Australia[145] rejected the doctrine of prospective overruling in 1997 as being contrary to fundamental principle:

> A hallmark of the judicial process has long been the making of binding declarations of rights and obligations arising from the operation of the law upon past events or conduct. The adjudication of existing rights and obligations distinguishes the judicial role from non-judicial power. Prospective overruling is thus inconsistent with judicial power on the simple ground that the new regime that would be ushered in when the overruling took effect would alter existing rights and obligations. If an earlier case is erroneous and it is necessary to overrule it, it would be a perversion of judicial power to maintain in force that which is acknowledged not to be the law.[146]

The question of prospective overruling was addressed by the Law Lords in *In re Spectrum Plus Ltd* [2005] UKHL 41, [2005] 2 AC 680. The question was whether the Court of Appeal's decision in *Siebe Gorman & Co Ltd v Barclays Bank Ltd* [1979] 2 Lloyd's Rep 142 should be overruled and if so, whether the overruling should be prospective only. The issue was whether the debt was secured by a fixed or a floating charge. All seven judges agreed that the Court of Appeal's decision should be overruled but that although prospective overruling might be appropriate in some exceptional cases, this was not such a case. They differed, however, as to when it might be appropriate. Lord Nicholls of Birkenhead, giving the lead judgment, said it might be appropriate even in a case of statutory interpretation:

> 40 Instances where this power has been used in courts elsewhere suggest there could be circumstances in this country where prospective overruling would be necessary to serve the underlying objective of the courts of this country: to administer justice fairly and in accordance with the law. There could be cases where a decision on an issue of law, whether common law or statute law, was unavoidable but the decision would have such gravely unfair and disruptive consequences for past transactions or happenings that this House would be compelled to depart from the normal principles relating to the retrospective and prospective effect of court decisions.
>
> 41 If, altogether exceptionally, the House as the country's supreme court were to follow this course I would not regard it as trespassing outside the functions properly to be discharged by the judiciary under this country's constitution. Rigidity in the operation of a legal system is a sign of weakness, not strength. It deprives a legal system of necessary elasticity. Far from achieving a

[144] Ibid, 35.

[145] Australia's highest court.

[146] *Ha v New South Wales* [1997] HCA 34 aff'd *Bell Lawyers Pty Ltd v Pentelow* [2019] HCA 29 at [55], [94]–[98].

> constitutionally exemplary result, it can produce a legal system unable to function effectively in changing times. 'Never say never' is a wise judicial precept, in the interest of all citizens of the country.
>
> 42 Moreover, in one particular context the courts' ability to give a ruling having only prospective effect seems irresistible. As noted above, at times the Strasbourg court interprets and applies the European Convention on Human Rights with prospective effect only. It would be odd if in interpreting and applying Convention rights the House was not able to give rulings having a comparable limited temporal effect: see Lord Rodger of Earlsferry, 'A Time for Everything under the Law: Some Reflections on Retrospectivity' 121 *LQR*, 2005, 57, 77.

Lord Hope, Lord Walker and Lady Hale agreed with Lord Nicholls. Lord Scott agreed that prospective overruling might exceptionally be appropriate in a case where the court was changing the common law. He (and Lord Steyn), however, did not agree that that could be so if the case concerned interpretation of a statute:[147]

> It may be a function of judges incrementally to develop the common law, but it is a duty of judges faithfully to interpret and apply the statutory law. This duty applies as much to the 'always speaking' statute as to other statutes. The notion that a judge could decide what a statute meant and required and then announce that the effect of the ruling would be postponed for some period or other seems to me inconsistent with that duty. It is for Parliament, not judges, to decide when statutes are to come into effect. It is for judges to interpret and apply the statutes. Where interpretation and application of a statute is the issue, a prospective ruling would, absent legislative authority ...,[148] appear to constitute an improper usurpation by the judiciary of the role of the legislature.

The jurisprudence of the European Court of Justice in Luxemburg regarding prospective decisions was considered by Silber J in the case of *Richards* (p 358 n 117 above, at [68]–[78]).

See further on this subject MDA Freeman, 'Standards of adjudication, judicial law-making and prospective overruling' 26 *Current Legal Problems*, 1973, 166, 200–07 and Samuel Beswick, 'Prospective overruling unravelled' 41 *Civil Justice Quarterly*, 2022, 29–53, both against prospective overruling; Robert Traynor, 'Quo vadis, prospective overruling: a Question of Judicial Responsibility' 28 *Hastings Law Journal*, 1979, 533, which supports the case for prospective overruling; and G Tedeschi, 'Prospective revision of precedent', 8 *Israel Law Review*, 1973, 173. Tedeschi suggests that 'prospective revision' is a better term than 'prospective overruling', since if it is prospective it technically does not amount to overruling. See also RHS Tur, 'Time and Law' 22 *Oxford Journal of Legal Studies*, 2002, 463.

The concept of prospective decisions has been used by the English courts on occasion in the context of remedies in administrative law – for instance, by granting a declaration prospectively. Professor Jeremy Horder argues that declarations should be used more often to seek needed improvements in criminal law. ('In particular, courts should be more open to actions for declarations as to the scope of criminal offences brought by a broader range of

[147] The seventh judge, Lord Brown, did not express a view as to whether prospective overruling could extend to statutory interpretation cases.

[148] Lord Scott here referred to the devolution legislation cited by Lord Nicolls in his judgment: 'The Scotland Act 1998, section 102, provides that where a court decides that a provision in an Act of the Scottish Parliament is not within the legislative competence of the Parliament the court may make an order removing or limiting any retrospective effect of the decision or suspending the effect of the decision to enable the defect to be corrected. Comparable provisions appear in the Government of Wales Act 1998, section 110, and the Northern Ireland Act 1998, section 81. These provisions show that Parliament does not perceive non-retroactive rulings by courts as being of their nature inconsistent with the judiciary's proper function.' (per Lord Nicholls at [17]) (ed.).

third parties, such as third sector organisations devoted to exposing wrongdoing' by powerful private entities. (Jeremy Horder, 'The courts development of the criminal law and the role of declarations', 40 *Legal Studies*, 2020, 42–54.)

The Judicial Review and Courts Act 2022 gives courts making quashing orders the power to provide that they take effect from a date specified in the order and to remove or limit any retrospective effect of the quashing.[149]

See further Clive Lewis, 'Retrospective and prospective rulings in administrative law' *Public Law*, 1988, 78–105; Harry Woolf, *Protection of the Public – A New Challenge* (Stevens, 1990) 52–55; and 'The additional responsibilities of the judiciary in the new millenium' in B Markesinis (ed), *The Millenium Lectures* (Hart Publishing, 2000) 142–48. See also JF Avery-Jones, 'Decisions with prospective effect: a less drastic solution for the House of Lords, *British Tax Review*, 1984, 203.

7.8. Legal Argument by Non-Parties

One of the differences between the English and the United States systems used to be that the English did not have anything comparable to the United States practice of allowing non-parties to participate in litigation so as to provide the court with additional material on the legal issues under consideration. In recent years, however, the English system has developed the third-party intervention on a considerable and growing scale. (But see pp 371–73 below.)

The United States procedure was based on the traditional English concept of the *amicus curiae* ('friend of the court'). The Attorney-General has had the right to intervene as *amicus* in a private suit whenever it might affect the prerogatives of the Crown or where the action raised a question of public policy on which the executive might have a view.[150] The Attorney-General equally has had the right, either at the invitation of the court or with leave of the court, to intervene as *amicus* in litigation.[151] It is normally used when the court would not otherwise hear all relevant legal argument – for instance, to represent unborn children. An example was the case of the conjoined twins heard by the Court of Appeal in September 2000 when two counsel were appointed to assist the court as to whether the operation to separate them would involve the commission of a criminal offence. The then Attorney-General wrote in 2002 that in the three previous years such appointments had been made in 31, 22 and 26 cases.[152]

In the same article he explained new guidance being issued to the judges as to the circumstances in which an Advocate to the Court (as it was to be called) could assist and those in which it would not be appropriate. The role of the Advocate to the Court, he said, was to

[149] Judicial Review and Courts Act 2022, s 1 inserting new s 29A in Senior Courts Act 1998. The court must take into account (a) the nature and circumstances of the relevant defect; (b) any detriment to good administration that would result from exercising or failing to exercise the power; (c) the interests or expectations of persons who would benefit from the quashing of the impugned act; (d) the interests or expectations of persons who have relied on the impugned act; (e) so far as appears to the court to be relevant, any action taken or proposed to be taken, or undertaking given, by a person with responsibility in connection with the impugned act;(f)any other matter that appears to the court to be relevant.

[150] *Adams v Adams* [1971] P 188.

[151] *Adams v Adams*, 576–77, per Simon P. See also *Re James* [1977] Ch 41.

[152] Lord Goldsmith, 'Friend of the court', *Counsel*, February 2002, 30–32, fn 4.

act impartially – not to represent the interests of any party to the proceedings. Litigants in person often failed to understand this. The role of the Advocate was to assist the court not the litigants. It was part of the Attorney-General's role as guardian of the public interest in the proper administration of justice. ('An important aspect is that the court should hear all relevant legal argument before arriving at a decision. There is a public interest in the highest quality of decision-making, particularly in those cases that will set precedents.'[153]) Once appointed, the Advocate receives their instructions from the Treasury Solicitor.

The United States development of this concept has taken it from neutral 'friendship' to committed partisanship. The extract that follows, written more than fifty years ago, explains:

Ernest Angell, 'The amicus curiae: United States developments of English institutions' 16 *International and Comparative Law Quarterly*, 1967, 1017

> The *amici* whose names appear in the printed columns of reported decisions fall into three general categories. First, there are … the legal representatives of the government, federal or state, counties, municipalities, government agencies and bodies. Secondly, there are private organisations of professional or other occupational membership; employers, business, commercial and industrial entities; labour unions; government and private industry employees by occupational class; bar associations and many others. In this category there should be included, though less common, a business unit which does not appear as part of an organised group and, rarely, an individual person. Thirdly, there are innumerable private associations, in general formally organised, which purport to speak for non-occupational, non-governmental, broad public interests; churches and religious bodies; minority groups … the range is almost unlimited …
>
> *Some reasons for the multiplicity of appearances of amicus curiae in United States courts*: avoiding dogmatic assertion of any single factor, one can state that several have disparately combined, without overall shaping by the courts. What does appear to be the most obvious is the United States legal habit of presenting printed or typed 'briefs', to marshal the acts and cite the pertinent authorities of cases, statutes and texts: (1) at the conclusion of a trial and often in support of a motion on evidence or for interlocutory remedy; and (2) universally on appeal to the reviewing court. In the absence of special leave granted to counsel for the *amicus* to make oral argument, the judges thus avoid the necessity of listening to expanded oratory of the intervenor, but do have the advantage of being able to study his written argument which may range beyond the industry and legal knowledge of counsel for the parties of record. Some judges give only perfunctory attention to oral pleading from any but the most persuasive advocates and rely much more heavily on the written word.
>
> The universality of the written brief seems to have been born from the enormous sheer volume of United States law – the decision of well over 100 federal courts and of several hundred courts of the 50 states; statutes, rules and regulations beyond the possibility of count; innumerable texts, the 'model' codes of the United States Law Institute and 100 or so law 'journals' or law 'reviews' published by bar associations, learned societies and the many schools of law. No judge or lawyer can know or without immense labour pinpoint *ad hoc* anything more than a small fraction of the 'law' in America, compared with the wider familiarity of the English barrister with his own far more restricted volume of law. United States counsel for a party of record may overlook what the court later finds to be the key point at issue and the available authorities. Our judges need more frequent and informed advice from the barristers before them; sometimes, perhaps frequently, this comes from the 'friend' …
>
> Finally, the growth has been favoured by the proliferation in our society of the private non-profit organisations which exist to promote at the bar or courts, before legislatures and in public opinion, the interests of a class group and their convictions about the values of some social interest

[153] Ibid, 32.

> – the Red Indian, the conscientious objector, tighter control over excesses of the 'free press', the economic interest of railway clerks. Newspapers, magazines, television and radio abound with the highly vocal claims of conflicting legal interests put forward by organised groups alert for every occasion to speak publicly.
>
> The courts cannot operate in an Olympian remoteness from the social scene; they must perforce listen to what class interest claims are laid upon the bench for judicial digestion. Moreover, the judges seek information and informed opinion by inviting such appearances by those believed to be able to render such assistance – by no means confined to law officers of government. It has become inevitable that the threads of argument spun by these intervening 'friends' are woven into the fabric of formal decisions, sometimes visible to the inquiring eye outside the judicial chamber and, occasionally if more rarely, openly acknowledged in the formal opinion …
>
> *Procedure*
>
> … the court rules provide that *amicus* briefs may be filed merely with the consent of counsel for the formal parties to the cases then pending; if consent is refused – as sometimes happens – then a motion may be made and the court passes upon this, generally granting it.

See also GA Gadeira and JR Wright, '*Amici curiae* before the Supreme Court: who participates, when and how much?' 52 *Journal of Politics*, 1990, 782; and K O'Connor and L Epstein, 'Amicus curiae participation in US Supreme Court litigation: an evaluation of Hakman's "Folklore"' 16 *Law and Society Review*, 1990–91, 311. As has been said, 'In the United States much of the successful and groundbreaking civil rights litigation of the 1960s was supported by enormously influential third party interventions, which in several instances played a decisive role in shaping the developing jurisprudence of the Supreme Court.'[154]

For the Canadian experience see, for instance, B Dickens, 'A Canadian development: non party intervention' 40 *Modern Law Review* 1997, 666. Such interventions have sometimes played a major role there in the law-making process.

In England, until the 1990s, third-party intervention to argue points of law was rare but, exceptionally, bodies such as the Law Society, the Motor Insurer's Bureau, the Commission for Racial Equality were given the right to make oral submissions in cases concerning their field of concern.

In *Gillick v West Norfolk and Wisbech Area Health Authority and DHSS* [1986] AC 112 the House of Lords had to rule on the problem of contraceptive advice given by doctors to girls under sixteen. Mrs Gillick challenged the legality of a DHSS circular to doctors stating that in some circumstances it might be legitimate to give such advice to under sixteen-year-olds. The parties to the case were Mrs Gillick and the DHSS. No one was there to represent the position of minor girls. The Children's Legal Centre sought permission either to lodge a written case and make oral submissions, or to instruct counsel as *amicus curiae*, or to make only written submissions. The House of Lords refused the request, without giving reasons.

But gradually, the English courts accepted the validity of the concept of third-party intervention for the purpose of assisting the court with the legal issues. In 2003, a study was published of petitions for leave to intervene in cases before the House of Lords in the years from 1997 to 2002[155] with a table distinguishing between cases in which leave to

[154] M Arshi and C O'Cinneide, 'Third party interventions: the public interest re-affirmed' *Public Law*, 2004, 69, 76.

[155] S Hannett, 'Third party intervention: in the public interest' *Public Law*, 2003, 128, 147–49.

intervene fully was granted[156] and cases in which leave was restricted to making only written submissions.[157] Interventions by third parties in all varieties of litigation had increased dramatically in the previous five years. Of equal note had been the shift in the qualitative nature of intervention – 'from invitation by court, to application to the court; from official or statutory body, to lobbying group, commercial organisation or professional body; and from ostensibly neutral submissions, to rather more partisan argument'.[158] The Human Rights Act 1998 had accelerated the rate of intervention, with 'more people with more rights' seeking adjudication on polycentric issues and legal questions with a decidedly political hue.

Support for the increased use of third-party intervention had been wide-ranging: 'from the cautious approval of the House of Lords in its judgment in *Re Northern Ireland Human Rights Commission*,[159] to comments made by the Lord Chancellor during the House of Lords debate on the Human Rights Act 1998,[160] to the tentative endorsement by an eminent working party set up under the auspices of JUSTICE and the Public Law Project.'[161]

Confirmation that there was a statistically significant increase in third-party interventions post-HRA came in a study of all House of Lords decisions from 1994 to 1999. In the pre-HRA period (January 1994–October 2000), third-party interventions occurred in only 7 per cent of the 343 cases heard by the HL. Post-HRA, the Law Lords heard from interveners in 23 per cent of the 571 cases in the period.[162] Unsurprisingly, the highest rate of interventions was in human rights and rights related cases.

Permission to intervene is normally required.[163] The study found that the great majority of applicants were granted permission to intervene.

The two surprising findings in the study related to the effect of third party interventions. It was found that there was no correlation between third-party interventions and the likelihood of separate judgments or dissents. Secondly, the study did not find any

[156] They included the *Pinochet* case [2000] 1 AC 61, Amnesty International and a number of other organisations, as well as the Government of Chile; *Hamilton v Al Fayed (No 1)* [2001] 1 AC 395, the Speaker and Authorities of the House of Commons; *Hall v Simons* [2002]1 AC 615, the Bar Council; *R v Kansal (No 2)* [2002] 2 AC 69, three convicted defendants in the Guiness case; in *R v Crown Court at Manchester, ex p McCann* [2002] UKHL 39, Liberty; *R v Shayler* [2002] 2 WLR 754, *The Times*, *Guardian* and other newspaper and television companies.

[157] They included, again, the *Pinochet* extradition case, n 156 above, Human Rights Watch; *Horvath v Secretary of State for the Home Department* [2001] 1 AC 489, the Refugee Legal Centre; *R v Smith (Morgan)* [2001] 1 AC 146, Southall Black Sisters, Justice for Women and Liberty; *R v DPP, ex p Pretty* [2002] 1 AC 800, Canon Gill, Archbishop Smith, Medical Ethics Alliance and the Society for the Protection of the Unborn Child; *R v Lambert* [2001] 3 WLR 206, JUSTICE; *R v A* [2001] 1 AC 45, Rape Crisis Federation of England and Wales, Campaign to End Rape, Child and Women Abuse Studies Unit.

[158] Hannett (n 155 above) 128.

[159] [2002] UKHL 25. (For comment on the decision see L Blom-Cooper, 'Third party intervention and judicial dissent' *Public Law*, 2002, 602–3 (ed)). The Commission was subsequently given permission to intervene in an important Human Rights Act 1998 case – *R (on the application of Amin) v Secretary of State for the Home Department* [2003] UKHL 51, [2003] 3 WLR 1169. For a further example of such intervention see *Ghaidan v Godin Mendoza* [2002] EWCA Civ 1533, [2002] 4 All ER 1162.

[160] HL, *Hansard*, vol 583, col 834, 24 November 1997.

[161] See also approving comment by A Loux, 'Hearing a "different voice": third party intervention in criminal appeals' 53 *Current Legal Problems*, 2000, 449; and S Fredman, 'Judging democracy: the role of the judiciary under the Human Rights Act 1998' 53 *Current Legal Problems*, 2000, 99.

[162] S Shah, T Poole and M Blackwell, 'Rights, interveners and the Law Lords' 34 *Oxford Journal of Legal Studies*, 2014, 295, 307.

[163] There are a few statutory exceptions. Section 5 of the HRA gives the Crown a right to intervene in cases to which it is not party where a declaration of incompatibility is being contemplated by the courts. Section 30 of the Equality Act 2006 provides for the Equality and Human Rights Commission to intervene in legal proceedings that relate to the Commission's remit, which includes the HRA. Section 11 of the Scottish Human Rights Commission Act 2006 gives that body a similar power.

statistically significant correlation between the presence or absence of third party interventions and the result. Litigants who were supported by interventions were not more (or less) likely to win.

Sarah Hannett, author of the 2003 study, had serious misgivings about this procedural development. In her view 'an expansive intervention regime shifts the courts towards a legislative function, by allowing intervention to operate as one of several tactics in a campaign strategy and by permitting political battles lost elsewhere to be revisited'.[164] There were adverse effects for the parties to litigation as well – 'intervention moves the courts from an adjudicative to an expositive function, and risks shifting the case beyond the parameters presented by the parties'.[165] The courts had neither justified nor explained the reasons for, nor the need for, the rise in the use of third-party intervention. Moreover, the procedural rules were widely drafted and vague. ('They provide no assistance as to whom may intervene, when and why.'[166]) It was impossible to assess why some interventions were permitted and others were denied.

Her views were strongly contested by Mona Arshi, a solicitor with Liberty, and Colm O'Cinneide of University College, London.[167]

> ... third party intervention can inject otherwise marginalised or absent perspectives, expertise and data into the decision-making process and this appears to be enriching and enabling the work of the courts.[168]

Intervention, they said, was always subject to the approval of the court. It was allowed because the court took the view that the intervenor would be able to provide a relevant perspective that would otherwise not be available to the judges. The objection that it was liable to lead to politicisation of the judicial process ignored the fact that since the advent of the Human Rights Act 1998 the judiciary's task was broader and deeper than before:

> The Human Rights Act has changed the legal landscape, or to be more precise has introduced an explicit and broader dimension of rights adjudication to supplement the time-honoured role of the judiciary under the common law in making decisions as to the scope of fundamental rights. In carrying out this enhanced role, the judiciary have inevitably to adopt a more complex and contextually sensitive approach than hitherto, as suggested by Lord Steyn in *R (on the application of Daly) v Secretary of State for the Home Department*.[169] None of this makes the judicial process more 'political' than it has been hitherto: the task of the court remains to address the issue at stake through the legal framework within which they operate, informed by a full contextual understanding which may only be possible if third party intervention has occurred.[170]

In 2009, JUSTICE produced a 68-page report, *To Assist the Court* – accessible on its website, www.justice.org.uk.

— Part 1 looked at the third party interventions in UK courts, their development, and the procedural rules governing them.

— Part 2 identified key issues with the law and practice relating to third party interventions.

[164] Hannett (n 155 above) 129.
[165] Ibid.
[166] Ibid.
[167] Arshi and O'Cinneide, 'Third party interventions' (n 154 above) 69–77.
[168] Ibid, 69.
[169] [2001] UKHL 26, [2001] 2 AC 532, 548.
[170] Hannett (n 155 above) 73.

— Part 3 provided a brief comparative survey of third party interventions before the Supreme Courts of other common law jurisdictions, and discussed the future role of third party interveners before the UK Supreme Court.

The report concluded with a series of recommendations – for the UK Supreme Court, the Court of Appeal and the European Court of Human Rights – aiming to ensure interventions in the public interest are not unduly restricted. The report's annex gave details of twenty of JUSTICE's then most recent interventions in the UK courts.[171]

In 2017, Dr Alec Samuels gave this very positive assessment of interveners in the Supreme Court:[172]

> Traditionally the judges did not like intervention, for fear of irrelevant or academic or hypothetical material being introduced, of lengthening the proceedings and increasing the costs, and of imposing an unfair disadvantage on one of the parties. This fear has passed … An intervener appears in up to a third of Supreme Court cases. No difficulties seem to have arisen. Hearings have not been unduly extended. The parties have not complained. The presence and participation of the intervener has been beneficial. Additional experience and expertise has been contributed, e.g. research, statistics, social material, foreign and comparative law, legal history. Judicial discussion on highly important matters involving the constitution, devolution, human rights, EU law, public law and fundamental social policies has been greatly enriched by intervention. The Supreme Court has become much more of a forum for discussion of contemporary socio-legal issues. Problems requiring the attention of the Law Commission and Government and Parliament have received useful publicity. Progressive and socially-minded judges, such as Lady Hale, have seized on the intervener submissions. Intervention is here to stay.

In the six years 2019 to 2024, the Supreme Court allowed intervenors in 37 per cent, 20 per cent, 35 per cent, 23 per cent, 21 per cent and 19 per cent of cases. In some cases there were several intervenors.[173]

Civil Procedure Rule 54.17 gives the court power to grant 'Any person … permission: (a) to file evidence or (b) to make representations at the hearing of the Judicial Review' whether in support of, or in opposition to the claim.[174] Reservations about the way this had developed were expressed by the Independent Review of Administrative Law (IRAL) IRAL's report (March 2021) said (para 4.108):

> The Panel is concerned that this development is the product of unfettered judicial discretion. Promptness aside, CPR 54 is silent about the relevant criteria and judicial failure to explain when, why, by whom and in what form intervention will be permitted is a major point of criticism. The courts have effectively adopted a policy of drift. Intervention as a lobbying tactic also raises concerns for the integrity of the adjudicative process and separate identity of courts. The Panel therefore recommends that criteria for permitting intervention should be developed.

Can Intervenors for one party be liable for the costs of the other party?

The Criminal Justice and Courts Bill introduced by the Conservative-Liberal Democrat Coalition Government in February 2014 had provisions on interveners and costs in cl.86

[171] See also H Brooke, 'Interventions in the Court of Appeal' *Public Law,* 2007, 401–09. Sir Henry, former Lord Justice of Appeal, proposed that at least some interveners should be charged a moderate fee of say £200.

[172] A Samuels, 'The intervener is here to stay', *New Law Journal*, 6 October 2017, 17.

[173] Figures reported by Brice Dickson in his annual report in the *New Law Journal* on the previous year's Supreme Court's caseload.

[174] For consideration of the issues raised in deciding whether to allow an intervention *see R (British American Tobacco Ltd v Secretary of State for Health)* [2014] EWHC 3515 (Admin).

(originally in cl 53), that would likely have a serious negative impact on the possibility of intervention. The original clause provided:

- — The High Court or the Court of Appeal cannot order a party to judicial review proceedings to pay the intervener's costs in connection with the proceedings, unless there are exceptional circumstances making it appropriate to do so (subss.(2) and (3));
- — Where a party to the judicial review proceedings applies, the court *must* order the intervener to pay any costs that the court considers have been incurred by that party as a result of the intervention, unless there are exceptional circumstances making it inappropriate to do so (subs.4).
- — Rules of Court would indicate the factors to be taken into account when considering whether there were exceptional circumstances (subs.(6))

These new costs rules would apply to interveners who asked for permission to intervene. They would not apply to persons or bodies invited to intervene by the court.

The Joint House of Lords and House of Commons Committee on Human Rights, commenting, said: 'The evidence we have received from many organisations with experience of interventions suggests that this risk of exposure to a costs liability will deter many of those organisations from intervening in future, because as relatively small charitable organisations they could not take the risk of being landed with a large costs bill as a result of their intervention.' The Committee called for the clause to be taken out of the Bill.[175] This did not happen. But the clause was amended, first by the House of Lords. On the Report stage of the Bill, 27 October 2014, the Lords, defeating the Government by 219 votes to 186, approved an amendment changing 'must' in subs.(4) to 'may', thereby giving the court a discretion as to whether to order an intervener to pay costs.[176] However, when the Bill returned to the Commons, 1 December 2014, Mr Chris Grayling, Lord Chancellor and Secretary of State for Justice, moved an amendment inserting new ss (6). The amendment restored 'must' if any of four conditions exist: (a) that the intervener acted 'in substance, as the sole or principal applicant, defendant, appellant or respondent'; (b) the intervener's 'evidence and representations, taken as a whole, have not been of significant assistance to the court'; (c) a significant part of the intervener's evidence and representations relates to matters that it is not necessary for the court to consider'; (d) that 'the intervener has behaved unreasonably'.

When the Bill came back to the Lords this time the government prevailed – by 190 to 160. Under what is now s 87 the courts are obliged to order interveners to pay costs if any of the four conditions apply.[177] It is not known how often that has occurred but it is rare. Interveners generally inform the parties of the intention to intervene and often seek their agreement not to ask for or enforce costs. They obviously pay their own costs. The court

[175] HL, HC Joint Committee on Human Rights, *The implications for access to justice of the Government's proposals to reform judicial review*, 13th Report 2013–14, HL 174, HC 868, April 2014, pp 28–29.

[176] Lord Woolf, who moved the amendment, said (col 959) '[I]t is dangerous to go down the line of telling the judges what they have got to do. Everybody accepts that the independence of our judiciary is important. I emphasise the importance of that independence not because it is some right of the judiciary; it is important because the citizens know that a matter in issue, particularly in these important areas, will be considered by a judge who is independent.

[177] HL, *Hansard*, 9 December 2014, col 1783. See A Miller 'Reforms to judicial review in the Criminal Justice and Courts Act 2015: promoting efficiency or weakening the rule of law?' *Public Law*, 2015, 583–95.

determines whether they are permitted to make oral, in addition to written, submissions and, if so, will indicate their length.

7.9. Interaction between the Judge and the Advocate

It is an axiom of the adversary system that the judge sits more or less silently as a kind of umpire whilst the battle rages between the lawyers in the case. But while this model may be broadly accurate in regard to the process of establishing the facts, it does not do justice to the role of the judge in the process of establishing the law. Here the judge tends to be very much more active. They commonly see it as their job to challenge the propositions of law advanced by counsel and to test them by detailed questioning and probing. The higher in the courts system, the more the exchanges between counsel and the court are apt to resemble a seminar, with the judges firing questions at counsel.

In a curious way the result of this process is that the contest is in a sense between counsel and the court rather than between the lawyers for the two sides. Lord Kilbrandon expressed this in Alan Paterson's 1982 book, *The Law Lords*, based on interviews with judges of the House of Lords. From the dialectic between Bench and Bar which resembled nothing so much as 'conversation between gentlemen on a subject of mutual interest', 'the judge is forced to come to terms, openly and explicitly, with the views of counsel; to present, in short, his own assessment of them and, where necessary, his counter-argument' (p 50). Often, in fact, the judges are using their exchanges with counsel to advance their own thoughts in order to attempt to persuade one or more doubters amongst their brother judges.[178]

Paterson pointed out (p 82) that these exchanges between counsel and the bench are not recorded in the way that the questioning of witnesses and the summing-up or judgments are taken down, by tape-recorder or shorthand writer. The law reported in the Law Reports gave only an abbreviated version of counsel's arguments and judicial ininterventions. But this is far from the whole of the oral exchanges that take place.The result was that only those who were present could gauge what really happened between counsel and the judges and to what extent oral argument by the lawyers for the winning party had a role in the process that led to the court finding for their side. Paterson commented:

> Inevitably, this means that significant aspects of the decision-making process are lost to posterity. Judicial interjections which change the course of appeals go unreported … Equally the persuasive influence of counsel's submissions, the pictures they paint, the baited analogies they proffer, the avenues they close in their arguments – all these are left neglected. Worst of all, the lack of proper transcripts helps perpetuate the notion amongst academic scholars that the real work of the Law Lords and the only important aspect of appeals … are the speeches produced at the end of the day. This concentration on the end product, to the exclusion of the process by which it was arrived at, is intellectually dangerous and academically unsound.[179]

As will be seen below, written argument now plays a significant role but oral argument remains central to the process of law-making by the judges.

[178] Professor Paterson made the same point in the later book, *Final Judgment* (n 108 above) 76–81.
[179] Paterson, *The Law Lords* (n 106 above) 82–83.

7.9.1. The Quality of Oral Argument in the Court of Appeal

English lawyers incline to the view that the quality of oral argument by barristers is high – and that view is shared by lawyers from overseas. In the early 1990s, Professor Robert Martineau, an American scholar who had written extensively on appellate processes in the United States, came to London to undertake research on the English system with a view to comparing the two systems. He sat over a period of months in the Court of Appeal, Civil Division. He had been expecting to find our appellate oral advocacy of a calibre distinctly superior to that in the United States. To his surprise he found that in his opinion it was not. 'Most English barristers', he said, 'are not effective appellate advocates'. They took an inordinate time to identify what their appeals were about, what the issues were and what were their contentions. Most appeals began at 10.30 am. 'It was often 2.30 or 3 pm before [the author] could ascertain what the key issues were.' By contrast, in the United States, it only required fifteen minutes to ascertain the key issues and some thirty minutes to come to a conclusion. The English oral tradition, he suggested, 'rather than forcing counsel to focus on the key facts and legal arguments, has allowed [barristers] to argue *ad infinitum* and often *ad nauseam* without the discipline of the written word or a time limit'.

Professor Martineau strongly urged the merit of the United States system combining a written brief with severely restricted oral argument. English advocates and judges ridiculed the idea that oral argument could be reduced to half an hour or so for each side[180] and still remain a useful tool. But in his view it gave the best result both in terms of efficiency and effectiveness – 'oral argument based on a written brief becomes an intense exercise in advocacy in which the lawyers and the judges immediately confront the key issues of dispute that require resolution by the judges'.[181]

Time limits on oral argument The English courts have not adopted the radical United States approach to time limits[182] but at the appellate level they do now require that counsel give an estimate of the time they require for their argument. The 1995 Practice Note on appeals in the Civil Division of the Court of Appeal stated that 'the court and its listing officers place considerable reliance on advocates' time estimates'.[183] The 1997 Bowman Review of the Court of Appeal (Civil Division) said that although there were no formal limits on oral arguments, in some cases, especially heavy cases, 'the CA does seek to impose limits' based on the parties' estimates (p 88). It was the experience of the court that time limits were 'often over-estimated and that where the CA imposes time limits, they are usually not exceeded' (ibid). The Bowman Report said:

> The oral tradition is an important part of the legal system of England and Wales. We fully support that and believe that there must always be a right to oral argument on appeal. We are also satisfied that there is no need to impose strict mandatory time limits on oral argument in appeals. We know

[180] Oral argument in the US Supreme Court was unrestricted until 1849 when it was changed to two hours per side. In 1925 this was changed to one hour per side. In 1970 it was reduced to 30 minutes per side.

[181] Robert Martineau, *Appellate Justice in England and the United States* (WS Hein, 1990). For an article on the book see M Zander, 'A brief encounter' *New Law Journal*, 12 April 1991, 491.

[182] 'In our informal discussions with Lords Justices of Appeal there was no dissent from the general proposition that … there should be no time limits placed on oral arguments by counsel.' (G Drewry, L Blom-Cooper, C Blake, *The Court of Appeal* (Hart Publishing, 2007) 126.) Professor Paterson in *Final Judgment* (n 108 above) 64 said the same: '[F]ew of the Law Lords, Justices and counsel favoured' constraints on the length of oral argument as in the US Supreme Court.'

[183] [1995] 1 WLR 1191, para 16.

> that this would not receive widespread support. However, we do consider that there is a greater need to impose appropriate time limits for individual appeals, although we are not suggesting that they should be anywhere near as short as those imposed in the United States. That would be entirely opposed to the oral tradition of England and Wales. In Ontario there was a member of the provincial Court of Appeal with particular responsibility for overseeing time limits. It is that sort of judicial oversight that we would like to build on in our jurisdiction.

Bowman recommended that appeals should normally require leave (as has been seen, that was implemented from May 2000) and thought that in most cases the Lord Justice who granted leave to appeal could estimate a time limit for oral argument. In practice, the Lord Justice who grants permission to appeal, having considered the parties' time estimates, indicates how much time they will be allowed. This indication is treated as the expected length of the oral hearing, subject to whatever adjustment the court is prepared to allow.

In 1991 the House of Lords issued a Procedure Direction[184] that, subject to any directions during the hearing, counsel would be 'expected to confine the length of their submissions to the time indicated in the estimates'. This remains the position in the Supreme Court. Parties are required to give advance notice of the time they consider they will need for their oral argument and are expected to keep to that estimate.[185] The Practice Direction states that an appeal is normally expected to take no longer than two days.[186]

But granted that written advocacy has become much more present and important, oral argument is still highly valued. It is highly valued in the sense that it is highly paid.[187] And it is highly valued in the sense that the judges believe it to be important. Professor Paterson reports that the judges were generally positive about oral advocacy in his research for both his 1982 and his 2013 books.

> All of them told me that they had changed their mind during the oral argument and not that infrequently in some cases. This was true 40 years ago and remains true today.[188]

Few of those he interviewed favoured greater constraints on the length of oral argument, such as exist in the United States.[189]

> The dramatic curtailment of oral advocacy in the final court would reduce costs but only at the expense of the efficacy and impact of oral advocacy, and the loss of a nuanced refining process for ideas.[190]

[184] [1991] 3 All ER 608, (1991) 93 Cr App R 356.

[185] Supreme Court Practice Direction, para 6.2.2.

[186] Ibid. Paterson states that cases determined by the Supreme Court between October 2009 and July 2012 lasted 2.18 days on average (*Final Judgment* (n 108 above) 82). Forty years before they lasted twice as long.

[187] Having reported the self-deprecating views of counsel as to the impact they could make as advocates, Professor Alan Paterson wrote (in 2013): 'These relatively modest assessments by counsel of what advocacy can achieve in the final court might, if they were the whole story, make clients wonder why they pay out sometimes in excess of £20,000 a day for the QC of their choice' (Paterson, *Final Judgment* (n 108 above) 50).

[188] Paterson, *Final Judgment* (n 108 above) 50. But judges differ in the way they approach written and oral advocacy: 'Lord Diplock, for example, made up his mind on the basis of the written material and had no time for oral argument and Lord Atkin was sometimes not much better. Lord Hoffmann, in contrast, usually reached a firm conclusion based on the written matter but could be moved off by oral argument. Lords Reid, Radcliffe, Devlin, Hope and Bingham, on the other hand, would leave it until the oral argument stage before reaching preliminary conclusions' (ibid, p 76).

[189] Paterson, *Final Judgment* (n 108 above) 64.

[190] Ibid, 65.

7.10. The Trend Toward Written Argument

One of the clear differences between the English and the American systems used to be in respect to the role of written argument. At the appellate level in the United States, the key role was played by the written brief with oral argument severely limited. By contrast, in England, legal argument was wholly oral.[191] Today the difference has narrowed.

In 1953 the Evershed Committee considered but rejected the idea that our system should adopt the American-style written brief at the appellate level – not least because no one seemed to want it:

Final Report of the (Evershed) Committee on Supreme Court Practice and Procedure, Cmd 8878, 1953.

> 572 ... it seemed to some of us, at first sight, that the American system [of written briefs] possesses certain marked advantages over the procedure for hearing appeals in this country, at any rate from the point of view of the saving of costs. These apparent advantages may be briefly summarised as follows:
>
> (a) Since the grounds of appeal are precisely stated and the authorities relied on are cited in the written 'brief', there is no room for surprise. Not only are the members of the court apprised at once of the point that is to be decided, but the other side are fully aware, before the hearing, of what is going to be said against them.
>
> (b) Formulation beforehand of the precise grounds of the appeal makes it possible in many cases to eliminate much of the evidence, both oral and documentary, which came before the trial Judge but which is not relevant to the particular question that forms the subject of appeal. This enables considerable economies to be made in the transcribing of evidence and duplication of documents.
>
> (c) The 'brief' constitutes a permanent record of the argument on either side, which the judges can take away and consider at leisure. They are not so dependent therefore, on the notes which they are themselves able to make during the hearing or on their fleeting recollection of counsel's oral argument.
>
> (d) Above all, at the cost of preparing the written argument, there is, at any rate in all but the smallest cases, an immediate economy in relation to the time occupied in the hearing of the appeal. As already pointed out, the consumption of time, involving as it does the payment of refresher fees to counsel, is the most expensive feature of our English appellate procedure.
>
> 573. Whatever may be thought to be the advantages of the American system of 'briefs', however, we found singularly little enthusiasm for it amongst the witnesses whose opinions we sought. The members of the Court of Appeal whom we consulted were emphatically opposed to the adoption of such a system in this country as also were the representatives of the Bar Council and Law Society.

[191] The writer, a non-practising solicitor, can claim to have presented the first and perhaps the only American style written brief in an English case – representing Mr Norbert Fred Rondel in the case of *Rondel v Worsley* [1966] 3 WLR 950, as to whether a barrister could be sued for negligence. I acted for Rondel but instead of instructing counsel I submitted a 110-page written brief which was accepted and read ahead of the hearing by the three Court of Appeal judges and which was referred to frequently in the course of the 10-day legal argument. The court also had the benefit of counsel instructed by the Official Solicitor acting as *amicus*. One of the judges, Lord Justice Danckwerts, did not approve. He said in his judgment that this had been 'wholly irregular and contrary to the practice of the court and in my opinion should not be allowed as a precedent for future proceedings' (p 968).

The Evershed Committee gave various reasons for its view that (the then unrestricted) oral argument was preferable to a combination of written briefs and drastic time limits on oral argument:

— The parties' arguments could be fully tested by the judges
— The judges had the benefit of hearing the testing of the arguments by their fellow judges which was more likely to produce unanimous decision. In the US there were more dissents. ('It has seemed to us that the members of the appellate court, reading the 'briefs' and documents for themselves, and without the advantage of hearing unrestricted oral argument together, must tend to bring their individual minds to the case rather than work as a team.'[192])
— Written briefs caused delay in the preparation of cases, the handling of trials and in the delivery of judgment.

Today however written argument is a familiar (and indeed required) part of the English system in the form of what is called 'skeleton arguments'. The story of skeleton arguments goes back to the 1980s. In April 1983, the then new Master of the Rolls, Sir John Donaldson, issued a Practice Note in which he set out the Court of Appeal's approach to the issue:

Practice Note (Presentation of Appeals) [1983] 1 WLR 1055

> As is well known, the judges of the Court of Appeal have been seeking new ways in which appeals can be presented and decided more quickly and at less expense to the parties. One innovation which has proved very successful in more complex appeals is the submission by counsel of what have been called 'skeleton arguments'.
>
> It would be quite inappropriate to use a practice direction in this context since whether skeleton arguments should be submitted, what form they should take and how they should be used will depend on the peculiarities of the appeal concerned. However, it may assist both branches of the profession if I mention the result of such experience as we have had of their use.
>
> Skeleton arguments are, as their name implies, a very abbreviated note of the argument and in no way usurp any part of the function of oral argument in court. They are an aide-mémoire for convenience of reference before and during the hearing and no one is inhibited from departing from their terms. Nevertheless experience shows that they serve a very real purpose.
>
> Before the appeal is called on, the judges will normally have read the notice of appeal, and the respondent's notice and the judgment appealed from. The purpose of this pre-reading is not to form any view of the merits of the appeal, but to familiarise themselves with the issues and scope of the dispute and thereby avoid the necessity for a lengthy, or often any, opening of the appeal. This process is assisted by the provision of skeleton arguments, which are much more informative than a notice of appeal or a respondent's notice, being fuller and more recently prepared.
>
> During the hearing of the appeal itself, skeleton arguments enable much time to be saved because they reduce or obviate the need for the judges to take a longhand note, sometimes at dictation speed, of the submissions and authorities and other documents referred to. Furthermore in some circumstances a skeleton argument can do double duty not only as a note for the judges but also as a note from which counsel can argue the appeal.
>
> The usual procedure is for the skeleton argument to be prepared shortly before the hearing of the appeal at the same time as counsel is getting it up. It should contain a numbered list of the points which counsel proposes to argue, stated in no more than one or two sentences, the object being to *identify* each point, not to argue it or to elaborate on it. Each listed point should be followed by

[192] Evershed Committee Report, para 574(b).

> full references to the material to which counsel will refer in support of it, i.e. the relevant pages or passages in authorities, bundles of documents, affidavits, transcripts and the judgment under appeal. It should also contain anything which counsel would expect to be taken down by the court during the hearing such as propositions of law, chronologies of events, lists of dramatis personae and, where necessary, glossaries of terms. If more convenient, these can of course be annexed to the skeleton argument rather than being included in it. Both the court and opposing counsel can then work on the material without writing it down, thus saving considerable time and labour.
>
> The document should be sent to the court as soon as convenient before the hearing or, if for some reason this is not possible, handed in when counsel rises to address the court. It is however more valuable if provided to the court in advance. A copy should of course at the same time be sent or handed to counsel on the other side.
>
> It cannot be over-emphasised that skeleton arguments are not formal documents to the terms of which anyone would be held. They are simply a tool to be used in the interests of greater efficiency. Experience shows that they can be a valuable tool. The judges of the court all hope that it will be possible to refine and extend their use.
>
> Finally, even in simple appeals where skeleton arguments may be unnecessary, counsel should provide notes (preferably typed) of any material such as I have mentioned which would otherwise have to be taken down by the court more or less at dictation speed, thereby saving considerable time and labour.

It would seem that Lord Donaldson thought that the balance between oral and written argument in the Court of Appeal was about right. In his 1986 review of the legal year, the Master of the Rolls said:

> The basis of the 1982 procedural reforms was a realisation that time spent in court was extremely expensive, because it occupied not only the judges, but also counsel, solicitors and sometimes the parties. Accordingly, it was thought that, even if there was no overall saving in the time taken to hear any given appeal, a change whereby part of the process could be undertaken by the judges reading in their rooms, instead of being read to in court, should effect a reduction in the cost of the proceedings to the parties. A secondary advantage would accrue if, as seemed likely, such a division between time spent in and out of court would lead to some slight reduction in the time occupied by each individual appeal. The latter expectation was based upon the fact that judges, like anyone else, can absorb written material more quickly if they read it to themselves than if it is read aloud to them. In the event there is every reason to believe that both advantages have been achieved, although it is difficult to measure the precise extent of the achievement.[193]
>
> In the light of four years' experience, the question has now to be asked whether more should be done to shift the process of hearing an appeal from oral argument in court to private study in the judges' rooms. There is no doubt that it could be done.
>
> The United States judiciary do it. They rely heavily on written 'briefs' prepared by the parties, they use legally qualified assistants ('law clerks') and they impose time limits on oral argument in court.
>
> The fact that in this country we have a specialist corps of advocates in the Bar, upon whom the judiciary can and do rely to do much of the work done by judicial law clerks in the United States, and that we have a long tradition of oral argument differentiates our position from that of the United States. It is, therefore, no criticism of that system if I say that in my opinion we have in general gone as far as we should in reducing court time. The judges' present aim is to enter court for the hearing of the appeal already knowing the background facts, the point or points in issue

[193] *New Law Journal*, 17 October 1986, 990.

> and the essence of the arguments to be advanced by the parties … If we were to go further, I think that we should lose the undoubted advantage of a dialogue between bench and Bar in detecting, refining and resolving the crucial point or points in the appeal and, although we should undoubtedly decrease the expense of time spent in court, we should considerably increase other costs in that the written arguments prepared by counsel would have to be far more elaborate …
>
> This is not to say that the system works perfectly in all cases. We have always recognised that there are a few cases in which written skeleton arguments may be unnecessary and others in which some degree of flesh may legitimately be put upon the bones, although obesity is never justified. Flexibility and tailoring the method of presentation to particular appeals is of the essence of the system. From this it follows inexorably that counsel may sometimes get the balance wrong, but in general the system works well. If I had one criticism to make, it would be that some skeleton arguments are submitted to the court too late. Judges, like counsel, have to plan their work and their personal lives. It is highly disruptive of both if a skeleton argument is delivered late in the afternoon of the day before an appeal is due to be heard first thing in the morning. Furthermore, the absence of the argument when the judge was reading the papers will probably have made his task substantially more difficult and time-consuming.

In March 1989, Lord Donaldson took the next step by issuing a Practice Note requiring skeleton arguments in all cases as from June 1989.[194] They would have to be lodged by both sides not less than four weeks before the date of the scheduled hearing. In May 1990, Lord Donaldson issued a further Practice Note reducing the period within which the skeleton arguments had to be lodged from four weeks to two weeks.[195] A much more radical change in regard to skeleton arguments came with a new Practice Direction, 1 January 1999.[196] Instead of requiring that they be delivered shortly before the hearing it required that they be delivered with the appeal bundle of documents within fourteen days after the appeal appeared in the list of forthcoming appeals.

Writing in *The Times* (26 January 1999) to protest about this new rule, Mr David Pannick QC (now Lord Pannick KC) said this meant they had to be filed months before the hearing. This would mean the case would have to be prepared twice over, once to prepare the skeleton argument and once for the hearing. More important, they would decline in quality and focus and would not provide as much assistance to the court as a skeleton argument filed close to the hearing date. Replying, Lord Woolf, the Master of the Rolls, said that early skeleton arguments were needed because of the new rule requiring leave to appeal in almost all cases. They were also needed as part of the new approach to case management. ('They are essential for the monitoring and management of appeals from the time of receipt. The Court of Appeal in a modern civil justice system must manage its workload.'[197])

A little later the thrust of the new rule was extended even further. This came about as part of the Court of Appeal's attack on hopeless appeals. As from May 2000, leave (now called 'permission') to appeal is required for almost all appeals.[198] See Civil Procedure Rules, CPR Pt 52 and the accompanying Practice Direction. The Practice Direction now requires that the would-be appellant (if legally represented) must file a skeleton argument together

[194] [1989] 1 WLR 281.
[195] [1990] 1 WLR 794.
[196] [1999] 1 WLR 2.
[197] *The Times*, 2 February 1999.
[198] The reform was based on the recommendations first of the Woolf Report on *Access to Justice* (1996) and then of the Bowman Report (*Review of the Court of Appeal (Civil Division)* (1997)).

with their notice requesting leave to appeal.[199] Respondents are required to provide a skeleton argument 'in all cases where he proposes to address argument to the court'.[200] Where the respondent's skeleton is not included with their notice, it must be lodged and served not later than 21 days after receipt of the appellant's skeleton.[201]

The Practice Direction states that skeleton arguments 'should be concise'[202] and not more than 25 A4 size pages long, 12-point font.[203] A reader of this admonition might imagine that the preparation of skeleton arguments would not be unduly costly. The reality is that advocates lavish immense time and effort on preparation of skeleton arguments. The costs appeal in *Hornsby v Clark Kenneth Leventhal*[204] offered a glimpse of this reality. Leading counsel claimed £30,000 for 'settling' (ie preparing) the skeleton argument; junior counsel claimed £6,650 for his part in drafting the skeleton argument. In addition they had claimed respectively another £30,000 and £20,000 for their 'brief fee'.[205] The initial costs assessment (then called 'taxation') by the court allowed them £6,000 plus £6,000 for the QC and £3,000 plus £3,000 for the junior. They appealed. The court accepted the QC's assertion that he spent 150 hours or twenty days in preparing the skeleton argument. This included time spent reading documents and transcripts of the trial, as well as time spent on legal research and drafting the skeleton. But the court held that this time was not 'reasonable and proportionate'. A reasonable amount of time would have been 75 hours – giving a proper fee of £15,000, rather than the £6,000 allowed on the initial taxation. The junior's fee it held should be £5,000 rather than the £3,000 allowed. As to the brief fees, the court said that they should not include any element of double payment for work already paid for in respect of preparation of the skeleton. On that basis the court allowed a brief fee of £25,000 for the QC and of £15,000 for the junior.

Skeleton arguments work to the benefit both of the parties and of the judges. The parties are given advance knowledge of the opponent's arguments and authorities and can prepare to meet them. The court can use the skeleton to pre-read so that they are prepared before the case opens. But it goes further. The skeletons can be used by the court to reach a preliminary view as to the result before either counsel has spoken a word. Professor Penny Darbyshire came across this in her observational study of judges:

> I noticed that judges could formulate an opinion on the skeletons, do their own research, draft judgments, deliberate/negotiate, refine their reasoning and even swap drafts or modify a single draft *before* the hearing.[206]

Writing about the Civil Division of the Court of Appeal Professor Darbyshire went so far as to say, 'Most judgments are reached before the hearing'![207]

[199] CPR 52 PDC, para 3(g).
[200] CPR 52 PDC, para 13.
[201] CPR 52 PDC, para 21.
[202] CPR 52 PDA, para 5.1.
[203] CPR 52 PDC, para 31(1).
[204] [2000] 4 All ER 567. (Comparable charges have no doubt risen considerably since 2000.)
[205] A barrister's brief fee covers preparation of the case and the first day in court. Thereafter they are entitled to a daily 'refresher'.
[206] P Darbyshire, *Sitting in Judgment The Working Lives of Judges* (Hart Publishing, 2011) 344. Her basic sample consisted of 40 judges of different levels: two Law Lords/Supreme Court Justices; four Lords Justices of Appeal; eight High Court judges; 16 Circuit judges; one High Court district judge; three district judges (magistrates' courts) and six county court district judges. The research method was direct observation, not only by sitting in court but, remarkably, by watching what the judges did out of court.
[207] Darbyshire (n 206) 344.

7.11. Interaction between the Judges and their Judicial Assistants

Law clerks, able young lawyers to assist the judges, have long been a familiar part of the US Supreme Court. They are a relatively new feature in English courts.[208] They have been employed in the Court of Appeal since 1996 and in the House of Lords since 2001. Paterson says that the post of judicial assistant in the House of Lords emerged 'under the aegis of Lord Bingham when he was translated from the position of Lord Chief Justice into that of senior Law Lord'.[209] In the House of Lords there was room only for four. In the Supreme Court, where there is much more space, there are currently eight. In the Court of Appeal there are also eight.

In the Lords their first primary role was to assist with managing petitions to appeal by writing neutral memos summarising in a few pages what the application was about. They would attend the hearing of the petition by three members of the court – and after the decision had been reached the author was typically asked for their view. However, according to Paterson, some of the Justices might ask their judicial assistant for a view *before* the hearing of the petition.[210]

With the establishment of the Supreme Court the judicial assistants had taken on a new role. The assistant of the Justice delivering the lead judgment assisted in the drafting of the brief press release about the decision that now goes on the Court's website. But the largest commitment of the judicial assistant's time was attending meetings and hearings of their Justice, taking notes, doing research on points of law requested by the Justice and generally acting as a sounding-board before, during and after the hearing on a case. ('Lords Bingham, Hope and Rodger, for instance, saw their assistants every morning (at 7.45 am, 8.30 am and 9 am respectively) when the Court was sitting to discuss the case that was coming up that day.'[211]) The way that Justices used their assistants varied considerably.

Paterson reports that gradually the role of the judicial assistants was expanding.

> The Law Lords and the Justices were well aware that, in the eyes of the US law clerks at least, the latter have a significant input to the first drafts of most Justices' judgments in the US Supreme Court.[212] This was not thought to be a good precedent to follow. Yet over the years the brilliance of some of the UK assistants has begun to push the boundaries. Discussions as to what happened at the first conference in key cases was the first to go (at least in the case of some Law Lords and Justices) leading – on occasion – to more general discussions of what other Justices were saying in their draft judgments, and the strengths and weakness of the same. The informality of the

[208] See T Nesterchuk, 'The View from Behind the Bench', ch 11 in A Burrows, D Johnston and R Zimmerman (eds), *Judge and Jurist: Essays in Memory of Lord Rodger of Earlsferry* (Oxford University Press, 2013); and R Munday, 'Of law clerks and judicial assistants' 171 *Justice of the Peace*, 2007, 455–50. Ms Nesterchuk's article was based on her personal experience. Dr Munday's article arose from reading *Sorcerer's Apprentices: 100 Years of Law Clerks at the United States Supreme Court* by Artemus Ward and David L Weiden (New York University Press, 2006).

[209] Paterson, *Final Judgment* (n 108 above) 247.

[210] Ibid 249.

[211] Ibid 251.

[212] Ibid 254. Ward and Weiden, *Sorcerer's Apprentices* (n 208 above) report that progressively the law clerks' contribution had increased from checking citations, to drafting opinions on the instructions of their Justice and often to actually drafting opinions in collaboration with the Supreme Court Justices.

> Court was such that the more inquisitive assistants would come to see, without any impropriety, some or all of the circulating drafts. From an early stage some Law Lords asked their assistants from time to time to research some factual or even legal issue for use in their judgments … In the Supreme Court, armed with the circulating drafts, some assistants may now find themselves expected not only to critique their own Justice's judgment but also to comment on the drafts of other Justices. Of course, this is not the same as drafting the judgments, but the input is growing. One of the questions facing today's Supreme Court is how much further these developments should go.[213]

The crunch question is whether law clerks will ever be involved in writing the first draft of judgments. This, Paterson says, was not a role assigned to judicial assistants or their equivalents in the UK Supreme Court, the Australian High Court or the Canadian Supreme Court. But it had become part of the role of law clerks in the US Supreme Court:

> It certainly seems to be the case that all or almost all of today's US Supreme Court Justices routinely allow their clerks … to do first drafts of judicial opinions, or to revise and edit such drafts. According to the authors of *Sorcerers' Apprentices*, a book on the influence of Supreme Court clerks, about 30 per cent of the opinions issued by the Supreme Court are almost entirely the work of law clerks.[214]

Paterson observes, 'All this seems very far removed from the judicial assistants of the UK Court. At present the consensus that their role does not and should not encompass the writing of judgments seems robust'. But, he warns, 'doubtless the same was true 70 years ago in the US Supreme Court'.[215]

7.12. The Interaction between the Judges

Perhaps the most interesting section of Professor Alan Paterson's 2013 book *Final Judgment: The Last Law Lords and the Supreme Court* is the chapter entitled 'Dialogues with colleagues – the stages for discourse'. Paterson identified four main stages: the Preparatory Stage, the Oral Hearing, the First Conference and Drafting the Judgment.

The Preparatory Stage is the selection of cases to be given permission to appeal (PTA).[216] The decision is made by a panel of three judges. Who gets to sit on the PTA panel may make a difference.[217] In the House of Lords, traditionally selection of judges for the panel was left to the Principal Clerk but in more recent years, 'the senior Law Lords came to take a more prominent role'[218] and 'by 2003-05 the senior Law Lords were carrying out most of the work'.[219] Also nowadays the panel usually consists of specialists in the relevant field.[220]

[213] Paterson, *Final Judgment* (n 108 above) 254.

[214] Ibid 255.

[215] Ibid 256. Munday, 'Of law clerks and judicial assistants' (n 208 above) raises the same concern.

[216] In the four years to 2023–24 the number of applications ran from a high of 217 to a low of 153. The percentage refused was 71, 78, 71, 72 per cent. (*Supreme Court Annual Report,* (2023–24, 28.)

[217] S Shah and T Poole, 'The impact of the Human Rights Act on the House of Lords' *Public Law*, 2009, 347, 356–61. See also B Dickson, 'The processing of appeals in the House of Lords' 123 *Law Quarterly Review,* 2007, 571, 576–84.

[218] Paterson, *Final Judgment* (n 108 above) 68.

[219] Dickson, 'The processing of appeals' (n 217 above) 579. Paterson said that the Registrar of the Supreme Court operated with four permission to appeal (PTA) committees, chaired by the four most senior Justices (*Final Judgment* (n 108 above) 69).

[220] 'Thus Lady Hale would be on the Family law petitions, Lord Walker on the Tax ones, Lords Scott and Neuberger on the Landlord and Tenant cases, Lord Bingham, Rodger, Carswell or Brown would do the Criminal petitions and Lords Bingham and Hope and Lady Hale got most of the Human Rights cases' (Paterson, *Final*

All the Justices receive notice of the pending petitions and the names of those on the panel, to whom comments could be sent in advance of the meeting at which the petition will be considered. But such communications are rare.[221]

The decision as to who sat on an appeal in the House of Lords was basically left to the Principal Clerk. In the Supreme Court, similarly, it is basically left to the Registrar under the supervision of the President and Deputy President. The decision is based on various criteria obviously including availability and workload. But specialism ('horses for courses' – see p 281 above) and having participated in the PTA meeting are nowadays very relevant.[222] (For recent research and consideration of its policy implications see D Fairgrieve, J Tomlinson and J Rylatt, 'Panel Size Determination in the UK Supreme Court; A Critical and Empirical Analysis' 39 *Civil Justice Quarterly* 2020 (2), 144–62.)

Brief pre-hearing meetings of the judges are usual in the Court of Appeal. Lord Bingham introduced them in the House of Lords when he became senior Law Lord in 2000 and they are common in the Supreme Court.

During the hearing of the appeal, as has already been noted, the judges may seek to influence each other through exchanges with counsel. One of the barristers quoted by Paterson said:

> Lots of the questions you get asked by the Lords are actually ways of scoring points off their colleagues whose position they know to be in some respect different … What they do is they ask the kind of question which they expect will provoke what they regard as the conclusive argument against a particular position that's been expressed outside the court by one of their colleagues.[223]

Another said:

> I can think of occasions where Lord X would be putting questions to the counsel and then he would look round to see whether his point had gone home with his colleague.[224]

Lord Hoffmann told Paterson,

> [The oral hearing] is the stage at which you make your view known both for the benefit of counsel and for the benefit of your colleagues. It's an opportunity not just for counsel to exercise advocacy on the bench but for the judges to exercise advocacy on each other.[225]

All the judges interviewed by Paterson said that they had changed their minds during the oral argument – 'though it was often unclear whether this was due more to the dialogue with counsel than that with their colleague'.[226]

After the oral hearing has ended, in both the House of Lords and the Supreme Court, the panel meets for what is usually their only conference. The tradition in the House of Lords was that the presiding judge would ask each of the judges, in reverse order of seniority, to give their views. Their remarks would be heard uninterrupted. At the end of the

Judgment (n 108 above) 68). The disadvantage is the danger that the other members of the panel may leave it to the specialist.

[221] Paterson, *Final Judgment* (n 108 above) 69.

[222] Of the 339 Justices who sat on 113 PTA hearings 2009–11, 230 (68 per cent) were on the eventual appeal panel (Paterson, *Final Judgment* (n 108 above) 72).

[223] Paterson, *Final Judgment* (n 108 above) 79.

[224] Ibid.

[225] Ibid 81.

[226] Ibid.

individual statements, unless they were unanimous,[227] there would be discussion ending with a decision as to who would write the lead judgment. The practice in the Supreme Court is much the same though Paterson reports a trend toward shorter set piece individual statements and more discussion.[228]

Lord Hope said,

> [It's] really a means of trying to develop some kind of position at the end of the hearing, because one of the things one has to realise is that getting the same group together again with all the papers in front of them is not going to be terribly easy.[229]

The fact that the first conference is usually the only one held and that it is not very long, typically under an hour,[230] means that the main interaction between the judges in regard to their judgments takes place after the first conference. Judges nowadays are comfortable with use of email and electronic exchange of draft judgments is common. Sometimes a draft will be sent only to some of the panel. In 2012 the Justices in the Supreme Court resolved that in general the lead judgment should be the first to be circulated to the whole panel.[231]

In 2000, the average delay between hearing and judgment was 95 days, with two cases taking a year and two others more than 250 days. Lord Bingham's period as Senior Law Lord led to a reduction in delay to an average of under two months. Under Lord Phillips the average rose again somewhat while under Lord Neuberger it again came down.[232]

At the time of Paterson's first study of the House of Lords he found that it was very rare for a Law Lord to comment in writing on the draft judgment of a colleague. ('At the stage where the opinions are circulated one's colleagues are very polite. If there is an obvious omission you draw attention to it, but you would seldom re-argue the merits.'[233]) But by the time of the second study forty years later, Paterson found that it had become quite common to exchange – often by email – comments on a draft circulated by a colleague or to circulate one's own draft.

> [I]t is becoming the norm for Justices to email the lead judgment writer to raise either particular points on an individual basis, or to email all of the panel with suggestions as to how the judgment might be amended. Similarly, where Justices are considering dissenting or putting in a concurring judgment they will often liaise with a like-minded colleague by a lateral email or in a conversation if their room is nearby.[234] A judgment that appears under the name of a single judge may in fact be the product of input from several.[235]
>
> Sometimes the process most resembles five individuals in action; sometimes it is genuinely collaborative; mostly it is somewhere in between the two.[236]

Comment in one judgment on the content of another judgment in the time of the House of Lords was rare. ('For the most part the published judgments in the House in its last 40 years

[227] Dissents typically have occurred in around one-fifth of cases, with single dissents in around one tenth of cases.

[228] Paterson, *Final Judgment* (n 108 above) 87.

[229] Ibid 86. Paterson (ibid) says that re-convened meetings in the House of Lords occurred only two or three times in a year. They have been rare in the Supreme Court too.

[230] As Paterson wrote, 'One of the curiosities of appellate decision-making is how little time is spent in collective deliberation.' (*Final Judgment* (n 108 above) 128.).

[231] Paterson, *Final Judgment* (n 108 above) 98.

[232] Ibid 120–21.

[233] Ibid 125, quoting an unnamed Law Lord.

[234] Ibid 127.

[235] Judgment in *Manchester City Council v Pinnock* [2010] UKSC 45 under the name of Lord Neuberger was 'the product of several meetings of the whole panel of nine Justices and multiple emails, with direct contributions from most of the Justices (in some cases quite substantial contributions) to the single judgment'. (Paterson, *Final Judgment* (n 108 above) 130–31.).

[236] Paterson, *Final Judgment* (n 108 above) 131.

resembled ships passing in the night. Only in the final few years of the House did direct references (in disagreement) become more common.'[237] But in the Supreme Court this has changed:

> Today in the Supreme Court engagement with the published judgment of one's colleagues is an everyday event where there is more than a single majority judgment. It has occurred in every case where there is a significant disagreement in the court, in almost all of the cases where there are any dissents at all and in many of the cases where there are multiple concurrences.

Paterson expressed satisfaction at this development:

> The key issue about the judicial dialogue of engagement in published judgments, however, is that not only does it demonstrate that the judges are working together more collectively in the final court, but also that the dialogues with the parties, academics and the lawyers and judges of the present and future are more effective. This is because the engagement reveals in a way that was all too frequently missing in the House of Lords, precisely which issues the Justices are in agreement about and those where they disagree and why.[238]

Under Lord Phillips and Lord Neuberger the Supreme Court engaged in team working to a far greater extent than was the case in the House of Lords – though it is not a team in the ordinary sense:

> It is a curious team because the value of the team depends on everybody using their own individual intelligence and their own experience and so forth and bringing all that to the party, but our working method is very collaborative.[239]

Or, as Professor Paterson put it:

> The Justices do not go on team building exercises, there is no manager, no opposing team, no team strips, no team mascot and no league table of supreme courts. However, there are other team-related characteristics … e.g. team selection, team-work, team leaders, team players and team spirit.[240]

The Court of Appeal, Paterson suggested, was an example of this collegiality:

> The English Court of Appeal is a highly collegial court in this sense. Its members regularly sit on the same panel for several weeks, they meet before cases to discuss points on which they wish to hear argument, to allocate who will write and to express preliminary views on the case.

An example of the effect of team-working in the Supreme Court, was the rise in the proportion of single majority judgments and a corresponding decrease in concurring judgments, which 'can only be achieved by the Justices working together (rather than as individuals)'.[241]

Reflecting on these developments in his concluding chapter Professor Paterson said that this kind of team-working required a different skill set in the participants than was once required of Law Lords:

> The ability to negotiate, to compromise, to persuade whilst robustly defending a position of principle are skills which until a few years ago were more associated with a member of the Law

[237] Ibid 136.
[238] Ibid 137–38.
[239] Ibid 141, per Lord Reed.
[240] Ibid 141.
[241] Ibid 144.

> Commission than a member of the final court, yet they are being actively applied in the pursuit of more collaborative judgments.[242]

But this came at a price:

> Team-working potentially has another drawback – a loss of individualism in our Justices. The glory of the common law and its final court has included the individuality and idiosyncrasy of its top judges …
>
> Single judgments representing the outcome of the internal debates within the Supreme Court which are not publicly rehearsed, remove the humanity of individual difference and potentially undermine transparency. For those who believe in the virtues of diversity (including diversity in thought) within the final court this is not necessarily a welcome development. Fewer dissents and concurrences in return for more single judgments mean more judgments devised by a committee and consequently more compromise.[243]

Alan Paterson wrote further on these developments in 'Creating a group oriented Supreme Court – Lord Neuberger's legacy' (28 *International Journal of the Legal Profession*, 2021 (1), 107–26:

> Eschewing the individualism of the Law Lords on the one hand and the European style judgments of the Court, on the other, Lord Neuberger produced a via media, unique in the common law world. He took the part-formed versions of team-working and group decision-making which had evolved between 2009 and 2012 and transformed them through an elliptical style of leadership by 'nudge' or example, into a thorough-going collegial form of team working. To achieve this Lord Neuberger was prepared to innovate eg pursuing balance in panel selection, boosting single judgments, using 600 word essays,[[244]] encouraging joint judgments, holding multiple conferences, facilitating remote decision making through email and multiple drafts, and taking the Court to the rest of the UK.

For a broader take on judicial leadership in the Supreme Court over its first six years see R Hunter and E Rackley, 'Judicial leadership in the UK Supreme Court' 38 *Legal Studies*, 2018 (2), 191–220. They examine the different leadership roles played by the twelve justices.

7.13. What about Judges' Biases?

The great American judge, Benjamin Cardozo, in a passage quoted above wrote:

> Every one of us has in truth an underlying philosophy of life. There is in each of us a stream of tendency, whether you choose to call it philosophy or not, which gives coherence and direction to thought and action.[245]

But does such 'stream of tendency' of the individual judge amount to a generalised bias of judges as a collective?

[242] Ibid 314–15.

[243] Ibid 315.

[244] At the end of the hearing in two cases each justice was asked to write a 600-word essay and to circulate it to the others by email. That had greatly reduced the time required for their first conference.

[245] Benjamin N Cardozo, *The Nature of the Judicial Process* (Yale University Press, 1921) 12.

It has been said that the narrow social-class background of English judges influences them, and in particular explained the alleged fact that the judges had historically shown themselves to be biased, for instance, against the trade unions. A study published in 1969 of judicial decisions affecting trade unions did not, however, bear out the claim that these decisions showed any clear bias.[246] The authors analysed every judicial decision arising out of disputes between groups of workers and employers or between groups of organised or unorganised workers. The cases in the study were those referred to in the three leading textbooks at that time concerned with industrial conflict (Citrine,[247] Grunfeld[248] and Wedderburn[249]). Between 1871 and 1966 there were seventy cases arising out of industrial conflict. Of these, fifty were civil and twenty were criminal. The article showed which side won in those seventy cases.

On the basis of the information in the article, the data is shown in tabular form (Table 7.2).[250]

Table 7.2 House of Lords Employment Law Cases 1997–2004

	Determined in favour of workers	**Determined against workers**
Civil courts:		
House of Lords and Privy Council	5	8
Court of Appeal	17	12
High Court	16	29
Divisional Court	4	1
Total	42	50
Criminal courts:		
Court of Criminal Appeal	1	1
Divisional Court	2	11
First instance	3	17
Total	6	29
Grand total	48	79

In a study of employment law cases heard by the House of Lords in the seven years May 1997 to June 2004 employers succeeded in almost twice as many cases as employees but the author did not detect any evidence of pro-employer bias. Critical comment was directed rather to the poor quality of the reasoning of some decisions.[251]

For an analysis of the male prejudices of English and United States judges in cases involving sex-equality issues, see Albie Sachs and Joan Hoff Wilson, *Sexism and the Law: A Study of Male Beliefs and Legal Bias in Britain and the United States* (Martin Robertson, 1978).

[246] P O'Higgins and M Partington, 'Industrial conflict: judicial attitudes' 32 *Modern Law Review*, 1969, 53.
[247] NA Citrine, *Trade Union Law*, 2nd edn (Stevens, 1960).
[248] C Grunfeld, *Modern Trade Union Law* (Sweet & Maxwell, 1966).
[249] KW Wedderburn, *The Worker and the Law* (Penguin, 1965).
[250] Based on the seventy cases decided between 1871 and 1966. The numbers exceed seventy because the article traced the fate of appeals and many cases are therefore counted more than once.
[251] S Honeyball, 'Employment law and the Appellate Committee of the House of Lords' 24 *Civil Justice Quarterly*, 2005, 364–87.

See also Zsuzsanna Adler, 'Rape – the intention of Parliament and the practice of the courts' 45 *Modern Law Review*, 1982, 664. For the suggestion that judges' attitudes to landlord–tenant issues were influenced by conscious or unconscious pro-landlord attitudes, see JI Reynolds, 'Statutory covenants of fitness and repair: social legislation and the judges' 37 *Modern Law Review*, 1974, 377. See also a reply by MJ Robinson, 'Social legislation and the judges: a note by way of rejoinder' 39 *Modern Law Review*, 1976, 43.

For a substantial study of judicial attitudes and their influence on decision-making see Robert Stevens, *Law and Politics: The House of Lords as a Judicial Body, 1800–1976* (Weidenfeld and Nicolson, 1979). The book is instructive, for instance, on the changing judicial attitudes to tax laws – see pp 170–76, 204–08, 312, 392–96, 411–14, 600–13.

In a provocative book, described in a review by the present writer when it was first published in 1977 as 'an instant classic', Professor John Griffith of the London School of Economics argued that judges generally were biased in their approach to certain issues not so much because of their social background as because of the nature of their function. According to this thesis the judge, by virtue of their office, is mainly concerned to uphold and maintain the status quo and therefore inevitably tends to find himself in conflict with any groups in society whose purpose is to seek change – the more so if they proceed by other than conventional methods:

JAG Griffith, *The Politics of the Judiciary*, 5th edn (Fontana, 1997) 336, 342–43

> [336] A central thesis of this book is that judges in the United Kingdom cannot be politically neutral because they are placed in positions where they are required to make political choices which are sometimes presented to them, and often presented by them, as determinations of where the public interest lies; that their interpretation of what is in the public interest and therefore politically desirable is determined by the kind of people they are and the position they hold in our society; that this position is a part of established authority and so is necessarily conservative not liberal. From all this flows that view of the public interest which is shown in judicial attitudes such as tenderness towards private property and dislike of trade unions, strong adherence to the maintenance of order, distaste for minority opinions, demonstrations and protests, support of governmental secrecy, concern for the preservation of the moral and social behaviour to which it is accustomed, and the rest …
>
> [342] Far more than on the judiciary, our freedoms depend on the willingness of the press, politicians and others to publicise the breach of these freedoms and on the continuing vulnerability of ministers, civil servants, the police, other public officials and powerful private interests to accusations that these freedoms are being infringed. In other words, we depend far more on the political climate and on the vigilance of those members of society who for a variety of reasons, some political and some humanitarian, make it their business to seek to hold public authorities within their proper limits. That those limits are also prescribed by law and that judges may be asked to maintain them is not without significance. But the judges are not – as in a different dispensation and under a different social order they might be – the strong, natural defenders of liberty.
>
> Judges are concerned to preserve and to protect the existing order. This does not mean that no judges are capable of moving with the times, of adjusting to changed circumstances. But their function in our society is to do so belatedly. Law and order, the established distribution of power both public and private, the conventional and agreed view amongst those who exercise political and economic power, the fears and prejudices of the middle and upper classes, these are the forces which the judges are expected to uphold and do uphold.
>
> In the societies of our world today judges do not stand out as protectors of liberty, of the rights of man, of the unprivileged, nor have they insisted that holders of great economic power, private or public, should use it with moderation. Their view of the public interest, when it has gone beyond the interest of the governments, has not been wide enough to embrace the interests of political,

> ethnic, social or other minorities. Only occasionally has the power of the supreme judiciary been exercised in the positive assertion of fundamental values. In both democratic and totalitarian societies, the judiciary has naturally served the prevailing political and economic forces. Politically, judges are parasitic.
>
> [343] That this is so is not a matter for recrimination. It is idle to criticise institutions for performing the task they were created to perform and have performed for centuries. The principal function of the judiciary is to support the institutions of government as established by law. To expect a judge to advocate radical change is absurd. The confusion arises when it is pretended that judges are somehow neutral in the conflicts between those who challenge existing institutions and those who control those institutions. And cynicism replaces confusion whenever it becomes apparent that the latter are using the judges as open allies in those conflicts.
>
> Thus it is usual for judges in political cases to be able to rely on the rules of law for the legitimacy of their decisions. As we have seen, there are innumerable ways – through the development of the common law, the interpretation of statutes, the refusal to use discretionary powers, the claims to residual jurisdiction and the rest – in which the judges can fulfil their political function and do so in the name of the law.

Griffith's thesis did not pass unchallenged. The first edition (substantially the same as the fifth) was discussed in a review article by retired Law Lord, Lord Devlin:

Lord Devlin, 'Judges, government and politics' 41 *Modern Law Review*, 1978, 505

> The professor begins with a concise and interesting account of how judges work, what they are paid, their social origins and so on. This covers a good deal more ground than is necessary for his conclusion which is that the judicial political outlook, while not extreme, is right of centre. Judges are 'neither Tories, nor Socialists, nor Liberals' but 'protectors and conservators of what has been, of the relationships and interests on which, in their view, our society is founded.'[252] He is talking chiefly of the small group, less than 30, of the senior judges in the House of Lords and the Court of Appeal whose views matter. 'These judges,' he writes, 'have by their education and training and the pursuit of their profession as barristers, acquired a strikingly homogeneous collection of attitudes, beliefs and principles, which to them represents the public interest.' Since he is writing of men in their sixties and seventies whose working life has given them a common outlook on many questions, by no means all political, I have very little doubt that he is right. I have very little doubt either that the same might be written of most English institutions, certainly of all those which like the law are not of a nature to attract the crusading or rebellious spirit …
>
> But the real question posed by the author is on other subjects. Do the judges allow their devotion to law and order to distort their application of the law when they apply it to those who do not think as they do? In exploring the cases to get the answer to this the author is faced with two difficulties. The first is the lack of discipline among the judges; they do not always toe what Professor Griffith declares to be their party line. The law lords are sometimes divided: more frequently they quarrel with the Court of Appeal. The second difficulty is that the scale of the work does not permit any analysis of the cases. Leaving Lord Halsbury to his own generation, it is difficult to get much from the modern cases without looking for the legal errors and examining them to see whether they disclose a pattern of thought. Without such an analysis the reader is left to go by the result: in the trade union cases, for example, the implication seems to be that a decision against the union cannot be in the public interest …
>
> It is this section containing the cases which is the core of the book. What matters after all is not whether judges have the political prejudices of their age and upbringing, but whether or to what extent they allow the prejudice to get into their judgments. Most people, including judges, are prejudiced against crime, but judges have to learn to keep that prejudice out of a trial. His purpose

[252] JAG Griffith, *The Politics of the Judiciary*, 1st edn (Fontana, 1977) 52.

> is to show that there are certain types of cases that the judges as a body do not decide fairly. I am not sure that in the end he proves much more than that there are cases which he, often in accord with dissenting judges, would have decided differently from the final court …
>
> What the book presents is not a major issue but a problem, or rather one facet of the universal problem caused by the fact that in any peaceful and law-abiding democratic society in which the mortality rate is constantly declining, government falls into the hands of the ageing. No doubt power rises upward from the people, who are of all ages, but it becomes effective only when it is channelled, and the controllers of the channels are, as Professor Griffith says, oligarchs. The oligarchs who rise to the top in the democratic society are usually mature, safe and orthodox men. Autocracy sometimes runs risks in selection, democracy hardly ever. So throughout the whole apparatus of the state, in every institution, whether it be the judiciary, the civil service or the political party, the men at the top, especially perhaps the senior judges because of their training, are seen by the young, among whom I count Professor Griffith because age has not wearied him nor the years condemned, as showing too much concern with stability and too little with movement. Of course the silent majority may see this as a very good thing: let the judges protect the laws and customs of the realm and the traditional values and leave movement to others.

Could it be argued that Professor Griffith and Lord Devlin are really saying much the same thing in different words? Professor Griffith argues that all judges, irrespective of their social class or the country in which they sit, are members of the Establishment who favour the status quo. Lord Devlin contends that judges tend to be 'mature, safe and orthodox men'.

See further and generally, John Bell, *Policy Arguments in Judicial Decisions* (Oxford University Press, 1983).

A different line of inquiry was opened by Rachel Cahill-O'Callaghan in her book *Values in the Supreme Court: Decisions, Division and Diversity* (Hart, 2020). Her aim was to challenge the 'myth of objectivity and impartiality' of the UK Supreme Court (Prologue). Her focus was values, which, she says, anchor all decision-making.

> Judges in the final courts of appeal exercise considerable discretion and it is the exercise of discretion which underpins judicial disagreement. It is the factors that influence the exercise of discretion, in the context of the uncertain decisions in the superior court, which are the subject of this book. The overarching hypothesis is that the exercise of judicial discretion, and ultimately judicial decisions, are influenced by personal values … [I]t is accepted that all judges are constrained by the judicial oath, which calls for fairness, impartiality and independence. A decision must also be exercised within the bounds of statutory and common law. Yet, uncertainty is inherent in the process of reducing the general to the particular and when the law is uncertain, judicial discretion necessarily plays a greater role in the decision-making process. (p 2)

When answering a legal question judges would *first* be guided by their personal values and would only then consider other factors. Social psychologist Shalom Schwartz had identified ten such factors including self-direction, power, conformity, tradition, and universalism. Most of the cases selected for analysis were ones in which there were majority and minority judgments. Each judgment in the selected cases was combed for usage of terms, phrases or expressions that Schwartz claims reveal personal values. The author (at p 181) sums up the result of her empirical work: 'The findings demonstrate that in hard cases, where the law is uncertain, Supreme Court Justices reach decisions which align with their values.'

The issue raised by Rachel Cahill-O'Callaghan was developed by Professor Kate Malleson in 'Values Diversity in the UK Supreme Court: Abandoning the "don't-ask-don't tell" philosophy', 49 *Journal of Law and Society* 2022 (1), 3–22:

> The emerging body of empirical research on judicial values in the UK is developing a fuller and more nuanced picture of the decision making of the Supreme Court. As this evidence base grows

> more rigorous, extensive, and specific, it raises normative questions about which values we want to see prioritized by the Justices. These vital but challenging questions have barely yet been asked. To date, the Court has adopted a don't-ask-don't-tell approach as an institutional response that sidesteps the implications of acknowledging that the Justices must draw on their values in their decision making. Justices do not explicitly deny that their values matter, any more than they deny that they make law. Instead, they try to hold two position that are inherently in tension: accepting that judges' values matter in general terms while continuing to insist on a judicial values blackout in relation to any individual judge in any specific case. This position requires an individual and collective silence about the values that judges hold and the effect that these values have in practice on their decision making. The maintenance of this values blackout is fostered by a fear that making explicit the role of Justices' values will open the door to a US-style partisan Court composed of politicians in wigs. To date, the danger of politicization has been raised as the standard response of the senior judiciary to any proposals that seek to make space in the judicial appointments process for consideration of the values of the Justices.
>
> Maintaining this judicial values blackout in the Supreme Court depends on continued public and political deference to, as well as disinterest in, the Court. Both are reduced when the Court is called upon to decide politically or socially sensitive issues that attract public attention. These cases often concern so-called 'lose–lose' controversial issues in which public opinion is polarized. Whatever decision the Court makes in such cases, it will attract hostility from the losing side, as it did in response to the Miller decisions in 2017 and 2019.[253] To date, the Court's response to these bouts of criticism has generally been to ride out the storm and continue to maintain its silence on the subject of judicial values. An alternative approach would be to address the problem proactively by lifting the judicial values blackout and engaging with the challenging question of how to promote a diversity of values on the Court …
>
> Values are not the only or even the most significant factor in appointing Supreme Court Justices, but they do and should come into play when choosing between those candidates who meet the exacting legal and intellectual selection criteria. The move from tacit to explicit consideration of values would ultimately strengthen the Court's legitimacy in making decisions in the fuzzy space between law and politics in which it must adjudicate. (pp 21–22)

Professor Malleson's argument is not that the values of potential candidates for appointment to the Supreme Court are unknown or regarded as irrelevant to appointment:

> [The values that they prioritize both collectively and individually have always been known to those who appoint them, whichever system is adopted – and nor could it be otherwise … The candidate pool for selection to the Court is made up of senior lawyers and judges with a substantial back catalogue of legal argument, judgments, articles, lectures, and talks, as well as longstanding reputations in a relatively small legal world. Their career choices, extra-curricular activities, character, and attitudes will be well known to the appointing commissioners, in particular the judicial members of the commission, whether directly through personal professional knowledge and experience or indirectly through the extensive consultations process. (p 18)

The question she raises is not whether their values should be taken into account, but whether value diversity should be a recognised part of the decision-making process. The desirability of judicial diversity was officially recognised[254] – though at present it was thought to mean in regard just to gender and race. It could – and, she urges – it should be broadened to include values.

[253] *R (on the Application of Miller and Another) v. Secretary of State for Exiting the European Union)* [2017] UKSC 5; *R (on the application of Miller) v The Prime Minister* [2019] UKSC 41.

[254] 'Each of the Lord Chancellor and the Lord Chief Justice of England and Wales must each take such steps as that office-holder considers appropriate for the purpose of encouraging judicial diversity.' (Constitutional Reform Act 2005, s 137A, inserted by Crime and Courts Act 2013, Sch 13, Pt 2, para.11.

The potential scope for judgments being influenced by the judges' personal values is obviously likely to be most significant where judges give their own judgment and, conversely, least significant where the court issues a single judgment. Single judgments now account for between a half and three-quarters of the decisions of the Supreme Court.[255]

Another relevant consideration is how could value diversity of the Justices be achieved? Professor Malleson is clearly right to say there would be little support for suggestions that might end with anything like the US system of selecting Supreme Court justices. She suggests however something may be learned from Canada, Australia, New Zealand and South Africa.[256]

7.14. Should Judges be Activist in Law-Making?

If judges are human beings who have private opinions or even prejudices, should their basic stance be activist or passive? Should they seek opportunities creatively to develop or even reform the law, or should they leave law reform to the legislature? Needless to say there are different schools of thought on this issue. The remainder of this chapter explores a range of these views through the writings – often eloquent writings – of judges and scholars.

A leading exponent of the 'passive' approach in the post-Second World War era was Lord Simonds, Lord Chancellor from 1951 to 1954 and who sat as a Law Lord for nearly twenty years from 1944 to 1962. Professor Robert Stevens wrote of him that 'during the time that the House was dominated by Simonds, its purpose, intellectually and practically, remained the preservation of the status quo'.[257] In one famous case, for instance, he rejected Lord Denning's invitation to overrule the ancient rule that a third party cannot sue on a contract with a resounding affirmation of the principle of judicial conformity to what has previously been decided:

> To that invitation I readily respond. For to me heterodoxy, or as some might say, heresy, is not the more attractive because it is dignified by the name of reform. Nor will I easily be led by an undiscerning zeal for some abstract kind of justice to ignore our first duty, which is to administer justice according to law, the law which is established for us by an Act of Parliament or the binding authority of precedent. The law is developed by the application of old principles to new circumstances. Therein lies its genius. Its reform by the abrogation of these principles is the task not of the courts of law but of Parliament … I would cast no doubt upon the doctrine of stare decisis without which law is at hazard.[258]

There are countless similar, if less vivid, statements in the law reports.

At the opposite end of the spectrum represented by Lord Simonds stood Lord Denning, who was a judge from 1944 for almost forty years and Master of the Rolls for twenty years from 1962 to 1982. For him certainty in the law was an overrated virtue and judges not only

[255] Professor Brice Dickson's annual report in the *New Law Journal* on the Supreme Court's output the previous year. In the six years 2019 to 2024 the proportion of cases decided by a single judgment was 69 per cent, 62 per cent, 72 per cent, 57 per cent, 54 per cent and 77 per cent.

[256] For contributions from Australia, Canada and South Africa and from the UK see Graham Gee and Erika Rackley (eds), *Debating judicial Appointments in an Age of Diversity* (Routledge, 2018).

[257] Stevens, *Law and Politics* (n 110 above) 342.

[258] *Midland Silicones Ltd v Scruttons Ltd* [1962] AC 446, 467–94.

did make law but should do so. On innumerable occasions, both on the bench and off, he proclaimed the law-making potential of the judiciary:

> The truth is that the law is uncertain. It does not cover all the situations that may arise. Time and again practitioners are faced with new situations, where the decision may go either way. No one can tell what the law is until the courts decide it. The judges do every day make law, though it is almost heresy to say so. If the truth is recognised then we may hope to escape from the dead hand of the past and consciously mould new principles to meet the needs of the present.[259]

For Lord Denning the function of the judge was to be active in reforming the law – 'if the law is to develop and not to stagnate, the House must, I think recapture this vital principle – the principle of growth. The House of Lords is more than another court of law … It acts for the Queen as the fountain of justice in our land'.[260] This statement was made whilst he was still in the House of Lords and before he returned to the Court of Appeal as Master of the Rolls – the better, as he said, to make a mark on the law. Lord Denning's book *The Discipline of Law* (Butterworths, 1979), published to mark his eightieth birthday, was a celebration of his reforming zeal – with chapter and verse. Lord Denning did not, however, express his passion for reform in a coherent philosophy. He never, for instance, formulated principles to guide judges as to the kind of cases in which they should intervene and when they should follow precedent and leave reform to the legislature. Over and over again he chipped away at doctrines that seemed to him to be wrong – on third-party beneficiaries to a contract,[261] sovereign immunity,[262] the doctrine of frustration in contract,[263] fundamental breach,[264] the right of married women to remain in the matrimonial home,[265] the action for negligent misstatement,[266] exclusion clauses in consumer contracts,[267] equitable estoppel[268] and many others.[269] But there was no very clear articulation of the proper relationship between law and justice – beyond the repeated assertion that precedent must not stand in the way of justice. In the final words of his book Lord Denning said only that while precedent was the foundation of our system of case law it must not be applied too rigidly. 'You must cut out the dead wood and trim off the side branches, else you will find yourself lost in thickets and brambles. My plea is simply to keep the path to justice clear of obstructions which would impede it.'[270] But we were not told how the path may be recognised.[271]

Between the two extremes of Lord Simonds and Lord Denning there are many other significant voices. One such was Lord Devlin, who to general surprise retired from the bench in 1964 at the early age of 59 after only three years in the House of Lords. His years on the bench coincided with the high-water mark of the Simonds era, and in 1962 Lord Devlin was despondent about the role of the judge. At that time he wrote: 'I doubt if judges will

[259] Lord Denning, 'The reform of equity' in CJ Hamson (ed), *Law Reform and Law-Making* (Heffer, 1953) 31.
[260] Lord Denning, *From Precedent to Precedent* (Clarendon Press, 1959) 34.
[261] *Midland Silicones Ltd v Scruttons Ltd* [1962] AC 446.
[262] *Rahimtoola v Nizam of Hyderabad* [1958] AC 379.
[263] *British Movietonews Ltd v London and District Cinemas Ltd* [1952] AC 166.
[264] *Karsales (Harrow) Ltd v Wallis* [1956] 1 WLR 936.
[265] *National Provincial Bank v Ainsworth* [1965] AC 1175.
[266] *Candler v Crane Christmas* [1951] 2 KB 164.
[267] *Adler v Dickson* [1955] 1 QB 158.
[268] *Central London Property Trust Ltd v High Trees House Ltd* [1947] KB 130.
[269] For an extended survey, see Stevens, *Law and Politics* (n 110 above) 488–505.
[270] Lord Denning, *Discipline of Law* (Butterworth, 1979) 314.
[271] See generally JL Jowell and JPWB McAuslan (eds), *Lord Denning: The Judge and the Law* (Sweet & Maxwell, 1984).

now of their own motion contribute much more to the development of the law.'[272] Even if the House of Lords changed the rule that it was bound by its own decisions 'it might do its own lopping and pruning … and perhaps even a little drafting, instead of leaving all that to the legislature. But it could not greatly alter the shape of the tree'.[273] By 1975, however, he had formed a rather different view. Delivering the Chorley Lecture at the London School of Economics, ('Judges and Law makers' *Modern Law Review*, 1975, 1) he expressed a conservative but by no means passive philosophy of the judicial role. He was against a judiciary that was dynamically activist, but on the other hand he saw a useful and quite considerable role for judges in shaping the common law. He later developed his views further.

Patrick Devlin, *The Judge* (Oxford University Press, 1979) 3, 5, 9, 17

> What is the function of the judge? Professor Jaffé has a phrase for it – 'the disinterested application of known law.'[274] He would put it perhaps as the minimal function. I should rank it as greater than that. It is at any rate what 90 per cent or more of English judges – and I daresay also of all judges of all nationalities – are engaged in for 90 per cent of their working lives. The social service which the judge renders to the community is the removal of a sense of injustice. To perform this service the essential quality which he needs is impartiality and next after that the appearance of impartiality. I put impartiality before the appearance of it simply because without the reality the appearance would not endure …
>
> The disinterested application of the law calls for many virtues, such as balance, patience, courtesy and detachment, which leave little room for the ardour of the creative reformer. I do not mean that there should be a demarcation or that judges should down tools whenever they meet a defect in the law. I shall consider later to what extent in such a situation a judge should be activist. But I am quite convinced that there should be no judicial dynamics.
>
> So much for the nature and function of the judge. I return to the lawmaker and consider what, if anything, judges and lawmakers have in common.
>
> The lawmaker takes an idea or a policy and turns it into law. For this he needs the ability to formulate principle, and a judge in common with any other trained lawyer should have that. Is the judge any different in this respect from a professor or a parliamentary draftsman? Yes, because he has experience of the administration of the law. So has the barrister and the solicitor, but it is an advantage to see it working from the Bench. So there is no reason why, given the policy, a judge should not be a good activist lawmaker. The question, to which I shall return, is whether he should be the complete lawmaker or whether he would not do better work in committee, pooling his judicial experience with the social, commercial and administrative experience of others.
>
> Let me repeat the distinction, since it may be one which I have freshly drawn, between activist and dynamic lawmaking. In activist lawmaking the idea is taken from the consensus and demands at most sympathy from the lawmaker. In dynamic lawmaking the idea is created outside the consensus and, before it is formulated, it has to be propagated. This needs more than sympathy; it needs enthusiasm. Enthusiasm is not and cannot be a judicial virtue. It means taking sides and, if a judge takes sides on such issues as homosexuality and capital punishment, he loses the appearance of impartiality and quite possibly impartiality itself … It is essential to the stability of society that those whom change hurts should be able to count on evenhanded justice calmly dispensed, not driven forward by the agents of change.
>
> It is this even-handedness which is the chief characteristic of the British judiciary and it is almost beyond price. If it has to be paid for in impersonality and remoteness, the bargain is still a good one … The reputation of the judiciary for independence and impartiality is a national asset of

[272] P Devlin, *Samples of Lawmaking* (Oxford University Press, 1962) 23.
[273] Ibid, 116.
[274] Jaffé, *English and United States Judges and Lawmakers* (n 143 above) 13.

> such richness that one government after another tries to plunder it. This is a danger about which the judiciary itself has been too easygoing. To break up the asset so as to ease the parturition of judicial creativity, an embryo with a doubtful future would be a calamity. The asset which I would deny to governments I would deny also to social reformers.
>
> I have made it plain that I am firmly opposed to judicial creativity or dynamism as I have defined it, that is, of judicial operations in advance of the consensus. The limit of the consensus is not a line that is clearly marked, but I can make certain what would otherwise be uncertain by saying that a judge who is in any doubt about the support of the consensus should not advance at all. This however leaves open quite a large field for judicial activity. In determining its extent it is, I think, necessary to distinguish between common law and statute law. This is because the requirement of consensus affects differently the two types of law. The public is not interested in the common law as a whole. When it becomes interested in any particular section of it, it calls for a statute; the rest it leaves to the judges. The consensus is expressed in a general warrant for judicial lawmaking. This warrant is an informal and rather negative one, amounting to a willingness to let the judges get on with their traditional work on two conditions – first, that they do it in the traditional way, i.e. in accordance with precedent, and second, that parliamentary interference should be regarded as unobjectionable. In relation to statute law, by contrast, there can be no general warrant authorising the judges to do anything except interpret and apply.

Although there was some scope for judicial activism, there were limits:

> In every society there is a division between rulers and ruled. The first mark of a free and orderly society is that the boundaries between the two should be guarded and trespasses from one side or the other independently and impartially determined. The keepers of these boundaries cannot also be among the outriders. The judges are the keepers of the law and the qualities they need for that task are not those of the creative lawmaker. The creative lawmaker is the squire of the social reformer and the quality they both need is enthusiasm. But enthusiasm is rarely consistent with impartiality and never with the appearance of it.
>
> Why is it, I ask in conclusion, that the denunciators of judicial inactivity so rarely pause to throw even a passing curse at the legislators who ought really to be doing the job. They seem so often to swallow without noticing it the quite preposterous excuse that Parliament has no time and to take only a perfunctory interest in an institution such as the Law Commission. Progressives of course are in a hurry to get things done and judges with their plenitude of power could apparently get them done so quickly; there seems to be no limit to what they could do if only they would unshackle themselves from their precedents. It is a great temptation to cast the judiciary as an elite which will bypass the traffic-laden ways of the democratic process. But it would only apparently be a bypass. In truth it would be a road that would never rejoin the highway but would lead inevitably, however long and winding the path, to the totalitarian state.[275]

For Lord Radcliffe, 'The law has to be interpreted before it can be applied and interpretation is a creative activity.'[276] But he preferred the judges to work creatively with caution and without alerting the populace to what they were about: '[I]f judges prefer to adopt the formula – for that is what it is – that they merely declare the law and do not make it, they do no more than show themselves wise men in practice. Their analysis may be weak, but their perception of the nature of law is sound. Men's respect for it will be the greater, the more imperceptible its development.'[277] If public opinion might lose respect for creative judges, Parliament certainly would: 'I think that the judge needs to be particularly circumspect in

[275] For an account of Lord Devlin's own notable decisions developing the common law, see Stevens, *Law and Politics* (n 110 above) 464–66.

[276] Lord Radcliffe, *Not in Feather Beds* (Hamish Hamilton, 1968) 213.

[277] Lord Radcliffe, *Law and Its Compass* (Faber, 1961) 39.

the use of his power to declare the law, not because the principles adopted by parliament are more satisfactory or more enlightened than those which would commend themselves to his mind but because it is unacceptable constitutionally that there should be two independent sources of law-making at work at the same time.'[278] He saw (and exercised) a modest creative role for the judges but without advertising the fact.

One of the most influential judges of the period was Lord Reid, who was a Law Lord from 1948 to 1974 and was senior judge in the House of Lords from 1962.

Lord Reid himself expressed his philosophy in a lecture to the Society of Public Teachers of Law entitled 'The judge as law maker':

Lord Reid, 'The judge as law maker' 12 *Journal of the Society of Public Teachers of Law*, 1972, 22, 24–27

> Some years ago we decided in the House of Lords that we would no longer regard previous decisions as binding. It is good constitutional doctrine that Parliament cannot bind its successors. So we saw no reason why a rule set up by our predecessors should not be altered by us. I am glad we did: we now have more freedom of movement. But it was never intended to lead to a legal revolution. We have got rid of one or two real blots like absolute Crown privilege and the paramountcy of domicile in divorce jurisdiction and there may be a few more to come – but not very many.
>
> Even if we do not greatly relax the doctrine of precedent and if we do not encroach on the sphere of Parliament there is still considerable scope for judges to mould the development of the common law. I propose now to say something of the way in which I think we should proceed in a case where we feel we have some freedom to go in one or other direction.
>
> We should, I think, have regard to common sense, legal principle and public policy in that order. We are here to serve the public, the common ordinary reasonable man …
>
> Sometimes the law has got out of step with common sense. We do not want to have people saying: 'if the law says that the law is an ass'. If they say that about a statute our withers are unwrung. But if they say it about the common law we can usually trace the trouble to one or other of two causes.
>
> Common sense is not static. What passed for common sense three hundred or even one hundred years ago sometimes seems nonsense today. I do not say that modern notions are necessarily better. We may fight against some of them but we can hardly help being influenced. *Communis error facit jus* may seem a paradox but it is a fact. Take for instance the doctrine of common employment – that a master is not liable to his servant for the fault of his fellow servant. That seems nonsense today. But look at the cases from Chief Justice Shaw in Massachusetts to the House of Lords just over a century ago. They thought it was plain good sense. But then in the 1870s the tide began to turn. But the doctrine was too strongly entrenched and we had to wait for Parliament to abolish it …
>
> But common sense alone is not enough. The law is or ought to be organised common sense and that brings me to my second guide, legal principle. That is not very easy to define. We have to avoid on the one hand the rock Scylla where sits the austere figure of Austin and on the other the whirlpool Charybdis where some modern theorists for ever go round in circles. But we must get rid of the idea which still seems to animate some of our pedestrian confreres, that law is a congerie of unrelated rules. That results in the dreary argument that the case is similar to *A v B* and *C v D*, but is distinguishable from *X v Y* and *In re Z* That way lies confusion and uncertainty. We must try to see what was the principle or reason why *A v B* should go one way and *X v Y* the other.
>
> One often says to oneself when some proposition is put forward: 'That just can't be right' and then one looks to see why it cannot be right. Sometimes it offends against common sense, sometimes against one's sense of justice, but more often it just will not stand with legal principles, though it

[278] Ibid, 216.

> may seem to be supported by some judicial observations read apart from their context. I would say that in dealing with precedents the most dangerous pitfall is to treat the words of eminent judges as if they were provisions in an Act of Parliament. You infer from the case the sort of circumstances the judge must have had in mind. There what he said is generally quite right. But you must be very careful when the circumstances are entirely different.
>
> People want two inconsistent things; that the law shall be certain, and that it shall be just and shall move with the times. It is our business to keep both objectives in view. Rigid adherence to precedent will not do. And paying lip service to precedent while admitting fine distinctions gives us the worst of both worlds. On the other hand too much flexibility leads to intolerable uncertainty …
>
> Now I must come to the vexed subject of public policy. Long ago it was said to be an unruly horse and elderly judges did not like unruly horses. That applied particularly to those who have led cloistered lives. But today they are a much smaller proportion than they used to be, thanks partly to most of us having had war service in the field and partly to the fact that economic circumstances prevent most of us from living in a world of our own.
>
> If the law is to keep in step with movements of public opinion then judges must know how ordinary people of all grades of society think and live. You cannot get that from books or courses of study. You must have mixed with all kinds of people and got to know them. If you only listen to those who hit the headlines you get quite the wrong impression. If we are to remain a democratic people those who try to be guided by public opinion must go to the grass roots. That is why it is so valuable for a judge to have given public service of some kind in his early days. I sincerely hope that the 'rat race' of today will not prevent our young men from acquiring the breadth of mind that comes from widespread personal contacts in different strata of society.

Lord Bingham expressed his philosophy in a few vivid words: 'the common law scores its runs in singles: no boundaries, let alone sixes. The common law advances … like one venturing onto a frozen lake, uncertain whether the ice will bear, and proceeding in small, cautious steps …'[279]

Widely regarded as the greatest English judge of his generation, Lord Bingham addressed the issue again in important lectures in 1977[280] and 2005.[281] The inadequacy of the declaratory principle as an explanation of the judicial role was evident, he said when one looked at the objective record of what judges had done:

> In England, the last quarter century has seen fundamental, Judge-made changes in the law relating to public interest immunity; sovereign immunity; forum non conveniens; restitution; tax avoidance schemes; pre-emptive interlocutory remedies; the currency in which judgment may be given; and, pre-eminently, judicial review.[282]

Lord Bingham, however, identified a number of situations in which most judges even of the reformist tendency would regard as apposite signs such as 'No entry', 'Stop', 'Give way' or 'Slow':

(1) Where reasonable and right-minded citizens have legitimately ordered their affairs on the basis of a certain understanding of the law …

[279] 'The way we live now: human rights in the new millenium' 1 *Web Journal Current Legal Issues*, 1998. See also Lord Bingham, 'The judge as lawmaker: an English perspective' in P Rishworth (ed), *The Struggle for Simplicity in the Law: Essays for Lord Cooke of Thorndon* (Butterworths, 1997) 3–12.

[280] 'The judge as lawmaker: an English perspective' in T Bingham, *The Business of Judging: Selected Essays and Speeches* (Oxford University Press, 2010) ch 2, 26–34.

[281] Lord Bingham, 'The judge: active or passive?' Maccabean Lecture, 139 *Proceedings of the British Academy*, 2006, 55.

[282] 'The judge as lawmaker' (n 280 above) ch 2, 29.

(2) Where, although a rule of law is seen to be defective, its amendment calls for a detailed legislative code, with qualifications, exceptions and safeguards which cannot feasibly be introduced by judicial decisions. Such cases call for a rule of judicial abstinence, particularly where wise and effective reform of the law calls for research and consultation of a kind which no Court of law is fitted to undertake.
(3) Where the question involves an issue of current social policy on which there is no consensus within the community.
(4) Where an issue is the subject of current legislative activity. If Parliament is actually engaged in deciding what the rule should be in a given legal situation, the Courts are generally wise to await the outcome of that deliberation rather than to pre-empt the result by judicial decision.
(5) Where the issue arises in a field far removed from ordinary judicial experience.[283]

Even where a judge recognised that a change in the law was called for, they were well advised, Lord Bingham said, to walk circumspectly.

> On the whole, the law advances in small steps, not by giant bounds. Many Judges will seek to adopt the approach of Bacon, in his declaration that 'The work which I propound tendeth to pruning and grafting the law, and not to ploughing up and planting it again'.[284]

In 2014 the Supreme Court had to decide whether the Suicide Act 1961 which made it a crime to assist another to commit suicide was compatible with the ECHR.[285] Lord Sumption was one of four Justices who thought the question was for Parliament rather than judges:

> 230 Where there is more than one rational choice the question may or may not be for Parliament, depending on the nature of the issue. Is it essentially legislative in nature? Does it by its nature require a democratic mandate? The question whether relaxing or qualifying the current absolute prohibition on assisted suicide would involve unacceptable risks to vulnerable people is in my view a classic example of the kind of issue which should be decided by Parliament. There are, I think, three main reasons. The first is that, as I have suggested, the issue involves a choice between two fundamental but mutually inconsistent moral values, upon which there is at present no consensus in our society. Such choices are inherently legislative in nature. The decision cannot fail to be strongly influenced by the decision-makers' personal opinions about the moral case for assisted suicide. This is entirely appropriate if the decision-makers are those who represent the community at large. It is not appropriate for professional judges. The imposition of their personal opinions on matters of this kind would lack all constitutional legitimacy.
>
> 231. Secondly, Parliament has made the relevant choice. It passed the Suicide Act in 1961, and as recently as 2009 amended section 2 without altering the principle. In recent years there have been a number of bills to decriminalise assistance to suicide, at least in part, but none has been passed into law …
>
> 232. Third, the Parliamentary process is a better way of resolving issues involving controversial and complex questions of fact arising out of moral and social dilemmas. The legislature has access to a fuller range of expert judgment and experience than forensic litigation can possibly provide. It is better able to take account of the interests of groups not represented or not sufficiently represented before the court in resolving what is surely a classic 'polycentric problem'. But, perhaps critically in a case like this where firm factual conclusions are elusive, Parliament can legitimately

[283] 'The judge as lawmaker' (n 280 above) 31–32.
[284] Ibid 32.
[285] *R (on the application of Nicklinson and another v Ministry of Justice* [2014] UKSC 38.

act on an instinctive judgment about what the facts are likely to be in a case where the evidence is inconclusive or slight.[286]

Lord Sumption developed his concerns in the 2019 Reith Lectures. Under the Freedom of Information Act 2000 ministers have a veto on disclosure if they consider it contrary to the public interest. The Attorney General decided that disclosure of letters written by Prince Charles to ministers was not in the public interest. The Supreme Court quashed the decision by a majority of five to two.[287] Lord Sumption, who did not sit on the case, criticised the decision which he thought was part of a pattern of decisions. ('For my part, I think that there is no reason why a statute should not say that on an issue like this a minister answerable to Parliament is a more appropriate judge of the public interest than a court.') He suggested that no other modern case revealed so clearly the judges' 'expansive view' of the rule of law:

> Whether the Prince of Wales' letters should be disclosed is not in itself a very important question. But the same technique has been applied more discreetly to sensitive issues of social policy about which the public feels more strongly. Examples over the past half century include education, subsidised fares on public transport, social security benefits, the use of overseas development funds, statutory defences to murder, the establishment of public enquiries and many others. On immigration and penal policy the courts have for years applied values of their own, which are at odds with the harsher policies adopted with strong public support by Parliament and successive governments. Most people's reactions to decisions like these depends on whether they agree with the result. But we ought to care about how our decisions are made, and not just about the outcome. We ought to ask whether litigation is really the right way to resolve differences of opinion about what are really questions of policy ...[288]

The judicial resolution of policy issues undermined the single biggest advantage of the political process which, Lord Sumption suggested, was 'to accommodate the divergent interests and opinions of citizens'. (p 41).

> Litigation can rarely mediate differences. It is a zero sum game. The winners carry off the prize, and the losers pay. Litigation is not a consultative or participatory process. It is an appeal to law. Law is rational. Law is coherent. Law is analytically consistent and rigorous. But in public affairs these are not always virtues. Opacity, inconsistency and fudge may be intellectually impure, which is why lawyers do not like them. But they are often inseparable from the kind of compromises that we have to make as a society if we are to live together in peace. (pp 41–42)

Ronald Dworkin describing his model judge, Hercules, as 'no activist', said that Hercules will refuse to substitute his judgment for that of the legislature when he believes the issue is primarily one of policy rather than principle, when the argument is about the best strategies for achieving the overall collective interest through goals like prosperity or the eradication of poverty or the right balance between economy and conservation. In his view courts are the forum of principle, whereas policy is properly the province of government.[289]

[286] See also J Sumption QC, 'Judicial and political decision-making the uncertain boundary', FA Mann Lecture 2011. The lecture, given after he had been appointed to the Supreme Court, provoked a strong critical response from former Lord Justice Sedley – 'Judicial politics' 34 *London Review of Books,* 23 February 2012, 15–16 – accessible via Google. For another view see J Jowell, 'Judicial deference: servility, civility or institutional capacity?' *Public Law*, 2003, 592.

[287] *R (on the application of Evans v Attorney General* [2015] AC 1787.

[288] Jonathan Sumption, *Trials of the State – Law and the Decline of Politics* (Profile Books, 2019) 38–39.

[289] R Dworkin, *Law's Empire* (Belknap Press, 1986) 398.

Patrick Atiyah contrasted the approach of English and American judges to law-making. 'English judges, he suggested, were much less adventurous than American judges. One reason he thought was that 'English judges do generally believe that law is a system of rules, and act on that belief to a greater degree than most American judges, particularly in courts of last resort':[290]

> A judge's duty, an English judge would say, is primarily to apply the law, and previous judicial decisions in the courts of last resort *are* the law. The judge does, of course, have a secondary, lawmaking function where there are no prior decisions, but these gaps in the law are relatively few and far between. Only in quite exceptional circumstances, therefore, should the judge's secondary, law-making function be permitted to operate where a clear prior decision already determines the rules. These perceptions of law, rules, and gaps in the system are, of course, open to philosophical challenge, but few observers of the English legal scene would dispute that they are held by an overwhelming number of judges, and indeed by most practicing lawyers too. Conversely, equally few observers of the American legal scene would doubt that, though similar perceptions are widely found in American courts, alternative perceptions also may be found. I would hypothesize that many American judges regard rules as having less importance than do English judges; that they see judicial decisions as illustrations of underlying principles (often seen as drawn from morality or natural law) rather than as rules in themselves and of themselves; that they see the law-making function of courts of last resort as more important than English judges do; and that they do not in consequence feel bound by prior decisions to the same degree as English judges.

Professor Atiyah thought that one reason was the different background of English and American judges, with the American judge being more likely to be and to see himself as part of the political process. English judges rely more on the argument of counsel than American judges who often do their own research. In United States courts the role of dissent is quite different. A dissenting judge in an English court will follow the majority view next time the issue comes up. American dissenting judges regard themselves as free to continue their disagreement with fellow judges from one case to the next.

Also, Atiyah noted, in United States cases, it was much more common for there to be a dissent. In the 1980 term, no fewer than 69 per cent of full opinions were subject to a dissent. In the House of Lords they varied from year to year from 10 per cent to 46 per cent. Even Lord Denning, a judge known to be a dissenter, dissented in only a small minority of cases – 4.7 per cent of 1,742 cases as compared with Justice William Douglas of the United States Supreme Court who dissented in 19.2 per cent of 6,863 cases.

In the first three years of the new UK Supreme Court one quarter of cases (24 per cent) had at least one dissent but the proportion of dissents went down significantly after Lord Neuberger became President in October 2012. Between mid-June 2013 and mid-February 2014 there was not one dissent![291] In the four years 2021–24, the proportion of UK Supreme Court cases in which there was one or more dissent was 7 per cent, 8 per cent, 12 per cent, 9 per cent.[292] The contrast with the US Supreme Court is very striking. In those

[290] P Atiyah, 'Lawyers and rules: some Anglo-American comparisons' 37 *Southwestern Law Journal*, 1983, 545.

[291] Giving the First Annual BAILII Lecture, Lord Neuberger said: '[W]hile I am emphatically not suggesting banning dissenting judgments, it may be that we could have fewer of them, and they could be shorter. Lord Ackner was supposed to have observed that one only dissents when one's sense of outrage at the majority decision outweighs one's natural indolence, so it could be said that I am recommending more indolence. Perhaps a judge who is considering dissenting should ask himself whether (i) they feel strongly enough, (ii) the point is important enough, (iii) it would help the development of the law, and (iv) it would help the understanding of the law, if there was a dissenting Judgment' ('No judgment – no justice', 20 November 2012, para 28).

[292] Professor Brice Dickson's annual report in the *New Law Journal* on the Supreme Court's output the previous year.

three years the proportion of cases with one or more dissent was 62 per cent, 88 per cent, 72 per cent.[293]

The significance of the greater frequency of dissents, Atiyah suggested, was that it reflected a different perception of the nature of the judicial role and even of the nature of law itself:

> First, judges who are more concerned to impress the public with the idea that law in some sense represents neutral and eternal values of truth and right may be more concerned to present a united front, and suppress their differences of opinion. Hence the infrequency of dissent in a particular jurisdiction may reflect 'acceptance of the notion that unanimity denotes precision and truth and, therefore, is more convincing.' I think English judges are more influenced than most American judges by a desire to promote this goal. By contrast, American judges often appear to have viewed dissent as a way of asserting 'a personal, or individual responsibility … of a higher order than the institutional responsibility owed by each to the Court, or by the Court to the public.'
>
> Second, as I have already suggested, judges who perceive the law as a system of rules binding on the judges as on everyone else are more likely to arrive at the same conclusion in a given case. For to put it at the lowest level, such a view of the nature of law and the judicial rule narrows the range of choice open to the judge and therefore makes unanimity more likely.

In France, Belgium, the Netherlands, Italy and most other civil law countries dissents are prohibited, though in Germany the highest constitutional court does now allow dissents.[294] Dissent is not permitted either in the Court of Justice of the European Union. Lord Neuberger said of this: 'One only has to look at some of the judgments of the [court] in Luxembourg to see how compulsory unanimity can result in decisions which (i) are incomprehensible, (ii) have internally inconsistent reasoning, (iii) do not answer the issue that has been referred, or (iv) manage to enjoy all these three regrettable characteristics.'[295]

One of the most sophisticated attempts to diagnose when courts should and should not legislate is that of Professor Michael Freeman of University College, London University.[296] He listed certain basic differences between courts and legislatures. First, judges were not democratically answerable to the electorate, which made it inappropriate for them to enact their own social policies. Secondly, courts had to justify their decisions by articulating reasons, whereas legislators were not under this constraint. Thirdly, judges came from a narrow social background and represented only one profession. The information available to a court when it was considering law reform was very limited. Also the range of options available to the courts was much more limited:

> When Parliament decides that something ought to be the law it can consider the different ways of achieving that goal. It might wish to stop policemen extracting confessions from suspects. It could do this in a number of ways. It could make such confessions inadmissible evidence. It could make the extraction of confessions a criminal offence and expose the offending police officer to a long term of imprisonment. It could set up a state board which paid compensation to victims of such police conduct. It could direct that offending police officers be dismissed or demoted. But the judge could only adopt the first of these steps. Or, to take a second example, the development

[293] The November (No 1) issue of the *Harvard Law Review* each year reports the Supreme Court statistics for the previous term.

[294] See generally M Kirby, 'Judicial dissent – common law and civil law traditions' 123 *Law Quarterly Review*, 2007, 379–400.

[295] Lord Neuberger, 'No judgment, no justice', First Annual BAILII Lecture, 20 November 2012.

[296] M Freeman, 'Standards of adjudication, judicial law making and prospective overruling' 26 *Current Legal Problems*, 1973, 166.

of a 'deserted wife's equity'[297] by the Court of Appeal was an attempt (some would say of dubious propriety) to ground protection for the deserted wife in legal principle. With its collapse in *Ainsworth*,[298] the legislature intervened and passed the Matrimonial Homes Act in 1967. This set up machinery whereby a spouse could gain protection by registering a charge on the other spouse's property. The Court of Appeal had suggested this might be the solution, but with a court's limited powers they were unable to initiate such a scheme.

Judges then do not have available to them the very important instruments of administrative enforcement, licensing or positive rewards. They can use only damages and specific orders, injunctions, specific performance, *certiorari*, *mandamus*, declaratory judgments and so on. And without this institutional machinery the steps they can undertake are limited. (p 178)

Another distinguishing feature had been seen by Lon Fuller in his *Anatomy of the Law* (Penguin, 1971). The rules applied by judges to individual cases must be 'brought into, and maintained in, some systematic interrelationship; they must display some coherent internal structure' (p 134). Parliament by contrast can take 'leaps into the dark'. If judicial decisions were to be predictable by practitioners and their clients, they must be grounded in principle. ('This means that judges develop the law incrementally' (Freeman, 'Standards of adjudication' (n 296 above) 179).) Society expected judges to decide disputes in a rational way. There was much room for creativity but the judge did not have a clean slate on which to write.

Freeman then illustrated what he regarded as good and bad examples of judicial activity and inactivity. He distinguished between judicial restraint, judicial cowardice, judicial boldness, and judicial creativity.

Judicial restraint was shown in *Morgans v Launchbury* [1973] AC 127 which raised for decision the question whether injured persons could sue a wife whose husband had taken her car with permission and then loaned it to a third person who caused the accident. On accepted principles prevailing at that time there was no doubt that no such action lay, but the House of Lords was urged to introduce a new rule. It refused to do so (the Court of Appeal had held for the plaintiffs): Lord Salmon recognised that

it is an important function of this House to develop and adapt the common law to meet the changing needs of time

however:

[i]n the present case … the proposed development constitutes such a radical and far-reaching departure from accepted principle that it seems to me to smack of naked legislation.[299]

There were similar sentiments in the judgments of Lord Cross and Lord Pearson.[300] But it was in Lord Wilberforce's judgment that one got the clearest exposition of the problem.

He was in no doubt that some adaptation of common law rules of agency could be made by the judges. He admitted that traditional concepts of vicarious liability might be proving inadequate. He saw some attractions in being creative. But he spurned any invitation to do so in this case. His reasons deserve careful examination. He said that the assumption was that it was desirable to fix liability in cases of negligent driving on the owner of the car. Such a policy was disputable, though His Lordship saw no need to discuss such a question. He rather averted his attention to the different systems that could be introduced. He catalogued four: a system of liability based on

[297] In *Bendall v McWhirter* [1952] 2 QB 466 and many other cases until 1965.
[298] [1965] AC 1175.
[299] [1973] AC 127, 151.
[300] Ibid, 142–43 and 146.

the concept of the 'matrimonial' car; one based on the 'family' car; one stating that any owner who permits another to use his car should be liable by the fact of permission; and possibly even a system of strict liability. But as Lord Wilberforce rightly said:

I do not know on what principle your Lordships acting judicially can prefer one of these systems to the others or on what basis any one can be formulated with sufficient precision or its exceptions defined. The choice is one of social policy; there are arguments for and against each of them.[301]

Freeman continued:

> … To summarise, *Morgans v Launchbury* shows judicial restraint at its best. It was a polycentric dispute *par excellence*. It involved a policy choice upon which the judges had no information or guidance. Law-making would have involved upturning the rightful expectations of thousands. The effect of a wider test on insurance, on premiums, on organisations like the Motor Insurers' Bureau could only be guessed at; and that is not an adequate basis for law-making. (pp 187–89)

To illustrate *judicial cowardice* Freeman used the case of *Myers v DPP* [1965] AC 1001. The question was whether the House of Lords would stretch the exceptions to the hearsay rule to include records kept in a mechanical way by a business. The prosecution wanted to introduce in evidence the numbers fixed on cars to show that the defendants had stolen and altered parts of cars in order to conceal their origin. Three Law Lords (Lords Morris, Hodson and Reid) held the evidence was inadmissible.

> Lord Morris stated that it had been decided eighty years earlier that hearsay is not admissible unless authority 'be found to justify its reception within some established … rule.'[302] Lord Hodson took the position that to create a new exception 'would be judicial legislation with a vengeance in an attempt to introduce reform of the law of evidence which if needed can properly be dealt with only by the legislature'.[303] Lord Reid believed that the 'common law must be developed to meet changing economic conditions and habits of thought … But there are limits … If we are to extend the law it must be by the development and application of fundamental principles … If an exception were created here, others should be created, and there would be a series of appeals … If we are to give a wide interpretation to our judicial functions questions of policy cannot be wholly excluded, and it seems to me to be against public policy to produce uncertainty.'[304] He too advocated legislation.
>
> Lord Pearce and Lord Donovan dissented. Lord Pearce's judgment is particularly persuasive. He showed that the admission of the evidence in question was fully in accordance with the shared principles and expectations of the legal profession. On a technical matter of 'lawyers' law' concerned with the machinery of justice this must be the appropriate audience. He demonstrated that they could admit the evidence in question without violating the substance of the rule purporting to exclude it. Indeed, that there were principles in the law which clamoured for its acceptance. Suppose, he argued, the anonymous workman could be identified. If he was dead, 'the records would be admissible as declarations in the course of duty.'[305]
>
> Legislation was in due course passed,[306] but judicial legislation was feasible and apposite. The laws of evidence are better developed by those who operate them than by Parliament, though radical policy changes even in this area must be left to the legislature. If Lord Pearce's reasoning had been followed it is difficult to see whose reasonable expectations could have been thwarted. (pp. 190–92)

[301] Ibid, 136.
[302] [1965] AC 1001, 1028.
[303] Ibid, 1034.
[304] Ibid, 1021–22.
[305] Ibid, 1036.
[306] Criminal Evidence Act 1965.

Judicial boldness, Freeman said, was exemplified by *Knuller v DPP* [1973] AC 435, which raised the question of extending the criminal law. *Shaw v DPP* [1962] AC 220, in which the House of Lords had in effect invented a new offence of conspiracy to corrupt public morals, had met with widespread opprobrium. But in *Knuller* the Law Lords went further and recognised another offence – of conspiracy to outrage public decency. The case was brought against the publisher of *International Times* in respect of small ads by homosexuals.

> The Lords in *Knuller* created new law ... Lord Diplock's judgment is an exemplary exposure of the illogical, unhistorical and often hypocritical reasoning underlying the judgments in *Shaw*'s case and those of his brethren in *Knuller*. But the other four Lords tied themselves into knots in their attempts to rationalise their judgments ...
>
> *Knuller* had injected uncertainty into criminal law and its administration. It flies in the face of legislative policy[307] and ministerial assurance.[308] If it endorses the values of certain sectional interests it flouts others. In a democratic society consensus demands compromise. Legislation embodies this: *Knuller* rejects it. It exemplifies judicial law-making at its worst. (pp 192–93, 194–95)

The final category identified by Freeman, that of *judicial creativity*, he illustrated by *British Railways Board v Herrington* [1972] AC 877, in which the House of Lords had to decide whether to overrule its own decision of *Addie v Dumbreck* [1929] AC 358 on the liability of occupiers towards trespassers. The most interesting judgment, Freeman thought, was that of Lord Wilberforce:

> He made his ideology clear. A law of tort based on fault liability was 'outdated'. '[C]ases such as these could be more satisfactorily dealt with by a modern system of public enterprise liability devised by Parliament.'[309] But such wholesale institutional change could not be devised by judges, even if it were desirable for them to do so. Parliament had, of course, passed in 1957 the Occupiers' Liability Act, and this had preserved the common law ruling on trespassers. This did not mean that 'the House was bound hand and foot by *Addie's* case at its narrowest.'[310]
>
> The common law, his lordship argued, 'always leaves a residue to be completed by common sense.'[311] Common sense dictated that the development of the law would best be served by concentrating on the particular type of case which worries the courts and on which the law has been tested by experience. Most twentieth-century litigation was brought against public utilities. A duty of care arises, he held, 'because of the existence, near to the public, of a dangerous situation.'[312] ...
>
> Law-making such as that perpetrated by Lord Wilberforce is a legitimate activity. It does not create injustice (the argument of 'system') as public utilities and, for example, farmers are not 'alike'. In one sense what is being done is classification of legal concepts on to a more factual basis. It is right for a judge to take the minor step taken by Lord Wilberforce. He knows that other judges now have a framework, that as new problems arise there is something against which to test the formulation. *Herrington* clears a lot of dead wood, and enables judges to focus on unresolved problems. It may be that as they do this, as the *Herrington* ruling is tested and re-tested, that a new principle will emerge. But for the present the common law has been developed to accommodate a social problem: the pre-existing rules have hardly changed yet the seed of public enterprise liability has been sown. (pp 198–200)

[307] Obscene Publications Act 1959; Theatres Act 1968.
[308] HC, *Hansard*, vol 695, col 1212, 3 June 1964.
[309] [1972] AC 877, 922.
[310] Ibid, 921.
[311] Ibid.
[312] Ibid.

Robert Stevens' study of the House of Lords' judges from 1800 to 1976 traced a succession of stages.[313] Stevens traced the gradual shift in the modern era from the period of the rigid and narrow formalism under Lord Simonds to a more open and policy-oriented period under Lords Reid, Wilberforce, Diplock, Salmon and Simon: 'By the mid-seventies it [the House of Lords] was no longer regarded as the restater of accepted doctrines, but rather as the incremental developer of new doctrines … [W]hile the belief in the predictability of "clear rules" was no doubt still stronger than in any other common law jurisdiction, the belief in the anonymity and irrelevance of the judicial contribution had largely evaporated.'[314] The 1966 Practice Statement (p 221 above) advising the world that the House of Lords might depart from its previous decisions added legitimacy to a process that had been going on since the late 1950s and was accelerating in the early 1960s.[315] The Statement seemed to confirm that Parliament had no objection to the judges making law in those areas of society primarily entrusted to dispute settlement in the courts. 'Thus it is not surprising that, although rarely mentioned, the statement encouraged a greater flexibility of approach and, in particular, an emphasis on principle rather than rule and precedent and a noticeably greater inclination to talk about policy.'[316]

It was true that the traditional view of the role of the courts had by no means disappeared. A substantial element in the profession still preferred to emphasise the role of logic, certainty and predictability, and to play down discretion and creativity. Thus Sir Henry Fisher, formerly a High Court judge, attacked the 1966 Practice Statement arguing that judges 'should refrain from broad statements on principle and from obiter dicta. They should be scrupulous to apply the law as it exists even if they think it to be wrong or unfair or unjust and should resist the temptation to twist the law to conform with their sympathies or theories, as the proper instrument for the reform of the law is Parliament, aided where necessary by the Law Commission, a Law Reform Committee, or Royal or departmental commission.'[317] Professor LCB Gower, a former Law Commissioner, urged the relative unsuitability of the House of Lords as a law-reform agency, and even the Law Commission had criticised the Law Lords' reform of the law on occupier's liability towards trespassers in *Herrington v British Railways Board* [1972] AC 877 because it had not produced 'a clear principle applicable to the generality of cases'.[318]

> Yet in spite of all these factors, by the mid-1970s forces were gathering and trends were developing that in the long run were likely to accentuate the creative force of the final appeal court … By English standards the approach to precedent evidenced rapid changes. After 1966 even the more conventional law lords began to talk the language, if not the litany, of judicial creativity. When overruling, the House talked less about the errors of legal logic made in the prior case and more about the underlying policies that had changed since the earlier decision.
>
> In 1955 … law-making by judges had been seen in simplistic terms – it either competed with Parliament or it did not, and it was either good or bad. That had been largely abandoned. Various North American influences helped inject into English thinking the American concepts of judicial

[313] Professor Alan Paterson similarly analysed the attitude of the Law Lords in terms of changes over time in his much more limited sixteen-year period – 1957–62, 1962–66, 1966–73 – A Paterson, *The Law Lords* (Macmillan, 1982) 132–53.

[314] Stevens, *Law and Politics* (n 110 above) 589.

[315] Ibid, 621.

[316] Ibid.

[317] 119 *Solicitors' Journal*, 1975, 854.

[318] *Report of the Law Commission on Occupiers' Liability* (Cmnd 6928, 1975).

> restraint and judicial activism[319] – that there are shades of desirability of law-making. Rather than the competition between the legislature and judiciary that had so concerned Radcliffe, it was increasingly argued that '[t]he organs of government are partners in the enterprise of lawmaking'. Out of this … grew a much greater awareness of when judicial legislation was appropriate.[320]

Judicial law-making in the field of criminal law seems to be especially problematic. ATH Smith, discussing the creative powers of the courts, listed the main objections to judicial law-making as the usurpation of Parliament's function, the creation of uncertainty and the retrospective effect of judge-made law.[321] The author suggested that waiting for reform of the criminal law through legislation was the lesser evil 'compared with judicial law-making which seems to create at least as many problems as it solves … and additionally is objectionable in point of principle as a means of law reform'. An example was the decision of the House of Lords in *C v DPP* [1996] AC 1 upholding the presumption that a person between the age of ten and fourteen is deemed not to have the intent to make their act criminal unless it can be positively proved by the prosecution that they knew what they did was seriously wrong. The Divisional Court ([1994] 3 WLR 888) had held that the presumption of *doli incapax* was outdated and no longer had any application in the changed conditions of society. The House of Lords agreed that the presumption had been 'subject to weighty criticism over many years by committees, by academic writers and by the courts'. Nevertheless it still represented the law. In a twenty-page judgment with which the four other Law Lords agreed, Lord Lowry said that if the rule was to be changed it should be done by Parliament. (The invitation was taken up and the rule was changed in the Crime and Disorder Act 1998, s 34.)

Professor, now Lord, Burrows, in his 2017 Hamlyn Lectures,[322] referred to Lord Goff's 'wonderful speech' in *Woolwich Equitable Building Society v Inland Revenue Commissioners*[323] in which the common law of unjust enrichment was developed to allow restitution as of right from a public authority that had obtained payments *ultra vires*. Lord Goff had pointed out there that if judges had held back 'we would not have had the modern law of negligence or freezing injunctions or the modern law of judicial review'. Burrows wrote:[324] 'One can add that we would also not have had other famous examples of common law developments such as the removal of the rule that a husband cannot rape his wife,[325] or the award of mental distress damages in contract,[326] or the removal of the mistake of law bar to restitution in the law of unjust enrichment.'[327]

Burrows contrasted the advantages and disadvantages of legislative as against judicial law reform:

> The advantages of legislative law reform include that one can deal with a wide area in precisely the way one wishes; there is no need to wait for a particular case to reach the highest court; the change can be, and almost always is, non-retrospective; the reform can be fully informed by

[319] Jaffé, *English and United States Judges as Lawmakers* (n 127 above) 28–29.

[320] Stevens, *Law and politics* (n 110 above) 624.

[321] ATH Smith, 'Judicial law-making in the criminal law' 100 *Law Quarterly Review*, 1984, 46. See to like effect Marianne Giles, 'Judicial law-making in the criminal courts: the case of marital rape' *Criminal Law Review*, 1992, 407.

[322] A Burrows, *Thinking About Statutes* (Cambridge University Press, 2018) 75.

[323] 1993 AC 70.

[324] Ibid.

[325] *R v R* [1992] AC 599 (HL).

[326] *Jarvis v Swan's Tours Ltd* [1973] QB 233.

[327] *Kleinwort Benson Ltd v Lincoln City Council* [1999] 2 AC 349.

> different points of view, research and consultation; and difficult decisions are ultimately legitimated because the process can be seen to reflect the democratic will. In contrast, the disadvantage of legislative law reform as against judicial law reform include that it is difficult to find time in the legislative programme for 'non sexy' technical law reform, there is a danger of legislation freezing the law so that 'mistakes' cannot be corrected so easily or, perhaps expressed more accurately, the law cannot so easily be adapted to changing circumstances and values; the very process of a bill going through Parliament can undermine and complicate its drafting and structure thereby producing law that is irrational and incoherent; and legislation can produce a clash between the common law and the statutory inroad which may produce costly and problematic demarcation issues.[328]

For more views on judicial attitudes to law-making see Anthony Lester, 'English judges as law-makers' *Public Law*, 1993, 269–90. See further Alan Paterson, *The Law Lords* (Macmillan, 1982) chapters 6 and 7; JAG Griffith, *Judicial Politics Since 1920* (Blackwell, 1993); Justice Michael Kirby, *Judicial Activism, Authority, Principle and Policy in the Judicial Method* (Sweet & Maxwell, 2004). Kirby's lectures, with special reference to Australia, traced how the traditional declaratory theory of law was vanquished by the Realist school – the teachings of Pound, Holmes, Cardozo, Learned Hand, Karl Llewellyn and others adapted and proclaimed by judges like Lord Reid and Lord Denning had led to what Kirby calls a Legal Reformation in virtually every country of the common law. But he warned that more recently, there had been a Counter-Reformation. The chief object of his lectures, he said, was 'to give a warning about the strategies of those who lead a call to return to the land of intellectual fairytales' (p 44). In the Counter-Reformation the expression 'judicial activism' was a term of abuse. Judges, especially in the United States and in Australia, had fallen victim to furious attack. A federal judge of the United States District Court wrote that 'judicial activism' had become a code word to induce public disapproval of a court action that a politician opposed but was powerless to overturn. In most cases, the mindless incantation of the phrase amounted to a political retrial which touched the congregation of voters on an emotional level without promoting any reasoned discourse amongst them (p 46). Kirby said that he had collected some of the more printable comments made by critics of 'judicial activism' in Australia. The courts and the justices had been labelled 'bogus', 'pusillanimous and evasive', guilty of 'plunging Australia into the abyss', a 'pathetic … self-appointed [group of] Kings and Queens', a group of 'basket weavers', 'purveyors of intellectual dishonesty …'[329]

For a recent significant contribution see Sir Philip (now Lord) Sales, 'The Common Law: Context and Method', 135 *Law Quarterly Review*, 2019, 47–66.

In a challenging article, Professor Danny Nicol of the University of Westminster, suggested that at least in the field of human rights fierce exchanges between politicians and the judiciary should be welcomed not deplored.[330] Judges and politicians, he said, were both engaged in decisions as to the good life or the public interest:

> In the 1940s and 1950s, judges located themselves on different terrain from politicians. Judicial activity was depicted as a technical specialism … inhabiting a world neutrally detached from the contests of political ideas and argument.

[328] A Burrows, *Thinking about Statutes* (Cambridge University Press, 2018) 78, fn 81.

[329] MD Kirby, 'Attacks on judges: a universal phenomenon' 72 *Australian Law Journal*, 1998, 599, 601. See also Allan C Hutchinson, 'Judges and politics: an essay from Canada' 24 *Legal Studies*, 2004, 275.

[330] D Nicol, 'Law and politics after the Human Rights Act' *Public Law*, 2006, 722.

In the era of the ECHR this was no longer plausible.

> Interpretation has become extremely flexible, not least because the Convention rights do not admit of a singular correct construction. Precedent has become unprecedently pliable. The subject-matter of cases focuses increasingly on the territory of the politicians ... Rather than seeing judges as operating on a higher plane, courts and politicians might more fruitfully be conceived as constitutional actors occupying the same territory and at the same level ... But whereas the positions advanced by politicians depend primarily on their place in the party spectrum, the courts present a more united ideology with a particular focus on the rights dimension of a constitutional conflict ... [C]ourts need to reconfigure themselves as ideological partisans who will lay down fearless challenges to legislators in defence of constitutional liberties. For its part, Parliament is entitled to reply with its view of how rights conflicts should be resolved. No doubt this will lead to tempestuous argument, but so much the better; argument would be the best possible sign that Britain takes rights seriously. Far from being condemned as 'constitutional crisis', disagreement should rather epitomise the nation's constitutional culture, a source of pride in the vibrancy of our political community.[331]

7.15. The Supreme Court

The UK Supreme Court was established in 2009.[332] This final section starts with an assessment two years later by Professor Kate Malleson of the significance and likely development of the new court.

Kate Malleson, 'The Evolving Role of the UK Supreme Court', *Public Law*, 2011, 754

> It is very likely that the Supreme Court will, in many respects, continue to follow the approach of the Appellate Committee given that its formal powers and its judicial personnel remain much the same. Yet because the judicial role which the new Supreme Court Justices have inherited has been a far more dynamic one than is generally acknowledged it is likely that the Supreme Court will evolve into a top court which more closely resembles the supreme courts or constitutional courts found in other parts of the world. The combined effects of the UK membership of the European Union in the 1970s, the development of judicial review in the 1980s and 1990s, the provisions of the Human Rights Act 1998 and the devolution settlement have transformed the functions of the UK's top court. By the time the Appellate Committee was reconstituted into the Supreme Court in 2009 it had come to engage with contentious social and political issues in a way that would have once been considered unthinkable ...
>
> Looking back at the development of the Appellate Committee over the last 40 years of its existence, it is in relation to the determination of rights-based core constitutional values that the role of the Court has changed most dramatically. This change has come about partly as a result of the powers which have been given to the Court by Parliament, most obviously through the Human Rights Act 1998. But of equal, if not greater significance, is the expansion in the role of the Appellate Committee brought about as a result of the choices the Court itself made as to what cases it would hear and what approach it would adopt to the exercise of its powers. The history of the development of other top courts around the world, most notably the US Supreme Court, reminds us that ultimately the future role of the UK Supreme Court lies in the hands of the Justices themselves. The fact that the power of constitutional review in the US was developed by the Supreme

[331] Ibid, 749–51.

[332] For references to the history see 4.1.1 and especially n 3.

Court suggests that there is little doubt that the UK Supreme Court, operating within the flexibility of an uncodified constitution, could similarly expand its powers if it so chose …

What is clear is that the Appellate Committee in 2008 was in many respects a very different body from the Court in, say, 1968.[333] Both in terms of the type of cases it heard and the effects of its judgments, the Court shifted quite radically over that forty year period from a body which dealt largely with private law cases often involving highly technical legal questions to one which tended to focus on public law cases some of which were highly controversial and many of which had an impact on an increasingly wide range of social and political issues.

While the significance of the careful crafting of the HRA to retain parliamentary sovereignty should not be underestimated, it is nevertheless the case that the consequence of the powers given to the higher courts under the Act are such that in many cases there is little difference, in practice, between their decision-making under ss. 3 and 4 HRA, and the judgments of the Canadian or US Supreme Courts exercised under their more extensive powers of constitutional review. As Lord Phillips has noted, referring to the 'remarkable' decision in *Ghaidan*:[334]

> '… the House held that the true interpretation of section 3 of the 1998 Act required, where necessary, that the courts, and indeed other public authorities, should give to provisions in subsequent statutes a meaning and effect that conflicted with the legislative intention of the Parliaments enacting those statutes.'[335]

The bold approach to s 3 adopted by the courts in cases such as *Ghaidan*, has been matched by an inverse timidity on the part of Parliament in relation to s 4. To date, Parliament has taken steps to amend legislation in all cases in which the courts have issued a declaration of incompatibility. In effect, therefore, the provisions of the HRA have meant that the higher courts in the UK have had the last word in relation to a number of key human rights issues over the last 10 years. The consequence of these developments is that the first cohort of Supreme Court Justices, all but one of whom were promoted from the UK appellate courts,[336] have sat on a wide range of controversial human rights cases and have been schooled in the notion that the top courts must, through the HRA and judicial review, engage fully with a complete range of social and political issues. There are no longer any 'no-go areas' for courts in the way that there once were.

Caseload

One very tangible piece of evidence demonstrating the evolving role of the Appellate Committee which the Supreme Court has inherited is the changing nature of the Court's caseload in its later years. A quantitative review of the work of the Appellate Committee carried out by Shah and Poole in 2004, concluded that public law issues had moved 'from the periphery to the centre of the business of our highest court'.[337] This development was, of course, a direct consequence of the provisions of the HRA, but it is also in line with a longer-term trend in the changing caseload of

[333] See M Beloff, 'The end of the twentieth century: the House of Lords 1982–2000' in L Blom Cooper et al (eds), *The Judicial House of Lords: 1876 to 2009* (Oxford University Press, 2009); B Dickson, 'A hard act to follow: the Bingham court, 2000–2008' in Blom-Cooper et al (eds), *The Judicial House of Lords: 1876 to 2009* (Oxford University Press, 2009).

[334] See p 228 above (ed).

[335] Lord Phillips, First Lord Alexander of Weedon Lecture, 19 April 2010, p 38.

[336] Not true in the case of Lord Sumption, who was appointed straight from the Bar. (ed) (It is said that eighteen months earlier Sumption's appointment was blocked by judges who objected to someone being parachuted into the highest court direct from practice.) Sumption's is the only such case in recent years. Two earlier precedents were Lord Reid in 1948 (previously Lord Advocate) and Lord Radcliffe in 1949. (In addition to his practice at the Bar, Radcliffe had chaired several high-profile public inquiries including the boundary commission which led to the independence of India and Pakistan.)

[337] S Shah and T Poole, 'The impact of the Human Rights Act on the House of Lords' (n 217) 347–71. See also, S Shah and T Poole, 'The Law Lords and human rights' 74 *Modern Law Review*, 2011, 79.

the Court away from relatively narrow commercial cases involving issues such as tax law, towards public law cases of wider general significance.[338] …

Just as the current cohort of Justices is well-versed in the role of human rights principles and provisions in the fabric of UK law, so EU law and the decisions of the ECJ are today normal and familiar elements of the legal landscape within which they work. While the power to strike down domestic legislation as being in breach of EU law has been used sparingly, it has, as Lord Neuberger has noted, set the context within which the new Court operates: '… the very forces which gave such a vital supporting wind to the creation of the Supreme Court, have already given the judges of this country their first taste of what it is to be a constitutional court.'[339]

At the other end of the constitutional spectrum, the Supreme Court has inherited the role more recently played by the Judicial Committee of the Privy Council in determining conflicts at the sub-national level between the central government at Westminster and the devolved regions.

Name and new building

The very fact of the Court's new title and new building is likely to impact both on how the Justices come to see themselves and how others see the Court … The debates during the passage of the Constitutional Reform Act 2005 suggest that the change in title in the UK from Appellate Committee to Supreme Court was not intended to grant it greater authority or a higher status. Yet in practice it is likely to have this effect. As Gavin Drewry has noted, the term 'Supreme Court' has particular resonance because of the significance of the US Supreme Court; the first judicial institution to be known by this title. For many in the UK, the US Supreme Court is the only body of that name with which they are familiar and may well associate that term with a constitutionally powerful institution.

The greater clarity in terms of identity which the court's new name will convey is reinforced by the fact that it now occupies its own building. Here too, the comparative experience of other top courts suggests that this move is likely to enhance its authority, since constitutional court and supreme court buildings generally acquire iconic status and come to be symbolic of a court's constitutional position …[340]

Lady Hale, for example, has quoted with approval the view of the former Chief Justice Barak of Israel that the job of a Supreme Court is: 'to bridge the gap between law and society and to protect democracy'.[341] It is very hard to imagine that the Law Lords thirty years ago would have seen such

[338] Between 1952 and 1968 tax cases represented a quarter (26 per cent) of the caseload of the House of Lords. By the decade from 2000–09 tax cases had fallen to 5 per cent and in the Supreme Court, 4 per cent of the caseload. ('Human rights and public law combined is currently close to half the caseload. (Paterson, *Final Judgment* (n 108 above) 288–89) (ed)) 'If it was only a slight exaggeration to suggest that the House of Lords in the 1950s and 1960s functioned substantially as a specialist tax tribunal, it is surely no more of an exaggeration to suggest that it has now become a court specialising in public law.' (G Drewry, L Blom-Cooper and C Blake, *The Court of Appeal* (Oxford, Hart Publishing, 2007) 147.).

[339] Lord Neuberger, 'Is the House of Lords 'losing part of itself?' Speech to the Young Legal Group of the British Friends of the Hebrew University Lecture, 2 December 2009, para 21.

[340] The Supreme Court has made a major effort to make itself accessible: 'Proceedings in the House of Lords took place tucked away in a room in that grand but labyrinthine building the location of which would have tested the most determined member of the public. By contrast, the UK Supreme Court puts a premium on public accessibility, and welcomed its 250,000th visitor last year – and currently we are receiving around 80,000 visitors per annum. Technology also provides a new means to reach a wider public audience, and our proceedings are streamed live online [on Sky News]. Summaries of every one of our judgments are read out and televised, and fuller printed summaries are available for anyone who wants them.' (Speech of Lord Neuberger, entitled 'Sausages and the judicial process: the limits of transparency', Annual Conference of the Supreme Court of New South Wales, Sydney, 1 August 2014, para 6 – accessible www.supremecourt.uk.) The Court was also the first Supreme Court to join Twitter (@uksupremecourt) (ed).

[341] Lady Hale, 'A Supreme Court for the United Kingdom?' 24 *Legal Studies*, 2004, 36, 42.

> a broad mission statement as an accurate or acceptable view of the role of the Appellate Committee of the House of Lords.
>
> Drawing together the legal and political context, both domestic and international, in which the Court was created, these arguments suggest that the new Supreme Court, renamed in its own prestigious, spacious and well-equipped building, will, in time, evolve into a different body from the Appellate Committee of the House of Lords.[342]

Professor Brice Dickson examined the first 350 or so decisions given by the Supreme Court in the five years after it was established (2009–14[343]). His purpose was to discover whether the court and the individual justices had been 'activist'. He looked at the degree to which the court and the justices: (1) departed from precedents, (2) interpreted legislation in unanticipated ways, (3) rejected the government's position on matters of social, economic or foreign policy and (4) developed the common law. His focus, he said, was 'the unexpectedness of decisions'. The abstract says:

> The article concludes that while the Supreme Court as a whole remained as conservative as the Appellate Committee of the House of Lords (with the possible exception of its approach to immigration law), there awere notable differences between the attitudes of individual Justices, one or two of whom appeared to be straining at the leash.[344]

Putting the then twelve Justices on what Brice Dickson called the activism-restraint spectrum, he thought (at p 14)

> six could be said to be restrained in their approach to judicial lawmaking (Lords Sumption, Clarke, Hughes, Toulson, Reed and Hodge), four are more willing to develop the law but are still mostly hesitant to do so (Lords Neuberger, Mance, Wilson and Carnwath), while two are very much in favour of doing so (Lord Kerr and Lady Hale).

During the battle over Brexit a great deal of controversy was generated over the Supreme Court's two decisions known as *Miller (1)* and *Miller (2)*. (Both were brought by Mrs Gina Miller. In both cases the Supreme Court sat with eleven Justices.) In the first,[345] the Court, upholding the Divisional Court,[346] held by a majority of eight to three, that starting the withdrawal process from the EU under Article 50 of the Treaty on European Union required authorisation by Parliament in a statute. In *Miller (2)* the issue was whether the Prime Minister, Boris Johnson, was legally entitled to prorogue Parliament in a patent manouevre in his battle 'To Get Brexit Done'. The Divisional Court ruled the

[342] See to similar effect, Lord Neuberger, then the President of the Court speaking (pre-Brexit) at a judicial conference in Australia: 'In the UK, for the first time, the courts have duties under the HRA which in many ways are those which would normally arise under a written constitution. The notion that the UK Supreme Court is almost drifting into being a constitutional court is reinforced by two further recent factors. The first is the UK's membership of the EU which, revolutionarily means that judges have to disregard statutes if they conflict with EU law; secondly, with the existence of Scottish, Welsh and Northern Irish parliaments, the Supreme Court has duties which are hard to characterise as anything other than constitutional, not least because they are super-parliamentary.' (Lord Neuberger, 'The role of judges in human rights jurisprudence: a comparison of the Australian and UK experience', speech at Supreme Court of Victoria, 8 August 2014, para 18.

[343] The first President of the Court was Lord Phillips (2009–12). He was succeeded by Lord Neuberger (2012–17), Baroness Hale (2017–20) and Lord Reed (2020–).

[344] B Dickson, 'Activism and Restraint within the UK Supreme Court' (2015) 21(1) *European Journal of Legal Issues* I, http://webjcli.org/article/view/399. See also B Dickson, *Judicial Activism in Common Law Supreme Courts* (Oxford University Press, 2007).

[345] *R (Miller) v Secretary of State for Exiting the European Union* [2017] UKSC 5.

[346] In a notorious *Daily Mail* front page, the three Divisional Court judges (Lord Thomas LCJ, Sir Terence Etherton MR and Lord Justice Sales) were pictured under the headline 'ENEMIES OF THE PEOPLE'.

prorogation was lawful. The 11 Justices of the Supreme Court unanimously ruled it was unlawful.

Commenting, Jack Caird, of the Bingham Centre for the Rule of Law, wrote:

> The High Court's judgment in *Miller (No 2)*, and the way it approached the key questions of constitutional interpretation, was just as political as the Supreme Court's judgment insofar as it relied on, and set out, a clear view on how the constitution should operate. In a sense, this reveals that the problem with characterising a judgment as 'political' is that there is no agreed definition of what the term means in this context. More often than not this accusation is used as a proxy for: 'I do not agree with the conclusions reached by the Court'... The independence of the judiciary does not mean that judges cannot take political positions on the meaning of the constitution. On the contrary, this is part of the core constitutional role of the courts as constitutional interpretation necessarily involves political judgments on the meaning of constitutional principles and the nature of institutional relationships ... One of the few positives of the Brexit process is that it has served to expose the myth that party politics is the only political arena in our constitution. Contestable constitutional decisions, which are by definition political, are a routine and necessary part of any constitutional system based on checks and balances.[347]

For an assessment of the allegation that since 2020 under Lord Reed the Supreme Court had taken a politically motivated step back, see Lewis Graham, 'Has the Supreme Court become more restrained in public law cases? 87 *Modern Law Review* 2024 (5), 1073–110. Dr Graham, of Cambridge University, assessed the quantitative and qualitative evidence for the proposition that in the crucial field of public law, the Supreme Court under Lord Reed was more restrained than the Court had been under his immediate predecessors, Lord Neuberger and Lady Hale. Voices had been raised about this. Professor Conor Gearty had accused the court of having a restrained disposition and 'a commitment to formalism';[348] Professor Adam Tomkins had noted the 'conservative turn' in the Court's recent jurisprudence;[349] Sir Jonathan Jones suggested that there was evidence of the Court's judges holding a 'conservative constitutionalist view';[350] and Professor Brice Dickson had identified 'a more restrained approach' in the Court's judgments compared to 'just a few years ago'.[351] A 2022 Report by the All-Party Parliamentary Group on Democracy and the Constitution alleged that the Court's recent judgments showed a trend towards restraint and deference, and created the impression of a Court which was 'more favourable to the executive' than it was before.[352]

Dr Graham found that that there was substance in these views – but not across the board. There were some areas in which the Court had been anything but restrained and deferential. He concluded his article (pp 1109-10):

> Whilst I submit that some clear patterns do emerge, and that there is positive evidence of the application of a notably more restrained approach than that which had previously been employed,

[347] JS Caird, 'Miller 2, the Supreme Court and the Politics of Constitutional Interpretation', *Counsel*, November 2019, 28–29.

[348] Conor Gearty, 'In the shallow end' (*London Review of Books*, Vol 44(2), 27 January 2022), at www.lrb.co.uk/the-paper/v44/n02/conor-gearty/in-the-shallow-end.

[349] Adam Tomkins, 'Why did the Tories retreat from taking on the Supreme Court judges?' (*The Herald*, 11 August 2021), at www.heraldscotland.com/opinion/19504394.adam-tomkins-tories-.

[350] Alex Dean, 'The government wanted to rein in the Supreme Court. Now it may not need to' (*Prospect*, 16 October 2021) at www.prospectmagazine.co.uk/politics/38065/the-government-wanted-to-rein-in-the-supreme-court.-now-it-may-not-need-to.

[351] Brice Dickson 'Judgement Day for the Supreme Court' (2022) *New Law Journal*, 28 January 2022.

[352] APPG on Democracy and the Constitution, 'An Independent Judiciary – Challenges since 2016', 8 June 2022 ('APPG Report') 49, available at www.icdr.co.uk/judicial-independence-inquiry.

accusations that the Court has in some way been totally supine, or that showing greater restraint evidences some abdication of constitutional duty, should be flatly rejected. Indeed, there are certain aspects of the Court's recent case law which point in quite the opposite direction. For example, statistically, the Court was more likely than not to find in favour of immigrants challenging removal during this period[353] and was responsible for a number of important decisions heralding significant successes for workers and employees.[354] The Court is clearly neither dogmatically conservative nor totally restrained.

Rather, what the Court's case law reveals is a commitment to a kind of legal conservatism, and in particular might be called a kind of political constitutionalist outlook, in which elected politicians get the last word. This can be seen through the Court's tendency to afford greater deference to the legislature and (especially) the executive, and its allergy to policy considerations, as well as in its general approach to human rights cases. The court adopts a wide understanding of forbidden 'political' territory and is anxious to stay away from it. There is also a renewed emphasis on the dualist nature of our constitution. Again, this is often linked with the idea that international commitments are merely a subspecies of politics, suitable for determination by politicians and not for adjudication by judges.

This explanation, focusing on the relationship between the Courts and political bodies, provides a more convincing account of the Court's restrained approach compared to other models. For example, there is little evidence that the Court is advocating for judicial restraint across the board, or a wholesale reduction of its powers or jurisdiction (there is little evidence, for example, of a general deference towards lower courts or a tightening of the Court's inherent jurisdiction); equally, it is not generally conservative when it comes to developing law, exercising discretion or departing from precedent *generally* – it is only really reluctant to do this when the outcome would intrude upon political issues upon which the executive has competence, or the sovereignty of the legislature, or the dualist nature of the constitution.[355] The Court *has* become more restrained, but only in certain respects. The Court is not a political court; it is a *political constitutionalist* Court.

For a radically different view of the Supreme Court's role see Richard Ekin's pamphlet *Protecting the Constitution, How and Why Parliament should Limit Judicial Power*, 2019, published by Policy Exchange, a right-leaning think-tank. As previously noted (pp 348–49) Richard Ekins, Professor of Law and Constitutional Government at Oxford University,

[353] See eg *AM (Zimbabwe) v Secretary of State for the Home Department* [2020] UKSC 17 (removal from UK prevented on medical grounds); *Re G* [2021] UKSC 9 (8-year old child of asylum seeker mother can rely on protection from removal notwithstanding abduction claim from father in South Africa); *SC (Jamaica) v Secretary of State for the Home Department* [2022] UKSC 22 (tribunal entitled to find that deportation would breach ECHR); *HA (Iraq) v Secretary of State for the Home Department* [2022] UKSC 22 (upheld challenge to deportation for one claimant and sent others back to tribunal for reconsideration). See similarly, in *R (DN) v Secretary of State for the Home Department* [2020] UKSC 7 (immigration detention found unlawful). There are exceptions, eg *Robinson v Secretary of State for the Home Department* [2020] UKSC] 22 (Court did not agree with lower court that immigration was prevented on EU law grounds); *Sanambar v Secretary of State for the Home Department* [2021] UKSC 30 (Court did not find that, in order to justify deporting a child, 'very serious reasons' need to be provided and removal of child approved).

[354] Examples include *Uber BV v Aslam* [2021] UKSC 5 (worker status for Uber drivers recognised); *Asda Stores v Brierley* [2021] UKSC 10 (retail workers at Asda could validly point to distribution depot workers as a valid comparator helping them continue their equal pay claim); *Kostal UK v Dunkley* [2021] UKSC 47 (worker protection and trade union statutes interpreted generously so as to prohibit employer's actions, which involved making an agreement with workers directly); *Basfar v Wong* [2022] UKSC 20 (wider protection for trafficked workers working for diplomats; immunity not arising for employer in claimant's case); *Harpur Trust v Brazel* [2022] UKSC 11 (more generous holiday pay scheme for music teacher). One of the only cases in this category to go in the other direction was *Royal Mencap Society v Tomlinson-Blake* [2021] UKSC 8.

[355] see eg Lord Sales: 'In addition to this functional constraint on the development of common law constitutional norms, there are constraints on judges in the development of such norms stemming from judges' position and limited authority in a democratic order': Lord Sales, 'Long waves of principle in the common law' (8 July 2022), 5, available at www.supremecourt.uk/docs/lord-sales-long-waves-of-constitutional-principle-lecture.pdf.

believes that the judges, especially of the Supreme Court, exceeded their proper role and that their powers should be curtailed. In the Introduction Ekins explains his programme of action:

> The report recommends enactment of legislation – which might be termed a Constitutional Restoration Act – to wind back the Supreme Court's prorogation judgment, restore other limits on the scope of judicial review, restore a measure of political control over senior judicial appointments, and reform the Supreme Court's institutional structure to minimise the risks of judicial overreach …[356]
>
> … Parliament should enact a Constitutional Restoration Act that would:
>
> - Rename the Supreme Court the Upper Court of Appeal in order better to indicate the Court's function and to address the symbolism of constitutional primacy;
> - Specify that the Upper Court of Appeal's responsibility is to adjudicate disputes in accordance with law and that the guardians of the constitution are Parliament and the electorate; and
> - Limit the Upper Court of Appeal's jurisdiction to questions involving matters of general legal importance rather than public importance simpliciter. (p 19)

In the five years of Conservative Governments following publication of Ekins' programme of action, there was no indication that it might one day be acted upon.

[356] Introduction, p 10.

8

Foreign and Other Sources of Law

Foreign law can be a source of law-making for English judges. Lord Reed, now President of the Supreme Court, spoke of this in a lecture in 2017.[1] The most familiar source of foreign law, he said, was judicial decisions from other common law countries:

> When we are dealing with problems in areas of the common law, we expect to be referred to the judgments of the highest courts of other common law jurisdictions, especially Australia, Canada, New Zealand, Hong Kong, Singapore and the United States, and we also consult their academic scholarship. In an English or Northern Irish appeal, we will also look at relevant Scottish cases, and vice versa.

By comparison, he said, apart from European Union and European Court of Human Rights law, the use made by English courts of legal reasoning in civil law jurisdictions was very limited:

> We sometimes refer to civilian codes and to the judgments of civilian courts, but we do not do so frequently and the material tends to be used in a different way. In general, this is partly because the law tends to be substantially different from our own, partly because of language issues, and partly because some civilian courts do not produce fully reasoned judgments.

At the most senior level, as Lord Reed explained, the judges nowadays have regular opportunity to meet each other:

> On the Supreme Court of the United Kingdom, we have contact with a large number of jurisdictions in all parts of the world. In recent years, our most frequent and regular contacts have been with the German Federal Constitutional Court the French Conseil d'Etat, the Canadian Supreme Court and the United States Supreme Court ... Another important development has been the establishment of annual seminars involving a group of judges and academic lawyers from a variety of European countries, with an interest in comparative public and constitutional law. They include judges from the French Conseil d'Etat and Cour de Cassation, the German Constitutional Court, the Italian Corte de Cassazione, the Norwegian and Swedish Supreme Courts, the European Court of Human Rights and the UK Supreme Court.

The most significant impact of foreign law, Lord Reed said, had occurred as a result of the United Kingdom's membership of the EU and its implementation of the European

[1] Lord Reed, 'Comparative Law in the Supreme Court of the United Kingdom', October 2017, lecture at the Centre for Private Law, University of Edinburgh accessible on the Supreme Court's website. See also Lord Reed, 'Foreign precedents and judicial reasoning: the American debate and British practice' 124 *Law Quarterly Review*, 2008, 253–73; K Stanton, 'Comparative law in the House of Lords and Supreme Court' 42(3) *Common Law World Review*, 2013, 269 and C Lienen, 'Judicial constitutional comparativism at the UK Supreme Court' 39 *Legal Studies*, 2019, 166–82.

Convention on Human Rights and Fundamental Freedoms by means of the Human Rights Act 1998:

> Both the establishment of the EU, and the task of interpreting and applying the ECHR, have depended on recognising and building on the fundamental values which the different national legal cultures have in common: values with their roots in a shared European cultural tradition. They include the values which find expression in the concepts of the rule of law, the Rechtsstaat, and the État de droit, such as the independence of the judiciary, the right of access to a court, and the right to a fair trial, and the other values which are reflected in the guarantees contained in the EU Charter of Fundamental Rights and the ECHR. These shared values also include basic constitutional principles, such as the separation of powers between the courts and the other institutions of government ...
>
> In addition to fundamental values held in common, and a shared understanding of the broad elements of constitutionalism, the successful implementation of EU law and the ECHR also requires the application by the national courts of some shared general principles of administrative law. Fortunately, the Court of Justice and the European Court of Human Rights have established some common principles, derived mainly from French and German administrative law, such as legal certainty, the protection of legitimate expectations, equality, non-discrimination, proportionality, and subsidiarity.

The Human Rights Act remains in place, but the effect of EU law in the UK has been drastically altered by Brexit. The only EU institution that can now have direct effect on UK law is the Court of Justice. As a result, of Brexit, this EU law section has been drastically altered.

8.1. European Union Law

The system that is now called the European Union began in 1957 with the treaty establishing the European Economic Community (EEC). The United Kingdom joined in 1972. Over the years the system went through many changes (including changes in what things are called[2] and the numbering of treaty provisions[3]). Important changes were made particularly by the Treaty on European Union (TEU) signed in Maastricht in 1992 and by the Treaty on the Functioning of the European Union (TFEU) signed in Lisbon in 2009.

Originally there were six Member States. Post-Brexit there are 27.

The European Communities Act 1972 The EU system took effect as part of United Kingdom law by virtue of the European Communities Act 1972 which made Community law part of national law.

Section 2(1) made both existing and future directly effective EU law part of national law:

> All such rights, powers, liabilities, obligations and restrictions from time to time created or arising by or under the Treaties, and all such remedies and procedures from time to time provided for by or under the Treaties, as in accordance with the Treaties, are without further enactment to be

[2] What is now called the European Union (EU) was originally called the 'European Economic Community' (EEC); and from 1993, the 'European Community' (EC). It became the European Union by virtue of the Treaty of Lisbon in 2009. Unless the context makes it inappropriate the phrase 'European Union' is used throughout.

[3] First by the Treaty of Amsterdam in 1999 and then by the Lisbon Treaty of 2009.

> given legal effect or used in the United Kingdom shall be recognised and available in law, and be enforced, allowed and followed accordingly …

Section 2(2) of the 1972 Act provided that implementation of any EU obligation could be by Order in Council – ie statutory instrument.

Section 2(4) of the 1972 Act required the courts in the United Kingdom, in their interpretation of both present and future statutes, to give full effect to s 2:

> [A]ny such provision (of any such extent) as might be made by Act of Parliament, and any enactment passed or to be passed … shall be construed and have effect subject to the foregoing provisions of this section.

In *Factortame Ltd v Secretary of State for Transport*,[4] the House of Lords held that by virtue of s 2(4) the relevant statutory provision of the Merchant Shipping Act 1988 took effect subject to directly enforceable Community rights.

Section 3 of the 1972 Act stated that questions as to the validity, meaning and effect of the treaties were to be determined in accordance with the jurisprudence of the European Court of Justice.

8.1.1. The Institutions of the European Union[5]

The European Council (Heads of State or Government)

The European Council[6] composed of Heads of State or Government was established in 1974 to provide political initiatives and to deal with issues on which there was policy deadlock.[7] It is responsible for setting the EU's strategic priorities. It meets four times a year in what are called European Summits. The Presidency of the European Council previously changed every six months but the Lisbon Treaty provided for the President to serve a term of two-and-a-half years renewable once. The European Council elects its President by a qualified majority (as to which see below).

The Council of the European Union or Council of Ministers

The Council consists of ministers in national governments. The Presidency of the Council of Ministers rotates every six months.

Most of the preparatory work and the negotiations are in fact done by full-time national representatives who form the Committee of Permanent Representatives (COREPER).[8] COREPER is an important part of the Council's decision-making process.

[4] [1990] 2 AC 85.

[5] Post-Brexit, the only EU institution with direct effect in UK law is the Court of Justice, but it nevertheless seemed right to continue to include most of this section.

[6] Not to be confused with the 'Council' – see below.

[7] Art 15 TEU states that the European Council will provide the EU with the necessary impetus for its development, and will define its general political directions and priorities.

[8] The workload is such that COREPER is divided into two. COREPER 1 is composed of deputy Permanent Representatives who deal with technical issues. COREPER 2 is composed of representatives of ambassadorial rank, who discuss the more political matters.

The Council can only act on a legislative proposal on the basis of a proposal from the European Commission.

Voting on procedural or administrative matters is by a simple majority. On important matters unanimity is required. Most matters are decided by what is called a qualified majority where states have weighted votes.

As from November 2014 the qualified majority voting (QMV) system has had only two requirements: 1) the states approving the proposal must constitute at least 55 per cent of the total number of Member States, comprising at least fifteen members; and 2) those Member States must have at least 65 per cent of the EU's total population.[9]

The European Commission

The Commission is the EU's executive branch, responsible for formulating and implementing policy on a day-to-day basis. It monitors compliance with EU law and can take action to enforce compliance. Each Member State has one Commissioner. The Commission has a very large staff, of some 10,000.

The President of the Commission is proposed by the European Council acting by qualified majority and then has to be elected, by secret ballot, by a majority of the European Parliament.

Commissioners do not represent their national governments. They are supposed to act independently of national interests.[10]

The Commission has the right of initiative to propose laws for adoption by the European Parliament and the Council of the EU. In most cases, the Commission makes proposals to meet its obligations under the EU treaties, or because another EU institution, country or stakeholder has asked it to act. From April 2012, EU citizens have also had the right to call on the Commission to propose laws.

The principles of *subsidiarity* and *proportionality* mean that the EU may legislate only where action is more effective at EU level than at national, regional or local level, and then no more than necessary to attain the agreed objectives.

In principle, the European Commission proposes new laws, but it is the Council together with the Parliament that adopts them.

The European Parliament (Formerly the Assembly)

Composition Members of the European Parliament (MEPs) are elected directly by national populations.

The European Parliament (EP) is primarily a forum for debating EU policies and problems. Initially, it had little real power other than the right to be consulted. It was known as mainly a talking-shop. But this is no longer entirely the case. Its powers have gradually increased.

Approval of the Commission EP elects the President of the Commission and the President and the Commission as a whole are subject to a vote of approval by the Parliament.

Consultation The usual procedure is that a proposal from the Commission is considered by the relevant standing EP committee which produces a report for the full Parliament. The Commission may (or may not) modify the proposal in light of EP's views.

[9] Art 16(4) TEU.

[10] Art 17(3) TEU provides: 'In carrying out its responsibilities, the Commission shall be completely independent ... [T]he members of the Commission shall neither seek nor take instructions from any Government, other institution, body, office or entity.'

The Ordinary Legislative Procedure There is an elaborate process for the creation of legislation involving the Commission, the Council and the Parliament.

The Court of Justice ('The European Court')

The Court has one judge from each of the Member States. Post-Brexit there are therefore now 27 judges. The result is that the Court is dominated by judges from the smaller countries. (There are nine countries with a population of under five million.)

The judges are nominated by their own countries and are normally then accepted by the other Member States. There is no retirement age.

The Court normally sits in Chambers, usually of three or five judges. A Grand Chamber consisting of fifteen judges, sits when requested by a Member State or a Union institution party to the proceedings.

There are also eleven Advocates General who have the same status as the judges. Their role in cases being heard by the Court is to make reasoned submissions by way of assistance to the Court.

The Court gives a single judgment. There are no concurring or dissenting judgments.

To relieve some of the burden of the case-load, the Single European Act in 1987 provided for a second court, originally called the Court of First Instance, renamed the General Court by the Treaty of Lisbon. It also has 27 judges, one from each Member State. It too normally sits in chambers of three and five judges. If it sits in Grand Chamber there are thirteen judges. It deals with a limited range of cases, mainly actions brought by individuals against the Union, especially competition, anti-dumping and intellectual property cases. Appeals are to the European Court and must be brought within two months. Appeals can only be brought on points of law.[11]

The European Court generally follows its own previous decisions but it is not bound to do so.

Decisions of the Court of Justice

Under Art 19 of the Treaty on European Union (TEU), the Court of Justice is required to 'ensure that in the interpretation and application of the Treaties the law is observed'. Decisions of the Court of Justice interpreting EU law have direct effect in Member States, and take precedence over anything in national law, including statutes, that may be contrary to such interpretation whether earlier or later. The Court established early the fundamental principle of membership of the EU that in case of conflict, EU law took precedence over national law.[12]

8.1.2. EU Law and the United Kingdom System Prior to Brexit

The effect of EU law on the United Kingdom system pre-Brexit depended on the type of law in question. Some EU law had direct effect, meaning that it was part of national law without need for anything more. In order for EU law to have direct effect it had to be clear and

[11] Appeals constitute as much as a quarter of the Court's caseload.
[12] Case 26/62 *Van Gend en Loos* [1963] ECR 1.

unambiguous, it had to be 'unconditional, not within the control of any other body and its operation must not be dependent on further action either by Union or national authorities.

The Treaties

It is the norm for Treaty provisions to be held directly applicable.

These directly applicable rights and obligations created by the Treaty, as well as secondary legislation made under it, took precedence over national provisions and as was held by the European Court in the case of *Simmenthal* [1979] ECR 777, 'by their entry into force render automatically inapplicable any conflicting provision of national law'. This principle was applied by the European Court in *R v Secretary of State for Transport, ex p Factortame & ors* [1992] QB 680, [1990] 3 CMLR 1. The Court ruled that where in a case involving EU law, a national court considers that the sole obstacle to the granting of interim relief is a rule of national law, Union law required it to set aside that law.

Regulations, Directives, Decisions, Recommendations and Opinions

Article 288 of the Treaty on the Functioning of the European Union (TFEU) states:

> A regulation shall have general application. It shall be binding in its entirety and directly applicable in all Member States.
>
> A directive shall be binding, as to the result to be achieved, upon each Member State to which it is addressed, but shall leave to the national authorities the choice of form and methods.
>
> A decision shall be binding in its entirety. A decision which specifies those to whom it is addressed shall be binding only on them. Recommendations and opinions shall have no binding force.

Regulations

Regulations normally require no national legislation to implement them.

Directives

Directives are the most usual channel for the translation of EU law into national law. Unlike a regulation, a directive does not normally in itself alter the national law. The directive will, however, always state the date by which national systems must have implemented it. The Member State is left with a discretion only as to how it will implement the directive. However, if it is not implemented properly or at all, it may be treated as directly applicable. The technical term is that a directive can have vertical (as opposed to horizontal) direct effect. This means that if the directive is clear, precise and unconditional it can have direct effect in the sense that it can be utilised by an individual against the State which has failed to implement the directive properly or in time

The Court has developed a principle (known as the principle of indirect effect) requiring national law to be interpreted in such a way as to conform to directives.[13] *Marleasing* (n 13) decided that a non-implemented directive could be relied on to guide the interpretation of national law in a case between individuals, even where the national law predated the

[13] Case 14/83 *Von Colson and Kamann v Land Nordheim-Westfalen* [1984] ECR 1891; Case C-106/89 M*arleasing SA v La Comercial Internacionale de Alimentacion SA* [1990] ECR I-4135, [1992] 1 CMLR 305.

directive. But the duty to conform to the directive where possible does not apply where such an interpretation is impossible.[14]

The Court's decision in *Francovitch v Republic of Italy*[15] took the doctrine further still by holding that an individual can sue the state for damages when it has failed to provide rights required under EU directives.

Decisions

As noted above, Art 288 TFEU states that 'A decision shall be binding in its entirety. A decision which specifies those to whom it is addressed shall be binding.'[16] Decisions may therefore be directly applicable, depending on how they are framed. They can be directed at individuals or companies as well as Member States.

There are many kinds of decisions. One sort is a decision authorising a Member State or individuals to do something. Some decisions place obligations on those to whom they are addressed. An example would be a decision requiring a Member State to modify a particular state regime because it infringes a prohibition in the Treaty.

Other decisions are merely declaratory.

Recommendations

Recommendations have no binding force and are therefore not directly a source of law. But national courts are required to interpret their own law in the light of recommendations, especially where the national law is implementing the recommendation or where the recommendation 'perfects' a directive.[17]

Opinions

Article 288 TFEU states 'Recommendations and opinions shall have no binding force'.

The Charter of Fundamental Rights

By virtue of the Treaty of Lisbon, the Charter of Fundamental Rights of the European Union, is the EU's own human rights text, with the same legal status as the Treaties.[18] The Charter is similar to, but not identical with, the European Convention on Human Rights. In particular it gives protection to various rights that are not to be found in the ECHR – including the right to education (Art 14), the right to engage in work (Art 15), the rights of the elderly (Art 25), the right of access to health care (Art 35).

The relationship between the two human rights systems is addressed in Article 52(3) of the Charter:

> Insofar as this Charter contains rights which correspond to rights guaranteed by the Convention for the Protection of Human Rights and Fundamental Freedoms, the meaning and scope of

[14] Case C 334/92 *Wagner Miret v Fondo de Garantia Salariel* [1993] ECR I-6911. And see also Case 80/86 *Kolpinghuis Nijmegen BV* [1987] ECR 3969, [1989] 2 CMLR 18; Case C-168/95 *Arcaro* [1996] ECR I-4705.

[15] Cases C-6/90 and C-9/90 *Francovich and Bonfaci v Italy* [1991] ECR I-5357, [1993] 2 CMLR 66.

[16] For an example see Case 9/70 *Franz Grad v Finanzamt Traunstein* [1970] ECR 825, [1971] CMLR 1.

[17] Case 322/88 *Grimaldi v Fonds des Maladies Professionelles* [1989] ECR 4407; Case 188/91 *Deutsche Shell-Hauptzollamt Hamburg-Harburg* [1993] ECR I-363.

[18] Art 6(1) TEU. The Charter was originally proclaimed in December 2000 by the Parliament, the Council and the Commission but at that time it had no legal force.

> those rights shall be the same as those laid down by the said Convention. This provision shall not prevent Union law providing more extensive protection.

8.1.3. Parliamentary Scrutiny of EU Legislation

Pre-Brexit, both Houses of Parliament had special machinery to assist in the process of keeping abreast of EU legislation.

The *House of Commons European Scrutiny Committee* was set up in 1974. Its terms of reference were:

> To consider draft proposals ... and to report their opinion as to whether such proposals or other documents raise questions of legal or political importance, to give their reasons for their opinion, to report what matters of principle or policy may be affected thereby, and to what extent they may affect the law of the United Kingdom, and to make recommendations for the further consideration of such proposals and other documents by the House.

Post-Brexit, the Committee continued in existence until after the 2024 General Election, at which point it was abolished.

The House of Lords EU Select Committee, which dated from 1973, had wider terms of reference:

> To consider Community proposals whether in draft or otherwise, to obtain all necessary information about them, and to make reports on those which, in the opinion of the Committee, raise important questions of policy or principle, and on other questions to which the Committee consider that the special attention of the House should be drawn.

The Committee worked through specialist sub-committees,[19] consisting of members of the Select Committee, co-opted members and specialist advisers.

Post-Brexit, in 2021, the Committee was dissolved. Most of its functions were allocated to the newly formed European Affairs Committee and the International Agreements Committee which had previously been one of its sub-committees. The role of the new European Affairs Committee is 'to consider matters relating to the United Kingdom's relationship with the European Union and European Economic Area'.

8.1.4. EU Law and the United Kingdom System after Brexit

Brexit – The History

On 23 June 2016, a referendum was held pursuant to the European Union Referendum Act 2015 initiated by Prime Minister, David Cameron. The question put was: 'Should the United Kingdom remain a member of the European Union or leave the European Union?' More than 33 million people, some 72 per cent of registered voters, voted in the referendum. A slender majority (51.9 per cent against 48.1 per cent) voted to leave the EU. Mr Cameron resigned and was replaced by Mrs Theresa May.

On 2 October 2016, Theresa May announced her intention to give notice of the intention to withdraw from the EU under Article 50 of the Treaty on European Union. That

[19] Economic and Financial Affairs; Internal Market, Infrastructure and Employment; External Affairs; Agriculture, Fisheries, Environment & Energy; Justice, Institutions and Consumer Protection; Home Affairs, Health and Education.

announcement led to a legal challenge. The Supreme Court held (by a majority of eight to three) that notification under Article 50 required the authority of an Act of Parliament.[20]

Parliament authorised the giving of that notice by the European Union (Notification of Withdrawal) Act 2017 and notice under Article 50 was given by the Prime Minister on 29 March 2017. That led to a long- drawn out saga of Theresa May's attempts, first to get an agreement with the EU and then to get the House of Commons to approve it.[21] Mrs May did eventually get a Withdrawal Agreement with the EU, but she could not get it approved by Parliament. The House of Commons rejected the Agreement three times.[22] In that process, the two-year period allowed under Article 50 for withdrawal had to be extended.

Article 50 provides that if there is no withdrawal agreement, withdrawal takes effect two years from the date of the Article 50 notification 'unless the European Council, in agreement with the Member State concerned, unanimously decides to extend this period'. Membership of the EU is a matter of international law. The provisions of Article 50, not UK law, determined whether and when the UK left the EU, regardless of any UK legislation. UK legislation was required not to effect withdrawal but to deal with its consequences.

Mrs May's European Union (Withdrawal) Act 2018 (at the start officially titled the Great Reform Bill), fixed 'exit day' as 29 March 2019. But it provided that this could be extended by statutory instrument.[23] Upon agreement with the EU, the date was first changed from 29 April to 31 October 2019 and subsequently to 31 January 2020.[24]

The European Union (Withdrawal) (No 2) Act 2019 (popularly referred to as 'the Benn Act' put forward by Labour MP Hilary Benn with cross-party support from other MPs) provided that if the Prime Minister was unable to reach a withdrawal agreement with the EU by 19 October 2019 or had Parliament's agreement to leave without a deal, he was required to write to the EU Council to request a further extension to 31 January 2020 or such other date agreed with the EU. The precise wording of the required letter from the Prime Minister was specified in the Act.

When Boris Johnson became Prime Minister in July 2019 he said there would be no further delays to Brexit and, famously, that he would 'die in a ditch' rather than ask for an extension. But on 19 October he sent the specified letter (admittedly unsigned!) asking for the extension required by the Benn Act and an extension to 31 January 2020 was duly granted by the EU.

On 17 October 2019, the EU and the UK Government published an updated and revised Withdrawal Agreement and Political Declaration.[25] Instead of, like Theresa May, asking parliament to approve the Agreement and the Declaration,[26] Boris Johnson asked the House of Commons to approve the legislation to give effect to the 541-page Withdrawal Agreement.[27]

[20] *R (Miller) v Secretary of State for Exiting the European Union* [2017] UKSC 5; [2018] AC 61.

[21] See Meg Russell and Lisa James, *The Parliamentary Battle Over Brexit*, 2023, OUP, 397pp; Meg Russell, 'Brexit and Parliament: The Anatomy of a Perfect Storm', 74 *Parliamentary Affairs*, 2021(2) 443–63.

[22] On 15 January 2019 by 432 to 202; on 12 March 2019 by 391 to 242; on 29 March 2019 by 344 to 286.

[23] 2018 EU Act, s 20(4).

[24] Reflected in UK law respectively by the European Union (Withdrawal) Act 2018 (Exit Day) (Amendment) (No 2) and (No 3) Regulations 2019 (SI 2019/859 and SI 2019/1423).

[25] HM Government, New Withdrawal Agreement and Political Declaration, 19 October 2019: www.gov.uk/government/publications/new-withdrawal-agreement-and-political-declaration. For an analysis of both documents see Lords European Union Committee, *Brexit: the revised Withdrawal Agreement and Political Declaration*, 1st Report, Session 2019–2020, HL Paper 4, 10 January 2020.

[26] Required by the 2018 EU Act, s 13 ('Parliamentary approval of the outcome of negotiations with the EU').

[27] Section 13 of the 2018 EU Act was repealed by the 2020 EU Act, s 31.

The European Union (Withdrawal Agreement) Bill providing for the implementation of the Withdrawal Agreement was introduced in the House of Commons on 21 October 2019.[28] The Commons gave the Bill its Second Reading the following day by a clear majority (329 to 299), but it then proceeded to defeat the very tight programme motion for the progress of the Bill (by 322 to 308). The Prime Minister thereupon stopped further proceedings on the Bill.

A week later, on 28 October, Mr Johnson sought the consent of Parliament to hold a General Election. The vote gave the government a majority of 299 to 70, but the decision of Labour MPs to abstain meant that it failed to get the approval of the two-thirds of all MPs required by the Fixed-term Parliaments Act 2011.[29] The next day, instead, the Prime Minister introduced the Early Parliamentary Election Bill providing for an election on 12 December. This time, goaded by derisive Tory accusations that they were scared to put the matter to the electorate, the Labour Party decided to approve. The House of Commons agreed the Third Reading by 438 to 20. The Bill completed all its stages in both Houses in two days and received Royal Assent the next day, 31 October.

The election on 12 December, known as 'the Brexit election', resulted in a decisive victory for Boris Johnson. The Conservatives were returned with a large overall majority. During the election campaign Johnson's constant refrain was 'Get Brexit Done'. His European Union (Withdrawal Agreement) Bill was reintroduced on 19 December and this time it went through. The Bill received Royal Assent on 23 January. On 29 January the Withdrawal Agreement and Political Declaration were approved by the European Parliament and at 11pm on 31 January 2020 – almost exactly three and a half years after the June 2016 referendum – the UK left the European Union.

***

The topic EU law in the UK after Brexit requires reference mainly to three pieces of legislation – Theresa May's European Union (Withdrawal) Act 2018,[30] Boris Johnson's European Union (Withdrawal Agreement) Act 2020[31] and Rishi Sunak's Retained EU Law (Revocation and Reform) Act 2023.[32] (They are referred to here as the '2018 EU Law Act', the '2020 EU Law Act' and the '2023 EU Law Act'.) Working with these three Acts is not for the faint-hearted – it is complicated.

[28] For commentary by the Lords Constitution Committee on Boris Johnson's first EU Withdrawal Agreement Bill see HL Paper 21, 2nd Report of Session 2019, published 5 November 2019.

[29] Under the Fixed-Term Parliament Act 2011, an election could be held other than at the prescribed five-year interval, with the approval of two-thirds of all MPs or after the government suffered a No-Confidence defeat) (The Fixed-Term Parliament Act was repealed by the Dissolution and Calling of Parliament Act 2022.).

[30] On the 2018 EU Act see. M Elliott and S Tierney, 'Political pragmatism and constitutional principle: The European Union (Withdrawal) Act 2018' *Public Law*. 2019, 37–60; and P Craig, 'Constitutional principle, the rule of law and political reality: the European Union (Withdrawal) Act 2018' 82 *Modern Law Review* 2019, 319–51.

[31] For a guide to the 2018 and the 2020 EU Acts see Eleonor Duhs and Indira Rao, *Retained EU Law*, 2021. See also Simon Winchester, 'Retaining European Law in the United Kingdom', 137 *Law Quarterly Review*, 2021, 477–502; A Hameed, 'UK Withdrawal from the EU: Supremacy Indirect Effect and Retained EU Law' 85 *Modern Law Review* 2022 (3) 726–54.

[32] At the time of writing there were not yet any academic texts on the 2023 EU Act but the House of Commons Library produced valuable papers accessible online:

- Commons Library Briefing, 'Retained EU Law (Revocation and Reform) Act 20'23, 28 July 2023
- Commons Library Insight, 'Which retained EU laws will be revoked at the end of 2023?', 30 November 2023
- Commons Library Insight, 'What powers do ministers have to reform retained EU laws?', 19 December 2023
- Commons Library Briefing, 'The end of REUL? Progress in reforming retained EU law', 2 February 2024

The basic approach to withdrawal from the EU was to repeal the European Communities Act 1972 from 'exit day' as to future effect, but to provide that the status quo at the time of exit be preserved as domestic law until decisions were made as to whether to keep, amend or repeal. The approach was explained in the White Paper issued by Theresa May's Government in March 2017:

> In order to achieve a stable and smooth transition, the Government's overall approach is to convert the body of existing EU law into domestic law,[33] after which Parliament (and, where appropriate, the devolved legislatures) will be able to decide which elements of that law to keep, amend or repeal once we have left the EU. This ensures that, as a general rule, the same rules and laws will apply after we leave the EU as they did before …
>
> Simply incorporating EU law into UK law is not enough, however. A significant amount of EU-derived law, even when converted into domestic law, will not achieve its desired legal effect in the UK once we have left the EU. For example, legislation may refer to the involvement of an EU institution or be predicated on UK membership of, or access to, an EU regime or system. Once we have left the EU, this legislation will no longer work. Government must act to ensure that the domestic statute book continues to function once we have left the EU.[34]

Professors Elliott and Tierney warned of the problem of this massive domestication project:

> This task of retaining EU law is however fraught with difficulty given the myriad ways in which EU law (per the [European Communities Act 1972 or] ECA) has taken effect in domestic law: primary legislation, secondary legislation (emanating not only from the ECA but many other parent Acts), the direct effect of EU treaty provisions, legislation and general principles, and the jurisprudence of domestic and EU judicial organs and regulatory agencies.[35]

Boris Johnson's 2020 EU Act provided that the continuing domestic effect of the European Communities Act 1972 post repeal would cease at the end of an 'implementation period', beginning on the day the UK would leave the EU and ending by default on 31 December 2020.[36] His Withdrawal Agreement with the EU (Art 132) allowed for an extension of up to two years which was reflected in the Withdrawal Agreement Bill when first introduced in October 2019. But when the Bill was re-introduced after the December general election, it contained a new clause making an extension unlawful.

The phrase 'exit day' used in the 2018 Act was replaced in the 2020 EU Act with the phrase 'implementation period (or IP) completion day'. The implementation period ended at 11pm on 31 December 2020, the day that the UK left the EU.

'Repeal' of the European Communities Act 1972

Section 1 of the 2018 EU Act provided that the European Communities Act 1972 (ECA), the Act which took the country into what became the European Union, was repealed as from exit day. This would have had the effect of removing the mechanism for the automatic flow of EU law into UK law which previously occurred through s 2(1) of the ECA. Despite

[33] It has been estimated that some 20,000 laws deriving from the EU were given effect in UK domestic law. (*Legislating for Brexit, directly applicable EU Law*, House of Commons Briefing Paper 7863, 12 January 2017.) (ed).

[34] *Legislating for the United Kingdom's Withdrawal from the European Union*, Cm 9446, March 2017, paras.1.12, 1.14.

[35] Elliott and Tierney (n 30 above) 39.

[36] 2018 EU Act, s 1A(6) inserted by the 2020 EU Act, s 1.

being repealed, it was given life after death, first by ss 2, 3 and 4 of the 2018 EU Act and then by new s 1A inserted by s 1 of the 2020 EU Act.

New s 1A provided that until IP completion date, 31 December 2020, 'The European Communities Act 1972, as it had effect in domestic law or the law of a relevant territory immediately before exit day, continued to have effect in domestic law'.[37] The definition of the EU Treaties was updated to include the Withdrawal Agreement and to reflect that EU law was being enforced because of the Withdrawal Agreement rather than because the UK was a Member State.[38] The references to 'EU law' in the devolution statutes continued to impose restrictions during the implementation period on the competence of the devolved administrations and legislatures, as they did during the period of the UK's membership of the EU.

New section 1B of the 2018 EU Act, inserted by s 2 of the 2020 EU Act, saved existing EU-derived domestic legislation during the implementation period.

Retained EU Law[39]

The domestication of EU law after the implementation period is founded on ss 2, 3 and 4 of the 2018 EU Act as amended by the 2023 EU Act.

Section 2 stated that existing EU derived domestic legislation[40] as it applied to the UK was preserved beyond IP completion day[41] by conversion into 'retained EU law'.[42] That applied equally to any new such law passed between exit day and the IP completion date. The legal status of all such law post-Brexit was the same as its status before Brexit.[43] It consisted mainly of statutes or statutory instruments bringing EU directives which are not directly applicable into domestic law.

Section 3 of the 2018 EU Act, subject to some exceptions, preserved 'direct EU legislation', defined as EU regulations, decisions or tertiary legislation.[44]

Section 4 of the 2018 EU Act, subject to exceptions in s 4(2), preserved rights, powers, liabilities, obligations, restrictions, remedies and procedures in EU law which are directly effective by virtue of s 2(1) of the ECA.

EU law retained under ss 3 and 4 was a new category with its own new rules as to how it could be modified, set out in s 7 and Schedule 8 of the 2018 EU Act. Section 7 created two new categories of EU legislation – 'principal' and 'minor'. The key difference was that whereas the 'minor' could be modified by ordinary secondary legislation, the 'principal' had to be modified by primary legislation unless and to the extent that the provisions under which secondary legislation was made provided otherwise – ie by 'Henry VIII' clauses.[45] Most EU regulations fall into the 'principal' category.[46]

[37] The 2018 EU Act, s 1A(2) inserted by the 2020 EU Act, s 1.

[38] The 2018 EU Act, s 1A(3) inserted by the 2020 EU Act, s 1.

[39] Defined in s 6(7) of the 2018 EU Act as 'anything, which on or after [IP completion day], continues to be, or forms part of domestic law by virtue of ss 2, 3 or 4 or subs (3) or (6) above (as that body of law is added to or otherwise modified by or under this Act, or by other domestic law from time to time'. (Words in square bracket substituted by s 26(1)(a) of the 2020 EU Act.)

[40] This mostly means legislation made under the ECA 1972, s 2(2).

[41] Substituted for 'on and after exit day' in s 2(1) of the 2018 EU Act by s 25(1)(a) of the 2020 EU Act. Section 25 made the similar replacement of 'exit day' in ss 3–5 of the 2018 EU Act. Section 26(1)(a) made the same provision in respect of s 6 of the 2018 EU Act.

[42] As to this new concept see the valuable 49-page House of Commons Library Briefing Paper *The status of 'retained EU law'* (No 08375) 30 July 2019.

[43] 2018 EU Act, s 7(1).

[44] 2018 EU Act, s 3(2).

[45] On 'Henry VIII clauses' see pp 120–22 above.

[46] For consideration of the problems created by s 7 see P Craig, 'Constitutional principle' (n 30 above) at 326–28.

The 2018 EU Act did not retain as domestic law the category of EU legislation called 'directives'. As seen above, these leave Member States with discretion as to how they are implemented – contrasted with 'regulations' which are directly effective across Member States. ('Directly effective' means that if they are sufficiently certain, precise and unconditional they can be enforceable by individuals.)

Retained EU Law (Revocation and Reform) Act 2023 ('the 2023 EU Act')

The 2023 EU Act made significant changes to the framework of retained EU law (REUL). The Explanatory Notes listed what it did:

- revokes all or part of 587 legislative instruments of EU-related origin (though thousands of other legislative instruments will now be kept)
- revokes all retained directly effective EU law (for example, rights and obligations formerly conferred directly under EU treaties or directives)
- revokes the modified principle of supremacy of EU law (which governs the hierarchy of laws passed before the end of the transition period)
- revokes the retained general principles of EU law (which govern the interpretation of REUL)
- renames 'retained EU law' so that it will be known as 'assimilated law'
- permits and encourages lower courts more often to depart from legacy caselaw of the Court of Justice of the European Union (CJEU)
- confers broad delegated powers to restate, replicate, revoke and replace REUL/assimilated law (those powers will expire after 23 June 2026)
- confers a power to update REUL/assimilated law in light of technological and scientific developments (these powers will not expire)
- relaxes the scrutiny rules for modifying or revoking REUL (making it easier to do using, among other things, pre-existing delegated powers)

Government's U-turn on the Sunset Clause

The bill had been fashioned by Brexiteer Jacob Rees-Mogg under Prime Minister Boris Johnson, but by the time it came before Parliament, Boris Johnson was no longer Prime Minister and Jacob Rees-Mogg was no longer a Minister.[47] The bill was intended to launch a bonfire of retained EU law. Clause 1 provided that, unless expressly preserved, swathes of retained EU legislation would be sunsetted (ie expire) at the end of 2023.

Clause 1 became the focus of massive opposition from civil society and proved an impossible burden for government, as civil servants tried to discover what would be sunsetted. The government first said there were some 2,400 retained EU law (REUL) statutory instruments, but in November 2022 it emerged that the National Archive had found another 1,400 pieces of REUL and eventually it turned out that there were some 5,000.[48] At Lords Report Stage,

[47] The bill had its second reading in the House of Commons on 25 October 2022, the day that Rishi Sunak became Prime Minister, succeeding Liz Truss, who had succeeded Johnson. Rees-Mogg resigned on that same day as the Minister in charge of the bill.

[48] Lord Callanan, the Government Minister, explained to peers why there was uncertainty as to the number. Legislation introduced by virtue of s 2(2) of the European Communities Act 1972 had been easy to locate. But, he explained: 'Government often did not want to say that legislation was introduced as a result of an EU obligation. It was therefore introduced under various instruments under either domestic legislation or normal domestic secondary legislation. Therefore, the difficulty departments faced was identifying what was an EU obligation.' (House of Lords *Hansard* 15 May 2023, col.46)

the Government announced a major change in approach. Instead of generically sunsetting a mass of legislation, sunsetting would only apply to items on a list. (Schedule 1 lists 587 instruments that would expire at the end of 2023.)

The government also agreed to report on further EU law reform. The Secretary of State is required to publish six-monthly updates on the EU law dashboard as to progress in revoking and reforming retained EU law and as to government's further plans. This obligation continues until 23 June 2026 – the tenth anniversary of the EU referendum.[49]

Abolition of the supremacy principle Section 3 of the 2018 EU Act (as amended) requires that, so far as possible, any provision of retained EU law has to be read and given effect in a way which is compatible with all domestic enactments.[50] As from 1 January 2024 the principle that UK law must give way to inconsistent EU law no longer applies, regardless of when it was made.[51]

Incompatibility orders Where a court concludes that a provision of retained EU law is incompatible with any domestic enactment, it must make an incompatibility order. This applies equally in the reverse case where the court finds that a domestic enactment is incompatible with a provision of retained direct EU legislation.[52]

Abolition of general principles of EU law as from 1 January 2024.[53] There is no definitive list of such general principles but they include proportionality, the protection of fundamental rights and the principle of equal treatment. For how English courts should approach interpretation of 'assimilated' (previously 'retained') EU law see Lord Sales, 'Retained EU law: purposive interpretation when the constitutional architecture changes' 49 *European Law Review*, 2024 (1), 3-14.

Retained EU law became 'assimilated' law as from 1 January 2024 The many different categories of assimilated law are identified in s 5 of the 2023 EU Act and on p 17 of the Explanatory Notes.[54]

Role of the courts[55]

(1) Courts and tribunals are not bound by any decision of the European Court of Justice (ECJ) made after 31 December 2020 ('IP completion day').[56]
(2) The UK Supreme Court, the High Court of Justiciary (Scotland) and 'relevant appeal courts'[57] are not bound by earlier decisions of the European Court of Justice.[58] (The 2018 EU Act provided that only the Supreme Court and the High Court of Justiciary were free to depart from decision of the ECJ. The 2020 EU Act, controversially, gave the minister the power by regulations to extend this right to *any* court or

[49] 2023 EU Act s 17.

[50] 2018 EU Act, s 5(A2) inserted by 2023 Act, s 3(1).

[51] This does not apply however to anything in the EEA-EFTA Separation Agreement and the Swiss Citizens' Rights agreement – see 2018 EU Act ss 7A, 7B and 7C inserted respectively by ss 6 and 26(2) of the 2020 EU Act.

[52] 2018 EU Act s 6D inserted by s 8 of the 2013 EU Act.

[53] Amendments to s 5 of the 2018 EU Act, made by s 4(2)–(7) of the 2023 EU Act.

[54] 2023 EU Act s 5 says that from the end of 2023 'the things listed in the left-hand column are to be known by the names in the right-hand column'. The difference is that in each case 'retained' is replaced by 'assimilated' and 'EU' as part of the description in the left-hand column does not occur in the right-hand column.

[55] 2018 EU Act s 6 as amended by the 2020 and the 2023 EU Acts.

[56] 2018 EU Act s 6(1)(a) as amended by s 26(1)(a) of the 2020 EU Act.

[57] Relevant appeal court includes the Court of Appeal of England and Wales and the Inner House of the Court of Session (Scotland)–2018 EU Act s 6 (6B) inserted by s 6(6) of the 2023 EU Act.

[58] 2018 EU Act s 6(4) as amended by s 6(2)(b) of the 2023 Act.

tribunal,[59] though before making such regulation, the minister would have had to consult the President of the Supreme Court, the Lord Chief Justices of England and Wales and of Northern Ireland, the Lord President of the Court of Session and the Senior President of Tribunals.[60] In the event, no such regulation was made and the 2023 EU Act provided for the more modest extension to include just the Court of Appeal level.)

(3) A court or tribunal that is not bound by a decision of the European Court of Justice may 'have regard to such decision so far as it is relevant'.[61]

(4) *Considerations regarding departing from a previous decision*

(1) When higher courts consider whether to depart from retained EU law they should (amongst other things) have regard to:

'(a) the fact that decisions of a foreign court are not (unless otherwise provided) binding;
(b) any changes of circumstances which are relevant to the retained EU case law;
(c) the extent to which the retained EU case law restricts the proper development of domestic law.'[62]

(2) When considering whether to depart from its own retained domestic case law, a court should have regard (among other things) to:

'(a) the extent to which the retained domestic case law is determined or influenced by retained EU case law from which the court has departed or would depart;
(b) any changes of circumstances which are relevant to the retained domestic case law;
(c) the extent to which the retained domestic case law restricts the proper development of domestic law.'[63]

(5) *Court's power to refer points of law* A lower court that is bound by a decision of retained EU case law can refer a point of law of general public importance to a higher court that is not bound. The court may refer the point of law of its own motion or following an application by a party to the proceedings. The reference must be made to the court to which an appeal would lie in the case unless it concerns a decision of the Supreme Court, in which case it must be referred to the Supreme Court. No appeal can be made from a decision to make or not to make a reference, or to accept or not accept a reference.[64]

Law officers can refer points of law The new reference procedure applies also to the law officers. A law officer of the UK Government or of the devolved administrations may refer a point of retained EU case law to a higher court. Such reference must be made within six months from the conclusion of the case where there has been no reference by the court and either there was no appeal or the appeal has been concluded or dismissed without being heard. A law officer of a devolved administration may only refer a point of law that relates

[59] 2018 EU Act s 6(4)(ba) inserted by 2020 EU Act s 26(1)(b).
[60] 2018 EU Act s 6(5A) inserted by 2020 EU Act s 26(1)(d).
[61] 2018 EU Act s 6(2).
[62] 2018 EU Act s 6(5) substituted by s 6(3) of the 2023 EU Act. These factors were taken into account by the Court of Appeal when considering whether to depart from retained EU case law in *Tuneln Inc v Warner Music UK Ltd* [2021] EWCA Civ 441. (The original version in the 2018 Act only required that the court apply the same test as it would apply when considering whether to depart from its own decision.)
[63] 2018 EU Act s 6(5ZA) inserted by s 6(4) of the 2023 EU Act.
[64] 2018 EU Act s 6A inserted by s 6(8) of the 2023 EU Act.

to the law in that jurisdiction. The higher court to which the reference is made must accept the reference.[65]

Law officers' intervention on retained EU law Law officers are entitled to receive notice of proceedings in which a higher court is considering argument that the court should depart from retained case law. On giving notice to the court, the law officer is entitled to be joined as a party.[66]

Modification of retained/assimilated law Changes made by the 2023 EU Act were aimed at downgrading assimilated EU law so that it could be amended as if it were domestic secondary legislation. The Explanatory Notes (para 45) say: 'In effect this ensures RDEUL [retained direct EU law] has a more appropriate status in UK law downgrading it from primary to secondary status for the purpose of amendment'. Restrictions on use of the power to make modifications have also been removed.[67]

Power to turn assimilated law into non-assimilated law The 2023 EU Act gives Ministers the power to use secondary legislation to restate provisions of 'secondary assimilated law'. Once restated, it would no longer be assimilated law and would therefore be subject to interpretation without any EU considerations, unless they had been expressly retained in the restatement. This provision expires on 23 June 2026.[68]

Power to revoke or replace The 2023 EU Act gives ministers the power to use regulations to revoke assimilated secondary EU law or to replace it with provisions to similar effect. But replacement provisions must not increase the regulatory burden. This power expires on 23 June 2026.[69]

Power to update The 2023 EU Act gives ministers the power to make regulations modifying any secondary assimilated law to take account of changes in technology or 'developments in scientific understanding'.[70]

Power to remove or reduce burdens The 2023 EU Act provides a power for ministers to issue Legislative Reform Orders (LROs) to amend any assimilated direct EU legislation. Such LROs would however be required to follow the standard procedure including consultation, committee reports and would be subject to either the negative, affirmative or super affirmative procedure.[71]

Conforming construction An article published just before the 2023 EU Law Act became law considered how it would affect the principle of 'conforming construction' which prescribed that EU derived domestic legislation, such as enactments implementing EU Directives, had to be interpreted, as far as possible, in accordance with EU law.[72] The conclusion:

> The 2023 EU Act does not explicitly address the question whether and to what extent it affects the principle of conforming construction. On the one hand, it abolishes retained EU treaty rights and obligations as well as the supremacy of EU law, which arguably both constitute the legal

[65] 2018 EU Act s 6B inserted by s 6 (8) of the 2023 EU Act.
[66] Section 6C of the 2018 EU Act inserted by s 6(8) of the 2023 EU Act.
[67] Section 9 of the 2023 EU Act amending provisions in Sch.8 of the 2018 EU Act.
[68] Sections 12 and 13 of the 2023 EU Act.
[69] Section 14 of the 2023 EU Act.
[70] Section 15 of the 2023 EU Act.
[71] Section 16 of the 2023 EU Act amending Part 1 of the Legislative and Regulatory Reform Act 2006.
[72] Fabian Barth, 'How will the Retained EU Law (Revocation and Reform) Act 2023 Affect the Principle of EU-Law Conforming Construction in UK law?' 44 *Statute Law Review*, 2023(3).

foundation for applying a conforming construction post-Brexit. On the other hand, it leaves intact the binding nature of most case law, including that which establishes those principles. Depending on how much emphasis is placed on each angle, one may read the 2023 EU Act as not affecting conforming construction, as radically abolishing it, or as somewhere in between.

In a nutshell, it appears on balance most likely and reasonable that the courts will find a middle-ground. This could be that a conforming construction will, in the future, only apply where it is already the subject of binding case law for the specific provision one seeks to construe, or where there is a genuinely identifiable intention by Parliament for the enactment to fully comply with EU law. In other cases however, the principle of conforming construction likely may no longer be available as a tool to interpret domestic statutes, not even for the ones which originate from EU law and will become 'assimilated law'.

The Charter of Fundamental Rights

Section 5(4) of the 2018 EU Act says: 'The Charter of Fundamental Rights is not part of domestic law on or after [IP completion day]'.[73] But confusingly, section 5(5) provided that 'this does not affect the retention in domestic law … of any fundamental rights or principles which can exist irrespective of the Charter

The Explanatory Notes to the 2018 EU Act (para 107) said:

> Given that the Charter did not create any new rights, subsection (5) makes clear that whilst the Charter will not form part of domestic law after [IP completion day], this does not remove any underlying fundamental rights or principles which exist, and EU law which is converted will continue to be interpreted in light of these underlying rights and principles.[74]

Schedule 1 para 2 of the 2018 EU Act said:

> No general principle of EU law is part of domestic law after [IP implementation day][75] unless it had previously been recognised as such by the European Court in a case decided before [IP completion day] (whether or not as an essential part of the decision in the case).

That left open the possibility that general principles of EU law *could* be considered if recognised by the Court before 31 December 2020. But para 2 of Schedule 1 was repealed by the 2023 EU Act s 4(6). So what use could the Charter of Fundamental Rights now be in litigation? This question was addressed by Sir Philip (now Lord) Sales. True, he wrote, the Charter of Fundamental Rights (CFR) was not part of UK law.[76]

> But to a large degree the CFR was a codification of the general principles of respect for fundamental rights and equality before the law, and the CFR also reflects the ECHR [European Convention on Human Rights] to which the UK is party and which it has adopted into national law under the HRA [Human Rights Act] … Where retained EU laws have the purpose of protecting fundamental rights, at least in the ECHR sense, that purpose will therefore continue to be relevant for their interpretation and with similar interpretative effect.[77]

[73] As amended by the 2020 EU Act, s 25(4)(a)].

[74] For critical consideration of the provisions regarding the Charter see Craig, 'Constitutional principle' (n 30 above) at 330–33. On Brexit and the Charter see generally C Barnard, *So Long, Farewell, Auf Wiedersehen, Adieu: Brexit and the Charter of Fundamental Rights*, 82 *Modern Law Review*, 2019 (2), 351–66.

[75] 31 December 2020.

[76] 2018 EU Act s 5(4).

[77] Lord Sales, 'Retained EU law: purposive interpretation when the constitutional architecture changes' 49 *European Law Review*, 2024 (1), 3–14, 8.

Parliamentary Oversight of the Brexit Withdrawal Process

The 2018 EU Act received Royal Assent at the end of June 2018, at which point the Prime Minister, Theresa May, was negotiating with the EU on a withdrawal agreement. Section 13 of the 2018 EU Act provided that the withdrawal agreement could only be ratified if it was approved by a resolution of the House of Commons. As noted above, Mrs May did not succeed in getting that parliamentary approval. The 2020 (Withdrawal Agreement) Act, as its title proclaimed, reflected approval of the Withdrawal Agreement reached by Boris Johnson. The Act (s 31) therefore repealed s 13 of the 2018 EU Act.

The first version of Boris Johnson's EU (Withdrawal Agreement) Bill, introduced in October 2019 included provisions for parliamentary oversight of the negotiations for the future relationship with the EU:[78] (1) within 30 days of 'exit day' a Minister had to lay a statement before the House of Commons outlining a statement of objectives for the forthcoming negotiations; (2) the statement required the approval of the House of Commons; (3) the government's approach to the negotiations had to be based on that statement of objectives; (4) the Minister had to report to Parliament every three months; and (5) the ultimate result in the form of a treaty required the approval of the Commons before it could be ratified.

The second version of Mr Johnson's EU (Withdrawal Agreement) Bill introduced in December 2019 after the general election had none of those provisions. All it had was a new s 13A of the 2018 EU Act ('Review of EU legislation during implementation period')[79] which merely provided for a measure of scrutiny of new EU legislation passed or pending during the implementation period. If either the European Scrutiny Select Committee of the House of Commons or the EU Select Committee of the House of Lords considered that such legislation raised a matter of 'vital national interest' and suggested a motion to be debated in that House, the government had to arrange for a debate and a vote on such motion within fourteen days.

There was nothing else regarding Parliamentary involvement. Lord Wallace of Saltaire (Liberal Democrat) told peers during the Second Reading debate on the Bill that he had been shocked when Liberal Democrats peers had been told in a ministerial briefing the previous week 'that there was now no need for the previous Bill's clause guaranteeing parliamentary scrutiny of future trade negotiations because the result of December's election had given the Government sufficient mandate to negotiate them in whatever form they may be able to agree'.[80]

However, the record shows that Brexit generated massive parliamentary concern. During the Committee stage of the Bill, Lord Bridges of Headley told the House that he had asked the Library to collect some statistics:

> In the calculation the Library made, it excluded the Bills we have debated, including the 650 hours this House has spent on debating EU-related issues. Let me give your Lordships the results of this exercise. Since the referendum, there have been, in Parliament as a whole: 10 Private Notice Questions related to Brexit; 32 Urgent Questions; 116 Oral Statements; 179 Select Committee reports; 743 Written Statements; 6,241 Oral Questions and supplementaries; and 15,366 Written Questions.[81]

[78] Clause 31 inserting new s 13B into the 2018 EU Act.
[79] Inserted by 2020 EU Act s 29.
[80] HL *Hansard*, 13 January 2020, col 470.
[81] HL *Hansard*, 20 January 2020, col 1001.

On EU law generally see Mark Dawson and Floris de Witte, *EU law and Governance* (Cambridge University Press, 2022).[82]

8.2. Scholarly Writings

According to orthodox traditional theory, the writing of scholars fell into two categories – the authoritative and the rest. In order to be treated as authoritative a writer had to be dead. The most authoritative were a select band of hallowed names such as Bracton, Glanvil, Littleton, Coke, Hale and Blackstone. Most practitioners go through their entire professional lives without ever having occasion to cite any of these giants.[83] But if their views are brought to the attention of a court, they have an extra patina of respectability not available to lesser writers. On the other hand, it is questionable whether in practice their views are treated as any more persuasive – this depends on what they said and what other authorities counsel has been able to deploy. These names certainly evoke in English lawyers a Pavlovian respectful response. But this does not mean that their views are more likely to be followed.

The rule that an author had to be dead before they could be cited as 'authority' was considered by Professor Neil Duxbury then of Manchester University in *Jurists and Judges: An Essay on Influence*.[84] Technically, he suggested, it was not so much a rule as a convention – and one that was sometimes honoured in the breach. Duxbury identified eight different reasons that had been advanced for the rule (all exceedingly feeble):

- The existence of law reports made textbooks unnecessary.
- The declaratory theory of law, subscribed to by most judges until at least the middle of the twentieth century seemed to preclude the possibility of treating textbooks as authorities since the judges 'found' rather than made the law.
- Offence might be caused to jurists who were not cited.
- It was not desirable to quote immature or unreflective commentary.
- Citation of text writers did not work well since a high proportion of judgments were given extempore at the end of the case.
- Academics, justifiably, had an inferiority complex.
- Commentators were not subject to stare decisis – an author might change their mind and thereby render the source of law uncertain.
- Judges should not rely on the work of living authors because the two groups inhabited different worlds and were engaged in very different enterprises.[85]

[82] The book has 10 chapters: Understanding EU Law and Governance; The EU as a Bureaucracy; The EU as a Political Union; The EU as a Regulator; The EU as a Legal Order; The EU as a Market; The EU as a Union of Citizens; The EU as a Union of Values; The EU as a Unity; The Future of EU Law and Governance.

[83] For examples of rare modern cases which dealt with these great names see, for instance, *Button v DPP* [1966] AC 591 or *L v K* [1985] 3 WLR 202.

[84] N Duxbury, *Jurists and Judges: An Essay on Influence* (Hart Publishing, 2001) 62 and especially fn 4.

[85] The work of jurists was basically one of criticism – 'and criticism comes cheap' – Duxbury, *Jurists and Judges*, ibid, 74.

If an advocate wanted to cite a living author they had to do so by the device of saying they were adopting the jurist's view 'as part of my argument'. Today, the rule is long dead.[86]

But the contribution of scholars has not had the same role in the English law-making process that it has in many other countries. In the United States or on the continent of Europe, for instance, no self-respecting practitioner would present an argument to the court on a point of law without directing the court's attention to the views of the leading academic commentators. The decisions of the Supreme Court of the United States as well as those of lower courts cite a mass of academic authority as a matter of course.

The fact is that, historically, academic law was not held in high esteem either by English practitioners or by the judges. For centuries the only two English universities, Oxford and Cambridge, did not even teach English law. They taught only Roman and Canon law, which were irrelevant to practitioners. Those who went into the profession as barristers learnt their law first at the Inns of Court and then in practice. Blackstone is said to have inaugurated the teaching of English law at the universities with his famous course on the Common Law from 1753, but the teaching of the subject lapsed after his resignation. In 1800 the Downing Chair of the Laws of England was founded in Cambridge, but the subject did not flourish there either. When in 1846 a Parliamentary Select Committee inquired into the state of legal education in this country, it reported that 'no legal education worthy of the name is at this moment to be had'.[87] Whereas in Berlin, for instance, there were fourteen professors teaching some thirty branches of law to hundreds of students, in Oxford and Cambridge there appeared to be neither lectures, nor examinations, nor for that matter any students.[88]

The Select Committee's Report led to changes. In 1852 Oxford established a BCL degree and in 1855 Cambridge started an LLB degree. Law faculties were created at London University and in provincial universities as they were set up. By 1908 there were eight law faculties. But they had to struggle to establish their academic respectability. It was still a moot point whether law was a fit subject for university legal education. (In 1996, Lord Diplock told the annual meeting of the Society of Public Teachers of Law that he had serious doubts on the question.[89] Lord Diplock was at the time not only chairman of the Council of Legal Education of the Inns of Court, but also chairman of the Institute of Advanced Legal Studies at London University!)

The acid test of whether law was suitable for inclusion in university courses was whether it was 'liberal'. A distinction was drawn for this purpose between liberal education on the one hand and practical, technical or vocational training on the other. The essence of the difference between the two, it was thought, lay in the different content of each. Thus Roman law, jurisprudence and legal history were thought to be suitable subject-matter for liberal education, whilst company, tax or labour law were not. The closer the subject came to being concerned with the affairs of the ordinary man or, worse, the marketplace, the less it qualified as 'liberal'. Common law subjects such as contract and tort and even property law were somehow exempted, even though they plainly had practical importance.

The fallacy that liberality of pursuit is limited to certain subject-matter is not a new one. A hundred years after Newton's *Principia*, Oxford and Cambridge were still making

[86] In his remarks at a memorial event for the late Dr David Thomas, 17 June 2014, Lord Judge, the former Lord Chief Justice, said that the idea that judges at the Judicial Studies Board should listen to the views of distinguished authors (such as Thomas on sentencing) but ignore them when sitting in judgment would have been farcical. So the old rule, he said, had withered and vanished.

[87] *Report of the Select Committee on Legal Education*, 1846, vol X, British Parliamentary Papers, p lvi, para 3.

[88] Ibid, para 2.

[89] *Journal of the Society of Public Teachers of Law*, 1966, 193.

virtually no contribution to scientific thought because they refused to accept that science was a proper subject for study. In the medieval university the seven liberal arts were grammar, rhetoric, dialectic, geometry, music, arithmetic and astronomy. After the Renaissance the emphasis shifted to the language and literature of the Hebrews, the Romans and above all of the Greeks. More recently the classics have receded, as the concept of liberal education has expanded to embrace the imaginative and philosophical literature of modern Europe. Today none but the most sheltered humanist would deny that science has an honoured place in this great tradition.

The view that regards the *content* of liberal education as crucial ignores the fact that the most liberal subjects can be (and often have been) taught in a narrow, pedantic and scholastic manner which is the very antithesis of the spirit of liberal education. It is not the content at a particular place or time which is fundamental, but rather the way in which that content is imparted. As Samuel Alexander said: 'Liberality is a spirit of pursuit not a choice of subject'. If a subject is one in which principles can be discovered and reasons for facts can be related to the principles, then such a subject can be made the basis for liberal education. A practical subject, such as company law, can be taught as a means to achieving technical proficiency, or alternatively as a means of studying the problems of business organisation as a phase of human experience to be appreciated and understood as part of the economic and social problems of a wider society.

As a result of their worries about the liberality of the subject-matter, the university law schools for decades failed to teach some of the most ordinary practical subjects which today are taken for granted. The result was that even the minority of practitioners who had read law at the university tended to regard their academic law studies as largely irrelevant to their professional work. They rarely read the academic journals and, when they did, they found their prejudices amply confirmed. Worse, the teaching of the subjects that were supposed to be liberal was frequently arid, technical and dull. The legal academic world, with few exceptions, was detached from the concerns of the real world and, understandably, was ignored by both practitioners and judges.

Over the past decades this all changed. The law faculties teach subjects of importance to practitioners; books and articles in academic journals are of direct relevance to them; the majority of practitioners have read law at university;[90] quite a few of the judges, especially at the senior level are themselves experienced authors, former Law Commissioners or even academics.[91] Contact between the two worlds is much more frequent and more on the basis of mutual respect rather than the old mutual disparagement. Not that the old divide between academic and practitioner has gone, but the role of the academic as a subsidiary contributor to the law-making process is nowadays fully established.[92]

[90] Between 1970 and 1978 the proportion of new solicitors who were law graduates rose from 40 per cent to 60 per cent – a remarkable rate of increase (*Report of the Royal Commission on Legal Services* Cmnd 7648, 1979, para 38.13, 609). In 1989, of those admitted to the Rolls as solicitors, 73 per cent were law graduates, 14 per cent were non-law graduates and the remainder were miscellaneous categories including 10 per cent who were overseas lawyers, most if not all of whom would have been law graduates.

In 2021–22, 77 per cent of newly admitted solicitors were law graduates, 2 per cent were non-law graduates and 15 per cent were overseas lawyers transferring. (Source: *Trends in the Solicitors' Profession Annual Statistical Report 2022*, Law Society, November 2023, Table 7.3.)

[91] Former full-time academics include Justice Brenda Hale and Lord Burrows of the Supreme Court, Lord Justice Beatson and Mr Justice Cranston.

[92] For an informative and rounded paper on this subject see P Birks, 'The academic and the practitioner' 18 *Legal Studies*, 1998, 397–414.

In his 1982 book, *The Law Lords*, Professor Alan Paterson noted the increase in citations of academic writings in decisions of the House of Lords.[93] In 1955 Appeal Cases, there had been only seven references by counsel to textbooks written by authors who were then alive, and two to articles. In the Law Lords' speeches there were six references to textbooks and none to articles. By 1961 the position had changed only marginally. In that year counsel cited textbooks by living authors only eleven times. But ten years later there had been a threefold increase (compared with 1955) in the number of such references by counsel and the Law Lords themselves. Paterson said that such references were by then a commonplace and that 'in some recent cases in the House of Lords the welter of academic references on both sides of the Bar has reached floodlike proportions which would have astounded their counterparts of twenty years ago'.[94]

In the 93 reported decisions in the 1985 volumes of the *All England Law Reports* there were a total of 72 citations to 'secondary authorities', an average of 0.77 per case. Of these, 66 were to textbooks, one was to a law review article, one to a case note and four to the reports of various commissions.[95]

In the 126 cases reported in the first two volumes of the 1999 *All England Reports* there were 200 references to secondary sources, a slightly increased average of 1.6 per case. Just over half (55 per cent) were textbooks, a tenth (11 per cent) were journal articles, a fifth (20 per cent) were reports by the Law Commission, Royal Commissions and other official bodies. The remainder were EU law, UN or other international sources (6 per cent), Parliamentary debates (3 per cent) and miscellaneous (4 per cent).[96]

There are a number of scholars whose books and articles are regularly cited both by counsel and by the judges in their decisions[97] and it is not just eminent authors that are cited. A study by Professor Keith Stanton of 104 tort cases decided by the House of Lords, 1990 to 2009, showed a considerable range of citations:

> The wide range of sources cited in the cases surveyed suggests that information technology is enabling counsel to find material of this kind which would have gone unnoticed in earlier years. While some eminent authors and venerable textbooks appear time and again, there is also significant use being made of the work of a wide range of little known authors publishing in periodicals which would not be available in many law libraries.[98]

The journals that received most mentions were the *Law Quarterly Review* (58), the *Cambridge Law Journal* (20) and the *Modern Law Review* (17). But the breadth of the material being fed into judicial decision-making was shown by the wide spread of journals that had only one mention.[99] Online access to journals will likely increase citation of academic writings year on year.

[93] For a case in which the Law Lords bandied conflicting academic views see *Hunter v Canary Wharf Ltd* [1997] AC 655, [1997] 2 WLR 684.

[94] A Paterson, *The Law Lords* (Macmillan, 1982) 16.

[95] H Kötz, 'Scholarship and the courts: a comparative survey' in DS Clark (ed), *Comparative and Private International Law: Essays in Honor of John Henry Merryman* (Duncker & Humblot, 1990) 188–89.

[96] Research conducted by the writer.

[97] The writings for instance of Professor Glanville Williams and Professor Sir John Smith on criminal law would be obvious examples.

[98] K Stanton, 'Use of scholarship by the House of Lords in tort cases' in J Lee (ed), *From House of Lords to Supreme Court* (Hart Publishing, 2011) 207.

[99] *Australian Bar Review*, *Brigham Young University Law Review*, *California Law Review*, *Canadian Bar Review*, *Canadian Journal of Law and Jurisprudence*, *Columbia Law Journal*, *Fordham Law Review*, *Journal of Applied Philosophy*, *Journal of Legal History*, *Juridical Review*, *Michigan Law Review*, *Monash Law Review*, *New Law Journal*, *Otago Law Review*, *Singapore Journal of Legal Studies*, *Tel Aviv University Studies in Law*, *Texas Law Review*, *The Times* (newspaper), and the *University of Western Australia Law Review*. (Stanton, 'Use of Scholarship' (n 99) p 225.)

So today the lawyers will bring academic writings to the attention of the courts and the judges will read these writings – with whatever effect. Sometimes it is clear that. the decision was influenced by a jurist's contribution. A famous example was an article in the *Law Quarterly Review* by the distinguished solicitor Dr FA Mann that led to two re-hearings before the House of Lords and changed the mind of the majority.[100] In *Shivpuri*, Lord Bridge explained that he had changed his mind as to how the case should be decided by reading, *after oral argument had concluded*, Professor Glanville Williams' fierce critique of his judgment in a then recent House of Lords decision. ('The language in which he criticises the decision in *Anderton v Ryan* is not conspicuous for its moderation, but it would be foolish, on that account, not to recognise the force of his criticism and churlish not to acknowledge the assistance I have derived from it.[101]) Former Lord Chief Justice, Lord Judge went so far as to admit that if in difficulties on a question of sentencing law, 'I would telephone David Thomas'.[102] In 1997, Lord Goff, originally an academic and himself a distinguished author, said in a lecture, 'It is difficult to overestimate the influence of the jurist in England today – both on the formation of the view of young lawyers and in the development of the law. Indeed, we now live in the age of the legal textbook. It is the textbook which provides the framework of principle within which we work'.[103]

Very occasionally a judge criticises counsel for *not* citing academic writings. Lord Steyn, in the Court of Appeal decision in *White v Jones* said that the court had been referred to about forty decisions of English and foreign courts. Pages and pages from judgments had been read to the court. 'But we were not referred to a single piece of academic writing'. Counsel, he said, were not to blame, 'traditionally counsel make very little use of academic materials other than standard textbooks'.[104] Lord Steyn continued:

> In a difficult case it is helpful to consider academic comment on the point. Often such writings examine the history of the problem, the framework into which a decision must fit and countervailing policy considerations in greater depth than is usually possible in judgments prepared by judges who are faced with a remorseless treadmill of cases that cannot wait. And it is arguments that influence decisions rather than the reading of pages upon pages from judgments …[105]

There can be no doubt that academic writing is much more present today in the courts' decisions than in former times. But assessing its impact is difficult.[106] In 1982, Professor

[100] FA Mann, 'The present validity of Nazi nationality laws' 89 *Law Quarterly Review*, 1973, 194. For its influence see *Oppenheimer v Cattermole* [1976] AC 249, 268.

[101] [1987] AC 1, 23.

[102] Remarks at the memorial event for Dr David Thomas of Cambridge University, the academic acknowledged as the leading authority on that subject.

[103] 'Judge, jurist and legislature' *Denning Law Journal*, 1997, 79, 92.

[104] Professor Basil Markesinis has observed, '[F]ormidable though the talents of English barristers are, fondness for academic research is not, I venture to suggest, one of them … one gets the impression that academic law is dismissed as too theoretical, avoided because it might leave the judges indifferent, and subconsciously played down because it undoubtedly involves a constructive use of national and international developments which successful practitioners do not have high on their list of priorities …' ('A matter of style' in *Foreign Law and Comparative Methodology* (Hart Publishing, 1997) 141).

[105] *White v Jones* [1993] 3 WLR730, 750–51 (CA). In *Spiliada Maritime v Cansulex Ltd* [1987] AC 460 (HL) Lord Goff concluded his twenty-page speech by paying tribute to the writings of jurists (notably Mr Adrian Briggs and Miss Rhona Schuz), which he said had assisted him in the preparation of his opinion. Even when he disagreed with them he had found their work to be of assistance – 'For jurists are pilgrims with us on the endless road to unattainable perfection and we have it on the excellent authority of Geoffrey Chaucer that conversations among pilgrims can be most rewarding' (487).

[106] For a somewhat pessimistic assessment of the future prospects of scholars influencing judicial decision-making see Jack Beatson, 'Legal academics: forgotten players or interlopers?' in A Burrows, D Johnston, R Zimmermann (eds), *Judge and Jurist: Essays in Memory of Lord Rodger of Earlsferry* (Oxford University Press, 2013) 523–42. (Lord Justice Beatson was formerly a member of the Law Faculty of Cambridge University.)

Paterson, on the basis of his study of the House of Lords' decisions, wrote, 'there seems little evidence that the Law Lords regard pronouncements of living academic writers (as a group) as having even persuasive authority. Their practice seems to be to accord such writings merely "permissive" status'.[107] In his subsequent study in 2013 Paterson gave examples of ways in which the situation had changed but concluded that, 'while the dialogue between jurist and judge on the final court has deepened in the last 40 years, its contribution to judicial decision-making still generally falls below that of the dialogues between counsel and judges and between the judges themselves'.[108]

Just how a judge should approach the writings of a jurist – in that instance his own writings cited by counsel in the case – was the subject of a characteristically elegant statement by Lord Justice Megarry:

> I would add one comment, in amplification of certain observations that I made when during the argument counsel cited a passage from the 3rd edition of Megarry & Wade's *Real Property*. It seems to me that words in a book written or subscribed to by an author who is or becomes a judge have the same value as words written by any other reputable author, neither more nor less. The process of authorship is entirely different from that of judicial decision. The author, no doubt, has the benefit of a broad and comprehensive study of his chosen subject as a whole, together with a lengthy period of gestation, and intermittent opportunities for reconsideration. But he is exposed to the perils of yielding to preconceptions,[109] and he lacks the advantage of that impact and sharpening of focus which the detailed facts of a particular case bring to the judge. Above all, he has to form his ideas without the aid of the purifying ordeal of skilled argument on the specific facts of a contested case. Argued law is tough law … I would therefore give credit to the words of any reputable author in book or article as expressing tenable and arguable ideas, as fertilisers of thought, and as conveniently expressing the fruits of research in print, often in apt and persuasive language. But I would do no more than that; and in particular I would expose those views to the testing and refining process of argument. Today, as of old, by good disputing shall the law be well known.[110]

8.3. Custom

There are several separate meanings of the word 'custom' as a source of law. The first is *general custom* in the sense of common usage. It seems possible that after the Norman Conquest this was a real source of some law. As the country was gradually reduced to centralised order by the judges travelling around the country, they must have based at least some of their decisions on the common custom of the realm. According to Sir Frederick Pollock, 'The common law is a customary law if, in the course of about six centuries, the undoubting belief and uniform language of everybody who had occasion to consider the matter were able to make it so'. Coke described custom as 'one of the main triangles of the laws of England', and for Blackstone, general customs were 'the universal rule of the whole kingdom and forms the common law in its stricter and more usual signification'. But

[107] Paterson, *The Law Lords* (n 94 above) 18–19.

[108] Paterson, *Final Judgment: The Last Law Lords and the Supreme Court* (Hart Publishing, 2013) 221.

[109] For the courageous suggestion that judges too may be captives of their preconceptions see 'Five days in the House of Lords: some comparative reflections on *White v Jones*' in BS Markesinis, *Foreign Law and Comparative Methodology* (Hart Publishing, 1997) 346–56.

[110] *Cordell v Second Clanfield Properties Ltd* [1968] 3 WLR 864, 872.

these claims are likely to be more poetic than historically accurate. In fact a high proportion of the so-called customs were almost certainly invented by the judges.

An article in the *Law Quarterly Review* in 1893 claimed, for instance, that there was 'a very strong presumption that the common law originated in the judicial adoption of the common customs of the realm'.[111] The evidence cited for the proposition, however, hardly bears the weight of the argument. Thus the man who so negligently looked after his house that it caught fire and the fire spread to his neighbour's house was liable 'by the law and custom of the realm'. But what sort of custom was this? Is the suggestion that it was customary for every man to look after his own property so that fires did not arise and spread? Or is it rather that when such fires occurred the house owner was customarily held liable? The custom was of the courts rather than of the people. Similarly, it is said that the law regarding the liability of carriers and innkeepers was founded on the custom of the realm. But what was the nature of the custom? Did the common carriers voluntarily pay their customers when goods entrusted to them were lost or damaged? It seems unlikely. Or did the populace demand that the rule be so? Even making the large and somewhat improbable assumption that the public did make such a demand, this hardly amounts to a popular custom but merely to popular pressure for a rule.[112] Although therefore, no doubt, general custom may have played some part in the early development of the law, it seems probable that even at that time the judges were the true originators of a good deal of 'the custom of the realm'.

The second main meaning of custom as a source of law is in the sense of *local custom* in contrast to the common law. From early times the judges, for obvious reasons, established a series of rigorous tests or hurdles that had to be met by anyone claiming the benefit of some exception to the common law. The judges were trying to impose the Westminster brand of justice and did not look benevolently on too many local variations. There were seven main tests for a local custom.

(1) It must have existed from 'time whereof the memory of man runneth not to the contrary', or from time immemorial. This concept was arbitrarily defined by statute to mean from 1189, the date of the coronation of King Richard 1. If proof could be brought that the custom did not exist in 1189, it was rejected. Thus in *Simpson v Wells* (1872) it was shown that the appellant could not have a customary right to set up a refreshment stall on a public footway as he claimed from 'statute sessions', because these were first authorised in the fourteenth century. More recently Mr Justice Lawton rejected a claim by a barrister that there was a customary rule that barristers could not be sued – on the ground that dicta in a case in 1435 suggested that at that time a barrister might be sued![113]
(2) The custom must have existed continuously since 1189 – any proved interruption defeated the claim.
(3) The custom must have been enjoyed peaceably without opposition.
(4) It must have been felt to be obligatory.
(5) It must be capable of being defined precisely – a requirement of certainty.
(6) Customs must be consistent one with another.

[111] FA Greer, 'Custom in the Common Law' 9 *Law Quarterly Review*, 1893, 157–60.

[112] I am indebted for these examples and the analysis presented to EK Braybrooke, 'Custom as a source of English law' 50 *Michigan Law Review*, 1951, 71, 74.

[113] *Rondel v Worsley* [1966] 2 WLR 300, 307. However, the judge was able to find other reasons to uphold barristers' immunity.

(7) Finally they must be reasonable – if it could be proved that it would have been unreasonable in 1189, again the claim would fail.

These formidable qualifying conditions gave the judges ample powers to reject any local custom they regarded as unsuitable for recognition.

Neil Duxbury has pointed out that judicial proclamations regarding immemorial general customs 'could sometimes seem rather eccentric'.[114] In 1606, for example, 'Coke declared digging for saltpetre for the manufacture of gunpowder to be a custom of the realm, even though gunpowder production in Britain did not start until around the mid-fourteenth century.'[115]

Though claims to local custom in modern times are rare, they do occasionally occur. In *Egerton v Harding* [1975] 2 QB 62 the courts upheld a customary duty on one of the parties to fence land against cattle straying from the common. Another case in the same year concerned the alleged right of the mayor, bailiff and burgess and others to indulge in lawful sports including shooting, on land in the centre of the borough of New Windsor.

New Windsor Corporation v Mellor [1974] 1 WLR 1504 (Ch D)

The respondent caused certain land in the centre of the borough of New Windsor to be registered in the register of town or village greens maintained by the registration authority under s 3 of the Commons Registration Act 1965, claiming that the inhabitants of the borough had by custom acquired the right to indulge in lawful sports and pastimes on it. The borough objected to the registration and an inquiry was held by the Chief Commons Commissioner. The evidence before the Commissioner showed that in 1651 a lease of the land had been granted by the borough for 40 years, the lease containing a covenant by the lessee that it should be lawful for the 'Mayor Bailiffs and Burgesses and ... all and every person and persons to have access' to the land 'as well as to exercise and use shooting or any other lawful pastime for their recreation at all convenient times'. The lessee also covenanted to set up a pair of butts 'for the inhabitants of the ... town to shoot at' and to repair and maintain them, and not to do anything which might be 'hurtful to the shooting or any other pastime then to be exercised for recreation of the people'. Further leases of the land for 40-year terms, containing similar covenants, were granted in 1704 and 1749. In 1819 the corporation granted a 3-year lease, the lease being made subject to the right 'of the Native Bachelors of Windsor in exercising all lawful sports games and pastimes' over the land, and, in 1822 a similar lease 'subject to the rights and privileges of the Bachelors of Windsor who are entitled to use the [land] for all lawful recreations and amusements'. After the Inclosure Act 1813 the borough held the land by virtue of their statutory title under that Act. Following an inclosure award in 1819, they held it free from any rights of common of pasture or turbary, but still subject to any rights to use it for lawful sports and pastimes to which it was formerly subject. The land was used annually for 'revels' until the 1840s. There were also in evidence extracts from newspaper reports and reports of meetings, a newspaper extract of October 1875 recording that the land had been used for sports by a large number of people and that the mayor had vetoed the holding of the sports, on wrong advice given to him by the town clerk on the legal effect of the inclosure award. From 1875 onwards the borough refused to recognise that the inhabitants had any right to use the land for recreation and accordingly it was no longer used for that purpose. At the time of the respondent's registration the land had for some

[114] N Duxbury, 'Custom as law in English law' 76 *Cambridge L.J.*, 2017, 337 at 354 n 88.

[115] *The Case of the King's Prerogative in Saltpetre* (1606) 12 Co. Rep. 12.

years been used partly as a school sports ground and partly as a car park. It was listed in the development plan for the borough as the site for a multi-storey car park. On the evidence the Commissioner confirmed the registration, holding that a customary right to indulge in lawful sports and pastimes on the land had been acquired by the inhabitants of the locality from time immemorial and that the land was therefore 'town or village green' within ss 1 and 22(1) of the 1965 Act. The borough appealed, contending, inter alia, (i) that the evidence did not support the conclusion of long usage since there was no direct evidence of any user and the Commission had found that there had been no such user since 1875, and (ii) that the user was incapable of existing as a custom since, from the terms of the covenants in the 1651 lease, the user was not confined to the inhabitants of the borough, ie, the 'Burgesses', but extended to 'all and every other person', ie, persons residing outside the borough.

Foster J stated:

> *Long usage*
>
> There was, in my judgment, ample evidence on which the Commissioner could come to the conclusion that there had been long usage, and I, for my part, on that evidence would have come to the same conclusion.
>
> *That the claim had been made as of right*
>
> The Commissioner came to the conclusion that the user has been as of right, in view of the leases granted, subject to the right and to the events in 1819 and 1822, to which I have referred. In my judgment, his conclusion was right.
>
> *That the right claimed is capable of existing as a custom*
>
> It is well established that to create a custom the user must have been, by the inhabitants of an area, defined by reference to the limits of some recognised division of land such as a town … This raises the question of construction of the words used in the lease of 1651. The Commissioner held that the words 'all and every other person or persons' and the words 'the people' must be read in their context and the covenant to set up a pair of butts 'for the inhabitants of the said town' to shoot at shows that those wide expressions should be limited to the inhabitants of the town. He therefore concluded that the custom was confined to the inhabitants of a particular locality.
>
> Counsel for the borough submitted that the word 'burgesses' included all the inhabitants of the town, and reliance was placed on the definition of 'burgesses' in Wharton's Law Lexicon: 'Generally the inhabitants of a borough or walled town'. In Stroud's Judicial Dictionary, 'Burgesses' is defined as referring to men of trade. Earlier in the lease there are found the words 'Mayor Bailiffs Burgesses and their Successors', showing that the words 'Mayor Bailiffs and Burgesses' refer to the body corporate rather than to every person living in the town. It might well be ultra vires for the corporate body to provide benefits for persons not living within its boundaries, and it may be, but this is pure surmise, since there is only an extract from the lease, and after the words 'all and every other person or persons' there may have followed some words such as 'being inhabitants of the town', which occur later. I have, however, come to the conclusion that the Commissioner was correct in confining the expressions used to the inhabitants of the town.
>
> *Does the custom arise from time immemorial?*
>
> Counsel for the respondent submitted that once the first three points were established the court should be astute to find that the origin of the custom was from time immemorial, and he relied for his submission on three cases: *Cocksedge v Fanshaw*,[116] *Malcomson v O'Dea*[117] and *Johnson v*

[116] (1779) 1 Doug KB 119.
[117] (1863) 10 HL Cas 593.

> *Barnes*.[118] Counsel for the borough referred me to a statute of Henry VIII[119] which was not cited to the Commissioner, to show that the origin of the usage stemmed from that statute and not from time immemorial. If it could be shown that the right to use Bachelor's Acre stems from a statute passed after 1189, then the claim of a custom would be defeated (see *Simpson v Wells*).[120]
>
> Section 4 of that statute is in these terms:
>
> … (4) and also that Butts be made on this Side the Feast of St. *Michael* the Archangel next coming, in every City, Town and Place, by the Inhabitants of every such City, Town and Place, according to the law of ancient Time used; (5) and that the Inhabitants and Dwellers in every of them be compelled to make and continue such Butts, upon Pain to forfeit for every three Months so lacking, (6) and that the said Inhabitants shall exercise themselves with Long-Bows in shooting at the same time, and elsewhere in holy Days and other Times convenient.
>
> But from the terms of s. 4(4) the words 'according to the Law of ancient Time used' show that the making of butts was not started by virtue of that Act. The provisions do not negative the right having existed from time immemorial.
>
> The Court should therefore be astute to find the origin from time immemorial and, in my judgment, the Commissioner was right to do so. For these reasons, in my judgment the appeal fails and I propose to dismiss it.

In 1992 the High Court held that anglers had a customary common law right to dig on the foreshore for worms as bait. The right to fish in tidal waters, dating back to Magna Carta, included the ancillary right to dig for bait. But the right did not cover digging for bait for sale or other commercial purposes.[121]

The question has been much canvassed as to whether a local custom is law regardless of the court's decision. If this is so, the court recognises the custom because it is already law. This represents the late Professor Rupert Cross's view.[122] But there is an inevitable circularity about the argument. If the custom is not recognised, it was not law; if it is recognised, it was. It seems more accurate to posit that the custom is authenticated by the judicial decision which upholds it. Professor Cross objected that this is the equivalent of saying that a statute is not law until it has been interpreted by a judge. But the two cases are very different. A statute is undeniably law – every word is law and there is no possibility of argument about it. The document is tangible and certain and the contents are known even if the meaning is in dispute. There could never be litigation testing whether a statutory provision is law. By contrast, the fact that there is litigation over the existence of the custom indicates that there are serious doubts as to whether a court will uphold the claim. An alleged custom, the validity of which is as yet unrecognised by a court, may be more than half way to being a law; but it lacks the accolade of recognition without which it is merely a claim.

Much the same is true of *mercantile custom*, which is often cited in the books as another instance of custom as a source of common law. The practices of merchants, it is said, were recognised by the courts and became rules of law because they were felt by the courts to be binding. But this is again to pay excessive regard to the rhetoric, and not to focus on the likely reality of the situation. The point has been made by a learned commentator, EK Braybrooke:

[118] (1872) LR 7 CP 592.
[119] 33 Hen 8 c 9.
[120] (1872) LR 7 QB 214.
[121] *Guardian*, 12 December 1992.
[122] R Cross, *Precedent in English Law*, 3rd edn (Oxford University Press, 1977) 162–63. The 4th edition (R Cross and JW Harris, Clarendon Press, 1991) was unchanged – see 170–71.

> If we take as typical of the custom of merchants the rule that if A draw upon B a bill payable to C, B (if he accept the bill) is bound thereby to pay C, we may readily see expressed in this rule the result of a long-continued course of practice among merchants; the crux of the matter is that acceptors of such bills have in the past acknowledged their liability to pay the payee, though there may be no privity of contract between them. All that remains to be done is for the courts to enforce this customary rule by allowing C to succeed in an action against B. But is the matter quite as simple as it looks? If acceptors of bills have customarily acknowledged their liability in the past, is it not because by all acknowledged *rules of contract* they are bound to A in any case. Certainly it may be the custom of merchants to *make* contracts of this kind; but how can the mere existence of this custom persuade a court to grant an action to the payee, in contradiction to its fundamental theories of the law of contract? This custom of merchants is a more complex affair than appears at first sight. The development of the bill of exchange in the form summarised above owes at least as much to the theories of lawyers as to the usages of merchants; and the notion of the direct liability of the acceptors to the payee is the end-product of a complex process of juristic reasoning on the part of … lawyers … The adoption of mercantile customs by the common law courts was the product of a deliberate decision, motivated by a desire to extend the jurisdiction of those courts, not by any belief that the law-creating effect of popular custom compelled them to apply the rules of the law merchant professed to be based on such custom.[123]

When, in 1657, Chief Justice Hobart said 'The custome of merchants is part of the common law of this kingdom, of which the judges ought to take notice',

> the operative part of the statement was not the semi-fictional statement that the custom of merchants was part of the common law of the kingdom but the assertion that the judges would take notice of it.[124]

The same was true, Braybrooke suggested, of the famous cases of the nineteenth and twentieth centuries concerning the attitude of the common law courts to mercantile custom:

> We find this fact of deliberate adoption readily deducible from the decisions … We may indeed see in the history of mercantile custom a reflection of the pattern which we may suppose the history of the general custom of the realm to have followed. No doubt at some early time the complex of popular and feudal practices and usages which was in fact, and not in name merely, the common custom of the realm, furnished a rich storehouse of rules and standards and principles from which the judges might draw the materials to lay down the foundation of fundamental rules and principles on which the common law was built. But once these fundamental rules and principles are established the same habit of mind which endows popular custom with what authority it possesses endows them with perpetual life; they become fixed, unalterable, fundamental. The general customs of the realm lose their law-creating force; they can no longer prevail against the fundamental rules which were their own creation … But the tradition that the common law is no other than the common custom of the realm survives as a fossilised doctrine long after it has ceased to correspond fully with the facts. Its survival may indeed become a source of embarrassment to those whose charge it is to lay down the common law; and so, we may conjecture, the doctrine becomes converted into a rule of pleading whose object is to prevent the judges, who are repositories of the common law, from possible coercion by evidence of a strong current of popular usage which they are unwilling to accept.[125]

[123] EK Braybrooke, 'Custom as a source of English law' 50 *Michigan Law Review*, 1951, 84–85, 86.

[124] Ibid, 87. There follows some discussion of the cases, which has been omitted here (ed).

[125] 'Custom as a source of English law' 50 *Michigan Law Review*, 1951, 87–88. For a masterly history see Ross Cranston, *Making Commercial Law through Practice, 1830–1970* (Cambridge University Press, 2021) 483pp.

What Braybrooke wrote of general, local and mercantile custom seems more convincing than the conventional theory that the courts were meekly following in the wake of the people in recognising the existence of the custom. It is the court, not the people, that exercises the decisive voice. In this sense it is possible to acknowledge that custom is, and always has been, a vital source of law. In a multitude of ways the courts are constantly referring to the actions and practices of the community as a point of reference in order to determine either rules or the application of existing rules. Thus in the whole field of negligence, the court has to determine whether conduct fell above or below the reasonable standard of performance required at any given time in the field in question. If the issue, for example, is whether a surgeon is negligent, the court hears expert evidence as to the practice of surgeons in regard to the procedure in question. It then decides that what was done by the defendant surgeon is acceptable and therefore free from liability, or not acceptable and therefore subject to liability. In making that judgment, the court may bear in mind amongst other things the state of development of medical knowledge, the difficulty and cost of taking the precautions that were not taken in that case, the differences that may exist between the level of practice to be expected in a London teaching hospital as against a small provincial one and a host of similar considerations. The practice of the community will be fed into the process of decision-making as among the factors to be taken into account. The court will not accept the particular procedure of surgeons as representing an acceptable standard unless it thinks it consistent with what can fairly be expected at that stage of development of medical practice. Custom in the sense of what the community does is therefore a potent living source of law in the sense that the courts draw upon it and rework it into the daily application of the common law. In this way the law is constantly renewed by contact with the life of the community and reflects back to the citizens the law's evaluation of what they do. Here again Benjamin Cardozo expressed the reality.

Benjamin N Cardozo, *The Nature of the Judicial Process* (Yale University Press, 1921) 62–63

> [62] It is, however, not so much in the making of new rules as in the application of old ones that the creative energy of custom most often manifests itself today. General standards of right and duty are established. Custom must determine whether there has been adherence or departure. My partner has the powers that are usual in the trade. They may be so well known that the courts will notice them judicially. Such for illustration is the power of a member of a trading firm to make or indorse negotiable paper in the course of the firm's business. They may be such that the court will require evidence of their existence. The master in the discharge of his duty to protect the servant against harm must exercise the degree of care that is commonly exercised in like circumstance by men of ordinary prudence. The triers of the facts in determining whether that standard has been attained must consult the habits of life, the everyday beliefs and practices, of the men and women about them. Innumerable, also, are the cases where the course of dealing to be followed is defined by the customs, or, more properly speaking, the usages, of a particular trade or market or profession. The constant assumption runs throughout the law that the natural and spontaneous evolutions of habit fix the limits of right and wrong. A slight extension of custom identifies it with customary morality, the prevailing standard of right conduct, the *mores* of the time.

But it is the judge who decides – not the people nor the custom.[126]

[126] See further N Duxbury, 'Custom as law in English law', 76 *Cambridge Law Journal*, 2017 (2), 337–59.

8.4. Quasi-legislation, Codes of Practice, Circulars, Guidance etc

The concept 'quasi-legislation' seems to have been identified first by RE Megarry in an article in 1944 – 'Administrative quasi-legislation'[127] – in which he pointed to law-which-is-not-law such as tax concessions and Practice Notes.

Since then there has been an explosion in the type and range of such semi-law-making. (It has also been called 'soft law'.) In a book on the subject published in 1987, Professor Gabrielle Ganz referred to 'an exponential growth of statutory and extra-statutory rules in a plethora of forms. Codes of practice, guidance, guidance notes, guidelines, circulars, White Papers, development control policy notes, development briefs, practice statements, tax concessions, Health Services Notices, Family Practitioner Notices, codes of conduct, codes of ethics and conventions are just some of the guises in which the rules appear'.[128]

One of the most remarkable examples of the potency of this form of 'soft law-making' was Ministry of Education Circular 10/65 which was the basis of the shift to comprehensive education, arguably one of the most radical changes ever made in British education.[129] Another is the so-called Concordat agreed between the Lord Chancellor and the Lord Chief Justice entitled: 'The Lord Chancellor's judiciary related functions: Proposals'.[130] The official Judiciary website said of the Concordat:

> As part of the process which led to the Constitutional Reform Act, in January 2004 the Government and the judiciary entered into a 'Concordat'. One essential purpose of this was to guarantee the continued independence of the judiciary. The Concordat also sets out which of the functions hitherto exercised by the Lord Chancellor were 'judicial' and now the province of the judiciary, which were 'administrative', and remain the province of government, and which are 'hybrid' and should be shared.

The Concordat was only an Agreement but the House of Lords Select Committee on the Constitution rightly referred to it as 'of great constitutional importance'.[131]

In 1986, Robert Baldwin and John Houghton wrote about the phenomenon – 'Circular arguments: the status and legitimacy of administrative rules' *Public Law*, 1986, 239.[132] They suggested that there were at least eight different categories.

(1) *Procedural rules* for example, rules for the guidance of applicants for licences to the Gaming Board; Prison Rules laying down disciplinary rules for prisoners; the Codes of

[127] 60 *Law Quarterly Review*, 1944, 125.

[128] G Ganz, *Quasi-Legislation: Recent Developments in Secondary Legislation* (Sweet & Maxwell, 1987) 1.

[129] We are told that the measure was mentioned in Cabinet only after it had been finalised in the Department – EC Page, *Governing by Numbers, Delegated Legislation and Everyday Policy-Making* (Hart Publishing, 2001) 12.

[130] See www.dca.gov.uk/consult/lcoffice/judiciary.htm.

[131] HL Select Committee on the Constitution, *Relations between the Executive, the Judiciary and Parliament*, 6th Report 2006–07, HL 151, 26 July 2007, para.13. Professor Robert Hazell of UCL told the Select Committee that in his view the Concordat had the status of a 'constitutional convention' (ibid, para 15).

[132] See also R Baldwin, *Rules and Government* (Oxford University Press, 1995) 81–85.

Practice under the Police and Criminal Evidence Act 1984,[133] etc. Practice Directions are a major component of the Civil Procedure Rules (CPR).[134]

(2) *Interpretative guides* Official statements of departmental or agency policy, explanations of how terms or rules will be interpreted or applied, expressions of criteria to be followed, standards to be applied or considerations to be taken into account.
(3) *Instructions to officials* Prison Department Circulars, Standing Orders and Regulations; Home Office Circulars to magistrates' courts; Home Office Circulars to Chief Constables etc.
(4) *Prescriptive/evidential rules* for example, the Highway Code, breach of which can be taken into account by a court; the Secretary of State's Code on Picketing under the Employment Act 1980 can be taken into account by the courts; under the Employment Protection Act 1975 the ACAS codes have evidential status; so too do the Codes under the Police and Criminal Evidence Act 1984, which therefore have dual status.
(5) *Commendatory rules* Commendatory rules simply or mainly recommend a course of action. An example is the guidance notes issued by the Health and Safety Commission and Executive advising on how safety objectives may be achieved. They overlap with prescriptive rules in that some rules of evidential significance might also be considered commendations – for example, the ACAS industrial relations codes. Another example of growing importance is that of specimen directions to juries formulated by the Judicial College (formerly the Judicial Studies Board) for the guidance of judges. At the time they were only available to the judges.[135] Today they are online.[136]
(6) *Voluntary codes* The City Code on Takeovers and Mergers or the former Press Complaints Commission are typical examples. Usually they are designed to stave off government regulation. Businesses often have voluntary labelling, codes of ethics and of good practice.
(7) *Rules of practice, management or operation* A new policy or enforcement practice would come under this heading. Extra-statutory concessions formerly made by the Revenue are in point. (The Revenue, for instance, agreed not to charge tax on cash payments to miners in lieu of free coal or on removal expenses borne by an employer where the employee has to change their residence to take up new employment.) The existing concessions are now accessible online.[137]

[133] See M Zander, 'If the PACE codes are not law, why do they have to be followed?' 176 *Criminal Law and Justice Weekly*, 2012, 713–14. The PACE Codes of Practice run to some 300 pages of material. See *Zander on PACE* (Sweet & Maxwell, 2018) 791–1071.

[134] See JA Jolowicz, 'Practice directions and civil procedure rules' 59 *Cambridge Law Journal*, 2000, 53–61; F Bennion, 'Practice directions: a need for order?' 170 *Justice of the Peace*, 2006, 508–10; and A Zuckerman, 'Rule making and precedent under the Civil Procedure Rules 1998 – still an unsettled field' 29 *Civil Justice Quarterly*, 2010, 1–12. For an important judgment on the legal status of Practice Directions see *Bovale Ltd v Secretary of State for Communities and Local Government* [2009] 1 WLR 2274; [2009] EWCA Civ 171. See also D Burrows, 'Precedent & practice' *New Law Journal*, 10 October 2014, 11. The Cabinet Office's *Guide to Making Legislation, Appendix D*, has seven pages on Codes of Practice. On the surprisingly late creation of the Criminal Procedure Rules, see Lord Chief Justice, Lord Thomas, 'The Criminal Procedure Rules: 10 Years On', *Criminal Law Review*, 2015 (6), 395–98.

[135] For the argument that they should be published and thereby be available to practitioners and scholars see R Munday, 'The Bench Books: can the judiciary keep a secret?' *Criminal Law Review*, 1996, 296; the reply by Lord Justice Kennedy, ibid, 529; and Dr Munday's riposte, ibid, 530.

[136] Now called the Crown Court Compendium. Previously called the Crown Court Benchbook. www.judiciary.uk/wp-content/uploads/2016/06/Crown-Court-Compendium-Part-I-December-2019.pdf – www.judiciary.gov.uk/training-support/judicial.college.

[137] www.gov.uk/government/collections/extra-statutory-concessions.

In 1979 it was argued in the *British Tax Review* that 'most of the extra-statutory concessions were illegal'.[138] Questions about them had been raised by the judges.[139] In the House of Lords decision of *R v Inland Revenue Commissioners, ex p Wilkinson*[140] Lord Hoffmann said that whilst the Revenue had a wide managerial discretion, it did not justify 'construing the power so widely as to enable the commissioners to concede, by extra-statutory concession, an allowance which Parliament could have granted but did not grant'. This decision caused HM Revenue and Customs to review all the extra-statutory concessions and to start a programme of withdrawing some and legislating others that fell outside the scope of its discretion as defined in the *Wilkinson* case.

(8) *Consultative devices and administrative pronouncements* This is a safety-net category that absorbs other pronouncements which do not fit into any of the previous groups but which have a significance beyond the individual case. One type of this category are consultative statements inviting comments on draft outlines or agency or departmental policy.

The attitude of the courts towards these various manifestations of rule-making has varied. To some they have given legal effect; to others they have denied it. Sometimes the same rules have legal effect for one purpose but not for another. (See four cases interpreting the Immigration Rules: *Ex p Bibi* [1976] 1 WLR 979; *Ex p Hosenball* [1977] 1 WLR 766; *Ex p Ram* [1979] 1 WLR 148; *Ex p Kharrazi* [1980] 1 WLR 1396.) Often the courts give the benefit of the doubt to the administrators by denying the rule legal effect. (See commentary by Baldwin and Houghton, above, pp 445–46.)

Among the important issues raised by such rule-making are the issues of control – by Parliament and by the courts – and the issue of consultation in such rule-making. The Lords Constitution Committee in its 2018 report on delegated powers said of official Guidance 'If there are policy lacunae in the legislation itself, it is unacceptable that guidance, which for the most part avoids parliamentary scrutiny, should serve to fill them.'[141] Sometimes there is also a question as to whether and if so, how the material is made available, though the existence of the internet has eased that issue very considerably

Daniel Greenberg, a former member of the Office of Parliamentary Counsel, has suggested that documents that are quasi-legislation are capable, in effect, of imposing or even modifying legal obligations and that it was therefore essential that they be drafted by people who understand the parameters of what is effective, just and proper legislation. But, he wrote, 'In reality, they are mostly drafted by administrators without legal training, and

[138] DW Williams, 'Extra statutory concessions' *British Tax Review*, 1979, 137–44. ('That they exist at all in either overt or covert form is a matter of concern. That they not only exist but grow regularly, in open contradiction to the rule of law, cannot but reflect on the quality of the executive that creates them, and the polity that tolerates them' (p 144).) See further GW Thomas, 'The constitutionality of extra-statutory concessions' *Law Society's Gazette*, 27 June 1979, 637–38; M Nolan, 'The unsatisfactory state of current tax law' *Statute Law Review*, 1981, 149–50; John Alder, 'The legality of extra-statutory concessions' *New Law Journal*, 21 February 1980, 180; A Rowland, 'Is the revenue being fair? Revenue statements and judicial review' *British Tax Review*, 1995, 115–21.

[139] In *Absalom v Talbot* [1943] 1 All ER 589, 598, Scott LJ said: 'No judicial countenance can or ought to be given in matters of taxation to any system of extra-legal concessions. Amongst other reasons, it exposes Revenue officials to temptation, which is wrong, even in the case of a service like the Inland Revenue, characterised by a wonderfully high sense of honour. The fact that such extra-legal concessions have to be made to avoid unjust hardships is conclusive that there is something wrong with the legislation.' See, to like effect, *Gleaner Co Ltd v Assessment Committee* [1922] AC 169, 175, per Lord Buckmaster; *IRC v Frere* [1965] AC 402, 429, per Lord Radcliffe; *Bates v IRC* [1968] AC 483, 516, per Lord Upjohn; *Vestey v IRC (No 2)* [1979] Ch.198, 203, per Walton J, [1979] AC 1148.

[140] [2005] UKHL 30, [2006] STC 270.

[141] Lords Constitution Committee, *The Legislative Process: The Delegation of Powers*, 16th Report, 2017–19, HL 225, November 2018, para 81.

without much or anything in the way of formal or effective oversight by legislative drafters. The result is an essentially unconstrained power for the Executive to use these wide-ranging documents to control the effect and application of legislation.'[142]

In a debate on codes of practice in the House of Lords[143] concern was expressed that the legal effect of failure to comply with codes of practice was uncertain and that they sometimes dealt with matters of importance but were not generally subject to parliamentary approval procedures.[144] As a result the government undertook to draft guidance for those involved in the policy and drafting of statutory provisions relating to codes of practice. See now the Cabinet Office, *Guide to Making Legislation* (2022), www.gov.uk/government/publications/guide-to-making-legislation – Appendix E. It states (p 352), 'This guidance refers to "codes of practice" but its comments apply equally to similar documents under other names.'

In *The Codes of the Constitution* (Hart, 2016) 260pp Andrew Blick examines the growth of codification of the working rules of the operation of the state. Examples include the Cabinet Manual, the Ministerial Code, the Civil Service Code, the Guide to Judicial Conduct, the Guide to Judicial Appearances before Select Committees. Originally these codes were unpublished; today, increasingly, they are available online. Codification of the substantive law may not have greatly advanced, but in the field of public governance, codification is of great significance.

See further generally C Harlow and R Rawlings, 'Rules and discretion', ch 5 of their Law and Administration (Cambridge University Press, 2021); G Weeks, *Soft Law and Public Authorities Remedies and Reform* (Hart Publishing, 2016). In regard to 'Soft Law' in the EU see L Senden, *Soft Law in European Community Law* (Hart Publishing, 2004); 25 *Leiden Journal of International Law*, 2012(2) (special issue on soft law); Fabien Terpan, 'Soft law in the European Union – the changing nature of EU law' 21 *European Law Journal*, 2015(1), 68–96.

[142] D Greenberg, 'Dangerous trends in modern legislation', *Public Law*, 2015 (1), 96–110, 99.

[143] *Hansard*, vol 469, cols 1075–104, 15 January 1986.

[144] The Codes of Practice under the Police and Criminal Evidence Act 1984 (PACE) are an exception. They do require parliamentary approval.

9

The Process of Law Reform

9.1. The History

The problem of keeping the law abreast of changing circumstances afflicts every system in every age. A brief history of the response to the problem in this country was given by Sir Michael Kerr, former Chairman of the Law Commission, in a lecture in 1980:

Lord Justice Kerr, 'Law Reform in Changing Times' 96 *Law Quarterly Review*, 1980, 515, 517–18

> SOME OF THE LANDMARKS
>
> As long ago as 1593 (and one could start earlier) Francis Bacon introduced a project in Parliament for reducing the volume of statutes, which were 'so many in number that neither the common people can practise [*sic*] them nor the lawyers sufficiently understand them.' This task was committed to all the lawyers in the House of Commons, but nothing came of it. In 1607 James I invited Parliament to scrape the rust off the laws so that they 'might be cleared and made known to the subjects.' The idea was to reconcile conflicting decisions, discard obsolete material and prepare an authoritative restatement of the law. In his 'Proposition touching the Amendment of the Law' in 1616, Bacon himself, by then Lord Chancellor, again called for digests of the common law and statute laws with 'law commissioners' to revise them and keep them up to date, but again nothing was done …
>
> Brougham's great speech on law reform on 7 February 1828, no doubt deserves to be considered as the greatest single landmark in our non-history of systematic law reform before 1965. The speech lasted 6 hours and 3 minutes, and he is reported to have sustained himself by consuming a hatful of oranges, 'which were all the refreshment then tolerated by the custom of the House.' …
>
> He ended with the greatest peroration in our legal history, paradoxically one of Lord Denning's favourite quotations, although it exhorted reform by legislation:
>
> > It was the boast of Augustus … that he found Rome of brick, and left it of marble … But how much nobler will be our Sovereign's boast, when he shall have it to say, that he found law dear, and left it cheap; found it a sealed book – left it a living letter; found it the patrimony of the rich – left it the inheritance of the poor; found it the two edged sword of craft and oppression – left it the staff of honesty and the shield of innocence,
>
> and then moved that
>
> > an humble Address be presented to His Majesty praying that he will graciously be pleased to issue a Commission for inquiring into the defects, occasioned by time and otherwise, in the Laws of this realm of England, as administered in the Courts of Common Law, and the remedies which may be expedient for the same.

> After a speech of this length it is not surprising that the Solicitor-General proposed an adjournment of the debate. It was resumed three weeks later and Brougham's motion was duly accepted, but again led to no result.
>
> After Brougham had become Lord Chancellor in 1830 the same fate befell a 'Royal Commission on the Consolidation of Statute Laws' which he set up in 1833. The Commission reported in 1835 but nothing was done to implement its recommendations. A further 20 years on, in 1853, when Lord Cranworth became Lord Chancellor, he wrote to the Chancellor of the Exchequer within three weeks of taking office to ask him for the necessary funds and facilities from the Treasury to appoint five Commissioners to compose a 'Board for Consolidating and Digesting the Statute Law.' He only asked for £3,400 per annum, a room, messenger, and 'two or three copies of the Statutes with Stationery, etc.' But again nothing came of it. In 1965, when a further 115 years of statutes and decisions had piled up, Lord Gardiner, the then Lord Chancellor, was armed with a copy of Lord Cranworth's letter during the House of Lords debate on the Law Commissions Bill!
>
> Nevertheless, Brougham's great speech and the many other pressures for reform during the first half of the nineteenth century left their mark, and the next hundred years did see a great deal of reform, but wholly piecemeal. The ancient system of causes of action and pleadings was simplified in 1852 and the common law and equity were fused in 1873. A number of important statutes codifying parts of the criminal law were passed in the 1860s; and towards the turn of the century there were codifying Acts dealing with negotiable instruments, arbitration, partnership, sale of goods and marine insurance. The law of property was finally reformed in 1925. But each initiative was piecemeal and in a strictly limited field; at no time was there any machinery for systematic reform across the board.
>
> The penultimate development in this brief survey of over three and a half centuries, in which only a few of the milestones have been mentioned, was a halting step towards a new regime: the establishment of two standing committees to advise on the reform of civil and criminal law topics as referred to them from time to time by the Lord Chancellor and Home Secretary of the day. In 1934 Lord Chancellor Sankey set up the Law Revision Committee, revived after the war in 1952 by Lord Simonds as the Law Reform Committee; and in 1959 the Home Secretary, (the late) Lord Butler, set up the Criminal Law Revision Committee. Both did and are doing invaluable work,[1] and many of our important law reform statutes during the last decades, civil and criminal, are due to their efforts. But both Committees are composed of members who give their services voluntarily part-time: judges, academics, barristers and solicitors meeting at intervals, usually after court hours. Moreover, the Committees only deal with specific topics referred to them by successive Lord Chancellors and Home Secretaries; they have no initiative of their own. Their establishment was therefore a step forward only to the extent that they marked the first formal recognition that some permanent machinery outside government was necessary to keep the law abreast of the time. Historically it was a typical compromise; a half-way house towards real change.

The idea of a permanent body to keep the whole of the law under review was articulated in 1921 in New York by the great American judge Benjamin Cardozo, later to become a Justice of the Supreme Court:

> The courts are not helped as they could and ought to be in the adaptation of law to justice. The reason they are not helped is because there is no one whose business it is to give warning that help is needed … We must have a courier who will carry the tidings of distress … Today courts and legislature work in separation and aloofness. The penalty is paid both in the wasted effort of production and in the lowered quality of the product. On the one hand, the judges, left to fight against anachronism and injustice by the methods of judge-made law, are distracted by the

[1] Neither was formally abolished but both have long been defunct (ed).

> conflicting promptings of justice and logic, of consistency and mercy, and the output of their labours bears the tokens of the strain. On the other side, the legislature, informed only casually and intermittently of the needs and problems of the courts, without expert or responsible or disinterested or systematic advice as to the workings of one rule or another, patches the fabric here and there, and mars often when it would mend. Legislature and courts move on in proud and silent isolation. Some agency must be found to mediate between them.[2]

9.2. The English and Scottish Law Commissions

Cardozo's call led in due course to an experiment in 1923 and to the setting up in 1934 of the New York Law Revision Commission.[3] Thirty years later Cardozo's plea was echoed in Britain by Gerald Gardiner QC in *Law Reform Now*, a book published in 1963 which Gardiner co-edited with Professor Andrew Martin. In the next year Gerald Gardiner (by then Lord Gardiner) became Lord Chancellor in Harold Wilson's first government. It was reported that he took the post on condition that his idea for a Law Commission was implemented, and shortly after the government came into office a White Paper was published describing the project:

9.2.1. The White Paper

White Paper, *Proposals for English and Scottish Law Commissions*, Cmnd 2573, 1965.

> One of the hallmarks of an advanced society is that its laws should not only be just but also that they be kept up-to-date and be readily accessible to all who are affected by them. The state of the law today cannot be said to satisfy these requirements. It is true that the administration of justice in our courts is highly regarded, and rightly so, in other countries beside our own; and it is also true that the spread of the ideas of personal liberty and respect for the rule of law which have been of such importance in the development of Western civilisation has been profoundly influenced by the importance which our law attaches to these concepts. But the very fact that English and Scottish law have a history stretching back for so many centuries is one of the reasons why the form of the law is now in such an unsatisfactory state.
>
> *England and Wales*
>
> English law today is contained in some 3,000 Acts of Parliament, the earliest of which dates from the year 1235, in many volumes of delegated legislation made under the authority of those Acts, and in over 300,000 reported cases. Although Parliament has been actively at work for so many years, much of the law is still to be found in the decisions of the courts operating in fields which Parliament has not entered. It is true that the law on certain subjects has from time to time been largely restated in codifying statutes, but these are few and far between and date mostly from the end of the nineteenth century. The result is that it is today extremely difficult for anyone without special training to discover what the law is on any given topic; and when the law is finally ascertained, it is found in many cases to be obsolete and in some cases to be unjust. This is plainly wrong. English law should be capable of being recast in a form which is accessible, intelligible and in accordance with modern needs …

[2] 'A Ministry of Justice' 35 *Harvard Law Review*, 1921, 113–14.
[3] John W Macdonald, 'The New York Law Revision Commission' 28 *Modern Law Review*, 1965, 1.

There is at present no body charged with the duty of keeping the law as a whole under review and making recommendations for its systematic reform.[4] Each Government department is responsible for keeping under review the state of the law in its own field and from time to time Royal Commissions or independent committees are set up to examine and make recommendations on particular subjects. There are standing bodies such as the Lord Chancellor's Law Reform Committee,[5] whose task it is to review such small fields of the civil law as may from time to time be referred to it, while a similar task is performed in the case of the criminal law by the Home Secretary's Criminal Law Revision Committee. While valuable work has been done by these means and important changes in the law have been made as a result of the recommendations of these and other bodies, this work has been done piecemeal and it is evident that comprehensive reform can be achieved only by a body whose sole task it is and which is equipped with a professional staff on the scale required.

The Government therefore propose, subject to the approval of Parliament, to set up a Law Commission for England and Wales. This will consist of five lawyers of high standing appointed by the Lord Chancellor with an adequate legal staff to assist them. The Commissioners will be required to keep the whole of English law under review and to submit to the Lord Chancellor programmes for the examination of different branches of the law with a view to its reform. The programmes will include recommendations on the best means of carrying them out. When a programme has been approved by the Lord Chancellor after consulting other Ministers concerned it will be laid before Parliament. It may be appropriate for some of the detailed projects for reform contained in the programmes to be undertaken by the Commissioners, for others to be referred to the Law Reform Committee or the Criminal Law Revision Committee, and others again to be undertaken by the Government department concerned; or, particularly, where important social questions may arise, for a topic to be referred to a Departmental Committee or a Royal Commission by, or at the instance of the appropriate Minister. The detailed proposals for reform prepared by the Commissioners or by those other bodies will be published, and if they are accepted by the Government the necessary legislation will be introduced.

The Commissioners will also be charged with the duty of pressing forward the task of consolidation and statute law revision. The object of the latter is to prune the statute book of dead and obsolete enactments, while consolidation consists of the bringing together in one Act of all the enactments on a particular branch of the law. It is true that some progress has been made with these tasks since the war, but much remains to be done.

It is generally agreed that in the field of law reform much valuable guidance can be obtained from the experience of other countries like the United States, the Commonwealth countries and the countries of Western Europe which have had to face problems similar to our own. While in some respects the insularity of English law has been one of the sources of its strength, there is no doubt that in other directions it is a source of weakness. There is much to be gained from comparative legal studies and this will be one of the tasks of the Law Commissioners. It is intended that the Commissioners should provide Government departments which are contemplating legislation with the research and advisory facilities which will be available to the Commissioners and this may well be of particular importance in enabling departments to take account of relevant Commonwealth and foreign experience. It is not, of course, proposed that the Commissioners should duplicate the work done by other bodies such as the British Institute of International and Comparative Law.

The Law Commissioners will be appointed by the Lord Chancellor for periods to be agreed upon at the time of their appointment. This will enable distinguished lawyers to be appointed to

[4] For a review of the then-existing machinery of law reform, see ECS Wade, 'The Machinery of Law Reform' 24 *Modern Law Review*, 1961, 3–17; Gerald Gardiner and Andrew Martin (eds), *Law Reform Now* (Gollancz, 1963) ch 1; JH Farrar, *Law Reform and the Law Commissions* (Sweet & Maxwell, 1974) chs 1 and 2 and Appendices A, B, C and D, setting out the achievements of the respective bodies (ed).

[5] See Michael C Blair, 'The Law Reform Committee: the first thirty years' *Civil Justice Quarterly*, 1982, 64 (ed).

> the Commission for a term of years before returning to work in their own field, whether on the Bench, in the practising legal profession or at the universities. It is likely that similar arrangements will be made in the case of some of the staff of the Commission so as to enable full advantage to be taken of the valuable work being done at the present time by academic lawyers in the field of law reform. The task of the Commission will be immense and will not be completed for many years.
>
> The Commissioners will be required to make an annual report to the Lord Chancellor, which will be laid before Parliament.

The White Paper was published in January 1965. The Law Commissions Bill was introduced the same month. It received the Royal Assent on 15 June and the names of the first Law Commissioners were announced the following day.[6]

The Commission consists of five Commissioners, appointed by the Lord Chancellor.[7] The chairman of the English Commission is a judge, appointed usually for three years.[8] The four other Commissioners are normally appointed for five years, sometimes extended for a second term. Usually there are two practitioners (one barrister and one solicitor) and two academic lawyers. All appointments, including that of the judge chair, are now by open competition.

The duties and functions of the Law Commissions are set out in s 3:

9.2.2. The Law Commissions Act 1965

> 3. (1) It shall be the duty of each of the Commissions to take and keep under review all the law with which they are respectively concerned with a view to its systematic development and reform, including in particular the codification of such law, the elimination of anomalies, the repeal of obsolete and unnecessary enactments, the reduction of the number of separate enactments and generally the simplification and modernisation of the law, and for that purpose—
>
> (a) to receive and consider any proposals for the reform of the law which may be made or referred to them;
>
> (b) to prepare and submit to the Minister from time to time programmes for the examination of different branches of the law with a view to reform, including recommendations as to the agency (whether the Commission or another body) by which any such examination should be carried out;
>
> (c) to undertake, pursuant to any such recommendations approved by the Minister, the examination of particular branches of the law and the formulation, by means of draft Bills or otherwise, of proposals for reform therein;
>
> (d) to prepare from time to time at the request of the Minister comprehensive programmes of consolidation and statute law revision, and to undertake the preparation of draft Bills pursuant to any such programme approved by the Minister;

[6] On the background and for an analysis of the Act, see Lord Chorley and G Dworkin, 'The Law Commissions Act 1965' 28 *Modern Law Review*, 1965, 675–88. For a study of the history of the establishment of the Law Commission 30 years later, based therefore on the departmental papers, see SM Cretney, 'The Law Commission: true dawns and false dawns' 59 *Modern Law Review*, 1996, 631–57.

[7] In the case of the equivalent Scottish body, the appointment is made by the Secretary of State for Scotland and the Lord Advocate.

[8] The Tribunals, Courts and Enforcement Act 2007, s 60 provides that the person appointed as chairman must either be a judge of the High Court or of the Court of Appeal. The tradition is that if the judge is a High Court judge, he or she is appointed, a Lord (or Lady) Justice of Appeal, latest on retirement as chairman and return to the bench.

(e) to provide advice and information to government departments and other authorities or bodies concerned at the instance of the Government with proposals for the reform or amendment of any branch of the law;

(f) to obtain such information as to the legal system of other countries as appears to the Commissioners likely to facilitate the performance of any of their functions.

(2) The Minister shall lay before Parliament any programmes prepared by the Commission and approved by him and any proposals for reform formulated by the Commission pursuant to such programmes.

The first chairman of the English Law Commission, Sir Leslie (later Lord) Scarman, emphasised the a-political nature of the project:

Sir Leslie Scarman, *Law Reform: The New Pattern* (Routledge and Kegan Paul, 1968).

> The Commission is an advisory body; Parliament is to be the source of any new law that may arise from proposals of the Commission. The Commission has been called into being to advise the government and Parliament, first in the planning of law reform; secondly, in the formulation of detailed proposals for the reform of the law. The theory that underlies the Act is that law reform should be the province of the legislature; that the legislature requires specialist advice in the planning and formulation of law reform; and that this advice should be provided by a body independent of the executive and of Parliament …
>
> It is clearly contemplated by the Act that, once the Lord Chancellor has approved a programme prepared by the Commission for the purpose of law reform, both the programme, and any proposals made by the Commission in the light of the programme, shall become public property. There is therefore a significant difference between government legislation and legislation based upon proposals by the Commission. It is the practice of governments to keep secret their detailed legislative proposals until the appropriate Bill is introduced. Law Reform Bills introduced pursuant to a Commission proposal are likely, however, to follow the draft of a Bill already published with the Commission's proposal.
>
> A plain implication of these provisions of the Act is that proposals for the reform of the law, though made to the legislature, ought to be kept outside the field of political controversy. They are to be carefully considered by an expert body before the introduction of legislation. The public is to be given an opportunity of debating them – also before the introduction of legislation. And, finally, when Parliament itself has to consider them, it should have the benefit of expert advice and prior public discussion.

9.2.3. The Commission's Method of Working

The description of the Commission's method of working by one of the first five Commissioners is still largely accurate:

Mr Norman Marsh, 'Law reform in the United Kingdom: a new institutional approach' 13 *William and Mary Law Review*, 1971, 263

> The process can best be illustrated by following the course of a project of the Law Commissions from the time that it appears as an item in an approved Programme until the stage when the completed report on the item is laid before Parliament with a draft Bill giving effect to the recommendations made in the report.
>
> First, a detailed Working Paper [now called a Consultation Paper (ed)] with provisional recommendations, usually including information about the relevant legal position in other countries,[9] is

[9] The Law Commissions are required by s 3(1)(f) of the 1965 Act to obtain information on the relevant law of other countries.

> prepared by a small team in the Law Commission, headed by one or two Commissioners. After the Working Paper has been discussed at length by the Commission as a whole and, as a result, often rewritten or amended, it is distributed in an edition of about 1500 copies, not only to the various interests in the legal sphere – the judiciary, practising and academic lawyers (the latter two categories have set up special committees to deal with Law Commission papers) – but also to many lay organisations particularly interested in the subject-matter. [Today it will be posted on the Commission's website. (ed)] Further, it is sent, as a matter of course, to the relevant government departments and to the national press, both general and legal. It is worthy of note that the Commissions, although they welcome informal oral consultations, do not hold anything in the nature of formal hearings. On the whole their experience is that the most satisfactory results are obtained from carefully prepared Working Papers which are not content to ask questions but which also set out in detail the basic material from which answers can be given, with some guidance as to the provisional thinking of the Commissioners, and a survey of other possible solutions with their accompanying advantages and drawbacks. It has been found that although this technique involves much work, in the long run it spares the Commission many irrelevant and time-wasting suggestions.
>
> After an interval of perhaps six months to a year the comments received on the Working [Consultation] Paper are considered, first by a specialist team within the Commission who, with or without a general consultation with the Commission as a whole depending on the tenor of the comments received, proceed to prepare a draft Report. This Report, generally at this stage without an accompanying draft Bill, is debated by the whole Commission and sent back for any necessary amendments and the addition of the Bill, which is supplied by Parliamentary draftsmen attached to the Commission, in often prolonged consultation with the Commissioners and their staff. The Report as presented to the Lord Chancellor (in the case of the Law Commission for England and Wales) will not only outline the present law in the area covered by the Report and set forth the recommendations therewith, together with the implementing draft Bill, but it will also deal in detail with the process of consultation, including the names of those consulted and (unless there is some problem of confidentiality) the views they have expressed. The Law Commissions see the ultimate object of the elaborate process of consultation as assisting Parliament on matters of often great technical detail which can seldom be adequately investigated in the course of Parliamentary debate. This assistance is ineffective unless the scope and nature of the consultation is clearly set out on the face of the Report.

More detail was given by Professor Martin Partington based on his experience as a Commissioner:

> In a normal project, therefore, having completed an analysis of the law in the research phase, the Law Commission formally sets out its proposals for reform in a consultation paper. In practice, however, the consultation process usually starts before any consultation paper is published. The Commissioners and their team of lawyers will have informal discussions with key stakeholders about how their thinking is developing and respond to the reaction of stakeholders to those ideas. In some projects, the Law Commission will establish an informal advisory or steering group, comprising representatives of key stakeholder bodies.
>
> Once the consultation paper is published, the Law Commission is now more proactive than it was in the early years about ensuring that it gets a good response to its consultation papers. Depending on the nature of the project, the relevant Commissioner and team lawyers will address meetings of practitioners, of special interest groups and of the public. They will also meet politicians and civil servants to seek their views.[10] All these responses are collated by the Law Commission and considered by the project team.[11]

[10] Regular meetings with relevant civil servants are now part of the Protocol – as to which see below.

[11] Martin Partington, 'Law reform: the UK experience' in M Tilbury, S Young and L Ng (eds), *Reforming Law Reform: Perspectives from Hong Kong and Beyond* (Hong Kong University Press, 2014).

The work on a project is done by a team led by a Commissioner. The team typically consists of three lawyers and three recently graduated research assistants. The drafter who will draft the resulting bill is normally not brought into the project until well into the third year – after the Commission has decided its response to the Consultation Stage. After publication of the report, there may be further consultation between the Commission and the relevant government department. When it comes to actual legislation, the Office of Parliamentary Counsel usually uses the drafter who prepared the Bill whilst attached to the Commission 'to avoid the unnecessary delay and duplication of resources' which had often happened in the past.[12]

In 2024, the Commission employed 25 qualified practitioner lawyers, 24 research assistants and three legal assistants employed on a project basis.[13] Emeritus Professor Martin Partington, a former Commissioner, writing about the Commission emphasised the importance of the young research assistants:

> A highly competitive recruitment exercise is run annually which attracts outstanding young law graduates, often before they have completed their professional legal qualification training. The research assistants undertake much of the basic research involved in developing law reform projects and play a full part in team discussions. These are posts that provide a demanding bridge between university and practice and/or teaching, and which have increased in importance during the life of the Law Commission. Many former research assistants have gone on to glittering careers in legal practice or in the academic world.[14]

The Commission also often appoints consultants ad hoc to work on specific projects or on particular aspects of projects. Many of the Commission's projects involve empirical research and impact assessments. The full-time staff includes an economist.

9.2.4. The Effect of the Lord Chancellor's Office becoming the Ministry of Justice

The Lord Chancellor has been the Minister responsible for the Law Commission from the start in 1965 to the present day. But what the Lord Chancellor presides over has not remained the same. In 2003, the Lord Chancellor's Office was abolished and replaced by the Department of Constitutional Affairs and in 2007 the Department of Constitutional Affairs was abolished and replaced by the Ministry of Justice. Its head was now titled not only Lord Chancellor, but Lord Chancellor and Secretary of State for Justice. The changes had nothing to do with the Law Commission, but the Law Commission was affected considerably. Sir Terence Etherton, chairman of the Commission in 2008, wrote of the effect of the changes. He was clearly very concerned. Lord Gardiner, he said:

> had a passionate and principled interest in the reform of the law to make it more modern, accessible and just. Critically, he was Lord Chancellor at a time when his Department (then called the Lord Chancellor's Office) was extremely small with few politically sensitive functions. At the same time, he combined the roles of Head of the Judiciary, the Speakership of the House of Lords, and membership of the executive with a senior Cabinet position. The Lord Chancellor was a highly influential member of the government, not by virtue of the size of his Department or the range of its functions and their political sensitivity, but by virtue of the constitutional significance of his office independent of party politics …

[12] Mr Justice Brooke, 'The role of the Law Commission in simplifying statute law' 16 *Statute Law Review*, 1995, 1–3.

[13] Information provided to the writer by the Law Commission.

[14] Partington, 'Law reform: the UK experience' (n 11 above).

> The political landscape has changed dramatically over time. Today, the reality is that the Lord Chancellorship is a facet of being the Secretary of State for Justice. As such, the Lord Chancellor is a fully fledged party politician, shorn of any independent judicial or legislative role. True it is that, under the Constitutional Reform Act 2005, and by virtue of his oath, the Lord Chancellor is bound to respect the rule of law, defend the independence of the judiciary and ensure the provision of resources for the efficient and effective support of the courts. Nevertheless, the political reality is that, unlike the Lord Chancellors of former times, he is wholly within the Cabinet and in no real sense detached from it. His influence is measured by the relative size and importance of his Department and his personal political standing. He does not therefore have the constitutional attributes of former Lord Chancellors, whose high standing and influence reflected the unique constitutional position and facets of the Lord Chancellor's Office.[15]

Those changes were part of a process of politicisation that could be traced back to the early 1970s and which gathered pace in the 1980s. Under the Courts Act 1971, the Lord Chancellor had taken over the running of the Court Service. In 1980 he assumed responsibility for criminal legal aid and in 1988 for civil legal aid. In 2005, the Department was given responsibility for the Magistrates' Court and, in 2007, by far the most weighty of all, for prisons and probation. The budget for the Department for 2006–07 was £3.49 billion of which 0.1 per cent was attributable to the Law Commission.

In addition, there had been an immense increase in legislation giving effect to party political manifesto obligations and general political policy initiatives resulting inevitably in less time for non-political, non-party Law Commission reports. Another problem, Sir Terence said, was the increased movement of junior ministers. In the fifteen months since he had been appointed Chairman of the Law Commission there had been no fewer than four junior ministers responsible for the Law Commission – averaging therefore less than four months each. Since a Law Commission bill generally took some three years from report to implementation there could be no assumption that a project supported or even promoted by the Department would be regarded with the same enthusiasm – 'or indeed any enthusiasm' – at its conclusion. (Rapid turn-over has applied since 2007 equally to the holders of the post of Lord Chancellor/Secretary of State. In the 38 years between the setting up of the Law Commission in 1965 and the abolition of the Lord Chancellor's Office, there were only four holders of the office – an average of 9.4 years.[16] In the 17 years between 2007 and 2024, there were eleven – an average of 1.5 years.[17])

Sir Terence Etherton lamented the downgrading of government's interest in law reform:

> Those changes have historically had an obvious harming effect on the sponsorship role of the [Department] for the Commission. The vision in [Lord Gardiner's] *Law Reform Now* of a strong unit in the Lord Chancellor's office headed by a Minister of State concerned exclusively with law reform has been translated into a very small Sponsorship team located in the HM Court Service section of the Department. That insouciant administrative pigeon-holding of the Commission within a court delivery service reflects both an awkward confusion or embarrassment as to how to

[15] Sir Terence Etherton, 'Law reform in England and Wales: a shattered dream or triumph of political vision', *Amicus Curiae*, Institute of Advanced Legal Studies, Spring 2008, 3–11.

[16] Lord Gardiner (1964–70), Lord Hailsham (1970–74 and 1979–87), Lord Elwyn Jones (1974–79) and Lord Mackay (1987–97). Lord Havers was also Lord Chancellor but only for four months in 1987. He was forced to resign because of ill health.

[17] Jack Straw (2013–15), Ken Clarke (2010–12), Chris Grayling (2012–15), Michael Gove (2015–16), Liz Truss (2016–17), David Liddington (2017–18), David Gauke (2018–19), Robert Buckland (2019–21), Dominic Raab (2021–22, 2022–23), Brandon Lewis (2022–22), Alex Chalk (2023–24).

deal with the Commission and, more particularly, a reflection of its low priority within a Department dealing with a wide range of highly politically charged and resource intensive functions.[18].

9.2.5. Threats to Independence and Funding

The Law Commission quickly established and has maintained an excellent reputation. As a public body, it is subject to periodic external review. The 2003 Quinquennial Review began, 'The Law Commission's contribution to improvements in the law is held in high esteem by the wide variety of its stakeholders who were consulted during this review'. Mr John Halliday, who carried out the Review, commended in particular: 'the high level of its expertise, and of its analytical and problem-solving skills; a strong tradition of openness and consultation; responsiveness to points made in consultation and to requests for new work; independence of judgment and integrity; an excellent peer review process; and an informal, engaging management style. Halliday also found that in general the Commission's staff were 'happy and motivated at work'.[19]

However, it has not always been smooth sailing. In 2010 the Commission faced a crisis arising from the sceptical attitude of the Conservative led Coalition Government toward quangos. Lord Justice Munby, the Commission's Chairman at the time, described what happened in his Denning lecture in 2011:[20]

> During the summer of 2010 we were presented with perhaps the biggest threats ever faced by the Commission, which put at risk not just our independence and our ability to function, but even our very existence. The Commission was examined as part of the Government's overall review of arms'-length bodies, the outcome of which is the Public Bodies Bill now making its way through Parliament. For a short period abolition seemed a possibility, though in time the Government decided that the Commission should continue to exist on the basis that there remains a need for a law reform body that is 'technically expert and independent'. Despite this, the Commission, with 150 other public bodies, was swept up into Schedule 7, perhaps the most controversial part of the Public Bodies Bill. This would have enabled the statutory provisions governing the Law Commission to be amended by secondary legislation, making it possible for the Government to adjust not just the composition but also the functions of the Law Commission by statutory instrument.
>
> Thankfully, on 28 February 2011, the Cabinet Office Minister, Lord Taylor of Holbeach, told the House of Lords that Schedule 7 would be dropped. He acknowledged that the Government 'absolutely recognises that some public functions need to be carried out independently of ministers'. Schedule 7, we were told, 'was never intended to hinder or threaten that independence'. Whatever the intention, it plainly did.[21]

The Law Commission's 2013–14 Annual Report expressed the Commission's relief that it had fought off the Ministry of Justice's plan to have the Commission included on the

[18] Sir Terence Etherton, 'Law reform in England and Wales: a shattered dream or triumph of political vision', *Amicus Curiae*, Institute of Advanced Legal Studies, Spring 2008, 3–11.

[19] Para 9.14. The Staff Attitude Survey in 2001 showed that 71 per cent were proud to work for the Commission – compared with an average of 47 per cent across the Lord Chancellor's Department.

[20] 'Shaping the Law: The Law Commission at the Cross-Roads', the 2011 Denning Lecture, p 5, The annual Denning Lecture is given under the auspices of the Bar Association for Commerce, Finance and Industry. The lectures can be accessed at www.bacfi.org.

[21] 'Shaping the Law: The Law Commission at the Cross-Roads', the 2011 Denning Lecture, p 5. Munby was Law Commission Chairman 2009–12.

Government's website. Retaining its separate website (www.lawcommission.justice.gov.uk) was an important indication of independence.

Lord Justice Munby said (at p 5) that having survived the threat to its independence, the Commission faced a serious threat to its funding:

> Simultaneously, and again in common with many other government bodies, we learned that the income we would receive from our sponsoring department, the Ministry of Justice, was to be very significantly reduced. There followed several months of hopeful attempts at negotiation on our part, which were met with a sympathetic but unbending response. Having already weathered a modest reduction in 2010–2011, we must now prepare ourselves for further, much deeper and more painful reductions over the next four years. Cuts that would otherwise have been insupportable and profoundly damaging to the Commission have been made tolerable only because we have been able to persuade a number of other government departments to contribute to the cost of the law reform projects they are sponsoring.

Over several years the funding situation was extremely difficult.[22] But in 2020–21 the government agreed to a new funding system. This was described in the Law Commission's annual report for 2021–22 (at p 7):

> One of the most significant developments during the course of 2020/21 was the creation of a new agreement reached with the Lord Chancellor to address concerns about the Law Commission's funding model. Without focusing in detail on the past, the Commission's funding model had over time developed into a hybrid model, whereby MoJ [Ministry of Justice] Core funding had been reduced by approximately 50%, with greater emphasis being placed on securing income-generating projects from other government departments so as to make up the shortfall. Not only was this model highly volatile, but it also risked skewing the type of work the Commission was asked to do. Numerous stakeholders were concerned that it affected our independence. We are grateful to those stakeholders for their support in setting out the arguments, most notably the Justice Select Committee, chaired by Sir Bob Neill MP.
>
> The new model can be viewed on our website. In short, it returns to full funding from the MoJ. It does bring with it an expectation that other government departments will continue to contribute towards the cost of law reform projects, however, the Agreement makes clear that the focus is on where law reform is most needed (against agreed criteria), rather than whether the finances are available. This should lead to a more balanced portfolio of work, together with more transparency about the work we are undertaking.
>
> During 2021/22, the new model has been implemented, with the Commission receiving its full budget from the Ministry of Justice.[23] This has greatly enhanced our ability to plan our work and staffing models. At the same time, we have been able to continue to source funding from other Whitehall Departments for a number of projects and have been able to return those funds to the MoJ as part of a year end planned underspend.
>
> The new model is working very well and we are pleased to see that the MoJ is particularly keen to make greater use of the Law Commission, while at the same time we continue to attract high quality work from across Whitehall.

In the 2022–23 annual report, the Law Commission's Chair confirmed that the new model was working well: '[I]n our view, it has proven to be a success and in many different ways

[22] In the five years from 2009–10 to 2013–14 income was £4.4m, £4.3m, £3.5m, £4.5m, £4.5m. In 2014–15 income was down to £2.9m, in 2017–18, £2.2m, in 2019–20, £2m. The figures are given each year in Appendix B of the annual report.

[23] In 2022–23 this amounted to £5.2m [ed].

has enhanced our ability to deliver law reform to a high quality, on time and which meets the needs of Government, the economy and society more broadly' (p 1).

9.2.6. The 2010 Protocol

The Law Commission works to a programme of projects agreed from time to time with the Lord Chancellor. (At the time of writing, late 2024, it was in the process of preparing the 14th programme.[24]) In regard to the work programme, the Law Commission Act 2009, amending the 1965 Act, inserted new s 3B, which provides:

> (1) The Lord Chancellor and the Law Commission may agree for the purposes of this section a statement (a 'protocol') about the Law Commission's work.
> (2) The protocol may include (among other things) provision about—
> (a) principles and methods to be applied in deciding the work to be carried out by the Law Commission and in the carrying out of that work;
> (b) the assistance and information that Ministers of the Crown and the Law Commission are to give each other;
> (c) the way in which Ministers of the Crown are to deal with the Law Commission's proposals for reform, consolidation or statute law revision.

The provisions of the Protocol were described in the Commission's introduction to its Eleventh Programme of law reform published in 2011:

> 1.7 The introduction to the Protocol sets out the joint aims of the Lord Chancellor and Chairman of the Law Commission to create law that is fair, modern, simple and accessible and to increase the momentum of law reform. The Protocol lays down the procedure for deciding on projects to be included in a programme of law reform; and on projects referred to the Commission by Ministers. It also sets out the role and procedures to be followed by both the sponsoring Government department and the Law Commission during the currency of a law reform project and after a project is completed.
>
> 1.8 This is the first programme of law reform to be developed under the terms of the Protocol.
>
> THE LAW COMMISSION'S PROJECT SELECTION CRITERIA
>
> 1.9 When considering whether to include a project in the next programme of law reform, the Law Commission assesses each proposal against the following broad selection criteria:
>
> (1) Importance: the extent to which the law is unsatisfactory (for example, unfair, unduly complex, inaccessible or outdated); and the potential benefits likely to accrue from undertaking reform.
> (2) Suitability: whether the reform would be suitable to be put forward by a body of lawyers after legal research and consultation (this would tend to exclude subjects where the considerations are shaped primarily by political judgements).[25]

[24] The Law Commission's annual report for 2023–24 explained (p 6) that preparation of the 14th programme had been paused in anticipation of the then forthcoming General Election.

[25] Commenting on this issue, Professor Martin Partington, a former Commissioner, wrote: 'This desire to deal with important areas of law that were not politically very controversial is in contrast to the experience of a number of other law commissions around the world that have ventured into far more politically sensitive areas. It is noteworthy that some of these arguably bolder law reform agencies have since disappeared, whereas the Law Commission continues to exist.' (Partington, 'Law reform: the UK experience' (n 11 above) fn 12 (ed).).

(3) Resources: internal and external resources needed, and whether those resources are likely to be available; and the need for a good mix of projects in terms of the scale and timing so as to enable effective management of the programme.

1.10 The Protocol also requires consideration of:

(1) whether project-specific funding is available (if relevant);
(2) the degree of departmental support;
(3) whether there is a Scottish or Northern Irish dimension to the project that would need the involvement of the Scottish and/or Northern Ireland Law Commissions; and
(4) whether there is a Welsh dimension that would need the involvement of the Welsh Government.

1.11 The Protocol has established a clearer system for ensuring that departments are supportive of the Law Commission's work in terms of future implementation. Where the Commission is considering including a project in a programme of law reform, the Commission notifies the Minister with relevant policy responsibility and, in deciding how to respond to the Commission, the Minister must bear in mind that, before approving the inclusion of the project in the overall programme, the Lord Chancellor will expect the Minister (with the support of the Permanent Secretary):

(1) to agree that the department will provide sufficient staff to liaise with the Commission during the currency of the project (normally, a policy lead, a lawyer and an economist); and
(2) to give an undertaking that there is a serious intention to take forward law reform in this area (if applicable in the case of the particular project).

1.12 In discussion between the department and the Commission, the department will, insofar as is possible at this stage, provide views to the Commission on:

(a) what it considers to be the most appropriate output for the project (for example, policy recommendations, a draft bill, draft guidance) and the likely method of implementation;
(b) any risks associated with that method of implementation which might lead to non implementation or significantly delayed implementation (for example, difficulties in obtaining legislative time if the method of implementation is legislation).

Lord Justice Munby, Law Commission chairman 2009-12, commenting on this development, said that the 2009 Act made the Commission less independent but he felt that pragmatism was needed to accomplish the Commission's aims. On the selection of topics for reform there were two alternative positions:

> At one end of the spectrum there is a free-wheeling body, reporting on what it thinks fit; at the other is a body bound by the Government's wishes and agenda. The attraction of the former is that it allows priority problems to be addressed, even if Government is not interested in them. It is a seductively pure existence. But the danger is that the work is not implemented, with all the lost opportunities, waste of resources and depression of morale that entails. The attraction of the latter option is that the Commission is working on an agenda that will actually change lives and the law; the danger is that it pushes us to take up projects that we would not have otherwise selected and which could damage the Commission's integrity.
>
> The Protocol puts the Commission more towards the latter camp. It remains extremely important that the Commission is independent of Government. This is a matter of fundamental importance; after all, we have built our reputation upon that independence. That we are able to do our work and make our recommendations free from any political influence is absolutely crucial and something on which the Commission will never compromise. But, in reality, our programmes of Law Reform have always had to be laid before the Lord Chancellor for his approval, and, while there

> may be great reform work to be done in many areas of law for their own sake, we must in today's climate be pragmatic if we are to achieve our essential aims.[26]

An assessment of this reform by Shona Wilson of Girton College, Cambridge, came to a mixed conclusion.[27] The new parliamentary procedure had 'given the Commission a useful tool to push through its more technical and controversial Bills'.[28] Acts had found their way onto the statute book which might otherwise have languished in Whitehall. The 2009 Act on the other hand was more problematic. There were worrying signs that it was not the fresh start that the Commission expected and needed. The reports from the Lord Chancellor required by the Act had not been very informative.[29] In some instances they had been deferred ie not made at all. Reasons for rejecting proposed projects had tended to say merely that the topic was not a government priority. The main potential problem identified by Shona Wilson was that of the possible compromise of the Commission's independence.

> The Commission has been fiercely proud of this independence. Does the 2009 Act jeopardise this by forcing it only to examine things which please the Government and, more worryingly preventing it from examining issues which the Government does not want explored? … Should independence be valued above all else, or should it be sacrificed in order to increase implementation? Implementation, after all, is not the only marker of the Commission's worth – its reports may have value in other ways, such as use by students, academics, legal practitioners, Parliament and the judiciary. Commissioners may also feel that their work whether implemented or not, examines an area of the law that should not have been left untouched and the report might be of use at some point in the future.[30]

Statute law revision The Law Commission, through its Statute Law Revision Bills, is responsible for the repeal, and therefore removal from the statute book, of over 3,000 whole statutes that no longer serve any useful purpose and the partial repeal of thousands of other statutes.[31] Since 1965, the Law Commission has also been responsible for over 200 consolidation statutes. In the 41 years between 1965 and 2006 there were 220 Consolidation Bills. In the seventeen years between 2006 and 2023 there were only three. The 2022–23 annual report said (p 69): 'This change reflects the fact that, in a time of reduced funding in most areas of public services, consolidation is perhaps seen by the Government to be a lower priority.'

9.2.7. Implementation of Law Commission Reports

The Law Commission's annual report has an appendix which states what happened (or is happening) to every report since the start of the Commission's existence. Appendix A shows: Pending/Implemented/Accepted and awaiting implementation/Accepted but not being implemented/Rejected/Superseded. If implemented, the table states the legislation.

Over the more than fifty years of the Commission's existence, two-thirds of its reports (66 per cent) have been implemented in whole or in part with 14 per cent rejected.[32]

[26] Sir James Munby, 'Shaping the Law: The Law Commission at the Cross-Roads', the 2011 Denning Lecture, p 5. Munby was Law Commission Chairman 2009–12.

[27] S Wilson, 'Reforming the Law (Commission): a crisis of identity?' *Public Law*, 2013, 20.

[28] Ibid, 28.

[29] Giving the 2011 Denning Lecture, Sir James Munby described the Lord Chancellor's report published in January 2011 as 'disappointing'. The second Lord Chancellor's report, published in March 2012, had followed the same pattern with many deferrals of decisions and statements about reforms not being Government priorities.

[30] Wilson, 'Reforming the Law (Commission)' (n 27 above) 27.

[31] The Statute Law (Repeals) Act 2013, for instance, repealed 817 whole Acts dating from 1322 to 2010.

[32] *Tailored Review of the Law Commission*, 2019, para 8.6.

It is often said that law reform proceeds at a very leisurely pace. In regard to Law Commission recommendations to government there are two stages – first, the preparation of the recommendations and then, waiting for the government to act.

As to the first stage, the 2003 Quinquennial Review of the Law Commission[33] stated that between 1997 and 2001 it took an average of five years and four months for the Commission to produce and publish a report – the average concealing a wide range of completion times. Between 1985 and 2001 it took an average of three years and one month between publication and implementation. The average time between publication and a Departmental decision to accept it was two years.[34]

The 2019 *Tailored Review of the Law Commission* (para 8.3) said on this topic:

> Stakeholders interviewed, particularly those from the legal sector, were not concerned with projects taking a long time as they recognised that the Law Commission is often dealing with challenging and complex areas of law reform that should not be rushed. Time is required to build consensus and generate implementable advice.

Once the Law Commission has delivered its recommendations, it awaits an indication of the Government's response. If the proposals are accepted in whole or in part, there is then the wait for acceptance to be translated into legislation. Because the Law Commission has drafters attached who are members of the Office of Parliamentary Counsel, it is able to accompany the recommendations with a draft bill. That will shorten or even avoid the need for a drafting stage. But the question for the government department that deals with the topic is whether the recommendations are acceptable in whole or at least in part and, if so, whether the government will include the bill in its legislative programme. Sometimes MPs who have drawn a slot in the ballot for Private Members' Bills agree to take forward a Law Commission bill that the government wish to see enacted but for which there is no room in its programme.

Another initiative aimed at improving the speed of implementation was the requirement introduced in 2009 that the Lord Chancellor lay before parliament an annual report (a) on the Law Commission proposals that have been implemented in whole or in part during the year and (b) on the Law Commission's proposals that have not been implemented, including plans for dealing with those proposals, any decisions not to implement any of those proposals taken and the reasons for the decision.[35]

This is not the previously mentioned report given in Appendix A of each year's annual report. That report gives only a one-line statement about more than 400 reports going back to 1967. This report gives quite lengthy explanations about each individual item. (The latest, at the time of writing, dated July 2023, ran to 39 pages.)

In his 2011 Denning lecture, Sir James Munby, Law Commission chairman, gave this then new requirement a mixed reception. On the one hand he said:

> This is a hugely important development, both for the Commission and for the public we serve. For the first time we shall have an annual report[36] produced by Government and presented to Parliament that explains what has happened and when action might be expected. This new statutory requirement on the Lord Chancellor increases the transparency of the Government's approach to

[33] The figures were mainly based on a survey of reports published between January 1985 and December 2001. In that period the Commission had published 91 law reform reports.

[34] Para 6.7.

[35] Law Commission Act 2009 s 1 inserting new s 3A into the Law Commissions Act 1965. The 2009 Act was a Private Members Bill introduced by a former Law Lord, Lord Lloyd of Berwick. The bill however was drafted by Parliamentary Counsel attached to the Law Commission. It would not have reached the statute book if its provisions were unacceptable to the Lord Chancellor's Department.

[36] The report published July 2023 stated that it was the eighth report, which means they have not been annual (ed).

> our work and is to be warmly welcomed, not least because of the pressure it puts on Government to respond to our reports.

But he found the actual content of the report a disappointment:

> The substance and detail of the report, however, was much less reassuring. While it showed that a number of the Law Commission's proposals had been implemented, of 20 during the preceding year, it was disappointing in the account it gave of those that have not been, or in some cases will now never be, implemented.
>
> The report listed fifteen Law Commission projects that had not yet been implemented and five that had been rejected. Of the fifteen projects that had not yet been implemented, a number had lain on Government shelves for far too long – in the case of our Partnership Law project, over seven years when the Lord Chancellor reported. Not only is this unsatisfactory. Delay of this kind means that the reports become out of date and may need a considerable amount of work to refresh, if the decision is ever taken to implement.
>
> But even worse, the delays continue. Although there was more or less positive progress reported in relation to four of these fifteen reports, in no fewer than nine cases, the best that the Lord Chancellor was able to say was that the Government aimed to respond or make an announcement 'early this year' or, in one case, 'in late Spring'. In the other two cases a much longer timescale was envisaged before any further consideration could be given.[37]

The 39-page report published in July 2023 gave an account of what had happened under four headings:

(1) Have been implemented: seven items flowing from Law Commission reports completed in 2014, 2015, 2017 (two), 2018, 2019 and 2022
(2) In the process of being implemented wholly or in part: eleven items flowing from Law Commission reports completed in: 2011, 2014 (two), 2016, 2017, 2018 (two), 2020 (three), 2022
(3) Awaiting a decision: 21 items flowing from Law Commission reports completed in: 2007, 2010, 2011, 2014 (five), 2015 (two), 2016 (two), 2017, 2019, 2020 (five), 2022 (two)
(4) Decision not to implement: one item

One entry reads: 'The Law Commission published a report and draft bill on 27 July 2010 and a draft bill making recommendations clarifying the limits on the availability of judicial review of decisions in a trial on indictment. The Government's interim response of 13 March 2015, noted that it was considering the Commission's recommendations and this work continues.'

If a Law Commission report published thirteen years previously is still under consideration, one wonders whether there is much difference between 'Not implemented' and 'Awaiting a decision'. That reports should be awaiting a decision for three or four years is perhaps understandable. That they should be waiting five to ten years is unacceptable. That they should be waiting for more than ten years is ridiculous – as well as insulting for the Law Commission.

The Tailored Review of the Law Commission, published in 2019, had this to say on implementation:

> 8.8 A key factor impacting the implementation rate is the parliamentary timetable which, at the time of writing, is largely occupied with EU Exit legislation; this is outside of the Law Commission's control. There are, however, some measures that the Law Commission can be taking to

[37] Lord Justice Munby, 'Shaping the Law – The Law Commission at the Crossroads', 2011 Denning Lecture.

increase the likelihood of government departments or Parliamentarians taking forward draft legislation.

8.9 For example, by networking and building closer relationships with Parliamentarians, policy colleagues and Ministers, the Commission may be able to find alternative ways to pass legislation outside of the normal departmental route, such as Private Members' Bills, inclusion in complementary bills or by building consensus around their existing Special Procedure process.[38] This would need to be done carefully to ensure that the Commission's independence is not impacted. As such, the review recommends the Commission considers drafting internal guidance to support this, as well as including it as a requirement in the job descriptions of the Chair and Commissioners.

9.3. Judicial Law-Making in Light of the Existence of the Law Commission

When the Law Commission was first set up, some took the view that this spelled the end for judicial law-making. One distinguished observer who expressed this opinion at an early stage was Lord Devlin:

Lord Devlin, 'The process of law reform' 63 *Law Society's Gazette*, 1966, 453–62

> There can be no doubt that the institution of the Law Commission marks a great step forward in the process of law reform. It has immediately and easily assumed command of the first stage of the process and its institution, taken in conjunction with other measures, holds out hope of widening the bottleneck in the second stage so that there is a much needed flow of beneficial reform. Its command of the first stage will mean that the importance of judicial law-making, which has been dwindling now for a century or more, will probably almost entirely vanish but without, I hope, dimming the name and reputation of Lord Denning, who will stand for future generations as the last great judicial innovator.
>
> The trouble about judicial law reform was never, as it is with parliament, lack of time but lack of opportunity – that and the multiplication of courts of appeal. When Lord Mansfield laid down the law, new law was created more or less from the moment he said it. But since his time the delay before a point of principle reaches the House of Lords may be so long as to outdistance by ten times or more the parliamentary process. With the Law Commission speeding the work of statutory reform and codifying the law, the day of the judicial law-maker is brought quite to an end.

Realisation of the concept of codification (as will be seen below), did not come to fruition. But, contrary to Lord Devlin's view, there is no evidence that the existence of the Law Commission altered the judges' attitude to law reform. They proved to be no less ready to undertake a role in the improvement of the law than before the Law Commissions were set up.

Moreover, law reform by judges is not to be dismissed as necessarily second-class by comparison with that of the legislature. Professor HK Lücke of the University of Adelaide made this point:

> Adjudication is the judge's most important function and the responsibility which it casts upon him is a personal and a heavy one. Like all human activity, adjudication must become routine to some

[38] Where Law Commission Bills are non-controversial, the Law Commission can introduce them directly to the House of Lords via Special Procedure. Details on the Special Procedure can be found here: http://researchbriefings.parliament.uk/ResearchBriefing/Summary/SN07156.

> extent, but it is difficult to see how the sense of occasion which affects every trial, civil or criminal, and to which barristers so readily testify, can ever be completely lost on the judge himself. Law, which grows out of adjudication, stems from a situation of judicial engagement much intensified by both proximity and the judge's special responsibility. Nothing comparable could exist in the remote atmosphere of ministries of justice, law reform commissions, or even of parliaments where statute law is prepared and made. A rule or principle which grows out of live adjudication differs from a legal opinion formed *in abstracto* in much the same way as a live performance differs from a mere rehearsal, real combat from a manoeuvre, the final race from a mere practice run.
>
> All this is unmistakably reflected in a fundamental feature of common law jurisprudence: hard, binding law emerges from judgments only to the extent to which the judge's faculties are sharpened and engaged by his duty to adjudicate a real dispute.[39]

The value of the common law as the method of developing the law slowly was emphasised by Lord Reid in a speech to teachers of law:

> Finally, may I make some comparison between the common law and statute law. I am tempted to take as an analogy the difference between old-fashioned, hand-made, expensive, quality goods and the brash products of modern technology. If you think in months, want an instant solution for your problems and don't mind that it won't wear well, then go for legislation. If you think in decades, prefer orderly growth and believe in the old proverb more haste less speed, then stick to the common law. But do not seek a middle way by speeding up and streamlining the development of the common law.[40]

Clearly though, judges cannot be regarded as sufficient law reformers. The reasons were considered by one of the original Law Commissioners.

Norman Marsh, 'Law reform in the United Kingdom: a new institutional approach' 13 *William and Mary Law Review*, 1971, 263

> Five considerations, some of which, if not entirely new, have at least intensified in recent years, and others, more or less inherent in a system of judge-made law, suggest that English law cannot, at least for the future, rely on that system as the main instrument of law reform.
>
> First, it is no longer possible for the judge in modern English society to make those bold assumptions about family life and about relations between landlord and tenant, employer and employee, citizen and the State which underlie many reforms of a seemingly legal character. On the one hand, he lives in an era where many value assumptions are being challenged; on the other, he does not enjoy quite the unquestioned prestige, the charismatic authority, enjoyed by his Victorian forbears. As the House of Lords recognised, after a decade or more of attempted judicial innovations designed to provide protection in the matrimonial home for the deserted wife, and after an even longer period of judicial experiments aimed at protecting the economically weaker party to a contract from unfair exemption clauses, reform of the law may raise issues which in present conditions are more appropriately dealt with by the legislature.
>
> Secondly, judge-made reforms are dependent on the issue coming before the courts, and more particularly on the issue reaching an instance which places the court in a position to overrule, ignore, or distinguish any awkward precedents which stand in the way of reform. This chance element is accentuated by another factor, namely, the respective means of the parties to the litigation in question. Between the litigant who qualifies for legal aid and the man, or more often the corporation or government body, for whom costs matter less than a satisfactory legal result, there

[39] 'The common-law: judicial impartiality and judge made law' 98 *Law Quarterly Review*, 1982, 29, 62.
[40] 'The judge as law maker' *Journal of the Society of Public Teachers of Law*, vol 12, NS, 1972, 28.

> is a large group of potential litigants deterred by lack of means from fighting a case through the courts and, if necessary, to the House of Lords. Sometimes it may profit a litigant with a business in which the same issue may reoccur, to settle a case in spite of a favourable ruling in, say, the Court of Appeal, in order to prevent a possible reversal in the House of Lords. Indeed, this is rather more likely since the House of Lords assumed power to overrule its own decisions. In such circumstances the average party to a case is likely to prefer the cash in hand to the doubtful distinction of running a large financial risk in the interests of a possible reform of the law.
>
> A third and even more important consideration may be summed up by a slight modification of a well-known aphorism: hard cases make not so much bad as unsystematic, incoherent and therefore, from the point of view of the law as a whole, uncertain law. In other words, the hard case invites an equitable decision, which is not bad in itself, but requires a broader base of principle than the judge in that particular case is entitled to provide. If he does reach a decision, he only prepares the way for a further spate of litigation which may ultimately have to be stemmed by legislation …
>
> Fourthly, it must be remembered that the reforming decision, which is welcomed by the critical academic lawyer, long familiar and impatient with some outdated but hitherto accepted piece of conventional legal wisdom, may be extremely unjust to the unsuccessful party. The latter is, in effect, the victim in a case of retrospective law-making. The danger of injustice by departing from the expected patterns of judicial behaviour was emphasised by the House of Lords when they announced in 1966 that they would no longer be necessarily bound by their own previous decisions. They would, they said, 'bear in mind the danger of disturbing retrospectively the basis on which contracts, settlements of property and fiscal arrangements have been entered into and also the especial need for certainty as to the criminal law'.
>
> There is a fifth consideration which it would, in the context of English law, seem natural to bear in mind when assessing the potentialities of the judiciary as a source of law reform. It concerns, of course, the important part played by *stare decisis* in the English legal system. Clearly there is less scope, at least for rapid change, where that principle prevails than by the clean-sweeping enunciation by the legislature of some new general principle.

A sixth consideration, not referred to by Mr Marsh, is that the courts are likely to be relatively ill-informed as to the background to the problem that is said to require reform. The court relies normally on the arguments presented by counsel for the parties. It has no opportunity to consult with other persons, interested bodies, government departments or experts, as to what kind of reform would be most beneficial.

The weaknesses of case-law as an instrument of reform were the subject of an article by Sir Richard Buxton, formerly a Lord Justice of Appeal. He identified four separate concerns:

(1) The purpose of any case is to decide the issue between the parties, and not to reform the law. The decision, and therefore the general shape of the law that is deduced from it, may be unduly influenced by a desire to do justice in the particular case, without appreciation of the wider implications of the way in which instant justice has been achieved.
(2) The glory of litigation, at least as practised in England and Wales, is the oral advocacy of counsel, and their ability seamlessly to reformulate a case to meet the exigencies of forensic debate. Moves that help to win the case may not help with the rational development of the law.
(3) There is no place in the English forensic process for the sort of review of opinion, practicalities and collateral damage that is undertaken by the Law Commission before it sets about changing the law,

(4) When an attempt is made to change the general law by the decision in a particular case, there may be prolonged uncertainty, often extending over a period of years, about the extent and generality of what the court has decided.[41]

On the other hand, if the court abdicates responsibility for improving the law, nothing may happen. Legislatures and government departments normally have more than enough to occupy their time and may not find time for a proposed project of reform. In particular they may lack both the time and the energy to conduct the necessary researches to formulate reform proposals that are well designed to meet the problem. It is this above all which justifies the existence of a full-time law-reform body such as the Law Commission.

See further on this issue the reflections of another Law Commissioner, Dr Peter North, 'Is law reform too important to be left to lawyers?' 5 *Legal Studies*, 1985, 119.

9.4. The Law Commission and the Codification Project

Codification was specifically referred to in s 3 of the Law Commission Act as one of the Commission's chief duties. The story of codification, however, is not a happy one. It began as the centrepiece of the Law Commission's project but the brave vision outlined by the first Chairman, Sir Leslie Scarman never materialised. He set out the vision in a lecture in 1966:

Sir Leslie Scarman, *A Code of English Law?* (Hull University, 1966)

> No one could suggest, without taking leave of his senses, that the present shape of English law is either simple or modern … English law lacks coherent shape, is inaccessible save to those with the training, the stamina, and the time to explore the jungle of case and statute law, and is unmanageable save by the initiated. It retains the mystical, priestly quality of early law: it has survived into the modern world only because of the tremendous quality of its high-priests – the judges who, from their seats of judgment, have from time immemorial – often in prose of striking beauty and clarity – declared its principles and solutions …
>
> But it may be that the quality of our judge-made law – its flexibility, its certainty, its capacity to develop in response to the stimuli of actual life conveyed through the channel of litigation to the minds of the judges – is such that its unmanageable bulk must be accepted. Can it be said that the refined gold of the common law is not to be had without the dust, darkness, and encumbrances of the mineworkings? I would not pretend in the time at my disposal to attempt an assessment of the value of our judge-made law, save to say that the achievements of the judges are immense. They have created one of the two great systems of jurisprudence existing today in the western world. Blessed as we have been with an unbroken legal development over a period of 600 years, we find in our judge-made law a wonderful consistency of legal thought and action, and a remarkable capacity for adjustment to changing social conditions. The risk exists that codification might well shatter it. Yet, if this is right, law reform by legislative process, even when it does not lead to codification, should in logic be abandoned as a danger to the unity of the common law. But no one suggests the need for so conservative an approach. And there are clear indications that under the strain of our times the courts, notwithstanding the quality of their work, can no longer be accepted as sufficient instruments for the reform or modernisation of the law …

[41] R Buxton, 'How the common law gets made: *Hedley Byrne* and other cautionary tales' 125 *Law Quarterly Review*, 2009, 60, 60. Sir Richard illustrated his concerns with the story of three House of Lords decisions: *Hedley Byrne & Co Ltd v Heller & Partners Ltd* [1964] AC 465; *Pepper v Hart* [1993] AC 593; and *Attorney-General v Blake* [2001] 1 AC 268.

> The basic weakness of a system of law which relies upon judicial precedent for its development is that it is not the primary function of courts or judges to legislate. This criticism may be put somewhat differently: development by judicial precedent is development of the law by lawyers – a practice against which man has protested with more or less success since the dawn of civilisation. One is back in the priestly atmosphere which bemuses and bewilders the ordinary citizen, which outraged Bentham. Codification is, however, a true law-making process – not merely an incidental benefit thrown up by another process, that of adjudication. It provides for study, research, consultation, planning – all essential to orderly development: it looks forward to the shape of things to come as well as back to the achievements of the past. Further, in an English context, it is a process which enables the layman's voice to be heard in the process of law-making. The community and its experts are involved: and the final stage is critical discussion of the proposed code in and outside Parliament during its passage into law. Codification as a process is thus responsive to modern ideas, and can be so managed as to be deliberate, scientific and representative. And as a process it can be kept in continuous action. It is true that a code begins to grow old, to become obsolete as soon as it is enacted. But if there be machinery for its continuous review, a code becomes not the last but the first stage in codification. The coalition of enacted code, judicial interpretation, probing and application, and continuous review by a commission such as the Law Commission Act creates, should ensure that codification continues, after as well as at the moment of the enactment of the code, to meet the endless challenge of simplification and modernisation …
>
> Let us assume it can be done. What would its impact be on the common law? We must face it: the impact would be immense. First, in the use of precedent. It would be inconceivable, upon the view I have put forward of the nature and objects of a code, that precedent earlier in date than the enacted code could be used as a source of law. It would, I suppose, be permissible to refer to earlier case law if it should be relevant to discover what the earlier law was: otherwise, with the enactment of the code, the curtain would drop for all save legal historians upon the earlier case law. Secondly, in the function of the judges. They would be interpreters of the law as found in the code. No doubt, as in France, a considerable judge-made jurisprudence carrying great authority would arise: for, as Aristotle once remarked, 'no piece of legislation can deal with every possible problem'.

The MacMillan Committee on Income Tax Codification (Cmnd 5131, 1936) described the relationship of code and judges in these words (p 17):

> Nothing short of omniscience would suffice to enable the draftsman to conceive and provide for every possible contingency … It is not practicable to pursue any given topic to its last details. There must always remain a margin within which the process of judicial interpretation and application is left to operate.

Thus, Scarman said, the judges would retain a vital legislative function when confronted with situations with which the code had failed to deal. Both as legislators, therefore, and as interpreters, their part in developing as well as applying the law would continue to be of immense importance. They would also fulfil a vital function as critics in continuous session.

> … [I]t will be the judges who will find the weaknesses, the ambiguities, the gaps, and so provide the opportunities and the incentive for keeping the code in 'efficient working order'.
>
> They would, however, have to be freed of the rigidities of our present 'stare decisis' rule; for though precedent would have a persuasive role to play of great importance, it could not be allowed to become sovereign. Code and persuasive precedent can co-exist to the advantage of law. Further, a code will require a 'fair, large and liberal' interpretation: the priorities now obtaining among the many rules of statutory interpretation, that at present our law offers, according to context, to the judge, would call for re-assessment. Further, it will be necessary to consider whether new aids to interpretation should not be made available: for example, a Law Commission memorandum or commentary on the code.

> All this may at first sight appear to portend legal revolution. But it is not so very drastic if viewed against the background of the legal development of the past 100 years. Much of our criminal law, our company law, our law as to competition and consumer protection, our planning and property law, our tax law is already embodied in statute: our judges already spend a great part of their time upon the interpretation of statute law. Even before the Law Commission Act, our law was on the move towards codification: a universal codification would not be such a strange new world as some lawyers fear. The observations that I have made do not enable a decisive answer to be given to the question – will English law become a codified system? I have endeavoured only to suggest grounds for believing that codification of our law – in part, if not in whole – is both desirable and possible. A final answer can be given only when its problems and implications have been subjected to more scientific study than has yet been thought necessary.

If one of the alleged virtues of codified systems is that they are easier to use than the common law system, the experience of practitioners is relevant. Dr Ernst Cohn was a lawyer who practised both in Germany and in England.

Dr Ernst Cohn, 'The German Attorney' *International and Comparative Law Quarterly*, 1960, 580, 586–87

> Codification renders the task of the practising lawyer very much easier than it is in an uncodified system. No code solves more than some problems. Freedom of interpretation and casuistry must remain and do remain. But only a very bad code would fail to deal clearly and succinctly with the vast majority of the day-to-day problems that are the bread and butter of the routine lawyer's life. These codes have been ably commented upon by numerous authors during the last sixty years. Commentators vary in size from a little one-volume pocket edition to huge standard works approximating in size to our 'Halsbury'. But it is believed that a good selection of pocket commentaries together with a more elaborate edition of one or two codes, plus the last fifteen years of the leading legal periodical, *Neue Juristische Wochenschrift*, and the current official Statute Book will do for the needs of a large percentage of attorneys in all but a fairly small number of cases, in particular if this 'library' is supplemented by some of the better-class students' textbooks from his university days.
>
> By the term 'codification' I mean, of course, what may well be styled the 'radical codification' which is the only form of codification known to the Continent of Europe. This type of codification differs from what is designated by the same term in this country by the fact that it will make recourse to all the accumulated mass of earlier material – whether statutes or decisions or other works of authority – completely unnecessary except perhaps in a case of the most extraordinary character. This radical codification furthermore differs from the common law type of codification by its attempt at laying down principles of a sweepingly wide and general character, rather than deciding in a binding manner typical cases as do so many common law statutes. This seemingly abstract type of code has the beneficial effect of drawing into its net a far larger number of actual cases. A practitioner who has grasped the rules of the first book of the German Civil Code and those of the first part of the second book of the German Civil Code is thereby alone well equipped to deal satisfactorily with an astonishingly large number of everyday problems. A question which would require a common law practitioner to search in books of reference for one or several quarters of an hour could be solved by his Continental colleague completely satisfactorily in as many minutes.

Dr Cohn's view was supported in his 1987 Chorley Lecture by Professor Hein Kötz, one of Germany's foremost comparative lawyers.[42] He quoted with approval Karl Llewellyn (a great Germanophile) who in 1938 had written:

> No one who has never seen a puzzled Continental lawyer turn to his little library and then turn out at least a workable understanding of his problem within half an hour will really grasp what the

[42] 'Taking civil codes less seriously' 50 *Modern Law Review*, 1987, 1, 14.

> availability of the working leads packed into a systematic Code can do to cheapen the rendering of respectably adequate legal service.

But that view was not shared by Professor Hahlo:

HR Hahlo, 'Here lies the common law' 30 *Modern Law Review*, 1967, 241

> Whether codification renders the routine work of legal practice and adjudication easier is a question on which opinions differ. Dr E. J. Cohn, who has practised in Germany and England, asserts … that
>
>> 'There can be no doubt at all … that codification renders the task of the practising lawyer very much easier than it is in an uncodified system'
>
> and that
>
>> 'A question which would require a common law practitioner to search in books of reference for one or several quarters of an hour could be solved by his Continental colleague completely satisfactorily in as many minutes.'
>
> referring in support to an article by Mr E. Moses on 'International Legal Practice'.[43]
>
> Other lawyers with experience of practice, both on the Continent and under an uncodified system, have been heard to assert, with equal assurance, that the task of a French, Dutch or German lawyer in arguing a legal point is not substantially easier than that of his English, American or Scottish colleague, and that there are as many points of controversy in modern Continental systems of law as there are in the common law.
>
> *Ex cathedra* statements of this sort, even if supported by an 'of course' or 'no doubt', are in the nature of things capable of neither proof nor disproof. Since a code wipes out the past, it generally obviates the need for historical research going back in time beyond the date of the code and, to this extent, it makes legal work easier, but how many cases arise, after all, in any system of law, in which deep historical research is required? In an uncodified as well as a codified system, it is rarely necessary to go beyond the last thirty years of law reports.
>
> Dr Cohn, after having told us that codification 'renders the task of the practising attorney very much easier …', goes on to say that the German codes 'have been ably commented upon by numerous authors during the last sixty years. Commentaries vary in size from a little one-volume pocket-edition to huge standard works approximating in size our *Halsbury*.' He then informs us that a library consisting of 'a good selection of pocket commentaries together with a more elaborate edition of one or two codes [one of the 'huge' standard works?], plus the last fifteen years of the leading legal periodical, *Neue Juristische Wochenschrift* [which contains, apart from articles, extensive case notes], and the current official Statute Book … supplemented by some of the better-class students' textbooks …' will 'do for the needs of a large percentage of attorneys in all but a fairly small number of cases.'
>
> Reading this, one cannot help wondering whether practice on the Continent can really be so very much easier than in England. How much more by way of materials does an English lawyer require in all 'but a fairly small number of cases?'

Another distinguished and experienced comparativist, Professor Basil Markesinis, took much the same view. In *The Gradual Convergence* (Clarendon Press, 1994, 19) he wondered whether Karl Llewellyn's statement quoted by Professor Kötz (above) was still true.

> Unless 'workable understanding of [the] problem' is taken at the most simple level, my own feeling is that a German lawyer asked to advise on the potential liability for negligent statements toward third parties, has to do almost as much research as an American lawyer to find the relevant case law and to come up with a moderately workable answer.

[43] 4 *Fordham Law Review*, 1935, 244.

Professor Markesinis later filled out this statement in an email to the writer:[44]

> Obviously, a complete and thorough advice can no longer be undertaken on the basis of consulting the Code alone. Typically, practitioners will cite commentaries such as Palandt or Staudinger etc to back up their assertions and provide illustrations. But in my opinion that is not enough if the case is a complex one and the point it raises is not subject to an obvious solution. Here the kind of research and conciliation of conflicting authorities that has to be undertaken must be complex and time-consuming if the advice is to be accurate.

This was especially so, Professor Markesinis added, where the advice concerned the larger international, financial, banking matters undertaken by sizeable law firms – a kind of practice that simply did not exist when Ernst Cohn wrote his piece.

For a sceptical view as to the advantages of codification see also Professor Aubrey Diamond in a lecture published three years before he became a Law Commissioner: 'Codification of the law of contract' 31 *Modern Law Review*, 1968, 361.

The rather dismal history of codification by the Law Commission was traced in a lecture by a former chairman of the Commission:[45]

Sir Michael Kerr, 'Law reform in changing times' 96 *Law Quarterly Review*, 1980, 527–29

> ... The experience of the Law Commission so far has certainly been that codification in the Continental sense is quite impracticable. It was first attempted in relation to Item I of the Commission's First Programme in 1965, 'Codification of the Law of Contract'. During the first six years of the Commission's existence this was one of its main priorities. Virtually all of our law of contract is governed by the common law; there are hardly any statutes. The Commission's objective was accordingly to produce a code of principles and rules which would cover the whole of the law of contract and to enact this in a single statute. However, by 1972 it had become clear that this was simply not practicable. Thus, it proved impossible to agree as between England and Scotland what should be the unified rules of contract for the whole of the United Kingdom. It then also proved impossible to produce a code for English law alone. It was found that agreement could not be reached on the formulation of rules and propositions to replace the immense body of case law in this field, as distilled in our text books, covering innumerable permutations of situations which a code would inevitably leave at large. In the result, this attempt at codification had to be suspended indefinitely,[46] and at present it has no prospect of realisation. What has been substituted for it is the objective of reforming specific parts of our law of contract by statutory reformulation where this seems particularly necessary.[47] Instead of having one all-embracing code of rules, as in other countries, we will therefore in the foreseeable future have no more than a number of statutes superseding those parts of our law of contract which appear to be in particular need of reform, leaving the rest to the common law as before.
>
> Very much the same fate befell the original scheme for the 'Codification of the Law of Landlord and Tenant', which was Item VIII of the Law Commission's First Programme. In the early years an attempt was made, with the assistance of outside specialists, to formulate a code. An experienced barrister did a great deal of work to evolve a set of propositions and rules intended to codify the whole of the present law of landlord and tenant apart from the Rent Act legislation.[48] However, it soon became clear, both inside the Commission and in consultation with others, that, at any rate for the present, any exercise on these lines had no realistic prospect of implementation

[44] Email of 11 May 2000, quoted here with his permission.

[45] See also AE Anton, 'Obstacles to codification' *Juridical Review*, 1982, 15; and P North, 'Problems of codification in a common law system' 46 *Rabels Zeitschrift*, 1982, 490.

[46] See Eighth Annual Report, 1972–73, Law Com No 58, paras 3–5.

[47] For example, the doctrine of consideration, the parol evidence rule, the law concerning minors' contracts, and parts of the law of insurance.

[48] The late LA Blundell QC. The code would have contained about 880 propositions, of which over 650 had been fully drafted by him before his death. The work was then suspended indefinitely.

> by legislation. Here again, therefore, the Commission had to compromise[49] by concentrating on the statutory restatement of a number of aspects of the law where reform appears particularly desirable, and this work is now proceeding.[50]
>
> The same problem faces the Commission in relation to the Criminal Law. There is hardly any legal system in the world without a comprehensive Criminal Code, but there is none in this country. The Commission is committed to the ultimate codification of the Criminal Law. With the assistance of the Criminal Law Revision Committee we are now well on the way towards the statutory restatement of all common law offences. This would be regarded as a self-evident necessity in virtually every other legal system, where it would be unimaginable that it should be left to the courts to decide *ex post facto* whether or not some particular course of conduct had or had not been criminal. We are now gradually approaching the stage when there will be a number of detailed statutes which, between them, will define all offences. However, this will still be a very long way from having anything in the nature of a comprehensive Criminal Code, such as exists in virtually all other jurisdictions, including the Commonwealth.

In 1986, Professor Hein Kötz, giving that year's Chorley Lecture ('Taking civil codes less seriously'[51]), accepted that codification was a dead issue in England. But he challenged some of the arguments that had been used to kill it off. The debate in England as to the vices and virtues of Continental codification, in Kötz's view, led nowhere and only obscured the basic problem that confronted all systems of finding an acceptable compromise between the values of experience and of order.[52]

The codification project that lasted longest was that in regard to criminal law. Its final demise only came in 2008. In its *Tenth Programme of Law Reform*, the Law Commission stated that it had removed the project from the Programme because codification had 'become ever more difficult'.[53] It blamed 'the complexity of the common law, the increased pace of legislation, layers of legislation on a topic being placed one on to another with bewildering speed, and the influence of European legislation'. The *Criminal Law Review*, in an editorial headed 'RIP: The Criminal Code (1968–2008)', wrote that this was 'a dispiriting and frustrating announcement of the death of a 40-year project':

> There is much that could be said about the reasons for the failure of what was once a flagship project for the Commission. While we can lament the largely fruitless expenditure of extensive time and resources on the project over many years, it is probably not profitable to embark on a full-scale inquest …

But, the Editor wrote, it was worth making three points.

> First, the Commission's conception of what codification means has shrunk to very modest proportions. In 1985 their view was expansive, 'codification … is essentially a task of restating a given branch of law in a single, coherent, consistent, unified and comprehensive piece of legislation'.[54]

[49] Eighth Annual Report, 1972–73, Law Com No 58, paras 3–5.

[50] The Law Commission published a Report and draft Bill on *Obligations of Landlords and Tenants* (HMSO, 1975) Law Com No 67; an unpublished draft Report on *Covenants against Dispositions, Alterations and Change of Use* is at present under consideration by the Department of the Environment; and the Commission will shortly produce a draft Report on *Termination of Tenancies* for consideration by this and other Departments.

[51] 50 *Modern Law Review*, 1986, 1.

[52] On misconceptions about codification see also Eva Steiner, 'Codification in England: the need to move from an ideological to a functional approach – a bridge too far?' 25 *Statute Law Review*, 2004, 209.

[53] *Tenth Programme of Law Reform*, Law Com No 311, HC 605, 2008, para 1.4.

[54] Introduction to Law Com No 143, *Codification of the Criminal Law*, 1985, para 16.

By 2008, however, codification for the Commission had become the reduction 'to one statute, or a small collection of statutes, of the whole of the law on any particular subject'. This seemed to imply an exercise that was 'little more than a consolidation of existing statutory sources (a useful but limited exercise), or a faithful restatement of the common law, which could be important and worthwhile, but is of dubious utility if it includes the warts and all'.[55]

> What the Commission doesn't say, and couldn't say, is that a root cause of the increased difficulty of codification is the way that the criminal law has become increasingly politicised over the last 15 years or so ... This generates two obstacles to codification. One is a reluctance on the part of government to contemplate any kind of legislation where this might stir up new controversy ... The other is that political pressures may distort schemes of principled and worthwhile law reform ... In these circumstances the achievement of codification aims of a coherent structure for the criminal law, with clear and consistent principles of liability, becomes almost impossible.

The third point made in the Editorial was that the Commission's strategy had shifted from era to era.[56] The Tenth Programme said that the Commission's new strategy was to focus on specific projects to reform and simplify the criminal law with the aim of returning to codify at some date in the future.

> No one will be holding their breath ... The Commission may now be realistic in finally conceding that codification is never going to happen, but this is nonetheless a sad end for a noble ideal.[57]

For categorical rejection of codification of the law on judicial review see TH Jones, 'Judicial review and codification' 20 *Legal Studies*, 2000, 517–37. The author's conclusion was that legislative attempts to constrain judicial review were misconceived and misguided. This was a field that should be left to the judges.

Sir Geoffrey Palmer, former New Zealand Prime Minister, Justice Minister and President of the New Zealand Law Commission, urged that codification should be an important part of the work of Law Commissions:

> While in large measure codification failed, I argue that it should be revived. New Zealand has had a criminal code since 1893 and Canada has one. In 2006, after more than a decade's work by the Law Commission, New Zealand passed the Evidence Act, a measure close to meeting Lord Scarman's definition of a code. Despite being leery about it, the judges would now not be without it .... An organisation with the characteristics of a law commission is the ideal one to engage in the drafting of codes. There should be a recommitment to that task everywhere in the common law world. Few measures would do more to assist the rule of law.[58]

9.4.1. The Sentencing Code

Codification in the fullest sense has not been a success in the UK, but the Law Commission's Sentencing Code published in 2018 is an important development.[59] The aim of the project

[55] *Criminal Law Review*, 2009, 1.

[56] There had been five. The first three were described by the editor, Professor Ian Dennis himself, in an article in 1997 'The critical condition of criminal law' *Current Legal Problems*, 1997, 213, 241–46.

[57] 'RIP: the criminal code (1968–2000)' *Criminal Law Review*, 2009, 1–2.

[58] Sir Geoffrey Palmer, 'The Law Reform Enterprise: Evaluating the Past and Charting the Future', 131 *Law Quarterly Review*, 2015, 402–23, 412–13.

[59] Law Commission Sentencing Code Pt 1 Report (310pp), Sentencing Code Pt 2 Draft Legislation (104pp). For an explanation of the project see Harry O'Sullivan and David Ormerod, 'Time for a Code: Reform of Sentencing Law in England and Wales', 19 *European Journal of Law Reform*, 2017, 285–305.

was to 'create a single sentencing statute … [to] bring together all of the existing legislation governing sentencing procedure within a single enactment' to resolve the complexity and inconsistency due to the multiple and overlapping sources of sentencing law.[60] The decision was made to limit the project by not going beyond the existing statutory law on sentencing– both to make it manageable in terms of time[61] and so that it would qualify for the expedited parliamentary procedure used for Bills that are 'mere' consolidations.[62] (See p 54 above.) It therefore does not include common law rules on sentencing.[63] It did not change any sentencing provisions. Its purpose was to alter the process by which sentencing decisions are made. As Roberts and Azmeh wrote:

> The benefits will include greater clarity and significant economic savings.[64] In addition the Code creates a vehicle for a more theoretically coherent and comprehensive sentencing regime for England and Wales. Henceforth, all changes to sentencing law will the Commission hopes, be made by way of amendment to the Code. In this respect, the Code represents the beginning of a new era, and not simply the successful conclusion to the Commission's consolidation project.[65]

The Sentencing Code Act 2020 came into force on 1 December 2020.

9.5. The Law Commission and Consultation

Consultation is central to the Law Commission's way of working. The 2022–23 annual report explains (p 8):

> We aim to consult fully with all those potentially affected by our proposals. We engage with stakeholders from the outset of a project, even before a piece of work is officially adopted, and conduct thorough, targeted consultations throughout. This allows us to acquire a good understanding of the issues that are arising in an area of law and the effect they are having, and gives us a clear picture of the context within which the law operates. We use this to assess the impact of our proposed policies and refine our thinking. Our consultations can include meetings with individuals and organisations, public events, conferences, symposia and other types of event, as well as interviews and site visits. We often work through representative organisations, asking them to help us reach their members and stakeholders.

Both the 2003 Quinquennial Review and the 2013–14 Triennial Review commended the Law Commission for the way it carried out consultation. The Commission's Evidence to the Triennial Review had given an example (p 24):

> Consultation is the fulcrum of our law reform projects. It is critical to the final outcome in that it allows us to gain an in-depth, up-to-date and thorough understanding of an area of law, the

[60] JV Roberts and U Azmeh, 'Cleansing the Augean Stables: A Commentary on the Law Commission's Sentencing Code for England and Wales', *Criminal Law Review*, 2019 (8), 694–705.

[61] It nevertheless took some three years.

[62] Implementation had two stages – a pre-consolidation Bill to make the necessary changes (47pp) and the consolidation bill itself. The Sentencing (Pre-consolidation Amendments) Bill had 2nd Reading, Committee stage and Report in the House of Lords on 16 October 2019 but made no further progress before Parliament was prorogued for the December General Election.

[63] Such as *Newton* [1982] 77 Cr App R. 13 or *Goodyear* [2005] EWCA Crim 888, [2005] 1 WLR 2532.

[64] Estimated by the Commission as being some £250m over ten years.

[65] JV Roberts and U Azmeh, 'Cleansing the Augean Stables: A Commentary on the Law Commission's Sentencing Code for England and Wales', *Criminal Law Review*, 2019 (8), 705.

problems that arise and how they are experienced by the courts, legal practitioners and other interested parties, be they business, the voluntary sector, private citizens or others. The result of our consultation process is virtually always to produce a more effective set of final recommendations.

A case study on how we consulted with providers and service users in our Adult Social Care project powerfully illustrates this point. The system of adult social care clearly needed improving. Our aim was to make sure that people who provide, deliver and use adult social care services have a say in how it should be changed for the better. Our public consultation on adult social care ran from 24 February until 1 July 2010. During this period, members of the Public Law team attended 72 consultation events across England and Wales.

Our programme included:

- a half-day workshop with deafblind people and carers, organised by Sense
- a joint conference organised by the Older People's Commissioner for Wales and Age Cymru for over 100 people in Cardiff, including service users, carers, professionals and academics
- a consultation stand at a Young Carers' Festival in Southampton
- a two-hour workshop with service users, carers, professionals and academics
- a two-hour workshop with service users, carers, service providers and local authority staff, organised by Reach in Newport
- a half-day workshop with over 40 family carers in Camden, London, and
- a blog that ran throughout the consultation period on which people could post their comments.

Through these events we were able to reach, and hear from, a wide audience with diverse views and experiences of the sector. Participants included service users, carers, social workers and members of safeguarding boards, community care lawyers, service providers and representatives from charities and campaigning organisations.

Sir Geoffrey Palmer, drawing on his experience as President of the New Zealand Law Commission and as Justice and Prime Minister, argued that law commissions should be the model for law-making by the executive:

> [L]aw commissions have forged superior methods of designing law compared with those employed by executive governments and parliaments. A robust set of transparent processes is bound to produce a better outcome that has been better tested than plans hatched by ministers and officials working behind closed doors. Furthermore, when the product comes to be considered by Parliament, there is a great deal more relevant information available to MPs and the public than is usually available on government bills. If these methods are superior, then the question has to be asked why are they not used for other legislation?[66]
>
> … The Commissions have added value. They have promoted, and quite often achieved, important legal reforms. But progress is not of the sort that would have impressed someone like Jeremy Bentham. No coherent philosophy for the law reform enterprise has emerged. Probably none can be devised because the Commissions occupy an awkward space between principle and expediency. We are still awaiting the golden age of law reform. While law commissions lifted law reform to a professional full-time activity, the vision has stalled …
>
> Law commissions' methods have shown up the flaws in the way the executive and parliament make law. Since providing the law is a fundamental constitutional duty of parliament, the remedy lies in reform of executive and parliamentary processes … New methods need to be devised to make statutes that involve openness, public participation, rigorous research and the systematic process

[66] Sir Geoffrey Palmer, 'The Law Reform Enterprise: Evaluating the Past and Charting the Future', 131 *Law Quarterly Review*, 2015, 402–23, 417.

> steps that law commissions have shown can produce more robust and durable laws. Those methods need to be adapted for use for all legislation and internalised within the executive government. Such a reform is a formidable undertaking, since it requires upending the whole method by which law is made by the executive and parliaments now. Fundamental revision is required within the executive and parliament as to how legislation is designed and enacted …
>
> Law making is a function of the utmost importance to a democratic society as a whole so it needs to be carried out as carefully and systematically as possible. Law commissions have pointed the direction for achieving better methods of making law generally. Executives and parliaments need to be persuaded they are not making law well and need to do better. To achieve such changes will require political leadership as there will be great resistance. In contemporary politics the fundamental features that matter most to the quality of governance tends to receive the least attention.
>
> Law commissions should be entrusted with wider responsibilities and their remits broadened to include big projects with social implications. Law commissions must cease being regarded as interesting appendages to the machinery of government and become central to legislative activities.[67]

For a discussion of the pros and cons of law reform by the four different possible actors (general legislative action/legislation based on Law Commission proposals/development of the law by the judges/and academic commentary) see P (now Lord) Sales, 'Law Reform Challenges: The Judicial Perspective' 39 *Statute Law Review*, 2018, 229–43. For the views of an academic, former member of the Law Commission, see S Cretney, 'The Politics of Law Reform – A View from the Inside' 48 *Modern Law Review*, 1985, 493–517.

The two joint Chief Executives of the Law Commission, in their introduction to the Commission's 2023–24 Annual Report, wrote:

> In December 2023, we published *Inside Modern Law Reform*,[68] a book explaining in detail how the law reform process really works. And in February this year we published an independent report assessing the *Value of Law Reform*, which updated a study originally carried out in 2019 by two independent economists. The report established that the Law Commission's projects make a difference in myriad ways: efficiency gains, technology driven growth, harm prevention, well-being improvement, rule of law, access to justice, modernising the legal system and thought leadership. Key findings included:
>
> - The estimated economic gains from the five highest value projects completed since 2019 is about £670 million over 10 years.[69]
> - Law reform can lead to positive impacts for significant numbers of people; two projects considered indicated a potential impact on 5.3 million people, and another project could positively impact 78 percent of households.
> - Within the four-year period, two of the five projects used as case studies have had their recommendations implemented in whole or in part.
> - The average annual number of reports published during the considerable disruption of the global pandemic was 5.8, which is higher than the Law Commission's historic average of 4.5 final reports per year.
> - A new key theme was identified in assessing the benefit of the Law Commission's work: the thought leadership offered by the Commission in national and international law reform.

[67] Ibid, 420, 421, 423.

[68] Available at www.lawcom.gov.uk (239pp).

[69] This is a conservative estimate as it does not include an additional £1.1 billion in net benefits to UK businesses from the Electronic Trade Documents Act, one of our case studies, a figure that was independently calculated by other Government analysts.

Index